Econometrics and Economic Theory in the 20th Century
The Ragnar Frisch Centennial Symposium

Ragnar Frisch (1895–1973) received the first Nobel Memorial Prize in Economic Science together with Jan Tinberger in 1969 for having played an important role in ensuring that mathematical techniques figure prominently in modern economic analysis. Frisch was also a co-founder of the Econometric Society in 1930, the inaugural editor of its journal *Econometrica* for more than 20 years, and a major figure in Norwegian academic life.

This collection of essays derived from the symposium that marked the centennial of Frisch's birth explores his contributions to econometrics and other key fields in the discipline, in addition to presenting findings from new research in areas that were of interest to Frisch. Contributors include eminent scholars from Europe and North America who investigate themes in utility measurement, production theory, microeconomic policy, econometric methods, macrodynamics, and macroeconomic planning.

Steinar Strøm is Professor of Economics at the University of Oslo. He has edited works on Knut Wicksell, energy economics, and environmental economics and has published books and papers on these subjects as well as on microeconometrics, labor supply, and taxation.

Econometric Society Monographs No. 31

Editors:
Peter Hammond, *Stanford University*
Alberto Holly, *University of Lausanne*

The Econometric Society is an international society for the advancement of economic theory in relation to statistics and mathematics. The Econometric Society Monograph Series is designed to promote the publication of original research contributions of high quality in mathematical economics and theoretical and applied econometrics.

Other titles in the series:
G. S. Maddala *Limited-Dependent and Qualitative Variables in Econometrics*, 0 521 33825 5
Gerard Debreu *Mathematical Economics: Twenty Papers of Gerard Debreu*, 0 521 33561 2
Jean-Michel Grandmont *Money and Value: A Reconsideration of Classical and Neoclassical Monetary Economics*, 0 521 31364 3
Franklin M. Fisher *Disequilibrium Foundations of Equilibrium Economics*, 0 521 37856 7
Andreu Mas-Colell *The Theory of General Economic Equilibrium: A Differentiable Approach*, 0 521 26514 2, 0 521 38870 8
Cheng Hsiao *Analysis of Panel Data*, 0 521 38933 X
Truman F. Bewley, Editor *Advances in Econometrics – Fifth World Congress (Volume I)*, 0 521 46726 8
Truman F. Bewley, Editor *Advances in Econometrics – Fifth World Congress (Volume II)*, 0 521 46725 X
Hervé Moulin *Axioms of Cooperative Decision Making*, 0 521 36055 2, 0 521 42458 5
L. G. Godfrey *Misspecification Tests in Econometrics: The Lagrange Multiplier Principle and Other Approaches*, 0 521 42459 3
Tony Lancaster *The Econometric Analysis of Transition Data*, 0 521 43789 X
Alvin E. Roth and Marilda A. Oliviera Sotomayor, Editors *Two-Sided Matching: A Study in Game-Theoretic Modeling and Analysis*, 0 521 43788 1
Wolfgang Härdle, *Applied Nonparametric Regression*, 0 521 42950 1
Jean-Jacques Laffont, Editor *Advances in Economic Theory – Sixth World Congress (Volume I)*, 0 521 48459 6
Jean-Jacques Laffont, Editor *Advances in Economic Theory – Sixth World Congress (Volume II)*, 0 521 48460 X
Halbert White *Estimation, Inference and Specification Analysis*, 0 521 25280 6, 0 521 57446 3
Christopher A. Sims, Editor *Advances in Econometrics – Sixth World Congress (Volume I)*, 0 521 56610 X
Christopher A. Sims, Editor *Advances in Econometrics – Sixth World Congress (Volume II)*, 0 521 56609 6
Roger Guesnerie *A Contribution to the Pure Theory of Taxation*, 0 521 23689 4, 0 521 62956 X
David M. Kreps and Kenneth F. Wallis, Editors *Advances in Economics and Econometrics – Seventh World Congress (Volume I)*, 0 521 58011 0, 0 521 58983 5
David M. Kreps and Kenneth F. Wallis, Editors *Advances in Economics and Econometrics – Seventh World Congress (Volume II)*, 0 521 58012 9, 0 521 58982 7
David M. Kreps and Kenneth F. Wallis, Editors *Advances in Economics and Econometrics – Seventh World Congress (Volume III)*, 0 521 58013 7, 0 521 58981 9
Donald P. Jacobs, Ehud Kalai, and Morton I. Kamien, Editors *Frontiers of Research in Economic Theory: The Nancy L. Schwartz Memorial Lectures, 1983–1997*, 0 521 63222 6, 0 521 63538 1
A. Colin Cameron and Pravin K. Trivedi, *Regression Analysis of Count Data*, 0 521 63201 3, 0 521 63567 5

Econometrics and Economic Theory in the 20th Century
The Ragnar Frisch Centennial Symposium

Edited by

Steinar Strøm

CAMBRIDGE UNIVERSITY PRESS
Cambridge, New York, Melbourne, Madrid, Cape Town, Singapore, São Paulo

Cambridge University Press
The Edinburgh Building, Cambridge CB2 8RU, UK

Published in the United States of America by Cambridge University Press, New York

www.cambridge.org
Information on this title: www.cambridge.org/9780521633239

© Steinar Strøm 1998

This publication is in copyright. Subject to statutory exception
and to the provisions of relevant collective licensing agreements,
no reproduction of any part may take place without the written
permission of Cambridge University Press.

First published 1998

A catalogue record for this publication is available from the British Library

Library of Congress Cataloguing in Publication data
Econometrics and economic theory in the 20th century : the Ragnar
Frisch Centennial Symposium / edited by Steinar Strøm.
p.   cm.
Includes index.
ISBN 0-521-63323-0. – ISBN 0-521-63365-6 (pb)
1. Frisch, Ragnar, 1895–1973. 2. Econometrics – History –
Congresses. 3. Econometric models – History – Congresses.
I. Strøm, Steinar.
HB139.E289   1998
330'.01'5195 – dc21
                                                                98-26460
                                                                        CIP

ISBN 978-0-521-63323-9 hardback
ISBN 978-0-521-63365-9 paperback

Transferred to digital printing 2007

Contents

Introduction	*page* ix
List of Contributors	xiii

PART ONE: RAGNAR FRISCH AND HIS CONTRIBUTIONS TO ECONOMICS

1	Ragnar Frisch at the University of Oslo JENS C. ANDVIG AND TORE THONSTAD	3
2	Ragnar Frisch and the Foundation of the Econometric Society and *Econometrica* OLAV BJERKHOLT	26
3	The Contributions of Ragnar Frisch to Economics and Econometrics JOHN S. CHIPMAN	58

PART TWO: UTILITY MEASUREMENT

4	Nonparametric Estimation of Exact Consumer Surplus and Deadweight Loss JERRY A. HAUSMAN AND WHITNEY K. NEWEY	111
5	Consumer Demand and Intertemporal Allocations: Engel, Slutsky, and Frisch RICHARD BLUNDELL	147

PART THREE: PRODUCTION THEORY

6	Production Functions: The Search for Identification ZVI GRILICHES AND JACQUES MAIRESSE	169
7	Investment and Growth DALE W. JORGENSON	204

PART FOUR: MICROECONOMIC POLICY

8	Evaluating the Welfare State JAMES J. HECKMAN AND JEFFREY SMITH	241

Contents

  9 Frisch, Hotelling, and the Marginal-Cost Pricing Controversy   319
      JEAN-JACQUES LAFFONT

PART FIVE: ECONOMETRIC METHODS

10 Scientific Explanation in Econometrics   345
      BERNT P. STIGUM

11 An Autoregressive Distributed-Lag Modelling Approach to Cointegration Analysis   371
      M. HASHEM PESARAN AND YONGCHEOL SHIN

12 Econometric Issues Related to Errors in Variables in Financial Models   414
      G. S. MADDALA

13 Statistical Analysis of Some Nonstationary Time Series   433
      SØREN JOHANSEN

PART SIX: MACRODYNAMICS

14 Frisch's Vision and Explanation of the Trade-Cycle Phenomenon: His Connections with Wicksell, Åkerman, and Schumpeter   461
      BJØRN THALBERG

15 Ragnar Frisch's Conception of the Business Cycle   483
      LAWRENCE R. KLEIN

16 Business Cycles: Real Facts or Fallacies?   499
      GUNNAR BÅRDSEN, PAUL G. FISHER, AND RAGNAR NYMOEN

PART SEVEN: MACROECONOMIC PLANNING

17 The Influence of Ragnar Frisch on Macroeconomic Planning and Policy in Norway   531
      PETTER JAKOB BJERVE

18 How Frisch Saw in the 1960s the Contribution of Economists to Development Planning   560
      E. MALINVAUD

19 On the Need for Macroeconomic Planning in Market Economies: Three Examples from the European Monetary Union Project   577
      A. J. HUGHES HALLETT

Author Index   619
Subject Index   625

Introduction

Ragnar A. K. Frisch was born March 3, 1895, and as 1995 approached, his former students and colleagues in the Department of Economics at the University of Oslo decided to celebrate the life and career of this remarkable and outstanding scientist with a centennial symposium. It was quite easy to get enthusiastic responses from those who were asked to take part.

One reason these participants so readily accepted the invitation most likely was the role Frisch had in the development of economic theory and econometrics in this century: He was the editor of *Econometrica* for more than 20 years and was one of the first (perhaps the very first) to use a new name for the blend of economics, mathematical modeling, and statistics: *econometrics*. That term appeared in his very first paper in economics in 1926: "Sur un problème d'économie pure," *Norsk Matematisk Forenings Skrifter* (series I, no. 16, 1926, pp. 1–40). Because it was written in French and was published in a Norwegian journal, that paper was less well known than it should have been, although at that time scientific writing was less strongly dominated by the English language than it is now. In that paper, translated and published in English in 1971, Frisch defined econometrics: "Intermediate between mathematics, statistics, and economics, we find a new discipline, which for lack of a better name, may be called *econometrics*."

Our main objectives in arranging this centennial symposium were, first, to review Ragnar Frisch's contributions to the development of econometrics and economic theory and, second, to invite essays that would reflect recent advances and ongoing research in fields to which Frisch had contributed. We had to be selective, for Frisch worked in many fields and left an impressive legacy of publications. In addition to his many published (165 titles) and republished articles and books, he left tons of unpublished material.

In the same year that Frisch published his first paper in economics, 1926, he published an agenda paper in which he formulated his own research program. His main concern was to lay a foundation for the quantification of economics, and clearly his efforts throughout his entire academic life were aimed at achieving that goal. Consequently, the topics selected for the centennial symposium had to be related to the quantification of economics.

In his first paper in economics, as cited earlier, Frisch stated that "the econometric study that I shall present is an attempt to realize the dreams of Jevons: to measure the variation in the marginal utility of economic goods." Thus it was natural to include a section of essays on *utility measurement* (Part II of this book) in the symposium. Frisch was convinced, throughout his career, that he would be able to estimate a cardinal utility function based on the assumption that individuals are able to rank *changes* in their consumption bundles. That idea has never been picked up by others in the profession. However, developments in the collection and processing of microeconomic data, together with the development of econometric methods, have made it possible to analyze rather complex models of individual behavior. The two essays herein that deal with this subject are good examples of how far the field of microeconometrics has now reached.

Another favorite topic of Frisch was *production theory* (Part III herein). In the late 1920s he began his work on the behavior of firms, with emphasis on a mathematical treatment of production and cost functions. His international publication record in this field was rather limited, but because his first unpublished draft of a textbook on production theory appeared in the late 1920s, Norwegian students have for decades been introduced to microeconomic theory through their reading of *Theory of Production* (the book's title when it was published in English in 1965 by D. Reidel Publishing Company). To represent this field we invited one essay dealing with the econometrics of production functions and one dealing with investment and growth, topics closely related not only to production theory but also to macroeconomic areas in which Frisch made numerous contributions.

As mentioned earlier, recent developments in data analysis and computer technology have made it possible to handle and analyze very complex microeconomic models and huge data sets containing masses of detailed information at the firm and household levels. Frisch had a real passion for computation, ranging from designing programming tools to developing optimization algorithms. It is a safe assumption that if he were still with us he would be deeply involved in the ongoing and rapidly expanding research in microeconometrics. In order to present research in the spirit of Frisch, we have included a section on *microeconomic policy* (Part IV). One essay deals with welfare evaluation, embedded in a microeconometric framework, and the second essay is inspired by the marginal-cost pricing controversy between Frisch and Hotelling from the late 1930s.

Frisch published only one technical paper on time series, despite the

Introduction

fact that the behavior of time series was central to his macrodynamics. His main contribution to *econometric methods* (Part V) was not this time-series analysis, but his development of tools for determining the interrelationships among stochastic variables, later most commonly known as his "confluence analysis." When measurement errors are present, this latter analysis has proved useful for finding consistent estimates for the bounds within which the true parameters will lie. Modern approaches to time-series analysis and errors-in-variables problems are presented in this econometric-methods section of this volume. Moreover, we have included an essay on scientific explanations in econometrics that stresses the importance of accounting carefully for the connection between theory and measurement – again, an issue whose importance Frisch stressed many times.

In a paper published in Norwegian in 1929, Frisch gave the following simple but sufficient definition of static and dynamic laws in economics: "If the formulation of an economic relationship requires both a variable and its rate of change (or lagged value), it is a dynamic relationship; if not, it is static." Because it was written in Norwegian, that early work on dynamic models, including the quoted definition, was not widely known. However, Frisch's most celebrated article was a discussion of dynamic laws and the stability of economic systems. His "propagation and impulse" article, published in 1933 as an essay in honor of the Swedish economist Gustav Cassel, presented the first self-contained model of the business cycle. Moreover, it was a business-cycle model with random disturbances that accounted for the shocks that can hit the supply side of the economy. Even judged by the macromodeling of today, that model is rather advanced. The links to the real-business-cycle (RBC) model of the 1980s are obvious. Of course, there are also major differences. Whereas the RBC models are stochastic, dynamic programming models in which instantaneous utility is derived from consumption and leisure, Frisch's ambition was to discuss the cycles through the specification and calibration of a rather small macroeconomic model that was meant to capture the dynamics of an economy. Frisch was awarded the Nobel Prize in economics primarily for his "propagation and impulse" article. Thus a section on *macrodynamics* (Part VI) was mandatory for this Frisch centennial symposium. Two essays present and discuss Frisch's conception of the business cycle.

After the Second World War, Frisch gave up most of his econometric research and small-scale macrodynamic modeling. Instead, he gave much attention to planning problems, including the programming and numerical solutions for extremely large planning models. At the beginning, his intention was to apply those models to solve Norwegian planning problems, but for a variety of reasons the focus of the applications was gradually shifted to solutions for planning problems in less developed countries like India and the United Arab Republic. In addition to two essays discussing Frisch's contributions to macroeconomic planning, we have included an essay on the need for planning in the European Monetary Union. In the section on *macroeconomic planning* (Part VII) we shall see that Frisch devoted an immense amount of energy to fighting that European project. He never wrote a scientific paper discussing the issue, but he took an active part, to say the least, in the public debate concerning the possible Norwegian membership in the European Monetary Union.

Is there anything to be learned from looking back? And would one not expect a history of economic thought to be a dry subject, particularly when the history is tied to the achievements of a single person? As demonstrated so brilliantly in the essay by John S. Chipman, the answers here would seem to be that much can be learned, and the history told may not be dull at all. In his essay in the first section of this book (*Ragnar Frisch and His Contributions to Economics*, Part I), Chipman takes us through some of the controversies in which Frisch participated. They were not few. But as emphasized by Chipman, "what makes the history of economic thought interesting, in my opinion, is how truth comes out of controversy."

Steinar Strøm

Contributors

Jens C. Andvig
Norwegian Institute of International
 Affairs
P. O. Box 8159 Dep.
0033 Oslo, Norway

Gunnar Bårdsen
Institute of Economics
Norwegian School of Economics and
 Business Administration
Helleveien 30
5035 Bergen-Sandviken, Norway

Olav Bjerkholt
Department of Economics
University of Oslo
P. O. Box 1095 Blindern
0317 Oslo, Norway

Petter Jakob Bjerve
Statistics Norway
P. O. Box 8131 Dep.
0033 Oslo, Norway

Richard Blundell
Department of Economics
University College London
Gower Street
London WC1E 6BT, United Kingdom

John S. Chipman
Department of Economics
University of Minnesota
271 19th Avenue South
Minneapolis, MN 55455

Paul G. Fisher
Bank of England
Threadneedle Street
London, EC2R 8AH, United
 Kingdom

Zvi Griliches
Department of Economics
Harvard University
125 Littauer Center
Cambridge, MA 02138

A. J. Hughes Hallett
Department of Economics
University of Strathclyde
100 Cathedral Street
Glasgow G4 0LN, United Kingdom

Jerry A. Hausman
Department of Economics
Massachusetts Institute of Technology
Cambridge, MA 02139-4307

James J. Heckman
Department of Economics
University of Chicago
1126 East 59th Street
Chicago, IL 60637

Søren Johansen
Institute of Mathematical Statistics
University of Copenhagen
Universitetsparken 5
2100 Copenhagen, Denmark

Dale W. Jorgenson
Department of Economics
Harvard University
122 Littauer Center
Cambridge, MA 02138

Lawrence R. Klein
Department of Economics
University of Pennsylvania
3718 Locust Walk CR
Philadelphia, PA 19104-6297

Contributors

Jean-Jacques Laffont
Institut d'Économie Industrielle
Université des Sciences Sociales de Toulouse
Place Anatole-France
31042 Toulouse Cédex, France

G. S. Maddala
Department of Economics
Ohio State University
1945 North High Street
Columbus, OH 43210-1172

Jacques Mairesse
Institut Nationale de la Statistique et des Études Économiques
CREST
15, Boulevard Gabrielle Péri
92245 Malakoff Cédex, Paris, France

Edmond Malinvaud
Institut Nationale de la Statistique et des Études Économiques
CREST
15, Boulevard Gabrielle Péri
92245 Malakoff Cédex, Paris, France

Whitney K. Newey
Department of Economics
Massachusetts Institute of Technology
Cambridge, MA 02139-4307

Ragnar Nymoen
Department of Economics
University of Oslo
P. O. Box 1095 Blindern
0317 Oslo, Norway

M. Hashem Pesaran
Faculty of Economics and Politics
University of Cambridge
Sidgwick Avenue
Cambridge CB3 9DD, United Kingdom

Yongcheol Shin
Department of Applied Economics
University of Cambridge
Sidgwick Avenue
Cambridge CB3 9DD, United Kingdom

Jeffrey Smith
Department of Economics
University of Western Ontario
London, Ontario, Canada N6A 5B8

Bernt P. Stigum
Department of Economics
University of Oslo
P. O. Box 1095 Blindern
0317 Oslo, Norway

Bjørn Thalberg
Department of Economics
Lund University (P. O. Box 7082)
220 07 Lund, Sweden

Tore Thonstad
Department of Economics
University of Oslo
P. O. Box 1095 Blindern
0317 Oslo, Norway

PART ONE

RAGNAR FRISCH AND HIS CONTRIBUTIONS TO ECONOMICS

CHAPTER 1

Ragnar Frisch at the University of Oslo

Jens C. Andvig and Tore Thonstad

1 A Difficult Decision?

During the spring and summer of 1931 Ragnar Frisch had to make one of the most difficult decisions of his life: Should he accept an offer from Yale University to become a full professor at that prestigious and internationally important university, or should he become a professor in economics at his old school, the provincial University of Oslo? He chose the University of Oslo. In this essay we shall indicate some reasons for that decision and record some of his more important activities influenced by or influencing that institution. In particular, some of the consequences of his choice for the subsequent teaching of economics and economic research in Norway will be described. The history of economics in Norway and Frisch's own research probably would have taken different directions had he remained at Yale.

In the spring of 1931, Dean Furniss at Yale sent Frisch a letter offering him a full professorship in economics, including a fairly large yearly grant that he might use for traveling and other research expenses.[1] Frisch was granted the summer before making his final decision. His answer was delayed until October:

> Shortly after I had returned to Oslo, in June this year, representatives of the Rockefeller Foundation came to Oslo to discuss with the University authorities and professor Wedervang and myself a plan for organizing an economic research institute at the University of Oslo. This plan had been outlined by Wedervang and myself already before I left the States in 1930, and it had been submitted to the Rockefeller Foundation by the Norwegian representative of the foundation, Professor Stang. This conversation, the subsequent correspondence and the attitude taken by Norwegian circles, both inside and outside the University, have given us the impression that there is a very real possibility for

---
[1] Letter from Furniss to Frisch, April 25, 1931; Frisch archives at the "Frisch Room," Department of Economics, University of Oslo, hereafter cited as "Frisch archives." There are also some Frisch archives in the main library at the University of Oslo.

organizing the institute. Needless to say such an institute would be of vital importance for Norwegian economic science and would offer great opportunities for quite a number of young economists. To some extent the chances for obtaining Rockefeller support for this depends, as I gathered from our conversation with the Rockefeller representatives, on my staying in Oslo.

On the other hand I have recently been brought in contact with the head of the Norwegian government in preliminary pourparlers regarding means and organs of creating unity in the work for better economic conditions in Norway.

This being the situation, I would feel it more or less as an act of disloyalty if I should at the present moment accept a permanent professorship at Yale.

2   The Student Years

Ragnar Frisch was born March 3, 1895. He completed his "examen artium" in 1913; it was also the entrance examination to the only university in Norway. He passed with excellent results.[2] However, he did not begin to study at the University of Oslo before 1917, or possibly 1916. His grandfather and father were both goldsmiths, and Frisch planned to follow them in the family firm (Frisch, 1970, p. 205):

> When I was planning my future it was more or less taken for granted that I should follow the gold and silver tradition. For that purpose I started as an apprentice in the workshop of the famous Oslo firm David Andersen, and at the end of the apprenticeship in 1920 I completed my handicraftsman's probation work as a goldsmith.
>
> After the beginning of my apprenticeship my mother got a strong feeling that the trade would not be satisfactory for me in the long run. She insisted that at the same time as I completed my apprenticeship I should take up a university study. We perused the catalogue of the Oslo University and found that economics was the *shortest* and *easiest* study. So therefore, economics it became. That is the way it happened.

However, even before entering the university, Frisch taught mathematics for the Student Union's socially oriented educational program. After entering the university as full-time student, while at the same time working as an apprentice, he still participated in student activities. Inter alia he was active in establishing an information office to inform foreign students about study conditions in Norway and Norwegian students about conditions abroad.[3] That information office evidently was part of an international movement that arose after World War I for strengthening intellectual links across borders. In 1919, Frisch was sent by the university to Copenhagen to study the organization of the Danish

---

[2] *Universitetets Matrikul 1913.*
[3] Frisch archives.

student-information office. He wrote a report and at once established a Norwegian office, which he managed until 1921.[4]

In the autumn of 1917 he passed the introductory examinations in Latin and philosophy, once more with outstanding marks. In the spring term 1919 he passed the final examination in economics. He was only the second student to pass that examination with "distinction" since the course was introduced in 1905.

At that time, the main task of the university was generally considered to be education of government officials and professionals: priests, medical doctors, lawyers, college teachers, and so on. Medicine and law were the large disciplines, registering about 500 students each in 1919. At that time there were 149 students in economics, a surprisingly large number compared with the 129 students of science. We should note that economics was an exceptionally short study in Oslo at the time, only 2 years of study, as compared with the normal 5–6 years or so for the other disciplines, where the students received an *embetseksamen* (literally, "the official's exam") as preparation for government positions.

As was the case in many universities in continental Europe, economics was organized as a part of the Faculty of Law.

Oscar Jaeger (1863–1933) was the most influential teacher in economics at that time. His doctoral thesis had been a study of Adam Smith, but he apparently had been strongly influenced by the Austrian version of neoclassical economics. Thorvald Aarum (1867–1926) had been educated as a lawyer, had written a doctoral thesis about wages, and seems to have been strongly influenced by Marshall. They were the only two professors in economics at the university in Frisch's student days. Neither was known outside of Scandinavia. The most intellectually demanding lecture series in economics in the years 1917–19 probably was a series conducted by Jaeger concerning interest on capital and rent on land.[5]

The regular curriculum consisted of five parts: theoretical economics, applied economics, public finance, descriptive statistics, and actuarial science. Actuarial science encompassed theoretical statistics and the mathematical theory of probability. The regular teacher was Alf Guldberg (1866–1936), who was an internationally active and competent mathematician. He was a specialist in difference equations. Guldberg evidently had a lasting effect on Frisch, for Frisch presented some of his ideas at the Econometric Society's meeting in Lausanne in 1931.[6] The economics examination was compulsory for the actuarial students. For

---

[4] Frisch archives.
[5] See *Det kgl. Frederiks Universitets Årsberetning* (*University of Oslo, Annual Report*) for the relevant years. Note that the report followed the academic year, which lasted from July 1 to June 30. Hereafter we shall call it *University of Oslo, Annual Report*. In that annual report, all the lectures had to be reported, with estimates of the average attendance.
[6] Frisch archives.

an economics student, the examination questions in actuarial science must have appeared quite difficult. It is conceivable that the study of actuarial science and statistics in Oslo was sufficiently inspiring to have turned Frisch's mind toward the mathematical aspects of economics.

His examination reports have survived. They are quite impressive, particularly the one on public finance, which inter alia contains a sharp criticism of Schønheyder's ideas about progressive taxation.[7] After Frisch had mentioned the need to measure the marginal utility of income in order to determine the rate of progressivity of the income tax, toward the end of that report he formulated his own overriding future research policy: "Man must not be afraid of what seems impossible to do. History has shown that the human beings possess a wonderful gift of being able to obey the saying of Aristotle: 'Measure the nonmeasurable' " (our translation). Somehow, during his 2-year study of economics at the University of Oslo, the young man who had entered that study through a random process had found a definite goal for his future career as an economic scientist, a goal he seemed to pursue from the day he finished his examinations in economics until the end of his life.

3   Advanced Studies Abroad

Frisch completed the apprenticeship as a goldsmith in 1920. In 1921 he began systematically to qualify himself for research. He followed in the footsteps of the many distinguished Norwegian mathematicians who during the preceding century had visited Paris in order to study and present their results. Frisch remained in Paris from the spring of 1921 until the spring of 1923. He then visited London and stayed there for most of the autumn, finally making brief visits to Germany and Italy. In the meantime he had received the so-called Manthey scholarship. Frisch made a report to the university.[8] He had studied the theory of functions and some mathematical statistics, and he conducted a rather extensive bibliographic study. Mathematical studies dominated, but he had at least begun two projects that would occupy his later research in economics: measurement of the marginal utility of income, and time-series analysis. By the end of that period he had become a competent mathematician and mathematical statistician, and he was soon to publish several articles in those fields.

What was remarkable about his career to that point was not those mathematical contributions, but rather the fact that he, despite his mathematical gifts and the intellectually inspiring environment of mathematicians to which he had been exposed both in Paris and in Oslo, still

---

[7] Schønheyder probably was theoretically the most ambitious Norwegian economist before Frisch. However, he was inadequately trained.

[8] Report from Frisch to the university, Frisch archives.

considered himself to be an economist and that he remained loyal to the fairly provincial group of economists in Oslo. Only 3 of his first 18 published works were in economics, however, and only one made a substantial contribution.

In the spring of 1924 Frisch was back in Oslo. In addition to research, he did some private tutoring. Some of Frisch's written preparations for that work have survived. They show how he used his teaching to educate himself more broadly in various fields ranging from mathematical statistics to economic history.[9]

4 Academic Positions at the University of Oslo

In 1925 Frisch became *universitetsstipendiat*[10] at the University of Oslo, thus joining the regular academic track at the university. In the autumn he lectured on graphical and analytical methods in economics.[11] In the spring of 1926 he organized classes in probability theory and mathematics. In the autumn he was exempted from regular lectures, but nevertheless held his first series of lectures in economics that were to become influential, namely, those in the mathematical theory of production.

In the autumn of 1925 Frisch actively participated in the Sixth Nordic Congress of Mathematicians, presenting two papers.[12] He was by then internationally recognized among European statisticians. Although he had not yet published internationally in economics, his interest in economics was already well known among the few mathematical economists in Europe.[13] In 1927 and the first part of 1928 Frisch toured the United States with a Rockefeller scholarship and became well known among American statisticians and mathematically inclined economists as well. Still the major bulk of his work was in mathematical statistics, but the focus had shifted from the study of mathematical distributions to time-series analysis.

In the meantime, Frisch received his doctoral degree from the Faculty of Science at the University of Oslo, October 16, 1926, published by the

---

[9] Frisch archives.
[10] Literally, "university scholarship," a scholarship that was granted by the university. In practice, it was not much different from an assistant professorship at an American university today. It was a temporary but very free position, with permission for travel and exemption from teaching duties being freely given.
[11] *University of Oslo, Annual Report 1925–26*. Students were not greatly interested in the lectures; only eight attended regularly, whereas 40–60 attended W. Keilhau's popular lectures.
[12] Frisch archives.
[13] Somewhat later, in July 1926, Slutsky wrote to Frisch that he had been told that in Italy, "pure economics is not studied eagerly any longer. It makes me happy to discover in your person an exponent of this science, since I am convinced that pure economics has a great future in store." Frisch archives (our translation from German).

Norwegian Academy of Sciences. The subject was mathematical statistics, and the title of his thesis was *Sur les semi-invariants et moments employés dans l'étude des distributions statistiques* (Frisch, 1926a). His formal qualification period had ended.

On March 16, 1928, Frisch was appointed *docent*[14] in economics and statistics at the University of Oslo. However, among his scientific contributions until then, as we have mentioned, the mathematical and statistical ones dominated. Except for the article about utility theory (Frisch, 1926b), an attempt to make one of Schønheyder's business-cycle theories precise (Frisch, 1927), and a methodological paper (Frisch, 1926c), Frisch had not published anything in economics. Nevertheless, the committee was not in doubt. Jaeger, who knew Frisch, wrote as follows:

> All Dr. Frisch's works indicate that however brilliant he masters his mathematics, it is for him only an instrument for solving the most difficult theoretical problems in economics. It is the questions of economics and statistics that have caught his scientific attention, and he possesses a thorough knowledge of both these sciences, where his knowledge of the literature is also very extensive.
>
> His output compared to his age bears witness to a passionate interest in science combined with an extraordinary working capacity.[15]

Frisch then, for the first time, remained for three semesters in a row at the university, giving lectures each semester. His lectures in basic economic theory were mimeographed (Frisch, 1929/30). Again the theory of production was central, but he also lectured extensively on the principles of stock-flow analysis. In addition, he shared with Schønheyder a series about business-cycle theory and statistics in the spring of 1929. During those three semesters he had some impact: Complaints were voiced that economics was becoming increasingly difficult.[16]

---

[14] *Docent* was a tenured position somewhat like an associate professorship. Frisch was competing with Kristian Schønheyder and Thomas Sinding. The evaluation committee was appointed by the Faculty of Law and consisted of O. Jaeger and I. Wedervang (who both taught economics at the university) and L. Birck (who was the only outsider, a professor in economics at the University of Copenhagen). The evaluation report probably was written mainly by Jaeger. The job description was changed from a position in "statistics" to "statistics and economics."

[15] *University of Oslo, Annual Report, 1927–28*, pp. 16–17 (our translation). Although Jaeger's evaluation proved to be true, it was not easy to reach that conclusion on the basis of Frisch's published works. Jaeger had read many of Frisch's unpublished works, however, including his examination reports, and knew about and believed in his aspirations.

[16] Ten years later, in a very polemic speech directed against the development that Frisch and Wedervang had headed, Sinding said that "after 1928 followed a gradual reshaping and extension of the '*statsøkonomisk*' exam. But this extension represents a dark chapter in the history of the University. From 1928 on, one breaks, without further ado, the law and the resolution addressed to the Faculty of Law, that regulate the size of the economics curriculum" (Sinding, 1939, p. 12, our translation). Sinding was then an associate professor with the special responsibility of teaching economics to law students.

Frisch again went abroad for the spring semester of 1930, serving as a visiting professor for one year at Yale University. He then taught at the University of Minnesota in the spring 1931. At Yale he experienced a burst of productive activity. In addition to all his research activities, he held at least four series of lectures: on the theory of production, methods of utility measurement, economic dynamics, and statistical verification. They were all typewritten and distributed, an output of more than 450 typewritten pages. In addition, he wrote articles and directed a research workshop on time-series analysis, where his own methods were applied to different kinds of data, including astronomic data.

While Frisch was abroad, Professor Jaeger and Professor Wedervang had begun an intensive campaign to establish a personal professorship for him in Oslo, a great honor.[17] Jaeger convinced Saeland, the *rektor* (president) of the university, to contact the prime minister to petition the government to establish a personal professorship for Frisch.[18] Jaeger and Wedervang succeeded. On June 5, 1931, Frisch was appointed professor at the University of Oslo, beginning July 1, 1931. He was elected a member of the Norwegian Academy of Sciences the same year.

Furthermore, early in 1932, the Institute of Economics at the University of Oslo was established, with Frisch and Wedervang serving as directors until 1941.

5 Organizational Aspects of Frisch's Research in the 1930s

Compared with an ordinary department, the Institute of Economics was a pure research entity, financed outside the university budget. Its main sponsor was the Rockefeller Foundation, which at a board meeting on December 15, 1931, granted $50,000 for the period 1932–37 (i.e., $10,000 per year, $5,000 being granted unconditionally, and $5,000 being granted on the condition that a similar amount be obtained from Norwegian sources).[19] At the time of the grant, the exchange rate was about 4 kroner

---

[17] In Norway, the procedure for appointing a professor used to be quite formal. In principle, there should be an open, public competition. Exemption would be granted only when a person was acknowledged to possess outstanding academic qualifications. Hence it was an extraordinary honor for Frisch to be appointed to a personal chair in economics and statistics.

[18] Letter from Jaeger to Frisch, December 19, 1930, Frisch archives. While not being a front-rank economist, Jaeger's openness of mind was exemplary. In the same letters in which he reported his efforts to have Frisch made a professor, he fiercely contested Frisch's criticism of the German economist Engländer. That criticism of Frisch was implicitly a criticism of Jaeger himself for lacking logical rigor. Furthermore, when Frisch was away, Jaeger actually lectured on Frisch's new theory of production for a whole semester.

[19] *University of Oslo, Annual Report, 1931–32.* Both Frisch and Wedervang had established good relations with central representatives of the Rockefeller Foundation, mainly because the foundation wanted to support modern, quantitatively oriented social sciences. A brief description of the major shifts in the research policies of the Rockefeller Foundation with respect to economics in the years between the wars has been presented

Norwegion (4NKr) to $1 (U.S.) so when a Norwegian research foundation, Norsk Varekrigsforsikrings Fond, granted 10,000 NKr, and its board assisted in getting a further 10,000 NKr from various private sources, the institute at the beginning was financed wholly from sources outside the university. That funding made it possible for Frisch to organize his empirical research as he desired. It required lots of calculations, and therefore, given the technology of the time, the process consumed much manpower.

The activity at the institute was often intense, but not yet on any large scale, as compared with other leading statistical laboratories at the time.[20] Partly through the efforts of the Rockefeller Foundation, the institute entertained a considerable number of foreign visitors, and some of them, such as T. C. Koopmans, stayed for fairly long periods. After 1937, activity increased further when the institute received new, additional funding from the Norsk Varekrigsforsikrings Fond and a few more economists had been trained and could be hired on a more permanent basis.

On October 15, 1936, the politically active industrialist Johan Throne Holst gave an important speech before The Norwegian Federation of Industries (Norges Industriforbund).[21] Holst repeated his proposal at a board meeting of the Norsk Varekrigsforsikrings Fond that "the board considers it to be of the utmost importance to acquire a survey of our production possibilities and their inner relationships" (our translation). The outcome of Holst's initiatives was that the Institute of Economics was asked to make such an overview and to initiate the first large-scale social-science research project in Norway, a project that was to become the starting point for the Norwegian national accounting system.

The institute received funds in 1936 for the purpose of developing a plan for the project, called "A Structural Survey of the Norwegian Economy" (Frisch, Keilhau, and Wedervang, 1936). The project started in earnest in 1937, when the private financing was matched by government funds. The total cost of the project was planned to be 200,000 NKr, a huge project for its time. The project was divided into four separate parts, where three were to investigate different industries and one was to be a coordination unit, headed by Frisch.[22] By March 4, 1938, 12

by Craver (1986), and for the social sciences in general, see Bulmer and Bulmer (1981). The policies of the Rockefeller Foundation were very important for the development of the social sciences in both Europe and the United States during the interwar years. We note that this foundation also showed up at the crossroads of Frisch's academic career.

[20] This is the impression gained from Koopmans's letter to Jan Tinbergen, August 21, 1935. Koopmans stayed in Oslo during the autumn semester, 1935. Albert Jolink, Erasmus Universiteit, Rotterdam, has kindly given us information on Koopmans's stay in Oslo.

[21] *Økonomisk orientering og videnskapelig forskning*, Norges Industriforbund, Oslo, 1936.

[22] The heads of the different departments were then Frisch, Keilhau, Wedervang, and Skaug. The project had a separate advisory board, appointed by Norsk Varekrigsforsikrings Fond, consisting mainly of leaders from various industries and a representative from the trade unions (Andvig, 1977, pp. 11–12).

economists were engaged in the project, in addition to the calculating staff.[23] This project bears witness to the entrepreneurial powers of both Wedervang and Frisch, although Throne Holst's contribution was also essential.

A later initiative by Throne Holst that eventually led to the creation of a separate Faculty of the Social Sciences, of which the Institute of Economics was to be a part, came to nothing at the time, largely because of the imminent threat of war.[24]

The Institute of Economics continued to receive support from the Rockefeller Foundation until the autumn of 1940, when Frisch and Wedervang had to ask the University of Oslo for money so that they would not have to discontinue work immediately.

6 Frisch's Teaching and the Study of Economics in Oslo in the 1930s

The first period when Frisch taught more or less continuously for a long period without any significant breaks was during the 1930s:

> When he started his work as professor at the University of Oslo ... it was as if the study of economics was shaken in its very foundations, at least when seen from the student's point of view.... In 1931 he thus began to lecture the partly bewildered students that if one would like to make any progress with economic analyses, one would first have to make the assumptions explicit, write down the model used for the reasoning, and stick to the assumptions throughout. [Haavelmo, 1974, pp. 2–3; our translation]

Frisch's lectures can be divided into at least two types. In one type he reported from his own research. Sometimes that produced excellent results. As an example, his lectures in macrodynamics, held in the autumn of 1933, were considered excellent and on the whole were accessible at

---

[23] "The Institute was to become a busy working place. As part of his work for the quantification of the economic relationships, Frisch needed to accomplish extensive numerical calculations. The calculation capacity was quite different from what the situation is today. At that time a large number of calculation assistants were sitting and turning the hand-driven calculator machines. Frisch even constructed a kind of weighing machine that could perform 180 multiplications simultaneously, a project worth a chapter on its own." (Haavelmo, 1974, p. 3; our translation).

[24] On November 1, 1938, Throne Holst (and other industrialists) asked the University of Oslo to appoint a committee to elucidate the future development of the social sciences in Norway. The university appointed a committee consisting of professors at the university and a secretary, Arvid Brodersen, on November 12, 1938 (*Universitetets Journal*, Universitetet i Oslos Arkiver, Journal nr. 2315–2629, Riksarkivet, Oslo). While Frisch was not formally a member of the committee, he became a consultant. According to Brodersen (interview with J. Andvig, February 1995), Frisch had a strong impact on the deliberations. The committee's report was delivered March 7, 1940, a month before the German occupation of Norway.

the level Frisch sought to develop among Norwegian students (Frisch, 1934b). They also made an impression at the international level, mainly through the leading Dutch economists, who picked up Norwegian easily. J. A. Schumpeter tried to learn Norwegian in order to read those lectures, but was less successful.[25]

However, sometimes his lectures could be very specialized and advanced. For example, Frisch began his lectures at the University of Oslo in the autumn of 1931 with a series on tensor analysis that continued in the spring and autumn of 1932.[26] In addition, that same autumn he gave a series of lectures on time-series analysis that were based on his own research efforts.

The last set of lectures that he started in the autumn of 1931, on the mechanics of markets, was somewhat different and marked the beginning of his teaching of basic microeconomic theory. Some of those lectures on microeconomics were also based on his own research, such as his axiomatic treatment of utility theory and his mathematical studies in the theory of production. But most of the lectures were based on the way Frisch himself had learned economic theory: He chose a couple of classic economic texts and formalized the more verbal parts in order to make them more accessible to students. The work he presented that way was mainly Marshall's *Principles* and Wicksell's *Lectures*. In the spring of 1932 he lectured on choice theory, and in the autumn on "polypoly" theory (i.e., the theory of different forms of noncompetitive markets). Later he lectured on Wicksell I, functional income distribution, tax incidence, Marshall, and so on. Most of the lectures were collected in mimeographed form (Frisch, 1939).

With regard to macroeconomics, his students were brought to the research frontier when Frisch, in the autumn of 1934 and the spring of 1935, discussed the recent works of Lindahl, Myrdal, Robertson, and Keynes. Those lectures probably were much more difficult, though they did not contain much mathematics (Andvig, 1986, ch. 6–8).

In addition to the traditional types of lectures, Frisch organized workshops for students involving computational exercises and even organized seminars in his home, where students were confronted with sets of written problems.[27]

---

[25] In a letter dated May 10, 1935, Schumpeter told Frisch that he had tried to learn Norwegian in order to understand Frisch's lectures: "With my teacher [of Norwegian] I read your lectures and I like them immensely. They open up an aspect of your scientific personality which is quite new to me, for one is a different man in one's papers and in one's lectures. They are, however, not mathematical enough to be understood without understanding the language, and as I never had the requisite time to do any exercises, my progress is very slow."

[26] Tensor analysis is based on a generalization of vectors. It had already been applied in the relativity theory of modern physics when Frisch lectured about it, but has only recently been applied in economics.

[27] One such set of tasks, to be discussed on the night of November 22, 1933, is found in the Frisch archives.

However pedagogical the major core of his lectures, the study of economics gradually became more demanding. Partly because of the perceived need for better-educated economists, and partly in order to increase the prestige of the field, that new situation was codified through a basic change in economics studies.

The prescribed length of the economics program was to increase from 2 to 5 years, and economics was to become an *embetseksamen* – a study that would allow the graduates to reach the highest ranks among public officials, if they were otherwise qualified. Those ranks the economics graduates had earlier been denied. To some extent the change only codified informal changes that had already taken place. For example, the typical length of study had changed from 2 to 3 years in the latter part of the 1920s.

The new study program was basically patterned on a Danish model and made it possible for Frisch "legally" to introduce a much more demanding curriculum, making the distance to the research frontier for the ablest students much shorter than before. The plans were accepted by the Norwegian parliament in 1934,[28] and the first cohort of students completed their final exams in 1939. The output of students dropped for a while, and only seven passed the test, less than one-third of the output in preceding years. Their education was much better, however.

Compared with the subjects contained in the older *statsøkonomisk eksamen*, the changes were not dramatic, but with respect to content they were considerable. First, the requirements for the compulsory introductory examination in mathematics were increased significantly. The same applied to the compulsory examinations in mathematical probability theory and statistics. Econometrics was formally introduced, and the student had to write a short econometric thesis before being allowed to pass the final examination. Some law studies were introduced, but kept to a minimum.

Finally we should note that parts of the study of economics could not cover the requirements for other degrees, so exit was costly. That made for student groups with rather dense internal networks and close and long-run student–teacher interactions. The qualification level of the graduates probably was somewhat above a master's degree at one of the better American universities at the time.

Those changes in examinations and curricula taking place during the 1930s after Frisch had become a full professor were very important in the longer run for the development of economics in Norway.

---

[28] The change in the study of economics at the University of Oslo was described in Ot. prp. nr. 15 (1934). In an addendum, Wedervang described the Swedish and Danish systems of university education in economics. See also Bergh and Hanisch (1984, ch. 4).

7 The War Years (1940–45)

During the first wartime years the university was harassed in various ways by the Nazi authorities. In 1941 the rector was removed from office and sent to prison, being replaced by a Nazi official. Despite such interference, the university functioned reasonably well until the fall of 1943. So in the first wartime years Frisch continued his research and teaching.

In the fall of 1940 he lectured on monetary theory and national accounting and also held an econometric seminar, where the students had their compulsory research papers in econometrics evaluated. In the spring of 1941 he lectured on macrodynamics and on regression and confluence analysis.[29] During the academic year 1940/41 he revised some earlier mimeographed student texts and completed mimeographed lecture notes on regression and confluence analysis.

In the fall of 1941 he lectured on optimum population, polypoly theory, and market operations. He also held an econometric seminar.[30] A treatise on optimum population was published in 1940, in Norwegian, and has not been translated into English (Frisch, 1940).

In the spring of 1942 he lectured on macroeconomics for a small group of students, but in the fall of 1942 the students stayed away from the university. Frisch then lectured for a small group of associates at the institute on the "ecocirc system,"[31] his national accounting system. In the spring of 1943 the students returned, and Frisch lectured on demand analysis (local and interlocal choice axioms, and so on).

In some departments of the university, admission was restricted by *numerus clausus*. The main criterion for admission was based on grades at the university entrance examination. In 1942 and 1943 the Ministry of Education decided that some Nazi students should be admitted, although they were not admitted, because of their low grades. In the fall of 1942 the deans of two faculties protested strongly against admissions according to political views. The issue was discussed in all faculties, and it was decided to urge the ministry to reject demands that were unacceptable to the university.

In the summer of 1943 the ministry announced new rules for student admission, rules that were not accepted by the university staff, and protests were sent to the ministry. On September 24, 1943, the deans were summoned to a meeting with the Nazi minister Skancke. He claimed that the deans had threatened a strike against the new admission regulations.

Frisch, being the dean of the Faculty of Law, 1942–44, was present

---

[29] *University of Oslo, Annual Report, 1940–41*, pp. 52–3.
[30] *University of Oslo, Annual Report, 1941–42*, p. 98.
[31] *University of Oslo, Annual Report, 1942–43*, p. 208.

at the meeting. From the minutes of the meeting[32] we quote the following:

> *Skancke*: I don't have to use the word "strike," I can use "sabotage." What's your stand, Professor Frisch?
> *Frisch*: First, regarding "strike" or "sabotage." Those who at the moment dispose of the instruments of power are of course in a position to interpret these notions quite at their own discretion and to act accordingly. They may treat those present as they see fit. We have to take the consequences of that and answer according to our conscience. We are convoked to this meeting in the capacity of deans, but are now requested to answer what we will do as individuals. This is a somewhat strange procedure, but all the same I will give you my personal answer. To me the essential point in this matter is not the detailed regulations in the statutes. I can very well imagine the possibility of statutes prescribing importance being attached also to other things than a certain score at the final secondary school examinations. But I lay stress on the point that all such considerations be expressed in the statutes, and in such a way that as far as possible personal judgments are eliminated.... But one has to see that whole matter in the context of the way it was forced through. We have seen how the ministry has tried to take into account political considerations, and we see today how the deans are submitted to interrogations, ascribing to us intentions we don't have. This is a procedure not warranted in a society governed by law. All this together makes me realize that the university, as a free, scientific and scholarly institution, is in danger. Thus the matter is turned into a question of conscience. The basis of my life's work is taken away, and then I cannot fail to draw the consequences, regardless of the results concerning my own person.
> *Skancke*: You know what you expose yourself to, Professor Frisch, you are a lawyer.
> *Frisch*: I am not a lawyer.

In October–November 1943 the Germans arrested some 1,100 to 1,200 students, of whom 700 were sent to German concentration camps. Many university professors were also arrested, but most of them were kept in prison camps in Norway. The university was closed. Frisch was arrested by the Germans on October 17, 1943.[33] He spent most of the time, together with other university staff members, in the large prison camp (concentration camp) Grini outside of Oslo, where he stayed until October 8, 1944. Grini was a place of torture and execution, but the university professors seem to have been treated comparatively well. At Grini, Frisch was in excellent company. Many of the university professors were there, including Odd Hassel, who in 1969 received the Nobel

---

[32] Elling (1961, pp. 176ff). The quotation is translated by Eilert Struksnes.
[33] He stayed October 17 to November 22, 1943, at Bredtvedt, November 22 to December 8, 1943, at Berg, and December 8, 1943 to October 8, 1944, at Grini. (Giertsen, 1946).

Prize in chemistry (Lange and Schreiner, 1946, p. 223). Some of the foremost Norwegian authors and artists were also at Grini. Several imprisoned professors gave lectures, often outdoors, and a type of "people's university" was created behind the prison walls (Lange and Schreiner, 1946, pp. 224–5).

8 A Plan for Postwar Training and Research

Soon after liberation from the German occupation, in December 1945 Frisch gave a speech that presented an ambitious plan for the future training of economists and future economic research in Norway (Frisch, 1945). The plan was developed in cooperation with some of his previous associates, Petter Jacob Bjerve, Stein Johnsen, Knut Getz Wold, and Olav Reiersøl.

He pointed out that when Norway was liberated, there was a group of young, highly qualified economists who could be allocated to important government posts, including reconstruction work. But the demand for well-trained economists far exceeded the supply, because of the overwhelming demands of reconstruction. First and foremost, that applied to the central-government administration, where they were needed for analysis and planning. It should be noted that among the main reasons for that situation was that Frisch had trained a new generation of economists with much better qualifications than earlier generations. Supply had created its own demand.

In the plan, Frisch outlined how this excess demand could be met. However, he asserted very strongly that it was necessary to take a longer perspective by ensuring satisfactory conditions for young economists to obtain scientific qualifications: "If we do not maintain the research activity, the source of new knowledge would dry up very quickly" (Frisch, 1945, p. 103; our translation).

He concluded that "an important element in the reconstruction in Norway today is as soon as possible to educate a sufficiently large and sufficiently well qualified group of young people who can devote themselves to free economic research and have at their disposal the necessary infrastructure at research institutes. This is necessary even from a very shortsighted evaluation of what is 'useful' for the society. It is hardly an exaggeration to say that the efficiency of this work will be decisive for how our economic and social future will materialize" (Frisch, 1945, p. 104; our translation).

Frisch went on to give his advice on establishing or strengthening research departments outside of the University of Oslo (e.g., at the Central Bureau of Statistics). However, his plans for research activity at the University of Oslo were his most far-reaching plans. For example, he suggested that about 15 percent of the students graduating with the *candidatus oeconomiae* degree should be given an opportunity to work for a period of 2–5 years as research associates at the Institute of Economics. There should be 2 years at the lowest level, and the best should be promoted to 3 more years at the higher level. That program probably was inspired by U.S. graduate-training programs.

He mentioned (Frisch, 1945, p. 107) that the institute owed a debt of gratitude to the Rockefeller Foundation and the Norsk Varekrigsforsikrings Fond. Some support had been obtained from the government for specific projects, and considerable sums had been received from private sources. However, he knew that such financing could not continue and that the financing had to be brought to a firmer basis.

He emphasized that a considerable part of the activity at the institute should concentrate on topics chosen by the institute. That would be necessary in order to stimulate and renew other parts of the institute's activities and to keep in close contact with international research. He mentioned that before the war, many foreign researchers had visited the institute for up to a year to study and do research, and that had provided mutual stimulation and should be encouraged again.

As will be seen in the following, most of the plans outlined by Frisch in that speech were actually carried out in the postwar period.

9   The Decision Models

In this essay we are not going to discuss Frisch's postwar scientific contributions, but only his role as a research director, heading a group of associates at his institute. During the postwar period Frisch concentrated on the development of multisectoral decision models for managing the economy, as well as the principles of economic planning. He outlined the mathematical structures for the models and used his staff to modify the models and provide estimates for the coefficients. The first model was the sub-model (see Section 11), which was a fairly well aggregated model to be applied for short-term policy.

The kernel for all of Frisch's later multisectoral models was an input–output model of the Leontief type.[34] He built his models around that kernel, extending it in different directions. Every extension resulted in a particular version of his decision model (Edvardsen, 1970, pp. 189ff.). Let us briefly indicate the main features of his subsequent decision models.

The Median Model. The median model was an input–output model expanded by income flows and consumer demand. It gave inspiration for construction of the MODIS models of the Central Bureau of Statistics that have been much used in planning work in Norway.

---

[34] A simple forerunner of the Leontief model was included in "circulation planning" (Frisch, 1934a).

The Refi Model. In this model, real and financial flows were integrated into one model structure. The focus was on the financing of real investment. The model was constructed before the later rapid development of portfolio theory, and many of its behavioral assumptions can be questioned.

Oslo Channel Model. The purpose of this model was to develop an instrument for optimal national-investment planning, taking into account that investment projects compete for the same scarce resources and create new production capacities.

Present at meetings for planning the model research was the research staff, including some student members. In addition, various specialists were sometimes invited (e.g., economists from the Ministry of Finance and from the Central Bureau of Statistics, or from various industries or industrial organizations). Records of the meetings have been kept.[35] Each participant had to report on work done since the last meeting, on problems encountered in the empirical work, and so on. Each meeting concluded with Frisch drawing up a plan for further work.

The attempts at calibration of the coefficients for the aforementioned models kept many researchers and research assistants busy during the period from around 1950 into the 1960s. In many cases the models needed data that could not be extracted from the national accounts, and a variety of sources and calibration techniques had to be used. Some of the work was tedious, but nevertheless represented an important part of the postgraduate training for those who would later become economics professors, researchers, or government economists. Other types of work for Frisch provided a different type of training (e.g., writing memoranda based on his lectures, or assisting him in preparing his scientific publications). Some of the assistants also worked for Haavelmo or had scholarships under his guidance. And it should not be forgotten that the postgraduate training at the institute was supplemented by participation in the extremely inspiring Saturday-morning seminars in economics and econometrics in Haavelmo's office, where no stone was left unturned.

In addition to outlining the models and directing his crew of model workers, Frisch was very much occupied with the philosophy of planning, with study of politicians' preferences, and with optimization techniques. Of these three areas, it was only in the last that he cooperated with collaborators to any great extent, at the institute and at the Norwegian Computing Center.

Frisch was an inspiring but also a very demanding research director. He was so enthusiastic a scientist that he worked almost day and night.

---

[35] See, e.g., "Forskningsplanmøte 26. juni 1953 om desisjonsmodellen" (research-plan meeting, June 26, 1953, about the decision model), memorandum, September 4, 1953, from the Institute of Economics, University of Oslo.

He did not always understand that his assistants and secretaries did not necessarily fully share his enthusiasm and were not always eager to extend the workday at the institute into the late evening or even into the night. There are also many stories about Frisch inviting his collaborators to his home for nighttime work.

Most of the time, four to seven economists worked on his model projects. That was not nearly enough to cover the vast data needs of his models, but it still required more financing than most other economics projects, at least in Norway.

10 Improved Funding for Research

The Rockefeller Foundation continued to play an important role in financing research projects at the institute in the postwar period. From the fiscal year 1946/47 onward, until 1960/61, the foundation gave an annual grant for research on repercussion studies and decision models. The size of the contribution was at the outset $10,000 annually, and in later years slightly lower.[36] That does not appear a sizable amount of money today, but at the time it sufficed to pay the wages of several research assistants. In addition, the Rockefeller Foundation provided scholarships for study and research in the United States for many of Frisch's and Haavelmo's associates. The last grant was in 1964–65.

In fiscal year 1945/46 the Institute of Economics received its first regular allocation on the university budget. But in all the years since its establishment in 1932 it had de facto operated as a university institute. The research was mainly privately financed, but some research projects at the institute had received government support. In addition, the institute was located in university buildings, and the wages of some of the staff members of the institute (e.g., Professor Frisch) were paid by the university. However, the institute was not represented in the annual reports of the university prior to 1945/46.

The Norwegian Council for Research in Science and the Humanities was established in 1950 and supported Frisch's work on repercussion studies and decision models every year from 1950 until he retired in 1965.[37] Most of the support went to the collection and processing of the data needed as inputs in his large-scale multisectoral models. Some funds also went to computational work. The annual funding varied, but usually was of the order of financing two researchers or research assistants and one clerical or computational assistant, plus some overhead.

After his retirement in 1965, Frisch continued his work on decision models, including study of the preferences of politicians. However, his research focused increasingly on nonlinear programming problems that

---

[36] Institute archives: "Instituttets Rockefeller-prosjekter."
[37] Institute archives: 57.0, "Instituttets NAVF-prosjekter."

arose in connection with seeking optimal solutions to his decision models. He was so fascinated with these optimization problems that they occupied most of his time. From 1965 until his death in 1973 he worked on these problems, in cooperation with assistants at the institute and in particular with mathematicians and programmers at the Norwegian Computing Center, which had installed some of the first electronic computers in Norway. The Norwegian Council for Research in Science and the Humanities supported his projects on nonconvex programming methods and macroeconomic decision analysis.[38] In 1966 and 1967 the council provided funds for one economist, one programmer, and one calculation assistant. The funding continued until his death in 1973, but on a gradually reduced scale. Much of his work on optimization methods was left unpublished. There is a possibility that the rapid advances in computer technology have made some of his results obsolete.

The research activity at the institute was also funded in part by a number of paid research projects and consultations on economics and statistics. Two projects deserve particular mention. In 1945, the main labor union (Landsorganisasjonen i Norge) carried out a household-consumption study, and the institute was made responsible for processing and analyzing the raw data. It was before the age of electronic computers and modern data processing, and up to 100 students were engaged in the data extraction and processing.[39] That was a way of providing the students with some income as well as some training in data processing and statistical work.

In 1956 the institute was asked by a group of Norwegian hydroelectric companies to analyze the optimal use of electricity in Norway, and an elaborate programming model was designed and calibrated.[40]

11   Postwar Teaching

When the German occupation ended in May 1945, the University of Oslo was reopened. The teaching of Frisch in the postwar period (i.e., in the 20 years until he retired in 1965) can roughly be classified into three main areas:

1. research-based teaching on the design of macroeconomic models and planning
2. various topics in economic theory (e.g., revisiting some of his main research areas of the 1930s)
3. mathematical statistics

A considerable part of Frisch's teaching was based on the main research projects at the institute (i.e., the building of large-scale multisectoral

---

[38] Institute archives: 57.1, "Professor Frisch's NAVF-prosjekter etter 1965."
[39] *University of Oslo, Annual Report, 1945–46*, p. 336.
[40] *University of Oslo, Annual Report, 1955–56*, p. 885.

models, so-called decision models) and on the use of optimization methods in economic planning.

In the spring term of 1947 and in both terms of 1949 he lectured on repercussion problems. To a large extent those lectures were based on his model work for the United Nations on price-wage-tax policies as instruments in maintaining optimal employment (Frisch, 1949). That was the so-called *sub-model*, a fairly well aggregated macroeconomic model with many degrees of freedom and many policy instruments. He performed experiments by dividing the students into groups, each representing the viewpoint of a different political party. He asked each group to present a policy menu (e.g., tax rates and subsidies) and then used the model to derive the implications of the choices of instruments for prices, employment, and so on. That was described in a number of memoranda from the Institute of Economics during October and November of 1949.

Later his attention shifted to the multisectoral planning models mentioned earlier. He lectured on applications of standard input–output models, as well as a variety of much more sophisticated planning models (median model, channel model, and refi model).[41] He talked enthusiastically about how the models could be used for economic planning using an optimization approach.

Sometimes he revisited the research areas where he had made pioneering contributions in the 1920s and early 1930s. One of those areas was utility theory and demand theory, to which he returned in the fall of 1946 and the spring of 1958. Another such area was macrodynamics – following up on his work in the 1930s on propagation and impulse problems (lectures in the fall of 1945 and fall of 1955). Some of those lectures were at a very advanced level, and many students felt that those lectures were beyond their comprehension and probably beyond what would be required at examination. Therefore, attendance was not very high.

Students often asked Frisch to lecture on the basis of some of the textbooks on their reading lists. At times he agreed to do so; however, he rarely followed the text of the textbook, but used it as an inspiration for his own ideas. Occasionally he took off in very special directions. In 1947 he gave lectures based on Oscar Lange's book *Price Flexibility and Employment*, and we have been told that it was a memorable experience. But at the end of the term he had reached only page 7 of Lange's book.

After Haavelmo's appointment in 1948, he covered more and more of the general economic theory and econometrics, with Frisch concentrating mainly on teaching related to his own research on macroeconomic decision models.

In the early 1950s the students were using rather outdated textbooks in mathematical statistics. It was decided that Frisch and Haavelmo should give lectures on modern statistical theory and have the lectures

---

[41] Lectures in fall 1951, spring 1952, fall 1952, fall 1953, fall 1954, fall 1958, and so on.

mimeographed. Frisch laid out a plan for the contents of a textbook in mathematical statistics and statistical inference, adapted for students of economics. However, he became so interested in particular problems that his writings on the various topics did not always match the needs of the students. Instead of covering each subject in a textbook style adapted to students who needed to know the basics of statistics and statistical inference, he wrote extensive memoranda on each subject. Some of those gave excellent expositions of the most modern statistical theory at that time, but they went too far for his audience.

At his best, Frisch was an eminent teacher, at least for the better students, but very often the teacher had to give way to the scientist, always on the outlook for solutions to intricate theoretical problems. A lecture could then slide so close to the research frontier and so deeply into specialties that, at best, only the brightest in the audience could follow him. In his later years it happened that the lecture was moved to his office with his dictaphone and a few surviving students.

In the first postwar years, a number of foreign scholars stayed for longer periods at the institute. One of them was Lawrence Klein, who stayed for most of the academic year 1947–48. Among them were also the Danes Poul Nørregaard Rasmussen (September 1947–June 1948) and Sven Danø (January–June 1950). They have described Frisch as a teacher (Danø/Nørregaard Rasmussen, 1973, p. 7; our translation):

> As a teacher he could be unbelievably inspiring. In some periods he could minimize teaching, and even neglect it if his bees in southern Norway (a dear hobby) needed him. But suddenly he was there and announced a lecture. It could start at 9 o'clock and continue during most of the day. Big, heavy, and enthusiastic, he was sitting at the edge of the desk – or standing at the blackboard, gradually quite white from chalk – and he hammered interest and enthusiasm for the topic into the audience. None who has ever witnessed it will ever forget it. On such a day he could easily lecture for 8 hours with one short break. And he could finish with a message that his assistants at the institute should meet him in an hour. After that he could continue untiring until late, when public transport had long since discontinued service.

12   From Institute and Section to Department of Economics

During most of Frisch's time as professor (1931–65) an important characteristic of the organizational pattern for economics at the University of Oslo was that the main research unit (the Institute of Economics) operated relatively independently of the teaching unit.

Economics belonged to the Faculty of Law until July 1, 1963, when the Faculty of Social Sciences was established. The main decisions regarding the teaching of economics, doctoral degrees, appointments, and so on were taken by the Faculty Council at the Faculty of Law. However, as the number of students of economics increased, it became necessary to organize a separate administrative unit.

On October 21, 1947, the four professors of economics decided to establish an Economics Section of the Faculty of Law, to provide preparatory treatments of issues relevant to the economists before they were handled by the Faculty Council, and to treat other matters of interest to economists and students of economics.

The Institute of Economics provided the section with secretarial assistance, but apart from that the Economics Section and the Institute of Economics remained two separate units, the institute being almost exclusively a research unit. But there were many types of overlap (e.g., the institute produced teaching materials, and some of the teachers took part in institute research projects).

The first meeting of the Economics Section was held February 2, 1948, with Frisch writing the minutes! Professor Einarsen was elected chairman and remained chairman as long as the section existed (October 1966), at which time the research unit was merged with the section into a Department of Economics.

The Institute of Economics (established in 1932) was a separate entity with its own administration. Frisch and Wedervang were both directors until 1941, and from 1941 until he retired from his professorship in 1965 Frisch was the sole director.

There is no doubt that having a separate research institute alongside the unit responsible for teaching and other matters suited Frisch very well and permitted him to carry out his large research projects relatively undisturbed by bureaucratic regulations. In the administration of the institute he benefited in the 1930s from Professor Wedervang's organizatorial talents, and during and after the war from office manager Sven Vigger's eminent administrative capabilities.

13   Concluding Remarks

We began this essay by discussing Frisch's decision in 1931 to stay at the provincial University of Oslo rather than accept a professorship at Yale. Looking back, that does not seem to have hampered his scientific career. First, it by no means cut off his international contacts and engagements. With Oslo as his base, he was extremely active in establishing the Econometric Society and *Econometrica*, and he was the editor of *Econometrica* from 1933 to 1955, only interrupted by a period during World War II.

Second, whereas in his younger days he had to go abroad to meet colleagues, after 1932 many of the best scholars visited his institute in Oslo. But in addition to that he traveled widely, giving lectures and attending conferences in many countries, and in his later years working as an expert in developing countries.

Third, his choice for Oslo did not cut him off from research funding. His ties with the Rockefeller Foundation, which began with a scholarship in 1927, continued through most of his lifetime.

While keeping up his intensive international activities, at the same time he succeeded in revolutionizing the curricula in economics at the University of Oslo, educating a new breed of economists trained in quantitative methods. In addition, he supplied postgraduate training for the best students at his large-scale research projects. Through his own writings, and even more through his pupils, he had a strong impact on economic policy-making in Norway. It is conceivable that the influence also went in the opposite direction: that the Norwegian economic, social, and cultural environment influenced his choice of research areas (e.g., his strong emphasis on economic planning).

References

Andvig, J. C. (1977). *Den historiske bakgrunnen til Frisch's analyse av forholdet sak og vurdering*. Memorandum fra Sosialøkonomisk Institutt, Universitetet i Oslo, 21. april.
  (1986). *Ragnar Frisch and the Great Depression*. Oslo: Norwegian Institute of International Affairs.
Bergh, T., and Hanisch, T. J. (1984). *Vitenskap og politikk*. Oslo: Aschehoug.
Bulmer, M., and Bulmer, J. (1981). Philanthropy and social science in the 1920s: Beardsley Ruml and the Laura Spelman Rockefeller Memorial, 1922–29. *Minerva* 19:347–407.
Craver, E. (1986). Patronage and the direction of research in economics: the Rockefeller Foundation in Europe, 1924–1938. *Minerva* 24:205–22.
Danø, S., and Nørregaard Rasmussen, P. (1973). Ragnar Frisch, 3. marts 1895–31. januar 1973. *Nationaløkonomisk Tidsskrift* 11:3–8.
Edvardsen, K. (1970). A survey of Ragnar Frisch's contributions to the science of economics. *De Economist* 118:175–208.
Elling, J. (1961). Universitetet under okkupasjonen. In: *Universitetet i Oslo 1911–1961*, vol. 2. Oslo: Universitetsforlaget.
Frisch, R. (1926a). Sur les semi-invariants et moments employés dans l'étude des distributions statistiques. *Skrifter utgitt av Det Norske Videnskapsakademi i Oslo, II*, Hist. Filos. Klasse no. 3, pp. 1–87.
  (1926b). Sur un problème d'économie pure. *Norsk Matematisk Forenings Skrifter*, series I, no. 16, pp. 1–40.
  (1926c). Kvantitativ formulering av den teoretiske økonomikks lover. *Statsøkonomisk Tidsskrift* 40:299–334.
  (1927). Sammenhaengen mellem primaerinvestering og reinvestering. *Statsøkonomisk Tidsskrift* 41:117–52.
  (1929/30). Referat av Dr. Frisch's forelesninger over teoretisk økonomikk. Høstsemestret 1928 og vårsemestret og høstsemestret 1929. Mimeographed manuscript.
  (1934a). Circulation planning. *Econometrica* 2:258–336, 422–38.

(1934b). Forelesninger holdt 1933 II og 1934 I over makrodynamikk. Mimeographed manuscript. Oslo: Ssss-trykk.
(1939). Notater til grunnkursus i økonomisk teori. Mimeographed manuscript. Oslo: Ssss–trykk.
(1940). Befolkningsoptimum. *Statsøkonomisk Tidsskrift* 54:157–219.
(1945). Økonomisk forskning og undervisning i Norge. *Statsøkonomisk Tidsskrift* 59:101–12.
(1949). Price-wage-tax policies as instruments in maintaining optimal employment. Memorandum, March 28. Institute of Economics, University of Oslo.
(1970). From Utopian theory to practical applications: the case of econometrics. In: *Les Prix Nobel en 1969*. Stockholm: Nobel Foundation.
Frisch, R., Keilhau, W., and Wedervang, I. (1936). *Plan til økonomisk strukturoversikt for Norge*. Oslo: Fabritius & Sønners Boktrykkeri.
Giertsen, B. R. (1946). *Norsk fangeleksikon. Grinifangene*. Oslo: Cappelen.
Haavelmo, T. (1974). Minnetale over professor, dr. philos. Ragnar Frisch. In: *Det Norske Videnskapsakademi i Oslo, Årbok 1973*.
Lange, E., and Schreiner, J. (eds.) (1946). *Griniboken*, vol. 1. Oslo: Gyldendal Norsk Forlag.
Sinding, T. (1939). Det socialøkonomiske studium – kritikk og forslag. *Statsøkonomisk Tidsskrift* 53:11–29.

CHAPTER 2

Ragnar Frisch and the Foundation of the Econometric Society and *Econometrica*

Olav Bjerkholt

1 Introduction

The Econometric Society was founded December 29, 1930. The constitutional assembly, or organization meeting, was held in the Statler Hotel, Cleveland, Ohio, during the annual joint meeting of American academic associations.[1] Sixteen persons who were participating in one or another of the professional-association meetings took part in the organization meeting. The organizing group comprised 11 Americans (Harold Hotelling, Frederick C. Mills, William F. Ogburn, J. Harvey Rogers, Charles F. Roos, Malcolm C. Rorty, Henry Schultz, Walter A. Shewhart, Carl Snyder, Norbert Wiener, Edwin B. Wilson) and 5 Europeans, of whom 3 were Norwegians (Ragnar Frisch, Oystein Ore, Ingvar Wedervang) and two Austrians (Karl Menger, Joseph Schumpeter).[2] The Americans present were all prominent members of the American Economic Association, the American Statistical Association, or the American Mathematical Society. Ragnar Frisch was associate professor of economics and statistics at the University of Oslo and had spent 1930 as a visiting professor at Yale University. Oystein Ore, a brilliant Norwegian mathematician affiliated with Yale University since 1929, had earlier in the same day chaired a joint session of the American

---

With kind permission from the publisher, I have borrowed freely from my introduction to *The Foundations of Modern Econometrics: The Selected Essays of Ragnar Frisch* (Frisch, 1995). I am most grateful for numerous suggested improvements from an anonymous referee. All letters quoted are from the Ragnar Frisch correspondence deposited at the Department of Manuscripts of the University of Oslo Library, to whose librarians I owe sincere thanks. Letters are referred to as "sender/addressee, date."

[1] There is no comprehensive source for the events that led to the foundation of the Econometric Society. Some of those who took part in the preparation of the new organization have left incomplete memoirs of the events: Divisia (1953), Frisch (1970), and Roos (1948). A brief history is given by Christ (1983). The foundation is also mentioned in recent works on the history of econometrics, e.g., Morgan (1990).

[2] According to Christ (1983) and Roos (1948), there were 12 Americans present; the discrepancy must have been due to Oystein Ore being counted as an American.

Mathematical Society and the American Statistical Association where Ragnar Frisch had presented a paper (Frisch, 1931). Ingvar Wedervang was one of only two full professors of economics in Norway at the time. Joseph Schumpeter was visiting at Harvard University, preparing for his move to the United States 3 years later. Karl Menger, mathematician and economist, was the son of Carl Menger.

Joseph Schumpeter was elected chairman of the meeting. Ragnar Frisch had drafted a constitution that was adopted with minor revisions, the draft being "based on ideas which had been obtained in an extensive correspondence carried on by himself, Professor Fisher, and Professor Roos, with economists and statisticians throughout the world" (*Econometrica* 1:71). Schumpeter's motion that the society be considered as founded was accepted unanimously at 10:00 P.M. The meeting proceeded to elect the first president and council of the society. Irving Fisher, notably absent from the meeting, was elected president. Apparently Fisher had expected Schumpeter to become the first president.[3] Frisch reported to Divisia that "the meeting played a trick on [Fisher] by electing him president" (Frisch/Divisia, January 13, 1931).

The council members elected were seven Europeans and three Americans. In addition to Fisher, the first council consisted of Charles F. Roos and Edwin B. Wilson from the United States and the European members Luigi Amoroso, Ladislaus von Bortkiewicz, Arthur L. Bowley, François Divisia, Ragnar Frisch, Joseph Schumpeter, and Wl. Zawadzki.

Was the founding of the Econometric Society an important event in the history of econometrics (apart from the consideration that the term "econometrics" might not have achieved quite the same general usage without the foundation of the society)? An unusual feature of the founding of the Econometric Society as an international scientific association was that the very discipline to be promoted (i.e., econometrics) was not well defined. The word "econometrics" was not in the dictionaries, and few had come across the word in writing. The society was at the outset without any financial resources apart from membership fees, and it failed in its first efforts at finding sponsors for a worthy cause.

The founders and early members of the new organization may have had somewhat different visions and aims for the new vehicle, and perhaps also different motives for joining. In the midst of the new society was a small but dedicated group of economists who had a view of the future development of economics as a science that in the ensuing years would come to exert a strong influence. One of those was Ragnar Frisch.

Ragnar Frisch played an important role in the development of the new organization in three major ways: First, Frisch had played an important role in promoting the idea of an econometric association since 1926,

---

[3] Some still think that he was; see Hendry and Morgan (1995, pp. 4, 8).

and he had an active part in preparing the ground for the foundation. Second, Frisch played a major role in the organization of the early Econometric Society meetings in Europe and was an energetic participant at most of them. Third, Frisch was elected the first editor-in-chief of the society's journal *Econometrica*, and he held that influential position throughout the formative years of the new association and journal.

Frisch was, perhaps more than anyone else, a forceful initiator of the new international organization and journal and was recognized as such by his co-founders. The period in which Frisch gave much of his time and energy to further the econometric cause through organizational and editorial efforts (i.e., from 1926 until the outbreak of World War II) coincided with his most productive period as an econometrician. His contribution to the foundation of econometrics is well recognized and has received increasing attention over the past decade.[4]

In the following sections we shall review some aspects of the foundation and the formative years of the Econometric Society and *Econometrica* and the role of Ragnar Frisch in those endeavors, paying only incidental attention to his scientific contributions in those years.

2   The Birth of Econometrics

What was the discipline to be promoted by the newly founded society? The constitution adopted at the organization meeting carried the subtitle that would forever accompany the name of the society as a motto and explanation of the meaning of econometrics: "... the advancement of economic theory in its relation to statistics and mathematics." Regarded as a definition, that hardly mediated a perfectly clear concept of what econometrics was to be. It established, however, the priority of economic theory over mathematics and statistics within the new interdisciplinary field.

Paragraph one of the constitution elaborated upon the motto by stating that the object of the society should be to "promote studies that aim at a unification of the theoretical-quantitative and the empirical-quantitative approach to economic problems and that are penetrated by constructive and rigorous thinking similar to that which has come to dominate in the natural sciences. Any activity which promises ultimately to further such unification of theoretical and factual studies in economics shall be within the sphere of interest of the Society."

The meaning of "econometrics" as stated in the constitution drafted by Ragnar Frisch bears a striking resemblance to formulations used by Frisch in 1926, when he was drafting his ideas for research in economics. In that year he also coined the term "econometrics." The essay "*Sur un*

---

[4] See, e.g., Epstein (1987), de Marchi and Gilbert (1989), Morgan (1990), and Hendry and Morgan (1995).

problème d'économie pure" by Ragnar Frisch appeared in a series issued by the Norwegian Mathematical Association (and would hardly have reached many within the profession without Frisch's own initiative in distributing it to a large number of international contacts in a dozen countries). It was Frisch's first published article in economics and a forceful demonstration of his econometric ideas. The essay had been largely completed in Paris in 1923, but not published, as Frisch's intention was to gather more statistical material for application of the theoretical methods for measuring utility expounded in the essay.

The essay would deserve a place in the history of economics solely on the basis of its opening paragraph, which introduced the first of Frisch's many contributions to the terminology of the discipline:

> Intermédiaire entre les mathématiques, la statistique et l'économie politique, nous trouvons une discipline nouvelle que l'on peut, faute de mieux, désigner sous le nom de *l'économétrie*. L'économétrie se pose le but de soumettre les lois abstraites de l'economie politique théorique ou l'économie 'pure' à une vérification expérimentale et numeriques, et ainsi de constituer, autant que cela est possible, l'economie pure en une science dans le sens restreint de ce mot. [Frisch, 1926a, p. 1][5]

From then on, Frisch began to introduce "econometric" and "econometrics" in his communications with economists and statisticians, while at the same time trying to delineate the proper meaning of "econometrics."[6]

2.1 *The Roots of Econometrics*

In his draft for paragraph one of the constitution of the Econometric Society Frisch had distinguished between the theoretical-quantitative and the empirical-quantitative approaches to economic problems. In that context the theoretical-quantitative approach meant something more precise than mathematically formulated economic theory, and the meaning was clearly related to what was at the time subsumed under "mathematical economics," a term that had been in use for decades. Frisch had identified himself as a mathematical economist in 1926 and

---

[5] The essay was translated into English by John S. Chipman (Frisch, 1971); the quoted passage is rendered as follows: "Intermediate between mathematics, statistics, and economics, we find a new discipline, which for lack of a better name, may be called *econometrics*. Econometrics has as its aim to subject abstract laws of theoretical political economy or 'pure' economics to experimental and numerical verification, and thus to turn pure economics, as far as possible, into a science in the strict sense of the word" (Frisch, 1971, p. 386).

[6] To the history of the term "econometrics" belongs the discovery in 1934 that it had been coined in German (*Oekonometrie*) by Pawel Ciompa in 1910 in the sense of bookkeeping (*Econometrica* 4:95). It may nevertheless seem like a mild anachronism when Hendry and Morgan (1995) refer to the "econometrics fraternity" of 1910 (p. 12).

had established contacts with many of the same designation through correspondence and his travels in France, Great Britain, and Switzerland.

Frisch was well versed in the major works of the pioneers in mathematical economics, on the foundations of which he wanted to build. The predecessors he would most frequently refer to were Augustin Cournot, Léon Walras, Stanley Jevons, Vilfredo Pareto, Knut Wicksell, Alfred Marshall, and Irving Fisher. Frisch had particularly strong affinity and admiration for Sweden's Knut Wicksell (whom he never met, although he once had heard Wicksell lecture in Oslo). Irving Fisher's doctoral thesis *Mathematical Investigations in the Theory of Value and Prices* from 1892 exerted great influence on Frisch, who had acquired the French edition in Paris in 1922 as a guide for theoretical-quantitative investigations. Fisher was thus a forerunner and a generation older than Frisch, but he became a friend and colleague with whom Frisch did joint research at Yale in 1930, and they worked closely in conducting the affairs of the Econometric Society and *Econometrica*. Fisher's thesis was not simply a great work in mathematical economics; it also included a history of mathematical economics and a bibliography, building on earlier efforts by Jevons. Fisher's hero, above others, was Augustin Cournot, whose 1838 treatise Fisher had supervised the translation of in the United States in 1897 and supplied with a 37-page bibliography of mathematical economics from 1711 until 1897.

When Fisher reissued Cournot's book in 1927, he wrote in the foreword that "since the book first appeared in English, the mathematical method has become so general in economic and statistical studies that no attempt has been made to bring the bibliography down to date by adding the many items which would be necessary; and there is today little need, as there was then, to emphasize the value of the method, as it is now seldom, if ever, challenged" (Cournot, 1927, p. vii).

In spite of that remark to the effect that the promotion of mathematical economics was a battle already won, it was regarded as a major problem by mathematical economists in several countries that the use of mathematics was severely restricted in the economic journals and in the teaching of economics. Many mathematical economists also shared the opinion that much of the nonmathematical economics, as printed and taught, did not meet a scientific standard with regard to theoretical rigor and logical consistency.

With regard to the empirical-quantitative approach, there were few historical antecedents. Frisch clearly had, in 1926, a conception of method and direction in empirical research. In the "*Sur un problème*" essay he characterized his effort as "an attempt to realize the dream of Jevons" in measuring marginal utility. He argued that economic theory needed to be restated by means of mathematics, both to be given a higher level of precision and as a prerequisite for quantitative analysis by means of statistical methods. The "*Sur un problème*" essay was a powerful demonstration of Frisch's unification ideas. The problem was to define "utility," as introduced by Jevons, in sufficiently operational terms to allow quantitative estimation from available data.

But also on the empirical side Frisch may have got a cue from Fisher, who showed in his 1892 thesis how the marginal-utility curve (for sugar) could be constructed from a series of hypothetical observations, adding "to do this statistically is of course quite a different thing and more difficult though by no means hopeless proceeding" (Fisher, 1892, p. 20). In Frisch's copy (of the French edition) the latter part of the sentence is underlined!

Frisch ended his *"Sur un problème"* essay programmatically as follows:

> It is to be hoped that there will be an ever increasing amount of research on utility curves as well as on the laws of production. I believe that economic theory has arrived at a point in its development where the appeal to quantitative empirical data has become more necessary than ever. At the same time its analyses have reached a degree of complexity that require the application of a more refined scientific method than that employed by the classical economists. [Frisch, 1971, p. 417]

2.2   *The Making of an International Organization*

As early as 1912, while he was vice-president of the American Association for the Advancement of Science, Irving Fisher apparently had made an attempt at establishing a group of economists interested in mathematics, but without success.[7] In 1926 both Fisher and Frisch, independently of each other, took initiatives to promote contacts among mathematical economists, which prepared the ground for the foundation of the Econometric Society. Fisher wrote in early 1926 to the heads of all departments of economics he could think of, asking for the names of "young mathematical-economists," and he prepared a list on the basis of the material he received.[8]

During his stay in Paris in 1921–23 Frisch had become acquainted with François Divisia, 11 years his senior, and the two continued to correspond.[9] Frisch had sent Divisia his *"Sur un problème"* essay, and Divisia

---

[7] According to Roos (1948, p. 127), Fisher wanted a group that would "stimulate the development of economic theory in its relation to statistics and mathematics," while Christ (1983, p. 3) states that Fisher had attempted to organize "a society to promote research in quantitative and mathematical economics." Both formulations may have been influenced by hindsight, and Fisher's initiative remains obscure.

[8] What Fisher did with the list in 1926 is unknown. He sent the list to Frisch in 1931 during the drive to enroll charter members in the Econometric Society. The list comprised 261 names, of which only a few, the foremost being Alvin H. Hansen (Minnesota) and Jakob Marschak (Heidelberg), became members of the society.

[9] Divisia was a prolific letter writer. It was not unusual for him to write Frisch two letters on the same day. He had a peculiar habit of first filling the page and then adding extra sentences around the margins.

was one of those who had responded to Fisher's letter with a list of names. Fisher's initiative may have led Divisia to raise with Frisch the possibilities for providing better means for communication among mathematical economists. Frisch was very enthusiastic about Divisia's suggestions and wrote back to Divisia in September 1926 proposing both a new organization ("Association internationale d'économie pure") and a journal. Frisch mentioned names of economists in Spain, Germany, Hungary, Sweden, Denmark, the United States, Russia, Greece, Bulgaria, Belgium, the United Kingdom, Italy, France, and Czechoslovakia whom he had met, corresponded with, or exchanged papers with. He would move ahead by asking their opinions about an organization and a journal.[10]

Divisia suggested a more stepwise approach, by first establishing a "cercle restraint" of interested mathematical economists for communication among themselves, and later considering the creation of an international association. Divisia expressed enthusiasm for Frisch's suggested name for a journal. Divisia set out his views and ideas at some length and so convincingly that Frisch translated into English a long excerpt from Divisia's letter and enclosed it with his own letter to four other economists he decided to consult.

The four economists who in November 1926 received similarly phrased letters from Frisch (in three different languages!) were Ladislaus von Bortkiewicz in Berlin, Arthur L. Bowley in London, Charles Jordan in Budapest, and Eugen Slutsky in Moscow. They were all Frisch's seniors, Slutsky by 15 years, the others by around 25 years. Why these men? Why no others? Frisch may have wanted to probe his and Divisia's ideas with these four men whose work he knew and admired and whom he must have regarded as quite influential in their respective countries. He did not write to anyone in the United States, as he was about to leave for New York with a fellowship from the Laura Spelman Rockefeller Memorial. He mentioned in the letter to his four chosen correspondents his hopes for finding support among American economists for the idea of taking organizational steps to promote mathematical economics or "pure economics," as he then preferred. He may also have nurtured a hope of eliciting financial support for the idea of a journal from one of the American research foundations.

L. von Bortkiewicz was a well-known figure in Scandinavia, as he and the Russian statistician Alexander Chuprov had been the main theoretical contributors to the *Nordic Statistical Journal* in the 1920s. Eugen Slutsky had visited Oslo and met with Frisch. He knew enough about Scandinavian languages to write occasionally in Swedish to Frisch and claimed to be able to read – with some difficulty – papers in

---

[10] The correspondence referred to in this and the following paragraph is quoted in extracts by Divisia (1953) and Frisch (1970).

Norwegian.[11] Frisch probably had sought out Arthur Bowley during his visit to Great Britain in 1923 and may have met Charles Jordan, a Hungarian economist of strong mathematical leanings, in Paris. The reactions he got were positive, but not overwhelmingly enthusiastic, except from the youngest one of the four, Eugen Slutsky. Arthur Bowley responded quickly, but uncommittingly, preferring "to take no part until a year has elapsed" (Bowley/Frisch, November 8, 1926). Both von Bortkiewicz and Bowley were elected to the first council of the Econometric Society, and Bowley became its fourth president.

Slutsky was very positive toward the idea of establishing a circle of econometricians immediately, but advised Frisch that the further goals of an association and a journal should be kept in view from the very beginning. "If we do not consider these important goals as *the* goals of the circle, then our undertaking will lack soul."[12]

Frisch left for the United States early in 1927 and stayed for more than a year. His main research project in that period was the analysis of time series. A manuscript he had prepared (Frisch, 1927) was widely distributed with the help of Wesley C. Mitchell. Frisch's main purpose may have been, however, to seek potential econometricians, both for scientific reasons and to gather support for an organization and a journal. Before he left he had corresponded with Irving Fisher and Allyn Young, and from them he obtained the names of other mathematical economists. From Allyn A. Young, Frisch got, in June 1927, a list of "practically everyone in the field of mathematical economics." The list comprised only eight names, and not many could have been new to Frisch.[13] Frisch visited

---

[11] Frisch had earlier sent his *Sur un problème* essay to all four, and Slutsky sent in return one of his five spare copies of the famous 1915 paper *Sulla teoria del bilancio del consumatore*, rediscovered by Henry Schultz and others in the mid-1930s.

[12] Slutsky/Frisch, December 17, 1926 (my translation from German). Slutsky added further thoughts on the importance of planning a widely defined journal, while concentrating in few hands the organizational preparation: "Was die Gründing einer Zeitschrift betrifft, so wird sehr viel von den Abgrenzung des Terrains abhängen, die man zur Grundlage der Kraftsammlung legen wird. Wird man solche Arbeiden nicht ausschliessen, die mit gründlichen mathematisch-statistischen Methoden zur Kenntnis der empirischen Regelmässigkeiten der Wirtschaft beitragen, also nicht zur reinen Oek. angehören, – werden auch die nicht mathematischen Arbeiden zugelassen, die der exakten Forschung durch logische bzw. phänomenologische Analysen den Weg vorbereiten können, so wird der eigentliche mathematisch-theoretische Kern der Zeitschrift mit einer so umfassender 'Hülle' versehen, dass man in Betreff des Umfanges des möglichen Leserkreises keine pessimistischen Gedanken haben kann. . . .

Vielleicht wäre es angezeigt in der ersten Vorbereitungsphase die Grenzen des Personenkreises, die zur Berathung angezogen werden, so eng als möglich durch Idee des 'Kerns' unseres Programms bestimmen lassen, um nicht zu sehr der Gefahr ausgesetzt werden die nötigen Grenzen zu verlieren."

[13] The names given by Allyn A. Young were Irving Fisher, H. L. Moore, Warren M. Persons, Holbrook Working, Frank H. Knight, Frederick C. Mills, Mordecai Ezekiel, and E. H. Chamberlin (Young/Frisch, June 27, 1927). In addition, Young enclosed a list he had

several universities, seeking out those whose names he had gathered, discussing time-series analysis and other research topics, and probably often bringing up his ideas for a journal and an organization to promote a more scientifically founded discipline. In the spring of 1927 Frisch wrote a memorandum on the importance of establishing a journal, the opening paragraphs of which went as follows:

> Two important features in the modern development of economics are the application of mathematics to abstract economic reasoning ... and the attempt at placing economics on a numerical and experimental basis by an intensive study of economic statistics.
>
> Both these developments have a common characteristic: they emphasize the quantitative character of economics. This quantitative movement in our estimation is one of the most promising developments in modern economics. We also consider it important that the two aspects of the quantitative method referred to should be furthered, developed, and studied jointly as two integrating parts of economics.
>
> We therefore venture to propose the establishment of an international periodical devoted to the advancement of the quantitative study of economic phenomena, and especially to the development of a closer relation between pure economics and economic statistics.
>
> We believe that the scope of the new journal would be happily suggested if it is called "Oekonometrika." Accordingly, the quantitative study of economic phenomena here considered may be termed econometrics.[14]

The memorandum went on to discuss details concerning the organization of such a journal, inviting comments from readers. Clearly it was written to be distributed to many, and it was frequently referred to in personal communications in the ensuing years. In fact, as a result of the memorandum, the idea of a journal at that stage seems to have become better known than the idea of an association. Frisch is reported to have drafted paragraphs for the constitution of the intended association during that period.

In the late autumn of 1927 Frisch met with Joseph Schumpeter at Harvard University, after having been in correspondence for some time. Schumpeter became a strong supporter of Frisch's ideas for a journal. Frisch also attended the joint meeting of the American Economic Association and the American Statistical Association in Washington,

---

solicited from M. Ezekiel of eight persons "having done outstanding work in statistical economics during the past five years" (Ezekiel/Young, June 28, 1927). Apart from Henry Schultz, none of these, mostly former colleagues of Ezekiel from the Department of Agriculture, became prominent in econometrics. A "memorandum for Dr. Frisch" of "places and persons to be visited" (filed with Young/Frisch, June 27, 1927), probably prepared by the Laura Spelman Rockefeller Memorial, with Frisch's handwritten additions and comments, included about 50 names from universities, government, and private institutions, most of whom it seems that he may have met during his stay.

[14] Quoted by Divisia (1953, pp. 24–5).

D.C., in December 1927. During the meeting Frisch took part in a round-table discussion with, inter alia, H. Schultz and A. Burns on the present status and future prospects of quantitative economics. Frisch's introductory statement was prepared for publication, but not included in the proceedings.[15] His remarks reiterated viewpoints he had earlier expressed in Norwegian in (Frisch, 1926b):

> Quantitative economics is something more than economic statistics. There is a quantitative aspect of economics which is rational and in one sense more fundamental than the empirical manipulation of numerical data on economic phenomena; namely, that part of economic theory which is concerned with the logic of our quantitative notions....
>
> We speak of one statistical procedure as giving a better result than another.... But I cannot get rid of the impression that we engage ... in target shooting without any target to shoot at. The target has to be furnished by axiomatic economics.
>
> Clearing the ground in axiomatic economics is a job which will certainly not be accomplished within the first few years to come. Little has as yet been done. This long-time prospect of the problem might perhaps discourage those who want results from economic theory, and want them quickly. They will perhaps get the feeling that in axiomatic economics the rationalists are again playing with some of those empty boxes which have become quite famous in a certain other part of economic theory. It should be kept in mind, though, that it is not possible to keep boxes filled all the time while they are in the process of being made. At times during the manufacturing process we have to handle them just as empty boxes. And if it is true that some rationalists have been playing with their empty boxes too often, I think it is equally true that the empiricists have too often been trying to carry along an infinity of their small objects without having boxes at all to carry them in.[16]

It seems likely that the meeting provided an opportunity to discuss the plans for a journal with other participants. Frisch reported to Divisia after the conference, though, that the prospects were not bright and there might not be a journal for some years (Frisch/Divisia, January 6, 1928).

Edwin B. Wilson proposed, in the spring of 1928, to the Executive Committee of the American Association for the Advancement of Science (AAAS), of which he was a member, that they attempt to develop economics as a science. Wilson's proposal was adopted, and he was appointed chairman of a committee to develop economics and sociology

---

[15] F. C. Mills, who organized the round table, apologized to Frisch that the editor, for space reasons, would not include the remarks of those who were not on the official program, adding "the points you made were among the most important of those raised at the conference" (Mills/Frisch, February 21, 1928).

[16] Filed with Mills/Frisch, February 21, 1928.

as sciences. Wilson got Charles F. Roos, a pupil of Griffith C. Evans, to serve as secretary of the committee, which was designated as Section K of the AAAS, and adjoined Henry Schultz, Wesley C. Mitchell, and H. L. Rietz as members of the committee. Section K had its first meetings in December 1928 and December 1929, and in 1930 at Cleveland it held joint sessions with the American Economic Association, the American Statistical Association, and the American Mathematical Society.

Frisch visited Irving Fisher at Yale University in February 1928, and a little later he came to Princeton University to see Charles F. Roos, a mathematical economist and the author of several articles on dynamic economics. There may also have been a joint meeting among Fisher, Roos, and Frisch in Fisher's home in New Haven in April 1928, discussing names of prospective members and concluding that more effort was needed to solicit future members.[17] Frisch left the United States soon after. In the period after his stay in the United States he traveled in Europe, visited Italy, and discussed his ideas with Corrado Gini and other European economists and statisticians. In the period that followed, Frisch had to attend to family affairs after his father died and he inherited the family's silversmith business.

2.3 We Have Been Unable to Find Any Better Word than "Econometrics"

Early in 1930 Frisch returned to the United States as visiting professor at Yale. The renewed contact with Fisher and Roos finally resulted in a concrete effort to prepare a foundation. The three drafted a circular letter to be sent to a select group to ask their advice before a formal invitation. Shortly before the letter was sent out, Divisia suggested to Frisch a safer route of organizing econometrics under the umbrella of the International Congress of Mathematicians, but Frisch had already set his course: "what we want is more to penetrate the whole body of economic theory with the keenness of mathematical thought.... I therefore believe that by acting wisely now we could be able, so to speak, to swallow the whole body of economic theory."[18]

The circular letter was dated June 17, 1930, and was sent to 31 persons, including the signees. The addressees, by country of residence (the names were all given in the letter), were one from Austria (H. Mayer), one from Denmark (H. Westergaard), one from Egypt (U. Ricci), four from France (C. Colson, F. Divisia, J. Moret, J. Rueff), two from Germany (L. von

---

[17] The meeting is mentioned in anecdotal terms by Christ (1983) and Roos (1948). I have found no documentary evidence of the meeting and thus am unsure whether or not it took place and when it took place. Neither have I found any record of an invitation sent out in 1928, as mentioned by Christ (1983). I believe the meeting that produced a list of names took place in 1930 and that no invitation was sent out prior to June 1930.
[18] Divisia/Frisch, March 22, 1930, and Frisch/Divisia, June 26, 1930.

Bortkiewicz, J. Schumpeter), four from Italy (L. Amoroso, C. Gini, A. de Pietri-Tonelli, G. del Vecchio), one from Norway (R. Frisch), one from Poland (Wl. Zawadzki), two from Sweden (G. Cassel, B. Ohlin), three from the United Kingdom (A. L. Bowley, J. M. Keynes, A. C. Pigou), ten from the United States (T. N. Carver, J. B. Clark, J. M. Clark, G. C. Evans, M. Ezekiel, I. Fisher, H. L. Moore, W. M. Persons, C. F. Roos, H. Schultz), and one from Russia (E. Slutsky).[19]

The letter asked "your opinion as to a project we have been considering, namely the organisation of an international association for the advancement of economic theory." The letter did not mention econometrics, and it did not discuss the name of the new organization. It asked for advice and judgment from the selected group of addressees and promised a similar letter to a larger group if sufficient encouragement was received.

After that general approach to the need for a new association, the letter went into surprisingly concrete detail on the (conditional) publishing activity:

> If at first sufficient funds should be difficult to raise, the publishing activity of the association might be restricted to a yearly leaflet giving the names of the members with addresses brought up to date and a list of the recent publications of the members. Such a leaflet would stimulate, we believe, an informal private correspondence and exchanging of reprints between the members. [Divisia, 1953, p. 26]

On the other hand, if funds were available, a journal would be created:

> The scope of the journal might perhaps be happily suggested by calling it "Oekonometrika." Do you think, however, that this name would (by analogy with Biometrika and Metron) suggest the idea of economic statistics only? Do you think that in order to indicate the constructive theoretical scope of the journal, it should be given a name such as "Economic Theory" or "Economic Science"? Have you any other suggestions as to the name of the journal? [Divisia, 1953, pp. 26-7]

The response to the letter was more than positive enough for the signees to move ahead to the next stage (i.e., the invitation to found the Econometric Society). The invitational letter that announced the date and time at the Statler Hotel in Cleveland was dated November 29, 1930. It included unmistakably Frischian formulations, and Frisch's tentative draft of the constitution was enclosed with the invitation. With regard to the name of the new society, the letter stated:

---

[19] Of the addressees, J. B. Clark, who was 83 at the time, never joined. G. Cassel, E. Slutsky, and A. C. Pigou never became members. Cassel refused outright after the society was founded: "as I do not want to identify my strivings with those of [the society]" (Cassel/Frisch, September 14, 1931; my translation). Pigou may have expected to be offered a more honorary status than ordinary membership. Why Slutsky never joined seems more of a mystery.

As to the name of the society, we consider it essential that the name should indicate quite clearly the specific object which the society has in view. If the society is formed with the scope we have suggested, it seems advisable to coin a word, since no current single word will connote exactly the correct idea. So far, we have been unable to find any better word than "econometrics." We are aware of the fact that in the beginning somebody might misinterpret this word to mean economic statistics only. But if the complete subtitle of the society is always given in the official publication and in the letterheads of the society, and if the members and fellows of the Society persist in using the word "econometrics" and "econometric" in their proper sense, we believe that it will soon become clear to everybody that the society is interested in economic theory just as much as in anything else. [Divisia, 1953, p. 29]

3 The First Years of the Econometric Society

The immediate organizational tasks facing the officers and the council of the Econometric Society after its foundation were the election of members, the initiation of Econometric Society meetings, and the establishment of a journal for the society. F. Divisia was elected as vice-president, and Charles F. Roos as secretary and treasurer. Irving Fisher, the first president, was much concerned about achieving an established and respectable status for the society as soon as possible. Both the membership policy and the effort to initiate a journal would serve that purpose. Other members may have been more iconoclastic in emphasizing the *different* character of the new society.

None exerted stronger influence within the new society in the early years than Fisher, Frisch, and Schumpeter. They may at the outset have had diverging views on how to conduct the affairs of the society, but they never seemed to have much difficulty reaching agreement. They shared a common view of the primacy of economic theory in the definition of econometrics, and they also shared an interest in the history of economics and a common regard for their predecessors.

From the outset it was decided that the first two years of the Econometric Society would count as one with regard to the time in office. Frisch and others persuaded Fisher to sit as president beyond his first period, first for one year and then for another year. Hence there was no change of president until 1935. The choice seemed to be between Divisia and Schumpeter. Frisch had tried in vain to persuade Schumpeter to accept the presidency, as he found Divisia too indecisive to make a good president. In the end Frisch supported Divisia, however, with Schumpeter as vice-president. After Divisia, the pressure was on Schumpeter, who absolutely refused to accept the presidency while he was still working to complete *Business Cycles*. Harold Hotelling was elected president for 1937, with Arthur Bowley as vice-president, followed by Bowley as president and Schumpeter as vice-president in 1938 and 1939. In 1940

Schumpeter was finally elected president, with Jan Tinbergen as vice-president. Alfred Cowles had taken over as treasurer from 1932, and from 1937 also as secretary.

3.1 Members, Charter Members, and Fellows

According to its constitution, the society would have two classes of members: regular members and Fellows. Members of either class would be subject to election. The procedure for nomination and election of regular members was set out in the constitution: "To become a regular member, a person must be proposed to the Council by two members of the Society. Once a year the Council shall nominate new members and these nominations shall be voted upon by mail of all members. No person can be elected to membership unless he is nominated by the Council" (Constitution, par. 2, *Econometrica* 1:106).

The constitution furthermore gave the council the authority to invite eligible persons to become charter members during the first year of the society's existence. The idea for charter members had not been well thought out before the attempt at implementation. Some, including both Frisch and Schumpeter, wanted to see qualified econometricians as charter members, and Fisher, indeed, wanted the charter members "with few exceptions, [to] consist of those who are eligible to become Fellows" (which few of them did). Others, like Roos, tended to regard the extra offer of becoming a charter member as an incentive to enroll, while Fisher was open to the idea of accepting, as exceptions, charter members without economic qualifications if they would help the society attain respectability in the right circles (or money, which Fisher may have found to be needed even more than respectability, in particular to finance a journal). Roos had, in that vein, got Fisher's support for a plan "to invite about one thousand American millionaires to give $500.00 each to the ES. All gifts will of course have to be without strings. Circularizations of this kind usually bring forth a response of about one half of one per cent. In other words our circularization should result in about five responses."[20]

That was not much to Frisch's liking, and he vented his opposition to Divisia:

> My feeling has been that the Econometric Society should be first of all an *Economic Society*. This is the reason why I have thought there might be reason for not being quite as liberal in exempting economist members as in exempting other kinds of members.... Our difference on this point is not so much a question of some dollars more or less as a question of the general attitude towards the group of people whom

---

[20] Roos/Frisch, March 23, 1934. The plan apparently was not executed. It is not clear how Roos estimated the expected return.

we could designate under the name "men of fame and influence." ... I do not think we should go too far in the direction of seeking the protection of the generation which has now arrived at the stage of influence and power. If the idea of the Econometric Society has the right of life it will win with or without the protection of the older generation. And if it has not the right of life no amount of protection will save us. My feeling is therefore that we should rather trust our own power of doing good work. It is through the organization and coordination of the work of our group that we shall finally obtain recognition.... I am most emphatically against the Econometric Society seeking any sort of official recognition. I revolt against being patted kindly on the back. [Frisch/Divisia, October 12, 1931]

Schumpeter vented equally strong reactions when he learned that Roos found it a "healthy attitude" in new entrants to find "the old theory to be practically worthless." Schumpeter found "that there was nothing in common between myself and anyone who thought the work of Cournot, Walras, Pareto, Fisher, Marshall 'worthless.' ... I wish to do my best to keep our front united on a very broad line."[21] Also, A. Bowley found it a mistake to rally for a great number of charter members, adding "eminence, by definition is rare" (Bowley/Frisch, October 25, 1931). In the end it was decided that all members who joined, or, rather, were allowed to join, during the first year of the society would be counted as charter members. In addition to the 16 present at the organization meeting, 153 members joined as charter members during 1931. But the discussion of charter membership during 1931 had caused much agony and a lot of wasted time and energy as well. Frisch, Fisher, and Schumpeter felt called upon to protect the international character and the integrity of the venture. The candidates for charter membership were from about 15 countries. Fisher also felt the responsibility: "the real architects of the Society seem to be yourself, Frisch, Roos and myself" (Fisher/Schumpeter, June 16, 1931). But to agree on charter members was not an easy task. Schumpeter wanted to strike out a number of Fisher's proposed names, but Fisher defended them vehemently: E. Cannan ("an unusually clear-headed economist ... one of the first to distinguish between a stock and a flow"), T. N. Carver ("the only one which has developed certain points in the coordination of distribution"), J. M. Clark ("he has done some mathematical writing which has not been published"), R. Hawtrey ("a keen thinker"), E. W. Kemmerer ("has used a little bit of mathematics"), and W. F. Ogburn ("a man with a high-powered mind ... familiar with the application of correlation to economics"). On the other hand, Fisher felt that Schumpeter's candidate F. W. Taussig, "distinguished, able and sound as he is, ... should not be a

---

[21] Schumpeter/Frisch, October 28, 1931. The entrant promoted by Roos for having a "healthy attitude" was Frank A. Pearson.

charter member" (Fisher/Schumpeter, June 16, 1931). From the Department of Economics at Harvard University, Fisher's candidate thus was T. N. Carver, while Schumpeter promoted F. W. Taussig. Frisch discarded both and wanted John D. Black as "Harvard man" as he "certainly has the econometric attitude, even if he does not master much of the mathematical technique" (Frisch/Fisher, August 27, 1931). Fisher became exasperated at that stage: "Frankly speaking, I think I would be severely criticised as a Yale man if no Harvard man were included in the charter membership" (Fisher/Frisch, July 3, 1931). Harvard University, but not the Department of Economics, would in any case have been represented by the eminent statistician Edwin B. Wilson. In the end Frisch and Schumpeter accepted Carver.

After the first year a more relaxed attitude gained ground regarding the power given the council by the constitution in controlling the inflow of regular members, although it was clearly a firm opinion of most of the leading members of the society at the outset that certain qualifications were required to become members. It was also cumbersome to have members vote on all new entrants. Fisher had already, in 1931, suggested that the membership rules be applied so as to "gather into the fold all who have any likelihood of becoming proper timber for fellows," without requiring more at the outset than that the new entrants be "interested in economic theory" (Fisher/Schumpeter, June 16, 1931). Some of the European members where afraid that the scarcity value of membership in the society would get lost by allowing in unworthy members, as expressed by one of them: "I shall have less reason than before to be proud of being a member of the Econometric Society" (Staehle/Cowles, February 7, 1932). In 1933 the membership policy adopted by the council was to consider "as eligible for membership all serious students interested in the objectives of the Society, regardless of whether they have as yet achieved established reputation based on published works. Membership should be considered an honor, especially to young men, but it means merely that they have shown an understanding of the problems with which our Society deals" (Econometric Society minutes book, 1933). Frisch and Schumpeter had a more restrictive attitude toward membership, but realized that the battle was lost: "I agree with you that the membership has now been extended beyond any limits compatible with standing. There does not seem to be any way back now, so we shall probably have to accept the situation that the membership will be a large group giving financial and moral support only. It is all the more necessary to establish a hard and fast organisation of the fellows. The outlook now seems that we shall have, when the machinery has finally begun to function, an outer circle of between 500 & 1,000 ordinary members. Then a group of fellows between 30 & 40 and finally a council of 7 or 8. The pyramid does not seem to be so bad after all" (Frisch/Schumpeter, January 11, 1933).

Fellowship was another matter. The constitution's requirement of one year's membership prior to Fellowship implied that the election of Fellows could not take place in the first year. The Fellowship issue is discussed later in Section 6.

Frisch had the idea of publishing the list of members of the society every year in *Econometrica*. Over the mild protest of his assistant editor, he put it into effect from the second volume: "I am thinking of the historians of the future who would be delighted to find the membership list in 'Econometrica'." (Frisch/Nelson, March 23, 1934).

3.2 *Que dites-vous d'une* Econometrica?

There can be little doubt that Frisch deserves more credit than anyone else for the idea of founding *Econometrica*, as well as for the name the journal was given. The idea of a journal was first put forward by Frisch in a letter to Divisia in 1926. Frisch not only suggested a journal but also named it, suggesting parenthetically to Divisia: "que dites-vous d'une Econometrica?, la sœur du Biometrika" (Frisch/Divisia, September 4, 1926).

L. von Bortkiewicz observed that it would be more correct to write "Oekonometrika." Divisia pointed to the Greek roots $οικος$, $νομος$, and $μετρον$ and offered on etymological grounds "Oeconomometrika" or "Oeconommetrika" as alternatives, but adding "vous avez la paternité du terme; a vous donc de façonner votre enfant à votre guise" (Divisia/Frisch, December 16, 1926). In a delayed reaction, Slutsky expressed his dislike of "Econometrica" and suggested "Economometrika," "every philologist will find the omission of one 'm' impossible and the word itself *barbarous*" (Slutsky/Frisch, July 4, 1927). Frisch pondered that and tried out different spellings before settling for von Bortkiewicz's suggestion of "Oekonometrika," and he used that in his 1927 memorandum, a name that, he argued, hinted at parallelism with *Biometrika* and avoided confusion with *Economica*.

After the founding of the society there still was no financial basis for a journal. Even with considerably increased membership fees there simply were not enough members. The 173 charter members at the end of 1931 (paying a membership fee of $2 in the United States and $1 elsewhere) hardly warranted the establishment of a journal. The salvation came in the shape of Alfred Cowles, III, who wrote to Fisher in August 1931 and offered to finance a journal for the society. In Fisher's home in New Haven he put his offer in writing on October 18, 1931: "I am ready to make up any deficit in the proposed journal, 'Econometrica', including all the expenses of editing, printing etc." (Cowles/Fisher, October 18, 1931).

Fisher wrote that same day to Frisch: "It is exceedingly wonderful to have an 'angel' suddenly fall down from the sky to supply us with the one thing needful to make our Society a huge success. Without financing we can never amount to a great deal but with financing we can leap years ahead of what we otherwise would.... I would not like to take the responsibility, even if I were sure that as President I had the power, to decide this without consulting you as the original founder of the Society" (Fisher/Frisch, October 18, 1931).

The question of the editor for the journal was also discussed at the meeting between Cowles and Fisher. Cowles had suggested Frisch as editor in his written offer to finance the journal, although the two had never met. Frisch was positively inclined toward Cowles's offer to finance a journal, but refused to consider himself as a candidate for editor. The European council members, however, were hesitant about the offer from an unknown American businessman, Divisia, for example, was worried that "l'affaire Cowles" could lead to lack of control over the journal and give Cowles a monopoly on the publication of econometric works (Divisia/Frisch, November 26, 1931). The European part of the council authorized Frisch to decide on their behalf after a meeting with Cowles. Cowles's offer was accepted early in 1932 (*Econometrica* 1:109). Frisch yielded under pressure from both Fisher and Schumpeter and agreed to become editor. He was elected by the council in February 1932 as editor-in-chief, with power to select his own editorial board and assistant editor.[22]

At the Econometric Society meeting in New Orleans in January 1932 the name issue had come up, and "Econometrika" won through as a name avoiding confusion with *Economica*. Cowles, who may have had the businessman's sense for a good name, seems to have stuck consistently to "Econometrica" and found the change of only one "c" to "k" as "inconsistent and...the spelling 'Ekonometrika'...bizarre" (Cowles/Roos, February 9, 1932). The council meeting that elected Frisch editor-in-chief reconsidered the name issue and decided that the name should be "Econometrica."

Frisch did not regard the name issue as settled by the council decision, and he brought it up again under his plenipotentiary mandate as editor-in-chief. Frisch's favored choice was still "Oekonometrika," and he decided to put the spelling of the name to a vote, with other editorial matters, in a questionnaire to the council members. After having got the returns, while the first issue was already being prepared, Frisch (in spite of support from Schumpeter) yielded. It had to be *Econometrica*.

4   The First Meetings

The Econometric Society meetings started in the first year after the founding of the society, with regional meetings held in Europe and in the United States. Travel time and costs hardly allowed even the thought of

---

[22] More details on the choice of editor and the name issue are given by Bjerkholt (1995, pp. 758–9).

having cross-Atlantic meetings. The first Econometric Society meeting ever was held at the University of Lausanne, September 22–24, 1931. The venue was deliberately chosen to commemorate Léon Walras.

The European meetings were held thereafter as one annual meeting in September or October. After Lausanne, there followed, in the next five years, Paris in 1932, Leyden in 1933, Stresa in 1934, Namur in 1935, and the famous Oxford meeting in 1936. In the United States the meetings were held regularly in December/January. For some years there was also a June meeting in the United States, but after being held in 1932–35 and 1937, it gave way to the Cowles Commission Seminars.

The different characters of the European meetings and the American meetings should be recognized. The American meetings were fitted into an established framework of national joint meetings among the American Economic Assocation (AEA), the American Statistical Association (ASA), and other scientific associations. The Econometric Society meetings were also, to begin with, held as joint sessions with either the AEA or the ASA. Several of the leading figures in the Econometric Society were prominent members of one of the other associations.[23]

In Europe, on the other hand, there existed no regular common conference ground in economics; hence the meetings became major innovations in the scientific exchange among economists. There were also great differences in style. The American meetings were well prepared ahead of time and may also have observed more formalities than the early European meetings, which, more often than not, were hastily prepared but had intense and informal discussions. At a decennial luncheon (to commemorate the founding of the Econometric Society) in New Orleans in December 1940, Jakob Marschak spoke about the European meetings in the preceding decade and referred to the "fruitfulness of frank and energetic discussions [that] found expression in the customary rule of the meetings of the European branch: everyone may interrupt the reading of a paper to ask the author to repeat or clarify a definition – a rule which has probably prevented many a discussion at cross purposes, so common in economics" (*Econometrica* 9:179, 1941).

The responsibility for the first European meeting fell to the vice-president, F. Divisia, and the other European members of the council, among whom Frisch was by far the most vigorous force. Before the meeting in Lausanne, Divisia was hesitant about many aspects of the meeting, leaning toward a restrictive attitude with regard to who should be allowed to take part in the proceedings. Four weeks before the meeting, no preparations had been made, apart from the invitation of papers. Frisch showered Divisia with advice, and with regard to admittance he wrote that "it would be possible for us to give the meeting more

---

[23] I. Fisher even held the presidency of the American Statistical Association while he was still president of the Econometric Society.

'ampleur' by inviting a larger number of people. The more I have thought of it the more convinced I have become that the number of attendants at the meeting should not be too small. . . . In the sessions devoted to modern investigation, the larger crowd would do no harm at all. On the contrary the fact that a larger crowd could be brought together to listen to a series of econometric papers, even if everybody in the meeting should not understand all that have developed, would be a very significant achievement, quite in the spirit of the Econometric Society" (Frisch/Divisia, August 25, 1931).

Schumpeter was taken ill before the Lausanne meeting, and Divisia was, for family reasons, also unable to take part. Frisch had to step in. He told Schumpeter, long after the event, that "at the last minute [Divisia] had to write to Staehle asking him to carry through the Lausanne Organisation, and on the evening before the opening of the Lausanne meeting there actually did not exist any programme. Staehle and I were working practically the whole night to bring things in order" (Frisch/Schumpeter, February 25, 1933).

The meeting was a great success, although the attendance was not large. Frisch gave the opening address and the closing address, presented 3 out of the 19 papers, and took an active part in every discussion. The papers were fairly evenly divided among the history of economics (including papers on Walras, Cournot, and Wicksell), methods in econometric analysis, and application of mathematical methods in economics. The speakers were Frisch, J. Åkerman, Boninsegni, G. Darmois, M. Fanno, P. Le Corbeiller, J. Marschak, P. N. Rosenstein-Rodan, R. Roy, P. Sraffa, J. Tinbergen, H. Staehle, G. del Vecchio, and O. Weinberger. Frisch's papers were "New Methods of Measuring Marginal Utility," "The Use of Difference Equations in the Study of Statistical Distributions," and "Tensor Calculus as a Tool for the Formulation of Invariance in Economic and Statistical Laws." The meeting was reported, with much detail of the discussion, by Hans Staehle (*Econometrica* 1:73–86).

Again at the 1932 meeting in Paris Frisch had to step in at short notice to take over from Divisia the arrangement of the program. Frisch was no less active than the year before and presented 2 out of the 22 papers.[24] The Leyden meeting in 1933, with Tinbergen in charge, had only slightly more than 30 participants, but it became a meeting often referred to later. The study of business cycles was the key topic: Frisch presented his propagation model, and Kalecki his own model. Both resulted in very active discussion. J. Hicks and H. Schultz took part in a society meeting for the first time. The Leyden meeting had only 15 papers (and Frisch only 1), but time was set aside for three night-session colloquia, and one full day for an 8-hour lecture by Frisch on the algebra of linear

---

[24] The report from the Paris meeting was written by G. Lutfalla and was not published in *Econometrica*, but in *Revue d'Economie Politique*, vol. 47 (April 1933), pp. 173–92.

transformations and quadratic forms (sessions were 10:00–12:30, 14:30–17:30 and 19:30–22:00)!

Frisch did not go to the Stresa meeting in 1934, but attended the Namur meeting in 1935. The Oxford meeting in 1936 was an event he eagerly anticipated. He reported to Hotelling and others after the event that it had been the best meeting thus far. The attendance had increased to between 40 and 50. The centerpiece of the meeting was a special symposium, "General Theory," with papers by Hicks, Harrod, and Meade. Frisch spoke on "Macrodynamic Systems Leading to Permanent Unemployment," in a quite non-Keynesian vein. Frisch also presented a paper on the measurement of money flexibility and lectured at a colloquium session that also included Jerzy Neyman presenting the Neyman-Pearson theory, T. Haavelmo's first paper at an Econometric Society meeting, and papers by A. P. Lerner and others.

Eyewitness accounts from some of those meetings indicate that Frisch made a lasting impression because of his indefatigable energy and exuberant spirits, but he could also deliver sharply formulated criticism against what he regarded as faulty reasoning. The energy be expended during the conference days did not prevent him from night work, bringing new results the next morning (Tinbergen, 1974).

5   Editorial Policy in the Early Years

As soon as Frisch had accepted the editorship, he set to work with enormous energy. He visited Cowles in Colorado Springs in June 1932. It was their first meeting, and they got on well from the start. Frisch involved himself not only in the editorial planning but also, during the initial phase, with every detail that had to do with layout, typesetting, printing, and so forth.

His view of the role of an editor-in-chief required almost superhuman effort by an editor. He would write, he would solicit, he would referee, and he would decide. He would even rewrite submitted papers when that was called for! In the middle of his planning he expressed his feeling to Divisia: "I have a policy of doing things as well as I can *from the beginning* giving the thing a good start. And then later trying to let it go by itself. So also with 'Econometrica.' The associate and assistant editors will I hope do the routine work. And there will certainly not be any 'Chasse aux manuscripts'" (Frisch/Divisia, August 13, 1932).

Frisch appointed three associate editors, representing economics (Alvin H. Hansen), statistics (Frederick C. Mills), and mathematics (Harold T. Davis). Frisch's first choice had been H. Schultz rather than Hansen, but Schultz declined, as he was already involved with two other journals. As the associate editor for mathematics Frisch tried to enlist his Norwegian friend Oystein Ore. That would have been an odd choice, as Ore's mathematics expertise (number theory, algebra) was not greatly applicable to economics. Ore, who was an eminent mathematician, declined. Frisch may have valued excellence above specialization. J. Schumpeter took over in 1938 after Hansen withdrew. An Advisory Editorial Board was also appointed, remaining unchanged until it was replenished during the war. Frisch may have thought of the associate editors primarily as potential contributors, but he got, to his disappointment, very few contributions from them.

The first assistant editor was William F. C. Nelson, an associate of Cowles, who died at age 36 years in 1936. He was replaced by Dickson H. Leavens, who lasted until after the war. Frisch was, to begin with, not inclined to use outside referees. He took much upon himself and might enter into considerable editing of submitted manuscripts, such as changing the system of notation. The burden on the editor-in-chief occasionally resulted in severe delays. The managing editor could be driven to despair waiting to get Frisch's decisions on manuscripts he was reviewing. Both Nelson and Leavens occasionally had to put it to Frisch in straight words, and Frisch would respond with a series of quick decisions and some good-natured and appreciative comments.

As editor, Frisch generated innovative ideas about what the journal ought to contain. He took a number of initiatives to make the journal known and fill its pages. In the first 10 years or so there seldom was a significant backlog of submitted articles for *Econometrica*, except in the first couple of years. It happened that issues sometimes were published smaller in size than planned, because of lack of approved manuscripts. The volumes started out large, with four issues of 112 pages each in the first two years, growing to close to 500 pages in 1935, a size not exceeded until well into the 1950s.

Econometrica worked on meager resources for many years, although Cowles extended his financial support much beyond his initial commitment of three years of financing. The membership fee had been increased to include journal subscription and was set to $6 for U.S. residents and $3 for the rest of the world. Frisch was paid, for his editorial services, $500 per year. He sent repeated appeals to Cowles in 1933 and 1934 to find means to offer honoraria for accepted papers, at least for solicited articles, but to no avail. The financial control rested firmly with Cowles.

5.1 *Features and Innovations*

Frisch had the idea of soliciting survey articles at an early stage, and he introduced it in his editorial statement in the first issue. There would be four different annual surveys on general economic theory (including pure economics), business-cycle theory, statistical techniques, and statistical information, to be published in successive issues. The specification of those surveys also says something about how Frisch viewed the priorities in econometrics in the early 1930s: that business-cycle studies were particularly important for econometrics and that better statistical information was an important concern.

In the first volume, A. Hansen and H. Tout wrote the first survey on business-cycle theory; W. A. Shewhart covered statistical techniques, and J. Marschak statistical information. The first survey on general economic theory was written by J. Tinbergen for the second volume. The third volume contained J. Hicks's survey of economic theory (on the theory of monopoly) and J. Tinbergen's survey of business-cycle theory. Frisch contributed his famous index number article as a survey of economic theory in the fourth volume.

It turned out to be too difficult to elicit four surveys each year. Only three business-cycle surveys were written. General economic theory (a wide category!) got six surveys. In some cases Frisch inventively redefined submitted articles as surveys to uphold the idea. The other two categories got four and five each, of somewhat mixed quality. Frisch tried hard to solicit surveys from the members, but to no avail. After some years the surveys dwindled. Originally Frisch's idea had been to have someone do the same survey each year for several years, assisted by a specialist if needed, but that idea failed from the start.

Another feature initiated by the editor was to have articles, both commemorative and theoretical, about the great pioneers in the econometric field. In the first volume, Johan Åkerman wrote on Wicksell, and René Roy on Cournot. The second volume contained Bowley on Edgeworth, Schneider on von Thünen, Hicks on Walras, and the Jevons children (H. Winefrid and H. Stanley) on their father. More followed in the ensuing volumes, but Amoroso on Pareto in 1938 became a slight scandal because of the homage to the Italian fascist state that came with it (Bjerkholt, 1995, p. 761, n. 6). Frisch included in *Econometrica* other documents of historical interest.

From the beginning, *Econometrica* allowed articles in French and English and also in German.[25] Language was not much of a problem for the early econometricians, at least not on the European side of the Atlantic. Not everyone was – like Frisch – fluent in English, French, and German, and reading Dutch and Italian as well, but an ability to read the major western European languages was taken for granted. Russian was, of course, another matter. In the early years of the journal Frisch arranged to have Russian articles translated and reissued in *Economet-*

---

[25] German was cut out lest the Italians should claim their rights to publish in their own language, but also for economic reasons. Cowles worked out that if the journal could be considered an English-language journal, i.e., with only occasional French contributions, 300 libraries would subscribe. A multilanguage journal would be limited to less than 25 academic libraries. What could be gained in Europe would not in any way outweigh the loss in the United States.

rica. Those included E. Slutsky's famous article on the random causes of cyclic processes, from 1927, which Frisch had embraced in his celebrated Cassel *Festschrift* contribution.

Frisch's ideas about what *Econometrica* ought to contain thus extended in many directions and were also influenced by ideas put forward by others. He was concerned about the role of *Econometrica* as a medium for communication among members. For that purpose the programs for coming meetings of the Econometric Society and reports from past meetings served an important function. The list of members, with addresses, also facilitated communication. The prime concern, papers representing what Frisch called "real econometric work," continued to be in short supply in the first 10 years or so of the journal's existence. When Paul A. Samuelson submitted his first papers in 1940, Frisch was enthusiastic: They were "first-rate stuff," much to his liking (Frisch/Leavens, December 22, 1940).

Frisch suggested innovations and improvements to produce a modern, up-to-date journal. A major project from the beginning was to include bibliographic notes about econometric work. Frisch had done much preparatory work on a classification system for econometric literature, but for lack of space and other reasons it was never published, nor was a survey of current literature according to the new classification system. Frisch suggested as early as 1934 that the submission date should be given when an article was printed, but met with opposition from the assistant editor (that practice was not introduced until 1970). Lists of forthcoming papers were included from the first issue, but disappeared after 1934, apparently because of failure to meet deadlines. Another idea that seems to have originated with Frisch was to establish a monograph series for the Econometric Society.

Frisch published a number of articles in *Econometrica* (not counting entries signed "Editor") varying in length from 1 to 93 pages. Many of those were comments and clarifying notes regarding articles he had accepted for publication. A more peculiar habit was to insert editorial notes in articles by other authors, often to comment on or to relate the content or assertions in the article to his own work.[26]

5.2   *Criticism*

Frisch's editorial policy and decisions elicited criticism on many occasions. Frisch either fought it off or, when he found it justified, did his best to change his ways. After the first couple of issues, complaints and criticisms about the style and content of *Econometrica* began to emerge, but often the editor would not be the first to hear about it.

---

[26] Some examples can be found (Bjerkholt, 1995, p. 763, n. 7).

When Frisch responded to early criticism demanding a change in editorial policy to recruit more new members, he explained to Divisia that *Econometrica* ought to remain a different kind of journal:

> However, I believe that we must be on our guard not to let "Econometrica" lose its characteristic features and become similar to the other economic journals now published. You know that all of them publish occasionally mathematical papers, but try to keep the bulk of the articles in a more literary style. No doubt some new subscribers could be acquired by letting "Econometrica" evolve more in the general direction of these types of journals. But I believe that a considerable number of our members would lose that interest and enthusiasm which they have now shown. I think therefore, that we must now and in the future always try to preserve this feature which makes "Econometrica" different from the rest of the journals. This applies both to the particular way in which we propose to apply statistics to economic theoretical problems and to our readiness in using mathematics whenever necessary. [Frisch/Divisia, May 25, 1933]

But criticism continued. After Fisher had attended the International Statistical Institute meeting in Mexico in 1933, he reported to Frisch that C. Gini was disappointed with *Econometrica*: "it was good, but not good enough." (Fisher/Frisch, January 18, 1934). Gini had also written to Frisch that *Econometrica* did not meet the criterion that Gini followed as editor of *Metron* that accepted papers ought to "contain some new contribution in the theory or in the applications." Gini furthermore objected to the surveys on the ground that to let just a few persons "review all the field of econometrics is rather dangerous. It is very difficult that a person knows sufficiently all the languages in order to be acquainted with all the contributions, without speaking of the impartiality of the reviewers towards all other contributors, which is not easy to realize" (Gini/Frisch, January 4, 1934). Frisch asked Gini which articles he had in mind, but Gini declined to elaborate.

Frisch's highly mathematical approach in many of the papers he presented at the European Econometric Society meetings offended the timid. Again it was Fisher who brought back the complaints: "Recently, I had Bousquet here at Yale. He was critical of you at the meetings in trying to use too strong-armed methods. Evidently, Bousquet is somewhat sensitive, but such men are good thermometers. I am therefore passing this criticism on to you for what it may be worth, for Bousquet seems to me a fine fellow and one worth placating" (Fisher/Frisch, January 18, 1934). Frisch's comment to the complaints from Gini and Bousquet was that "I have for a long time thought of trying to arrange in *Econometrica* a series of papers that may build a bridge between those who appear as using 'strong armour' methods and the more general group of economists." Frisch wrote to Bousquet and asked for "a paper along these lines," telling him that he would of course be quite free to express any criticisms he wanted. "I am not quite sure, however, that

Bousquet has sufficient power to exact a clear reasoning, but anyhow we shall see" (Frisch/Fisher, March 26, 1934).

Frisch's 93-page article in the second volume, "Circulation Planning," brought severe reactions from some of the members for its length as well as for misuse of editorial prerogative, and perhaps also for its content. Frisch accepted the criticism and promised to refrain from publishing his own works in the journal.[27]

Frisch's old Swedish friend, J. Åkerman, whose thesis had inspired Frisch to develop the propagation model, submitted, after his Wicksell paper and an annual theory survey, a paper to *Econometrica* in 1938 and had it turned down by Frisch, stating that "we have gradually constrained acceptance to works of definite mathematical and statistical character." Åkerman may have felt snubbed, and he retorted with a rather negative assessment of *Econometrica*: "too many treatises in Econometrica seem to me to be built on foundations that are not corroborated and are felt missing." Frisch responded in a jocular mode: "Don't shoot at the actors, they do as best they can.... It is important *to a certain degree* to give mathematical formulations precedence.... It is, of course, our wish that this could take place as a specialization without isolation."[28]

Most of the objections to Frisch's "strong-armour" methods and sharp polemical style may have derived more from his performance at the early Econometric Society meetings and some polemical articles than from his editorial practice. Schumpeter advised Frisch to adopt a softer touch in dealing with opponents, and he referred to "Anti-Frisch Currents" in the economic community in the United States, while at the same time expressing his wholehearted agreement with Frisch in substantial matters.[29]

Anecdotal accounts related to Frisch's handling of submitted manuscripts seem to have survived his 22 years as editor, but are hardly reliable sources. Complaints by snubbed authors are, almost by definition, one-sided.[30] In controversies that arose in the journal, such as the fierce

---

[27] Frisch/Roos, March 21, 1935. Roos also criticized in equally strong terms Tinbergen's business-cycle survey, which appeared in 1935 and ran to more than 60 pages.

[28] Frisch/Åkerman, October 1938, and Frisch/Åkerman, November 1938 (my translation).

[29] Schumpeter/Frisch, November 2, 1934. The worst incident was Frisch's rather unpleasant rebuke of W. Leontief in the *Quarterly Journal of Economics*, vol. 48 (1934), the last paragraph of which Schumpeter characterized as "a slap in the face you gave the whole [Harvard Economics] department."

[30] Evidence given decades later may be even less reliable! J. S. Gans and G. B. Shepherd (*Journal of Economic Perspectives*, vol. 8, no. 1, 1994, pp. 165–79) survey rejections of papers by well-known economists, including one from Frisch's period as editor of *Econometrica*. The authors quote F. Modigliani concerning that rejection, but from the filed evidence I have been able to retrieve, Modigliani gives a somewhat erring account about when the paper was submitted (1946, rather than 1949), about the reasons given for rejecting it (suppressing that the article came to more than 50 *Econometrica* pages, at a time when manuscripts piled up, and that he was, in fact, offered the opportunity to publish a briefer version), and about who rejected it (T. Haavelmo was not involved).

Lotka-Preinreich affair, Frisch seems to have steered a middle, just, and fairly liberal course. In matters of what constituted good econometrics (and good notation!) he held strong views and did not spare others' feelings.

6 The Election of Fellows

Fellows were to be elected by Fellows, by means of a mail vote. To be elected, a nomination by the council was required. The constitution stated the qualifications: "To be eligible for such nomination a person must have published original contributions to economic theory or to such statistical, mathematical, or accounting analyses as have a definite bearing on problems in economic theory, and must have been a member of the Society for at least one year." Further, the members would each year be offered "an opportunity to suggest nominees for fellowships" (Constitution, par. 3, *Econometrica* 1:106). To get the election of Fellows started, the constitution allowed the first group of Fellows to be elected by the council.

How the nomination and election process should be conducted was nevertheless quite open to interpretation. The core of the matter was, of course, how many Fellows and with what qualifications. The preparation for election of the first lot of Fellows by the council started soon after the first year of the society had passed, but turned out to become a drawn-out affair. Fisher sounded out the council members by having them fill out a preliminary ballot for Fellows in 1932. More than 50 names had been proposed by council members. The official ballots were distributed by the president in December 1932, accompanied by a letter stating that "the policy being followed is to have a large membership but a very select list of Fellows, so that there may be an ambition among a larger number (especially among the rising generation of economists) to become qualified for Fellowship, i.e. to become scientific economists." The vote was cast as first, second, and third choices, weighed together with weights 3-2-1. After the official ballot the final number of Fellows to be elected was decided. Some deviations from the order given by the summary of ballots were negotiated, taking the country distribution into consideration. E. Schneider and N. D. Kondratieff were thus elected, although W. M. Persons and W. Leontief had received more votes.

The first lot of 29 Fellows were notified of their election in August 1933. They were the following (*Econometrica* 1:445):

Professor Luigi Amoroso, Rome
Professor Oskar N. Anderson, Varna
Dr. Albert Aupetit, Paris
Professor Boninsegni, Lausanne
Professor A. L. Bowley, London
Professor Clément Colson, Paris

Professor Gustavo Del Vecchio, Bologna
Professor François Divisia, Paris
Professor Griffith C. Evans, Houston
Professor Irving Fisher, New Haven
Professor Ragnar Frisch, Oslo

Professor Corrado Gini, Rome
Dr. Gottfried Haberler, Vienna
Professor Harold Hotelling, New York
Professor John M. Keynes, Cambridge
Dr. N. D. Kondratieff, Russia
Professor Wesley C. Mitchell, New York
Professor H. L. Moore, Cornwall, N. Y.
Professor Umberto Ricci, Giza

Dr. Charles F. Roos, Washington
M. Jacques Rueff, London
Dr. Erich Schneider, Dortmund
Professor Henry Schultz, Chicago
Prof. Joseph A. Schumpeter, Cambridge, Mass.
Dr. J. Tinbergen, Scheveningen
Professor Felice Vinci, Bologna
Professor Edwin B. Wilson, Boston
Professor Wl. Zawadzki, Warsaw
Professor F. Zeuthen, Copenhagen

The first lot of Fellows included, naturally, the entire council elected at the organization meeting (apart from L. von Bortkiewicz, who died in 1931). The selection of the additional 20 Fellows was a matter of much difficulty for the council in reaching collective agreement. Some elder statesmen were included (i.e., Colson, Mitchell, Gini). A major concern was the number from each country. U.S. residents constituted the largest group, followed by Italians, while only two were included from the United Kingdom. Another was the order of promotion to Fellowship within each country: Divisia succeeded in trading G. Darmois, who had got two more votes, for C. Colson "le chef d'économistes 'scientifiques' français." Kondratieff was elected, although it was not known whether or not he was still alive.[31]

Frisch and Schumpeter may have been the two with the greatest personal acquaintance with prospective candidates across national boundaries, and also the most outspoken in their views. Schumpeter spoke warmly in favor of W. Leontief, and also for W. L. Crum, but had to yield on both. Schumpeter also wanted M. Fanno, but the Italians, represented by Amoroso, wanted their own ranking order respected, with Vinci appointed before Fanno. Frisch seems to have been concerned about convincing the majority of the council that the number of Fellows should be kept low.

The next (and the first proper) nomination for Fellowship took place in 1933. About 40 names had been suggested in 1933. Frisch was at the outset inclined to vote for only one of the suggested names: Jakob Marschak.[32] The nomination by the council reduced the number of nom-

---

[31] Nikolai Dmitrievich Kondratieff (born 1892), head of the famous Institute of Conjunctures at Narkomfin (Ministry of Finance), was alive but was imprisoned at the time of his election as Fellow. He was indicted and sentenced together with, inter alia, the agricultural economist A. V. Chayanov at one of the early Stalinist trials on (needless to say) trumped-up charges. He was "rehabilitated" after his death in prison in 1938.

[32] Frisch told Fisher that he would have supported Marschak for the first group of Fellows were it not for a remark by Divisia that Marschak did not know what a partial derivative was. Frisch had later met and read Marschak and knew that there was nothing to Divisia's remark (Frisch/Fisher, December 6, 1933).

inees to 18. That eliminated J. Hicks, P. Sraffa, F. Hayek, O. Morgenstern, and others. The 18 nominees were R. G. D. Allen, C. Bresciani-Turroni, G. Darmois, A. de Pietri-Tonelli, M. Ezekiel, M. Fanno, L.-V. Furlan, A. H. Hansen, R. Hawtrey, W. Leontief, J. Marschak, F. C. Mills, G. Mortara, C. Snyder, O. Weinberger, E. J. Working, and H. Working. At that time some guidelines for qualification for Fellowship had been suggested by the council (Econometric Society minutes book, 1933):

1. He should be an economist.
2. He should be a statistician.
3. He should have some knowledge of higher mathematics.
4. He should have made some original contributions.
5. Some of these contributions should be in economic theory.

The preliminary voting procedure was very elaborate and was designed to reveal both knowledge of the nominees' works and marginal preferences. For each candidate the electors (Fellows) would indicate a vote under five columns:

(a) Votes for nominees considered to have at least as high qualifications for fellowship as the average of the present Fellows
(b) Votes for the better half for those already marked in column (a)
(c) Votes for those nominees in column (b) who it is *very strongly* felt should be elected
(d) Votes against those nominees whose election is *very strongly* opposed

In each of the columns the votes were divided in two by "Have read works/Have not read works." An additional column (e) asked whether or not the electors had "critically scrutinized representative works of Nominees." The blackballing column (d) was from the outset meant to exclude candidates having been blackballed by a sufficient number, regardless of the score in the vote. It was not clear whether one or two (or even more) blackballs would be needed to disqualify a nominee.

The votes cast under (a), (b), and (c) were added up, with weights 1, 3, and 5. The highest scores went to Allen, Bresciani-Turroni, Ezekiel, and Marschak, followed by Mills, Hansen, Fanno, and Snyder. The four with the highest scores were elected.[33]

---

[33] The election of R. G. D. Allen, C. Bresciani-Turroni, M. Ezekiel, and J. Marschak was announced in *Econometrica*, vol. 3, pp. 477–8, accompanied by the following note by the council: "A surprising result of the vote was the discovery that works of several well-known nominees had been read by only a few Fellows. Indeed, the ballots show that some nominees failed of election primarily because their work was to a large extent unknown to the Fellows. This indicates how difficult it was to keep abreast of new developments in econometric research throughout the world when publication was as widely scattered as it was before the founding of Econometrica. In some instances the writings of a nominee were widely read by Fellows in his own country but were unknown to

In the third election of fellows in 1937 the following five were admitted: A. Cowles, J. Hicks, G. Mortara, R. Roy, and H. Staehle.

The experience thus far with the cumbersome nomination and voting procedures was not too good. The next time around was in 1938, and A. L. Bowley, the president, worked out new rules with Cowles that set the maximum number of Fellows at 7 percent of the number of members. The crucial nomination by the council would be conducted by having each council members approve or disapprove of each suggested name and rank all the approvals. Of those who had been approved by a majority, a number not exceeding twice the number to be elected would be sent to the Fellows for the final vote.

Frisch was opposed to the new rules, but he was the only one who voted against adopting them in the council. Frisch would have preferred a more sophisticated system, with both positive and negative votes in the nomination process. The new system turned out to be a flop. The number of new Fellows should, according to the percentage rule, be five, but only four candidates passed the nomination process; hence there was nothing to be voted on. Those who passed were O. Lange, W. Leontief, J. C. Stamp, and T. O. Yntema.

Cowles explained to Bowley: "an unexpected, and I think, unfortunate situation has developed.... The Fellows are thus given no opportunity to indicate a preference.... It seems to me that this outcome is contrary to the intent of the Constitution and I suggest that we at once set about revising the rules which will govern the next election" (Cowles/Bowley, December 29, 1938).

Frisch's alternative system could hardly have done worse. After that election Keynes was indiscrete enough to inform Piero Sraffa that Cowles has "disapproved" of him. Sraffa withdrew immediately from the society and asked for a partial return of his subscription payment.[34]

7 The War Years

The war years brought hard times for the society and *Econometrica*. The annual meetings were mostly canceled, and the volumes became considerably slimmer. The outbreak of the war in Europe isolated one country after another. Communication with the editor-in-chief became

---

Fellows in other parts of the world. It appears, therefore, that authors of works which are not published in Econometrica should endeavor to send out large numbers of reprints. In this way, members and Fellows of the Society can be kept constantly apprised of new discoveries in the rapidly growing field of econometrics" (*Econometrica* 3:479).

[34] The rules and procedures for nominating and electing Fellows were changed repeatedly in the years that followed. The current rules, simple by comparison, have a Nominating Committee, appointed by the president, preparing a list of nominees, limited to 50 each year. Fellows vote by mail for any number of candidates. At least 30 percent of the ballots are needed for election.

more difficult after the German attack on Norway in April 1940 and was completely broken off when the United States entered the war in December 1941.

The 10-year anniversary of the Econometric Society was celebrated with a decennial luncheon during the society meeting in New Orleans in December 1940. F. C. Mills, J. Marschak, and J. Schumpeter spoke at the event. Schumpeter appeared to be in a somber mood and appealed to the members "to stand by the Society."

Frisch was arrested in October 1943 when the Nazi authorities closed the University of Oslo, and he sat imprisoned for about a year. He had been reelected in 1940 for this third 4-year term as editor and was also reelected to the council in 1943. His return to the editor's chair was marked by his programmatic article "The Responsibility of the Econometrician," opening the first issue of 1946.

Frisch's last letter to Schumpeter before the wartime isolation set in was written in mid-October 1939. World War II had begun. Hitler's troops had crushed Poland, but closer to Frisch was the ominous development that Stalin had presented Finland threatening demands. In that somber moment he received the two volumes of Joseph Schumpeter's *Business Cycles*. Frisch had more than an inkling of what the book had cost Schumpeter to finish. Since Schumpeter's article "The Common Sense of Econometrics" in the first issue of *Econometrica* Frisch had not managed to get one single contribution from Schumpeter, not even a preview or excerpt from his book. Frisch congratulated Schumpeter "on the completion of your magnum opus" and continued as follows:

> This is a sad morning. Outside it is raining and the wind is blowing, and inside the air is filled with thoughts of the negotiations between Finland and Russia which have just begun. We follow them with extreme attention, and also with apprehension because of our deep sympathy with the Finnish people.... But at my table I have your book. And so nevertheless this is a cheerful morning. Your book has brought me a greeting from a world of intellect and kindness and beauty where the course of affairs is not determined by motorized armies. Will this tell you what feelings your book has released with me.
>
> Please drop just one word, or let your secretary do so, that I may know that this letter has reached its destination. I am sure you are tremendously busy these days – as I am myself – so don't sit down and write a long letter. One word is enough. I am only anxious to know that what I intend to be a token of warm friendship and admiration has been brought across. [Frisch/Schumpeter, October 13, 1939]

References

Bjerkholt, O. (1995). Ragnar Frisch, editor of *Econometrica* 1933–1954. *Econometrica* 63:755–65.

Christ, C. F. (1983). The founding of the Econometric Society and *Econometrica*. *Econometrica* 51:3–6.
Cournot, A. (1927). *Researches into the Mathematical Principles of the Theory of Wealth*. New York: Macmillan.
de Marchi, N., and Gilbert, C. (eds.) (1989). *History and Methodology of Econometrics*. Oxford: Clarendon Press.
Divisia, F. (1953). La Société d'Économetrie a Atteint sa Majorité. *Econometrica* 21:1–30.
Epstein, R. J. (1987). *A History of Econometrics*. Amsterdam: North Holland.
Fisher, I. (1892). Mathematical investigations in the theory of value and prices. *Transactions of the Connecticut Academy of Arts and Sciences* 9:1. (Reprinted and published as a monograph by Yale University Press, 1925.)
Frisch, R. (1926a). Sur un problème d'économie pure. *Norsk Matematisk Forenings Skrifter*, series I, no. 16, pp. 1–40.
  (1926b). Kvantitativ formulering av den teoretiske økonomikks lover [Quantitative formulation of the laws of theoretical economics]. *Statsøkonomisk Tidsskrift* 40:299–334.
  (1927). The analysis of statistical time series. Mimeographed manuscript.
  (1931). A method of decomposing an empirical series into its cyclical and progressive components. *Journal of the American Statistical Association* 26:73–8.
  (1970). From utopian theory to practical applications: the case of econometrics. In: *Les Prix Nobel en 1969*, pp. 213–43. Stockholm: Nobel Foundation.
  (1971). On a problem in pure economics. In: *Preferences, Utility, and Demand. A Minnesota Symposium*, ed. J. S. Chipman, L. Hurwicz, M. K. Richter, and H. F. Sonnenschein, pp. 386–423. New York: Harcourt Brace Jovanovich.
  (1995). *Foundations of Modern Econometrics. The Selected Essays of Ragnar Frisch*, ed. O. Bjerkholt. London: Edward Elgar.
Hendry, D. F., and Morgan, M. S. (eds.) (1995). *The Foundations of Econometric Analysis*. Cambridge University Press.
Morgan, M. S. (1990). *The History of Econometric Ideas*. Cambridge University Press.
Roos, C. F. (1948). A future role for the Econometric Society in international statistics. *Econometrica* 16:127–34.
Tinbergen, J. (1974). Ragnar Frisch's role in econometrics. *European Economic Review* 5:3–6.

CHAPTER 3

The Contributions of Ragnar Frisch to Economics and Econometrics

John S. Chipman

Ragnar Frisch opened his 1926 article "On a Problem in Pure Economics" with the following statement:

> Intermediate between mathematics, statistics, and economics, we find a new discipline which, for lack of a better name, may be called *econometrics*.
>
> Econometrics has as its aim to subject abstract laws of theoretical political economy or "pure" economics to experimental and numerical verification, and thus to turn pure economics, as far as possible, into a science in the strict sense of the word.

Thus we are here to celebrate the centennial of the birth of the founder of our subject, who gave it its name[1] and founded its journal.

Rather regrettably, but perhaps inevitably, the term "econometrics" has come to have a narrower meaning than Frisch originally intended: the study of statistical methods for the application of economic models. For that reason, the title of this chapter, instead of referring just to Frisch's contributions to econometrics in the narrower sense – which were many and profound – also refers to his contributions to economics, by which may be understood economic theory and policy, to which he made a large number of important contributions. I shall necessarily be quite selective, and rather than try to survey his huge output, which could be done only in a superficial way, I shall concentrate on what seem to me the most important and lasting of his contributions.

The history of economic thought can be, and often is, a dry subject, and if one limits oneself to the works of a single person, out of the context in which that person lived and worked, it can be dull. What is really much more interesting is how such a person interacted with others and with

---

This work was supported by a Humboldt Research Award for Senior U.S. Scientists. I wish to thank Dale Jorgenson for valuable discussions and Olav Bjerkholt for his valuable bibliographic help. Thanks are also due to the referee for helpful comments.

[1] This notwithstanding the fact that an earlier use of the term was subsequently made known to Frisch (1936c).

the economic environment. While I do not pretend to subscribe to, let alone understand, all of Hegelian philosophy, I believe that Hegel had an enormous insight into how knowledge progresses: by conflict. What makes the history of economic thought interesting, in my opinion, is the study of how truth comes out of controversy. In addition, conflict in itself is always interesting and makes the subject come alive. I shall therefore be especially interested in recounting the controversies in which Frisch was engaged, and in showing how they led to important advances in the subject.

I shall look at four fields in which Frisch made major contributions: (1) utility theory, index numbers, and welfare economics, (2) estimation of demand and supply functions, and statistical confluence analysis, (3) capital theory and dynamic economics, and (4) depression and circulation planning.

1 Utility Theory, Index Numbers, and Welfare Economics

1.1 *Measurable Utility, Price Indices, and Homothetic Preferences*

Frisch's first work on utility theory (1926a) was, in his words, an attempt to "realize the dream of Jevons." Jevons had stated (1911, pp. 146–7; 1871, p. 140) that

> the price of a commodity is the only test we have of the [marginal] utility of the commodity to the purchaser; and if we could tell exactly how much people reduce their consumption of each important article when the price rises, we could determine, at least approximately, the variation of the final degree of utility – the all-important element in Economics.

Frisch set himself the problem of objectively defining utility as a quantity. "The real advances in a science," he said, "begin on the day that it is realized that vague common sense notions must be replaced by notions capable of objective definition." He noted that while that had been the object of works by Edgeworth (1881), Fisher (1892), and Pareto (1906), definitive results had not been obtained. Indeed, those authors had provided the basic idea that Frisch was to use. Edgeworth postulated (1881, p. 99) that "just perceivable increments of pleasure are equatable." An alternative approach was followed by Fisher (1892, p. 17n). Pareto was still more explicit (1906, p. 252; 1909, p. 264):

> Moreover, man may know approximately whether in passing from combination I to combination II he experiences greater pleasure than in passing from combination II to another combination III. If this judgment could be made sufficiently precise we could, in the limit, determine whether passing from I to II provides equal pleasure to passing

from II to III; in which case, passing from I to III provides double the pleasure that is obtained in passing from I to II. This would suffice to enable us to consider pleasure or ophelimity as a quantity.

Frisch proceeded to formulate his axioms of the first kind (comparisons of commodity bundles) and of the second kind (comparisons of pairs of commodity bundles) and sketched a proof of the measurability of utility. Some years later this was followed by Alt (1936).

Proceeding to the "marginal utility of money" he added some further (and more controversial) assumptions for tractability, notably that it would remain unchanged if prices varied in such a way as to leave "the mean value of its components" (i.e., the price level) unchanged. He therefore expressed it as a function of income (Y) and price level (P) (on the legitimacy of this step, more later). He assumed further that it would approach infinity for minimum-subsistence income, would approach zero for infinite income, and would be decreasing in income — all reasonable assumptions. However, he added the more questionable assumptions that the elasticity of the marginal utility of income is greater than unity (in absolute value) for sufficiently small incomes and approaches zero for indefinitely large incomes. This led him to a formula for the marginal utility of income that I shall write in the form[2]

$$\frac{\partial \overline{V}}{\partial Y} = \frac{c(P)}{\log Y - \log a(P)} \tag{1.1}$$

where I have replaced his parameters a (representing subsistence income) and c by functions of P. Since $\overline{V}_Y(Y, P)$ must be homogeneous of degree -1 in its two arguments, $a(P)$ and $c(P)$ must be homogeneous of degree 1 and -1, respectively. Assuming additively separable utility, that is,

$$U(x_1, x_2, \ldots, x_n) = \sum_{i=1}^{n} u_i(x_i) \tag{1.2}$$

since the marginal utility of commodity i is proportional to its price, the factor of proportionality being the marginal utility of income, Frisch noted that

$$u_i'(x_i) = \overline{V}_Y(Y, P) p_i = \frac{p_i}{P} \overline{V}_Y\left(\frac{Y}{P}, 1\right) = \frac{p_i}{P} \frac{c(1)}{\log(Y/P) - \log a(1)}$$

expressing a relation among the three variables x_i (quantity of a commodity), p_i/P (its relative price), and Y/P (real income). Using French

---

[2] He specifically rejected Bernoulli's (1738) formula in which Y takes the place of $\log Y$ in (1.1), as well as a squared variant suggested by Jordan (1924) – see Frisch (1932c, p. 31).

sugar data, he developed a method for estimating the coefficients $c(1)$ and $a(1)$.[3]

Stimulated by Fisher's 1927 paper, Frisch undertook a more extensive investigation in his *New Methods of Measuring Marginal Utility* (1932c). Influenced by Birck's concept of a "general commodity" (1922, p. 53), he formulated the marginal utility of income more explicitly as a function of income and the "general price level" P. Defining "real income" by $R = Y/P$, because of homogeneity of degree 0 of the function $\bar{V}(Y, P)$ (Frisch dealt not with this function but only with its partial derivative with respect to income, Y) we have

$$\bar{V}(Y, P) = \bar{V}(Y/P, 1) = \bar{V}(R, 1) \equiv W(R) \tag{1.3}$$

Hence

$$W'(R) = \bar{V}_Y(Y/P, 1) = P\bar{V}_Y(Y, P)$$

leading to Frisch's basic formula [1932c, p. 16, formula (3.2)]

$$\frac{\partial \bar{V}(Y, P)}{\partial Y} = \frac{W'(R)}{P} = \frac{u'_i(x_i)}{p_i} \tag{1.4}$$

where x_i is the amount of the "commodity of comparison" (1932c, p. 8), and p_i is its price. He called $W'(R)$ the "real money utility," in contrast to the "nominal money utility" $\bar{V}_Y$ (1932c, p. 14). "Real income" R, according to this formula, may be interpreted as the quantity of the "general commodity," and P its price.

Frisch's formulation came under the forceful criticism of R. G. D. Allen (1933), whose paper, while ostensibly a review article of Frisch's work, was a very important contribution on its own. For the first time since (and independently of) Antonelli (1886), Allen formulated the concept of an "equilibrium utility function" (now known as "indirect utility function")

$$V(Y, p_1, p_2, \ldots, p_n)$$

and the accompanying partial differential equation[4]

$$\frac{\partial V}{\partial p_i} = -\frac{\partial V}{\partial Y} h_i \tag{1.5}$$

(1933, p. 190), where $h_i(Y, p_1, p_2, \ldots, p_n)$ is the Marshallian demand function for commodity i. Allen pointed out that whereas in equilibrium it is necessarily true that

---

[3] For good expositions of the procedure used by Frisch, see Marschak (1931, pp. 128–35), as well as the reviews of Frisch (1932c) by Bowley (1932) and Schultz (1933).

[4] Usually attributed to Roy (1942, p. 21). Roy (pp. 38–9) referred to Frisch but not to Allen. For the earliest derivation of (1.5), see Antonelli [1886, p. 17, equation (24)], or page 349 of the English translation.

$$\frac{\partial V}{\partial Y} = \frac{\sum_{i=1}^{n} u_i'(x_i)x_i}{\sum_{i=1}^{n} p_i x_i} \tag{1.6}$$

where the numerator on the right is the equilibrium marginal utility of the composite commodity and the denominator is its equilibrium amount, they cannot legitimately be interpreted as structural parameters; therefore the device of introducing a composite commodity entails a restrictive assumption on consumer behavior. In his words (p. 193):

> Professor Frisch's analogy with the marginal utility of a consumer's good and his introduction of a composite commodity only serve to hide the serious assumption that must be made before his statistical methods can be applied.

Unfortunately, however, Allen did not attempt to find out what that assumption was. It was left for Frisch himself to do so in his famous "Annual Survey" of the theory of index numbers (1936a), a paper subsequently characterized by Bergson (1936, p. 34n; 1966, p. 94n) as "chiefly a response to criticisms by Allen." Bergson himself set out to tackle this same problem.

The reasoning in these two papers is extremely difficult to follow, but I shall try to restate what is apparently claimed and sketch a supporting argument. The argument is entirely in terms of a single individual; the problem of aggregation over individuals is not taken up. The claim concerns two conditions:

1. Individual preferences can be represented by an additively separable, monotonic, and strongly concave utility function (1.2) (i.e., $u_i' > 0, u_i'' < 0$).
2. Denoting the demand functions generated by (1.2) by $h_i(Y, p)$, where p denotes the price vector, the indirect utility function obtained by composing (1.2) with these demand functions is separable as between income and the commodity prices; that is,

$$V(Y, p) \equiv \sum_{i=1}^{n} u_i[h_i(Y, p)] = \overline{V}[Y, P(p)] \tag{1.7}$$

The claim is that these two conditions together imply that individual preferences are homothetic. This is what Frisch described as "expenditure proportionality."[5]

---

[5] The superficial resemblance of this theorem to that of Houthakker (1960) and Samuelson (1965) – as amended by Hicks (1969) and Samuelson (1969) – requires some comment. The Houthakker-Hicks-Samuelson theorem states that (barring the exceptional cases brought to light by Hicks) condition 1 combined with the condition that the indirect utility function can be written in the form *(continued)*

Frisch's Contributions to Economics and Econometrics

In terms of concepts developed since Frisch's time, but undoubtedly influenced by and indeed implicit in Frisch's own work, we can define his concepts of price index and real income as follows. Let the *expenditure function* be defined as[6]

$$e(u, p) = \min\{Y: V(Y, p) \geq u\} \tag{1.8}$$

Note from this definition that since $V(Y, p)$ is homogeneous of degree 0, $e(u, p)$ is homogeneous of degree 1 in p. Frisch (1936a, p. 11) then defines the general price or cost-of-living index at time t, following Bowley (1928, p. 223), as the proportionate "change in expenditure ... necessary, after a change of prices, to obtain the same satisfaction as before," that is (pp. 15–16),

$$P(u; p^0, p^t) \equiv \frac{e(u, p^t)}{e(u, p^0)} \tag{1.9}$$

We verify that $P(u; p^0, \lambda p) = \lambda P(u; p^0, p)$, so (1.9) satisfies the property of the aggregator function $P(p)$ required for $\bar{V}(Y, P)$ to be homogeneous

---

$$V(Y, p) = \sum_{i=1}^{n} v_i(p_i/Y)$$

implies that preferences are homothetic. (The exceptional cases involve "parallel preferences.") In Frisch's theorem the second condition states that the indirect utility function can be expressed in the form

$$V(Y, p) = \bar{V}[Y, P(p)]$$

In one sense this is a weaker condition, since all that is involved is separability (not even additive) as between the income variable and the set of price variables. If $P(p)$ is homogeneous of degree 1, then

$$\bar{V}[\lambda Y, \lambda P(p)] = \bar{V}[\lambda Y, P(\lambda p)] = V(\lambda Y, \lambda p) = V(Y, p) = \bar{V}[Y, P(p)]$$

Hence $\bar{V}(Y, P)$ is homogeneous of degree 0. Conversely, if $\bar{V}(Y, P)$ is homogeneous of degree 0, then

$$\bar{V}[\lambda Y, \lambda P(p)] = \bar{V}[Y, P(p)] = V(Y, p) = V(\lambda Y, \lambda p) = \bar{V}[\lambda Y, P(\lambda p)]$$

which can hold for all λ if and only if $P(\lambda p) = \lambda P(p)$. Thus one need only require that the function $P(p)$ in (1.7) be positively homogeneous of degree 1. The conclusion of Frisch's theorem states that the preference ordering must be homothetic. But Bergson's extension of Frisch's theorem (shown later) proves as a consequence that the indirect utility function is *additively* separable as between income and the set of prices [see (1.19), where for $\beta \neq 0$ one can replace the indicated indirect utility function by its logarithm] and, in the Cobb-Douglas case ($\beta = 0$), additively separable in income and the individual prices.

[6] If p^t is the price vector in period t, then Frisch's notation for $e(u, p^t)$ is $\rho_t(I)$, where ρ denotes income and I ("indicator") denotes utility. Thus the concept is present in all but name.

of degree 0 (see footnote 5). The case of *expenditure proportionality* occurs when this function is independent of u. Frisch also defines *real income* in period t (p. 32) as money income in period t deflated by the above cost-of-living index; that is,

$$R(u; p^0, p^t) = \frac{Y^t}{P(u; p^0, p^t)} = e(u, p^0),$$

since $Y^t = e(u, p^t)$ (1.10)

Thus, real income, according to this definition, is independent of current prices and coincides with the expenditure function evaluated at base-year prices, $e(u, p^0)$.

Now the relation $R = e(u, p^0)$ from (1.10) can be inverted (because of monotonicity) to

$$u = W(R, p^0), \quad \text{where } R = e[W(R, p^0), p^0]$$ (1.11)

and the relation

$$Y^t = e(u, p^t) = e(u, p^0) P(u; p^0, p^t)$$

yields

$$\hat{Y}(R; p^0, p^t) = R\hat{P}(R; p^0, p^t)$$ (1.12)

where

$$\hat{Y}(R; p^0, p^t) = e[W(R, p^0), p^t] \quad \text{and} \quad \hat{P}(R; p^0, p^t) = P[W(R, p^0); p^0, p^t]$$

Differentiating (1.12) we obtain

$$\frac{\partial \hat{Y}}{\partial R} = \hat{P}\left(1 + \frac{R}{\hat{P}} \frac{\partial \hat{P}}{\partial R}\right)$$

Thus the marginal utility of income is

$$\frac{\partial V}{\partial Y} = \frac{\partial W/\partial R}{\partial \hat{Y}/\partial R} = \frac{\partial W/\partial R}{\hat{P}\left(1 + \frac{\partial \log \hat{P}}{\partial \log R}\right)}$$ (1.13)

This agrees with (1.4) if and only if

$$\frac{\partial \hat{P}}{\partial R} = \frac{\partial P}{\partial u} \frac{\partial W}{\partial R} = 0$$ (1.14)

which occurs if and only if $\partial P(u; p^0, p^t)/\partial u = 0$ (expenditure proportionality). Thus, homotheticity of preferences is implied by (1.4), which is in turn implied by (1.7).[7] Conversely, if preferences are homothetic, the formula

$$\frac{u_i'(x_i)}{p_i} = \frac{\partial W(R, p^0)/\partial R}{\hat{P}(R; p^0, p^t)}$$

holds, where $\hat{P}$ is now independent of R.[8]

Now the assumptions of homotheticity and additive separability of the direct preference relation together have very stringent implications, as shown by Bergson (1936, p. 45; 1966, p. 111). Since homotheticity and separability imply that the marginal rates of substitution

$$R_{ij}(x_i, x_j) = \frac{\partial U(x)/\partial x_i}{\partial U(x)/\partial x_j} = \frac{u_i'(x_i)}{u_j'(x_j)}$$

are homogeneous of degree 0 in the quantities x_i, x_j, it follows by Euler's theorem that

$$0 = \frac{\partial R_{ij}}{\partial x_i} x_i + \frac{\partial R_{ij}}{\partial x_j} x_j = \frac{u_i''(x_i)}{u_j'(x_j)} x_i - \frac{u_i'(x_i) u_j''(x_j)}{u_j'(x_j)^2} x_j$$

whence, multiplying through by $u_j'(x_j)/u_i'(x_i)$, we obtain

$$\frac{x_i u_i''(x_i)}{u_i'(x_i)} = \frac{x_j u_j''(x_j)}{u_j'(x_j)} \quad \text{for all } i, j \tag{1.15}$$

Thus, each of the two expressions in (1.15) is a (negative) constant. This can be written as

$$-\frac{d \log u_i'(x_i)}{d \log x_i} = -\frac{x_i}{u_i'(x_i)} u_i''(x_i) = 1 + \beta \tag{1.16}$$

where $\beta > -1$. Integrating (1.16) for each i gives the marginal utility

$$u_i'(x_i) = A_i x_i^{-1-\beta} \quad (A_i > 0)$$

and integrating this equation once again gives

---

[7] For the equivalence of homotheticity and expenditure proportionality, see Samuelson and Swamy [1974, p. 570, equation (2.5)] and Chipman and Moore (1980, p. 939, Proposition H6).

[8] This provided Frisch's answer to Allen's objection that equation (1.6) was only an equilibrium condition and not a structural relationship. In his words (1936a, p. 34n): "(1.13) – here derived as a theoretical consequence – should completely meet Allen's objection.... (1.13) shows that my original formula does hold under expenditure proportionality, which was assumed in the statistical work in New Methods...."

$$u_i(x_i) = \begin{cases} a_i x_i^{-\beta} + \gamma_i & \text{for } \beta < 0 \text{ and } a_i = -A_i/\beta \\ -a_i x_i^{-\beta} + \gamma_i & \text{for } \beta > 0 \text{ and } a_i = A_i/\beta \\ a_i \log x_i + \gamma_i & \text{for } \beta = 0 \text{ and } a_i = A_i \end{cases}$$

Summing these over all n commodities and dropping the spurious constant terms γ_i, we obtain for the utility function (1.2)

$$U(x) = \begin{cases} -(\operatorname{sgn}\beta) \sum_{i=1}^{n} a_i x_i^{-\beta} & \text{for } \beta \neq 0 \\ \sum_{i=1}^{n} a_i \log x_i & \text{for } \beta = 0 \end{cases} \quad (1.17)$$

The first of these, of course, will be recognized, after taking its absolute value and raising it to the power $-1/\beta$, as the Arrow–Solow constant-elasticity-of-substitution (CES) function introduced by Arrow et al. (1961, p. 226n) for the two-commodity case and generalized by Uzawa (1962) and McFadden (1963) to the n-commodity case, where the elasticity of substitution is $\sigma = 1/(1 + \beta)$.[9] The exponential of the second is the "Cobb-Douglas" function to which the CES reduces as $\beta \to 1$. We verify that

$$\frac{\partial U}{\partial x_i} = |\beta| \frac{a_i}{x_i^{1+\beta}} > 0 \quad \text{and} \quad \frac{\partial^2 U}{\partial x_i^2} = -|\beta|(1+\beta) \frac{a_i}{x_i^{2+\beta}} < 0 \quad \text{for } \beta \neq 0$$

as well as

$$\frac{\partial U}{\partial x_i} = \frac{a_i}{x_i} > 0 \quad \text{and} \quad \frac{\partial^2 U}{\partial x_i^2} = -\frac{a_i}{x_i^2} < 0 \quad \text{for } \beta = 0$$

as desired. Equating the ratios of these marginal utilities to the corresponding price ratios and substituting in the budget equation $\sum_{i=1}^{n} p_i x_i = Y$, we obtain, upon adopting the normalization $\sum_{i=1}^{n} a_i = 1$, the demand functions

$$x_i = h_i(Y, p) = \frac{Y}{a_i^{-\frac{1}{1+\beta}} p_i^{\frac{1}{1+\beta}} \sum_{j=1}^{n} a_j^{\frac{1}{1+\beta}} p_j^{\frac{\beta}{1+\beta}}} \quad \text{for } i = 1, 2, \ldots, n, \ -1 < \beta < \infty \quad (1.18)$$

Substituting (1.18) into (1.17), we obtain the indirect utility function

$$V(Y, p) = \begin{cases} -(\operatorname{sgn}\beta) Y^{-\beta} \left(\sum_{i=1}^{n} a_i^{\frac{1}{1+\beta}} p_i^{\frac{\beta}{1+\beta}} \right)^{1+\beta} & \text{for } \beta \neq 0 \\ \log Y + \sum_{i=1}^{n} a_i \log a_i - \sum_{i=1}^{n} a_i \log p_i & \text{for } \beta = 0 \end{cases} \quad (1.19)$$

---

[9] It is also the same as the "generalized weighted mean" of Hardy, Littlewood, and Pólya [1934, p. 13, formula (2.2.5)].

The marginal utility of income then becomes

$$\frac{\partial V}{\partial Y} = \begin{cases} \dfrac{|\beta| \left(\sum_{i=1}^{n} a_i^{\frac{1}{1+\beta}} p_i^{\frac{\beta}{1+\beta}} \right)^{1+\beta}}{Y^{1+\beta}} & \text{for } \beta \neq 0 \\ \dfrac{1}{Y} & \text{for } \beta = 0 \end{cases} \quad (1.20)$$

It follows from (1.20) that under the conditions implied by Frisch's assumptions, his functional form (1.1) for the marginal utility of income is inadmissible. Since this form no longer appears in the "Annual Survey" (Frisch, 1936a), it can be assumed that he became aware of this inconsistency.

The hypothesis of additively separable utility adopted by Fisher and Frisch came under strong criticism by Samuelson (1947), who noted that the hypothesis had strong empirical implications, namely (p. 177),

> if we are given as empirical observational data the two expenditure paths corresponding to the changes in quantities with income in each of two respective price situations, then from these observations, and these alone, the whole field of indifference curves can be determined by suitable extrapolation.

However, Arrow (1960) later came to Frisch's defense: "The sharpness of the implications of a hypothesis are a virtue, not a vice, provided of course the implications are not refuted by evidence" (p. 177). Samuelson returned to this subject in his obituary article (1974, pp. 11–15): "Arrow's 1960 appreciation of Frisch suggests that my own earlier criticisms have been too strong. He may well be right."

1.2 Laspeyres and Paasche Bounds to the Cost-of-Living Index

One of the most important contributions of Frisch's paper on index numbers was his analysis of inequalities bounding the cost-of-living index by the Laspeyres and Paasche price indices. Not having access to the original article in Russian by Konüs (1924), first brought to light by Bortkiewicz (1928), hence basing himself on the subsequent detailed exposition by Bortkiewicz (1932, pp. 18–20), he set forth and proved the following propositions attributed to Konüs by Bortkiewicz:

1. If $x^1 = h(Y^1, p^1)$ and $p^1 \cdot x^0 = p^1 \cdot x^1 = Y^1$, then denoting $u^1 = U(x^1) = V(Y^1, p^1)$ we have

$$P(u^1; p^0, p^1) \leq \frac{p^1 \cdot x^0}{p^0 \cdot x^0} \quad (1.21)$$

That is, the "true" cost-of-living index is bounded above by the Laspeyres price index.

2. If $x^0 = h(Y^0, p^0)$ and $p^0 \cdot x^1 = p^0 \cdot x^0 = Y^0$, then denoting $u^0 = U(x^0) = V(Y^0, p^0)$ we have

$$P(u^0; p^0, p^1) \geq \frac{p^1 \cdot x^1}{p^0 \cdot x^1} \tag{1.22}$$

That is, the "true" cost-of-living index is bounded below by the Paasche price index.

Frisch noted that if both inequalities are satisfied simultaneously, then under the stated conditions the Laspeyres and Paasche indices are necessarily the same, and moreover x^1 and x^0 must lie on the same indifference surface (and indeed, if the demand function is single-valued, $x^1 = x^0$); consequently (p. 25), "the simultaneous fulfillment of both Konüs conditions is, therefore, a trivial case, when the points compared lie in the same indifference map."

Frisch contrasted this with the limits obtained by Haberler (1927, pp. 89–92), which he interpreted (rightly, in my opinion) as follows:

1. If $x^0 = h(Y^0, p^0)$, then, denoting $u^0 = U(x^0) = V(Y^0, p^0)$,

$$P(u^0; p^0, p^1) \leq \frac{p^1 \cdot x^0}{p^0 \cdot x^0} \tag{1.23}$$

That is, the change in the cost of living from situation (Y^0, p^0) to situation (Y^1, p^1), defined as the ratio $\bar{Y}^1/Y^0$, where $\bar{Y}^1$ is the hypothetical expenditure in period 1 that would make $(\bar{Y}^1, p^1)$ indirectly indifferent to (Y^0, p^0), is bounded above by the Laspeyres price index.

2. If $x^1 = h(Y^1, p^1)$, then, denoting $u^1 = U(x^1) = V(Y^1, p^1)$,

$$P(u^1; p^0, p^1) \geq \frac{p^1 \cdot x^1}{p^0 \cdot x^1} \tag{1.24}$$

That is, the change in the cost of living from situation (Y^0, p^0) to situation (Y^1, p^1), defined as the ratio $Y^1/\bar{Y}^0$, where $\bar{Y}^0$ is the hypothetical expenditure in period 0 that would make $(\bar{Y}^0, p^0)$ indirectly indifferent to (Y^1, p^1), is bounded below by the Paasche price index.

He noted that under expenditure proportionality – an assumption that originally was only implicit (Haberler, 1927), but which was subsequently made explicit (Haberler, 1929, p. 8) in response to Bortkiewicz's charge that the result was simply fallacious (1928, pp. 428–9) – because $P(u; p^0, p^1)$ is then independent of u, the two limits reduce to the double limit

$$\frac{p^1 \cdot x^1}{p^0 \cdot x^1} \leq P(u;\, p^0, p^1) \leq \frac{p^1 \cdot x^0}{p^0 \cdot x^0} \tag{1.25}$$

That (1.25) holds when x^0 and x^1 lie on the same indifference surface, and hence $u = U(x^0) = U(x^1)$, as is immediately obvious from (1.23) and (1.24), was shown by Keynes (1930, I, p. 110) [who referred to Haberler (1927) and Pigou (1929)], Bortkiewicz (1932, p. 21), and Allen (1933, p. 204), but as Frisch (1936a, p. 26) pointed out, "none of these three authors noted the perfectly trivial character of" (1.25) in this case. Because $e(u;\, p^0) = p^0 \cdot x^0$ and $e(u;\, p^1) = p^1 \cdot x^1$ we then have simply $P(u;\, p^0, p^1) = p^1 x^1 / p^0 x^0$, and the bounds (1.25) are superfluous. Even Staehle (1935, pp. 169, 172), who had provided a detailed exposition of Haberler's 1927 and 1929 contributions (Staehle, 1934, pp. 76–9), thought that the condition $U(x^0) = U(x^1)$ was *necessary* as well as sufficient for (1.25) to hold. In this he was influenced by Bortkiewicz (1928). Writing decades later, Allen (1949, 1975, pp. 65–72) showed no evidence of having assimilated the results discovered by Haberler (1929) and proved by Frisch (1936a), namely, that homotheticity of preferences is necessary and sufficient for (1.25) to be true for any two arbitrary equilibrium situations (p^0, x^0) and (p^1, x^1).

A signal service to the profession was provided by Schultz (1939a) in arranging for the publication of an English translation of Konüs's 1924 article and pointing out that its contents had been greatly distorted by Bortkiewicz (1928, 1932). It turned out that Konüs had in fact obtained the Haberler conditions (1.23) and (1.24) three years before Haberler. He had also sought conditions under which the standards of living would be equivalent in two different situations (the part of his treatment summarized by Bortkiewicz), but had himself pointed out, as Frisch later showed, that the true cost-of-living index in such a situation would be simply the ratio of expenditures. He went further, however, in seeking conditions under which (1.25) would hold for some standard of living u^t intermediate between $u^0 = U(x^0)$ and $u^1 = U(x^1)$. He did not, however, obtain the general Haberler-Frisch homotheticity result. The closest he came to this was a characterization, in collaboration with Buscheguennce (1925) (Konüs and Buscheguennce, 1926), of preferences under which Fisher's "ideal index" (the square root of the products of the Laspeyres and Paasche indices) would be an exact cost-of-living index – preferences generated by a homogeneous quadratic utility function of the form $U(x) = (x'Ax)^{1/2}$ – as well as conditions (Cobb-Douglas preferences) under which a geometric price index would be an exact cost-of-living index (cf. Diewert, 1976; Afriat, 1977). In these cases the Laspeyres-Paasche bounds would of course be unnecessary.

Schultz's 1939 exposition (1939a) was astonishing in one respect. It praised Konüs's work as a forerunner of the results of Allen and Staehle – results that (at least in the case of Allen) Frisch had characterized as "perfectly trivial" (1936a, p. 26). On the other hand, it made no mention of Frisch (1936a) or of Haberler (1927, 1929) (except as the subject of Bortkiewicz's 1928 review). From then on, it seems that the most important contributions to index-number theory – the Haberler-Frisch propositions concerning the implicit assumption of homotheticity underlying the *economic* theory of index numbers – were buried alive, so to speak, and had to be rediscovered.

Rediscoveries there were, because truth always waits to be discovered. One was that of Malmquist (1953, p. 215) – though only a very acute reader would be able to discern homotheticity in the purely technical assumption he provided. The first systematic rediscovery appears to have been that of Pollak (1971), which was not published until 1983 (in a very obscure volume), and again in 1990. Shortly after came that of Afriat (1972). Resurrection of the idea came with Samuelson and Swamy (1974) and Samuelson (1974), although Frisch and Haberler still were not given their full due. The Laspeyres and Paasche bounds (1.23) and (1.24) were attributed by Diewert (correctly, as original discoverer) to Konüs (Diewert, 1981, p. 168; 1990, p. 85); the condition for the double inequality (1.25) to hold was correctly attributed to Frisch (Diewert, 1981, p. 168), though no mention was made of Haberler. The theorem that the cost-of-living function $P(u; p^0, p^1)$ is independent of u if and only if the preference ordering is homothetic was attributed to Malmquist (1953), Pollak (1971), and Samuelson and Swamy (1974) by Diewert (1981, p. 166), though in a footnote (p. 200) he remarked as follows: "It seems clear that earlier researchers such as Frisch (1936, p. 25) also knew this result, but they had some difficulty in stating it precisely, since the concept of homotheticity was not invented until 1953 (Shephard, 1953; Malmquist, 1953)." It is perhaps true that the *word* "homotheticity" did not enter the vocabulary until 1953, but the concept was surely well understood by Haberler (1929), Frisch (1936a), Bergson (1936), and Samuelson (1942). But the bulk of the profession apparently was not ready to accept the need to postulate severe restrictions on preferences in order to justify the use of index numbers in economic analysis. Thus it was the fate of this true genius, Frisch, that much of his work was misunderstood and buried by his contemporaries because it was too advanced for that time and had to await rediscovery.

1.3 The Double-Expenditure Method

One of the most novel ideas presented in Frisch (1936a) was the double-expenditure method (pp. 27–30). The problem posed was this: Suppose we are given data on a quantity vector $x^0 = (x_1^0, x_2^0, \ldots, x_n^0)$ and a price vector $p^0 = (p_1^0, p_2^0, \ldots, p_n^0)$ observed at time 0, where x^0 is consumed at prices p^0. This is called the base-period quantity and price. Suppose we are also given a price vector p^1. The problem is to find a commodity bundle x^1 consumed at prices p^1 that is indifferent to the bundle x^0. Stimulated by a formulation of Bowley (1928), Frisch took a second-order Taylor approximation of a utility function around the point x^0:

$$U(x^1) - U(x^0) = \sum_{i=1}^{n} U_i(x^0)(x_i^1 - x_i^0) \\ + \frac{1}{2}\sum_{i=1}^{n}\left[\sum_{j=1}^{n} U_{ij}(x^0)(x_j^1 - x_j^0)\right](x_i^1 - x_i^0) \quad (1.26)$$

where $U_i(x) = \partial U(x)/\partial x_i$ and $U_{ij}(x) = \partial^2 U(x)/\partial x_i \partial x_j$. Noting that the quadratic term in the Taylor expansion of $U_i(x^0)$ is

$$U_i(x^1) - U_i(x^0) = \sum_{j=1}^{n} U_{ij}(x^0)(x_j^1 - x_j^0) \quad (1.27)$$

and substituting the left member of (1.27) into the bracketed term of (1.26), we obtain

$$U(x^1) - U(x^0) = \frac{1}{2}\sum_{i=1}^{n}[U_i(x^0) + U_i(x^1)](x_i^1 - x_i^0) \\ = \frac{1}{2}\sum_{i=1}^{n}(\omega^0 p_i^0 + \omega^1 p_i^1)(x_i^1 - x_i^0) \quad (1.28) \\ = \omega^1 Y^1 + \omega^0 Y^0 + \omega^0 \sum_{i=1}^{n} p_i^0 x_i^1 - \omega^1 \sum_{i=1}^{n} p_i^1 x_i^0$$

where

$$\omega^t = V_Y(Y^t, p^t) \quad \text{where} \quad V_Y(Y, p) = \frac{\partial V(Y, p)}{\partial Y} \quad (1.29)$$

is the marginal utility of income in period t, and Y^t is period-t income, the quantities consumed satisfying the budget constraint $\sum_{i=1}^{n} p_i^t x_i^t = Y^t$. To obtain x^1, the expression (1.29) must be set equal to zero.

Now Frisch introduces another approximation, namely, $\omega^1 Y^1 = \omega^0 Y^0$, and notes that it is satisfied exactly if preferences are homothetic ("expenditure proportionality"), appealing to formula (1.13). Adopting this assumption, (1.28), when set equal to zero, becomes, using the budget constraint,

$$\sum_{i=1}^{n} p_i^1 x_i^1 \cdot \sum_{i=1}^{n} p_i^0 x_i^1 = \sum_{i=1}^{n} p_i^0 x_i^0 \cdot \sum_{i=1}^{n} p_i^1 x_i^0 \quad (1.30)$$

The term on the left Frisch denotes D_{01} and calls the *double expenditure along Engel curve 1* $(\{x: (\exists Y)x = h(Y, p^1)\})$, with Engel curve 0 $(\{x: (\exists Y)x = h(Y, p^0)\})$ as a base. Likewise the term on the right, D_{10}, is the double expenditure along Engel curve 0, with 1 as a base. Intuitively, at any point along Engel curve 1 we may ask the following: (1) What is the cost of purchasing this bundle at prices p^1? (2) What would be the cost of purchasing this bundle at prices p^0? The product of these costs is the double expenditure. A point x^1 on path 1 is indifferent to a point x^0 on path 0 if and only if (under this approximation) its double expenditure D_{01} relative to path 0 is equal to the double expenditure D_{10} of point x^0 relative to path 1. The concept can be applied to different markets (e.g., different countries) in place of different time periods with suitable interpretations (cf. Menderhausen, 1938; Frisch, 1937). Frisch subsequently (1938), following some further comments by Bowley (1938), carried out some simulations with some two-commodity utility functions to see how good an approximation his method gave; the results were certainly very favorable.

The following year, Wald (1939) raised an objection to Frisch's method. He pointed out that taking a Taylor approximation of the utility function to two terms amounted to assuming that the utility function was quadratic; hence "it is superfluous to make additional assumptions, because the polynomial assumption already suffices for the unique determination of the index" (p. 329). He proceeded to carry out this determination and showed that the utility function could be approximated by a quadratic function in the neighborhood of comparison points. Frisch, in a footnote to Wald's paper (p. 329n), made the point that "my additional 'superfluous' assumption may indeed in many cases correct for part of the error committed by assuming the indicator as a polynomial" and reported that he had experimented with Wald's method and found that the goodness of approximation was about the same for the two methods, but that "Dr. Wald's method proved to be much more laborious." Except for some interesting comments by Samuelson and Swamy (1974), that appears to be where the subject has rested![10]

1.4 Fisher's Tests for Internal Consistency of Index Numbers

An important early contribution of Frisch was his demonstration (1930) that if prices and quantities are chosen arbitrarily, there exists no relative index number (comparing situations at two points of time) that satisfies simultaneously several of Fisher's (1922) tests. That paper drew the attention of Subramanian (1934), who found technical problems with Frisch's proofs, but Frisch's reply (1934d) seemed to put the matter at rest. The issue was revived by Swamy (1965), who provided a rigorous proof of the incompatibility of four of Fisher's tests. Eichhorn (1976) subsequently furnished proofs that dispensed with continuity and differentiability assumptions, and the topic has been treated at length by Eichhorn and Voeller (1976). A recent survey has been provided by Balk (1995).

Samuelson and Swamy (1974), by removing the assumption that prices

---

[10] An interesting discussion of Wald's approach and its relation to that of Buscheguennce (1925) has been provided by Afriat (1977, pp. 133–40).

and quantities can be chosen arbitrarily, and taking account of the fact that quantities are chosen optimally at given prices, were able to find index-number formulas that satisfied "the spirit" of Fisher's tests "in the only case in which a single index number of cost of living makes economic sense – namely the 'homothetic' case" (p. 567). A valuable discussion has been provided by Samuelson (1974, pp. 15–21).

Going back to Allen (1933), it is clear that from a welfare point of view what is really sought is an indirect utility function, and it is only in the case of homothetic preferences that such a function has the form $V(Y, p) = Y/C(p)$, where $C(p)$ can be interpreted as a cost-of-living function. There are other cases where it makes more sense to *subtract* a cost-of-living index from income.[11] It is ironic that Frisch's 1936 approach to index-number theory, combined with his criterion of "expenditure proportionality," should in the end have furnished the required solution to his 1930 impossibility theorem!

1.5   *Taxation and Welfare*

Fisher (1927) constructed an ingenious example of three households, with households 1 and 3 living in the same district and thus facing the same prices but having different incomes, and household 2 facing different prices. He assumed that all three had identical preferences, representable by an additively separable utility function, and moreover that for each of two commodity groups the shares of expenditure were constant irrespective of prices and income [so that we are in the case $\beta = 0$ of (1.17)]. By assuming that households in a sample could be found such that households 1 and 2 consumed the same amount of food and households 2 and 3 consumed the same amount of housing, he was able to show that from this information one could deduce the marginal utility of income and the income of each household, and thus the elasticity of the marginal utility of income with respect to income. The object of this exercise was to determine the just degree of progression of an income tax. By the "principle of equal sacrifice" he meant that the subjective sacrifices of different households should be equated, these being defined as the product of the marginal utility of income and the amount of the tax payment. This kind of welfare economics has, of course, been pretty much discredited since the time of Lionel Robbins, but even if it is accepted, Fisher's assumption that the taxes are sufficiently small so as not to appreciably affect income and thus the marginal utility of income, even if realistic in 1927, would certainly not be so today. In any case, Fisher used this principle to show how one could calculate the optimal

---

[11] If preferences are of the "parallel" form with respect to commodity 1, then a representation of indirect preferences is given by $V(Y, p) = [Y - C(p)]/p_1$. Cf. Chipman and Moore (1980, p. 941).

rates at different incomes given information on prices and consumption of different households.

In "*Sur un problème*" (Frisch, 1926a) there is no indication that Frisch's research had similar goals; rather, it was a study in positive economics, with much of it devoted to the problem of statistical estimation of the marginal utility of income as a function of income and the price level. He had, in that paper, referred to Jordan (1924), who had associated mathematical expectation with equal taxes, Bernoullian moral expectation with proportional taxes, and his proposed "harmonic expectation" with progressive taxes. However, Frisch was interested only in the empirical realism of the functional forms. In *New Methods* (1932c), however, he devoted an entire chapter (ch. 11) to "Money Utility and the Income Tax." But he was far more cautious than Fisher, considering in turn the principles of equal sacrifice and proportional sacrifice and several others, ending with a Rawlsian "minimum-sacrifice" principle. Finally he insisted on specifying a particular "justice-definition" and insisted that "our statistically determined money utility curve *in itself* neither proves nor disproves the 'justice' of a progressive income tax, it will do so only when a particular form of [justice-definition] is used" (p. 133).

An important controversy in which Frisch was engaged was his 1939 debate with Hotelling about the welfare effects of excise taxes. Following Marshall (1890), but using a more sophisticated argument, Hotelling (1938) claimed that any system of ad-valorem excise taxes would be worse than a proportional income tax. Frisch objected to this conclusion and found a slip in Hotelling's argument. The argument, like all the previous ones discussed in this section, is stated in terms of a single consumer:

Suppose our single individual consumes n commodities in amounts x_i with prices p_i. Prior to the imposition of excise taxes, the individual consumes a bundle x^0 at prices p^0 and income Y^0 so as to maximize a utility function $U(x)$ subject to the budget constraint $p^0 \cdot x^0 = Y^0$. After the introduction of taxes, market (tax-inclusive) prices and after-tax income are p^1 and Y^1, respectively, and a bundle x^1 is chosen that maximizes $U(x)$ subject to $p^1 \cdot x^1 = Y^1$. The government collects $R = (p^1 - p^0) \cdot x^1 - (Y^1 - Y^0)$ in net revenues. Because the government is assumed by Hotelling to collect $(p_i^1 - p_i^0)x_i^1$ in taxes on commodity i, p_i^0 must be identified with the production cost after the tax as well as with the market price (= production cost) before the tax, that is, the tax does not affect pre-tax unit production costs, so that supplies are infinitely elastic; perhaps there is a single factor of production in the economy.[12]

---

[12] This results, as is well known, when there are constant returns to scale and no joint production; cf. Samuelson (1951), and for an elementary exposition, Chipman (1953).

Let the *ad valorem* excise-tax rate on commodity i and a proportional income-tax rate be denoted

$$t_i = p_i^1/p_i^0 - 1 \quad \text{and} \quad t_0 = 1 - Y^1/Y^0 \tag{1.31}$$

respectively (negative taxes are interpreted as subsidies). The government's net revenues are

$$R = \sum_{i=1}^{n} t_i p_i^0 x_i^1 + t_0 Y^0 = 0 \tag{1.32}$$

assumed zero because the government distributes the entire proceeds of these excise taxes back to the consumer (or taxes the consumer if these are negative). The consumer's budget constraint after the imposition of the taxes is

$$\sum_{i=1}^{n} (1 + t_i) p_i^0 x_i^1 = p^1 \cdot x^1 = Y^1 = (1 - t_0) Y^0 \tag{1.33}$$

Equations (1.33) and (1.32) together imply

$$Y^0 - \sum_{i=1}^{n} p_i^0 x_i^1 = \sum_{i=1}^{n} t_i p_i^0 x_i^1 + t_0 Y^0 = R = 0$$

that is, that x^1 satisfies the budget constraint

$$p^0 \cdot x^1 = Y^0 \tag{1.34}$$

and hence x^1 was in the consumer's original budget set.

According to Hotelling (1938, p. 252), setting aside the "infinitely improbable ... contingency" that x^0 and x^1 lie on the same indifference surface, it follows that "if a person must pay a certain sum of money in taxes, his satisfaction will be greater if the levy is made directly on him as a fixed amount than if it is made through a system of excise taxes which he can to some extent avoid by rearranging his production and consumption."

It was pointed out by Frisch (1939a,b) that Hotelling implicitly assumed that $x^1 \neq x^0$, whereas if the system of excise taxes were *uniform* (i.e., $t_i = t$ for $i = 1, \ldots, n$), then it would follow that $x^1 = x^0$, and Hotelling's conclusion would not follow. The reason for this is that under a system of *uniform (ad-valorem)* excise taxes, the consumer's post-tax budget constraint (1.33) becomes

$$(1+t) p^0 \cdot x^1 = (1 - t_0) Y^0, \quad \text{hence } p^0 \cdot x^1 = \frac{1 - t_0}{1 + t} Y^0 \tag{1.35}$$

On the other hand, the government's budget constraint (1.32) becomes

$$t p^0 \cdot x^1 = -t_0 Y^0, \quad \text{hence } p^0 \cdot x^1 = -\frac{t_0}{t} Y^0 \tag{1.36}$$

Putting (1.35) and (1.36) together, we conclude that

$$\frac{1-t_0}{1+t} = -\frac{t_0}{t}, \quad \text{implying } t_0 = -t \tag{1.37}$$

Substituting (1.37) back into the consumer's post-tax budget constraint (1.35), we obtain

$$(1+t)p^0 \cdot x^1 = (1+t)Y^0$$

which is a multiple of, *hence identical with*, his pre-tax budget constraint (1.34). Therefore, so long as demand is single-valued (as Hotelling assumed), it must follow that $x^1 = x^0$. Therefore, a system of *uniform (ad-valorem) excise taxes* is equivalent to a proportional income tax. Hotelling (1939) conceded the point.

1.6 The "Complete Scheme"

In a return to utility theory, Frisch (1959) developed his "complete scheme" for computing own- and cross-elasticities of demand in a complete system of demand functions. He observed that it was generally more difficult to estimate cross-elasticities than own-elasticities and that the imposition of restrictions on the forms of preference relations would facilitate the drawing of conclusions concerning these price elasticities from information about budget shares and income elasticities. The two principal restrictions were (1) the assumption that market demand is derivable from aggregable rational preferences and (2) the assumption of "want-independence" as between certain groups of commodities.

To formulate the concept of want-independence, Frisch proceeded as follows. Let the system

$$v_i = \frac{\partial}{\partial x_i} U(x_1, x_2, \ldots, x_n) \quad (i = 1, 2, \ldots, n) \tag{1.38}$$

be regarded as a mapping from the n commodity quantities x_i to the n marginal utilities v_i. The elasticities

$$v_{ij} = \frac{\partial v_i(x)}{\partial x_j} \cdot \frac{x_j}{v_i(x)} = \frac{\partial^2 U(x)}{\partial x_i \partial x_j} \cdot \frac{x_j}{\partial U(x)/\partial x_i} \tag{1.39}$$

are called the "utility accelerations." Frisch then considered the mapping inverse to (1.38). This involves the implicit assumption that such an inverse exists. For example, if (to fulfill his first criterion) individual preferences are assumed to be identical and homothetic, then a homogeneous-of-degree-1 utility indicator $\bar{U}(x)$ representing these preferences must be ruled out, since its Hessian determinant – which is the Jacobian determinant of the mapping (1.38) – would then vanish. Consequently, Frisch implicitly had to assume that these preferences are represented by a strongly increasing and concave function $U(x) = f[\bar{U}(x)]$, where $f(u)$ is such that $f'(u) > 0$ and $f''(u) < 0$. In the case, for example, of the homogeneous-of-degree-1 CES utility function $\bar{U}(x) = (\Sigma_{i=1}^n a_i x_i^{-\beta})^{-1/\beta}$ (where $\beta > -1$ and $\Sigma_{i=1}^n a_i = 1$), one could choose $f(u) = -(\text{sgn}\,\beta) u^{-\beta}$ for $\beta \neq 0$ and $f(u) = \log u$ for $\beta \to 0$ to obtain the Bergson family $U(x)$ given by (1.17). With this assumption, the conditions of Gale and Nikaido (1965) are satisfied, and one can define the inverse mapping

$$x_i = \xi_i(v_1, v_2, \ldots, v_n) \qquad (i = 1, 2, \ldots, n) \tag{1.40}$$

and the corresponding elasticities

$$\xi_{ij} = \frac{\partial \xi_i(v)}{\partial v_j} \cdot \frac{v_j}{\xi_i(v)} \tag{1.41}$$

which Frisch described as the "want elasticities."

Frisch stated (1959, p. 182) that "although not invariant under a general transformation of U, the magnitude ξ_{ij} expresses a very realistic fact: It answers the question: *is the want for good j elastic or not with respect to the quantity i?*" Frisch also defended his adherence to a particular cardinal utility indicator in the following terms (p. 178):

> To proceed from assumptions about an abstract theoretical set-up and from them to draw conclusions about the observable world and to test – by rough or more refined means – whether the conformity with observations is "good" enough, is indeed the time honoured procedure that all empirical sciences, including the natural sciences, have used. I shall therefore not plead guilty of heresy even if I do work with choice-theory concepts that are not invariant under a general monotonic transformation of the utility indicator.

There Frisch was absolutely on firm ground. As Debreu (1960) showed, and indeed as Samuelson unwittingly showed in his early criticisms of Frisch cited earlier, the property that there exists a utility indicator $U(x)$ such that $\partial U/\partial x_i > 0$ and $\partial^2 U/\partial x_i^2 < 0$ for $i = 1, 2, \ldots, n$, and $\partial U/\partial x_i \partial x_j = 0$ for $i \neq j$, has strong empirical implications (in particular, that all goods are normal, as Pareto had shown as early as 1892), yet this assumption is not invariant with respect to monotone transformation of the utility function.[13] Frisch proceeded to adopt the assumption of *want-independence* as between certain commodities; in the special case in which the cross-elasticities (1.41) vanish for *all* $i \neq j$ (which Frisch did not assume), the Jacobian matrix of the inverse mapping (1.40) – hence that of the original mapping (1.38) – is diagonal, and the cross-utility accelerations (1.39) vanish for $i \neq j$. But the latter assumption is equiv-

---

[13] For further discussion and references, see Chipman (1977a).

alent to the assumption of independent commodities, $\partial^2 U/\partial x_i \partial x_j = 0$ for $i \neq j$. Combined with the assumption of identical homothetic preferences needed for aggregation, this brings us right back to Frisch's original assumptions analyzed earlier in Section 1.1: Homotheticity plus universal want-independence implies that utility functions are of the Bergson form (1.17).

The foregoing conclusions (which are stronger than warranted by Frisch's actual assumptions) still do not detract from the usefulness of Frisch's 1959 analysis, however, which rests largely on the interrelations developed among his many new concepts. For example, defining the price elasticity of demand by $\pi_{ij} = \partial h_i/\partial p_j \cdot p_j/h_i$, the income elasticity of demand by $\eta_i = \partial h_i/\partial Y \cdot Y/h_i$, the budget share by $\theta_i = p_i x_i/Y$, and the flexibility of the marginal utility of income (or "money flexibility") by

$$\check{\omega} = \frac{\partial \omega}{\partial Y} \frac{Y}{\omega}, \quad \text{where} \quad \omega(Y,p) = \frac{\partial V(Y,p)}{\partial Y}$$

Frisch presented formulas relating the price elasticities to the remaining concepts.[14] Under the assumptions of the Bergson family of utility functions (1.17), the own-utility accelerations and the money flexibility coincide:

$$v_{ii} = \check{\omega} = -(1+\beta) = -\frac{1}{\sigma} \quad (i = 1, 2, \ldots, n)$$

hence the own-want elasticities are the reciprocals of these.

2 Estimation of Demand and Supply Functions, and Statistical Confluence Analysis

2.1 Estimation of Demand and Supply Functions

In the early part of his career Frisch had been devoting a great portion of his energies to statistical methods, particularly to the study of multicollinearity (Frisch, 1929a). During that decade, considerable progress

---

[14] These were

$$\pi_{ii} = -\eta_i \left(\theta_i - \frac{1-\theta_i \eta_i}{\check{\omega}} \right) \quad \text{and} \quad \pi_{ij} = -\eta_i \theta_j \left(1 + \frac{\eta_j}{\check{\omega}} \right) \quad (i \neq j)$$

(assuming want-independence between i and all other goods for π_{ii} and assuming want-independence between i and j for π_{ij}). Unfortunately I have been unable to reconcile these formulas with those that apply in the case of the Bergson family (1.18), which yield, for $i \neq j$,

$$\pi_{ij} = -\frac{\beta}{1+\beta} \alpha_j^{1/(1+\beta)} p_j^{-1/(1+\beta)} \bigg/ \sum_{k=1}^{n} \alpha_k^{1/(1+\beta)} p_k^{\beta/(1+\beta)}$$

had been made in developing methods to estimate demand and supply curves, following the seminal paper by Working (1927), who showed by simple geometric arguments that "statistical demand curves" could be fitted to intersections of shifting demand and supply curves and that they could legitimately be interpreted as demand curves only if supply curves shifted much more than demand curves over the sample period. During that period, Schultz (1925, 1928) was the most notable contributor to the literature on statistical estimation of demand and supply curves; his work took advantage of the fact that because foodstuffs entered into international trade, the relevant data needed to estimate a demand function (consumption) were different from the relevant data needed to estimate a supply function (production). However, there was considerable uncertainty as to the proper procedure to follow in the case of a closed economy.

It was during that same period that Leontief (1929) proposed a solution to the problem. He assumed that demand and supply relations were linear in the logarithms, with constant slopes (elasticities) over time, and were subject to random shifts that were independent as between demand and supply relations. His method (1929, p. 29*) was to divide the time series into two periods and perform regressions in each of the two periods, and then solve the resulting equations jointly to obtain two elasticity estimates, one of which would be interpreted as a demand elasticity, and the other as a supply elasticity.

Leontief's article, which had already been criticized by Schultz,[15] provoked Frisch into writing his *Pitfalls* monograph (1933b). He formulated the model as (p. 11)

$$\begin{aligned} x_t &= u_t + \alpha p_t \quad \text{(demand)} \\ x_t &= v_t + \beta p_t \quad \text{(supply)} \end{aligned} \qquad (2.1)$$

where x_t and p_t stand for the logarithms of the observed quantity and price of a commodity at time t (I have added the time subscripts) and u_t and v_t are unobserved shifts. He then (p. 12) restated equations (2.1) with the variables x_t, p_t, u_t, and v_t expressed as deviations from their sample means; consequently, he took the sums of squares and cross-products of

---

[15] Cf. Schultz (1930, app. II), as largely reproduced later (Schultz, 1938, pp. 83–95). Schultz's criticism rested mostly on the *results* of Leontief's procedure. For example, he applied Leontief's method to data on U.S. *consumption* and prices of sugar that he had used earlier (Schultz, 1928) (where he had employed consumption data only for estimation of the demand curve, and production data for the supply curve), saying (p. 87n): "This example is not unfair to Leontief, for in his own examples he derives both coefficients of elasticity sometimes from the statistics of consumption and prices, and sometimes from the data of production and prices, without considering the problems which arise when the economy under consideration is not a self-contained economy." He then ridiculed the resulting estimate of the supply elasticity of 15.0. However, this leaves open the question whether the mistake was to apply the method to a commodity that enters strongly into international trade or whether it was in the statistical method itself.

the deviations of u_t and v_t from their means, expressed as sample moments

$$m_{uu} = \sum_{t=1}^{n}(u_t - \bar{u})^2, \quad m_{vv} = \sum_{t=1}^{n}(v_t - \bar{v})^2, \quad m_{uv} = \sum_{t=1}^{n}(u_t - \bar{u})(v_t - \bar{v})$$

(where n is the sample size) with similar definitions for m_{xx}, m_{pp}, m_{xp} leading to the three equations

$$\begin{aligned} m_{uu} &= m_{xx} - 2\alpha m_{xp} + \alpha^2 m_{pp} \\ m_{vv} &= m_{xx} - 2\beta m_{xp} + \beta^2 m_{pp} \\ m_{uv} &= m_{xx} - (\alpha + \beta)m_{xp} + \alpha\beta m_{pp} \end{aligned} \quad (2.2)$$

Taking the ratios of the first two and the last two equations of (2.2), he obtained the two "fundamental equations"

$$\begin{aligned} (\alpha\beta - h\beta^2) - (\alpha + \beta - 2h\beta)H + (1 - h)K &= 0 \\ (\alpha^2 - k\beta^2) - 2(\alpha - k\beta)H + (1 - k)K &= 0 \end{aligned} \quad (2.3)$$

where

$$H = \frac{m_{xp}}{m_{pp}}, \quad K = \frac{m_{xx}}{m_{pp}}, \quad h = \frac{m_{uv}}{m_{vv}}, \quad k = \frac{m_{uu}}{m_{vv}} \quad (2.4)$$

He solved these equations for α and β. He then gave precision to Working's conclusions: In particular, if the parameter k expressing the relative variance of u and v (Frisch used the more colorful terminology "relative violence") goes to zero, then the demand elasticity α can be determined uniquely from the moments (p. 15), but the supply elasticity β will be indeterminate. Today we would say that α is "identifiable" and β "unidentifiable." Frisch described this case as one exhibiting a "Cournot effect on the demand side." Likewise, if $k \to \infty$ (a "Cournot effect on the supply side"), β is identifiable, and α not.

Frisch proceeded to spell out his objections to Leontief's procedure. Because Leontief assumed that the u_t and v_t series were uncorrelated (i.e., $h = 0$), the first of Frisch's fundamental equations (2.3) would reduce to (p. 21)

$$\alpha\beta - (\alpha + \beta)H + K = 0 \quad (2.5)$$

Thus, if one of the elasticities is given, the other is determined. Because Leontief's method consisted in dividing the sample period into two subperiods (in Frisch's terminology, two "materials," i.e., samples or data sets), the foregoing equation is replaced by two, where H and K are subscripted according to the data set. These two equations are then solved simultaneously for the two variables $\alpha\beta$ and $\alpha + \beta$, which is possible provided $H_1 \neq H_2$ and $K_1 = K_2$. Frisch carried out an exhaustive classification of cases, culminating in a table (p. 30). His general conclusion was that there were only three cases in which Leontief's method would give correct results under his assumption of uncorrelated shifts: (1) The two elasticities are known to be equal in magnitude, but of opposite signs; but in that case an ordinary regression would give the elasticities. (2) There is a pronounced Cournot effect on the demand side in one data set, and a pronounced Cournot effect on the supply side in the other; but in that case, too, straightforward regression would give the correct result. (3) Both the "relative violence" and the correlation have significantly different values in the two data sets. Only in the third case would Leontief's method do better than straight regression. But, he reasoned, for Leontief's method to have any raison d'être, it would have to give good results in other cases.

Leontief (1934) vigorously defended himself against those criticisms. He accepted the foregoing case (3) (including uncorrelated shifts) and stated (p. 357) that "these assumptions are essentially identical with the fundamental properties of the supply and demand relations which I have derived from a detailed discussion of the economic aspect of the problem," and because the other cases were "mathematical configurations which do *not* comply with the fundamental economic assumptions, ... Professor Frisch is tilting at windmills." He then (p. 358) defended the assumption of uncorrelated shifts by the argument that if the shifts were *perfectly* correlated, the concepts of supply and demand functions would make no sense. (Of course, the shifts will generally be correlated, but not perfectly so, and so this argument appears to be irrelevant.) But finally he came to a technical argument that, although arcane, seems worth describing in detail, because he made it his main point.

Frisch (1933b, p. 12) had expressed the parameters H and K of (2.4) as

$$H = rl, \quad K = l^2, \quad \text{where } r = \frac{m_{xp}}{(m_{xx}m_{pp})^{1/2}} \quad \text{and} \quad l = \left(\frac{m_{xx}}{m_{pp}}\right)^{1/2} \quad (2.6)$$

That is, r is the correlation between x and p, and l is the "relative violence" of x over p, that is, "the intensity (the amplitude) of fluctuations in x as compared with the intensity of fluctuations in p" (p. 11). Accordingly, under Leontief's assumption $h = 0$, the fundamental equations (2.5) for the two data sets become

$$\alpha\beta - (\alpha + \beta)r_1 l_1 + l_1^2 = 0$$
$$\alpha\beta - (\alpha + \beta)r_2 l_2 + l_2^2 = 0 \quad (2.7)$$

which, when summed, give, in Leontief's notation (1934, p. 360),

$$-(\alpha + \beta)r_1 l_1 + l_1^2 = -(\alpha + \beta)r_2 l_2 + l_2^2 \quad (2.8)$$

from which Leontief concluded the following: "Now it is evident that if $l_1 = l_2$ it follows that $r_1 = r_2$ and, on the other hand, if $r_1 \neq r_2, l_1 \neq l_2$." He went on to say that "any judgment concerning the 'significance' of the numerical inequality (or equality) $r_1 \neq r_2 \ldots$ necessarily implies a judgment about the 'significance' of the corresponding inequality (or equality) $l_1 \neq l_2$."

Frisch (1934c) began his reply by arguing that the whole intent of his monograph had been to show that Leontief's assumptions concerning independent shifts, however compelling they might be from the economic point of view, were disconfirmed by Leontief's own data. He pointed out, rewriting (2.8) as

$$l_1^2 - l_2^2 = (\alpha + \beta)(r_1 l_1 - r_2 l_2) \tag{2.9}$$

that while it implies, as Leontief noted, that $l_1 = l_2$ and $\alpha + \beta \neq 0$ imply $r_1 = r_2$, it does not show the converse. Setting $r_1 = r_2 = r$ yields $l_1^2 - l_2^2 = (\alpha + \beta)(l_1 - l_2)r$, so that either $l_1 = l_2$ or $l_1 + l_2 = (\alpha + \beta)r$, and the second of these equations can be satisfied in an infinite number of ways; he proceeded to illustrate this with a detailed numerical example. Frisch interpreted the first implication to mean that if uncorrelated shifts are assumed, and data sets are found with $r_1 \neq r_2$ and (approximately) $l_1 = l_2$, then the assumption must be accepted that $\alpha = -\beta$; otherwise the assumption of uncorrelated shifts must be rejected. But as for the converse, Frisch ended his discussion with the following statement:

> One cannot help feeling that the prestige of economics as a science must suffer when papers containing such mistakes and oversights as Dr. Leontief's last paper, appear in a journal of high international standing.

Leontief's rejoinder (1934) was unrepentant. He reiterated the argument that the alternative to perfect independence was perfect correlation, and, as for his slip, he stated that Frisch only "proves, with the help of an elaborate numerical example, that a quadratic equation has more than one solution."

Presumably at the editor's behest, Marschak (1934), who had previously discussed Leontief's work in his own study (1931, pp. 23–8), was brought in as an arbiter. He pointed out that both demand and supply were related to other common variables such as population and price level. He suggested introducing other variables [anticipating the method of instrumental variables introduced by Reiersøl (1945a) and the methods introduced by Koopmans (1949) to overcome the identification problem], as well as choosing the data sets in such a way as to make the independence assumption more likely to be satisfied, rather than arbitrarily.

Frisch's *pitfalls* monograph (1933b) not only had tremendous influence on the development of the simultaneous-equations approach in econometrics but also affected many subsequent developments that did not employ this approach, such as the consumer-demand studies of Wold and Juréen (1953) and Stone (1954), which relied basically on the type of reasoning introduced by Frisch.

Finally, it may be supposed that the interchange with Leontief, who had appealed to Marshall (1890) to support his assumptions, had something to do with Frisch's penetrating lectures during that period on Marshall's theory of value, which were later made available in English translation (1950). Frisch was not one to leave any stone unturned.

Almost 50 years after the Leontief–Frisch controversy, Leamer (1981) returned to the subject with a fresh look. Instead of concentrating on consistency of estimates, he approached the problem from the point of view of maximum-likelihood estimation subject to inequality constraints. He assumed the disturbances to be independently (serially and contemporaneously) normally distributed. The inequality constraints were that the demand curve have negative slope, and the supply curve positive slope. He showed that the set of maximum-likelihood estimates of the two elasticities consisted of a hyperbola whose two branches were separated by a horizontal line and a vertical line going through the points $(b, 0)$ and $(0, b)$, respectively, where b is the least-squares estimate. Leamer showed – where I use Frisch's notation α and β in place of Leamer's notation for the demand and supply elasticities – that under the assumptions $\alpha < 0$ and $\beta > 0$,

$$b > 0 \quad \text{implies} \quad \hat{\alpha} < 0, \quad 0 < b < \hat{\beta} < b_r$$

where b_r is the reverse least-squares estimate (obtained by regressing price on quantity and taking the reciprocal of the regression coefficient), and that, alternatively,

$$b < 0 \quad \text{implies} \quad b_r < \hat{\alpha} < b < 0, \quad 0 < \hat{\beta}$$

Leamer concluded as follows:

> The method ... rests on the unlikely assumption that the slopes α and β are constant over time but the variances are not. Still, Leontief did have the hyperbola properly defined,[16] which is only one short step from the results of this paper. It is therefore surprising that Leontief's contribution has been so completely ignored by the post-1940 econometrics literature. The fault seems to me to lie with excessive attention to

---

[16] I have not been able to find this hyperbola in Leontief (1929), though a similar hyperbola can be found in Allen (1939). Leontief did not assume normality; rather, as Schultz (1930, app. II; 1938, p. 84) explained, Leontief (1929, p. 24*) fitted the demand curve (a straight line on double-logarithmic scale) by minimizing the sum of squares of deviations measured parallel to the (unknown) supply curve, and *vice versa*. See also Schultz (1939b).

84   John S. Chipman

asymptotic properties of estimators and insufficient interest in the shapes of likelihood functions.

It would seem appropriate to add that the independence between demand and supply disturbances is crucial to this result, as Frisch stressed (and Leamer acknowledged).

2.2   The Frisch-Waugh Theorem

In the course of his investigations of the relationship between sugar consumption and sugar prices, Frisch had to face up to the problem that, as was contended by a number of authors at that time, if there were a strong upward trend in consumption accompanied by a strong downward trend in price, it would be a mistake to de-trend the data series and then perform a regression on the de-trended series [called the "individual trend method" by Frisch and Waugh (1933)], as opposed to including time explicitly as one of the explanatory variables (called the "partial time regression method"). It was the accomplishment of the paper by Frisch and Waugh (1933) to show that so long as the relations are assumed to be linear, both methods give exactly the same result. The Frisch-Waugh theorem was generalized by Reiersøl (1945b) to any instrumental set of variables and was applied by Lowell (1963) to seasonal adjustment. It has been given prominence in a recent text (Davidson and MacKinnon, 1993, pp. 19–24) and has been further developed and generalized by Fiebig, Bartels, and Krämer (1996), who point out that the result has also been implicitly derived and used by a number of authors.

The problem can be formulated in terms of the simple regression model

$$y = X\beta + \varepsilon = [X_1\ X_2]\begin{bmatrix}\beta_1\\ \beta_2\end{bmatrix} + \varepsilon = X_1\beta_1 + X_2\beta_2 + \varepsilon$$

where the $n \times k$ matrix X (assumed of rank k) is partitioned into $n \times k_1$ and $n \times k_2$ matrices. According to the individual-trend method, one first regresses both y and X_1 on the trend term X_2 to obtain

$$b_2^* = (X_2'X_2)^{-1}X_2'y \quad \text{and} \quad B_2^* = (X_2'X_2)^{-1}X_2'X_1$$

The deviations of y and X_1 from their trends (the de-trended series) are then

$$y^* = y - X_2 b_2^* = (I - H_2)y \quad \text{and} \quad X_1^* = X_1 - X_2 B_2^* = (I - H_2)X_1 \tag{2.10}$$

respectively, where we define $H_i = X_i(X_i'X_i)^{-1}X_i'$ for $i = 1, 2$. The estimate of β_1 by the individual-trend method is then

$$b_1^* = \left(X_1^{*'}X_1^*\right)^{-1} X_1^{*'}y* \qquad (2.11)$$

The estimate of β_1 by the partial-time-regression method is b_1, where

$$b = \begin{bmatrix} b_1 \\ b_2 \end{bmatrix} = \begin{bmatrix} X_1'X_1 & X_1'X_2 \\ X_2'X_1 & X_2'X_2 \end{bmatrix}^{-1} \begin{bmatrix} X_1' \\ X_2' \end{bmatrix} y = (X'X)^{-1}X'y \qquad (2.12)$$

The expression for b_1 can be obtained from standard formulas for inverses of partitioned matrices, but Frisch and Waugh showed that there is a simpler, direct approach. Defining $H = X(X'X)^{-1}X'$, and observing that

$$X_1 = X\Phi_1 = [X_1 \ X_2]\begin{bmatrix} I_{k_1} \\ 0 \end{bmatrix} \text{ and } X_2 = X\Phi_2 = [X_1 \ X_2]\begin{bmatrix} 0 \\ I_{k_2} \end{bmatrix} \qquad (2.13)$$

we see easily that $H_iH = HH_i = H_i$ for $i = 1, 2$; hence

$$(I - H_i)(I - H) = (I - H)(I - H_i) = I - H \qquad (i = 1, 2) \qquad (2.14)$$

consequently, from (2.13) and the definition of H,

$$(I - H)X_i = (I - H)X\Phi_i = 0 \text{ and } (I - H_i)X_i = 0 \qquad (i = 1, 2) \qquad (2.15)$$

Therefore, denoting the residual from the regression (2.12) by $e = y - Xb = (I - H)y$, we have

$$y = Xb + e = X_1b_1 + X_2b_2 + (I - H)y \qquad (2.16)$$

Now we observe from (2.14) and (2.13) that premultiplication of (2.16) by $X_1'(I - H_2)$ annihilates the last two terms on the right, leaving

$$X_1'(I - H_2)y = X_1'(I - H_2)X_1b_1$$

hence

$$b_1 = [X_1'(I - H_2)X_1]^{-1} X_1'(I - H_2)y \qquad (2.17)$$

Given the definitions (2.10), and using the idempotency and symmetry of H_2, it follows that the estimators (2.11) and (2.17) of β_1 are precisely the same. This is the Frisch-Waugh theorem.

Frisch and Waugh also proved the identity of the residuals

$$e = y - Xb = y - X_1b_1 - X_2b_2 \text{ and } e* = y* - X_1^*b_1^*$$

This follows from (2.10) and the fact that

$$e^* = (I - H_2)(y - X_1b_1) \qquad \text{(since } b_1^* = b_1\text{)}$$
$$= (I - H_2)(y - X_1b_1 - X_2b_2) \qquad [\text{since } (I - H_2)X_2 = 0]$$
$$= (I - H_2)(y - Xb)$$
$$= (I - H_2)(I - H)y$$
$$= (I - H)y = e \qquad [\text{from (2.14)}]$$

2.3 Statistical Confluence Analysis

Frisch's work on what he called "confluence analysis" stemmed from the anomalous results obtained when statistical methods such as multiple regression were extended from experimental applications to applications involving nonexperimental observations of the type studied by economists. That work consists largely of two main publications (Frisch, 1929a, 1934a). The Introduction to the second of these states (p. 9): "The present study has been undertaken as an indispensable preliminary step for certain projects, namely statistical productivity studies and statistical construction of econometric functions (demand and supply curve and the like)...."

Frisch formulated the regression problem in econometrics in terms of a model $y = X\beta$, in which both the $n \times 1$ vector y and the $n \times k$ matrix X of observations on explanatory variables consisted of sums of two terms: a systematic part and a disturbance. "Multicollinearity" refers to linear dependence among the systematic parts of the columns of X; owing to the disturbances, the observed matrix X can always be assumed to have full rank k even if the underlying systematic part of X has rank less than k, which leads to the danger that an investigator may erroneously infer a causal or structural relationship between X and y when there is none. Specifically, he laid down the hypothesis (1934a, p. 85) that the addition of a new explanatory variate was likely to exacerbate the multicollinearity problem, increasing the likelihood that there would be linear dependence among the systematic parts of the explanatory variates. To guard against this, Frisch suggested that it would be preferable to deliberately omit some explanatory variables that *a priori* would be considered relevant. In a passage that is strikingly prophetic of recent developments in statistics that emphasize sacrificing unbiasedness in order to improve mean-square error, Frisch stated (1934a, pp. 86–7) that

> in target shooting the result depends, not only on the correct aiming but just as much on the steadiness with which one pulls the trigger. If for some particular reason it is impossible to pull the trigger steadily when one aims *exactly* at the target, it is quite conceivable that it would be better deliberately to aim a little on the side of the target. And so in statistical analysis it may be found safer deliberately to leave some bias

in the regression coefficients by not including a certain variate in the analysis.

Frisch (1934a, p. 60) based his approach on his theorem – which had previously been proved by Gini (1921) and later was generalized by Koopmans (1937, pp. 98–115), Reiersøl (1941), and Willassen (1987) – that the "true" linear-regression coefficient between two variates lies between the two elementary regressions (the regression coefficient of x_1 on x_2 and the reciprocal of the regression coefficient of x_2 on x_1). In order to draw inferences concerning multicollinearity among the systematic parts of the variates, Frisch (1934a) took pairs, triples, and so forth, of these variates and considered the regressions within each l-tuple in all possible directions. If adding a third variate to a pair, say, increased the stability of the regressions in the sense that the regression coefficient of x_1 on x_2 and the inverse of the regression coefficient of x_2 on x_1 were closer together when x_3 was an additional explanatory variable, that was taken as an indication that the disturbances were major parts of these variates; if adding a third variate had the opposite effect, that was taken as an indication of multicollinearity. This is the basic idea of Frisch's "bunch analysis" (1934a, pp. 86–106), closely related to his method of "optimum regression" (1931d) and the theory of "cluster types" in Frisch and Mudgett (1931); a good exposition of his "bunch map" technique was provided by Haavelmo and Staehle (1951, pp. 16–21).

Frisch's work had a strong influence on Koopmans (1937), who provided a probabilistic formulation of Frisch's model, as well as on Reiersøl (1941, 1945a), who introduced the method of instrumental variables. And his formulation of the regression model in terms of errors in both dependent and independent variables led to a flurry of contributions culminating in the surprising finding of Wald (1940) that a consistent estimator of the slope of a straight line $y = \alpha + \beta x$ in a sample of even size n when both variables are subject to error is given by

$$b = \frac{\sum_{t=1}^{m} y_t - \sum_{t=m+1}^{n} y_t}{\sum_{t=1}^{m} x_t - \sum_{t=m+1}^{n} x_t}$$

where $m = n/2$.

It is natural to ask what influence Frisch's confluence analysis had on the development of simultaneous-equations models. Because the stimulus for the latter was mainly due to Haavelmo (1943, 1944), although Frisch (1993b) certainly played a part, as did Marschak and Andrews (1944), it is instructive to consider Haavelmo's retrospective assessment (1950). His basic point was that there was no reason to believe that a "true" structural relationship would hold exactly, as Frisch posited; rather, it would hold only stochastically. Thus, in a negative sense (but very positive for the progress of econometrics), Haavelmo's dissatisfaction with Frisch's formulation probably was the most important factor in the development of the simultaneous-equations approach.

3 Capital Theory and Dynamic Economics

Frisch's earliest work on capital theory was his 1927 article on primary investment and reinvestment. The problem he considered was this: Suppose that at an initial time an investment is made in a number of different goods with different durabilities, and assume that each of these goods has a definite durability and is replaced as soon as it wears out. What will be the subsequent pattern of total reinvestment over time? He gave examples (such as the production of a wooden hammer, iron hammer, and steel hammer with respective durabilities of one, two, and three years) that would give rise to a very marked subsequent limit cycle, but showed that this was atypical (resulting from the distribution of prime numbers from 1 to 6); with finer class intervals, he showed that fluctuations in reinvestment will be damped, so that a smooth flow of reinvestment will be approached asymptotically. This approach to production theory was first made known to English-speaking readers with the 1965 translation of his book *Theory of Production* – a work that has not received the attention that it deserves (cf. Frisch 1965, ch. 16–19, pp. 293–345).

A few years later, Frisch presented his methodological approach to static and dynamic economics in a penetrating Norwegian paper (1929b), of which unfortunately only the introductory sections are available in English.

Shortly thereafter, during a visit to the University of Minnesota, a lively discussion in the Campus Club with Alvin Hansen prompted Frisch to make his first well-known contribution to business-cycle theory (1931e). Not surprisingly, in view of his previous investigation, he again turned his attention to the cyclical nature of replacement investment. The occasion for the discussion was Hansen's treatment (1927, p. 113) building upon the "acceleration principle" introduced by Clark (1917, 1923), among others.[17] Clark had stated (1917, p. 220) that "the demand for maintenance and replacement of existing capital varies with the amount of the demand for finished products, while the demand for new construction or enlargement of stocks depends upon whether or not the

---

[17] Including Aftalion (1909a, pp. 219–20; 1909b, pp. 71–2; 1913, II, pp. 371–3) and Bickerdike (1914). Earlier hints of the acceleration principle are contained in Cassel (1904, pp. 76–7; 1918, §70, pp. 510–11; 1927, §70, pp. 527–9; 1932a, §70, pp. 528–30; 1932b, II, §69, pp. 596–8) and Bouniatian (1908, pp. 109–10; 1915, p. 172; 1922, p. 236; 1930, p. 266). Curiously, Frisch (1931e, p. 646n) cited Bickerdike's article and attributed it to Clark, evidently mistaking it for Clark (1917); but it seems that his criticisms of Clark were based entirely on Clark (1923).

sales of the finished product are growing." Thus, "if demand be treated as a rate of speed..., maintenance varies roughly with the speed, but new construction depends upon the acceleration." From this he had concluded (pp. 222–3) that "in order to bring about an absolute shrinkage in the demand for the intermediate product, all that may [sic] be needed is that the final demand should slacken its rate of growth." However, he subsequently (1923, p. 390) stated (less cautiously) that "the makers of capital equipment are bound, in the nature of the case, to suffer an absolute decline in the demand for their products... whenever ultimate demand slackens its rate of growth," and further, "once demand for finished products starts growing it cannot pause or else the derived demand for means of production will [sic] shrink...."

Frisch (1931e) set out to correct that formulation by introducing the model

$$I = \delta K + \dot{K} = \varkappa(\delta C + \dot{C}); \quad \text{hence} \quad \dot{I} = \varkappa(\delta \dot{C} + \ddot{C}) \quad (3.1)$$

where C is the rate of consumption, K is the aggregate capital stock, and I is the rate of gross investment. It assumes that capital must maintain a fixed ratio $\varkappa$ to consumption (i.e., $K = \varkappa C$), so that net investment must retain the corresponding relation to the rate of change of consumption (i.e., $\dot{K} = \varkappa \dot{C}$), and replacement investment is a fixed proportion of the capital stock (i.e., $R = \delta K$). Thus, a slowdown in the rate of growth of consumption, though it necessarily entails a fall in *net* investment $\dot{K}$, need not lead to a fall in *gross* investment I. Moreover, Frisch observed (p. 649) that

> the system is, so far, quite indeterminate. In the reduced form [(3.1)] of the relationship, we have two variables but only one equation. It would be attempting the logically impossible if, from the conditions here considered, we should try to demonstrate that the system must after a while turn into depression.

He followed with numerous numerical examples illustrating this point.

Clark, in his reply (1931), essentially admitted his error, but without missing the opportunity to retort that while Frisch's point was mathematically correct, his own treatment still had "the legitimacy of sound formulations adapted to the thinking of the majority who are laymen in mathematics" – evidently because replacement investment was, in his opinion, a small proportion of total investment. In his rejoinder, Frisch (1932a, p. 254) pointed out that if consumption is assumed to move cyclically, there is a small interval of time after the point of fastest increase in consumption during which investment continues to rise:

> This little interval of time around the turning-point in capital production is the critical interval in the business cycle. It is here that the enigma of business cycles lies. And in this critical interval capital production

> for expansion purposes *is not the dominating element in total capital production.*

That is, replacement is not a small proportion of investment as Clark claimed. In his "Further Word," Clark (1932, p. 692) agreed that

> for a full explanation... one must take account of factors acting in the reverse direction, namely, the fact that actual movements of consumer demand depend on the movements of purchasing power; and these in turn are governed by the rate of production in general....

And Clark expressed the "hope that this discussion may stimulate some mathematical economist to produce a solution" (p. 693). As we shall see, his hope was soon fulfilled; and for his part, most of his later (1935) treatise on the business cycle may be regarded as his own attempt to meet Frisch's challenge.

Prior to developing his business-cycle model, Frisch (1928) had developed a method to extract cyclical and trend components from economic time series in such a way as to allow for variable amplitudes and phases, and he announced (1931b) a forthcoming monograph in which these methods would be further developed and applied to business-cycle research; unfortunately that never appeared. Subsequently he presented his vision (1931c) of future business-cycle research at a conference in Stockholm, including even a proposed model containing some 38 variables and equations. He also carried out a detailed empirical study of price and quantity fluctuations in several countries (1932d), with data in some cases going back as far as the fourteenth century.

Frisch (1933c) proceeded to develop a self-contained model of the business cycle in a brilliant contribution incorporating ideas from his early 1927 work, as well as his controversy with Clark. His first task was to generalize (3.1), and the next was to add enough suitable equations to make the model self-contained and determinate. The generalization consisted mainly in taking account of the fact that capital is needed to produce not only consumer goods but also more capital goods. In the following exposition I shall fill in some details that Frisch left to the reader and replace Frisch's notation with the more common Keynesian type of notation that has become customary in the macroeconomic literature.

Let K_C and K_I denote the stocks of capital in the consumer-good and investment-good industries, respectively. Overlooking, at first, the length of time needed to produce capital (or, alternatively, interpreting K_C and K_I as the desired stocks of capital in the respective industries), these are related to production (and consumption, because there are no inventories) of consumer and producer goods by

$$K_C = \varkappa_C C \quad \text{and} \quad K_I = \varkappa_I I$$

where $\varkappa_C$ and $\varkappa_I$ are fixed coefficients. Next, denoting by δ_C and δ_I the rates of depreciation of capital in the respective industries (the reciprocals of their durability), replacement investment is given by

$$R = \delta_C K_C + \delta_I K_I = \delta_C \varkappa_C C + \delta_I \varkappa_I I = \delta_C \varkappa_C C + \delta_I \varkappa_I (R + \dot{K}) \quad (3.2)$$

which is equal to gross investment I when net investment $\dot{K}$ is zero. Thus, under stationary conditions (cf. Frisch 1933c, pp. 176–7) replacement investment is[18]

$$R = \frac{\delta_C \varkappa_C}{1 - \delta_I \varkappa_I} C \quad (3.3)$$

Now imagine that the level of consumption moves from one stationary level C to another $C + \Delta C$; then formula (3.3) shows that replacement investment must rise from the indicated level to the one in which the factor on the right is $C + \Delta C$. Thus, net investment is

$$\begin{aligned}\dot{K} &= \dot{K}_C + \dot{K}_I = \varkappa_C \dot{C} + \varkappa_I \dot{I} \\ &= \varkappa_C \dot{C} + \varkappa_I \frac{\delta_C \varkappa_C}{1 - \delta_I \varkappa_I} \dot{C} \\ &= \left(1 + \frac{\delta_C \varkappa_I}{1 - \delta_I \varkappa_I}\right) \varkappa_C \dot{C}\end{aligned} \quad (3.4)$$

It follows from (3.3) and (3.4) that gross investment is

$$I = R + \dot{K} = \frac{\varkappa_C}{1 - \delta_I \varkappa_I} \{\delta_C C + [1 + \varkappa_I (\delta_C - \delta_I)]\dot{C}\} = mC + \mu\dot{C} \quad (3.5)$$

where m and μ are the symbols used by Frisch to denote the more complicated coefficients of C and $\dot{C}$ shown in (3.5). Note that if the durability of capital is the same in the two industries ($\delta_C = \delta_I$), then (3.5) reduces formally to (3.1).

Frisch next took into account the production lag in construction of capital. The actual capital formation at time t is the result of activities that have taken place in the past and that continue up to time t; these activities Frisch called "production starting" or "capital starting," as opposed to the capital formation itself, which he called the "carry-on activity." The latter is determined from the former by the convolution operation

$$I_t = \int_0^\infty D(\tau) J_{t-\tau} d\tau \quad (3.6)$$

---

[18] More generally, one would have to add to the right side of (3.3) the term $[\delta_I\varkappa_I/(1 - \delta_I\varkappa_I)]\dot{K}$, introducing an unpleasant complication into formula (3.4).

where J_t is the investment starting at time t, and $D(t)$ is the delay function or, in Frisch's terminology, the "advancement function." Frisch chose, for simplicity, the function

$$D(t) = \begin{cases} 1/\theta & \text{for } 0 < t < \theta \\ 0 & \text{for } t \geq \theta \end{cases} \tag{3.7}$$

Defining the average period of production as $\int_0^\infty D(\tau)\tau/d\tau$,[19] this becomes $\theta/2$ for the foregoing special function. Differentiating (3.6) with respect to time, and employing (3.7), we obtain

$$\dot{I}_t = \frac{1}{\theta}\int_0^\theta \dot{J}_{t-\tau}d\tau = \frac{1}{\theta}[-J_{t-\tau}]_0^\theta = \frac{1}{\theta}(J_t - J_{t-\theta}) \tag{3.8}$$

Frisch attributed this idea to Aftalion.[20]

Formula (3.5) now needs to be adjusted to take account of production lags. Frisch did that by replacing the actual capital formation or "carry-on activity" I on the left by the "starting investment" J:

$$J = mC + \mu\dot{C} \tag{3.9}$$

Equations (3.9) and (3.8) are two of the fundamental equations of Frisch's system – one a differential equation and the other a difference equation – involving the three variables I, J, and C. One more equation is needed to close the system.

For that, Frisch got his idea (or at least the terminology) from Walras (1926, ch. 29, §275, p. 305; 1954, p. 321); the desired cash balance (*encaisse désirée*), $\alpha C + \beta I$, where α and β are constants, consists in amounts of money needed for both consumption and investment purposes, which are assumed to rise during the boom faster than the money supply M. An excess of money demand over money supply is assumed to have its greatest impact on consumption (Frisch, 1933c, p. 179), causing it to contract; thus, the third equation of the system is[21]

---

[19] This appears to be Frisch's implicit definition, and it is suitable for the case of a stationary (i.e., nongrowing) economy. In the case of an economy growing at the rate r, one would want to include the factor e^{-rt} in the integrand; cf. Chipman (1977b, p. 301).

[20] Cf. Aftalion (1908, p. 703; 1909b, p. 11; 1913, II, ch. VII, pp. 113ff.), who in turn attributed the idea to Böhm-Bawerk and Jevons. This formulation had already been anticipated in Frisch (1931e, p. 652): "In Aftalion's manner we could distinguish between capital goods *ordered* and capital goods *delivered*." Frisch apparently was unaware that formula (3.1) also goes back to Aftalion; see footnote 17.

[21] Frisch multiplies the *encaisse désirée* by a factor λ, which he describes (p. 189) as its "reining-in effect," but it seems to me simpler to absorb this factor in the coefficients α and β. Further, Frisch, in place of M in (3.10), writes c (a constant); but it seems easier to understand the model if this is interpreted as the money supply. However, it is treated as a (constant) parameter to be estimated, rather than as a variable.

$$\dot{C} = M - (\alpha C + \beta I) \tag{3.10}$$

Frisch made the important observation (p. 180) in connection with his previous controversy with Clark that if there is no production lag (3.6), so that J is replaced by I in (3.9), as in (3.5), then equations (3.9) and (3.10) together imply a linear relation between C and I; substitution of this relation in either (3.9) or (3.10) yields a first-order linear differential equation in a single variable, whose solution is a path of steady growth or contraction.[22] This proved, he observed, that contrary to Clark's claim, (3.1) was not sufficient by itself to explain turning points in the business cycle.

Frisch's model of the "propagation" process thus consists of the three equations (3.8), (3.9), and (3.10). He assumed that its solution would be of the form[23]

$$i_t = a_{i0} + \sum_{k=1}^{\infty} a_{ik} e^{\rho_k t} \quad \text{for } i = C, I, J$$

where the ρ_k are complex numbers, and found that the ρ_k must be roots of the characteristic equation

$$\frac{\theta \rho}{1 - e^{-\theta \rho}} = -\beta \frac{m + \mu \rho}{\alpha + \rho}$$

He studied the solutions for the choices $\theta = 6, m = 0.5, \mu = 10, \alpha = 0.1$, and $\beta = 0.05$ (p. 186). One curious but extremely interesting feature of the model, which might have been better clarified if prices and incomes

---

[22] Specifically, it yields the differential equation

$$(1 - \beta \mu)\dot{C} + (\alpha - \beta m)C - M = 0$$

which has the solution

$$C = \frac{M}{\alpha - \beta m} + k e^{\lambda t}$$

(for some arbitrary constant k), where $\lambda = -(\alpha - \beta m)/(1 - \beta \mu)$. If $\lambda > 0$, this gives a path of steady growth; for the numerical coefficients supposed by Frisch (see the later text), $\lambda < 0$, and the solution converges to $C = M/(\alpha - \beta m)$.

[23] It seems to be an open question whether or not this gives the correct general solution for Frisch's system. It is based on the Herz–Herglotz method adopted by Alfred Lotka in the 1930s for solving the integral equation of renewal theory. Following an acrimonious controversy between him and Gabriel Preinreich, the dispute was finally settled by Feller (1941) in favor of Preinreich's criticism (but not in favor of Preinreich's own method). For instance, Frisch (1965, p. 323) derived the renewal equation and tried to solve it by Lotka's method, with mixed success, whereas the solution by Laplace transforms is known from Feller (1941). On this, see Chipman (1977b), as well as the comments by Samuelson (1974, pp. 8–10).

had been incorporated in the analysis, is that during an upswing workers are being paid for production of capital that will be completed in time to produce more consumer goods only several years hence; because inventory accumulation or decumulation is not allowed, equation (3.10) must bring about *forced saving* (likewise, forced dissaving during a downswing).

Frisch's business-cycle model was an extraordinary achievement. It was the first self-contained model of the cycle. Moreover, he found three cycles, of durations 8.57, 3.50, and 2.20 years, in conformity with much statistical data. Some observers have criticized it for exhibiting contrafactual symmetry between upswings and downswings (Blatt, 1980), and no doubt it has many other faults that Frisch would readily have conceded; but it was a first, and it still compares very favorably with other models that have been developed. Kalecki's (1935) model, for which Frisch and Holme (1935) provided a solution, was followed by those of Samuelson (1939a, 1939b), Kaldor (1940), Hicks (1950), and Goodwin (1951). Except for Kalecki's model, none of those allowed for replacement investment, which Frisch considered of such importance. By allowing for nonlinearities such as capacity constraints and nonnegativity constraints, Hicks and Goodwin were able to generate persistent limit cycles. But Frisch accomplished the same thing by his idea, stimulated by Wicksell (1907, 1918), of subjecting his model – which he regarded as a model of the "propagation" process, leading to damped cycles – to random shocks or "impulses" so as to obtain persistent cycles – an approach that found justification in the work of Slutsky (1927, 1937), Yule (1927), and Hotelling (1927). His strong belief that economic cycles were basically damped may have been formed by the findings of his early 1927 article on replacement cycles. In Frisch and Holme (1935), Frisch criticized Kalecki for forcing the roots of his system to lie on the unit circle in order to obtain persistent cycles, a procedure that was further criticized by Haavelmo (1940).

Frisch (1933c), toward the end of his paper, illustrated his method for a model of the pendulum. He showed by means of simulation that application of random shocks to a pendulum would give rise to what he called a "changing harmonic" (already defined in his 1928 paper), namely "a curve that is moving more or less regularly in cycles, the length of the period and also the amplitude being to some extent variable, these variations taking place, however, within such limits that it is reasonable to speak of an *average* period and an *average* amplitude" (p. 202). For the case of his business-cycle model (for which simulations would not have been possible in 1933), he identified the random shocks with innovations in Schumpeter's (1926) theory. Subsequently, in replying to a criticism of Tintner (1938), Frisch (1939c) elaborated by explaining that "a shock is any event which contradicts the assumptions of some pure economic theory and thus prevents the variables from following the exact course implied by that theory." He agreed with Tintner that Slutsky had not explained "in terms of economic theory how the effects of the shocks are 'summed'," but went on to point out that his paper was precisely intended to fill that gap:

> I showed that if a set of variables are defined by a linear system..., the time shape of one of the variables, *when hit by shocks*, is obtained by extending to the shock series a moving summation whose weight system is exactly the same sort of curve as that which would have given the time evolution of this variable, if no shocks had occurred. Thus economic theory furnishes the weight system, statistical theory does the rest.

In his article on Wicksell, Frisch (1952, pp. 698–9) quoted a very revealing passage from Wicksell outlining this approach to business-cycle theory, in which the shocks were identified with technical progress. In fact, this article reveals the profound influence that Wicksell's work must have had on Frisch, and in particular there is probably more of Wicksell behind (3.10) than Walras.

Not until 1990 did it occur to anybody to take the logical step of using a computer to simulate Frisch's model – which of course was impossible in 1933. Thalberg (1990) carried out such simulations and found that fluctuations were persistent and that "the amplitude of the fluctuations increases with the disturbances [which he added to (3.9) and (3.10)], while the length of the fluctuations is more or less strongly tied to the propagation mechanism" (p. 108). But "the generated fluctuations become irregular and unpredictable," precluding forecasting more than two years ahead. Furthermore, the three variables of the model did not move in tandem, which he attributed to the omission from the model of any feedback from investment to consumption. He therefore added another independent variable $\dot{J}_{t-\xi}$ to (3.10) so as to approximate the Keynesian multiplier.[24] He also replaced the advancement function by $D(\tau) = \omega^2 \tau e^{-\omega \tau}$. Although the modified system exhibited instability for some values of the parameters, in the contrary case it appeared to reproduce observed cycles in a satisfactory way.

4   Depression and Circulation Planning

One of Frisch's most striking contributions (1934b) was born out of the experience of the Great Depression; it might have had greater impact if it had not been overshadowed by Keynes's *General Theory*, which

---

[24] Another choice, which would bring the model closer to that of Samuelson (1939a, 1939b), would be $\dot{C}_{t-\xi} + \dot{J}_{t-\xi}$ (the rate of increase of gross national product at factor cost), whose coefficient would be the marginal propensity to consume. The pre-Keynesian nature of Frisch's model is brought out by the fact that Frisch never thought to sum consumption and investment to obtain national income.

appeared two years later.[25] Frisch opened his book-length article with the following passage:

> The most striking paradox of great depressions, and particularly of the present one, is the fact that poverty is imposed on us in the midst of a world of plenty. Many kinds of goods are actually present in large quantities, and other kinds could without any difficulty be brought forth in abundance, if only the available enormous productive power was let loose. Yet, in spite of this technical and physical abundance, most of us are forced to cut down consumption. We are compelled to make real sacrifices in order to economize in the use of these very goods and services that *could* easily be produced in abundance if we would only use our resources.

He attributed the problem to a defect in the form of organization and to a situation in which groups "are forced *mutually to undermine each other's position....* This meaningless vicious circle is what I understand by the incapsulating phenomenon." The picture he painted was of a game that ended up in a sub-Pareto-optimal situation and even a prisoner's dilemma. But in some respects it also is a picture of *unstable equilibrium*.

The problem was well expressed in a subsequent publication (1963, p. 2) as follows:

> To illustrate . . . we may think of the tailor and the shoemaker who were standing looking at each other with sorrowful faces. The sorrow stemmed from the fact that the tailor did not *dare* to order the shoes he needed because he was not sure that he would be able to sell any suit to the shoemaker, while the shoemaker did not *dare* to order the suit he needed because he was not sure that he would be able to sell any shoes to the tailor. If we include also the baker, the fisherman and a few others in the picture we have a good illustration of what is meant by the multilateral balancing problem, and in particular we get an illustration of the need for a system which can *assure* everybody that he is taking part in a game where a multilateral balancing is *automatically provided for*.

One way to interpret these passages is that Frisch is showing the failure of Walras's law to hold in a dynamic economy. The worker, according to this law, will effectively demand the goods which he would purchase if he were to get the job he is looking for. The essential asymmetry between the buying and selling sides of the transaction is what leads to the breakdown; the selling must take place first. And all proofs of stability of competitive equilibrium assume Walras's law.[26]

---

[25] It was preceded by an equally striking little book, *Saving and Circulation Control* (1933a), in which he traced the mechanism by which a rise in saving, instead of leading to increased investment, would lead to decreases in output and employment.

[26] I have discussed this question in greater detail elsewhere (Chipman, 1965).

Frisch's Contributions to Economics and Econometrics

In his 1934 paper, Frisch set forth a schematic model of the tailor-shoemaker problem, with "coefficients of optimism" in the difference equations. He showed in this schematic model how fluctuations could result merely from the nature of the trading game. He then introduced a model of "planned exchange" in which warrants were issued in order to reestablish equilibrium, then destroyed when no longer needed. The scheme is, of course, very close to the idea of the role of a central bank as lender of last resort.

In later years Frisch extended these ideas to the problem of international equilibrium (1947, 1948b). He extended his 1934 idea of a "request matrix" to that of a "trade matrix" whose typical element a_{ij} represented the value of country i's exports to country j, where the term "exports" is used in a very broad sense to include long-term capital transactions; thus, a sustained capital movement from i to j would be included among the exports from j to i. Frisch's object was to devise a scheme to prevent a vicious circle from developing in which, starting from unbalanced trade, each country would successively reduce its imports to the level of its exports until an equilibrium would be reached with a very low level of trade. He distinguished (1947, p. 537) between the "specialization effect" of trade (the mutual advantage of international specialization and trade) and the "payment effect" referred to earlier, which he attributed to the failure of Say's law (which I have always considered to be the proposition that a full-employment competitive equilibrium exists, whereas the failure of Walras's law does not preclude the existence of such an equilibrium, but results in its being dynamically unstable). He took as his "rough indicator of the welfare created by international trade" the *total* volume of international transactions in goods and services (p. 545); however, because this is later identified with the sum of all the elements of the trade matrix, it is really the total *value* of international transactions, capital as well as current.[27] The other concept Frisch introduces is the *skewness* of the matrix: If the ith-row sum (country i's total exports) exceeds the ith-column sum (country i's total imports), the amount is entered to the right of the ith row as a surplus; in the contrary case the amount is entered at the bottom of the ith column as a deficit. The sum of all the surpluses (which is, of course, equal to the sum of all the deficits) is the skewness. The mathematical policy problem is to reduce the skewness to zero with minimum reduction in the total value of transactions.

Frisch noted correctly that a one-country-at-a-time policy of reduction of deficit countries' imports to the levels of their exports, by *pro-*

---

[27] Frisch subsequently insisted (1963, p. 5) that he did mean volumes, and that "this can be made tangible through the medium of value figures expressed in base year prices." However, very few countries have price indices of imports and exports, and the available unit-value data are regarded with much suspicion by many experts.

rata proportional reduction of imports from all countries, was a pessimal solution to this problem, that a balancing of accounts with much less drastic reduction in total transactions could be accomplished by discriminatory reduction in imports as between different countries. The algorithm used by Frisch to obtain the optimal solution was that developed in his earlier paper (1934b).

Frisch's 1947 paper was greeted with respectful skepticism on the part of Polak (1948) and Meier (1948). Polak pointed out that the beneficial effect of discrimination rested on the assumption of asymmetry in the behaviors of surplus and deficit countries, deficit countries reducing their imports to the levels of their exports, but surplus countries not increasing their imports to the levels of their exports. This asymmetry, he thought, was realistic in 1947, but not in the period of the Great Depression with reference to which Frisch made his case. In that period, he stated, countries' imports depended on their national income and relative prices, and there was no reason to believe that the marginal propensities to import for different countries were different. His second main point was that if countries were forced to switch their sources of imports to other countries, "they would have to accept a commodity structure of imports which might be quite incompatible with full national output" unless there were considerable multilateral negotiations; but then if one is to have negotiation, why not use it to increase world trade rather than mitigate its decline? Finally, he pointed out that

> if serious disequilibria in international trade and payments were dealt with, not by the necessary fundamental adjustments, but by successive doses of discrimination, the "specialization" advantages of the remaining international trade would continually decline and the volume of international trade would lose all value as an indicator of national welfare.

Meier (1948) made the additional point that Frisch's analysis

> makes the further assumption that when the active balance of a surplus country is reduced by the import restrictions of the deficit countries, the former country will retain its imports from all countries at the initial level in spite of the fact that its national income will be falling due to the decline in its export balance.

Frisch offered no response to those criticisms. In his second formulation (1948b) he broke each country's trade accounts down into 10 categories, numbered from 0 to 9. However, those numbers represented not SITC categories, but rather the "export priority numbers" fixed by the authorities in exporting countries. An importer in country A would contact an exporter in country B, who would file an application with its export authority, which would assign the export priority number and return the application to the importer, who would file an application with his own country's import authority, which would in turn assign an import priority number to the application. Finally, an international "bureau of compensation" would consider all these applications, each with two priority numbers, to decide which ones to accept. It would compute the mean of the export priorities by weighting them by the total amount of exports applied for, and similarly for the mean of the import priorities. For each country, the import average would have to exceed the export average. The bureau of compensation would then maximize the "global priority surplus" (the sum of countries' average import priorities minus the sum of countries' average export priorities) subject to balanced trade for each country.

Hinshaw's (1948) discussion, following Frisch's, consisted largely in a very useful exposition of Frisch's earlier (1947) article, but with respect to the new formulation he pointed out that it would require utmost cooperation among countries and that "if this almost utopian degree of international cooperation were to be attained, it would be just as easy to follow a more rational criterion of trade policy than the essentially restrictive goal of minimum-contraction-via-discrimination" (p. 274). Furthermore, "the scheme involves a much more comprehensive supervision and control of international transactions than is the case even at the present time."

With the Mexican debacle so fresh in our memories,[28] we can appreciate the need for new approaches to the problem of attaining international equilibrium. Frisch's scheme had definite drawbacks, but the problem it addressed is very real, one that was even addressed by a very classic economist, the young John Stuart Mill (1844). There can be no doubt that the problems to which Frisch drew attention urgently need the continued attention of theoretical economists.

References

Afriat, S. N. (1972). The theory of international comparisons of real income and prices. In: *International Comparisons of Prices and Output*, ed. D. J. Daly, pp. 13–69. New York: Columbia University Press.
  (1977). *The Price Index*. Cambridge University Press.
Aftalion, A. (1908). La réalité des surproductions générales. *Revue d'économie politique* 22:696–706.
  (1909a). La réalité des surproductions générales. *Revue d'économie politique*. 23:81–117, 201–29, 241–59.
  (1909b). *Essai d'une théorie des crises périodiques de surproduction. La réalité des surproductions générales*. Paris: Librairie de la Société du Recueil J.-B. Sirey et du Journal du Palais, Ancien Maison L. Larose & Forcel.
  (1913). *Les crises périodiques de surproduction*, 2 vols. Paris: Marcel Rivière et Cie.
Allen, R. G. D. (1933). On the marginal utility of money and its application. *Economica* 13:186–209.

---

[28] These words were written in 1995, but they apply with still greater force to the 1997–8 crisis in Southeast Asia.

(1935). Some observations on the theory and practice of price index numbers. *Review of Economic Studies* 3:57–66.

(1939). The assumptions of linear regression. *Economica, N.S.* 6:191–201.

(1949). The economic theory of index numbers. *Economica, N.S.* 16:197–203.

(1975). *Index Numbers in Theory and Practice*. Chicago: Aldine.

Alt, F. (1936). Über die Meßbarkeit des Nutzens. *Zeitschrift für Nationalökonomie* 7:161–9. English translation (1971): On the measurability of utility. In: *Preferences, Utility, and Demand*, ed. J. S. Chipman, L. Hurwicz, M. K. Richter, and H. F. Sonnenschein, pp. 429–31. New York: Harcourt Brace Jovanovich.

Antonelli, G. B. (1886). *Sulla teoria matematica della economia politica*. Pisa: Tipografia del Folchetto. English translation (1971): On the mathematical theory of political economy. In: *Preferences, Utility, and Demand*, ed. J. S. Chipman, L. Hurwicz, M. K. Richter, and H. F. Sonnenschein, pp. 332–64. New York: Harcourt Brace Jovanovich.

Arrow, K. J. (1960). The work of Ragnar Frisch, econometrician. *Econometrica* 28:175–92.

Arrow, K. J., Chenery, H. B., Minhas, B. S., and Solow, R. M. (1961). Capital–labor substitution and economic efficiency. *Review of Economics and Statistics* 43:225–50.

Balk, B. M. (1995). Axiomatic price index theory: a survey. *International Statistical Review* 63:69–93.

Bergson (Burk), A. (1936). Real income, expenditure proportionality, and Frisch's "New methods of measuring marginal utility." *Review of Economic Studies* 4:33–52. Reprinted in Bergson, A. (1966). *Essays in Normative Economics*, pp. 93–122. Cambridge, MA: Harvard University Press (Belknap Press).

Bernoulli, D. (1738). Specimen theoriae novae de mensura sortis. *Commentarii academiae scientiarum imperialis Petropolitanae* 5:175–92. English translation (1954): Exposition of a new theory on the measurement of risk. *Econometrica* 22:23–6.

Bickerdike, C. F. (1914). A non-monetary cause of fluctuations in employment. *Economic Journal* 24:357–70.

Birck, L. V. (1922). *The Theory of Marginal Value* (translated from the Danish *Læren om Grænseværdien*). London: George Routledge & Sons.

Blatt, J. M. (1980). On the Frisch model of business cycles. *Oxford Economic Papers, N.S.* 32:467–79.

Bortkiewicz, L. von (1928). Review of *Der Sinn der Indexzahlen* by Gottfried Haberler. *Magazin der Wirtschaft* 4:427–9.

(1932). Die Kaufkraft des Geldes und ihre Messung. *Nordic Statistical Journal* 4:1–68.

Bouniatian, M. (1908). *Wirtschaftskrisen und Ueberkapitalisation*. Munich: Ernst Reinhardt.

(1915). *Ekonomicheskie krizisy*, 2nd ed. Moscow: Tip. Mysl'.

(1922). *Les crises économiques* (French translation of 2nd edition). Paris: Marcel Giard.

(1930). *Les crises économiques*, 2nd French edition. Paris: Marcel Giard.

Bowley, A. L. (1928). Notes on index numbers. *Economic Journal* 38:216–37.

(1932). Review of *New Methods of Measuring Marginal Utility* by Ragnar Frisch. *Economic Journal* 42:252–6.

(1938). Note on Professor Frisch's "The problem of index numbers." *Econometrica* 6:83–4.

Buscheguennce (Byushgens), S. S. (1925). Sur une classe des hypersurfaces (a propos de "l'index idéal" de M. Irv. Fischer.). *Matematicheskii sbornik (Recueil mathématique de la Société Mathématique de Moscou)* 32:625–31.

Cassel, G. (1904). Om kriser och dåliga tider (On crises and bad times). *Ekonomisk Tidskrift* 6:21–35, 51–81.

(1918). *Theoretische Sozialökonomie*. Leipzig: C. F. Wintersche Verlagshandlung.

(1927). *Theoretische Sozialökonomie*, 4th ed. Leipzig: A. Deichertsche Verlagsbuchhandlung Dr. Werner Scholl.

(1932a). *Theoretische Sozialökonomie*, 5th ed. Leipzig: A. Deichertsche Verlagsbuchhandlung Dr. Werner Scholl.

(1932b). *The Theory of Social Economy*, 2 vols. (English translation by S. L. Barron from the manuscript of the 5th edition). London: Ernest Benn.

Chipman, J. S. (1953). Linear programming. *Review of Economics and Statistics* 35:101–17.

(1965). The nature and meaning of equilibrium in economic theory. In: *Functionalism in the Social Sciences*, pp. 35–64. Monograph no. 5. Philadelphia: American Academy of Political and Social Science.

(1977a). An empirical implication of Auspitz-Lieben-Edgeworth-Pareto complementarity. *Journal of Economic Theory* 14:228–31.

(1977b). A renewal model of economic growth: the continuous case. *Econometrica* 45:295–316.

Chipman, J. S., Hurwicz, L., Richter, M. K., and Sonnenschein, H. F. (eds.) (1971). *Preferences, Utility, and Demand*. New York: Harcourt Brace Jovanovich.

Chipman, J. S., and Moore, J. C. (1980). Compensating variation, consumer's surplus, and welfare. *American Economic Review* 70:933–49.

Clark, J. M. (1917). Business acceleration and the law of demand: a technical factor in economic cycles. *Journal of Political Economy* 25:217–35.

(1923). *Studies in the Economics of Overhead Costs*. University of Chicago Press.

(1931). Capital production and consumer-taking – a reply. *Journal of Political Economy* 39:814–16.

(1932). A further word. *Journal of Political Economy* 40:691–3.

(1935). *Strategic Factors in Business Cycles*. Washington, DC: National Bureau of Economic Research.

Davidson, R., and MacKinnon, J. G. (1993). *Estimation and Inference in Econometrics*. Oxford University Press.

Debreu, G. (1960). Topological methods in cardinal utility theory. In: *Mathematical Methods in the Social Sciences, 1959*, ed. K. J. Arrow, S. Karlin, and P. Suppes, pp. 16–26. Stanford University Press.

Diewert, W. E. (1976). Exact and superlative index numbers. *Journal of Econometrics* 4:115–45.

(1981). The economic theory of index numbers: a survey. In: *Essays in the Theory and Measurement of Consumer Behaviour: In Honour of Richard Stone*, ed. A. Deaton, pp. 163–208. Cambridge University Press.

(1983). The theory of the cost-of-living index and the measurement of welfare change. In: *Price Level Measurement*, ed. W. E. Diewert and C. Montmarquette, pp. 163–233. Ottawa: Ministry of Supply and Services Canada. Reprinted (1990) in *Price Level Measurement*, ed. W. E. Diewert, pp. 79–147. Amsterdam: North Holland.

Edgeworth, F. Y. (1881). *Mathematical Psychics*. London: C. Kegan Paul & Co.

Eichhorn, W. (1976). Fisher's tests revisited. *Econometrica* 44:247–56.

Eichhorn, W., and Voeller, J. (1976). *Theory of the Price Index*. Berlin: Springer-Verlag.

Feller, W. (1941). On the integral equation of renewal theory. *Annals of Mathematical Statistics* 12:243–67.

Fiebig, D. G., Bartels, R., and Krämer, W. (1996). The Frisch-Waugh theorem and generalized least squares. *Econometric Reviews* 15:431–43.

Fisher, I. (1892). Mathematical investigations in the theory of value and prices. *Transactions of the Connecticut Academy* 9:1–124. Reprinted (1925) by Yale University Press.

(1922). *The Making of Index Numbers*. Boston: Houghton Mifflin.

(1927). A statistical method for measuring marginal utility and testing the justice of a progressive income tax. In: *Economic Essays, Contributed in Honor of John Bates Clark*, ed. J. H. Hollander, pp. 157–93. New York: Macmillan.

Frisch, R. (1926a). Sur un problème d'économie pure. *Norsk Matematisk Forenings Skrifter* serie I, no. 16, pp. 1–40. Reprinted (1957) in *Metroeconomica* 9:79–111. English translation (1971): On a problem in pure economics. In: *Preferences, Utility, and Demand*, ed. J. S. Chipman, L. Hurwicz, M. K. Richter, and H. F. Sonnenschein, pp. 386–423. New York: Harcourt Brace Jovanovich.

(1926b). Kvantitativ formulering av den teoretiske økonomikks lover. *Statsøkonomisk Tidsskrift* 40:299–334.

(1927). Sammenhengen mellem primærinvestering og reinvestering. *Statsøkonomisk Tidsskrift* 41:117–52. English translation by Einar Hope (1965): The relationship between primary investment and reinvestment (mimeographed). Economics Translation Series, no. 8, ed. J. S. Chipman. University of Minnesota.

(1928). Changing harmonics and other general types of components in empirical series. *Skandinavisk Aktuarietidskrift* 11:220–36.

(1929a). Correlation and scatter in statistical variables. *Nordic Statistical Journal* 8:36–102.

(1929b). Statistikk og dynamikk i den økonomiske teori. *Nationaløkonomisk Tidsskrift* 67:321–79. English translation of sections 1–3 (1992): Statics and dynamics in economic theory. *Structural Change and Economic Dynamics* 3:391–401.

(1930). Necessary and sufficient conditions regarding the form of an index number which shall meet certain of Fisher's tests. *Journal of the American Statistical Association* 25:397–406.

(1931a). Der Einfluß von Veränderungen des Preisniveaus auf den Grenznutzen des Geldes. *Zeitschrift für Nationalökonomie* 2:625–31.

(1931b). A method of decomposing an empirical series into its cyclical and progressive components. *Journal of the American Statistical Association (Suppl.)* 26:73–8.

(1931c). Konjunkturbevegelsen som statistik og som teoretisk problem. In: *Förhandlingar vid Nordiska Nationalekonomiska Mötet i Stockholm 15–17 juni 1931*, pp. 127–68, 224–34. Stockholm: Ivar Hæggströms Boktryckeri och Bokförlags A. B.

(1931d). The optimum regression (mimeographed). Department of Economics, University of Minnesota.

(1931e). The interrelation between capital production and consumer-taking. *Journal of Political Economy* 39:646–54.

(1932a). A rejoinder. *Journal of Political Economy* 40:253–5.

(1932b). A final word. *Journal of Political Economy* 40:694.

(1932c). *New Methods of Measuring Marginal Utility*. Tübingen: Verlag von J. C. B. Mohr (Paul Siebeck).

(1932d). Konjunkturene. In: *Verdensøkonomien i efterkrigstiden*, ed. W. Keilhau, I. Wedervang, and R. Frisch, pp. 79–139. Universitetets Radioforedrag, serie B, no. 6. Oslo: Forlagt av H. Aschehoug & Co. (W. Nygaard).

(1933a). *Sparing og circulasjons regulering*. Oslo: Fabritius & Sønners Forlag.

(1933b). *Pitfalls in the Statistical Construction of Demand and Supply Curves*. Veröffentlichen der Frankfurter Gesellschaft für Konjunkturforschung, Herausgegeben von Dr. Eugen Altschul, Neue Folge, Heft 5 (16. Heft der ganzen Reihe). Leipzig: Hans Buske Verlag.

(1933c). Propagation problems and impulse problems in dynamic economics. In: *Economic Essays in Honour of Gustav Cassel*, pp. 171–205. London: George Allen & Unwin.

(1934a). *Statistical Confluence Analysis by Means of Complete Regression Systems*. Publikasjon no. 5. Oslo: Universitetets Økonomisk Institutt.

(1934b). Circulation planning: proposal for a national organization of a commodity and service exchange. *Econometrica* 2:258–336, 422–35.

(1934c). More pitfalls in demand and supply curve analysis. *Quarterly Journal of Economics* 48:749–55.

(1934d). Reply to Mr. Subramanian's note. *Journal of the American Statistical Association* 29:317.

(1936a). Annual survey of general economic theory: the problem of index numbers. *Econometrica* 4:1–38.

(1936b). Errata. *Econometrica* 4:192.

(1936c). Note on the term "econometrics." *Econometrica* 4:95.

(1936d). On the notion of equilibrium and disequilibrium. *Review of Economic Studies* 3:100–5.

(1937). Price index comparisons between structurally different markets. In: *Comptes rendus du Congrès International des Mathématiciens Oslo 1936*, tome II (Conférence de Sections), pp. 220–1. Oslo: A. W. Brøggers Boktrykkeri.

(1938). The double-expenditure method. *Econometrica* 6:85–90.

(1939a). The Dupuit taxation theorem. *Econometrica* 7:145–50.

(1939b). A further note on the Dupuit taxation theorem. *Econometrica* 7:156–7.

(1939c). A note on errors in time series. *Quarterly Journal of Economics* 53:639–40.

(1947). On the need for forecasting a multilateral balance of payments. *American Economic Review* 37:535–51.

(1948a). Overdeterminateness and optimum equilibrium. *Nordisk Tidsskrift for Teknisk Økonomie* 12:95–105.
(1948b). Outline of a system of multicompensatory trade. *Review of Economics and Statistics* 30:265–71.
(1950). Alfred Marshall's theory of value. *Quarterly Journal of Economics* 64:495–524.
(1951). Knut Wicksell. A cornerstone in modern economic theory. Memorandum from the Institute of Economics, University of Oslo. Reprinted (1952): Frisch on Wicksell. In: *The Development of Economic Thought. Great Economists in Perspective*, ed. H. W. Spiegel, pp. 652–99. New York: Wiley.
(1959). A complete scheme for computing all direct and cross demand elasticities in a model with many sectors. *Econometrica* 27:177–96.
(1963). A multilateral trade clearing agency. *Statsøkonomisk Tidsskrift* 77:1–10.
(1964). Dynamic utility. *Econometrica* 32:418–24.
(1965). *Theory of Production*, translated from the 9th Norwegian edition of *Innledning til Produksjonsteorien*. Chicago: Rand McNally.
Frisch, R. and Holme, H. (1935). The characteristic solutions of a mixed difference and differential equation occurring in economic dynamics. *Econometrica* 3:225–39.
Frisch, R., and Mudgett, B. D. (1931). Statistical correlation and the theory of cluster types. *Journal of the American Statistical Association* 26:375–92.
Frisch, R., and Mudgett, B. D. (1932). A correction. *Journal of the American Statistical Association* 27:187.
Frisch, R., and Waugh, F. V. (1933). Partial time regressions as compared with individual trends. *Econometrica* 4:387–401.
Gale, D., and Nikaido, H. (1965). The Jacobian matrix and global univalence of mappings. *Mathematische Annalen* 159:81–93.
Gini, C. (1921). Sull'interpolazione di una retta quando i valori della variabile indipendente sono affeti da errori accidentali. *Metron* 1:63–82.
Goodwin, R. M. (1951). The nonlinear accelerator and the persistence of business cycles. *Econometrica* 19:1–17.
Haavelmo, T. (1940). The inadequacy of testing dynamic theory by comparing theoretical solutions and observed cycles. *Econometrica* 8:312–21.
(1943). The statistical implications of a system of simultaneous equations. *Econometrica* 11:1–12.
(1944). The probability approach in econometrics. *Econometrica (Suppl.)* 12:1–118.
(1950). Remarks on Frisch's confluence analysis and its use in econometrics. In: *Statistical Inference in Dynamic Economic Models*, ed. T. C. Koopmans, pp. 258–65. New York: Wiley.
Haavelmo, T., and Staehle, H. (1951). The elements of Frisch's confluence analysis. Memorandum fra Universitetets Socialøkonomiske Institutt, Oslo, serie 5, no. 6.
Haberler, G. (1927). *Der Sinn der Indexzahlen. Eine Untersuchung über den Begriff des Preisniveaus und die Methoden seiner Messung*. Tübingen: Verlag von J. C. B. Mohr (Paul Siebeck).
(1929). Der volkswirtschaftliche Geldwert und die Preisindexziffern. Eine Erwiderung. *Weltwirtschaftliches Archiv* 30:6**–14**.
Hansen, A. H. (1927). *Business-Cycle Theory*. Boston: Ginn & Co.

Hardy, G. H., Littlewood, J. E., and Pólya, G. (1934). *Inequalities.* Cambridge University Press.
Hicks, J. R. (1950) *A Contribution to the Theory of the Trade Cycle.* Oxford: Clarendon Press.
  (1969). Direct and indirect additivity. *Econometrica* 37:353–4.
Hinshaw, R. (1948). Professor Frisch on discrimination and multilateral trade. *Review of Economics and Statistics* 30:271–5.
Hotelling, H. (1927). Differential equations subject to error, and population estimates. *Journal of the American Statistical Association* 22:283–314.
  (1938). The general welfare in relation to problems of taxation and of railway and utility rates. *Econometrica* 6:242–69.
  (1939). The relation of prices to marginal costs in an optimum system. *Econometrica* 7:151–5, 158–9.
Houthakker, H. S. (1960). Additive preferences. *Econometrica* 28:244–57.
Jevons, W. S. (1871). *The Theory of Political Economy.* New York: Macmillan. Second edition 1897, third 1888, fourth 1911.
Johansen, L. (1969). Ragnar Frisch's contributions to economics. *Swedish Journal of Economics* 71:302–24.
Jordan, C. (1924). On Daniel Bernoulli's "moral expectation" and on a new conception of expectation. *American Mathematical Monthly* 31:183–90.
Kaldor, N. (1940). A model of the trade cycle. *Economic Journal* 50:78–92.
Kalecki, M. (1935). A macrodynamic theory of business cycles. *Econometrica* 3:327–44.
Keynes, J. M. (1930). *A Treatise on Money,* 2 vols. London: Macmillan.
  (1936). *The General Theory of Employment, Interest and Money.* London: Macmillan.
Klein, L. R., and Rubin, H. (1948). A constant-utility index of the cost of living. *Review of Economic Studies* 15:84–7.
Konüs (Konyus), A. A. (1924). Problema istinnovo indeksa stoimosti zhizni *Konyunkturnyi institut. Ekonomicheskii byulleten' (Economic Bulletin of the Conjuncture Institute) (Moscow)* 9–10:64–71. English translation (1939): The problem of the true index of the cost of living. *Econometrica* 7:10–29.
Konüs (Konyus), A. A., and Buscheguennce (Byushgens), S. S. (1926). K probleme pokupatelnoi cili deneg (On the problem of the purchasing power of money). *Voprosi Konyunkturi (Problems of Economic Conditions)* (supplement to the *Economic Bulletin of the Conjuncture Institute*) 2:151–72.
Koopmans, T. (1937). *Linear Regression Analysis of Economic Time Series.* Haarlem: De Erven F. Bohn N. V.
  (1949). Identification problems in economic model construction. *Econometrica* 19:125–44. Reprinted (1953) in *Studies in Econometric Method,* ed. W. C. Hood and T. C. Koopmans, pp. 27–48. New York: Wiley.
Leamer, E. E. (1981). Is it a demand curve, or is it a supply curve? Partial identification through inequality constraints. *Review of Economics and Statistics* 63:319–27.
Leontief, W. W. (1929). Ein Versuch zur statistischen Analyse von Angebot und Nachfrage (with an appendix, Mathematische Ableitung der Berechnungsformeln, by Robert Schmidt). *Weltwirtschaftliches Archiv* 30:1*–53*.
  (1934). Pitfalls in the construction of demand and supply curves: a reply. *Quarterly Journal of Economics* 48:355–61, 755–9.

Lovell, M. C. (1963). Seasonal adjustment of economic time series and multiple regression analysis. *Journal of the American Statistical Association* 58:993–1010.

McFadden, D. (1963). Further results on CES production functions. *Review of Economic Studies* 30:73–83.

Malmquist, S. (1953). Index numbers and indifference surfaces. *Trabajos de Estadistica* 4:209–42.

Marschak, J. (1931). *Elastizität der Nachfrage*. Tübingen: Verlag von J. C. B. Mohr (Paul Siebeck).

(1934). More pitfalls in demand and supply curve analysis: some comments. *Quarterly Journal of Economics* 48:759–66.

Marschak, J., and Andrews, W. H., Jr. (1944). Random simultaneous equations and the theory of production. *Econometrica* 12:143–205.

Marshall, A. (1890). *Principles of Economics*. London: Macmillan.

Meier, G. M. (1948). The trade matrix: a further comment on Professor Frisch's paper. *American Economic Review* 38:624–6.

Menderhausen, H. (1938). The definition of "equal well-being" in Frisch's double-expenditure method. *Econometrica* 6:285–6.

Mill, J. S. (1844). On the influence of consumption on production. Essay II in: *Essays on Some Unsettled Questions of Political Economy*, pp. 47–74. London: John W. Parker.

Pareto, V. (1892). Considerazioni sui principi fondamentali dell'economia politica pura. *Giornale degli Economisti* 5:119–57.

(1906). *Manuale di economia politica, con una introduzione alla scienza sociale*. Milan: Società Editrice Libraria. French translation (1909): *Manuel d'Économie politique*. Paris: V. Giard et E. Brière.

Pigou, A. C. (1912). *Wealth and Welfare*. London: Macmillan.

(1926). *The Economics of Welfare*. London: Macmillan. Second edition 1924, third 1929, fourth 1932.

Polak, J. J. (1948). Balancing international trade: a comment on Professor Frisch's paper. *American Economic Review* 38:139–42.

Pollak, R. A. (1971). The theory of the cost-of-living index. Research discussion paper no. 11, Office of Prices and Living Conditions, U.S. Bureau of Labor Statistics. First published (1983) in *Price Level Measurement*, ed. W. E. Diewert and C. Montmarquette, pp. 87–161. Ottawa: Ministry of Supply and Services Canada. Also published (1990) in *Price Level Measurement*, ed. W. E. Diewert, pp. 5–77. Amsterdam: North Holland.

Reiersøl, O. (1941). Confluence analysis by means of lag moments and other methods of confluence analysis. *Econometrica* 9:1–24.

(1945a). Confluence analysis by means of instrumental sets of variables. *Arkiv för Matematik, Astronomi och Fysik*, 32A:1–119.

(1945b). Residual variables in regression and confluence analysis. *Skandinavisk Aktuarietidsskrift* 28:201–17.

Roy, R. (1942). *De l'utilité. Contribution à la théorie des choix*. Paris: Hermann & Cie.

Samuelson, P. A. (1939a). Interactions between the multiplier analysis and the principle of acceleration. *Review of Economics and Statistics* 21:75–8.

(1939b). A synthesis of the principle of acceleration and the multiplier. *Journal of Political Economy* 47:786–97.

(1942). Constancy of the marginal utility of income. In: *Studies in Mathematical Economics and Econometrics, in Memory of Henry Schultz*, ed. O. Lange, F. McIntyre, and T. O. Yntema, pp. 75–91. University of Chicago Press.
(1947). *Foundations of Economic Analysis*. Cambridge, MA: Harvard University Press.
(1951). Abstract of a theorem concerning substitutability in open Leontief models. In: *Activity Analysis of Production and Allocation*, ed. T. C. Koopmans, pp. 142–6. New York: Wiley.
(1965). Using full duality to show that simultaneously additive direct and indirect utilities implies unitary price elasticity of demand. *Econometrica* 33:781–96.
(1969). Corrected formulation of direct and indirect additivity. *Econometrica* 37:355–9.
(1974). Remembrances of Frisch. *European Economic Review* 5:7–23.
Samuelson, P. A., and Swamy, S. (1974). Invariant economic index numbers and canonical duality: survey and synthesis. *American Economic Review* 64:942–52.
Schultz, H. (1925). The statistical law of demand as illustrated by the demand for sugar. *Journal of Political Economy* 33:481–504, 577–637.
(1928). *The Statistical Laws of Demand and Supply, with Special Application to Sugar*. University of Chicago Press.
(1930). *Der Sinn der statistischen Nachfragekurven*. Veröffentlichen der Frankfurter Gesellschaft für Konjunkturforschung, Herausgegeben von Dr. Eugen Altschul, Heft 10. Bonn: Kurt Schroeder Verlag. 1930. [German translation of The meaning of statistical demand curves (mimeographed), University of Chicago, 1930].
(1933). Frisch on the measurement of utility. *Journal of Political Economy* 41:95–116.
(1938). *The Theory and Measurement of Demand*. University of Chicago Press.
(1939a). A misunderstanding in index-number theory: the true Konüs condition on cost-of-living index numbers and its limitations. *Econometrica* 7:1–9.
(1939b). The assumptions of linear regression: comments. *Economica, N.S.* 6:202–4.
Schumpeter, J. A. (1926). *Theorie der wirstchaftlichen Entwicklung. Eine Untersuchung über Unternehmergewinn, Kapital, Kredit, Zins und der Konjunkturzyklus*, 2nd ed. Munich: Duncker & Humblot. English translation (1934): *The Theory of Economic Development: An Inquiry into Profits, Capital, Credit, Interest, and the Business Cycle*. Cambridge, MA: Harvard University Press.
Shephard, R. W. (1953). *Cost and Production Functions*, Princeton, N.J., Princeton University Press.
Slutsky, E. (1927). The summation of random causes as the source of cyclic processes (in Russian). *Voprosi ekonomiky* 3. English translation, revised by the author (1937): *Econometrica* 5:105–46.
Staehle, H. (1934). International comparison of food costs, part I. In: *International Comparisons of Cost of Living*. Studies and reports of the International Labour Office, series N (statistics), no. 20. Geneva: International Labour Office.

(1935). A development of the economic theory of price index numbers. *Review of Economic Studies* 2:163–88.

(1936). Further notes on index numbers. *Review of Economic Studies* 3:153–5.

Stone, R. (1954). *The Measurement of Consumer Expenditure and Behaviour in the United Kingdom 1920–1938*, vol. I. Cambridge University Press.

Subramanian, S. (1934). On a certain conclusion of Frisch's. *Journal of the American Statistical Association* 29:316–17.

Swamy, S. (1965). Consistency of Fisher's tests. *Econometrica* 33:619–23.

Thalberg, B. (1990). A reconsideration of Frisch's original cycle model. In: *Nonlinear and Multisectoral Macrodynamics. Essays in Honour of Richard Goodwin*, ed. K. Velupillai, pp. 96–117. New York University Press.

Tintner, G. (1938). A note on economic aspects of the theory of errors in time series. *Quarterly Journal of Economics* 53:141–9.

Uzawa, H. (1962). Production functions with constant elasticities of substitution. *Review of Economic Studies* 29:291–9.

Wald, A. (1937). Zur Theorie der Preisindexziffern. *Zeitschrift für Nationalökonomie* 8:179–219.

(1939). A new formula for the index of cost of living. *Econometrica* 7:319–31.

(1940). The fitting of straight lines if both variables are subject to error. *Annals of Mathematical Statistics* 11:284–300.

Walras, L. (1926). *Éléments d'économie politique pure, ou Théorie de la richesse sociale*. Paris: R. Pichon et R. Durand-Auzias. English translation by W. Jaffé (1954): *Elements of Pure Economics, or The Theory of Social Wealth*. London: George Allen & Unwin.

Wicksell, K. (1907). Krisernas gåta. *Statsøkonomisk Tidsskrift* 21:255–86.

(1918). Ett bidrag till krisernas teori (review of *Goda och dårliga tider* by Karl Petander). *Ekonomisk Tidskrift* 20:66–75.

Willassen, Y. (1987). A simple alternative derivation of a useful theorem in linear "errors-in-variables" regression models together with some clarifications. *Journal of Multivariate Analysis* 2:296–311.

Wold, H., and Juréen, L. (1953). *Demand Analysis*. New York: Wiley.

Working, E. J. (1927). What do statistical "demand curves" show? *Quarterly Journal of Economics* 41:212–35.

Yule, G. U. (1927). On a method of investigating periodicities in disturbed series, with special reference to Wolfer's sunspot numbers. *Philosophical Transactions of the Royal Society of London* [A] 226:267–98.

PART TWO

UTILITY MEASUREMENT

CHAPTER 4

Nonparametric Estimation of Exact Consumer Surplus and Deadweight Loss

Jerry A. Hausman and Whitney K. Newey

1   Introduction

Nonparametric estimation of regression models has gained wide attention in econometrics in the past few years. Nonparametric models are characterized by very large numbers of parameters. Often they may be difficult to interpret, and their usefulness in applied research has been demonstrated in a limited number of cases. We apply nonparametric regression models to estimation of demand curves of the type most often used in applied research. After estimation of the demand curves, we then derive estimates of exact consumer surplus and deadweight loss, which are the most widely used welfare and economic-efficiency measures in areas of economics such as public finance. We also work out asymptotic normal sampling theory for the nonparametric case, as well as the parametric case (where, except in certain analytic cases, the results are not known).

This study includes an application to gasoline demand. Empirical questions of interest here are the shape of the demand curve and the average magnitude of welfare loss from a tax on gasoline. In this application we compare parametric and nonparametric estimates of the demand curve, calculate exact measures of consumer surplus and deadweight loss, and give estimates of standard errors. We also analyze the sensitivity of the welfare measures to components of nonparametric regression estimators such as window width and number of terms in a series approximation.

The definition of exact consumer surplus (CS) is based on the expenditure function

---

This research was supported by the National Science Foundation. Helpful comments were provided by D. Collins, T. Gorman, I. Jewitt, A. Pakes, R. Porter, the referees, and participants at many seminars. Sarah Fisher-Ellison and Christine Meyer provided able research assistance.

This is a revised version of an article that appeared in *Econometrica* in November 1995 (63:1445–76).

$$CS(p^1, p^0, u^r) = e(p^1, u^r) - e(p^0, u^r)$$

where p^0 are initial prices, p^1 are new prices, and u^r is the reference utility level. The case $r = 1$ corresponds to the case we focus on here, equivalent variation:

$$EV(p^1, p^0, y) = e(p^1, u^1) - e(p^0, u^1) = y - e(p^0, u^1)$$

where y denotes income, fixed over the price change. It is also easy to carry out a similar analysis for compensating variation.

The measure of exact deadweight loss (DWL) used corresponds to the idea of the loss in consumer surplus from imposition of a tax less the compensated tax revenue raised, under the implicit assumption that it is returned to the consumer in a lump-sum manner. See Auerbach (1985) for a discussion of the various definitions of DWL (also called the excess burden of taxation). Here we use the Diamond-McFadden (1974) definition of DWL, where $p^1 - p^0$ is the vector of taxes. Then, for equivalent variation, the definition of exact DWL is

$$\begin{aligned}DWL(p^1, p^0, y) &= EV(p^1, p^0, y) - (p^1 - p^0)'h(p^1, u^1)\\ &= y - e(p^0, u^1) - (p^1 - p^0)'q(p^1, y)\end{aligned}$$

where $h(p, u)$ is the compensated, or Hicksian, demand function, and $q(p, y)$ is the Marshallian (market) demand function. Thus, to estimate exact consumer surplus or exact DWL it is necessary to estimate the expenditure function and the compensated demand function, which are related by the equation

$$\partial e(p, u)/\partial p_j = h_j(p, u) \quad \text{(Shephard's lemma)}$$

The expenditure function and compensated demand curve are estimated from observable data on the market, or Marshallian, demand curve, $q_j(p, y)$.

Various approximations have been proposed for estimation of the exact welfare measures. Willig (1976) demonstrated that the Marshallian measure of consumer surplus is often close to the exact measure, and he derived bounds as a function of the income share. Various authors have also recommended higher-order Taylor-type approximations to the exact welfare measures. Limitations of the approximation approach are that they do not yield measures of precision, given that they are based on estimated coefficients in most cases, and the approximations may do poorly in some situations that are difficult to specify a priori. Deaton (1986) discussed these problems in more detail. Also, Hausman (1981) demonstrated that whereas the approximations may often do well for the consumer-surplus measure, they often do very poorly in measurement of DWL; Small and Rosen (1981) demonstrated a similar proposition in the discrete-choice situation.

Two approaches have been proposed for estimation of the exact welfare measures from estimates of ordinary demand functions. Hausman (1981) demonstrated that for many widely used single-equation demand specifications, the necessary differential equation could be integrated to derive the expenditure function and also the compensated demand function. He was also able to derive the sampling distribution for the measures of consumer surplus and DWL, given the distribution of the estimated demand coefficients. Vartia (1983), instead of using an analytic solution to the differential equations, proposed a variety of numerical algorithms that estimate consumer surplus and DWL to any desired degree of accuracy. Whereas the Vartia approach can be applied to a wider range of situations, no correct sampling distribution has been derived for the estimated welfare measures, although some approximate results have been given by Porter-Hudak and Hayes (1986).

Both the Hausman approach and the Vartia approach can be applied to multiple price changes and are path-independent for the true demand function. The various approximation approaches do not share the path-independence property, which can lead to perplexing computational results and has led to much theoretical misunderstanding in the appropriate literature. Here, we consider nonparametric estimation via an unrestricted estimator that uses some, but not all, the implications of path independence. Our approach allows us to test path independence (i.e., symmetry of compensated demands) and impose further implications of path independence to construct more efficient estimators.

The Hausman and Vartia approaches begin with Roy's identity, which links the ordinary demand function with the indirect utility function:

$$q_j(p, y) = -[\partial v(p, y)/\partial p_j]/[\partial v(p, y)/\partial y]$$

where $v(p, y)$ is the indirect utility function. The partial differential equation derived from this equation can be solved along an indifference curve for a unique solution so long as the initial values are differentiable. Let $p(t)$ denote a price path, with $p(0) = p^0$ and $p(1) = p^1$, and let $y(t)$ be compensated income, satisfying $V(p(t), y(t)) = V(p^1, y)$. Differentiating with respect to t gives

$$[\partial V(p(t), y(t))/\partial p]' \, \partial p(t)/\partial t + [\partial V(p(t), y(t))/\partial y]\partial y(t)/\partial t = 0$$

Hausman notes that this equation can be converted into an ordinary differential equation by use of the implicit-function theorem and Roy's identity. Let $S(t, y) = y - e(p(t), u^1)$ denote the equivalent variation for a price change from $p(t)$ to p^1. Then, because compensated income is $y - S(t, y)$,

$$\partial S(t, y)/\partial t = -q(p(t), y - S(t, y))' \, \partial p(t)/\partial t, \quad S(1, y) = 0 \qquad (1.1)$$

Alternatively, this equation follows immediately from Shephard's lemma and the definition of $S(t, y)$. Hausman solved this equation for some widely used demand curves. The solution gives both the expenditure function and indirect utility function, and the right-hand side of this equation gives the compensated demands.

Vartia's numerical solutions to the differential equation also arise from equation (1.1). To solve it, Vartia used a numerical method of Collatz. He orders $t_s = 1 - s/N$ $(s = 0, \ldots, N)$ and defined S iteratively by

$$\begin{aligned}S(t_{s+1}) = S(t_s) &- 0.5[q(p(t_{s+1}), y - S(t_{s+1})) \\ &+ q(p(t_s), y - S(t_s))]' \times [p(t_{s+1}) - p(t_s)]\end{aligned}$$

This algorithm consists in averaging demand at the last price and demand at the current price and multiplying this average by the change in price. By the envelope theorem, the product of the price change times the quantity equals the additional income required to remain on the same indifference curve. Intuitively, $dy = q \cdot dp$, where y is updated at each step of the process, rather than being held constant as in the Marshallian approximation to consumer surplus. There are alternative numerical algorithms to solve equation (1.1) that may lead to faster results. We use a Buerlisch-Stoer algorithm from *Numerical Recipes* that does not require solution of the implicit equation in Vartia's algorithm, has a faster (quintic) convergence rate than Vartia's (cubic), and in our empirical example leads to small estimated errors with few demand evaluations.

The possible shortcoming of all applications to date of both the Hausman approach and the Vartia approach is that the parametric form of the demand function is required. In most applied situations, the exact parametric specification of the demand curve (up to unknown parameters) will not be known. Thus, commonly used demand-curve specifications may well lead to inconsistent estimates of the welfare measures if the demand curve is misspecified. This problem is potentially quite important, especially in the case of measuring DWL, which depends on "second-order" properties of the demand curve. See Hausman (1981) for a discussion of the second-order properties and their effects on estimates of DWL.

Varian (1982a–c) has proposed an alternative approach, based on the revealed-preference ideas of Samuelson (1948) and Afriat (1967, 1973), that is nonparametric, but is able to estimate only upper and lower bounds on the welfare measures. That approach is quite different from the approach taken here, because we estimate a nonparametric demand function, whereas that alternative approach considers inequality restrictions on observations. Varian's nonparametric-approximation approach is very interesting, but it often yields rather wide bounds, because many price observations per individual are required for tight bounds. Furthermore, use of sampling distributions to measure the precision of the estimate is problematical. Here we use a nonparametric cross-section demand analysis, imposing enough homogeneity across individuals and smoothness of the demand function that we can estimate it by nonparametric regression. We construct point estimates of exact consumer surplus and DWL, as well as precision estimates of the welfare measures. The sensitivity of the welfare measure to the amount of smoothing used in the nonparametric regression can be analyzed straightforwardly. Our estimates also allow for a straightforward test of the integrability conditions using the path-independence property of our welfare measures and the downward-sloping characteristic of compensated demand.

2   Estimation

Our estimator of consumer surplus is obtained by solving equation (1.1) numerically, with $q(p, y)$ replaced by an estimator obtained from nonparametric regression. We also allow covariates w to enter the demand function $q(p, y, w)$. In our empirical work these covariates are region and time dummies. In other contexts they might be demographic variables. We try to minimize the dimension of this nonparametric function by restricting w to enter in a parametric way. Let $x = (\ln p', \ln y)'$, where $\ln p$ represents the vector of natural logs of prices, and assume that the true value of the demand function satisfies

$$q_0(p, y, w) = \exp(g_0(x, w)), \quad g_0(x, w) = r_0(x) + w'\beta_0 = E[\ln q|x, w] \tag{2.1}$$

where q denotes observed quantity and the expectations are taken over the distribution of a single observation from the data. This is a log-linear demand specification that is common in applications and will be considered in ours. The theory of Section 6 will allow for a somewhat more general specification, where the demand function is $T(E[T^{-1}(q)|x, w])$ for some transformation $T(q)$, and x is any invertible transformation of p and y.

Equation (2.1) specifies the true demand function to be the exponential of a partially linear regression of $\ln q$ on $\ln p$, $\ln y$, and w. A corresponding estimator of the demand function will be

$$\hat{q}(p, y, w) = \exp(\hat{g}(x, w)) = \exp(\hat{r}(x) + w'\hat{\beta}) \tag{2.2}$$

where $\hat{g}$ is an estimator of g_0, such as the kernel or series estimator discussed later. We estimate exact consumer surplus nonparametrically by substituting $\hat{q}(p, y, w)$ for $q(p, y)$ in equation (1.1) and solving numerically. This estimator depends on the value of w, so we consider fixing w at a particular value and averaging over different values. The empirical results reported here set w equal to its sample mean, because averaging across different values for the covariates is computationally too demanding for our application.

A kernel estimator is a locally weighted average that can be described as follows. Let k denote the dimension of the price vector, equal to the number of goods minus 1 (to allow for a numeraire good). Let $\mathcal{K}(v)$ be a kernel function of a $(k + 1)$-dimensional argument, satisfying $\int \mathcal{K}(v)dv = 1$ and other regularity conditions discussed later. Let $\sigma > 0$ be a bandwidth parameter, and $K_\sigma(v) = \sigma^{-k-1}\mathcal{K}(v/\sigma)$. Also, let the data be denoted by $z_1, \ldots, z_n$, where z includes q, y, w, and possibly other variables. For a matrix function $B(z)$, a kernel estimator of $E[B(z)|x]$ is

$$\hat{E}[B(z)|x] = \sum_{j=1}^{n} B(z_j) K_\sigma(x - x_j) \bigg/ \sum_{j=1}^{n} K_\sigma(x - x_j)$$

To estimate the partially linear specification in equation (2.1), we "partial out" the coefficients of w in a way analogous to that of Robinson (1988). Let $\tau(x)$ be a trimming function that is zero for outlying values for x. In the application, we set $\tau(x) = 1$ for the observations, with $(x - \bar{x})'\hat{\Sigma}^{-1}(x - \bar{x})$ less than or equal to its 0.95 quantile and $\tau(x) = 0$ otherwise, which leaves 95 percent of the observations in the sample. This trimming function depends on the data through $\hat{\Sigma}$, although the theory requires that it not depend on the data. The estimator of g_0 is

$$\hat{g}(x, w) = \hat{r}(x) + w'\hat{\beta}, \quad \hat{r}(x) = \hat{E}[\ln q|x] - \hat{E}[w|x]'\hat{\beta}$$

$$\hat{\beta} = \left[\sum_{i=1}^{n} \tau_i(w_i - \hat{E}[w|x_i])(w_i - \hat{E}[w|x_i])'\right]^{-1} \quad (2.3)$$

$$\times \sum_{i=1}^{n} \tau_i(w_i - \hat{E}[w|x_i])(\ln q_i - \hat{E}[\ln q|x_i])$$

where $\tau_i = \tau(x_i)$. The kernel that we consider in the empirical work, where k is 1, so that v is two-dimensional, is

$$\mathcal{K}(v) = a(\hat{\Sigma}^{-1/2}v)$$

$$a(u) = \begin{cases} (1 - u'u)^3 [3 - 21(u'u) + 28(u'u)^2], & u'u \leq 1 \\ 0, & u'u > 1 \end{cases} \quad (2.4)$$

where $\hat{\Sigma}$ is the sample covariance of x. This kernel is three times continuously differentiable and has moments that are zero up to the fifth order, as required for the asymptotic theory. In practice it is common to make the estimator invariant to linear transformations of x by scaling by $\hat{\Sigma}^{-1/2}$, as is done here, although we do not allow for an estimated variance matrix in the theory. Figure 4.1 shows the shape of this kernel as a function of $(v'\hat{\Sigma}^{-1}v)^{1/2}$, the distance of $\hat{\Sigma}^{-1/2}v$ from zero in the Euclidean metric.

It is well known that the choice of bandwidth σ can have important effects on nonparametric regression. In the empirical work we consider a data-based choice of σ, equal to the value that minimizes a cross-validation criterion, and also check sensitivity to bandwidth by considering more than one bandwidth. The cross-validation criterion takes the form

$$CV = \sum_{i=1}^{n} \tau_i (\ln q_i - \hat{g}_i)^2$$
$$\hat{g}_i = w_i'\hat{\beta} + \sum_{j \neq i} \{\ln q_j - w_j'\hat{\beta}\} K_\sigma(x_i - x_j) \Big/ \sum_{j \neq i} K_\sigma(x_i - x_j)$$
(2.5)

Here $\hat{g}_i$ is the predicted value of $\hat{g}(x, w)$ for the ith observation computed from all but the ith observation. Of course, CV depends on σ through both $\hat{\beta}$ and the sums in equation (2.5). In the application, we compute $\hat{\beta}$ and CV for a grid of different σ values, as described in Section 5. Choosing σ to minimize CV is known to lead to an estimator that minimizes the mean square error asymptotically (e.g., Hardle and Linton, 1994). However, the theory here requires that σ be smaller than the mean-square minimizing value, so we also compute results for smaller σ.

A series estimator is the predicted value from a regression on some approximating functions for p and y and on w. For $x = (\ln p', \ln y)'$, let $(\phi_{1K}(x), \ldots, \phi_{KK}(x))$ be a vector of K approximating functions, and let $\phi^K(x) = I_k \otimes (\phi_{1K}(x), \ldots, \phi_{KK}(x))$ be the block diagonal matrix of k copies of these functions. The idea here is that the vector of k functions $r(x)$ is to be approximated by a linear combination of $\phi^K(x)$, with its Kronecker-product form allowing each element of $r(x)$ to be separately approximated by a linear combination of $(\phi_{1K}(x), \ldots, \phi_{KK}(x))$. The number of approximating functions K will be allowed to grow with the sample size, in order that $r(x)$ be approximated arbitrarily well no matter what its form. Power-series and spline examples of such approximating functions are discussed later.

Let $\phi^K(x, w) = (\phi^K(x)', w')'$ and

$$\hat{\gamma} = \left[\sum_{i=1}^{n} \phi^K(x_i, w_i) \phi^K(x_i, w_i)'\right]^{-1} \cdot \sum_{i=1}^{n} \phi^K(x_i, w_i) \ln q_i$$

be the coefficients from a regression of $\ln q_i$ on $\phi^K(x_i, w_i)$. A series estimator of g_0 is

$$\hat{g}(x, w) = \phi^K(x, w)'\hat{\gamma} = \phi^K(x)'\hat{\eta} + w'\hat{\beta} \qquad (2.6)$$

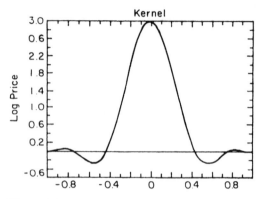

Figure 4.1

where $\gamma = (\eta', \beta')'$ is partitioned conformably with $\phi^K(x, w)$. This estimator can also be interpreted as "partialling out" w, satisfying equation (2.3) with $\tau_i \equiv 1$ and the kernel-conditional expectation estimator replaced by $\hat{E}[B(z)|x] = \phi^K(x)'\hat{\eta}_B$ where $\hat{\eta}_B$ are the coefficients of the least-squares regression of $B(z_i)$ on $\phi^K(x_i)$.

Two important types of approximating functions are power series and regression splines. Power series are formed by choosing the elements of $\phi^K(x)$ to be products of powers of the individual components of x. Power series are easy to compute and have good approximation rates for smooth functions, although they may be sensitive to outliers in x and local behavior of the approximation, and can be highly collinear. The collinearity problem can be overcome to some extent by replacing the powers of individual components with orthogonal polynomials, which does not affect the estimator but may lead to easier computation. Regression splines are piecewise polynomials of order s with fixed join points referred to as knots. For univariate x in $[0, 1]$ with evenly spaced knots, regression-spline approximating functions are $a_{jK}(x) = x^{j-1}$ ($j = 1, \ldots, s+1$), $(x - (j - s - 1)/[K - s])_+^s$, $j \geq s + 2$, where $(v)_+^s = 1(v \geq 0)v^s$. For multivariate x, a regression spline can be formed from all cross-products of univariate splines in the components of x. Splines are less sensitive than power series to discontinuities in the function being approximated and its derivatives and to outliers in x. Unlike the case for power series, the range of x must be known in order to place the knots. In practice, such a known range can be constructed by dropping from the data any observation where x is not in some prespecified range. Also, the foregoing power-spline sequence can be highly collinear, but this problem can be alleviated by replacing them with their corresponding B splines (e.g., Powell, 1981).

Series estimators are sensitive to the number of terms K in the

Exact Consumer Surplus and Deadweight Loss

approximation. In the empirical work, we choose the number of terms to minimize a cross-validation criterion that takes the form in equation (2.3), with τ_i the same as for kernel estimators and $\hat{g}_i = \phi^K(x_i, w_i)'\hat{\gamma}_{-i}$, where $\hat{\gamma}_{-i}$ is the least-squares coefficient computed from all the observations except the ith.[1] Cross-validation is known to lead to a mean-square-error-minimizing choice of number of terms (Li, 1987). We also try different numbers of terms, because our theory requires that the number exceed the minimum mean-square-error value, as well as to see how the results are affected.

Returning now to estimation of consumer surplus, our estimator is constructed by substituting the estimated demand function in equation (1.1) and integrating numerically. As in Section 1, let $p(t)$ be a price path, with $p(0) = p^0$ and $p(1) = p^1$. Also, let $S(y, w, g)$ denote the solution to equation (1.1), with demand function $q(p, y) = \exp(g(x, w))$, where $x = (\ln p', \ln y)'$. Then consumer surplus at particular income and covariate values y_0 and w_0, respectively, with a corresponding estimator, is

$$S_0 = S(y_0, w_0, g_0), \quad \hat{S} = S(y_0, w_0, \hat{g}) \tag{2.7}$$

where $\hat{g}$ is a kernel, series, or other nonparametric estimator. A corresponding DWL value and associated estimator can be formed by subtracting the "tax receipts," as in

$$L_0 = S_0 - (p^1 - p^0)'q_0(p^1, y_0, w_0), \quad \hat{L} = \hat{S} - (p^1 - p^0)'\hat{q}(p^1, y_0, w_0) \tag{2.8}$$

for q_0 and $\hat{q}$ from equations (2.1) and (2.2), respectively.

A summary measure for consumer surplus can be obtained by averaging over income values. In addition, it may sometimes be of interest to average over different prices, to reflect the fact that individuals face different prices. To set up such an average, let u index price paths, so that $p(t, u)$ is the price at $t \in [0, 1]$ for price path u, with initial and final prices $p(0, u)$ and $p(1, u)$, respectively. Also, let z denote a single data observation that includes u and values y_0 for income and w_0 for covariates. For example, u, y_0, and w_0 might be drawn (simulated) from some distribution, or y_0 and w_0 might be the actual observations. Let $S(z, g)$ be the solution to equation (1.1) for the price path $p(u, t)$ at y_0 and w_0, with demand $q(p, y) = \exp(g(x, w))$. The average surplus and DWL we consider are weighted means across z, of the form

---

[1] Well-known recursive residual formulas can be used to simplify calculation of the cross-validation residuals $y_i - \hat{g}_i$.

$$\mu_0 = E[\omega(z)S(z, g_0)]/E[\omega(z)], \quad \hat{\mu} = \overline{\omega}^{-1}\sum_{i=1}^{n}S(z_i, \hat{g})/n$$

$$\overline{\omega} = \sum_{i=1}^{n}\omega(z_i)/n$$

$$\lambda_0 = \mu_0 - E[\omega(z)\{p(1,u) - p(0,u)\}'q_0(p(1,u), y_0, w_0)]/E[\omega(z)]$$

$$\hat{\lambda} = \hat{\mu} - \overline{\omega}^{-1}\sum_{i=1}^{n}\omega(z_i)\{p(1,u_i) - p(0,u_i)\}'\hat{q}(p(1,u_i), y_{0i}, w_{0i})/n$$

(2.9)

The weights $\omega(z)$ are useful for the theory of Section 6, where they are required to be zero for income values that are too extreme. Also, they provide a method of selecting the weights assigned to individuals in these average welfare measures.

It is interesting to note that the consumer-surplus estimator may converge faster than the DWL estimator. In particular, $\hat{S}$ is like an integral over one dimension [the variable t in $p(t)$], and so has a faster convergence rate than $\hat{L}$, which depends on the value of $\hat{g}$ at a particular point.[2] Similarly, average consumer surplus and DWL may have different convergence rates. One important case where their convergence rates will be the same, both being the parametric $1/\sqrt{n}$ rate, is when the initial and final prices and income have sufficient variation. An example is that in which the initial price for each individual is the price actually faced, and the tax rate is the same across individuals. In this case, averaging will take place over all the arguments of the nonparametric estimates, and it is known from the semiparametric-estimation literature to result in $\sqrt{n}$ consistency (under appropriate regularity conditions).

So far, our nonparametric consumer-surplus estimators have ignored the residual $\varepsilon = \ln q - g_0(p, y, w)$. This approach is consistent with current practice in applied econometrics and is difficult to improve without more information about the residual. One can ignore the residual if it is all measurement error, but not if it contains individual heterogeneity. Hausman (1985) showed that it is possible to separate out measurement error and heterogeneity in parametric, nonlinear models, but the amount of heterogeneity is not identified in our nonparametric, linear-in-residual specification. Even when ε is all heterogeneity, it may be possible to interpret the demand function as corresponding to a particular consumer type. Suppose that $\varepsilon = \varepsilon(p, y, w, v)$ for some function $\varepsilon(p, y, w, v)$ of prices, income, covariates, and a taste variable v, where v is independent of price and income. In general, $\varepsilon(p, y, w, u)$ will depend on p and y, as shown by Brown and Walker

---

[2] It is known from the work on semiparametric estimation that integrals or averages converge faster than pointwise values (e.g., Powell, Stock, and Stoker, 1989). The fact that one-dimensional integrals converge faster than pointwise values has recently been shown by Newey (1994a) for kernel estimators.

(1989).[3] Nevertheless, if $\varepsilon(p, y, w, v)$ is identically zero for some value of v [e.g., if $\varepsilon = \sigma(p, y, w)v$], then $g(p, y, w)$ can be interpreted as the demand function for that value of v. In the rest of this study we stay with the specification of demand as $\exp(g_0(p, y, w))$, corresponding to an interpretation of ε as measurement error or to evaluation at a particular consumer type.

3 Asymptotic Variance Estimation

Under the regularity conditions given in Section 6, all of the estimators will be asymptotically normal. To be specific, let $\hat{\theta}$ denote any one of the estimators previously presented. For a kernel estimator there will be V_0 and $\alpha \geq 0$ such that

$$\sqrt{n}\sigma^\alpha(\hat{\theta} - \theta_0) \xrightarrow{d} N(0, V_0) \tag{3.1}$$

The "full-average," $\sqrt{n}$-consistent case corresponds to $\alpha = 0$, whereas in other cases the convergence rate for $\hat{\theta}$ will be $1/(\sqrt{n}\sigma^\alpha)$, which is slower than $1/\sqrt{n}$ by $\sigma \to 0$. For a series estimator there will be V_n such that

$$\sqrt{n}V_n^{-1/2}(\hat{\theta} - \theta_0) \xrightarrow{d} N(0, 1) \tag{3.2}$$

In the $\sqrt{n}$-consistent case the series and kernel estimators will have the same asymptotic variance, with V_n converging to V_0 from equation (3.1). In other cases the two estimators generally will not have the same asymptotic variance, and the series estimator will satisfy the weaker property of equation (3.2) that does not specify a rate of convergence. Exact convergence rates for series estimators are not yet known, except for $\sqrt{n}$ consistency, although it is possible to bound the convergence rate. Despite this lack of a convergence rate, equation (3.2) can still be used for asymptotic inference.

For large sample inference, suppose that there is an estimator $\hat{V}_n$ of V_n in equation (3.2). If $(V_n/\hat{V}_n)^{1/2} \xrightarrow{p} 1$, then it follows by equation (3.2) (and the Slutzky theorem) that

$$\sqrt{n}\hat{V}_n^{-1/2}(\hat{\theta} - \theta_0) \xrightarrow{d} N(0, 1) \tag{3.3}$$

Consequently, a $1 - \alpha$ large-sample confidence interval will be

$$\hat{\theta} \pm x_{\alpha/2}\sqrt{\hat{V}_n/n} \tag{3.4}$$

where $x_{\alpha/2}$ is the $1 - \alpha/2$ quantile of the standard normal distribution. One could also use equation (3.3) to form large-sample hypothesis tests.

---

[3] Strictly speaking, these results apply only to a linear specification, but Brown has indicated to us in private communication that the residual in a log-linear regression must be functionally dependent on prices.

122   Jerry A. Hausman and Whitney K. Newey

To form large-sample confidence intervals, as in equation (3.4), an estimator $\hat{V}_n$ of V_n is needed. For kernel estimators, one method of forming $\hat{V}_n$ would be to derive a formula for V_0 and then substitute estimators for unknown quantities to form $\sigma^{-2\alpha}\hat{V}_0$. This procedure is not very feasible, because the asymptotic variances are quite complicated, as described in Section 6. Instead, we use an alternative method, from Newey (1994a), that requires knowing only the form of $\hat{\theta}$. For series estimators we also use a method based only on the form of $\hat{\theta}$.

The asymptotic variance estimators for kernel and series estimators have some common features. In each case,

$$\hat{V}_n = \sum_{i=1}^{n} \hat{\psi}_{ni}^2 / n \qquad (3.5)$$

where the estimates $\hat{\psi}_{ni}$ are constructed in a way described later. Also, in each case, the variance will be based on the common form of the estimator, which is

$$\hat{\theta} = \bar{\omega}^{-1}\sum_{i=1}^{n} a(z_i, \hat{g})/n, \quad \bar{\omega} = \sum_{i=1}^{n} \omega(z_i)/n \qquad (3.6)$$

where $a(z, g)$ is a function of a single observation z and the partially linear specification $g = g(x, w) = r(x) + w'\beta$, $\hat{g}$ is the kernel or series estimator described earlier, and $\omega(z)$ is a weight function. The specification of $a(z, g)$ and $\omega(z)$ corresponding to each case is

$$\begin{aligned}
\hat{\theta} = \hat{S}: \quad & a(z_i, g) = S(y_0, w_0, g), \quad \omega(z) = 1 \\
\hat{\theta} = \hat{L}: \quad & a(z_i, g) = S(y_0, w_0, g) \\
& \quad - (p^1 - p^0)'\exp(g(p^1, y_0, w_0)) \\
\hat{\theta} = \hat{\mu}: \quad & a(z_i, g) = \omega(z_i)S(z_i, g) \\
\hat{\theta} = \hat{\lambda}: \quad & a(z_i, g) = \omega(z_i)\{S(z_i, g) - [p(1, u_i) - p(0, u_i)]' \\
& \quad \times \exp(g(p(1, u_i), y_i, w_i))\}
\end{aligned} \qquad (3.7)$$

where $g(p, y, w)$ denotes $g(x, w) = r(x) + w'\beta$ for $x = (\ln p', \ln y)'$. For both kernel and series estimation, $\hat{\psi}_{ni}$ will have two components, one of which accounts for the variability of z_i in $a(z_i, g)$ and $\omega(z_i)$, and the other for the variability of $\hat{g}$. The first component is the same for both kernel and series, so that we can specify

$$\hat{\psi}_{ni} = \hat{\psi}_i^z + \hat{\psi}_i^g, \quad \psi_i^z = \bar{\omega}^{-1}a(z_i, \hat{g}) - \hat{\theta} - \bar{\omega}^{-1}\hat{\theta}[\omega(z_i) - \bar{\omega}] \qquad (3.8)$$

where an n subscript on $\hat{\psi}_i^z$ and $\hat{\psi}_i^g$ is suppressed for notational convenience. The $\hat{\psi}_i^z$ term is an asymptotic approximation to the influence on $\hat{\theta}$ of the ith observation in $\bar{\omega}^{-1}\Sigma_{i=1}^{n}a(z_i, g)$. The term $\hat{\psi}_i^g$ will account for the estimation of g. It can be constructed from an asymptotic approximation to the influence of $\hat{\theta}$ of the ith observation in $\hat{g}$, taking different forms for kernel and series estimators.

For kernel estimators, the idea for forming $\hat{\psi}_i^g$, developed by Newey (1994a), is to differentiate with respect to the ith observation in the kernel estimator. This calculation amounts to a "delta method" for kernels and leads to an estimator that is robust to heteroskedasticity and has the same form, no matter what the convergence rate of $\hat{\theta}$ is. To describe the estimator, let δ denote a scalar, and

$$\hat{h}^r(x) = \sum_{j=1}^{n} \{\ln q_j - w_j'\hat{\beta}\} K_\sigma(x - x_j)/n,$$

$$\hat{f}(x) = \sum_{j=1}^{n} K_\sigma(x - x_j)/n$$

$$\hat{A}_i = \partial\bigg[n^{-1}\sum_{j=1}^{n} a(z_j, \{\hat{f} + \delta K_\sigma(\cdot - x_i)\}^{-1}\{\hat{h}^r + \delta\{\ln(q_i) - w_i'\hat{\beta}\}\}$$

$$\times K_\sigma(\cdot - x_i) + w_i'\hat{\beta})/n]/\partial\delta|_{\delta=0} \qquad (3.9)$$

$$\hat{G}^\beta = \partial\bigg[\sum_{j=1}^{n} a(z_j, \hat{g}_\beta)/n\bigg]\bigg/\partial\beta\bigg|_{\beta=\hat{\beta}}$$

$$\hat{g}_\beta(x,w) = \hat{E}[\ln q - w'\beta|x] + w'\beta$$

$$\hat{M} = \sum_{i=1}^{n} \tau_i(w_i - \hat{E}[w|x_i])(w_i - \hat{E}[w|x_i])'/n$$

$$\hat{\psi}_i^g = \bar{\omega}^{-1}\bigg\{\hat{A}_i - \sum_{j=1}^{n}\hat{A}_j/n + \hat{G}^\beta \hat{M}^{-1}\tau_i(w_i - \hat{E}[w|x_i])$$

$$\times (\ln(q_i) - \hat{g}(x_i, w_i))\bigg\}$$

The term $\hat{A}_i$ is an asymptotic approximation to the influence of the ith observation in $\hat{r}(x)$ on the average of $a(z_j, \hat{g})$, and the second term in $\hat{\psi}_i^g$ is a fairly standard delta-method term for estimation of β.

For series estimators, the idea is to apply the delta method as if the series approximation were exact. This results in correct asymptotic inference because it accounts properly for the variance, while the bias is small under appropriate regularity conditions. To describe the estimator, let

$$\hat{G}^\gamma = \partial\bigg[\sum_{j=1}^{n} a(z_j, g_\gamma)/n\bigg]\bigg/\partial\gamma\bigg|_{\gamma=\hat{\gamma}}, \qquad g_\gamma(x,w) = \phi^K(x,w)'\gamma$$

$$\hat{\psi}_i^g = \bar{\omega}^{-1}\hat{G}^\gamma \hat{\Sigma}^{-1}\phi^K(x_i, w_i)[\ln(q_i) - \hat{g}(x_i, w_i)] \qquad (3.10)$$

$$\hat{\Sigma} = \sum_{i=1}^{n} \phi^K(x_i, w_i)\phi^K(x_i, w_i)'/n$$

Here $\hat{\psi}_i^g$ is a standard delta-method term for ordinary-least-squares estimation of γ.

For either kernels or series, the main difficulty in computing $\hat{\psi}_i^g$ is calculating the derivatives $\hat{A}_i$ and $\hat{G}^\beta$ or $\hat{G}^\gamma$. For each of the estimators described in Section 2, it is possible to derive analytical expressions for these derivatives, but the expressions are so complicated as to make them almost useless for calculation. Instead, these derivatives can be calculated by numerical differentiation. This calculation requires only evaluation of $\Sigma_{i=1}^n a(z_i, g)/n$ for many different values of g, which is quite feasible, particularly for series estimators.

A procedure analogous to that for the series estimator can be used to construct a consistent asymptotic variance estimator for exact consumer surplus for any parametric specification of the demand function. For a parametric specification, $a(z, \gamma)$ will depend on the parameters γ of the demand function. In this case, $\hat{G}^\gamma = \partial[\Sigma_{i=1}^n a(z_i, \gamma)/n]/\partial \gamma|_{\gamma=\hat{\gamma}}$ can be calculated by numerical differentiation. Then, supposing that $\sqrt{n}(\hat{\gamma} - \gamma_0) = \Sigma_{i=1}^n \Psi^\gamma(z_i)/\sqrt{n} + o_p(1)$ and that $\hat{\Psi}_i^\gamma$ is an estimator of $\Psi^\gamma(z_i)$, we can form

$$\hat{\psi}_i = \hat{\psi}_i^z + \overline{\omega}^{-1} \hat{G}^\gamma \hat{\Psi}_i^\gamma \tag{3.11}$$

Asymptotic inference for parametrically estimated exact consumer surplus could then be carried out as described earlier for $\hat{V}_n$, as in equation (3.4).

4 Testing Consumer-Demand Conditions

Tests of the downward slope and symmetry of Hicksian (compensated) demands provide useful specification checks for consumer-surplus estimates and are of interest in their own right as tests of demand theory. Here we consider tests that are natural by-products of consumer-surplus estimation. An implication of symmetry is that consumer surplus is independent of the price path, which can be tested by comparing estimates based on different price paths. The downward-sloping property can be tested by comparing the demand at the new price with compensated demand at the initial price, which is easily computed from the consumer-surplus estimate.

Path independence can be tested by comparing consumer surplus for the same income and covariates but different price paths. To describe this test, let j index a price path $p^j(t)$, with $p^j(0) = p^0$ and $p^j(1) = p^1$. Let $\hat{S}_j$ denote the equivalent variation estimator described earlier for the price path $p^j(t)$, income y_0, and covariates w_0. An implication of symmetry of compensated demand is that all $\hat{S}_j$ ($j = 1, \ldots, J$) should converge to the same limit. This implication can be tested by comparing the different estimators. A simple way to construct this test is by minimum chi-square. Let $\hat{\psi}_i^j$ denote the corresponding influence estimator from equation (3.8), and

$$\hat{\Pi} = (\hat{S}_1, \ldots, \hat{S}_J)', \quad \hat{\Psi}_i = (\hat{\psi}_i^1, \ldots, \hat{\psi}_i^J)', \quad \hat{\Omega} = \sum_{i=1}^n \hat{\Psi}_i \hat{\Psi}_i'/n \qquad (4.1)$$

Here $\hat{\Omega}$ is an estimator of the joint asymptotic variance of $\hat{\Pi}$. Let e denote a $J \times 1$ vector of 1's. Then the test statistic is given by

$$T = n(\hat{\Pi} - \tilde{S} \cdot e)'\hat{\Omega}^{-1}(\hat{\Pi} - \tilde{S} \cdot e), \quad \tilde{S} = \left(e'\hat{\Omega}^{-1}e\right)^{-1} e'\hat{\Omega}^{-1}\hat{\Pi} \qquad (4.2)$$

Under the symmetry hypothesis, the asymptotic distribution of this test statistic will be $\chi^2(J - 1)$.

The estimator $\tilde{S}$ may be of interest in its own right. By the usual minimum-chi-square estimation theory, under symmetry of compensated demands it will be at least as asymptotically efficient as any of the estimators $\hat{S}_j$, with an estimated asymptotic variance matrix $(e'\hat{\Omega}^{-1}e)^{-1}$.

The downward slope of compensated demands can be tested by testing for nonnegativity of $(p^1 - p^0)'[\exp(g_0(p^1, y_0, w_0)) - \exp(g_0(p^0, y_0 - S(y_0, w_0, g_0), w_0))]$ over several different prices, incomes, and covariates. To describe this test, let p_j^0, p_j^1, y_{0j}, and w_{0j} ($j = 1, \ldots, J$) denote different values, let $\hat{S}_j$ denote the corresponding equivalent variation estimates, and

$$\hat{\theta}_j = (p_j^1 - p_j^0)'[\exp(\hat{g}(p_j^1, y_{j0}, w_{j0})) - \exp(\hat{g}(p_j^0, y_{j0} - \hat{S}_j, w_{j0}))] \qquad (4.3)$$
$$(j = 1, \ldots, J)$$

An implication of convexity of the expenditure function is that each of these estimators should have a nonnegative probability limit. This hypothesis can be tested using an estimator of the asymptotic variance matrix of $\tilde{\theta} = (\hat{\theta}_1, \ldots, \hat{\theta}_J)'$ that can be constructed via the approach of Section 4. Let $\hat{\psi}_i^j$ be as described in equation (3.8), for $a(z, g) = (p_j^1 - p_j^0)'[\exp(g(p_j^1, y_{j0}, w_{j0})) - \exp(g(p_j^0, y_{j0} - S_j(y_{j0}, w_{j0}, g), w_{j0}))]$, $w(z) = 1$, and let $\hat{\Omega} = \Sigma_{i=1}^n (\hat{\psi}_i^1, \ldots, \hat{\psi}_i^J)'(\hat{\psi}_i^1, \ldots, \hat{\psi}_i^J)/n$. Alternatively, if the income values y_{j0} are mutually distinct, then the asymptotic covariances between the $\hat{\theta}_j$ will be zero, so that $\hat{\Omega} = \Sigma_{i=1}^n \text{diag}((\hat{\psi}_i^1)^2, \ldots, (\hat{\psi}_i^J)^2)/n$ will suffice. The asymptotic approximation to the distribution of $\tilde{\theta}$ is then that $\tilde{\theta}$ is normal, with variance $\hat{\Omega}/n$. Thus the hypothesis that the limit of $\tilde{\theta}$ is a nonnegative vector can be tested by applying multivariate tests of inequality restrictions developed in the statistics literature. A particularly simple test would be to reject if $\min_j \{\sqrt{n}\hat{\theta}_j / \hat{\Omega}_{jj}\} \leq k$ for some k. The size of this test could be calculated by simulating the distribution of the minimum of a vector of mean-zero normals with variance matrix equal to the correlation matrix implied by $\hat{\Omega}$.

It should be possible to combine these two types of tests, of symmetry and of downward-sloping compensated demand, into a single test of consumer-demand theory and to consider versions of these tests based on the consumer-surplus averages of equation (2.9). Furthermore, it should be possible to give these tests some asymptotic power against any alternative to demand theory by letting J grow with the sample size in such a way that different price paths and income and covariate would "cover" all values in their support. These extensions are beyond the scope of this chapter.

5   An Application to Gasoline Demand

To estimate the nonparametric and parametric demand functions for gasoline, we use data from the United States Department of Energy. The first three waves of the data were collected in the Residential Energy Consumption Survey conducted for the Energy Information Agency of the Department of Energy. Surveys were conducted in 1979, 1980, and 1981 at the household level. Gasoline consumption was kept by diary for each month; in our analysis we use average household gallons consumed per month. The gasoline price is the weighted average of purchase price over a month. Note that gasoline prices were quite high during most of that period in the United States because of the second (Iranian) oil shock. Gasoline prices averaged between $1.34 and $1.46 for those 3 years, where we use 1983 dollars. Income is divided into 12 categories, with the highest category being over $50,000 (in 1983 dollars). We used the midpoint for each income category, and for the highest category we used the conditional median for national household income above $50,000. Lastly, geographic information is given by eight census regions. Average driving patterns differ significantly across regions of the United States. The last three waves of data were collected by the Energy Information Agency in the Residential Transportation Energy Consumption Survey for the years 1983, 1985, and 1988. (The upper limit on income changed in the surveys; however, the technique used to estimate income in the top category remained the same.) Note that the (real) gasoline price in the United States fell throughout that period, so that by 1988 it had decreased to levels, about $0.83, approximately equal to prices before the first oil shock in 1974. Thus, we have both time-series variation and cross-sectional variation due to differences in state and city taxes for gasoline. In the latter surveys, nine, rather than eight, census divisions were used. Because we are unable to map the earlier eight-region breakdown into nine regions, or vice versa, in the empirical specifications we use different sets of indicator variables, depending on the survey year.

Overall, we have 18,109 observations, which should provide sufficient data to do nonparametric estimation and achieve fairly precise results. Our empirical approach is to do both the nonparametric and parametric estimations with indicator variables both for survey year and for region.

Exact Consumer Surplus and Deadweight Loss

Table 4.1. *Cross-Validation*

| Kernel || Cubic spline || Power series ||
σ	CV	Knots	CV	Order	CV
1.6	4621	1	4546	1	4534
1.9	4516	2	4543	2	4539
2.0	4508	3	4546	3	4512
2.1	4700	4	4551	4	4505
		5	4545	5	4507
		6	4552	6	4507
		7	4546	7	4500
		8	4551	8	4493
		9	4552	9	4494

Thus, we have 20 indicator variables in our specifications. In the parametric specifications, we allow for interactions, most of which are found to be statistically significant, which is to be expected given our very large sample. However, we decided to use the same set of indicator variables in both the nonparametric and parametric specifications to make for easier comparisons.

We give three types of nonparametric estimates, using the kernel from equation (2.4), a cubic regression spline with evenly spaced knots, and power series. We use a log-linear demand specification, as previously described. Also, the covariates w are 20 indicator variables that allow for different region and survey-year effects. In the results we present, we evaluate demand and consumer surplus at a fixed value for w equal to its sample mean.

We used cross-validation to help choose the bandwidth for the kernel estimator and the number of terms for the series estimators, as described in Section 2.[4] Table 4.1 reports the criteria. The power series and spline terms do not include any interactions between log-price and log-income, because tests for exclusion were insignificant, and the cross-validation criteria were not lowered by their inclusion. Thus, the series estimates were additive in log-price and log-income. The theory suggests that the bandwidth should be chosen smaller and the number of terms larger than the mean-square-error-minimizing number that is obtained by cross-validation, so that the bias goes to zero faster than the variance. For this reason we prefer $\sigma = 1.6$ or $\sigma = 1.9$, eight or nine knots, and an eighth-order or ninth-order polynomial. The results for nine knots were similar to those for eight, except that the estimated standard errors were very

---

[4] The minimizing kernel bandwidth was obtained from a grid of 0.05 width, by minimizing over such a grid for subsamples of increasing size.

large, so we do not report them. Instead, we give results for six to eight knots.

For purposes of comparison we also report results for standard parametric forms for the demand function. The specification of the demand function is

$$\ln q = \eta_0 + \eta_1 \ln p + \eta_2 \ln y + w'\beta + \varepsilon \tag{5.1}$$

where y is household income, p is gasoline price, and w are the 20 region and time dummies discussed earlier. The estimated income elasticity is 0.37, with standard error 0.01, and the estimated price elasticity is -0.81, with standard error 0.09. To check on the sensitivity of our estimates, we also estimated a "translog" type of parametric specification, where we allow for quadratic terms in log-income and log-price as well as an interaction term between log-income and log-price. The income–price interaction term has no estimated effect, but the quadratic terms do have an effect on the estimates. The sum of squared errors decreases from 8,900.1 to 8,877.0 which is a decrease of 0.26 percent, but a traditional F statistic is calculated to be 16.1, with three degrees of freedom, because of the large sample size. The estimated elasticities for the log-linear and log-quadratic models are quite similar at the median gasoline price, $1.23: The log-linear price elasticity is -0.81 at all income levels, and the log-quadratic-model price elasticity is approximately -0.87, with very little variation across income levels. The two specifications do have different elasticities at lower and higher gasoline prices. The log-linear-model price elasticity, because it is estimated as a single parameter, remains at -0.81 across all gasoline prices, whereas the log-quadratic model, which has a variable price elasticity, has an estimated elasticity of approximately -0.64 at a gasoline price of $1.08 (the first-quartile price), and an estimated elasticity of -1.14 at a gasoline price of $1.43 (the third quartile). Because the results for the log-quadratic translog specification are different from those for the simpler linear specification, we present results for both of the parametric specifications in what follows.

Our estimated elasticities are well within the range of recent surveys of gasoline demand price elasticities. Dahl (1986), in a recent survey, found estimated long-run elasticities in the range of -0.60 for log-time-series estimates to -1.02 for cross-section estimates. Our results, which are estimated from a time series of cross sections, fall almost exactly at the midway point of Dahl's range. Gately (1992) gave a more recent long-run estimate of -0.75, which is again quite close to our estimates.

Figures 4.2–4.4 show the estimated nonparametric log-demand with respect to log-price, evaluated at mean income, for the parametric, kernel, and spline specifications. We do not give graphs for other income values, because the lack of significance of price and income interactions strongly suggests that the log-demand function is additive in log-price and log-income, in which case the shape of log-demand will not depend

Exact Consumer Surplus and Deadweight Loss

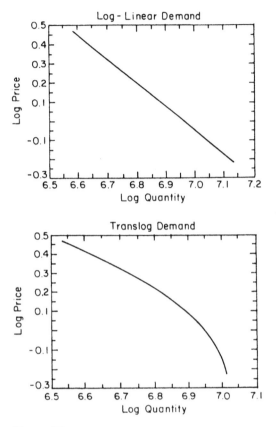

Figure 4.2

on income. There are interesting differences between the parametric and nonparametric estimates, with the nonparametric estimates having a much more complicated shape than the parametric ones. The kernel and spline estimates generally have similar shapes. There is some tendency for an upward slope over a small range of prices. For the spline estimator, we tested whether or not this upward slope indicates a failure of demand theory, using the test of downward-sloping compensated demand described earlier. For eight knots (our preferred number) and a price change from $1.39 to $1.46, which is the range over which the demand curve slopes up, our $N(0, 1)$ statistic is 0.90. This value is not statistically positive at any conventional (one-sided) significance level.[5]

---

[5] The conventional significance levels may not be appropriate here, because we have chosen the interval based on the estimated demand function. However, the conventional critical values should provide a bound when the test statistic is maximized over choice of interval, with our test being an approximate maximum.

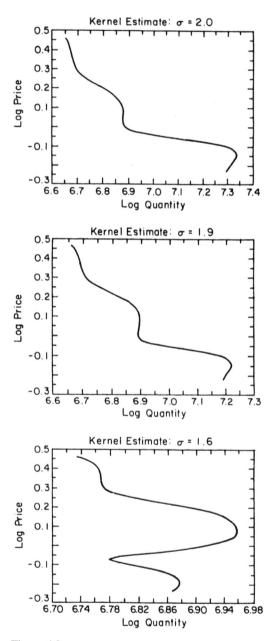

Figure 4.3

Exact Consumer Surplus and Deadweight Loss

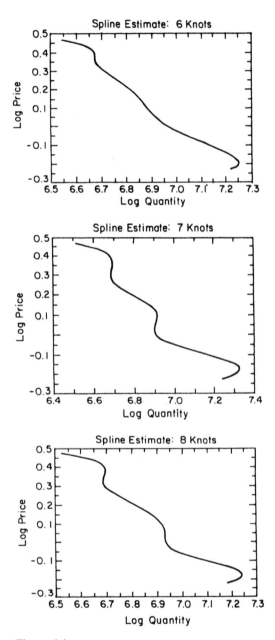

Figure 4.4

Table 4.2. *Yearly Equivalent Variation Estimates (in 1983 dollars)*

Estimates	$1.00–1.30	$1.00–1.50
Parametric estimates		
1. Log-linear model	282.34	442.00
	(2.07)[a]	(2.31)
2. Translog quadratic model	285.44	444.16
	(3.03)	(3.90)
Kernel estimates		
3. $\sigma = 1.6$	302.75	475.91
	(5.58)	(5.19)
4. $\sigma = 1.9$	284.79	446.94
	(5.38)	(5.34)
5. $\sigma = 2.0$	278.94	438.01
	(5.42)	(5.82)
Cubic-spline estimates		
6. 6 knots	284.58	444.63
	(4.93)	(6.31)
7. 7 knots	282.30	441.72
	(4.68)	(5.82)
8. 8 knots	287.12	447.80
	(4.77)	(6.04)
Power-series estimates		
9. 8th order	287.31	448.64
	(4.76)	(5.91)
10. 9th order	287.27	448.55
	(4.75)	(5.88)

[a] Standard errors in parentheses.

We next estimated the exact consumer surplus, here the equivalent variation, across our different estimated demand curves. We considered two sets of price changes for gasoline: an increase from $1.00 to $1.30 (in 1983 dollars) per gallon and an increase from $1.00 to $1.50 per gallon. The starting price of $1.00 corresponds roughly to 1992 gasoline prices, and a 50-cent increase is well within the range of the data. We estimated the equivalent variation for these price changes at the median of income. We present the estimates in Table 4.2. Estimated standard errors are given in parentheses and were calculated using the formulas given earlier. All the nonparametric estimates are quite close, although the kernel estimates exhibit some sensitivity to the choice of band-width. Surprisingly, although the graphs show quite different shapes for parametric and nonparametric estimates, the welfare estimates are quite similar. We also computed a Hausman statistic, equal to the difference of the spline estimate with eight knots and the log-linear estimator divided by the square root of the difference of the asymptotic variance estimates, for the larger price change. This statistic will converge in distribution to a standard normal, because the convergence rate for the parametric estimator is faster than that for the nonparametric.[6] The value of the resulting statistic is 1.04, which is not significant for a two-tailed test based on the normal distribution.

We also estimated the DWL from a rise in the gasoline tax of either $0.30, or $0.50, which would induce the corresponding rises in gasoline prices. We based our estimate of DWL on the equivalent variation measures of the compensating variation. The results are given in Table 4.3. The estimates of DWL are very similar across bandwidths for the kernel estimator, but are somewhat smaller than the series estimates for the smaller price change. The spline results are sensitive to the number of knots. We prefer the results for the larger number of knots, because they are theoretically preferred and the results seem to be less sensitive to choice between seven and eight knots than between six and seven knots.

We do find rather large differences between the nonparametric and parametric estimates of DWL. The estimated differences between the nonparametric estimates and the log-linear parametric estimates are in the range of 40–50 percent. In particular, the nonparametric estimates seem to be somewhat smaller for the larger price change and larger for the smaller price change. These are economically significant differences, with the ratio of DWL to tax revenue varying widely between parametric and nonparametric specifications. The differences are also statistically significant: The Hausman statistic, given by the difference of the log-linear and spline estimates with eight knots, is 2.07 for the smaller price change and -3.35 for the larger. Thus, efficiency decisions on which commodities to tax and the size of the tax might well depend on the rather sizable differences in the estimated efficiency cost changes from the increased taxes.

6 Asymptotic Distribution Theory

In this section we give results for the kernel estimator of consumer surplus at particular income and covariate values, and for power series. The conclusions for other cases will be described, without full sets of regularity conditions. These results show that the standard-error formulas given earlier are correct and describe the asymptotic properties of the estimators, without overburdening the reader.

---

[6] Dividing by the standard deviation of the nonparametric estimator would also give a standard normal statistic, but we felt that dividing by the difference might lead to a better approximation, because the estimated variances for the nonparametric and parametric estimators have similar magnitudes.

Table 4.3. *Yearly Average DWL Estimates (in 1983 dollars)*

Estimates	$1.00–1.30	$1.00–1.50
Parametric estimates		
1. Log-linear model	26.92	62.50
	(3.13)[a]	(6.77)
2. Translog quadratic model	27.07	75.30
	(3.15)	(7.24)
Kernel estimates		
3. $\sigma = 1.6$	33.36	44.40
	(7.69)	(10.45)
4. $\sigma = 1.9$	30.75	46.72
	(6.81)	(9.41)
5. $\sigma = 2.0$	29.19	45.80
	(6.54)	(9.29)
Cubic-spline estimates		
6. 6 knots	28.60	51.05
	(5.03)	(8.65)
7. 7 knots	38.68	46.84
	(5.37)	(8.77)
8. 8 knots	35.72	46.95
	(5.27)	(8.94)
Power-series estimates		
9. 8th order	34.92	48.66
	(5.21)	(8.80)
10. 9th order	34.86	48.74
	(5.38)	(8.86)

[a] Standard errors in parentheses.

In this section we generalize the log-linear regression previously considered to allow other transformations. Here let $T(q)$ denote an invertible transformation with inverse $T^{-1}(q)$. Also let $x(p, y)$ be an invertible function of (p, y). The demand function will be modeled as $T(E[T^{-1}(q)|x, w])$. This generalizes the previous results, where $T(q) = \exp(q)$ and $T^{-1}(q)$ and $\ln q$.

Precise conditions are needed for stating the results. Let $p_t(t, u) = \partial p(t, u)/\partial t$, and $g(p, y, w)$ denote $r(x(p, y)) + w'\beta$. Let $\mathcal{U}$ be the support of u, $\mathcal{P} = p([0, 1] \times \mathcal{U})$ be the image of $p(t, u)$ on $[0, 1] \times \mathcal{U}$, and $\mathcal{W}$ be the support of w. Also, let $\mathcal{Y} = [\underline{y}, \bar{y}]$ be a set of y values that includes those where the demand function is evaluated in solving equation (1.1). The conditions will involve supremum norms for the demand function over the set $\mathcal{Z} = \mathcal{P} \times \mathcal{Y} \times \mathcal{W}$. Let $\|g\|_j = \sup_{z \in \mathcal{Z}, l \leq j} \|\partial^l g(p, y, w)/\partial(p, y, w)^l\|$, where for a matrix function $B(z)$, $\partial^l B(z)/\partial z^l$ denotes any vector of all dis-

Exact Consumer Surplus and Deadweight Loss

tinct lth-order partial derivatives of all elements of $B(z)$. Let "a.e." denote "almost everywhere" with respect to Lebesgue measure.

Assumption 1. $\mathcal{W}, \mathcal{U}$ and $\mathcal{Y}$ are compact, $\mathcal{Z}$ is contained in the support of z_i, $\|g_0\|_2 < \infty$, $T(g)$ and $x(p, y)$ are invertible and three times continuously differentiable with nonsingular Jacobians on their respective domains, $p(t, u)$ is twice continuously differentiable on $[0, 1] \times \mathcal{U}$, and $\mathcal{P}$ does not include zero. Also $\omega(y)$ is bounded and continuous a.e. and for $\bar{C} = \sup_{[0, 1] \times \mathcal{U} \times \mathcal{Y} \times \mathcal{W}} |T(g_0(p(t, u), y, w))' p_t(t, u)|$, $\omega(y) = 0$ for y outside $\mathcal{Y}_\varepsilon = [\underline{y} + \bar{C} + \varepsilon, \bar{y} - \bar{C} - \varepsilon]$, for some $\varepsilon > 0$.

We shall derive the results under an i.i.d. assumption and certain moment conditions specified in the following result. Let $\tau(x)$ be a trimming function that will be identically equal to 1 for series estimators.

Assumption 2. z_i is i.i.d., $E[\|T^{-1}(q)\|^4] < \infty$, x is continuously distributed with bounded density $f_0(x)$, and $E[\tau(x)(w - E[w|x])(w - E[W|x])']$ is nonsingular.

Assumptions 1 and 2 are useful for both the kernel and series results. Following the earlier format, we first give results for kernel estimators. The next three assumptions are more or less standard conditions for kernel estimators.

Assumption 3. $E[\|T^{-1}(q)\|^4 |x] f_0(x)$ is bounded, $\tau(x)$ is bounded, bounded away from zero on $z \in \mathcal{Z}$, and zero outside a compact set on which $f_0(x)$ is positive.

Assumption 4. There is a positive integer s such that $\mathcal{K}(u)$ is twice continuously differentiable, with Lipschitz derivatives, $\mathcal{K}(u)$ is zero outside a bounded set, $\int \mathcal{K}(u)\, du = 1$, and for all nonnegative integers $j_1, \ldots, j_{k+1}$ such that $j_1 + \cdots + j_{k+1} < s$, $\int \mathcal{K}(u) \prod_{l=1}^{k+1}(u_l)^{j_l}\, du = 0$.

Assumption 5. There is a nonnegative integer d and extensions of $E[T^{-1}(q)|x]$ and $E[w|x]$ to all of $\mathbb{R}^{k+1}$ such that $f_0(x)$, $f_0(x)r_0(x)$, and $f_0(x)E[w|x]$ are continuously differentiable to order $d \geq s + 2$ on $\mathbb{R}^{k+1}$.

Assumption 4 requires that the kernel be a higher-order, bias-reducing type. An example of such a kernel is the Gaussian one used in the application. These kernels are useful for making sure that the limiting distribution of the estimator is centered at the true value, because they reduce the bias of the estimator. In practice, the bias of low-order kernel estimators often seems to be quite small, and the higher-order kernel tends to have substantially larger variance; see the discussion by Robinson (1988).

To describe the result for the kernel estimator of consumer surplus at particular income and covariate values, it is necessary to introduce a little more notation. Let $S(t)$ denote the solution to equation (1.1) at the truth, that is, the solution to $dS/dt = -T(g_0(p(t), y_0 - S(t), w_0))'p_t(t)$, $S(1) = 0$, where $p_t(t) = \partial p(t)/\partial t$. Let $x(t) = x(p(t), y_0 - S(t))$, and partition $x(t) = (x_1(t), x_2(t)')'$, where $x_1(t)$ is a scalar. Let

$$\zeta(t) = \xi(t) \cdot \exp\left\{-\int_0^t \xi(v)'[\partial g_0(p(v), y_0 - S(v), w_0)/\partial y]dv\right\}$$
$$\xi(t) = T_g(g_0(p(t), y_0 - S(t), w_0))'p_t(t)$$

Let $t(\tau)$ be the inverse function of $x_1(t)$ (which will exist by the following Assumption 6), $x(\tau) = x(t(\tau)) = (\tau, x_2(\tau))'$, and $\zeta(\tau) = \zeta(t(\tau))$.

Assumption 6. *(i) There is $\eta > 0$ such that $p(t)$ can be extended to a function with domain $\mathcal{D} = [-\eta, 1 + \eta]$ such that $x_1(t)$ is invertible, with derivative bounded away from zero; (ii) $E[\varepsilon\varepsilon'|x]$ is continuous a.e., and for some $\eta > 0$ and $(0, \gamma')$ partitioned conformably with $x(\tau) = (\tau, x_2(\tau)')$,*

$$\int_{x_1(\mathcal{D})} \left\{\sup_{\|\gamma\| \leq \eta}\left(1 + E[\|\varepsilon\|^4 | x = x(\tau) + (0, \gamma)]\right) f_0(x(\tau) + (0, \gamma))\right\} d\tau < \infty$$

(iii) f_0 is bounded away from zero on $x(p(\mathcal{D}), [\underline{y}, \bar{y}])$, for $\underline{y}$ and $\bar{y}$ from Assumption 1.

Note that $x_2(\tau)$ is differentiable by the inverse-function theorem and the chain rule, and let $\tilde{\mathcal{K}}(\tau) = \int[\int \mathcal{K}(v, u + [\partial x_2(\tau)/\partial \tau]v)dv]^2 du$. The asymptotic variance of consumer surplus at a point will be

$$V_0 = \int 1(0 \leq t(\tau) \leq 1)\tilde{K}(\tau)f_0(x(\tau))^{-1}|\partial t(\tau)/\partial \tau|^2$$
$$\times E\left[\{\zeta(\tau)'\varepsilon\}^2 | x = x(\tau)\right] d\tau$$

Let $1(A)$ denote the indicator function for the set A. The following result gives the asymptotic distribution of the kernel estimator of consumer surplus evaluated at particular income and covariate values.

Theorem 1. *If Assumptions 1–6 are satisfied, for $\omega(y) = 1(y = y_0)$, $\sigma = \sigma(n)$ with $n\sigma^{2k+4}/[\ln(n)]^2 \to \infty$, and $n\sigma^{2s} \to 0$, then $\sqrt{n\sigma^{k/2}}(\hat{S} - S_0) \xrightarrow{d} N(0, V_0)$. If in addition $n\sigma^{3k+7}/\ln(n) \to \infty$, then for $\hat{V}$ in equation (3.5), $\sigma^k \hat{V} \xrightarrow{p} V_0$.*

For our application, where $k = 1$, the conditions on the bandwidth σ are that $n\sigma^{10}/\ln(n) \to \infty$ and $n\sigma^{2s} \to 0$. These conditions require that $s > 5$ (i.e., that the kernel be at least sixth order). The normal kernel used in the application is such a sixth-order kernel.

The asymptotic distribution of a kernel estimator of DWL at particular income and covariate values is straightforward to derive. Because the "tax-receipts" term $(p^1 - p^0)'T(\hat{g}(p^1, y_0, w_0))$ depends on the demand function evaluated at a particular point, it will have a slower convergence rate than the consumer-surplus "integral" and hence will dominate the asymptotic distribution. Then standard results on pointwise convergence of kernel regression estimators can be applied to obtain, for $x^1 = x(p^1, y_0)$,

$$n^{(k+1)/2}(\hat{L} - L_0) \xrightarrow{d} N(0, V_0)$$

$$V_0 = \left[\int \mathcal{K}(u)^2 du\right] f_0(x^1)^{-1} \cdot E\left[\{(p^1 - p^0)'T_g(g_0(x^1, w_0))\varepsilon\}^2 | x = x^1\right]$$

Also, it is straightforward to show consistency of the asymptotic variance estimator, by means like those used to prove Theorem 1.

As previously noted, average consumer surplus and DWL will be $\sqrt{n}$-consistent if initial and final prices are allowed to vary. In this case the asymptotic distribution will be the same for both kernel and series estimators. This asymptotic distribution will be described later.

Some of the conditions need to be modified for series estimators. For simplicity we give results for only the scalar price case, where there is a single demand function being estimated.

Assumption 7. $E[\varepsilon_i^4|x_i, w_i]$ *is bounded, and* $E[\varepsilon_i^2|x_i, w_i]$ *is bounded away from zero.*

Let $\|g\|_j$ be as defined earlier, except that the supremum is taken over the support of (x, w), and let $\mathcal{X}$ denote the support of x.

Assumption 8. $\phi_{kK}(x)$ *consists of products of powers of the elements of x that are nondecreasing in order as K increases, with all terms of a given order included before the order is increased, $\mathcal{X}$ is a compact rectangle, and the density of x is bounded away from zero on $\mathcal{X}$.*

The condition that the density is bounded away from zero is useful for controlling the variance of a series estimator. The next condition is useful for controlling the bias.

Assumption 9. $r_0(x)$ *is continuously differentiable of all orders on $\mathcal{X}$ and there is a constant C such that for all integers d the partial derivatives of order d are bounded in absolute value by C^d on $\mathcal{X}$.*

This smoothness condition is undoubtedly stronger than necessary. It is used in order to apply second-order Sobolev-norm approximation rates (i.e., approximation of the function and derivatives up to order 2), where a literature search has not yet revealed such approximation rates for power series except under this hypothesis. Also, results for regression splines are not given here because multivariate Sobolev approximation rates do not seem to be readily available for them.

Average equivalent variation and DWL will be $\sqrt{n}$-consistent under certain conditions that we now describe. Let t_i denote a random variable that is uniformly distributed on $[0, 1]$ and independent of z_i, $\tilde{p}_i = p(t_i, u_i)$, $\tilde{y}_i = y_i - S(t_i, z_i, g_0)$, and $\tilde{x}_i = x(\tilde{p}_i, \tilde{y}_i)$. Let $S(t, z) = S(t, z, g_0)$, and

$$\zeta(t, z) = \xi(t, z) \cdot \exp\left\{-\int_0^t \xi(v, z)' g_{0y}(p(v, u), y - S(v, z), w) dv\right\}$$

$$\xi(t, z) = T_g(g_0(p(t, u), y - S(t, z), w))' p_t(t, u)$$

Assumption 10. *Conditional on w, $\tilde{x}$ is continuously distributed with bounded density $f^\mu(x|w)$, and for the density $f(x|w)$ of x_i given w, $a(x, w) = E[\omega(y_i)\zeta(t_i, z_i)|\tilde{x}_i = x, w_i = w]$ is zero outside the support of $f(x|w)$, and $f(x|w)^{-1}a(x, w)$ is bounded.*

Let $\bar{\omega} = E[\omega(y_i)]$ and

$$\tilde{\xi}^\mu(x, w) = f(x|w)^{-1} \tilde{f}^\mu(x|w) E[\omega(y_i)\zeta(t_i, z_i)|\tilde{x}_i = x, w_i = w]$$
$$\bar{\xi}^\mu(x, w) = E[\tilde{\xi}^\mu(x, w)|x]$$
$$\qquad + (w - E[w|x])' M^{-1} E[(w - E[w|x])' \tilde{\xi}^\mu(x, w)]$$
$$\psi_i^\mu = \bar{\omega}^{-1} \omega(y_i) S(0, z_i, g_0) - \mu_0 + \bar{\omega}^{-1} \mu_0 [\omega(y_i) - \bar{\omega}]' + \bar{\omega}^{-1} \bar{\xi}^\mu(x_i, w_i)' \varepsilon_i$$

Then the asymptotic variance of $\hat{\mu}$ will be $E[\psi_i^\mu \psi_i^{\mu\prime}]$.

Under an additional condition we can also derive the asymptotic variance of DWL. We consider here only the case where there is sufficient variation in the final price to achieve $\sqrt{n}$ consistency. The next assumption embodies this requirement, by the condition that the final price is continuously distributed.

Assumption 11. *Conditional on w, $\bar{x}_i = x(p^1(u_i), y_i)$ is continuously distributed with bounded density $f^\lambda(x|w)$, and $\omega(y) f^\lambda(x|w)$ is zero outside the support of $f(x|w)$.*

Let $T_i = \bar{\omega}^{-1} \omega(y_i)(p^1 - p^0)' T(g(p^1(u_i), y_i))$ and

$$\tilde{\xi}^\lambda(x, w) = f(x|w)^{-1} \tilde{f}^\lambda(x|w)$$
$$\qquad \times E[\omega(y_i)(p^1 - p^0)' T_g(g_0(x_i, w_i))|\bar{x}_i = x, w_i = w]$$
$$\bar{\xi}^\lambda(x, w) = E[\tilde{\xi}^\lambda(x, w)|x]$$
$$\qquad + (w - E[w|x])' M^{-1} E[(w - E[w|x])' \tilde{\xi}^\lambda(x, w)]$$
$$\psi_i^\lambda = \psi_i^\mu - \{T_i - E[T_i] - E[T_i]\bar{\omega}^{-1}[\omega(y_i) - \bar{\omega}] + \bar{\omega}^{-1} \bar{\xi}^\lambda(x_i, w_i)' \varepsilon_i\}$$

Then the asymptotic variance of $\hat{\lambda}$ will be $E[(\psi_i^\lambda)^2]$.

The next result shows asymptotic normality of the power-series estimators.

Theorem 2. *Suppose that Assumptions 1, 2, and 7–9 are satisfied, with $\tau(x) = 1$, and $K = K(n)$ satisfies $K^{22}/n \to 0$ and $Kn^{-\gamma} \to \infty$ for some $\gamma > 0$. Then for $\hat{\theta} = \hat{S}$ or $\hat{\theta} = \hat{L}$, equation (3.3) will be satisfied, and $\hat{\theta} = \theta_0 + O_p(K^5/\sqrt{n})$. If Assumption 10 is also satisfied and $V_0 = E[(\psi_i^\mu)2] < 0$, then $\sqrt{n}(\hat{\mu} - \mu_0) \xrightarrow{d} N(0, V_0)$ and $\hat{V} \xrightarrow{p} V_0$. If Assumption 11 is also satisfied and $V_0 = E[(\psi_i^\lambda)^2] > 0$, then $\sqrt{n}(\hat{\lambda} - \lambda_0) \xrightarrow{d} N(0, V_0)$ and $\hat{V} \xrightarrow{p} V_0$.*

Appendix: Proofs of Theorems

Throughout the Appendix, C will denote a generic positive constant that may take different values in different uses.

One intermediate result that is needed for both kernel and series estimators is a linearization of the solution to equation (1.1) around the true demand function. Some additional notation is needed to set up this linearization. Let z be a data observation that includes u, and $S(t, z, g)$ denote the corresponding solution to equation (1.1), that is, the solution to $\partial S/\partial t = -T(g(p(t, u), y - S, w))$. Let $g_y(p, y, w)$ denote the derivative of $g(p, y, w)$ with respect to y, and

$$\zeta(t, z, g) = \xi(t, z, g) \cdot \exp\left\{-\int_0^t \xi(v, z, g)' g_{0y}(p(v, u), y - S(v, z, g), w) dv\right\}$$

$$\xi(t, z, g) = T_g(g(p(t, u), y - S(t, z, g), w))' p_t(t, u) \tag{6.1}$$

Under conditions specified later, when g is near the truth g_0, equivalent variation can be approximated by the linear functional

$$\Delta(z, g; \tilde{g}) = \int_0^1 g(p(t, u), y - S(t, z, \tilde{g}), w)' \zeta(t, z, \tilde{g}) dt \tag{6.2}$$

evaluated at $\tilde{g} = g_0$.

Lemma A1. *If Assumption 1 is satisfied, then there is an $\varepsilon > 0$ and a constant C such that for all $z \in \mathcal{Z}_v$, $\|g - g_0\|_2 < \varepsilon$, and $\|\tilde{g} - g_0\|_2 < \varepsilon$, it is the case that*

$|\omega(y)S(0, z, \tilde{g}) - \omega(y)S(0, z, g) - \omega(y)\Delta(z, \tilde{g} - g; g)| \leq C\|\tilde{g} - g\|_0\|\tilde{g} - g\|_1$

$|\omega(y)\Delta(z, g; g_0)| \leq C\|g\|_0$

$|\omega(y)S(0, z, g) - \omega(y)S(0, z, g_0)| \leq C\|g - g_0\|_0$

and for any $\bar{g}$ with $\|\bar{g}\|_1 < \infty$,

$|\omega(y)\Delta(z, \bar{g}; g) - \omega(y)\Delta(z, \bar{g}; g_0)| \leq C(\|\bar{g}\|_0 \|g - g_0\|_1 + \|\bar{g}\|_1 \|g - g_0\|_0)$

Proof of Lemma A1. By Assumption 1, it suffices to prove the result when $\omega(y) = 1$ for all $y \in \mathcal{Y}_\varepsilon$. We use standard results on existence and continuity of solutions of differential equations (e.g., Finney and Ostberg, 1976). Let $q(t, y, z, g) = T(g(t, u), y, w))'p_t(t, u)$. By $T(g)$ thrice continuously differentiable, its derivatives up to order 2 are bounded and Lipschitz on any bounded set. Then by $p_t(t, u)$ bounded, we can choose ε so that for $\|\tilde{g} - g_0\|_2 < \delta$, $\|g - g_0\|_2 < \delta$, and δ small enough,

$$\sup_{[0,1]\times\mathcal{Y}\times\mathcal{Z}} |\partial^j q(t, y, z, \tilde{g})/\partial y^j - \partial^j q(t, y, z, g)/\partial y^j| \leq C\|\tilde{g} - g\|_j \quad (A.1)$$
$$(j = 0, 1, 2)$$

In particular, for δ small enough, $\sup_{[0,1]\times\mathcal{Y}\times\mathcal{Z}}|q(t, y, z, g)| \leq \bar{C} + \varepsilon$. Also, by construction of $\mathcal{Y}_\varepsilon$, $(p(t, u), y - s) \in \mathcal{P} \times \mathcal{Y}$ for $(t, u, y, s) \in [0, 1] \times \mathcal{U} \times \mathcal{Y}_\varepsilon \times [-\bar{C}, \bar{C}]$. Then by Theorem 12-6 of Finney and Ostberg (1976) there exists a solution $S(t, z, g)$ to $\partial S(t, z, g)/\partial t = -q(t, y - S(t, z, g), z, g)$, $S(1, z, g) = 0$, for $t \in [0, 1]$, $z \in \mathcal{Z}_\varepsilon$, and y now included in z. Furthermore, by integration of equation (1.1) on $t \in [0, 1]$, $|S(t, z, g)| < \bar{C} + \varepsilon$, so that $y - S(t, z, g) \in \mathcal{Y}$ for $z \in \mathcal{Z}_\varepsilon$. Also, the same existence and boundedness properties hold for $\tilde{g}$ replacing g in q and S.

Next, $\|g\|_2 < \infty$ by $\|g_0\|_2 < \infty$ and $\|g - g_0\|_2 < \delta$. Also, by $p(t, u) \in \mathcal{P}$ and $y - S(t, z, g) \in \mathcal{Y}$ for $t \in [0, 1]$ and $z \in \mathcal{Z}_\varepsilon$, it follows that $g(p(t, u), y - S(t, z, g), w)$ and $g_y(p(t, u), y - S(t, z, g), w)$ are bounded on this set. Then boundedness of $\zeta(t, z, g)$ follows by $T_g(g)$ bounded on any compact set and boundedness of $p_t(t, u)$, giving the second conclusion.

Next, it follows by Theorem 12-9 (equation 12-22) of Finney and Ostberg (1976), and from $T(g)$ Lipschitz on any bounded set, $p_t(t, u)$ bounded, and equation (A.1), that

$$\sup_{t\in[0,1], z\in\mathcal{Z}_\varepsilon} |S(t, z, \tilde{g}) - S(t, z, g)| \leq C\|\tilde{g} - g\|_0 \quad (A.2)$$

which implies the third conclusion.

Next, for all $t \in [0, 1]$, $z \in \mathcal{Z}_\varepsilon$, by $|S(t, z, g)| \leq \bar{C} + \varepsilon$ and $|S(t, z, g_0)| < \bar{C}$, it follows that $\|\bar{g}(p(t, u), y - S(t, z, g), w)\| \leq \|\bar{g}\|_0$, and by mean-value expansion and equation (A.2) that

$$\|\bar{g}(p(t, u), y - S(t, z, g), w) - \bar{g}(p(t, u), y - S(t, z, g_0), w)\|$$
$$\leq \|\bar{g}_y(p(t, u), y - \bar{S}(t, z, g, g_0), w)\| \|S(t, z, g) - S(t, z, g_0)\|$$
$$\leq \|\bar{g}\|_1 \|g - g_0\|_0$$

for an intermediate value $\bar{g}$ and a value $\bar{S}(t, z, g, g_0)$ between $S(t, z, g)$ and $S(t, z, g_0)$. Then by boundedness of $\zeta(t, z, g_0)$,

$$|\Delta(z, \bar{g}; g) - \Delta(z, \bar{g}; g_0)| \leq \|\bar{g}\|_0 \sup_{t\in[0,1], z\in\mathcal{Z}_\varepsilon} \|\zeta(t, z, g) - \zeta(t, z, g_0)\|$$
$$+ C\|\bar{g}\|_1 \|g - g_0\|_0 \quad (A.3)$$

Exact Consumer Surplus and Deadweight Loss

Also $\tilde{g}(p(t, u), y - S(t, z, g), w)$, $\tilde{g}_y(p(t, u), y - S(t, z, g), w)$, and $\tilde{g}_{yy}(p(t, u), y - S(t, z, g), w)$ are all bounded uniformly in $t \in [0, 1]$, $z \in \mathcal{Z}_\varepsilon$, $\|\tilde{g} - g_0\|_2 < \varepsilon$, and $\|g - g_0\|_2 < \varepsilon$, as are the same expressions with $S(t, z, g)$ replaced by a value in between $S(t, z, g)$ and $S(t, z, g_0)$. Also, it then follows by mean-value expansion arguments similar to those given earlier, including expansions of $S(t, z, g)$ around $S(t, z, g_0)$, that uniformly in $\|g - g_0\|_2 < \varepsilon$,

$$\sup_{t\in[0,1],\, z\in\mathcal{Z}_\varepsilon} \|\zeta(t, z, g) - \zeta(t, z, g_0)\| \leq C\|g - g_0\|_1 \tag{A.4}$$

For example, for a value $\bar{S}(t, z, g, g_0)$ in between $S(t, z, g)$ and $S(t, z, g_0)$,

$$\|g_y(p(t, u), y - S(t, z, g), w) - g_{0y}(p(t, u), y - S(t, z, g_0), w)\|$$
$$\leq \|g_y(p(t, u), y - S(t, z, g), w) - g_{0y}(p(t, u), y - S(t, z, g), w)\|$$
$$+ \|g_{0y}(p(t, u), y - S(t, z, g), w) - g_{0y}(p(t, u), y - S(t, z, g_0), w)\|$$
$$\leq \|g - g_0\|_1 + \|g_{0yy}(p(t, u), y - \bar{S}(t, z, g, g_0), w)\|$$
$$\cdot \|S(t, z, g) - S(t, z, g_0)\| \leq C\|g - g_0\|_1$$

The fourth conclusion then follows by equation (A.3).

Finally, to show the first conclusion, let $D(t, z, \tilde{g}, g) = S(t, z, \tilde{g}) - S(t, z, g)$. For notational convenience, suppress the t and z arguments, and let $\tilde{S} = S(t, z, \tilde{g})$ and $S = S(t, z, g)$. Differencing the differential equation gives

$$\partial D/\partial t = -q(y - \tilde{S}, \tilde{g}) + q(y - S, g)$$
$$= -[q(y - S, \tilde{g}) - q(y - S, g)] - [q(y - \tilde{S}, g) - q(y - S, g)]$$
$$\quad - \{q(y - \tilde{S}, \tilde{g}) - q(y - \tilde{S}, g) - [q(y - S, \tilde{g}) - q(y - S, g)]\}$$
$$= -\xi(g)'\{\tilde{g}(y - S) - g(y - S)\} - q_y(y - S, g)D - R(g, \tilde{g})$$
$$R(g, \tilde{g}) = [q(y - S, \tilde{g}) - q(y - S, g) - \xi(g)'\{\tilde{g}(y - S) - g(y - S)\}]$$
$$\quad + [q(y - \tilde{S}, g) - q(y - S, g) - q_y(y - S, g)D]$$
$$\quad + [q(y - \tilde{S}, \tilde{g}) - q(y - \tilde{S}, g) - q(y - S, \tilde{g}) + q(y - S, g)]$$
$$= R_1(g, \tilde{g}) + R_2(g, \tilde{g}) + R_3(g, \tilde{g}) \tag{A.5}$$

The first equation here is an inhomogeneous linear differential equation, with final condition $D|_{t=1} = 0$, nonconstant coefficient $-q_y(y - S, g)$, and nonconstant shift $-\xi(g)'\{\tilde{g}(y - S) - g(y - S)\} + R(g, \tilde{g})$. Let $v(t, z, g) = \exp[-\int_0^t q_y(r, y - S(r, z, g), z, g)'\xi dr]$. Then the solution to this linear equation at $t = 0$ is

$$D\big|_{t=0} = \int_0^1 [\xi(g)'\{\tilde{g}(y - S) - g(y - S)\} + R(g, \tilde{g})]v(t, z, g)dt$$
$$= \Delta(z, \tilde{g} - g) + \int_0^1 R(g, \tilde{g})\xi(t, z, g)dt \tag{A.6}$$

By $\tilde{g}(y - S)$ and $g(y - S)$ bounded and T_g twice continuously differentiable, the elements of $\partial^2 T(\bar{g}(y - S))/\partial g^2$ will be bounded on $t \in [0, 1]$, $z \in \mathcal{Z}_\varepsilon$, for any $\bar{g}$ on a line joining $\tilde{g}$ and g [that may differ from element to element of $\partial^2 T(g)/\partial g^2$]. Then by a mean-value expansion, for all $t \in [0, 1]$, $z \in \mathcal{Z}_\varepsilon$,

$$|R_1(g, \tilde{g})| \leq C\|p_t\| \|\partial^2 T(\bar{g})/\partial g^2\| \|\tilde{g}(y - S) - g(y - S)\|^2 \tag{A.7}$$
$$\leq C\|\tilde{g} - g\|_0^2$$

By $|\tilde{S}| < \bar{C} + \varepsilon$ and $|S| < \bar{C} + \varepsilon$, $q(y - s, \tilde{g}) - q(y - s, g)$ is differentiable in an open interval containing $\tilde{S}$ and S. Let $\bar{S} = \bar{S}(t, z, \tilde{g}, g)$ be the mean value for an expansion of $q(y - \tilde{S}, g)$ around S, with $\bar{S}$ between S and $\tilde{S}$, so that $y - \bar{S} \in \mathcal{Y}$ and $|\bar{S} - S| \leq |D|$. A similar statement holds for the mean value S^* of an expansion of $q_y(y - \bar{S}, g)$ around S. Then for all $t \in [0, 1]$, $z \in \mathcal{Z}_\varepsilon$,

$$|R_2(g, \tilde{g})| \leq |q_y(y - \bar{S}, g) - q_y(y - S, g)| |D| \tag{A.8}$$
$$\leq |q_{yy}(y - S^*, g)| |D|^2 \leq C\|\tilde{g} - g\|_0^2$$

Similarly, for a mean-value expansion of $q(y - \tilde{S}, \tilde{g}) - q(y - \tilde{S}, g)$ around S, for all $t \in [0, 1]$, $z \in \mathcal{Z}_\varepsilon$,

$$|R_3(g, \tilde{g})| \leq |q_y(y - \bar{S}, \tilde{g}) - q_y(y - \bar{S}, g)| |\tilde{S} - S| \tag{A.9}$$
$$\leq C\|\tilde{g} - g\|_1 \|\tilde{g} - g\|_0$$

where $\bar{g}$, $\bar{S}$, and $\tilde{S}$ denote mean values. Then combining equations (A.7)–(A.9) and noting that $\xi(t, z, g)$ is bounded uniformly in $t \in [0, 1]$, $z \in \mathcal{Z}_\varepsilon$, and $\|g - g_0\| < \varepsilon$, we have $\int_0^1 R(g, \tilde{g}) \xi(t, z, g) dt \leq C\|\tilde{g} - g\|_1 \|\tilde{g} - g\|_0$, so the first conclusion follows by equation (A.6). □

Proof of Theorem 1. We first consider $\hat{S}$, and proceed by using the lemmas of Section 5 of Newey (1994a) (N henceforth). Let f, h^q, and h^w denote possible values for the functions $f(x)$, $f(x)E[T^{-1}(q)|x]$, and $f(x)E[w|x]$, respectively, and $h = (f, h^q, h^w)$. Let $g(z; \beta, h) = f(x)^{-1}[h^q(x) - \beta' h^w(x)] + \beta' w$, and for any $\tilde{h}$ let $L(x, h; \beta, \tilde{h}) = \tilde{f}(x)^{-1}[h^q(x) - \beta' h^w(x)] - \tilde{f}(x)^{-2}[\tilde{h}^q(x) - \beta' \tilde{h}^w(x)] f(x)$. Let β and h in N equal $(\theta, \beta')'$ and h here. Let $m(z, \beta, h) = (m_1(z, \beta, h), m_2(z, \beta, h)')'$ where $m_1(z, \beta, h) = S(0, y_0, w_0, g(\cdot; \beta, h)) - \theta$ and $m_2(z, \beta, h) = \tau(x)[q - g(z; \beta, h) \otimes [w - f^{-1}(x)h^w(x)]$. For $\Delta(z, g; \tilde{g})$ from equation (A.2) let

$$D_1(z, h; \tilde{h}, \beta) = \Delta(z, L(\cdot, h; \beta, \tilde{h}); g(\cdot; \beta, \tilde{h}))$$
$$D_2(z, h; \tilde{h}, \beta) = -\tau(x)\tilde{f}(x)^{-1}[q - g(z, \beta, h)]$$
$$\otimes [h^w(x) - \tilde{f}^{-1}(x)\tilde{h}^w(x) f(x)]$$
$$-\tau(x) L(x, h; \beta, \tilde{h}) \otimes [w - \tilde{f}^{-1}(x)\tilde{h}^w(x)]$$

By Assumption 1 with $\omega(y) = 1(y = y_0)$ it follows that $y_0 \in \mathcal{Y}_\varepsilon$. Let $\|g\|_j$ be as defined preceding Assumption 1, and $\|h\|_j = \sup_{x \in x(\mathcal{P} \times [\underline{y}, \overline{y}]), l \leq j} \|\partial^l h(x)/\partial x^l\|$. Then by the hypothesis that the density of x is bounded away from zero on $x(\mathcal{P} \times [\underline{y}, \overline{y}])$, it follows by a straightforward application of the quotient rule for derivatives that if $\|h - h_0\|_j$, $\|\tilde{h} - h_0\|_j$, and $\|\beta - \beta_0\|$ are small enough, then $\|g - \tilde{g}\|_j \leq C\|h - \tilde{h}\|_j$ for $g = g(\cdot; h, \beta)$ and $\tilde{g} = g(\cdot; \tilde{h}, \beta)$. Also it follows by the usual mean-value expansion for ratios that for such h and $\tilde{h}$, $\|g - \tilde{g} - L(\cdot, h - \tilde{h}; \beta, \tilde{h})\|_0 \leq \|h - \tilde{h}\|_0^2$. Then by the conclusion of Lemma 1 and by $\|h - \tilde{h}\|_0 \leq \|h - \tilde{h}\|_1$ for $\|\tilde{h} - h_0\|_2$ and $\|h - h_0\|_2$ small enough,

$$\begin{aligned}
&|m_1(z, \beta, h) - m_1(z, \beta, \tilde{h}) - D_1(z, h - \tilde{h}; \beta, \tilde{h})| \\
&\leq |\Delta(z, g - \tilde{g}; \tilde{g}) - \Delta(z, L(\cdot, h - \tilde{h}; \beta, \tilde{h}), \tilde{g})| \\
&\quad + C\|g - \tilde{g}\|_0 \|g - \tilde{g}\|_1 \leq C\|g - \tilde{g} - L(\cdot, h - \tilde{h}; \beta, \tilde{h})\|_0 \\
&\quad + C\|h - \tilde{h}\|_0 \|h - \tilde{h}\|_1 \leq C\|h - \tilde{h}\|_0 \|h - \tilde{h}\|_1
\end{aligned} \quad (A.10)$$

It also follows by similar reasoning that for $\|\beta - \beta_0\|$ and $\|\tilde{h} - h_0\|_2$ small enough,

$$\begin{aligned}
|D_1(z, \overline{h}; \beta, \tilde{h})| &= |\Delta(z, L(\cdot, \overline{h}; \beta, \tilde{h}); \tilde{g})| \\
&\leq C\|L(\cdot, \overline{h}; \beta, \tilde{h})\|_0 \leq C\|\overline{h}\|_0 \\
|D_1(z, \overline{h}; \beta, \tilde{h}) - D_1(z, \overline{h}; \beta_0, h_0)| &= C\|\overline{h}\|_0 \|\tilde{h} - h_0\|_1 \\
&\quad + C\|\overline{h}\|_1 (\|\tilde{h} - h_0\|_0 + \|\beta - \beta_0\|) \\
|m_1(z, \beta, h) - m_1(z, \beta_0, h_0)| &\leq C\|h - h_0\| + C\|\beta - \beta_0\|
\end{aligned} \quad (A.11)$$

It also follows by straightforward algebra that for $\|\beta - \beta_0\|$, $\|h - h_0\|_0$, and $\|\tilde{h} - h_0\|_2$ small enough, there is $b(z) = C(1 + \|q\|)$ such that

$$\begin{aligned}
&\|m_2(z, \beta, h) - m_2(z, \beta, \tilde{h}) - D_2(z, h - \tilde{h}; \beta, \tilde{h})\| \\
&\leq b(z)(\|h - h_0\|_0)^2 \\
&|D_2(z, \overline{h}; \beta, \tilde{h})| \leq b(z)\|\overline{h}\|_0 \\
&\|D_2(z, \overline{h}; \beta, \tilde{h}) - D_2(z, \overline{h}; \beta_0, h_0)\| \leq b(z)\|\overline{h}\|_0 \|\tilde{h} - h_0\|_0 \\
&\|m_2(z, \beta, h) - m_2(z, \beta_0, h_0)\| \leq b(z)(\|h - h_0\|_0 + \|\beta - \beta_0\|)
\end{aligned} \quad (A.12)$$

Furthermore, $E[b(z)^4] < \infty$, and for $\eta_n^j [\ln(n)/(n\sigma^{k+2j})]^{1/2} + \sigma^s$ and $\alpha = m/2$, we have $\eta_n^2 \to 0$, $\sqrt{n}(\eta_n^0)^2 \to 0$, $\sqrt{n}\sigma^\alpha \eta_n^0 \eta_n^1 \to 0$, implying that $1/(\sqrt{n}\sigma^k) \leq \ln(n)/(\sqrt{n}\delta^k) \to 0$. Therefore, the hypotheses of Lemma 5.4 of N are satisfied, giving

$$\sqrt{n}\sigma^\alpha l \sum_{i=1}^n [m_l(z_i, \hat{h}, \beta_0) - m_l(z_i, h_0, \beta_0)]/n \\ = \sqrt{n}\sigma^\alpha l[m_l(\hat{h}) - m_l(h_0)] + o_p(1) \quad (l = 1, 2) \quad (A.13)$$

for $\alpha_1 = \alpha$ and $\alpha_2 = 0$, and $m_1(h) = \int D_l(z, h; h_0, \beta_0)dF(z)$.

Next, by hypothesis, $m_2(h) = 0$. Let $\zeta(\tau) = \zeta(t(\tau), y_0, w_0, g_0)$ and $f_\tau(\tau) = 1(0 \le t(\tau) \le 1)|\partial t(\tau)/\partial \tau|$ denote the density of τ when t is uniformly distributed on $[0, 1]$. By the inverse-function theorem, $f_\tau(\tau)$ is bounded and continuous a.e. with compact support. Then by the definition of Δ and L,

$$m_1(h) = \int \Delta(z, L(\cdot, h; \beta_0, h_0); g_0)dF(z) = \int \omega(t)h(x(t))dt$$
$$\omega(\tau) = f_0(x(\tau))^{-1}\zeta(\tau)'[-r_0(x(\tau)), I, -\beta_0']f_\tau(\tau)$$
(A.14)

By Assumptions 5 and 6, $\omega(\tau)$ is bounded, continuous almost everywhere, and zero outside $\tau([0, 1])$. Also, by the inverse-function theorem and the chain rule, $x_2(\tau)$ is continuously differentiable, with bounded derivatives on $\tau(\mathcal{D})$, a compact convex set containing $\tau([0, 1])$ in its interior. By the previously shown conditions, $n\sigma^{2k} \to \infty$ and $n\sigma^{2s} \to 0$. Then it follows by Lemma 5.4 of N that $\sqrt{n}\sigma^a[m_1(\hat{h}) - m_1(h_0)] \xrightarrow{d} N(0, V_0)$. It then follows by equation (A.13), $\sigma \to 0$, and the triangle inequality that $\sqrt{n}\sigma^a\Sigma_i m_1(z_i, \beta_0, \hat{h})/n \xrightarrow{d} N(0, V_0)$. Furthermore, by equation (A.13), $m_2(\hat{h}) = 0$, and $m_2(h_0) = 0$, it follows that $\sqrt{n}\sigma^a\Sigma_i m_2(z_i, \beta_0, \hat{h})/n \xrightarrow{p} 0$.

Next, note that by Lemma A1, for $\|\beta - \beta_0\|$ and $\|h - h_0\|_2$ small enough, $m_1(z, \beta, h)$ is differentiable in β, with derivative that is bounded uniformly in β and h, and derivative with respect to θ equal to -1. Also, $m_2(z, \beta, h)$ is linear in β, and it is straightforward to show that $n^{-1}\Sigma_{i=1}^n \partial m_2(z_i, \beta, \hat{h})/\partial\beta$ converges in probability to $E[\partial m_2(z, \beta_0, h_0)/\partial\beta]$, with a first column being zeros, and the remaining columns being nonsingular by Assumption 2. The first conclusion then follows by a Taylor expansion.

To show the second conclusion it is useful to verify Assumption 5.2 of N for both m_1 and m_2. For m_1, parts (i)–(iii) of Assumption 5.2 follow by equations (A.10) and (A.11), with $\Delta = 0, \Delta_1 = \Delta_2 = 1$, and $\Delta_3 = 0$. Also, part (iv) is satisfied with $\delta_{\beta n} = \frac{1}{2}$, by the conditions that $n\sigma^{3k+4}/\ln(n) \to \infty$ and $n\sigma^{2s} \to 0$. It then follows by Lemma 5.5 of N that $\sigma^{2a}\Sigma_{i=1}^n \hat{U}_i^2/n \xrightarrow{p} V_0$ for $\hat{U}_i = \hat{\psi}_i^z + \hat{A}_i - \Sigma_{j=1}^n \hat{A}_j/n$. Also, it is straightforward to check that Assumption 5.2 of N is satisfied for m_2, so that for $\bar{\psi}_i = \tau_i(w_i - \hat{E}[w|x_i])(T^{-1}(q_i) - \hat{g}(x_i, w_i))$, $\sigma^{2a}\Sigma_{i=1}^n \|\bar{\psi}_i\|^2/n \xrightarrow{p} 0$. Also, by arguments similar to those for asymptotic normality, $\hat{G}^\beta$ is bounded in probability and $\hat{M} \xrightarrow{p} M$, so the second conclusion follows by the triangle inequality. □

Proof of Theorem 2. The proof proceeds by verifying the hypotheses of Theorem 2 of Newey (1995) for $\hat{S}$ and $\hat{L}$ and Theorem 6.2 of Newey (1994b) for $\hat{\mu}$ and $\hat{\lambda}$. Assumptions 1 and 4 of Newey (1995) and Assumption 6.1 of Newey (1994b) follow from Assumption 7. Assumptions 2 of Newey (1995) and 6.2 of Newey (1994b) follow by Assumption 8, with P^k equal to products of orthogonal polynomials and $\zeta_d(K) = K^{1+2d}$, as discussed in the proof of Theorem 4 of Newey (1995). Also, Assumption 9 implies Assumption 3 of Newey (1995) and Assumption 6.3 of Newey (1994b), for any $\alpha > 0$, by an argument similar to that in the proof Theorem 7.2 of Newey (1994b). Also, by Lemma A1 and $K^{22}/n \to 0$, Assumption 4 of Newey (1995) and Assumption 6.4 of Newey (1994b) are satisfied with $d = 2$ (and hence $\zeta_d(K) = K^5$). Furthermore, Assumption 6.5 of Newey (1994b) holds with $d = 0$ by Lemma A1. Also, for $\hat{S}$ and $\hat{L}$, Assumption 5 of Newey (1995) is straightforward to show, using an argument similar to that in the proof of Theorem 4 of Newey (1995). Furthermore, for $\hat{\mu}$ and $\hat{\lambda}$, Assumption 6.6 of Newey (1994b) follows by choosing α big enough. Finally, Assumption 6.7 of Newey (1994b) follows by $K^{22}/n \to 0$ and choosing K large enough. The conclusions for $\hat{S}$ and $\hat{L}$ then follow by the conclusion of Theorem 2 in Newey (1995), and the conclusion for $\hat{\mu}$ and $\hat{\lambda}$ follow by the conclusion of Theorem 6.1 of Newey (1994b). □

References

Afriat, S. (1967). The construction of a utility function from expenditure data. *International Economic Review* 8:67–77.
— (1973). On a system of inequalities on demand analysis: an extension of the classical method. *International Economic Review* 14:460–72.
Auerbach, A. (1985). The theory of excess burden and optimal taxation. In: *Handbook of Public Economics*, vol. 1, ed. A. Auerbach and M. Feldstein. Amsterdam: North Holland.
Bierens, H. J. (1987). Kernel estimators of regression functions. In: *Advances in Econometrics, Fifth World Congress*, vol. 1, ed. T. Bewley. Cambridge University Press.
Brown, B. W., and Newey, W. K. (1992). Efficient semiparametric estimation of expectations. Working paper, Department of Economics, Rice University.
Brown, B. W., and Walker, M. B. (1989). The random utility hypothesis and inference in demand systems. *Econometrica*, 47:815–29.
Burman, P., and Chen, K. W. (1989). Nonparametric estimation of a regression function. *Annals of Statistics* 17:1567–96.
Dahl, C. (1986). Gasoline demand survey. *Energy Journal* 7:67–82.
Deaton, A. (1986). Demand analysis. In: *Handbook of Econometrics*, vol. 3, ed. Z. Griliches and M. Intriligator. Amsterdam: North Holland.
Diamond, P., and McFadden, D. (1974). Some uses of the expenditure function in public finance. *Journal of Public Economics* 3:3–21.
Finney, F. L. and Ostberg, D. R. (1976). *Elementary Differential Equations with Linear Algebra*. Reading, MA: Addison-Wesley.
Gately, D. (1992). Imperfect price-reversibility of US gasoline demand. *Energy Journal* 13:179–207.
Hardle, W., and Linton, O. (1994). Applied nonparametric methods. In: *Handbook of Econometrics*, vol. 4, ed. R. Engle and D. McFadden. Amsterdam: North Holland.

Hausman, J. (1981). Exact consumer's surplus and deadweight loss. *American Economic Review* 71:662–76.
  (1985). The econometrics of nonlinear budget sets. *Econometrica* 53:1255–82.
Li, K. C. (1987). Asymptotic optimality for C_p, C_L, cross-validation, and generalized cross-validation: discrete index set. *Annals of Statistics* 15:958–75.
Newey, W. K. (1994a). Kernel estimation of partial means and a general variance estimator. *Econometric Theory* 10:233–53.
  (1994b). The asymptotic variance of semiparametric estimator. *Econometrica*, 62:1349–82.
  (1995). Convergence rates and asymptotic normality of series estimators. Working paper, Department of Economics, Massachusetts Institute of Technology.
Porter-Hudak, S., and Hayes, K. (1986). The statistical precision of a numerical methods estimator as applied to welfare loss. *Economics Letters*, 20:255–7.
Powell, J. L., Stock, J. H., and Stoker, T. M. (1989). Semiparametric estimation of index coefficients. *Econometrica* 57:1403–30.
Powell, M. J. D. (1981). *Approximation Theory and Methods*. Cambridge University Press.
Robinson, P. (1988). Root-N-consistent semiparametric regression. *Econometrica* 56:931–54.
Samuelson, P. A. (1948). Consumption theory in terms of revealed preference. *Economica* 5:61–71.
Small, K., and Rosen, H. (1981). Applied welfare economics with discrete choice models. *Econometrica* 49:105–30.
Varian, H. (1982a). The nonparametric approach to demand analysis. *Econometrica* 50:945–74.
  (1982b). Nonparametric tests of models of consumer behavior. *Review of Economic Studies* 50:99–110.
  (1982c). Trois evaluations de l'impact "social" d'un changement de prix. *Cahiers du Seminar d'Econometrie* 24:13–30.
Vartia, Y. (1983). Efficient methods of measuring welfare change and compensated income in terms of ordinary demand functions. *Econometrica* 51:79–98.
Willig, R. (1976). Consumer's surplus without apology. *American Economic Review* 66:589–97.

CHAPTER 5

Consumer Demand and Intertemporal Allocations: Engel, Slutsky, and Frisch

Richard Blundell

1 Introduction

Individual consumers often are assumed to follow certain relatively simple budgeting rules when making expenditure decisions. For example, how much to save may be decided upon almost separately from decisions on how much to spend on food, services, and other day-to-day consumables. Of course, it is well known that such "decentralized" budgeting decisions can fit well within standard consumer theory. Indeed, the sequential nature of consumer budgeting decisions not only makes tractable the decision-making problem for the consumer but also makes it possible for the empirical microeconomist to build up a picture of consumer behaviour from a sequence of relatively straightforward estimation steps.

In his 1959 *Econometrica* paper "A Complete Scheme for Computing All Direct and Cross Demand Elasticities," drawing on his earlier 1932 study, Frisch saw the power of the sequential approach to analysis of consumer demand. He also developed a method for interpreting demands directly in terms of the marginal utility of money and prices when studying the analysis of allocations across groups. In particular, he considered the case in which groups were additively separable – what he termed *want-independent* – in which case these "Frisch" demands depended simply on own prices and marginal utility. Because marginal utility is equated across groups, the allocations between and across groups are cleverly simplified. Marginal utility is recovered up to scale from a simple within-group demand analysis – to quote Frisch (1959, p. 186), "detail

This essay was prepared for the Ragnar Frisch Centennial Symposium in Oslo, March 1995. Thanks are due to James Banks, Martin Browning, James Heckman, Arthur Lewbel, Ian Preston, Costas Meghir, and an anonymous referee for discussion of this work. This study is part of the research program of the Economic and Social Research Council (ESRC) Centre for the Microeconomic Analysis of Fiscal Policy at the Institute for Fiscal Studies. Material from the United Kingdom Family Expenditure Survey made available by the CSO through the ESRC data archive has been used by permission of the controller of Her Majesty's Stationery Office.

about the way in which the distribution of consumption within the group depends on the price differentials within the group and the group expenditure datum." Across-group preferences are then recovered from the marginal-utility condition.

Additive separability is a highly restrictive assumption. However, it is often considered to be more reasonable in the intertemporal analysis of expected-utility maximization. Frisch did not apply these ideas to the intertemporal problem, but instead to the study of broad groups of goods. Thus it could be argued that the simplifying approach he developed has rather more appeal in the intertemporal model. Of course, with expected-utility maximization in a world in which individuals have less than perfect foresight, the estimation and interpretation of the model and its elasticities require further development and cannot rely exclusively on that presented by Frisch. However, his elasticity decomposition and the usefulness of his marginal-utility constant demands still give remarkable insight.

These important developments by Frisch took place at the same time that Gorman (1959) and Strotz (1957) were developing the ideas of separability and two-stage budgeting, with the same simplifying motivation in mind – witness the lively interchange between Strotz (1959) and Gorman. That work complemented Frisch's analysis by focusing, especially in the case of Gorman, on the grouping of prices under separability. Gorman showed that, in general, homothetic separability was a necessary and sufficient condition for two-stage budgeting. That was the requirement that a single price index be used to allocate across groups of goods. As a consequence, two-stage budgeting placed heavy restrictions on within-group preferences – in particular, the homothetic-preference assumption that restricted all within-group Engel curves to be rays through the origin. Under additive separability, that could be relaxed, but only within the generalized Gorman polar-form class. In the nonparametric analysis to be described here, those restrictions are shown to be rejected for individual-level consumer expenditure data. However, later work by Gorman (1981) showed how such preferences could be generalized in a way that would retain the simplicity of groupwise price indices while allowing for quite general Engel curves. These Engel curves, in contrast, are shown to fit the data rather well.

For intertemporal allocations, the approach of Frisch has turned out to be extremely attractive. Additive separability over time is commonly assumed and can easily be extended to account for uncertainty. Moreover, the price elasticities from the Frisch demands are identical with the good-specific intertemporal substitution elasticities of Heckman (1974) and Hall (1978). It is important to point out that where we relax the perfect-foresight assumption and allow for uncertainty, the Frisch elasticities have to be interpreted as price responses along an *anticipated* price path. As such, they do not necessarily correspond to the intertemporal elasticities needed for policy analysis. Policy changes often are unexpected and therefore involve an *unanticipated* income or wealth effect.

It is easy to see that writing Frisch demands as linear or loglinear in marginal utility, though allowing estimation of intratemporal and intertemporal preferences together in one step (e.g., Browning, Deaton, and Irish, 1985), imposes unnecessarily strong restrictions on within- and between-period utilities. This has been pointed out in a number of papers, including those by Nickell (1988), Browning (1986), and Blundell, Fry, and Meghir (1989).

The sequential approach offers an attractive alternative. It is consistent with a flexible representation of consumer behaviour. It allows within-period preferences to be determined up to scale from "standard" within-period Marshallian demand analysis. The duality between these and Frisch demands means that Frisch elasticities can then be used to interpret intertemporal allocations.

This duality is most easily seen from the following relationship between the various elasticities of demand that dates back to Frisch's 1959 paper:

$$e_{ij}^f = e_{ij}^s + \sigma \eta_i \eta_j w_j \qquad (1.1)$$

where e_{ij}^f is the Frisch elasticity that holds the marginal utility of money constant, e_{ij}^s is the Slutsky[1] compensated substitution elasticity between goods i and j, σ is the intertemporal substitution elasticity for total consumption, η_i is the Engel budget elasticity, and w_i is the budget share of good i. It is clear from (1.1) that only *one* additional parameter (σ) is needed to determine intertemporal allocations over and above the within-period elasticities e_{ij}^s and η_i. That is, once e_{ij}^s and η_i are determined, knowledge of σ completes the description of preferences over time periods and goods. I shall argue here that building up the components of (1.1) from an analysis of within-period behaviour, coupled with a separate analysis of intertemporal behaviour to recover σ, is the most effective way of allowing the data the greatest flexibility in determining the underlying preference parameters. Clearly, it would be sensible for the σ elasticity (and other elasticities) to be allowed to vary across individuals with different demographic characteristics and different levels of overall consumption. What is surprising is that in many specifications used in empirical applications the Frisch elasticities are completely determined by within-period elasticities, leaving very little flexibility for intertemporal behaviour.

The aim of this essay, therefore, is to use the link between Frisch

---

[1] A series of letters from Slutsky to Frisch in 1926, while Slutsky was in Moscow, provided Frisch with the Slutsky decomposition of uncompensated elasticities into Engel and compensated elasticities.

demands and Marshallian demands to provide an attractive strategy for estimating income effects, price effects, and intertemporal substitution effects in consumer demand. The Frisch approach, together with the two-stage budgeting results of Gorman, are shown to provide a natural set of building blocks for analysis of consumer demand. Indeed, the first stage in estimating within-period demands is shown to break down conveniently into two steps: First, the Engel-curve relationship can be analysed for given price regimes giving the η_i elasticities in (1.1). At the second step, relative-price effects and the corresponding Slutsky elasticities e_{ij}^s in (1.1) are estimated by looking at demand shifts over time as relative prices change. It is then a simple matter to use the marginal-utility-of-money relationship over time to recover the remaining intertemporal-demand parameter σ in (1.1).

This chapter is organized to facilitate free-flowing interplay between theory and application – true to the spirit of Frisch. In the next section, the recovery of within-period demands is separated, as mentioned earlier, into a general nonparametric discussion of the Engel curve. That is followed in Section 3 by a discussion of the incorporation of relative-price effects. These results draw on a series of detailed studies based on the individual data in the United Kingdom Family Expenditure Survey. They use new results that derive an integrable parameterisation of preferences that corresponds to the empirically coherent quadratic logarithmic Engel-curve system. In Section 4, intertemporal demands are analysed using a synthetic cohort panel drawn from the long time series of family-expenditure data available for Britain. In Section 5, some conclusions are drawn, and a comparison with some alternative approaches in the literature is made.

2   Engel Elasticities and Nonparametric Regression

The Engel curve has been at the centre of applied microeconomic research since the early studies of Working (1943) and Leser (1963) uncovered the stability of the expenditure-share–log-income specification for food expenditures. Frisch himself used a cross-section study of budget proportions drawn up by Leif Johansen and the Central Bureau of Statistics in Oslo and quoted results that closely accorded with the Working-Leser model. Recently, attention has focused on Engel curves that have a greater variety of curvature than is permitted by the Working-Leser form underlying the "Translog" and "Almost Ideal" models of Jorgenson, Christensen, and Lau (1975), Jorgenson and Lau (1975), and Deaton and Muellbauer (1980a,b). This reflects growing evidence from a series of empirical studies suggesting that quadratic logarithmic income terms are required for certain expenditure-share equations; see, for example, Atkinson, Gornulka, and Stern (1990),

Bierens and Pott-Buter (1990), Hausman, Newey, and Powell (1995), Hardle and Jerison (1988), Lewbel (1991), and Blundell, Pashardes, and Weber (1993).

To analyse empirically the Engel curve, data from the United Kingdom Family Expenditure Survey (UK FES) are used. The data are split into relatively homogeneous demographic groups, and the results presented here refer to a sample of some 23,000 working-age households that are characterized by the presence of one male adult and one female adult, both being between the ages of 18 and 65. Five broad nondurable and service groups of commodities are chosen: food, fuel, clothing, alcohol, and other nondurable nonhousing goods.[2] Households are further split according to the number of children. A detailed description of these data and a comparison with other demographic groups are provided by Banks, Blundell, and Lewbel (1997). The broad results to be reported here carry over to the other main demographic groups in the population. In Section 4, when we come to analyse intertemporal behaviour by following date-of-birth cohorts over time, the demographic groups are pooled so as to get an accurate picture of the demographic changes that occur as a cohort ages.

Although our data set comes from a pooled household survey covering some 20 years, in order to focus on the shape of the Engel-curve relationship we initially consider subsamples by year and by demographic group. In this analysis, each expenditure share is defined over the logarithm of deflated income or total expenditure. Figures 5.1 and 5.2 present kernel regressions, quadratic polynomial regressions, and pointwise confidence intervals for the Engel curves for two commodity groups in a three-year period in the middle of our sample for households without children. Although from Figure 5.1 the linear formulation appears to provide a reasonable approximation for the food-share curve, for some groups (particularly alcohol and "other goods") distinct nonlinear behaviour is evident, at least in the raw data.

To construct these figures, the Gaussian kernel is used with a mean integrated-square-error optimal smoothing parameter (Hardle, 1990), but the overall shape is little affected by variations in the choice of kernel or smoothing parameter. It is interesting to focus on a comparison with the simple second-order-polynomial fit given by the dashed lines in the

---

[2] These groups were chosen primarily to be consistent with earlier studies on UK FES data. However, the results appear robust to further disaggregation of commodities (Blundell and Robin, 1997). Commodities like clothing and alcohol have significant numbers of zero values reported for expenditures in the FES diaries. In this chapter, such zeroes are treated as if they were generated through an independent infrequency-of-purchase process (Blundell and Meghir, 1997). In this case the instrumental-variable procedure can be shown to be valid. This is probably a reasonable modelling framework for clothing expenditures, but not necessarily for alcohol.

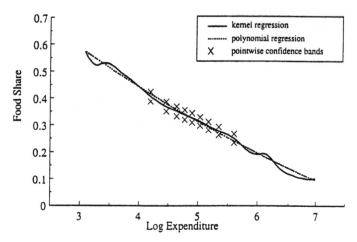

Figure 5.1. Nonparametric Engel curve: food share.

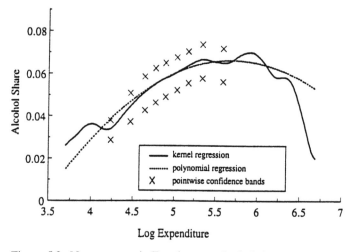

Figure 5.2. Nonparametric Engel curve: alcohol share.

figures. Some guide to the reliability of this approximation can be drawn from the pointwise confidence intervals (evaluated at the second-to-ninth decile points) also shown in the figures. It is only where the data are sparse and the confidence bands relatively wide that the paths diverge. For most goods it appears that expressing the budget share as a second-order polynomial in log total expenditure provides a very reliable approximation to Engel-curve behaviour.

These pictures are drawn from the study of Banks et al. (1997), where further kernel regressions are presented that indicate stability in the

Consumer Demand and Intertemporal Allocations

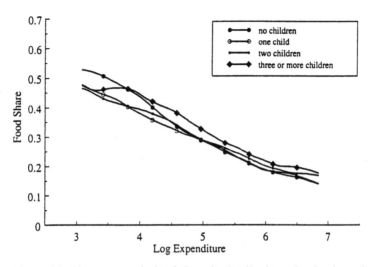

Figure 5.3. Nonparametric food share by family size: adaptive kernel.

overall patterns across time and different demographic groups. For example, Figure 5.3 plots the food-share Engel curve by household size. The linear relationship can be seen to hold across a wide range of the total-expenditure distribution. In this figure an adaptive kernel regression is used (e.g., Hardle, 1990). This allows the bandwidth to vary inversely with the density of the regressor variable so as to reduce the "wiggles" in the kernel regression line that occur where the density of log total expenditure is sparse.

These raw-data analyses should, of course, be viewed with caution, for a number of reasons. Most obviously, one would expect additional covariates. This point is largely accounted for by the selection of a homogeneous subsample. In addition, we trim any observations that lie outside three standard deviations of the mean for either log total expenditure or any of the five commodity-expenditure shares. More important are assumptions about the stochastic specification underlying the kernel regressions. The explanatory variable is the logarithm of (deflated) total expenditure on the sum of the five consumption categories. For obvious reasons this is likely to be endogenous, and it may well suffer from measurement error. The Banks, Blundell, and Lewbel study provides a detailed assessment of the extent to which the rejection of linearity can be attributed to one of these stochastic problems. In all cases the strong nonlinearity of the Engel curve is preserved, and there is found to be little evidence against the quadratic log specification.

These Engel-curve investigations suggest two distinct features of our expenditure data. For certain goods, such as food, the linear logarithmic expenditure-share model provides a robust description of behaviour.

Second, for certain other goods, such as alcohol, the linear model needs to be supplemented by a quadratic term.

3 Slutsky Elasticities and Marshallian Demands

Given the exploratory analysis of the shape of the Engel-curve relationship, attention in this section turns to the derivation of a class of consumer preferences that support these results. The baseline model in which expenditure shares that are linear in log total expenditure (hereafter referred to as log income) alone has been called PIGLOG (Muellbauer, 1976), and arise from indirect utility functions that are themselves linear in log total expenditure. These preferences underlie the Almost Ideal model of Deaton and Muellbauer. Our aim here is to consider extensions of PIGLOG demands that will yield models sufficiently flexible to capture our empirical evidence on the shapes of Engel curves.

In what follows, we use w_{it} to refer to the budget share for good i at observation t, p_t to refer to the n-vector of prices, z_t to refer to the k-vector of demographic controls, and $\ln c_t$ to refer to the log of total real expenditure. Working from our preferred form for the Engel curves (Banks et al., 1997), we prove the following lemma.

Lemma. *Consider all demand systems that are consistent with utility maximization and have Engel curves linear in a constant, log total expenditure, and some other function of total expenditure. If these also have coefficients of rank 3, then they are rank-3 quadratic logarithmic budget-share systems of the form*

$$w_{it} = a_i(p_t, z_t) + \beta_i(p_t, z_t)\ln c_t + \psi_i(p_t, z_t)\ln c_t^2 \quad (3.1)$$

□

Quadratic models that preserve sufficient flexibility under integrability must have the specific form of (3.1). It is worth noting that an implication from Gorman (1981) is that expenditure-share models that are higher-order polynomials in $\ln c$ will always require some rank reduction in the polynomial coefficients to achieve integrability.

To construct a simple quadratic logarithmic specification that does not impose the empirically rejected proportionality (rank-2) restriction, we consider a quadratic generalization of Deaton and Muellbauer's Almost Ideal Demand System:

$$w_{it} = a_i(z_t) + \sum \gamma_{ij} \ln p_{jt} + \beta_i(z_t)\ln c_t + \frac{\psi_i(z_t)}{b(p_t, z_t)}\ln c_t^2 \quad (3.2)$$

where

$$b(p_t, z_t) = \Pi p_{jt}^{\beta_i(z_t)} \quad (3.3)$$

and where, defining x_t to be total nominal expenditure, log total real expenditure is given by

$$\ln c_t = \ln\left(\frac{x_t}{a(p_t, z_t)}\right) \tag{3.4}$$

with

$$\ln a(p_t, z_t) = \alpha_0 + \sum_{k=1}^{n} \alpha_k(z_t) \ln p_{kt} + \frac{1}{2}\sum_{k=1}^{n}\sum_{j=1}^{n} \gamma_{kj} \ln p_{kt} \ln p_{jt}. \tag{3.5}$$

This has been shown (Banks et al., 1997) to correspond to an explicit indirect utility function that is a direct generalization of Deaton and Muellbuaer's LAIDS model – the QUAIDS model – given by

$$V_t(x_t, p_t, z_t) = \frac{b(p_t, z_t)}{\ln c_t} + \phi(p_t, z_t) \tag{3.6}$$

where

$$\phi(p_t, z_t) = \Pi p_{jt}^{\psi_i(z_t)}. \tag{3.7}$$

To estimate this model, data are again drawn from the UK FES. The exact same procedures of sample selection and separation into demographic groups are used as in the discussion of the Engel-curve relationship in Section 2. Estimation of the model takes place over the 20-year period for the five categories of expenditures described earlier – food, fuel, clothing, alcohol, and other goods – with monthly price variations.

The system is nonlinear, and estimation follows in two stages. First, the unrestricted estimates for the nonlinear system are calculated allowing for endogeneity of the total-real-expenditure variable $\ln c$; then symmetry-restricted parameter estimates are derived using a minimum-distance procedure. In the first stage, an "iterated moment estimator" is adopted that exploits the conditional linearity of the QUAIDS model (3.2), in which budget shares are linear in unknown parameters, given the nonlinear functions $a(p)$ and $b(p)$. The consistency of this procedure and its asymptotic efficiency properties have been described by Blundell and Robin (1997). To allow for the endogeneity of $\ln c$, a Wu-Hausman augmented regression model is adopted in which a reduced-form residual for $\ln c_t$ is added to each budget-share equation.[3] This technique preserves the adding-up and invariance properties of the demand system. The parameter α_0 is chosen by grid search using the conditional log likelihood of the system as the criterion. This turns out to be a well-behaved function with a unique maximum. At the second stage, to derive the

---

[3] The log of disposable non-asset income is used as an identifying instrument.

symmetry-restricted estimates, the optimal minimum-distance estimator is used; see Blundell (1988) and Browning and Meghir (1991) for a full description of this technique.

In what follows, we present the symmetry-restricted parameter estimates together with a table of compensated price and budget elasticities for the quadratic specification. The full results have been presented (Banks et al., 1997). Given the homogeneity of each of our sample splits, we choose to allow only a limited number of additional factors [z in equation (3.2)] to influence preferences (i.e., age, seasonal dummies, and a time trend). Table 5.1 presents the symmetry-restricted results for the sample of married couples without children. The real-expenditure terms here correspond (after scaling) to the unconditional, nonparametric Engel curves shown previously, and one can clearly see the importance of quadratic terms in the real expenditures (particularly for clothing and alcohol), as the nonparametric analysis suggested. The coefficients on the quadratic terms in the food- and fuel-share equations have been set to zero, as suggested by the nonparametric regression analysis. These restrictions are not rejected using conventional statistical criteria in the parametric QUAIDS demand system.

In Table 5.2 we report the corresponding within-period elasticities. These elasticities are first calculated for each household individually, and a weighted average is constructed, with the weights being equal to the households' shares of the total sample expenditure for the relevant good. The corresponding Slutsky matrix has eigenvalues of -0.2267, -0.1223, -0.0739, and -0.0087, confirming the negativity prediction of consumer theory.

Given these estimates for within-period behaviour, it is possible to engage in a static analysis of tax reforms, particularly reforms to the indirect-tax system. A detailed analysis of indirect-tax reform in this model was presented by Banks, Blundell, and Lewbel (1996), where the value of estimating elasticities in terms of the accuracy of welfare measurement was also assessed.

These estimates now allow us to go on to complete the picture of consumer preferences by considering intertemporal allocations. We have now determined the Engel elasticities η_i and η_j, as well as the Slutsky substitution elasticities e_{ij}^s. All that remains is to determine the intertemporal elasticity σ. In the next section we shall consider how to do this using the information from the repeated cross sections in the FES data.

4   Frisch Elasticities and Intertemporal Allocations

Our approach in deriving intertemporal allocations is based on the Hall (1978) Euler equation, which has been extensively implemented on microeconomic data, following the work of Heckman and MaCurdy (1980). Consider the behaviour of an individual or household who max-

Table 5.1. *Demand-System Parameter Estimates*

Variable		S.E.	t		S.E.	t		S.E.	t		S.E.	t
Constant	0.868	0.036	24.11	0.255	0.016	16.02	−0.383	0.088	−4.33	−0.400	0.065	−6.18
Pfood	−0.103	0.035	−2.95	−0.011	0.016	−0.68	0.123	0.033	3.70	0.128	0.021	5.96
Pfuel	−0.011	0.016	−0.68	0.005	0.015	0.31	−0.018	0.016	−1.12	0.055	0.012	4.48
Pcloth	0.123	0.033	3.70	−0.018	0.016	−1.12	−0.091	0.033	−2.72	−0.082	0.020	−4.10
Palc	0.128	0.022	5.95	0.055	0.012	4.48	−0.082	0.020	−4.10	−0.115	0.024	−4.80
Trend	0.010	0.012	0.84	−0.003	0.006	−0.60	−0.009	0.012	−0.71	0.005	0.007	0.69
S1	−0.003	0.003	−0.95	0.006	0.001	4.74	−0.006	0.003	−1.87	−0.005	0.002	−2.41
S2	−0.002	0.003	−0.65	−0.003	0.001	−1.84	−0.008	0.003	−2.39	−0.003	0.002	−1.27
S3	−0.007	0.003	−2.13	−0.011	0.001	−7.60	0.003	0.003	0.84	−0.002	0.002	−0.74
Age1	0.010	0.001	10.29	0.006	0.000	14.84	−0.004	0.001	−4.36	−0.006	0.001	−9.47
Age12	−0.000	0.001	−0.52	−0.002	0.000	−4.44	0.002	0.001	2.65	0.001	0.001	1.02
LogEx	−0.125	0.006	−21.34	−0.035	0.002	−14.85	0.184	0.032	5.71	0.173	0.024	7.13
LogEx2	—			—			−0.018	0.003	−5.24	−0.017	0.003	−6.52
V_Hat	−0.029	0.007	−4.32	−0.007	0.003	−2.51	0.028	0.006	4.28	−0.009	0.004	−2.16

Notes: Sample selection is for married couples without children living in London and the Southeast. Symmetry test = 12.5388; Wald 1 = 24.65; $\chi^2(6, 0.99)$ = 16.80; $\chi^2(16, 0.99)$ = 32.03.

Table 5.2. *Estimated Compensated Demand Elasticities*

	Food		Fuel		Clothing		Alcohol		Budget	
Compensated										
Food	−0.780	(0.15)[a]	0.108	(0.06)	0.292	(0.13)	0.297	(0.08)	0.5638	(0.11)
Fuel	0.471	(0.29)	−0.762	(0.22)	−0.471	(0.29)	0.645	(0.19)	0.4653	(0.20)
Clothing	1.074	(0.41)	−0.372	(0.17)	−1.012	(0.42)	0.063	(0.23)	1.1634	(0.38)
Alcohol	1.567	(0.42)	0.766	(0.21)	0.079	(0.41)	−1.692	(0.44)	1.2594	(0.38)
Uncompensated										
Food	−0.959	(0.16)	0.067	(0.06)	0.249	(0.13)	0.267	(0.08)		
Fuel	0.319	(0.31)	−0.800	(0.21)	−0.504	(0.29)	0.620	(0.19)		
Clothing	0.735	(0.44)	−0.448	(0.17)	−1.109	(0.41)	−0.059	(0.23)		
Alcohol	1.194	(0.44)	0.681	(0.21)	−0.092	(0.40)	−1.764	(0.44)		

[a] Standard error.

imizes the expected sum of discounted future utilities subject to a lifetime budget constraint.[4] Expected lifetime utility is given by

$$U = E_0 \sum_{t=1}^{T} U_t \tag{4.1}$$

or, in the particular specification used later,

$$U = E_0 \sum_{t=1}^{T} \frac{1}{1+\rho_t} \left(\frac{V_t(x_t, p_t, z_t)}{\delta_t(z_t)} \right)^{1+\rho_t} \tag{4.2}$$

where $V_t(x_t, p_t, z_t)$ is the within-period indirect utility derived from the QUAIDS model (3.6).

Under an assumption of perfect capital markets, period-t assets A_t are given by

$$A_t = (1 + r_t)A_{t-1} - x_t + y_t \tag{4.3}$$

where r_t is the period-t interest rate, and y_t is exogenous earned or transfer income in period t. Following the Frisch rule for the optimal allocation across additively separable groups, we find

$$E_t(1 + r_t)\lambda_{t+1} = \lambda_t \tag{4.4}$$

where

$$\lambda_t = \frac{\partial U_t}{\partial x_t} \tag{4.5}$$

This is typically referred to as the Euler condition for intertemporal allocations; see Nickell (1988) or Altonji (1986), for example.

---

[4] It is easy to incorporate a bequest motive into this model, as the terminal conditions may be quite general.

The intertemporal elasticity, or (minus) the inverse of Frisch's money flexibility, is given by

$$\sigma_t = \left(\frac{x_t}{\lambda_t}\frac{\partial \lambda_t}{\partial x_t}\right)^{-1} \leq 0 \tag{4.6}$$

This describes the impact on period-t consumption of a fully anticipated change in period-t prices (or real interest). For the chosen specification of preferences given earlier, this becomes

$$\sigma_t = \left(\frac{\rho_t b_t - 2\phi_t \ln c_t}{b_t + \phi_t \ln c_t} - 1\right)^{-1} \tag{4.7}$$

With values of $\rho_t \leq 0$, $\phi_t \geq 0$, and $b_t \geq 0$, this shows a willingness to substitute that is higher for the better-off, as hypothesized by Frisch (1959).

To estimate the intertemporal parameters that govern the evolution of dynamic expenditure paths, we assume that ρ_t is independent of demographics, which allows us to write down the intertemporal-allocation rule as

$$\Delta \ln c_t = \rho \Delta \ln(\ln c_t) - (2 + \rho) \ln \Delta\left(1 + \phi_t \ln \frac{c_t}{b_t}\right)$$
$$- (1 + \rho)\Delta \ln \delta_t - (1 + \rho)\Delta \ln b_t + r_{t-1} + \varepsilon_t \tag{4.8}$$

where we have used a loglinear approximation and entered a stochastic term ε_t to reflect the approximation error as well as the expectation error that enter after removal of the conditional expectation; see Banks, Blundell, and Preston (1994) for a detailed derivation.[5] In the intertemporal equation, it is only the δ_t and ρ parameters that are unknown. The rest are determined from the demand analysis described already; see (3.2)–(3.7). The δ_t parameter is specified as

$$\Delta \ln \delta_t = \delta_0 + \sum \delta_j \Delta z_{jt} \tag{4.9}$$

These remaining intertemporal parameters are therefore estimated from constructed cohort data from the 20 years of FES data described earlier. This follows the methodology of Blundell, Browning, and Meghir (1994) and recovers δ_t and ρ conditional on the Marshallian demand parameters.

Cohorts are constructed on the basis of the birth dates of heads of households. We construct 11 cohorts, each covering a five-year band, resulting in group sizes between 200 and 500 households, with a mean of 354 observations in each cohort. Of these cohorts, five are present for

---

[5] The degree of risk aversion directly enters the Euler equation for consumption growth and tilts consumption toward the future. Here it is implicitly being assumed that the degree of risk aversion is constant over time or is characterized through the demographic and labour-market variables included in the regression.

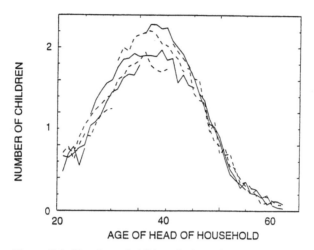

Figure 5.4. Number of children in household over the life cycle.

the full sample (i.e., 20 years), whereas young and old cohorts exist only for shorter periods at the ends of the sample. Within-period sampling errors in the construction of cohort averages lead to a resulting framework econometrically equivalent to errors-in-variables models (though with an estimatable variance-covariance structure for the measurement errors), as outlined by Deaton (1985). With sufficiently large cohort sizes, such as those here, it nevertheless becomes permissible to disregard this sampling error and treat the data as genuine panel data. After allowing for the different periods during which each cohort is observed and the loss of observations due to lagging the instrument set and taking first differences, the resulting data set comprises 133 data points. For the (individual-specific) real interest rate we take the after-tax "building-society" lending rate if the household has a mortgage, and the borrowing rate if it does not. This interest rate is then deflated by inflation – which we define as the change in the cohort average of the nondiscounted value of the individual-specific linear homogeneous price index.

Cohort-average data for number of children and total expenditure are illustrated in Figures 5.4 and 5.5. The pattern of child-bearing over the life cycle appears to be fairly stable across cohorts, with little variance over the business cycle. This contrasts somewhat with the expenditure profiles, in which the 1981/82 recession, for instance, is clearly visible. It should be noted that conditioning, as we do, on labour-market status in the estimation of both the demand system and the Euler equation may capture some of these business-cycle effects.

The orthogonality condition (4.4) is used to define a generalized-method-of-moments estimator (Hansen and Singleton, 1982) for the

Figure 5.5. Real expenditure over the life cycle.

intertemporal relationship (4.8). The terms in the intertemporal allocation rule are nonlinear and are constructed directly by consistent aggregation in each period of individual-level data. First differences are taken at the cohort level. The specification includes demographic and labour-market-status variables that have been shown to be important in recent studies (e.g., Blundell et al., 1994; Attanasio and Weber, 1989). We also include the levels of these demographics at time t.

This method relies on following a cohort of individuals over time and modelling the average behaviour of the group. Thus, consider the expected value of the Euler equation, conditional on a date-of-birth cohort and on time period t. For consistent estimation to be possible, we need to impose certain conditions. First, because prices and interest rates vary only with time t, our estimation procedure (for both the demand system and the Euler equation) assumes asymptotics on both N (individuals) and T (time periods). Given this, the average innovations $\{\varepsilon_t\}$ are zero unless there are aggregate shocks affecting all members of the cohort. Moreover, any idiosyncratic random preference errors entering through the discount factor at the individual level average out at the cohort level. Thus the only sources of stochastic variation are the aggregate shocks; these are assumed to average out over our 20 years of data.

The nature of the model is such that $\{\varepsilon_t\}$ will be correlated with consumption, prices, and most choice variables dated t (unless they are subject to relatively long decision lags). Moreover, time aggregation can induce moving-average errors, and hence $\{\varepsilon_t\}$ may also be correlated with (recent) past values of the decision variables and prices. Hence instrumental variables must be appropriately lagged. The instruments involve the second lags of the growth rates of income and consumption, the inter-

Table 5.3. *Intertemporal Allocations*

	(1)	(2)	(3)	(4)
Constant	0.0435	0.0606	0.0402	0.0219
	(0.0117)	(0.0300)	(0.0095)	(0.0071)
ΔTotkids	0.2629	0.1685	0.1903	0.1802
	(0.1022)	(0.0766)	(0.0826)	(0.0792)
ΔHunemp	−1.2745	0.0531	−1.4135	
	(0.6282)	(0.7170)	(0.4562)	
ΔWWife	0.5734			
	(0.4397)			
ΔMortg	−0.3612			
	(0.3758)			
TotKids		−0.0039		
		(0.0177)		
Hunemp		−0.3721		
		(0.1718)		
ρ	−2.5817	−1.3357	−2.2264	−1.4775
	(0.86337)	(0.9731)	(0.7165)	(0.6475)
σ	−0.6511	−0.7771	−0.6827	−0.7604
	(0.1716)	(0.1914)	(0.1445)	(0.1309)
δ_1	0.1662	0.5019	0.1551	0.3774
	(0.0776)	(1.3387)	(0.0804)	(0.4458)
Sargan	18.4270	24.0889	24.7710	37.3044
d.f.	16	16	18	19
S.E. of eq.	0.0070	0.0042	0.0059	0.0054

Notes: Standard errors are given in parentheses. Variables are levels at time t, or first differences (indicated by Δ). Hunemp is a dummy for head of household unemployed; WWife is a dummy for working female; Mortg is a dummy for presence of a mortgage; Totkids is the total number of children of all ages. Instruments are number of children in each of four age groups, age of head, age of spouse, working-male and working-female dummies, lending and borrowing interest rates, tenure and region dummies; all instruments are dated $t - 2$. σ is calculated at the mean $\ln c_t$ for the sample of 4.76714 (at January 1987 prices).

actions of the latter with characteristics, and the characteristics themselves. The latter are either dated $t - 2$ (labour-market status) or dated t (all other demographic variables). Consistency requires the grouped instruments to be orthogonal to the grouped error term over time. This will be true if each member of the cohort has in his information set the average cohort values of the variables we use as instruments. If the individuals' information sets contain only values relating to themselves, then this orthogonality condition will not be satisfied, and cohort aggregation will not lead to consistent parameter estimates, despite our exact aggregation procedure (Pischke, 1991).

Table 5.3 reports a sequence of alternative models taken from the Banks et al. (1994) study, with the first two columns containing the most general specifications. Column 3 presents a more parsimonious representation of these results, which, as can be seen, would not be rejected by the data, and also allows us to focus on the effects of children on the change in δ_t. This retains the influence of head unemployed, and column 4 shows that the ρ parameter in particular is sensitive to the exclusion of this variable, although the overall impact on the intertemporal elasticity σ is negligible. This intertemporal substitution elasticity is evaluated at the sample mean level.

The presence of a term like δ_t is attractive because we may wish to allow for the possibility that the presence of children in certain periods may make spending in those periods more or less appealing independently of the impact of children on the within-period composition of spending. Such an effect cannot be picked up by traditional Marshallian demand analysis. The term ρ is included to allow us to estimate the degree to which families are prepared to substitute expenditure away from the relatively expensive periods.

The results of Table 5.3 complete the analysis of household expenditure patterns. Having determined σ – which will vary across households depending on their demographic, labour-supply, and consumption patterns – we can return to the Frisch elasticity decomposition (1.1) described in the Introduction. The estimated Engel, Slutsky, and Frisch elasticities provide a complete picture of substitution across time and across goods. Naturally, the interpretation of estimated elasticities depends on the theoretical assumptions required to identify them as parameters of interest. Such assumptions are fairly innocuous for Engel elasticities, but require optimizing agents behaving according to the predictions of demand theory. For the Slutsky elasticities, this requires weak separability between these within-period decisions and decisions over other goods that do not enter the modelled demand equations. For the intertemporal elasticities, we also require additive separability over time and the rational use of information, as given by the stochastic Euler or marginal-utility condition (4.4). Lying behind this first-order condition is the assumption of perfect credit markets, which implies that the real interest rate is independent of the amount of borrowing or saving that a consumer does in transferring resources optimally across time so as to satisfy the marginal-utility condition.

5 Summary and Conclusions

The approach in this chapter has been to exploit the two-stage budgeting properties of an intertemporally separable model under uncertainty to simplify the estimation of consumer preferences. That has enabled us first to identify the characteristics of within-period behaviour from a detailed microlevel demand analysis on pooled cross-section data; and then to estimate the remaining parameters that identify intertemporal behaviour using a panel of cohort data constructed from our repeated cross sections. The sequential approach has exactly mirrored the Frisch decomposition of elasticities into Engel effects, Slutsky terms, and intergroup allocations. In contrast to the work of Frisch, however, the intergroup allocations in this study are the allocations of consumption over time under uncertainty.

The advantage of the approach followed in this chapter can be seen from the invariance of the resulting within-period preference estimates to assumptions concerning the degree of intertemporal substitution. Indeed, the Engel-curve relationship was examined using nonparametric regression and using the very minimum of economic assumptions – suggesting a quadratic Engel-curve relationship between budget shares and log total expenditure. Within-period preferences were estimated using a QUAIDS demand system consistent with the finding of quadratic Engel curves. These estimates, based on a long time series of repeated cross sections, were found to be both data- and theory-coherent. The full specification of life-cycle preferences was then completed with an intertemporal analysis of consumption growth following date-of-birth cohorts through their life-cycles. Intertemporal allocations were found to depend on labour-market variables and the numbers of children, as well as the consumption level itself.

References

Altonji, J. G. (1986). Intertemporal substitution in labour supply: evidence from micro-data. *Journal of Political Economy* 94:S176–215.

Atkinson, A. B., Gomulka, J., and Stern, N. H. (1990). Spending on alcohol: evidence from the Family Expenditure Survey 1970–1983. *Economic Journal* 100:808–27.

Attanasio, O. P., and Weber, G. (1989). Intertemporal substitution, risk aversion and the Euler equation for consumption. *Economic Journal (Suppl.)* 99:59–73.

  (1993). Consumption growth, the interest rate and aggregation. *Review of Economic Studies* 60:631–50.

Banks, J., Blundell, R. W., and Lewbel, A. (1996). Tax reform and welfare measurement: Do we need demand system estimation? *Economic Journal* 106:1227–42.

  (1997). Quadratic Engel curves and consumer demand. *Review of Economics and Statistics* 79:527–39.

Banks, J., Blundell, R. W., and Preston, I. (1994). Life-cycle expenditure allocations and the consumption costs of children. *European Economic Review* 38:1391–410.

Bierens, H. J., and Pott-Buter, H. A. (1990). Specification of household Engel curves by nonparametric regression. *Econometric Reviews* 9:123–84.

Blundell, R. W. (1988). Consumer behaviour: theory and empirical evidence. *Economic Journal* 98:16–65.

Blundell, R. W., Browning, M. J., and Meghir, C. (1994). Consumer demand and the life-cycle allocation of household expenditures. *Review of Economic Studies* 61:57–80.

Blundell, R. W., Fry, V., and Meghir, C. (1989). λ-constant and alternative empirical models of life-cycle behaviour under uncertainty. In: *Advances in Microeconometrics*, ed. J.-J. Laffont et al. Oxford: Blackwell.

Blundell, R. W., and Meghir, C. (1997). Bivariate alternatives to the Tobit model. *Journal of Econometrics* 34:179–200.

Blundell, R. W., Pashardes, P., and Weber, G. (1993). What do we learn about consumer demand patterns from micro data? *American Economic Review* 83:570–97.

Blundell, R. W., and Robin, J.-M. (1997). Estimation in large disaggregated demand systems: an iterated linear least squares estimator. UCL working paper 97-5.

Blundell, R., and Walker, I. (1986). A life-cycle consistent empirical model of family labour supply using cross-section data. *Review of Economic Studies* 53:539–58.

Browning, M. J. (1986). The costs of using Frisch demand functions that are additive in the marginal utility of expenditure. *Economics Letters* 21:205–9.

Browning, M. J., Deaton, A. S., and Irish, M. (1985). A profitable approach to labour supply and commodity demands over the life-cycle. *Econometrica* 53:503–44.

Browning, M., and Meghir, C. (1991). The effects of male and female labor supply on commodity demands. *Econometrica* 59:925–51.

Chamberlain, G. (1984). Panel data. In: *Handbook of Econometrics*, ed. Z. Griliches. Amsterdam: North Holland.

Deaton, A. S. (1985). Panel data from time series of cross sections. *Journal of Econometrics* 30:109–26.

Deaton, A. S., and Muellbauer, J. (1980a). An almost ideal demand system. *American Economic Review* 70:312–26.

(1980b). *Economics and Consumer Behaviour*. Cambridge University Press.

Duncan, A. S., and Jones, A. S. (1992). NP-REG: an interactive package for kernel density estimation and non-parametric regression. IFS working paper W92/07.

Frisch, R. (1932). *New Methods of Measuring Marginal Utility*. Tübingen: Mohr.

(1959). A complete scheme for computing all direct and cross demand elasticities in a model with many sectors. *Econometrica* 27:177–96.

Gorman, W. M. (1959). Separable utility and aggregation. *Econometrica* 27:469–81.

(1981). Some Engel curves. In: *Essays in the Theory and Measurement of Consumer Behaviour*, ed. A. S. Deaton. Cambridge University Press.

Hall, R. E. (1978). Stochastic implications of the life-cycle permanent income hypothesis: theory and evidence. *Journal of Political Economy* 86:971–88.

Hansen, L. P., and Singleton, K. J. (1982). Generalised instrumental variable estimation of non-linear rational expectations models. *Econometrica* 50:1269–86.

Hardle, W. (1990). *Applied Nonparametric Regression*. Cambridge University Press.
Hardle, W., and Jerison, M. (1988). The evolution of Engel curves over time. Discussion paper no. A-178, SFB 303, University of Bonn.
Hausman, J. A., Newey, W. K., Ichimura, H., and Powell, J. L. (1991). Identification and estimation of polynomial errors in variables models. *Journal of Econometrics* 50:273–96:
Hausman, J. A., Newey, W. K., and Powell, J. L. (1995). Nonlinear errors in variables: estimation of some Engel curves. *Journal of Econometrics* 65:205–34.
Heckman, J. J. (1974). Life-cycle consumption and labour supply: an explanation of the relationship between income and consumption over the life-cycle. *American Economic Review* 64:188–94.
Heckman, J. J., and MaCurdy, T. E. (1980). A life-cycle model of female labour supply. *Review of Economic Studies* 47:47–74.
Jorgenson, D. W., Christensen, L. R., and Lau, L. J. (1975). Transcendental logarithmic utility functions. *American Economic Review* 65:367–83.
Jorgenson, D. W., and Lau, L. J. (1975). The structure of consumer preferences. *Annals of Social and Economic Measurement* 4:49–101.
  (1979). The integrability of consumer demand functions. *European Economic Review* 12:115–47.
Jorgenson, D. W., Lau, L. J., and Stoker, T. M. (1980). Welfare comparison and exact aggregation. *American Economic Review* 70:268–72.
Leser, C. (1963). Forms for Engel curves. *Econometrica* 31:694–703.
Lewbel, A. (1991). The rank of demand systems: theory and nonparametric estimation. *Econometrica* 59:711–30.
MaCurdy, T. E. (1983). A simple scheme for estimating an intertemporal model of labour supply and consumption in the presence of taxes and uncertainty. *International Economic Review* 24:265–89.
Muellbauer, J. (1976). Community preferences and the representative consumer. *Econometrica* 94:979–1000.
Nickell, S. J. (1988). The short-run behaviour of labour supply. In: *Advances in Econometrics: Fifth World Congress*, vol. 2, ed. T. F. Bewley. Cambridge University Press.
Pischke, J.-S. (1991). Individual income, incomplete information, and aggregate consumption. Discussion paper no. 91-07, Zentrum für Europaische Wirtschaftsforschung, Mannheim.
Strotz, R. H. (1957). The empirical implications of the utility tree. *Econometrica* 25:269–80.
  (1959). The utility tree – a correction and further appraisal. *Econometrica* 27:482–8.
White, H. (1980). A heteroskedasticity-consistent covariance matrix estimator and a direct test of heteroskedasticity. *Econometrica* 48:817–38.
Working, H. (1943). Statistical laws and family expenditure. *Journal of the American Statistical Association* 38:43–56.

PART THREE

PRODUCTION THEORY

CHAPTER 6

Production Functions: The Search for Identification

Zvi Griliches and Jacques Mairesse

> We have here one of those cases – so frequent in economic practice – where it can be "proved" by abstract reasoning that a solution is not possible, but where life itself compels us nevertheless to find a way out.
>
> Frisch (1934, p. 274)[1]

1 Introduction

Econometric production functions, as we know them today, originated in the work of Douglas (Cobb and Douglas, 1928). They started out as tools for testing hypotheses about the workings of marginal-productivity theory and the competitiveness of labor markets, using macroeconomic data. After a number of withering attacks by critics, this line of work shifted from macroeconomic data to microeconomic data, especially in agriculture (e.g., Tintner, 1944; Mundlak, 1961; Heady and Dillon, 1961), where the assumptions necessary for estimating something sensible appeared to be more plausible. The increasing interest in growth and technological change brought production functions back as a measurement framework for productivity at the macroeconomic level. An important "dual" literature on cost functions, factor-demand systems, and flexible functional forms emerged somewhat later, but we shall comment on it only in passing here; see Jorgenson (1986) for a review. Both approaches have undergone significant econometric questioning, focused primarily on whether or not the relationship of

---

We are indebted to Aviv Nevo for able research assistance, to R. Blundell, G. Chamberlain, B. Crepon, B. H. Hall, T. J. Klette, Y. Mundlak, and A. Pakes for helpful comments, and to the Mellon Foundation, National Science Foundation, Sloan Foundation, and the Centre National de la Recherche Scientifique for financial support. This essay has also been published in Z. Griliches, *Practicing Econometrics: Essays in Method and Application*, Edward Elgar Publishing Ltd., Cheltenham U.K. (and Northampton MA), 1998. Reprinted by permission of the publisher.

[1] Quoted from Bjerkholt (1995).

interest has really been identified or is even identifiable with the data at hand.

During empirical implementation of econometric production functions we run into a number of difficult conceptual and data problems: (1) Is what we are looking for really out there? What is it that we are approximating when we write $Q = F(K, L, \ldots)$ and apply it to a particular data set across different firms and different time periods? Does the assumed functional form make sense? (2) Do we have the right data for this enterprise? Are all outputs and inputs accounted for and measured correctly? Have allowances been made for differences in the quality of labor and other resources across our units of observation? Have we accounted for differences in the utilization of capital? (3) How was the sample generated? Is it representative of the population of interest? (4) Is the proposed estimation procedure appropriate? Can we take all or most of the input variables as "independent," or should we embed this problem in a larger simultaneous-equations framework? Do the market structure and behavioral assumptions in this framework make sense? Can they be tested? And much more.

In this essay we shall limit ourselves to only the last question, even though some of the other questions, especially those concerned with data and sample construction, may be more important substantively.[2] We shall look at this question from a somewhat idiosyncratic historical perspective, tracing out the changing ideas and justifications offered in defense of the various suggested econometric procedures as they evolved alongside advances in data availability and computing ability. We shall reiterate an old observation that because we live in a second-best world, we should be careful in focusing on only one problem; fixing it may only aggravate other problems and may not necessarily lead us closer to the truth, wherever that may be (Griliches, 1977, pp. 12–13).

Before we turn to our discussion, a word should be said about why researchers are interested in estimating production functions. In most cases a production function is a tool that provides a framework for answering other questions that are only partially related to the production function itself. It is difficult even to pose some questions without embedding them in such a framework. For example, we may be interested in a range of questions: the presence or absence of economies of scale in production (Griliches and Ringstad, 1971; Mairesse, 1975); whether productivity differences are related to the quality of labor as measured by education (Griliches, 1964), to the efficiency of capital as measured by embodied technical progress (Mairesse, 1978), to differ-

---

[2] We shall ignore a large number of other interesting and related topics: alternative functional forms; estimation of cost functions and factor-demand structures; engineering production functions; frontier production functions; nonparametric measures of productivity. See Chenery (1949), Walters (1963), Nerlove (1968), Wibe (1984), Jorgenson (1986), Lovell (1993), and Mundlak (1996) for reviews of some of these topics.

ences in public and private investments in research (Griliches, 1980; Griliches and Mairesse, 1984), or to the diffusion of information technology (Brynjolfsson and Hitt, 1995; Lichtenberg, 1995; Greenan and Mairesse, 1996); whether or not marginal products are equated to the apparent factor prices (Hellerstein and Neumark, 1998); the market structures in various industries and the degrees of the markups there (Hall, 1988). Such questions require independent estimates of cost or production functions, and they are too interesting for us to give up trying to answer them, even though the estimation framework used for these purposes may itself be problematic. We have to start someplace.

2   The Basic Criticism

One of the first penetrating criticisms of Douglas's work came from Oslo. In 1938, in an article in *Econometrica*, Horst Mendershausen, after thanking Frisch, Haavelmo, and Reiersøl for their comments and referring to Frisch's then still unpublished *Theory of Production* (1965), argued that the data used by Douglas were too multicollinear to allow for reliable determination of the production-function coefficients. Though not saying so explicitly, he implied that the underlying production function is not identifiable because the input variables are determined simultaneously by the same forces.[3] He demonstrated the last point by computing the implicit coefficients from the "other-direction" regressions and showing that there was not enough independent variability in the data to determine them reliably.[4]

The first application of the simultaneous-equations method to production-function estimation, based explicitly on Haavelmo's earlier papers, is found in Marschak and Andrews's 1944 *Econometrica* article. Their formulation of the problem can hardly be improved upon:

> Can the economist measure the effect of changing amounts of labor and capital on the firm's output – the "production function" – in the same way in which the agricultural research worker measures the effect

---

[3] In the microeconomic language of the subsequent exposition, if all firms were on the same production function and faced the same prices, they would have the same input ratios, and there would be no relevant variability on which to base an estimate of the production function.

[4] His other major criticisms were as follows: (1) The capital variable should be capital used rather than capital in place (this issue of utilization is still with us). (2) Constant returns should be tested for, not imposed. (3) Technological change should not be ignored. His was only one voice in a chorus of criticisms. The work of Douglas was also criticized on a number of other grounds, among them disbelief in the existence and/or relevance of an aggregate production function (see, e.g., the discussion of intrafirm and interfirm industry production functions by Reder, 1943) and the importance of left-out variables: trends, technology levels, and capital utilization (e.g., Schultz, 1929; Durand, 1937; Smith, 1940, 1945). Douglas (1948) acknowledged most of those criticisms, but did not mention simultaneity nor the Marschak and Andrews paper.

of changing amounts of fertilizers on the plot's yield? He cannot, because the manpower and capital used by each firm [are] determined by the firm, not by the economist. This determination is expressed by a system of functional relationships; the production function, in which the economist happens to be interested, is but one of them. [Marschak and Andrews, 1944, p. 144][5]

Their main point can be illustrated with a simple two-equation model of producer behavior. The first is the production function

$$y = \alpha z + \beta x + u \tag{2.1}$$

where y is the logarithm of output, z is the logarithm of capital (or all fixed inputs), and x is the logarithm of labor input (or all variable inputs). This is just a logarithmic transformation of the simple Cobb-Douglas production function, where, ignoring the constant term, α and β are the elasticities of interest, and u represents all the "disturbances," namely, left-out factors, efficiency differences, functional-form discrepancies, and errors of measurement.[6] The critical point made by Marschak and Andrews, and by others, is that one cannot really treat the right-hand-side variables as independent variables and proceed with estimation by ordinary least squares (OLS) as was done originally by Douglas and is still being done by most applied practitioners of this genre of research. Because the inputs are not under the control of the econometrician, but are chosen in some optimal or behavioral fashion by the producers themselves, the usual exogeneity assumptions that are required for consistency in the OLS approach are unlikely to hold for the data at hand, at least not without further detailed analysis.

Even if we accept the notion that the fixed inputs (the z terms) are predetermined for the duration of the relevant observation period, the variable inputs (the x terms) may be adjusted by the decision-maker. A simple one-period profit-maximizing model for the joint determination of x and y, given z, product prices p (which, for now, will be assumed to be equal for different producers and hence normalized to unity), and factor prices w (e.g., wages, or rather their logarithms), implies the

---

[5] This passage was preceded by another similar and equally eloquent passage: "... the economist cannot perform experiments. That is, he cannot choose one variable as 'dependent,' and, while keeping the other, 'independent,' ones under control, ... watch the values taken by the dependent, i.e., uncontrolled variable. The economist has no independent variables at his disposal because he has to take the values of all the variables as they come, produced by a mechanism outside his control. This mechanism is expressed by a system of simultaneous equations, as many of them as there are variables. The experimenter can isolate one such equation, substituting his own actions for all the other equations. The economist cannot" (Marschak and Andrews, 1944, p. 143).

[6] In Marshak and Andrews's words, u (in their notation ε_0, the deviations in the constant-term parameter A_0 of the production function) "will depend on technical knowledge, the will, effort and luck of a given entrepreneur in a given year, as can be summarized in the words 'technical efficiency'" (p. 156).

Production Functions: Identification

following marginal-productivity condition (or variable-input demand function):

$$y = x + w + v - \ln(\beta) \qquad (2.2)$$

where v represents all deviations from the assumed conditions of perfect competition, perfect foresight, and absence of risk aversion, as well as the possible measurement errors in y, x, and w.[7] Ignoring constants, we can solve these two structural equations to yield the associated reduced-form equations

$$x = (1 - \beta)^{-1}(\alpha z - w + u - v) \qquad (2.3)$$

$$y = (1 - \beta)^{-1}(\alpha z - \beta w + u - \beta v) \qquad (2.4)$$

It is clear that if x is chosen even approximately optimally, then the production-function disturbance u is "transmitted" to this decision equation, and x is a function of it. Simple OLS estimates of the production function would be biased and would not possess the desired structural interpretation. This is the main and plain message of the Marschak and Andrews paper and of a large number of subsequent expositions of the same point (e.g., Hoch, 1962; Mundlak, 1963, 1996; Mundlak and Hoch, 1965).

The responses to that message have taken a number of forms. The most common has been and still is denial, either outright denial by ignoring it or denial by claiming that it does not seriously apply to the data at hand, that the simultaneity biases are relatively unimportant.[8] In the mid-1940s and 1950s, when much of the production-function work had shifted to microeconomic data, especially farm data, many of those criticisms seemed to have less force. (There were almost no comparable microeconomic data for industry available at that time.) In particular, it was possible to assert that much of what was contained in u, such as the factors of weather and pests, was unanticipated by farmers and that most of the resources used (land, machinery, family labor) were largely predetermined and hence were uncorrelated with it. That folklore position, expressed by Hoch (1962), was formalized by Zellner, Kmenta, and Dreze (1966) by putting the producer's decision within an uncertainty framework and having the producer maximize expected profits without

---

[7] Equation (2.2) can be rewritten as $x = \log(\beta) + y - w - v$, which is the demand function for x in the Cobb-Douglas case, or as $(x + w - y) = \log(\beta) - v$, which is the share equation in this case. If we allowed free coefficients on y and w, we would have the case of nonconstant returns to scale and constant (but nonunity) elasticity of substitution (Arrow et al., 1961; Griliches and Ringstad, 1971). The disturbance v is called by Marschak and Andrews the "economic efficiency" (in their notation, ε_1, the deviation in the constant term of the "firm's supply curve for labor" or the "outlay function for labor"), and it reflects the fact that "not all entrepreneurs may have the same urge, or ability, or luck to choose the most profitable combination of production factors" (p. 156).

[8] One could also do sensitivity analyses to support it (e.g., Griliches and Ringstad, 1971).

knowing the realization of u.[9] Under those circumstances there is no transmission of u to the inputs and hence no simultaneity bias. In spite of the eminence of those authors and the locus of publication (*Econometrica*), hardly anyone has been willing to offer that rationale for the use of OLS without feeling guilty about it. The weather aspect of the story seemed especially inapplicable to industrial data. Moreover, even within the agriculture scenario it was perceived that u also contained expected permanent components, such as land quality, and that the increasing availability of panel data allowed a somewhat better solution to the problem.

At the macroeconomic level, statistical estimation of production functions was largely abandoned for a while, with the emphasis shifting to the acceptance of marginal-productivity theory (and the competition and constant-returns-to-scale assumptions that went with it) and the use of factor shares as appropriate surrogates for the unknown elasticities (Klein, 1953; Solow, 1957). Somewhat later came the "duality revolution" in production-function theory, the associated functional-form generalizations, and the move toward estimation of cost functions and factor-demand systems; see Fuss and McFadden (1978) for reviews and references. In the rush to develop an exciting new field of research, the issue of simultaneity was largely ignored (with the notable exception of Nerlove, 1963), even though the problem is actually fully symmetric. Factor-demand functions, derived from the cost-function framework, interchange the roles of x and y. To estimate them by least squares or related methods requires the assumptions that y is exogenous, uncorrelated with v [which contradicts equation (2.4)], and that y is not subject to measurement error.[10] Moreover, the expected real factor prices w must also be measured correctly by the econometrician. In short, life is not any easier on the "other side."

In this chapter we focus primarily on estimation of the production function and the use of panel data to solve the simultaneity problem. Panel data allow the use of transformations (such as "within" and first differences), the use of lagged inputs as instrumental variables, and the use of additional proxies and equations to substitute for the unobserved disturbance u.[11] Many of these responses correspond to somewhat dif-

---

[9] "The investigator may attempt to rationalize the use of single equation estimates by arguing that firms do not maximize by differentiating current (money) output with respect to input but rather differentiate 'anticipated' money output with respect to input" (Hoch, 1962, p. 37).

[10] In his 1963 paper "Returns to Scale in Electricity Supply," Nerlove used the regulatory environment within which his electrical-utility firms operated to claim, quite reasonably, that in his case these assumptions did indeed hold.

[11] Another possible response, which we shall not discuss here explicitly, is to try to reduce the role and variance of u, and thus lower the remaining biases, by introducing additional variables into the equation, such as R&D stocks and labor-quality measures.

ferent interpretations about the potential components of u and hence also about the sources of their correlation with x. We need, therefore, to be more explicit about them.

3 The Anatomy of Error

To discuss the identification problem in greater detail, we have to specify the various potential components of u, the error in the production function, and how they affect the producer's input decision. We can write u tautologically as the sum of three such components:

$$u = a + e + \varepsilon \tag{3.1}$$

where a and e are components of the disturbance that are known, ultimately, by the producer, but not by the econometrician, and ε is the net error that is introduced by measurement, data collection, and computational procedures. (It is net in the sense that it combines the effects of measurement errors in output minus the measurement errors in all the specified inputs: $\varepsilon = \varepsilon_y - \alpha\varepsilon_z - \beta\varepsilon_x$.) The distinguishing characteristic of ε is that it is the econometrician's problem, not the producer's. It can have no effect on producer behavior, either currently or in the future. In the useful terminology of Mundlak and Hoch, ε is "never transmitted."[12]

The a and e components, on the other hand, are known to the producer, but are unobservable by the econometrician; a is known in time to affect the current x choice decisions, but e reveals itself only later on and is not predictable ex ante. That is, ignoring errors of measurement, we are describing the case of "partial transmission" of u, where a can affect current behavior, but e cannot, though it may have an effect on future behavior if its realization changes the producer's future expectations about a ("delayed transmission").[13]

Given this formulation, the e components should be serially uncorrelated, but a, and hence x (and possibly also z), can be affected by their past values. The e components represent unforeseen environmental

---

[12] This distinction is similar to the distinction made by Frisch (1938 and reprinted in Bjerkholt 1995) between *aberrations* and *stimuli*.

[13] The distinction we are making here (between a and e), though sufficient for our purposes, is not precise, because it encapsulates two different aspects of the problem: the distinction between the unpredictable ("news") components in u and its predictable part and whether or not such components are transmitted to current input decisions. Both distinctions depend on the length of the observational period and the persistence (serial correlation) of such components, whereas the latter also depends on the differential fixity (adjustment costs) of the various inputs. If a component in u is unpredictable, it cannot be transmitted; however, even when predictable it may not be currently transmitted. It is also imprecise, because when a is treated as fixed, we shall also want to allow for partial transmission of the news in e to the endogenous x variables.

changes, such as unusual weather conditions, and unanticipated changes in unmeasured "effort" due to unexpected demand conditions, and they are bona fide "disturbances," independent of the predetermined z and also of the currently more variable x.

The a components represent all the misspecifications made by the econometrician in describing the producer's situation, beyond the mismeasurement of the major observable variables already encapsulated in ε. They contain both important left-out variables and functional-form approximation errors. These would include unmeasured (by the econometrician) capital components such as R&D stocks and other intangibles, technology levels and managerial efficiency, unmeasured input quality (land, labor, and capital), unmeasured variables such as man-hours and capital-hours, and possibly higher-order terms (squares, cross-products, etc.) of x and z.[14] The main point about the a components is that they are known to the producer, and hence they are transmitted, to the extent that it is relevant, to the choice of x, and also, with some delay, to the longer-run choice of the level of z.[15] This is the essence of the simultaneity problem for production-function estimation.

Given these interpretations, equation (2.2) has to be rewritten as

$$y - \varepsilon_y - e = x - \varepsilon_x + w - \varepsilon_w + v - \ln(\beta) \qquad (2.2')$$

where ε_w is the measurement error in w. Equation (2.2') is the *expected* marginal-productivity condition, net of the unanticipated components e and the measurement errors ε, and is subject to the factor-allocation disturbance v. The reduced-form equations are now

$$x = (1 - \beta)^{-1}[\alpha(z - \varepsilon_z) - (w - \varepsilon_w) + a - v] + \varepsilon_x \qquad (2.3')$$

$$y = (1 - \beta)^{-1}[\alpha(z - \varepsilon_z) - \beta(w - \varepsilon_w) + a - \beta v] + e + \varepsilon_y \qquad (2.4')$$

and only the a component of u is transmitted to the input decision (2.3') in this model.

Note that the disturbance v can also be thought of as containing different components, such as $v = m + \omega$, where m reflects potentially permanent differences in markups and all other deviations from "simple" optimality, including risk-aversion factors and functional-form approximation errors, and ω represents individual differences in expected prices,

---

[14] The last two components represent individual deviations around the point of "average" behavior approximated by the fitted function. To the extent that they result from changes in factor and product prices, both anticipated and unanticipated, this may preclude the use of prices and demand-side variables as valid instrumental variables.

[15] To simplify the exposition, z is treated as predetermined in deriving equations (2.3) and (2.4). If z is also correlated with a, then these equations can hold only after some appropriate panel-data transformation (such as within-firm or first differences) and/or after an additional equation is appended for the now endogenous z (as in the work of Marschak and Andrews).

both product and input, and transitory errors in optimization.[16] Note also that it is doubtful that we can correctly assume independence between the a and the m components, though this is an assumption that is often made.

After this taxonomic digression, we are ready to consider the various suggestions that have been made for dealing with the possibility that some components of u may also appear in the reduced-form equation for x.

4 The Panel-Data Responses

The first major response to the Marschak and Andrews criticism arose from the newly increasing availability of panels of microeconomic data, especially in agriculture. In that context, it was possible to assert that the major misspecifications that are transmitted to the factor decisions, such as differences in land, entrepreneurial, and labor quality, are largely fixed over time (or at least over the length of the available panel) and hence can be eliminated by an appropriate within transformation (or covariance analysis).[17] With i and t being the subscripts for the individual and time dimensions of the panel ($i = 1, \ldots, N; t = 1, \ldots, T$), the production function (2.1) can be written as

$$y_{it} = \alpha z_{it} + \beta x_{it} + a_i + \lambda_t + e_{it} \tag{2.1'}$$

where the a components are treated as fixed (i.e., $a_{it} = a_i$). The λ_t values are time dummy variables that capture common technological-change shocks, deflator errors, aggregate R&D and other spillover externalities, and other common shocks, such as strikes and weather, and allow such aggregate shocks to have flexible effects on y and free correlations with x and z. Leaving aside the λ_t values to simplify the exposition (they can be subsumed within the z set of variables), and going "within" (subtracting appropriate individual means from the variables), we have

$$(y_{it} - y_{i.}) = \alpha(z_{it} - z_{i.}) + \beta(x_{it} - x_{i.}) + (e_{it} - e_{i.}) \tag{4.1}$$

where the $x_{i.}$ notation represents averaging over the time dimension for individual i. To the extent that e represents weather or other unexpected events, à la Zellner et al. (1966), and is not transmitted (uncorrelated with x and z), and ignoring errors of measurement for the time being, the problem of simultaneity has been solved.

---

[16] To the extent that these deviations are permanent, they imply a nonzero expectation for v and vitiate the attempt to estimate β from the factor-share or the extended factor-demand versions of this equation arising from more general translog and other types of cost functions.

[17] Going within is not the only way of eliminating fixed effects. Differencing over a single period or more would also accomplish that purpose. We shall return to this point later.

To the best of our knowledge, this approach was first stated briefly by Hoch (1955), based on a suggestion of Hildreth, with a fuller version appearing later (Hoch, 1962). It gained its popularity, however, from a series of remarkable papers by Mundlak (1961, 1963) and Mundlak and Hoch (1965). But as empirical work on production functions also began to move to the use of industrial microeconomic data panels (Krishna, 1967; Ringstad, 1971; Mairesse, 1978; Griliches, 1980; Griliches and Mairesse, 1984), two problems emerged, one empirical and the other theoretical.

In empirical practice, application of panel methods to microeconomic data produced rather unsatisfactory results: low and often insignificant capital coefficients and unreasonably low estimates of returns to scale. A second, not unrelated problem was the realization that the within transformation either was not doing enough, in the sense that there still were potential simultaneity problems, or was doing too much, in the sense that the transformation might be aggravating other preexisting problems, such as errors in variables.

The theoretical alarm was sounded by Chamberlain (1982), who pointed out that the within transformation that results in elimination of the a_i components introduces e_i into the equation and therefore requires strict exogeneity of the x and z variables, not just their being predetermined. That is, there can be no delayed transmission; the e_{it} components must be pure errors.

Chamberlain also provided a framework for specification testing and for a more efficient estimation of equation (2.1') in the context of heteroskedastic microeconomic data. His approach consists in considering a system of T-year equations, the so-called Π-matrix system, where all past and future values of the explanatory variables are included in each of the separate-year equations. Assuming the availability of a three-year panel, and ignoring the z and λ_t (year-constant) terms for simplicity, this system is written as

$$y_{1i} = \pi_{11}x_{1i} + \pi_{12}x_{2i} + \pi_{13}x_{3i} + u_{1i}$$
$$y_{2i} = \pi_{21}x_{1i} + \pi_{22}x_{2i} + \pi_{23}x_{3i} + u_{2i} \quad (4.2)$$
$$y_{3i} = \pi_{31}x_{1i} + \pi_{32}x_{2i} + \pi_{33}x_{3i} + u_{3i}$$

Under the hypothesis that there are no individual effects a_i (or that they are not correlated with x) in equation (2.1'), the expected Π-matrix equals

$$\Pi_0 = \begin{bmatrix} \beta & 0 & 0 \\ 0 & \beta & 0 \\ 0 & 0 & \beta \end{bmatrix} \quad (4.3)$$

Production Functions: Identification

But if there are individual a_i effects and they are correlated with the x variables, and if we write their expectation as $E(a_i|x_1, x_2, x_3) = \delta_1 x_{1i} + \delta_2 x_{2i} + \delta_3 x_{3i}$, the expected Π-matrix becomes

$$\Pi_c = \begin{bmatrix} \beta + \delta_1 & \delta_2 & \delta_3 \\ \delta_1 & \beta + \delta_2 & \delta_3 \\ \delta_1 & \delta_2 & \beta + \delta_3 \end{bmatrix} \qquad (4.4)$$

Each of these assumptions implies different restrictions (i.e., that the off-diagonal terms are all zero, or that they are all equal within each column) and can be tested by comparing the results to the estimated unrestricted Π-matrix. Furthermore, Chamberlain showed that if the relevant hypotheses are accepted, the parameters of interest [i.e., β in (4.3) and (4.4)] can be estimated in a more efficient manner (in the presence of heteroskedastic and serially correlated u terms).

Chamberlain also anticipated the new set of responses: first-differencing and using lagged values of x (and z) as instrumental variables. To get around the strict exogeneity requirements on x and z, we can proceed to the first differences (or longer differencs) of the available panel data, rather than going within. This also eliminates all individual fixed effects, yielding

$$y_{it} - y_{i(t-1)} = \alpha(z_{it} - z_{i(t-1)}) + \beta(x_{it} - x_{i(t-1)}) + e_{it} - e_{i(t-1)} \qquad (4.5)$$

which can be estimated consistently by OLS if e_{it} is untransmitted to x_{it} and $x_{i(t+1)}$ (and z_{it} and $z_{i(t+1)}$), even though it may affect subsequent decisions about x (and z).[18] If the "news" in e is transmitted to the current x, then the difference in x needs to be instrumented. Because the number of available instruments, lagged x and z terms, depends on the length of the panel and changes from cross section to cross section, the optimal estimation procedures become more complex, calling for the use of general-method-of-moments (GMM) estimators (e.g., Griliches and Hausman, 1986; Arellano and Bond, 1991; Keane and Runkle, 1992; Mairesse and Hall, 1996). It can be shown (Crepon and Mairesse, 1996) that all of these approaches are already implicit in Chamberlain's Π-matrix approach and the modeling possibilities contained therein.

A slightly more general specification of (2.1') allows for both fixed effects and additional serial correlation in the remaining disturbance. Keeping a fixed, and assuming that $e_{it} = \rho e_{i(t-1)} + \xi_{it}$, we can rewrite it as

$$y_{it} = \rho y_{i(t-1)} + \alpha(z_{it} - \rho z_{i(t-1)}) + \beta(x_{it} - \rho x_{i(t-1)}) + (1-\rho)a_i + \xi_{it} \qquad (4.6)$$

---

[18] If the e_{it} are transmitted to the subsequent x and z (for $t+2$ and further), first-differences-based estimates are still consistent, though the within estimates are not.

This is now an equation in levels, and if ρ is substantially less than 1, all the variables need to be instrumented, because only part of the a_i has been eliminated by the transformation. As before, first-differencing will take care of the a_i terms, but the lagged y terms and possibly the x terms will have to be instrumented by appropriately lagged x, y, and z values. In addition, under reasonable stationarity assumptions (that the covariances of x, z, and "fixed" a_i terms are constant over time), one can also use past *differences* in x and z as instruments for the *levels* in (4.6), keeping thereby some of the relevant information in them (Arellano and Bover, 1995; Blundell and Bond, 1995). Note that as ρ approaches 1, the distinction between a_i and e_{it} disappears, and u_{it} can now be interpreted as a not-so-fixed effect, declining at the rate $1 - \rho$. When $\rho = 1$, u_{it} becomes a random walk, and (4.6) becomes (4.5), with a serially uncorrelated error ξ_{it} instead of $e_{it} - e_{i(t-1)}$.

The difficulty with these new lines of attack is that such "internal" instruments (past levels for current differences and past differences for current levels) are likely to be quite poor and possess little resolving power. We shall return to this point later. It will suffice to note that many economic variables evolve in a random-walk-like fashion at the microeconomic level; that is, their growth rates (or log differences) are only weakly serially correlated. If the x and z terms were strictly random walks, there would be no power at all in their past levels as instruments for their current differences. Using past differences as instruments for current levels may be better. But in any case we must ask what behavioral theory implies the validity of such instruments. Lags in adjustments to shocks would do it, but even if valid, the available power is likely to be rather low. Ultimately, to do better will require bringing in some additional information from somewhere else: "external" instruments, more theoretical restrictions on the structure, and/or more equations. This is where the current frontier lies. But before we proceed to describe it, we need to indicate the magnitude of the empirical problem faced by researchers in this area.

5 The Empirical Experience

From the beginning, the within (covariance-analysis) results were not what one had hoped for. In the original 1955 note by Hoch, when farm effects were eliminated from the analysis, the estimated returns to scale fell from 1.0 to 0.6, forcing Hoch to interpret that "shortfall" as reflecting returns to unmeasured (fixed?) entrepreneurial capacity, but leaving him with unreasonably low estimated marginal returns to the relatively quasi-fixed labor and land inputs.[19]

---

[19] Similar results and a similar interpretation also appear in the original Mundlak (1961) study. See also Griliches (1957).

Production Functions: Identification 181

Similar, more recent examples of the same problem can be seen in Figure 5.1, based on 13 years of panel data for manufacturing firms in France, Japan, and the United States. It graphs different estimates of α and $\mu = \alpha + \beta$, the capital and scale elasticities in the Cobb-Douglas production function (2.1') derived from different cuts of the data: total pooled data, 13-year firm averages, firms' deviations from their averages, and a parallel set of estimates based on first differences in these same data sets.[20]

Whereas the first-differences transformation also eliminates whatever fixed individual effects a_i there might have been in the data, it also allows for not-so-fixed individual effects, and if they evolve as random walks, $\rho = 1$ in (4.6), then $u = u_{-1} + \xi$. We can also go further and consider the resulting $T - 1$ set of cross sections of differences as another panel, repeating the whole covariance-analysis partition into "between" and "within" once more. The major argument for this further step is that it allows us to consider individual effects that change smoothly over time, but at different rates.[21] These are eliminated by the "within differences." The "between differences," which in our data represent the average (log) growth rates of the various variables for the period as a whole, are just the normalized (divided by $T - 1$) long differences.[22] They can be viewed as a combination of first differences (with equal weights for all years), which also eliminates the individual effects, but does so, as we shall see later, with a different impact on the variances of the variables (and the error terms) than the various other within or difference transformations.[23]

Looking at Figure 6.1, we can see that the estimates of α and μ decline as we buy more protection, moving from the total and between estimates in levels to the between differences and within levels, and further to total and within differences. As we guard against various misspecifications by purging additional "components" from the available data, basing

---

[20] These different estimates are referred to in Figure 5.1 and Table 5.1 and subsequently in the text by the following shortcut expressions: "total levels," "between levels," "within levels," "total differences," "between differences," and "within differences." The former estimates (total and between in levels) are also referred to as cross-sectional-type estimates, and the latter (based on transformations of the data that eliminate the fixed effects) are referred to as time-series-type estimates.

[21] The idea of individual trends is not new and keeps reappearing in various forms. An early statement is that by Mundlak (1970).

[22] Obviously $\left[\sum_{t=2}^{T}(y_{it} - y_{i(t-1)})\right]/(T - 1) = (y_{iT} - y_{i1})/(T - 1)$.

[23] Under the hypothesis of fixed effects and identically independently distributed (iid) e_{it} values, the within-levels estimator is BLUE (best linear unbiased estimator), while first-differences and between-differences estimators are only consistent. Assuming random measurement errors, they are all inconsistent, but by different amounts. This is the basis for the specification tests suggested by Griliches and Hausman (1986).

182   Zvi Griliches and Jacques Mairesse

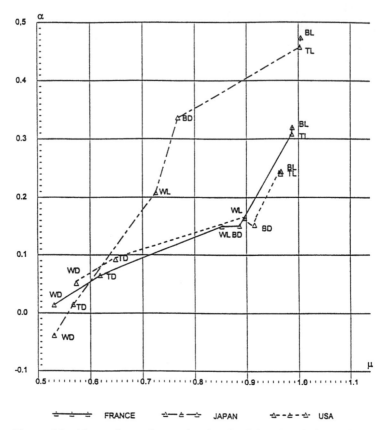

Figure 6.1. Alternative estimates for the elasticity of capital α and the elasticity of scale μ for three panel-data samples: French, Japanese, and American manufacturing firms, 1967–79 (N = 441, 845, and 462; T = 13). BL, between, in levels ($Y_{i.}$); TL, total, in levels (Y_{it}); BD, between, in differences ($\Delta Y_{i.}$); WL, within, in levels ($Y_{it} - Y_{i.}$); TD, total, in differences (ΔY_{it}); WD, within, in differences ($\Delta Y_{it} - \Delta Y_{.t}$). (From Mairesse, 1990.)

inference on progressively smaller fractions of the original data, both coefficients move toward zero, with the capital coefficient falling faster than the scale coefficient, often actually reaching zero. As the amounts of variance in x and z that are used to identify the relevant coefficients are continuously reduced, other misspecifications overwhelm the remaining signal in the data.[24] The simplest and oldest interpretation of

---

[24] Most of the variability in the levels of the data is in the cross-sectional dimension, while most of the variability in the first differences is in the time dimension. This explains the pairwise closeness of the total-levels and between-levels parameter estimates and also the total-differences and within-differences parameter estimates.

Table 6.1. *Alternative Estimates of the Elasticity of Capital α and Measurement-Error-Bias Multipliers: French Manufacturing Firms, 1967–79 (N = 441)*

Estimation method	Estimated α (1)	t_a (2)	Net variance of capital Absolute $\sigma^2_{z.x}$ (3)	Relative $m_{z.x}$ (4)	Measurement-error multipliers[a] Error variance m_ε (5)	Error bias m_b (6) = (5)/(4)
Total levels	0.304	34.8	0.3023	1	1	1
Between levels	0.315	10.1	0.2851	0.943	0.077	0.08
Within levels	0.146	12.0	0.0245	0.081	0.923	11.4
Total differences	0.061	3.4	0.0085	0.028	2	71.3
Long differences[b]	0.147	3.7	0.1282	0.424	2	4.7
Within differences	0.010	0.5	0.0074	0.024	1.986	80.9

[a] Under the assumption of random measurement errors in capital ε, the probability limit of the estimated α is given by

$$\text{plim } \hat{\alpha} = \alpha - \alpha \sigma^2_\varepsilon / \sigma^2_{z.x}$$

The error-bias multiplier m_b (column 6) taking total levels as a benchmark, is equal to $m_\varepsilon/m_{z.x}$, where m_ε and $m_{z.x}$ (in columns 4 and 5) are respectively the error variance and the net variance of capital multipliers.
[b] This line is in terms of the longest difference (1979–67). For the parallel between-differences calculation, the entries in columns 3 and 4 should both be divided by 144 (12 × 12).

this phenomenon is magnification of the role of random measurement errors as we reduce the identifying variance by the within or differencing transformations (or similarly by adding more variables to the estimating equation).[25]

Table 6.1 provides the ingredients for such an errors-in-variables interpretation of the results for the estimated capital elasticities in the sample of French firms (N = 441).[26] Columns 1 and 2 of this table give the estimated α values for the various methods and their corresponding t-ratios, and column 3 lists $\sigma^2_{z.x}$, the "net" variance of z (log of capital), net of its relationship to labor and time and industry dummies, with

---

[25] For repeated restatements of this point, see Griliches (1974, 1986), Mairesse (1978, 1990), and Griliches and Hausman (1986).
[26] This interpretation also works approximately for the estimated capital elasticities in the Japanese and U.S. samples. It does not carry over so neatly to the estimated labor elasticities. These do not decline as much as the capital elasticities when we move from between to within, and from level to difference estimates. The biases in the labor coefficients may be the results of convolution of the upward simultaneity bias and the downward measurement-error bias.

column 4, $m_{z.x}$, showing it as a ratio relative to the untransformed data variance (i.e., total levels). First, notice that the net variance of z declines roughly in parallel with the estimated α values and their t-ratios. In general, a lower net variance will give us more imprecise estimates, but that does not imply a larger downward bias per se.[27] The bias must come from some other source whose relative influence grows as the signal contained in the remaining variance of z keeps declining. A major suspect in this case is measurement error, because its variance σ_ε^2 does not decline in proportion to $\sigma_{z.x}^2$, making the standard assumption that it is not serially correlated, or weakly so (much less than z given x). Column 5 in Table 6.1 gives m_ε as the multiplier computed for uncorrelated errors, with $m_\varepsilon = 1$ in the untransformed data. For example, m_ε is 0.077 (i.e., 1/13) for the between levels, and 2 for the first-difference estimators, whereas $m_{z.x}$ is 0.943 and 0.028, respectively. The absolute random-measurement-error bias in α is $(\hat{\alpha} - \alpha) = -\alpha\sigma_\varepsilon^2/\sigma_{z.x}^2$ in large enough samples, and thus the multiplier for this bias is $m_b = m_\varepsilon/m_{z.x}$, given in column 6 of Table 6.1. It is about 11 times larger in the within levels than in the total levels, and 160 times larger than in the between levels, and it is 15–17 times larger in the total (first) differences and the within differences than in the long differences. We also see that long differences eliminate the fixed effects with the smallest magnification of the measurement-error bias, only about half of the bias in the within-levels estimator.

If we thought that random errors of measurement were the only problem with the data, we could infer both a consistent estimate of the true α and an estimate of σ_ε^2 from the numbers given in the first and last columns of Table 6.1. Using all six "estimates," a regression of the estimated α on m_b yields 0.244 and 0.0035 as the respective estimates for α and σ_ε^2. Dropping the first two observations, because they may be subject to correlated fixed-effects bias, gives 0.161 and 0.0031 as the respective estimates. The latter regression has an adjusted R^2 of 0.93 and a standard error of estimate 0.02, so this "model" fits rather well.[28] But, as we shall see later, it may not make much sense in this particular context.

We have made various attempts to eliminate such errors-in-the-variables (and simultaneity) biases in these particular samples, using lagged values of x and z (and y) as instruments for the first differences in equation (4.5) or (4.6) in a GMM framework, and/or using the lagged values of the first differences in x and z (and y) as instruments for the levels in these same equations. Most of the results were quite disap-

---

[27] The reason that the t-ratios decline is similar to the argument (given later) for the magnification of the measurement-error bias: The variance of the error in the equation σ_u^2 does not decline as fast as $\sigma_{z.x}^2$.

[28] Clearly, more efficient minimum-distance (or asymptotic least-squares) estimators could be computed if one believed it.

Table 6.2. *Alternative Estimates of Production-Function Parameters: U.S. R&D and Non-R&D Manufacturing Firms, 1982–87 (N = 676)*

	Levels					First differences		
	OLS		Instrumented by differences			OLS	Instrumented by levels	
Variable	(1)	(2)	(3)	(4)	(5)	(6)	(7)	(8)
Labor	0.567	0.616	0.665	0.750	0.652	0.613	0.611	0.705
	(0.008)[a]	(0.013)	(0.048)	(0.027)	(0.046)	(0.013)	(0.062)	(0.024)
Capital	0.402	0.122	0.277	0.289	0.314	0.114	0.110	0.084
	(0.007)	(0.012)	(0.036)	(0.027)	(0.031)	(0.012)	(0.037)	(0.019)
R&D stock	0.016	0.041	0.033	0.025	0.030	0.030	0.059	0.046
	(0.004)	(0.012)	(0.017)	(0.017)	(0.010)	(0.013)	(0.022)	(0.017)
Lagged output	0	0.981	0	0.573	0.654	1	1	1
		(0.004)		(0.023)	(0.031)			

Notes: Estimates in columns 2, 4, and 5 [equation (4.6)] are constrained to the same ρ coefficient in $(x - \rho x_{-1})$ and ρy_{-1}. Additional variables included in the equations: no-R&D dummy variable, year dummies, computer-industry dummy, and interaction with year. Instrument sets:

For levels:
  Columns 3 and 4: all differences as of $t - 2$ and earlier, for l, c, k, and y_{-1}
  Column 5: c and k treated as predetermined; only l and y_{-1} instrumented
For differences:
  Column 6: levels as of $t - 2$ and earlier for l, c, and k
  Column 7: c and k treated as predetermined; only l instrumented.

[a] Standard error.
Source: Adapted from Griliches (1998).

pointing. The resulting capital coefficient α was close to zero and usually was not statistically significantly different from it (in spite of the large number of degrees of freedom): Its implicit net variance (as computed from the estimated standard error) was minuscule. In the French sample, for example, instrumenting the first-differences equation by levels of labor, capital, and output lagged by two periods or more yielded an $\hat{\alpha} = 0.05$, with a t-ratio of 0.5, and an implicit net variance of capital of 0.0003.[29]

Somewhat better-looking GMM-based estimates are shown in Table 6.2, taken from Griliches (1998), who looked for the contributions of two capital stocks (physical and R&D) in a panel of U.S. firms; see also

---

[29] The implicit net variance $\sigma^2_{z \cdot x}$ is computed by analogy from $\hat{\sigma}^2_{\hat{\alpha}} = \hat{\sigma}^2_u / \mathrm{df}(\sigma^2_{z \cdot x})$, where $\hat{\sigma}^2_u$ is the estimated residual variance, $\hat{\sigma}^2_{\hat{\alpha}}$ is the estimated variance of the estimated coefficient, and df is the appropriate degrees of freedom.

Mairesse and Hall (1996) and Blundell and Bond (1996), who used similar panels extracted from the NBER manufacturing master file, as constructed by and updated by B. H. Hall (1990).[30] Columns 1 and 6 show the OLS estimates for levels and first differences, respectively [equations (2.1′) and (4.5)]. Column 2 allows for serial correlation [equation (4.6)] and shows it to be very high (as could be expected). Columns 3 and 4 repeat the level computations of columns 1 and 2 allowing for the endogeneity of all the input (and lagged output) variables, using past differences in these variables (from the years $t - 2$ and before) as instrumental variables.[31] Column 5 is similar, but it instruments only the labor and lagged output variables, treating the two capital stocks as predetermined.[32] Columns 7 and 8 present the corresponding estimates of this equation in first differences, instrumented by past levels. The first-differences transformation is optimal if the not-so-fixed effect is a random walk [$\rho = 1$ in (4.6)]. Column 7 uses past levels as instruments for all three variables, which is appropriate if there are random measurement errors in them or some remaining contemporaneous simultaneity. Column 8 instruments only the labor variable.

If we take column 5 as the preferred estimate, it indicates a large and plausible physical-capital coefficient of about 0.30 and a substantively and statistically significant R&D-capital coefficient of about 0.03. These results do not really change when we also instrument the two capital stocks (column 4), except for a large increase in the standard error of the R&D coefficient. As we approach the limit of $\rho = 1$ (first differences, columns 6–8) there is hardly any identifying variance left in the annual changes in our measures of physical and R&D capitals. Though the estimated R&D coefficient remains substantial and significant, the estimated physical-capital coefficient declines to the rather unlikely low value of 0.10. Measurement and timing errors now predominate, and the remaining information content in the instruments is too small to allow us to extract whatever signal is still left in these variables.

Using first differences and then instrumenting them to take care of errors of measurement does not really work for capital. Because measurement errors in capital are likely to persist, the within or difference transformations should have reduced their role, rather than magnified it![33] What might, then, be an alternative interpretation? The simplest explanation is that we have the timing of the influence of capital wrong.

---

[30] For a discussion of the concept of R&D capital, see Griliches (1995).
[31] Using instruments from $t - 3$ rather than $t - 2$ increases the standard errors but has little effect on the reported results.
[32] The argument here for not instrumenting the true capital stock is that in quasi differences (with ρ being large) the currently transmitted component of the error $(1 - \rho)a_i$ is small and can be neglected.
[33] This is particularly true when the capital stock (as in the case of R&D) is measured as the sum of depreciated past investments. If we assume, for example, a constant geometric depreciation pattern at the rate δ and uncorrelated (iid) measurement errors in invest-

If there are gestation lags, difference transformations could produce entirely irrelevant numbers, and the GMM estimates would not be of any help either. For example, consider the case in which investment has an assumed service life of six years, and let the weights of the past investments I in the true capital K^* be $(0, 1, 2, 2, 1, 0)$, instead of all being unity.[34] Assuming that the I values are serially uncorrelated and have a constant variance, the coefficient of the first-differenced incorrect capital measure K will then be exactly zero, and if we try the difference lagged one period, its coefficient will be approximately one-half the appropriate size.[35] It is not that capital does not matter; it is that our timing is wrong and may get worse as we apply various difference transformations.

Other sources of misspecification could also contribute to the observed results. (All could be guilty!) These include the omission of labor- and capital-utilization variables, such as hours of work per employee, and the use of sales rather than value added, or alternatively the omission of materials among the included factors. As shown by Griliches and Mairesse (1984), these omissions add to the content of the e terms [in (3.1)] and are the likely sources of upward biases in β. They will also show up as downward biases in α, because x and z are likely to be positively correlated.[36] Such biases are much more important in the time dimension of the data than in its cross-sectional dimension. Also, the maintained assumption of a perfectly competitive environment becomes more and more dubious as firms face a variety of shorter-run market imperfections. We shall come back to this last point later.

6   Other Approaches

One early "solution" to the simultaneity problem was to assume profit maximization (both ex ante and ex post) and perfect competition and

---

ment, the serial correlation of measurement errors on the resulting stock is $1 - \delta$, say 0.85 if $\delta = 0.15$, as assumed in the construction of R&D capital. This may be less true when the capital-stock measure is based on the gross or net book values of fixed assets in firms' balance sheets (with some adjustment for inflation, as in the case of our physical-capital variables). There are other sources of random errors arising from the actual bookkeeping procedures (e.g., in the assessment of retirements, maintenance costs, and reevaluations).

[34] One can find some evidence for such a pattern (Pakes and Griliches, 1984). Note that in this case the serial correlation of measurement errors in the capital stock would also be about 0.85 (i.e., $1 - 1/L$, where L is the service life).

[35] Under our assumption, we have $\Delta K_t = (I_{t-1} - I_{t-7})$ and $\Delta K_{t-1} = (I_{t-2} - I_{t-8})$, while $\Delta K_t^* = (I_{t-2} + I_{t-3} - I_{t-5} - I_{t-6})$, and hence, with constant variance and serially uncorrelated I terms, the coefficients of the auxiliary regressions of ΔK_t and ΔK_{t-1} on ΔK_t^* are respectively 0 and $\frac{1}{2}$. Note that these computations are only approximate, taking the production function to be linear (and not log-linear) in the capital stock (and considering the changes in capital to be uncorrelated with those in labor).

[36] See Appendix C of Griliches and Ringstad (1971) for an exposition of this point.

use the observed factor shares as estimates of the relevant production-function parameters. That was proposed by Klein (1953) for the Cobb-Douglas production function and was extended by Solow (1957), who used varying factor shares to compute the "residual" technical change without actually "estimating" (econometrically) the possibly more general underlying production function (Nerlove, 1968, ch. 4). The major difficulty with such a solution is that it begs some of the questions we might want to ask of the data, especially about the extent of profit maximization, competition, and economies of scale.[37] But it may prove adequate when applied to only some of the parameters of interest. Thus, Griliches and Ringstad (1971) used it to "solve" the simultaneity problem created by the endogeneity of the variable inputs x, estimating effectively a "partial-productivity" equation

$$y - s_x x = az + u \tag{6.1}$$

where s_x, the share of variable inputs in total sales, is taken as a consistent estimator of β, x is a similar share-weighted sum of all variable inputs (e.g., labor and materials), and z is assumed to be predetermined and to provide information on the scale parameter. Hall (1988) freed up the coefficient of s_x, assumed constant returns to scale, and estimated

$$y - z = m s_x (x - z) + u \tag{6.2}$$

to test the competitive assumption and estimate the "markup" coefficient m using a number of demand-side macroeconomic variables as instruments.[38] Klette (1994) followed a similar approach.

The obvious extension of the factor-shares solution is to use factor prices as instrumental variables to identify the parameters of interest. This is the essence of the "duality" approach to estimation. At the microeconomic level, the only factor prices available usually are average earnings of workers, and possibly also fuel prices. There are, however, several difficulties in using such price data as valid instruments. Why do wages differ across firms at a point in time and within firms over time? The first is likely to be related to unmeasured differences in the quality of labor,

---

[37] Equation (2.2) can be rewritten as $\ln(s_x) = \ln(\beta) - v$, where $s_x = (WX/PY)$ is the share of X in total revenue, and gives an estimate of β. The question of what average and transformation to use for this estimate depends on the assumed distribution of v (Is $Ev = 0$?) and on whether maximization is expected to be correct on the median, the arithmetic, or the geometric average. See Goldberger (1968) and Griliches and Ringstad (1971, p. 73) for additional discussion of this set of issues.

[38] Abbott, Griliches, and Hausman (1988) and Eden and Griliches (1993) raise questions about the validity of Hall's instruments. If u contains short-run specification errors, such as capital-utilization and labor-effort measures, that are related to expectational errors made by the decision-makers when choosing their desired capital and employment levels, then unanticipated macroeconomic shifts may cause such errors and cannot serve as valid instruments in this context.

and the second may fluctuate with unexpected shifts in the amount of overtime compensation. Even if there are aggregate time-series movements in the real wage and also valid regional wage differences, the use of time and firm dummies (i.e., estimating within or in differences) will eliminate their contribution from the data, leaving us mostly with inappropriate or erroneous variation in these numbers. Moreover, the right prices in such an analysis are "expected" prices, rather than the realized and possibly endogenous ones.[39]

As suggested by Mundlak (1963, 1996), a related (but also not very workable) solution idea is to use as an instrument the "whole" marginal-productivity equation (2.2) (i.e., $y - x = w + v$, ignoring the constant), because it contains both the factor prices w and the errors in optimization v. This assumes that all of u is transmitted to the x choice and thus does not enter this equation directly and that, in addition, u and v are independent, which might be reasonable after a within- or first-differences transformation that would eliminate firm effects. Under these conditions, labor productivity $(y - x)$ would be a valid instrument for x in the production function, and if there were more than one variable input, then the various input ratios $x_i - x_j$ would also be valid instruments. But the moment we introduce only partial transmission (i.e., non-negligible e and/or ε terms), that would no longer be legitimate. What may be possible is the use of lagged values of such terms (on the assumption that the currently untransmitted news e and errors of measurement ε are serially uncorrelated). Then we come back to the use of Chamberlain or GMM-type estimators (i.e., the use of lagged values of x and z and also possibly y as instruments), which we have already discussed.

Another related "semi-solution," proposed by Griliches and Mairesse (1984), proceeds to estimate the reduced-form equations (2.3) and (2.4), proxying the unavailable factor and product prices by time and individual-firm dummy variables (Hall and Mairesse, 1995). These semi-reduced-form equations may allow one to estimate $a/(1 - \beta)$ and, if there is more than one fixed input z, the relative sizes of the a terms (e.g., the relative sizes of the physical-capital and R&D-capital elasticities). These estimates will be unbiased to the extent that the residual variation in factor prices is uncorrelated with the fixed inputs z. This is plausible in the within or differences dimensions, because there is little relevant variance left in w (and p) after taking out their common time-series components with time dummies or a trend variable.[40]

---

[39] This criticism applies also to the literature on cost-function and factor-demand-system estimation, which leans rather heavily on the correctness and exogeneity of the price data used in the analysis.

[40] If factor prices w are available, the (full) reduced-form equations (2.3) and (2.4) are just identified, and estimating them is equivalent to estimating the production function directly using the w variables as instruments.

An interesting new approach, which we shall present at some length, is advocated by Olley and Pakes (1996) in their paper "The Dynamics of Productivity in the Telecommunications Equipment Industry." This paper deals with two topics: selectivity and simultaneity, in an intertwined fashion. The sample selectivity problem may be quite serious for panel data. If observations (and data) are not missing at random, estimates that are based on "clean" and "balanced" subsamples can be severely biased. For example, a bad draw of u may force a firm or plant to exit from the industry. Such a negative correlation between estimated productivity shocks and future probabilities of exit was observed by Griliches and Regev (1995) in their analysis of Israeli industrial firms. They called it "the shadow of death." If the impact of negative u values on exit is stronger for smaller firms (the larger ones having more resources to survive such impact), then that will induce a negative correlation between u and z (the stock of capital) among the surviving firms and bias the estimated capital coefficient downward in balanced samples.

To simplify our exposition, we consider the Olley and Pakes approach to the simultaneity problem first. Their major innovation is to proxy for a, the unobserved transmitted component of u, by bringing in a new equation, the investment equation.[41] Trying to proxy for the unobserved a (if it can be done right) has several advantages over the usual within estimators (or the more general Chamberlain and GMM-type estimators): It does not assume that a reduces to a "fixed" (over time) firm effect; it leaves more identifying variance in x and z and hence is a less costly solution to the omitted-variable and/or simultaneity problems; and it should also be substantively more informative.

Their argument is roughly as follows: The investment decision of a firm at time t can be viewed as a function of its predetermined capital z_t and of a_t, the transmitted component of u_t:

$$i_t = i_t(a_t, z_t) \tag{6.3}$$

where the function $i_t(\ )$ is allowed to change over time. Inverting this function, a_t can be written as a function of both capital z_t and investment i_t:

$$a_t = h_t(i_t, z_t) \tag{6.4}$$

where the potentially observable function h_t is now a perfect proxy for the unobserved a_t. Substituting h_t for a_t in $u = a + e + \varepsilon$ and the production function (2.1), and ignoring the measurement errors ε, leads to

$$y_t = \beta x_t + \phi_t(i_t, z_t) + e_t \tag{6.5}$$

where the function $\phi_t = \alpha z_t + a_t = \alpha z_t + h_t(i_t, z_t)$ "contains" the unobserved a_t variable. Because both i and z are observed, if the form of h or

---

[41] In their notation, a is ω, and they refer to it simply as "productivity."

Production Functions: Identification

ϕ were known, β could be estimated consistently by OLS. Note, however, that α is not identified at this point, because z_t is also in h_t. In practice, Olley and Pakes approximate ϕ_t by a third- or fourth-order polynomial in i and z to estimate β. Using the estimated β, we can now proceed to estimate α. If z_t and a_t were uncorrelated, we would simply use the partial-productivity equation

$$y_t - \hat{\beta}x_t = \alpha z_t + a_t + e_t \tag{6.6}$$

More reasonably, if we assume that z_t is uncorrelated only with the change in a_t, $\zeta_t = a_t - a_{t-1}$ (i.e., a_t is a random walk), we can estimate α from

$$y_t - \hat{\beta}x_t - \hat{\phi}_{t-1} = \alpha(z_t - z_{t-1}) + \zeta_t + e_t \tag{6.7}$$

where $\hat{\phi}$ is the estimated polynomial in i and z, and $(\hat{\phi}_{t-1} - \alpha z_{t-1})$ is proxying for a_{t-1}.[42]

Returning to the selectivity issue, Olley and Pakes add to equation (6.5) a probability-of-survival equation, which they estimate nonparametrically as a function of i_{t-1} and z_{t-1}. Using the estimated probability of survival λ_t [and the $\hat{\beta}$ and $\hat{\phi}_t$ estimated in equation (6.5)], they show that equation (6.7) becomes

$$y_t - \hat{\beta}x_t = \alpha z_t + g_t(\hat{\phi}_{t-1} - \alpha z_{t-1}, \hat{\lambda}_t) + \zeta_t + e_t \tag{6.8}$$

where the function g_t is approximated by a general polynomial (of order 3) in $\hat{\lambda}_t$ and $(\hat{\phi}_{t-1} - \alpha z_{t-1})$, and α is then estimated nonlinearly across all the terms that contain it.[43]

The main Olley-Pakes results are summarized in Table 6.3, and Table 6.4 presents an application of a simplified version of their model to U.S. data for firms that conduct R&D, focusing on the estimation of two

---

[42] This simplification (that a_t is a random walk) is made by us for expositional purposes. If it were an AR(1) process with the parameter ρ, a_t would be approximated by $\rho(\hat{\phi}_{t-1} - a_{t-1}z)$ in (6.6). More generally, Olley and Pakes (1996) assume only that a_t is an exogenous process and approximate it by a polynomial in $(\hat{\phi}_{t-1} - \alpha z_{t-1})$ [i.e., equation (6.8), where it is a function also of the estimated probability of survival] and estimate α nonlinearly across the various terms that contain it.

[43] The argument is approximately as follows: The probability of survival at time t, $\lambda_t = \lambda_t(a_{t-1}, \bar{a}_t)$, depends on a_{t-1} and $\bar{a}_t$, where $\bar{a}_t$ is the unobserved initial level of a_t that would cause the firm to exit. Assuming we know λ_t, this function can be inverted to yield an estimate of $\bar{a}_t$ as a function of λ_t and a_{t-1}, and thus of λ_t and $(\hat{\phi}_{t-1} - \alpha z_{t-1})$. Because $\bar{a}_t$ is itself a function of z_t, and hence of z_{t-1} and i_{t-1}, λ_t can be estimated by the equation $\hat{\lambda}_t = \lambda_t(z_{t-1}, i_{t-1})$, and

$$E(y_t - \beta x_t | a_{t-1} \text{ and survival}) = \alpha z_t + E(a_t | a_{t-1} \text{ and survival})$$
$$= \alpha z_t + g_t(a_{t-1}, \bar{a}_t)$$
$$= \alpha z_t + g_t(\hat{\phi}_{t-1} - \alpha z_{t-1}, \hat{\lambda}_t)$$

which is equation (6.8).

Table 6.3. *Alternative Estimates of Production-Function Parameters: U.S. Telecommunications-Equipment Plants, 1974–86*

	Sample					
	Balanced panel		Full sample[a]			
	(1)	(2)	(3)	(4)	(5)	(6)
Variables	Total	Within	Total OLS		Nonparametric F	
Labor	0.851	0.728	0.693	0.628	0.608	
	(0.039)[b]	(0.049)	(0.019)	(0.020)	(0.027)	
Physical capital	0.173	0.067	0.304	0.219	0.339	0.342
	(0.034)	(0.049)	(0.018)	(0.018)	(0.030)	(0.035)
Age	0.002	−0.006	−0.0046	−0.001	0.000	−0.001
	(0.003)	(0.016)	(0.0026)	(0.002)	(0.004)	(0.004)
Time	0.024	0.042	0.016	0.012	0.011	0.044
	(0.006)	(0.017)	(0.004)	(0.004)	(0.010)	(0.019)
Investment	—	—	—	0.130	—	
				(0.010)		
Other variables	—	—	—	—	Powers of h	Polynomial in P and h
No. of observations[c]	896		2,592		1,758	

[a] Consult the text for details of the estimation algorithm leading up to columns 5 and 6.
[b] Standard error.
[c] The number of observations in the balanced panel for regressions in columns 1 and 2 are the observations for those plants that have continuous data over the period, with zero-investment observations removed. Similarly, the 2,592 observations in columns 3 and 4 are all observations in the full sample, except those with zero investment. Approximately 8% of the full data set had observations with zero investment. The number of observations in columns 5 and 6 decreased to 1,758 because lagged values of some of the independent variables were needed in estimation.

Source: Adapted from Olley and Pakes (1996, table 6).

capital coefficients: physical and R&D.[44] The two sets of results tell largely the same story, though the selectivity problem matters only in the Olley-Pakes plant data. Its magnitude is reflected (Table 6.3) in the decline in the estimated capital elasticity α as we move from the unbalanced sample (column 3) to the balanced sample (column 1). Possibly because exit is often a success for R&D firms (being taken over), rather

---

[44] Our approach differs somewhat from that of Olley and Pakes (1996) because it uses data separated by five years, rather than adjacent cross sections and only quadratic and cross-product terms in the polynomial approximations and parametric assumptions (normality) for the selection equation.

Table 6.4. *Alternative Estimates of Production-Function Parameters: U.S. R&D-Performing Firms, 1973, 1978, 1983, 1988*

	\multicolumn{6}{c}{Sample}
	\multicolumn{2}{c}{Balanced Panel}	\multicolumn{4}{c}{Full Sample}
Variables	(1) Total	(2) Within	(3) Total OLS	(4)	(5) Nonparametric F^a	(6)
Labor	0.496 (0.022)[b]	0.685 (0.030)	0.578 (0.013)	0.551 (0.013)	0.591 (0.013)	
Physical capital	0.460 (0.014)	0.180 (0.027)	0.372 (0.009)	0.298 (0.012)	0.321 (0.016)	0.320 (0.017)
R&D capital	0.034 (0.015)	0.099 (0.027)	0.038 (0.007)	0.027 (0.007)	0.081 (0.016)	0.077 (0.019)
Investment	—	—	—	0.110 (0.011)	—	
Other variables[c]	—	—	—	—	Powers of h	Polynomial in P and h
No. of observations[d]		856		2,971		1,571

[a] Consult the text for details of the estimation algorithm leading up to columns 5 and 6.
[b] Standard error.
[c] All equations include "Year" and "Year × Industry 357" (i.e., computer) dummy variables.
[d] The number of observations in the balanced panel for regressions in columns 1 and 2 are the observations for those firms that have continuous data over the period. Similarly, the 2,971 observations in columns 3 and 4 are all observations in the full sample. (Only six observations had to be discarded because of zero investment.) The number of observations in columns 5 and 6 decreased to 1,571 because lagged values of some of the independent variables were needed in estimation.

than a failure, the selection problem is less severe in Table 6.4, and we find only a small increase in the estimated a. Once we shift to the unbalanced samples, the remaining selectivity (mainly attrition) does not appear to matter much (compare columns 5 and 6 in both tables).

As far as the simultaneity problem is concerned, either it is of no great import in these data or the introduction of investment and the associated Olley-Pakes procedure does not fully adjust for it. Looking at Tables 6.3 and 6.4, investment is highly significant in the production function, but at the end of the procedure (having allowed for sample selectivity and unbalance) the coefficients change only little (compare columns 3 and 5 or 6 in both tables). They change more in the Olley-Pakes data, where the labor coefficient is reduced by about 10 percent (from 0.69 to 0.61) and the capital coefficient is increased by about the same percentage (from 0.30 to 0.34), which goes in the "right" direction. In our own data, the changes are quite small and go slightly in the "wrong" direction (labor "up," and the sum of the "capital" coefficients down) and probably are not statistically significant.[45]

The Olley-Pakes solution to the simultaneity problem is a clever way to exploit the fact that the unobserved "productivity shocks" a_t are transmitted to more than just one equation and should be estimated within a system of behavioral equations. It does rest, however, on two very strong assumptions: that there is only *one* single-component unobservable in the system, the a_t, which follows a first-order Markov process and is fully transmitted to the investment equation, and that no other variables or errors appear in this equation. Macroeconomic variables are taken into account implicitly by letting the h and g functions change over time. Investment will, however, depend also on individual factors such as interest-rate expectations, tax treatments, and changes in future-demand prospects not yet captured in the state variable z_t. In principle, there may be additional instrumental variables and other indicators of a_t, such as R&D, that could help solve the errors in the investment-equation problem, except for the extreme nonlinearities introduced by the Olley-Pakes semiparametric approach.[46]

Even more problematic is the assumption that investment i_t depends on the whole of a_t. If a_t consists of both fixed and variable "omitted" components, i_t will not depend on the former if z_t has already fully adjusted to them, but only on the latter: the news in a_t, not on its level. Hence, investment may not be able to proxy well for all the various more or less permanent misspecifications of the production function and solve the bias problems created by their omission. A single first-order Markov unobservable cannot really capture a mixture of fixed and variable effects. This may explain why the "within" results that "do more" are so different. While being right on its own terms and making a significant contribution to the treatment of sample-selectivity and simultaneity problems, the Olley-Pakes model does not nest within it the standard fixed-effects model and leaves us with much of the original puzzle (the effect of un-accounted-for heterogeneity) still intact.

7   Other Problems

Besides simultaneity and selectivity, several other garden-variety problems arise when we try to estimate production functions: lack of information on the quality dimensions of labor and capital inputs, lack of

---

[45] The standard errors in columns 5 and 6 of Table 6.4 are too small because they do not allow for the fact that β and ϕ were estimated in the previous stage. For the correct way of deriving standard errors in such contexts, see Pakes and Olley (1995).

[46] The current state of our ability to estimate nonlinear errors-in-variables models is not completely hopeless, but neither is it easy.

Production Functions: Identification

utilization variables, and so forth. A major difficulty, largely ignored in the literature, is the fact that most often we do not have "quantity" measures of output, but rather simply nominal sales (or value added) that are deflated by a common industry price deflator.[47] The assumption is made that "the law of one price" holds: that all firms in an industry charge the same prices and that all these prices move in unison over time. That is wrong if different firms, even in a very well defined industry, produce different varieties of the product and operate within somewhat different, though possibly interconnected, markets. Examples would be cement plants that operate in different geographic markets, and plants in the computer-equipment industry, some of which produce mainframes, while others produce PCs or disc drives. The use of deflated revenue as a measure of output may have serious consequences for interpretation of the resulting estimates.

This can be illustrated using the simple model of Klette and Griliches (1996). To the production function (2.1) they add a function for the market share of the products of the ith firm in its industry I:

$$y_i - y_I = \eta(p_i - p_I) + d_i \quad (7.1)$$

where (with all variables in logarithmic form) y_i and y_I are the firm and industry outputs, respectively, p_i is the firm's own price or price index, p_I is the aggregate industry price index (relative to the overall economy price level), η is the elasticity of demand with respect to the firm's relative prices for its own products, and d_i represents all other (uncorrelated with p) demand shifters for the products of this firm. If the variable that we observe is not the real output y_i, but the deflated revenue $r_i = (y_i + p_i) - p_I$, then the revenue function (or pseudo–production function) is

$$r_i = \alpha z_i + \beta x_i + u_i + (p_i - p_I) \quad (7.2)$$

There would be no problem here if the p_i terms were random and exogenous (i.e., if $1/\eta$ were zero). But if firms have a modicum of market power, at least in the short run, p_i will be set by them and will be correlated with $u, x,$ and z. Using (7.1) and (7.2), we can solve for p_i and write the revenue function as

$$r_i = [\alpha z_i + \beta x_i + u_i]/m - (y_I)/\eta - d_i/\eta \quad (7.2')$$

where the markup coefficient $m = \eta/(1 + \eta)$ is likely to be larger than unity. It is clear, from (7.2'), that the estimates of α and β will be biased downward on the order of $1/m$, implying diminishing returns to scale in contexts where actually there may be increasing returns.[48] The size of the

---

[47] Though Marschak and Andrews were well aware of that. See also Griliches and Mairesse (1984) and Hall and Mairesse (1995).

[48] "They are estimates not of the output elasticities, but of the output elasticities corrected for monopoly" (Marschak and Andrews, 1944, p. 176).

Table 6.5. *Alternative Estimates of Production-Function Parameters: Norwegian Plants in Manufacture of Transport Equipment, 1983–89 (N = 409)*

	Basic model		Augmented model	
Variables	OLS	IV	IV	Implied elasticities[a]
Variable inputs	0.913	0.919	0.912	1.059
	(0.009)[b]	(0.013)	(0.013)	
Capital	0.005	0.005	0.005	0.006
	(0.003)	(0.003)	(0.003)	
Industry output	—	—	0.139	—
			(0.032)	
Intercept	0.001	0.001	−0.001	—
	(0.003)	(0.003)	(0.003)	
RMSE	0.165	0.165	0.164	—

Note: All estimates are based on first differences of the data. Instrumental-variable (IV) estimates use employment change as an instrument for the change in variable inputs.
[a] The implied input elasticities are computed by multiplying the values in column 3 by the estimated markup $m = \eta/(1 + \eta) = 1.16$, based on the implied demand-price elasticity $\eta = -1/0.139 = -7.19$.
[b] Standard error.
Source: Adapted from Klette and Griliches (1996, table 6).

bias (the size of the markup) may depend on the dimension of the data considered, being lower in the cross-sectional dimension in the longer run, because entry is more likely, and higher in the shorter-run time-series dimension. This may provide another explanation for the pattern of estimates reported in Figure 6.1.[49]

Klette and Griliches have shown that under certain conditions, using industry output y_I, we can identify all of the parameters in (7.2′).[50] An illustration of their analysis is given in Table 6.5, based on data for plants in the transportation-equipment industry in Norway ($N = 403$, $T = 6$). In their study, all the variable inputs are aggregated into one x (using factor shares as weights). When a production function is estimated by OLS on first differences (column 1), it yields a nonsignificant capital coefficient and a statistically significant estimate of decreasing returns to scale, a common result for such estimates. Using the more predetermined

---

[49] Also, there is a countervailing upward bias in β if u is transmitted to the x decision. It can be shown (Klette and Griliches, 1996) that the estimated β is bounded by β/m and 1.

[50] Assuming that other left-out components in the firm's production and demand functions are uncorrelated with the industry output y_I.

employment change as an instrument for x (column 2) does not change anything much, but when the industry output growth y_I is added to this equation (column 3), it is significant and provides for a reinterpretation of the results, implying a "reasonable" elasticity of demand, $\eta = -7.2$, and an associated estimate of mildly increasing returns, 1.06, rather than what appeared to be decreasing returns before.[51]

Although the solution offered by Klette and Griliches may be problematic, they have raised an important warning flag. Most microeconomic studies do not have detailed price data at the relevant level. To the extent that these missing prices are endogenous, the resulting estimates are likely to be biased, perhaps badly so, as estimates of the desired "pure" production-function parameters.

This reminds us that at the microeconomic level, the firms or plants we analyze differ a great deal, even within what we might think of as a relatively well defined industry (e.g., cement or bakeries). They differ in their geographic locations and in terms of potential for exercising market power; they differ in the particular assortments of products that they produce; and they may also differ in terms of the inputs and technologies that they use to produce their products.

Using the same data as in Figure 6.1 and Table 6.1, Mairesse and Griliches (1990) estimated separate capital coefficients α for each firm based on 13 years of data, assuming constant returns to scale. They found a great deal of heterogeneity in their estimates, much more than could be explained by sampling error and/or reasonable dispersion of the α values at the individual level. They concluded, not too surprisingly, that the simple production function must be seriously misspecified. The variegated world of plants and firms cannot really be summarized adequately by looking only at their capital–labor ratios and sizes. Things are much more complex than that. Unfortunately, standard census-type data do not provide enough additional information on relevant product and plant characteristics to allow us to pursue a substantive analysis of such differences much further.[52]

8 Coda as Prologue

We have surveyed one strand of research, the attempt to solve the simultaneity problem in estimating production functions from microeconomic data, perhaps at excessive length (but still leaving large areas uncov-

---

[51] Klette and Griliches (1996) found similar estimates for the other three industries they examined. They also presented parallel results for cost functions, showing that they were affected similarly by the use of the wrong output measure.

[52] Mundlak (1988) discussed a framework that had α terms as functions of other variables. In this work, those coefficient shifters were largely macroeconomic variables, which does not really fit into our world of microeconomic data very well.

ered). The main message has been that in trying to evade this problem, researchers have shifted their focus to thinner and thinner slices of data, leading to exacerbation of other problems and misspecifications. Much of this line of work has been guided, unfortunately, by what "econometrics," as a tool kit of techniques, could contribute, rather than by a focus on the more important but technically less appealing problems of data quality and more realistic model specification.

Instead of throwing away more of the data as "contaminated," the future, it is hoped, lies in finding circumstances and data that will provide credible identification.[53] What makes firms invest differently, hire more or less labor, or expand their R&D programs? Is it possible to look, for example, for periods of unexpected tax changes (or other regulatory-rule changes) that might impact firms differentially, depending on their previous histories and financial conditions? For that, we need to match detailed financial data to the standard census-type data. Data on capital subsidies in various countries could also help in the construction of differential cost-of-capital variables. Data on stock-market values may convey information on expectations about future-demand conditions and R&D opportunities, independent of current productivity disturbances. The challenge is to find (instrumental) variables that have genuine information about factors that affect firms differentially as they choose their input levels (their "locations on the isoquant").

Besides better data and more data, we need a richer theoretical framework to help us understand why firms are different, not only in their capital–labor ratios but also in terms of the product mixes produced, the quality of the workforce, the technologies used, the organizational structures, and the markets served. Our work with microeconomic data started with the hope that such data would provide solutions for the various difficulties encountered at the aggregate level, primarily because that is the level that our theories claim to comprehend, and because we believed that such data would provide us much more identifying variance and would reduce the multicollinearity problem. We also thought that we could reduce heterogeneity and the resulting aggregation biases by going down from such general mixtures as "total manufacturing" to something more coherent, such as "petroleum refining" or the "manufacture of cement." But something like Mandelbrot's fractals phenomenon seems to be at work here also: The observed variability/heterogeneity does not really decline as we cut our data finer and finer. There is a sense in which different bakeries are as different from each other as the steel industry is from the machinery industry.

This paradox arises in part from the fact that our theories, though

---

[53] The search for "natural experiments" has become important in labor economics, but has not yet caught on in the field of productivity analysis. For examples of the former, see Angrist (1990) and Angrist, Imbens, and Rubin (1996).

denominated in the microeconomic language of the firm or plant, were designed primarily with macroeconomic questions in mind. They deal with reasonably crude aggregates: output, labor, and capital, which turn out to be rather vague concepts when we go down to the microeconomic level and have to face large numbers of products, labor types, machines, and technologies. We have neither the data nor a convenient language and theory to describe all this variability effectively.

In spite of all these reservations, the production-function framework has been used widely in economics, and it does have its merits. It is a major tool for asking questions about rates of technological change, economies of scale, rates of return to R&D, the relevant productive qualities of labor, and so forth, and the answers may not be all that sensitive to the biases discussed here. Moreover, we are unlikely to give up this framework simply because it is imperfect. But to make further progress we need to infuse it with new data and more appropriate theoretical and econometric models that can better deal with the real heterogeneity that is the hallmark of the world in which we live.

References

Abbott, T. A., Griliches, Z., and Hausman, J. A. (1988). Short run movements in productivity: market power versus capacity utilization. Presented at NBER Summer Institute. Included in: Z. Griliches (1998), *Practicing Econometrics: Essays in Method and Application*, pp. 330–42. Cheltenham: Edward Elgar Publishing.

Angrist, J. (1990). Lifetime earnings and the Vietnam era draft lottery: evidence from Social Security administrative records. *American Economic Review* 80:313–35.

Angrist, J., Imbens, G. W., and Rubin, D. B. (1996). Identification of causal effects using instrumental variables. *Journal of the American Statistical Association* 91:444–72.

Arellano, M., and Bond, S. (1991). Some tests of specification for panel data: Monte Carlo evidence and an application to employment equations. *Review of Economic Studies* 58:277–97.

Arellano, M., and Bover, O. (1995). Another look at the instrumental-variable estimation of error-components models. *Journal of Econometrics* 68:29–52.

Arrow, K. J., Chenery, H. B., Minhas, B. S., and Solow, R. M. (1961). Capital–labor substitution and economic efficiency. *Review of Economics and Statistics* 43:225–50.

Bjerkholt, O. (1995). Introduction: Ragner Frisch, the originator of econometrics. In: *Foundations of Modern Econometrics: The Selected Essays of Ragnar Frisch*, vol. I, pp. xiii–lii. Aldershot, UK: Elgar Publishing.

Blundell, R. S., and Bond, S. (1995). Initial conditions and moment restrictions in dynamic panel data models. IFS working paper W95/17. London: Institute for Fiscal Studies.

(1996). GMM estimation with highly persistent panel data: an application to

production function estimation. Working paper, Department of Economics, University College, London.
Brynjolfsson, E., and Hitt, L. (1995). Information technology as a factor of production: the role of differences among firms. *Economics of Information and New Technology* 3:183–99.
Chamberlain, G. (1982). Multivariate regression models for panel data. *Journal of Econometrics* 18:5–46.
Chenery, H. B. (1949). Engineering production functions. *Quarterly Journal of Economics* 63:507–31.
Cobb, C. W., and Douglas, P. H. (1928). A theory of production. *American Economic Review (Suppl.)* 18:139–72.
Crepon, B., and Mairesse, J. (1996). Chamberlain and GMM estimates: an overview and some simulation experiments. In: *The Econometrics of Panel Data*, 2nd ed., ed. L. Matyas and P. Sevestre, Dordrecht: Kluwer, pp. 323–91.
Douglas, P. H. (1948). Are there laws of production? *American Economic Review* 38:1–41.
Durand, D. (1937). Some thoughts on marginal productivity, with special reference to Professor Douglas' analysis. *Journal of Political Economy* 45:740–58.
Eden, B., and Griliches, Z. (1993). Productivity, market power and capacity utilization when spot markets are complete. *American Economic Review, Papers and Proceedings* 83:219–23.
Frisch, R. (1934). Circulation planning. *Econometrica* 2:258–336.
   (1938). Statistical versus theoretical relations in economic macrodynamics. Memorandum prepared for the Business Cycle Conference at Cambridge, UK. In: *Foundations of Modern Econometrics: Selected Essays of Ragnar Frisch*, ed. O. Bjerkholt, 1995, pp. 272–87. Aldershot, UK: Elgar.
   (1965). *Theory of Production*. Dordrecht: Reidel.
Fuss, M., and McFadden, D. (1978). *Production Economics: A Dual Approach to Theory and Applications*, 2 vols. Amsterdam: North Holland.
Goldberger, A. S. (1968). The interpretation and estimation of Cobb-Douglas functions. *Econometrica* 36:464–72.
Greenan, N., and Mairesse, J. (1996). Computers and productivities: some evidence for France. NBER working paper no. 5836. Cambridge, MA: National Bureau of Economic Research.
Griliches, Z. (1957). Specification bias in estimates of production functions. *Journal of Farm Economics* 39:8–20.
   (1964). Research expenditures, education and the aggregate agricultural production function. *American Economic Review* 54:961–74.
   (1974). Errors in variables and other unobservables. *Econometrica* 42:971–98.
   (1977). Estimating the returns to schooling: some econometric problems. *Econometrica* 45:1–22.
   (1980). Returns to research and development expenditures in the private sector. In: *Studies in Income and Wealth*. Vol. 44: *New Developments in Productivity Measurement*, ed. J. W. Kendrick and B. Vaccara, pp. 419–54. University of Chicago Press.
   (1986). Data issues in econometrics. In: *Handbook of Econometrics*, vol. 3, ed. Z. Griliches and M. Intriligator, pp. 1466–514. Amsterdam: North Holland.
   (1995). R&D and productivity: econometric results and measurement issues.

In: *Handbook of the Economics of Innovation and Technological Change*, ed. P. Stoneman, pp. 52–89. Oxford: Blackwell.

(1998). R&D and productivity: the unfinished business. In: *R&D and Productivity: The Econometric Evidence*. Collected papers of Z. Griliches. University of Chicago Press. A preliminary version of the paper appears in *Conference Proceedings on Global Agicultural Science Policy for the Twenty-first Century: Invited Papers, August 26–28, 1996*. Melbourne, Australia: Conference Secretariat, Department of Natural Resources and Environment.

Griliches Z., and Hausman, J. (1986). Errors in variables in panel data. *Journal of Econometrics* 31:93–118.

Griliches, Z., and Mairesse, J. (1984). Productivity and R&D at the firm level. In: *R&D, Patents and Productivity*, ed. Z. Griliches, pp. 339–74. University of Chicago Press.

Griliches, Z., and Regev, H. (1995). Firm productivity in Israeli industry, 1979–1988. *Journal of Econometrics* 65:175–204.

Griliches, Z., and Ringstad, V. (1971). *Economies of Scale and the Form of the Production Function*. Amsterdam: North Holland.

Hall, B. H. (1990). The manufacturing master file 1959–87. NBER working paper no. 3366. Cambridge, MA: National Bureau of Economic Research.

Hall, B. H., and Mairesse, J. (1995). Exploring the relationship between R&D and productivity in French manufacturing firms. *Journal of Econometrics* 65:263–94.

Hall, R. E. (1988). The relation between price and marginal cost in U.S. industry. *Journal of Political Economy* 96:921–47.

Heady, E. O., and Dillon, J. L. (1961). *Agricultural Production Functions*. Ames: Iowa State University Press.

Hellerstein, J. K., and Neumark, D. (in press). Sex, wages and productivity: an empirical analysis of Israeli firm-level data. *International Economic Review*.

Hoch, I. (1955). Estimation of production function parameters and testing for efficiency. *Econometrica* 23:325–6.

(1962). Estimation of production function parameters combining time-series and cross-section data. *Econometrica* 30:34–53.

Jorgenson, D. W. (1986). Econometric methods for modelling producer behavior. In: *Handbook of Econometrics*, vol. 3, ed. Z. Griliches and M. Intriligator, pp. 1841–915. Amsterdam: North Holland.

Keane, M. D., and Runkle, D. E. (1992). On the estimation of panel-data models with serial correlation when instruments are not strictly exogenous. *Journal of Business and Economic Statistics* 10:1–14.

Klein, L. R. (1953). *A Textbook of Econometrics*. New York: Harper & Row.

Klette, T. J. (1994). Estimating price–cost margins and scale economies from a panel of microdata. Discussion paper 130. Oslo: Statistics Norway Research Department.

Klette, T. J., and Griliches, Z. (1996). The inconsistency of common scale estimators when output prices are unobserved and endogenous. *Journal of Applied Econometrics* 11:343–61.

Krishna, K. L. (1967). Production relations in manufacturing plants: an exploratory study. Unpublished Ph.D. dissertation, Department of Economics, University of Chicago.

Lichtenberg, F. R. (1995). The output contributions of computer equipment and personnel: a firm-level analysis. *Economics of Information and New Technology* 3:201–17.

Lovell, C. A. K. (1993). Production frontiers and productive efficiency. In: *The Measurement of Productive Efficiency: Technique and Applications*, ed. H. O. Fried, C. A. K. Lovell, and S. S. Schmidt. Oxford University Press.

Mairesse, J. (1975). Comparison of production function estimates on the French and Norwegian census of manufacturing industries. In: *On the Measurement of Factor Productivities*, ed. F. L. Altmann et al., pp. 434–62. Göttingen: Vendenbeck & Ruprecht.

(1978). New estimates of embodied and disembodied technical progress. *Annales de L'INSEE* 30–31:681–719.

(1990). Time-series and cross-sectional estimates on panel data: Why are they different and why should they be equal? In: *Panel Data and Labor Market Studies*, ed. J. Hartog et al., pp. 81–95. Amsterdam: North Holland.

Mairesse, J., and Griliches, Z. (1990). Heterogeneity in panel data: Are there stable production functions? In: *Essays in Honour of Edmond Malinvaud. Vol. 3: Empirical Economics*, P. Champsaur et al., pp. 192–231. Massachusetts Institute of Technology Press.

Mairesse, J., and Hall, B. H. (1996). Estimating the productivity of research and development in French and U.S. manufacturing firms: an exploration of simultaneity issues with GMM methods. In: *International Productivity Differences and Their Explanations*, ed. K. Wagner and B. Van Ark, pp. 285–315. Amsterdam: Elsevier Science.

Marschak, J., and Andrews, W. (1944). Random simultaneous equations and the theory of production. *Econometrica* 12:143–205.

Mendershausen, H. (1938). On the significance of Professor Douglas' production function. *Econometrica* 6:143–53.

Mundlak, Y. (1961). Empirical production function free of management bias. *Journal of Farm Economics* 43:44–56.

(1963). Estimation of production and behavioral functions from a combination of cross-section and time-series data. In: *Measurement in Economics*, ed. C. Christ et al., pp. 138–66. Stanford University Press.

(1970). Empirical production functions with a variable firm effect. Working paper 7005, Center for Agricultural Economic Research, Hebrew University, Rehovoth, Israel.

(1988). Endogenous technology and the measurement of productivity. In: *Agricultural Productivity: Measurement and Explanation*, ed. S. M. Capalbo and J. M. Antle, pp. 316–31. Washington, DC: Resources for the Future.

(1996). Production function estimation: reviving the primal. *Econometrica* 64:431–8.

Mundlak, Y., and Hoch, I. (1965). Consequences of alternative specifications of Cobb-Douglas production functions. *Econometrica* 33:814–28.

Nerlove, M. (1963). Returns to scale in electricity supply. In: *Measurement in Economics*, ed. C. Christ et al., pp. 167–200. Stanford University Press.

(1968). *Estimation and Identification of Cobb-Douglas Production Functions*. Chicago: Rand McNally.

Olley, S., and Pakes, A. (1996). The dynamics of productivity in the telecommunications equipment industry. *Econometrica* 64:1263–97.

Pakes, A., and Griliches, Z. (1984). Estimating distributed lags in short panels

with an application to the specification of depreciation patterns and capital stock constructs. *Review of Economic Studiesp* 51:165, 243–62.
Pakes, A., and Olley, S. (1995). A limit theorem for a smooth class of semiparametric estimators. *Journal of Econometrics* 65:295–332.
Reder, M. W. (1943). An alternative interpretation of the Cobb-Douglas function. *Econometrica* 11:259–64.
Ringstad, V. (1971). *Estimating Production Functions and Technical Change from Micro Data*. Economic studies no. 21, Central Bureau of Statistics of Norway, Oslo.
Schultz, H. (1929). Marginal productivity and the general pricing process. *Journal of Political Economy* 37:505–51.
Smith, V. E. (1940). An application and critique of certain methods for the determination of a statistical production function for the Canadian automobile industry, 1917–1930. Unpublished Ph.D. dissertation, Department of Economics, Northwestern University, Evanston, IL.
  (1945). The statistical production function. *Quarterly Journal of Economics* 59:543–62.
Solow, R. M. (1957). Technical change and the aggregate production function. *Review of Economics and Statistics* 39:312–20.
Tintner, G. (1944). A note on the derivation of production functions from farm records. *Econometrica* 12:26–34.
Walters, A. A. (1963). Production and cost functions: an econometric survey. *Econometrica* 31:1–66.
Wibe, S. (1984). Engineering production functions: a survey. *Economica* 51:401–11.
Zellner, A., Kmenta, J., and Dreze, J. (1966). Specification and estimation of Cobb-Douglas production function models. *Econometrica* 34:784–95.

CHAPTER 7

Investment and Growth

Dale W. Jorgenson

1 Introduction

The early 1970s marked the emergence of a rare professional consensus on economic growth, articulated in two strikingly dissimilar books. Simon Kuznets, the greatest of twentieth-century empirical economists, summarized his decades of research in *Economic Growth of Nations* (1971). The enormous impact of that research was recognized in the same year by the Royal Swedish Academy of Sciences in awarding the third Bank of Sweden Prize in Economic Science in Memory of Alfred Nobel to Kuznets "for his empirically founded interpretation of economic growth which has led to new and deepened insight into the economic and social structure and process of development" (Lindbeck, 1992, p. 79).

Robert Solow's book *Growth Theory* (1970), modestly subtitled *An Exposition*, contained his 1969 Radcliffe Lectures at the University of Warwick. In those lectures, Solow also summarized decades of research initiated by the theoretical work of Roy Harrod (1939) and Evsey Domar (1946). Solow's seminal role in that research, beginning with his brilliant and pathbreaking essay of 1956, "A Contribution to the Theory of Economic Growth," was recognized, simply and elegantly, by the Royal Swedish Academy of Sciences in awarding Solow the Nobel Memorial Prize in Economic Science in 1987 "for his contributions to the theory of economic growth" (Maler, 1992, p. 191).

After a quarter of a century, the consensus on economic growth reached during the early 1970s has collapsed under the weight of a massive accumulation of new empirical evidence, followed by a torrent of novel theoretical insights. The purpose of this essay is to initiate the

I have benefited greatly from the help of my colleague, Zvi Griliches, in exploring the recent empirical literature on investment in new technology. Susanto Basu and Charles Jones, as well as Griliches, have kindly provided me with access to unpublished material. Financial support was provided by the Program on Technology and Economic Policy of Harvard University. Responsibility for any remaining deficiencies rests solely with the author.

search for a new empirical and theoretical consensus. An attempt at this thoroughly daunting task may be premature, because professional interest in growth currently appears to be waxing rather than waning. Moreover, the disparity of views among economists, always looming remarkably large for a discipline that aspires to the status of a science, is greater in regard to the topic of growth than for most other topics.

The consensus of the early 1970s emerged from a similar period of fractious contention among competing schools of economic thought, and that alone is reason for cautious optimism. However, I believe that it is critically important to understand the strengths and weaknesses of the earlier consensus and how it dissolved in the face of subsequent theory and evidence. It is also essential to determine whether or not elements have survived that can provide a useful point of departure in the search for a new consensus.

Let us first consider the indubitable strengths of the perspective on growth that emerged victorious over its numerous competitors in the early 1970s. Solow's neoclassical theory of economic growth, especially his analysis of steady states with constant rates of growth, provided conceptual clarity and sophistication. Kuznets contributed persuasive empirical support by quantifying the long sweep of the historical experience of the United States and 13 other developed economies. He combined that with quantitative comparisons among a wide range of developed and developing economies during the postwar period.

With the benefit of hindsight, the most obvious deficiency of the neoclassical framework of Kuznets and Solow was the lack of a clear connection between the theoretical and the empirical components. That lacuna can be seen most starkly in the total absence of cross-references between the key works of these two great economists. Yet they were working on the same topic, within the same framework, at virtually the same time, and at the same geographic location – Cambridge, Massachusetts.

Searching for analogies to describe this remarkable coincidence of views on growth, we can perhaps think of two celestial bodies in different orbits, momentarily coinciding, from our earth-bound perspective, at a single point in the sky and glowing with dazzling but transitory luminosity. The indelible image of that extraordinary event has been burned into the collective memory of economists, even if the details have long been forgotten. The common perspective that emerged remains the guiding star for subsequent conceptual development and empirical observation.

In Section 2 we shall consider challenges to the traditional framework of Kuznets and Solow arising from new techniques for measuring economic welfare and productivity. The elaboration of production theory and the corresponding econometric techniques led to the successful implementation of constant quality measures of capital and labor inputs and investment-goods output. However, it was not until July 11, 1994, that the Bureau of Labor Statistics (BLS) incorporated those measures into a new official productivity index for the United States.

The recent revival of interest in economic growth by the larger community of economists can be dated from Angus Maddison's (1982) updating of Kuznets's (1971) long-term comparisons of economic growth among industrialized countries. That was followed by successful exploitation of the Penn World Table – created by Irving Kravis, Alan Heston, and Robert Summers – which provided comparisons among more than 100 developed and developing countries. Exploiting the panel-data structure of these comparisons, Nasrul Islam (1995) was able to show that the Solow model is the appropriate point of departure for modeling the endogenous accumulation of tangible assets.

The new developments in economic measurement and modeling summarized in Section 3 have cleared the way for undertaking the difficult, if unglamorous, task of constructing quantitative models of growth suitable for analysis of economic policies. Models based on the neoclassical framework of Kuznets and Solow determine growth on the basis of exogenous forces, principally spillovers from technological innovations. By contrast, models based on the new framework described in Section 4 determine the great preponderance of economic growth endogenously through investments in tangible assets and human capital.

Endogenous models of economic growth require the concepts of an aggregate production function and a representative consumer, concepts that can be implemented econometrically. These concepts imply measurements of welfare and productivity that can best be organized by means of a system of national accounts. The accounts must include production, income and expenditure, capital formation, and wealth accounts, as in the United Nations (1993) *System of National Accounts*. Alternative economic policies can then be ranked by means of equivalent variations in wealth, providing the basis for policy recommendations.

In Section 5 we shall consider quantitative models suitable for the analysis of economic policies. Econometric techniques have provided the missing link between the theoretical and empirical components of the consensus of the early 1970s. The development of those techniques was a major achievement of the 1970s, though successful applications began to emerge only in the 1980s. These techniques were unavailable when Solow (1970) first articulated the objective of constructing econometric models of growth for analysis of economic policies.

The growth of tangible assets is endogenous within a Solow (1956, 1970) neoclassical growth model. Kun-Young Yun and I constructed a complete econometric model for postwar U.S. economic growth with this feature in two papers published in 1986 (Jorgenson and Yun, 1986a,b). We have used this model to analyze the economic impact of fundamental tax reforms. Subsequently, Mun Ho and I extended this model to incorporate endogenous growth in human capital, and we have employed the extended model to analyze the impact of alternative educational policies (Jorgenson and Ho, 1995).

Although endogenous investment in new technology has been a major theme in growth theory for four decades, empirical implementation has foundered on an issue first identified by Zvi Griliches (1973): measuring the output of research-and-development activities. Until this issue has been resolved, a completely endogenous theory of economic growth will remain a chimera, forever tantalizing to the imagination, but far removed from the practical realm of economic policy. Section 6 assesses the prospects for endogenizing investment in new technology and concludes this chapter.

2 Sources and Uses of Growth

The objective of modeling economic growth is to explain the sources and uses of economic growth endogenously. National income is the starting point for assessment of the *uses* of economic growth through consumption and saving. The concept of "a measure of economic welfare," introduced by William Nordhaus and James Tobin (1972), is the key to augmenting national income to broaden the concepts of consumption and saving. Similarly, gross national product is the starting point for attributing the *sources* of economic growth to investments in tangible assets and human capital, but could encompass investments in new technology as well.

The allocation of the sources of economic growth between investment and productivity is critical for assessing the explanatory power of growth theory. Only substitution between capital and labor inputs resulting from investment in tangible assets is endogenous in Solow's neoclassical model of economic growth. However, substitution among different types of labor inputs is the consequence of investment in human capital, and investment in tangible assets also produces substitution among different types of capital inputs. These were not included in Solow's 1957 model of production.

Productivity growth is *labor-augmenting* or equivalent to an increase in population in the simplest version of the neoclassical growth model. If productivity growth greatly predominates among the sources of economic growth, as indicated by Kuznets (1971) and Solow (1957), most of growth is exogenously determined. Reliance on the Solow residual as an explanatory factor is a powerful indictment of the limitations of the neoclassical framework. This viewpoint was expressed by Moses Abramovitz (1956), who famously characterized productivity growth as "a measure of our ignorance."

The appropriate theoretical framework for endogenous growth is the

Ramsey model of optimal growth introduced by David Cass (1965) and Tjalling Koopmans (1965). A promising start on the empirical implementation of this model was made in my 1967 paper with Griliches (Jorgenson and Griliches, 1967). It appeared that 85 percent of U.S. economic growth could be made endogenous; determinants of the remaining 15 percent were left for further investigation, but might be attributable to investments in new technology.[1]

The conclusions of that paper (Jorgenson and Griliches, 1967) were corroborated in two subsequent studies (Christensen and Jorgenson, 1969, 1970). Those studies provided a much more detailed implementation of the concept of capital as a factor of production. We used a model of the tax structure for corporate capital income that had been developed in a series of papers with Robert Hall (Hall and Jorgenson, 1967, 1969, 1971). Christensen and I extended that model to noncorporate and household capital incomes in order to capture the impact of additional differences in returns to capital due to taxation on substitutions among capital inputs.

In 1973 we incorporated estimates of the sources of economic growth into a complete system of U.S. national accounts in our paper "Measuring Economic Performance in the Private Sector" (Christensen and Jorgenson, 1973).[2] Our main objective was the construction of internally consistent income, product, and wealth accounts. Separate product and income accounts were integral parts of both the U.S. National Income and Product Accounts and the United Nations (1968) *System of National Accounts* designed by Richard Stone.[3] However, neither system included wealth accounts consistent with the income and product accounts.

Christensen and I constructed income, product, and wealth accounts, paralleling the U.S. National Income and Product Accounts for the period 1929–69. We implemented our vintage accounting system for the United States on an annual basis. The complete system of vintage accounts gave stocks of assets of each vintage and their prices. The stocks were cumulated to obtain asset quantities, providing the perpetual inventory of assets accumulated at different points in time or different vintages employed by Raymond Goldsmith (1955–6, 1962).

The key innovation in our vintage system of accounts was the use of

---

[1] See Jorgenson and Griliches (1967, table IX, p. 272). We also attributed 13 percent of growth to the relative utilization of capital, measured by energy consumption as a proportion of capacity; however, this is inappropriate at the aggregate level, as Edward Denison (1974, p. 56) pointed out. For additional details, see Jorgenson, Gollop, and Fraumeni (1987, pp. 179–81).

[2] This paper was presented at the 37th meeting of the Conference on Research in Income and Wealth, held at Princeton, New Jersey, in 1971.

[3] The United Nations *System of National Accounts* (SNA) is summarized by Stone (1992) in his Nobel Prize address. The SNA has been revised (United Nations, 1993).

asset pricing equations to link the prices used in evaluating capital stocks and the rental prices employed in our constant quality index of capital input. In a prescient paper on the measurement of welfare, Paul Samuelson (1961, p. 309) had suggested that the link between asset and rental prices was essential for the integration of income and wealth accounting proposed by Irving Fisher (1960). Our system of accounts employed the specific form of this relationship developed in my 1967 paper "The Theory of Investment Behavior" (Jorgenson, 1967).

Christensen and I distinguished two approaches to the analysis of economic growth. We identified the production account with a production-possibilities frontier describing technology. The underlying conceptual framework was an extension of the aggregate production function – introduced by Paul Douglas (1948) and developed by Jan Tinbergen (1942) and Solow (1957) – to include two outputs, investment and consumption goods. These two outputs were distinguished in order to incorporate constant quality indices of investment goods.

We used constant quality indices of capital and labor inputs in allocating the sources of economic growth between investment and productivity. Our constant quality index of labor input combined different types of hours worked into a constant quality index of labor input, using the method Griliches (1960) had developed for U.S. agriculture. That considerably broadened the concept of substitution employed by Solow (1957) and altered, irrevocably, the allocation of economic growth between investment and productivity.[4]

Our constant quality index of capital input combined different types of capital inputs into a constant quality index. We identified input prices with rental rates, rather than the asset prices appropriate for the measurement of capital stock. For this purpose we used a model of capital as a factor of production that I had introduced in my 1963 article "Capital Theory and Investment Behavior" (Jorgenson, 1963). That made it possible to incorporate differences in returns due to the tax treatment of different types of capital income.[5]

Our constant quality measure of investment goods generalized Solow's (1960) concept of embodied technical change. My 1966 paper "The Embodiment Hypothesis" showed that economic growth could be interpreted, equivalently, as "embodied" in investment or "disembodied" in productivity growth (Jorgenson, 1966). My 1967 paper with Griliches removed that indeterminacy by introducing constant quality indices

---

[4] Constant quality indices of labor input are discussed in detail by Jorgenson et al. (1987, chs. 3 and 8, pp. 69–108, 261–300) and Jorgenson, Ho, and Fraumeni (1994).

[5] A detailed survey of empirical research on the measurement of capital input is given in my 1996 paper "Empirical Studies of Depreciation" (Jorgenson, 1996) and Jack Triplett's (1996) paper, "Measuring the Capital Stock: A Review of Concepts and Data Needs," both presented a meeting of the Confrence on Research in Income and Wealth, held at Washington, D.C., in May 1992.

for investment goods (Jorgenson and Griliches, 1967).[6] The Bureau of Economic Analysis (1986) has now incorporated a constant quality price index for investment in computers into the U.S. national accounts.[7]

Constant quality price indices for investment goods of different ages or vintages were developed by Hall (1971). That important innovation made it possible for Hulten and Wykoff (1982) to estimate relative efficiencies by age for all types of tangible assets included in the national accounts, putting the measurement of capital consumption onto a solid empirical foundation. Estimates of capital inputs presented in my 1987 book with Gollop and Fraumeni were based on the Hulten-Wykoff relative efficiencies (Jorgenson et al., 1987). The Bureau of Economic Analysis (1995) has incorporated these relative efficiencies into measures of capital consumption in the latest benchmark revision of the U.S. National Income and Product Accounts.[8]

Christensen and I identified the income and expenditure account with a social-welfare function. The conceptual framework was provided by the representation of intertemporal preferences employed by Ramsey (1928), Samuelson (1961), Cass (1965), Koopmans (1965), and Nordhaus and Tobin (1972). Following Kuznets (1961), we divided the uses of economic growth between current consumption and future consumption through saving. Saving was linked to the asset side of the wealth account through capital-accumulation equations for each type of asset. Prices for different vintages were linked to rental prices of capital inputs through a parallel set of capital-asset pricing equations.

The separation of production and welfare approaches to economic growth had important implications for the theory. The Ramsey model, so beautifully exposited by Solow (1970), had two separate submodels, one based on producer behavior, and the other on consumer behavior. The production account could be linked to the submodel of production, and the income and expenditure account to the submodel of consumption. That made it possible, at least in principle, to proceed from the

---

[6] A detailed history of constant quality price indices is given by Ernst Berndt (1991). Triplett's (1990) contribution to the jubilee of the Conference on Research in Income and Wealth discusses obstacles to the introduction of these indices into government statistical programs. Robert Gordon (1990) constructed constant quality indices for all types of producers' durable equipment in the national accounts, and Paul Pieper (1989, 1990) gave constant quality indices for all types of structures.

[7] Cole et al. (1986) reported the results of a joint project conducted by the Bureau of Economic Analysis (BEA) and IBM to construct a constant quality index for computers. Triplett (1986) discussed the economic interpretation of constant quality price indices in an accompanying article. Dulberger (1989) presented a more detailed report, while Triplett (1989) gave an extensive survey of empirical research on constant quality price indices for computers. Allan Young (1989) answered Denison's (1989) objections and reiterated the BEA's rationale for introducing a constant quality price index for computers.

[8] The method is described by Fraumeni (1997).

design stage of the theory of economic growth, emphasized by Solow, to econometric modeling, which he accurately described as "much more difficult and less glamorous."[9]

In summary, the dizzying progress in empirical work on economic growth by 1973 had created an impressive agenda for future research. Christensen and I had established the conceptual foundations for quantitative models of growth suitable for analyzing the impact of policies affecting investment in tangible assets. However, critical tasks, such as construction of constant quality indices of capital and labor inputs and investment-goods output, remained to be accomplished. The final step in this lengthy process was completed only with the benchmark revision of the U.S. National Income and Product Accounts in September 1995.

3   The Growth Revival

On October 16, 1973, the Organization of Petroleum Exporting Countries (OPEC), acting as a cartel, initiated sharp increases in world petroleum prices that led to a rapidly deepening recession in industrialized countries, accompanied by a rise in inflation. Because that contradicted one of the fundamental tenets of the reigning Keynesian orthodoxy in macroeconomics, it engendered a shift in the focus of macroeconomic research from economic growth to stagflation. Debates among Keynesians ("old" and "new"), monetarists, and "new classical macroeconomists" took center stage, pushing disputes among the proponents of alternative views on economic growth into the background.

In graduate courses in macroeconomics the theory of economic growth was gradually displaced by newer topics, such as rational expectations and policy ineffectiveness. The elementary skills required for growth analysis – national-income and national-product accounting, index-number theory, the perpetual-inventory method, and intertemporal asset pricing – were no longer essential for beginning researchers and fell into disuse. Even the main points of contention in the rancorous debates over growth in the early 1970s began to fade from the collective memory of economists.

Like a watercourse that encounters a mountain range, the stream of research on endogenous growth continued to flow unabated and unobserved, gathering momentum for its later reemergence into the light of professional debate. When it did erupt in the early 1980s, the initial impulse threatened to wash away the entire agenda that had been laboriously put into place, following the canonical formulation of the neoclassical framework in the early 1970s. The renewed thrust toward endogenizing economic growth acquired startling but illusory force by

---

[9] See Solow (1970, p. 105). He went on to remark, "But it may be what God made graduate students for. Presumably he had something in mind."

channeling most of its energy into a polemical attack on the deficiencies of the "exogenous" theories of growth of Kuznets and Solow.

The flow of new talent into research on economic growth had been interrupted for a decade, sapping the high level of intellectual energy that had fueled the rapid progress of the early 1970s. The arrival of a new generation of growth economists in the early 1980s signaled a feverish period of discovery and rediscovery that is still under way. That has been followed by a revival of the latent interest of many economists in economic growth, after a substantial time lapse. The consequence of that time lapse has been a form of amnesia, familiar to readers who recall Washington Irving's fictional character Rip Van Winkle. To remedy this collective lapse of memory, it is essential to bring our story of the dissolution of the neoclassical framework up to date.

We can fix the revival of interest in economic growth among the larger community of economists with some precision at Angus Maddison's (1982) updating and extension of Kuznets's (1971) long-term estimates of the growth of national product for 14 industrialized countries, including the United States. Maddison added Austria and Finland to Kuznets's list and presented growth rates covering periods beginning as early as 1820 and extending through 1979. Maddison (1991, 1995) has extended these estimates through 1992. Attempts to analyze Maddison's data led to the "convergence debate" initiated by Moses Abramovitz (1986) and William Baumol (1986).

Denison (1967) had compared differences in growth rates for national income per capita for the period 1950–62 with differences in levels in 1960 for eight European countries and the United States. He also compared the sources of these differences in growth rates and levels. The eight European countries as a whole were characterized by much more rapid growth and a lower level of national income per capita. However, that association was not monotonic for comparisons between individual countries and the United States. Nonetheless, Denison's conclusion was that "aside from short-term aberrations Europe should be able to report higher growth rates, at least in national income per person employed, for a long time. Americans should expect this and not be disturbed by it" (Denison, 1967, ch. 21).

Kuznets (1971) provided elaborate comparisons of growth rates for the 14 countries included in his study. Unlike Denison (1967), he did not provide comparisons of levels. Maddison (1982) filled that gap by comparing levels of national product for 16 countries. Those comparisons were based on estimates of purchasing-power parities by Irving Kravis, Alan Heston, and Robert Summers (1978).[10] Those estimates have been

---

[10] For details, see Maddison (1982, pp. 159–68). Purchasing-power parities were first measured for industrialized countries by Gilbert and Kravis (1954) and Gilbert et al. (1958).

updated by successive versions of the Penn World Table.[11] These data have made it possible to reconsider the issue of convergence of productivity levels raised by Denison (1967).

Abramovitz (1986) was the first to take up the challenge of analyzing convergence of productivity levels among Maddison's 16 countries. He found that convergence appeared to characterize the postwar period, whereas the period before 1914 and the interwar period revealed no tendencies for productivity levels to converge. Baumol (1986) formalized those results by running a regression of the growth rate of gross domestic product (GDP) per hour worked over the period 1870–1979 on the 1870 level of GDP per hour worked.[12]

In his notable paper "Crazy Explanations for the Productivity Slowdown," Paul Romer (1987) derived a version of the growth regression from Solow's (1970) growth model with a Cobb-Douglas production function. An important empirical contribution of the paper was to extend the data set for growth regressions from Maddison's (1982) group of 16 advanced countries to the 115 countries included in the Penn World Table (Mark 3), presented by Summers and Heston (1984). Romer's key finding was that an indirect estimate of the Cobb-Douglas elasticity of output with respect to capital was close to three-quarters. The share of capital in gross national product (GNP) implied by Solow's model was less than half as great on average.[13]

Gregory Mankiw, David Romer, and David Weil (1992) provided a defense of the neoclassical framework of Kuznets (1971) and Solow (1970). The empirical portion of their study is based on data for 98 countries from the Penn World Table (Mark 4), presented by Summers and Heston (1988). Like Romer (1987), Mankiw et al. (1992) derived a growth equation from the Solow (1970) model; however, they augmented that model by allowing for investment in human capital.

The results of Mankiw et al. (1992) produced empirical support for the augmented Solow model. There was clear evidence of the convergence predicted by the model; in addition, the estimated Cobb-Douglas elasticity of output with respect to capital was in line with the share of capital in the value of output. The rate of convergence of productivity

---

[11] A complete list through Mark 5 is given by Summers and Heston (1991), and the results for Mark 6 are summarized in the *World Development Report 1993* (World Bank, 1994).

[12] This "growth regression" has spawned a vast literature, summarized by Levine and Renelt (1992), Baumol (1994), and Barro and Sala-i-Martin (1994). Much of this literature has been based on successive versions of the Penn World Table.

[13] Unfortunately, this Mark-3 data set did not include capital input. Romer's empirical finding has spawned a substantial theoretical literature, summarized at an early stage by Lucas (1988) and, more recently, by Grossman and Helpman (1991, 1994), Romer (1994), and Barro and Sala-i-Martin (1994). Romer's own important contributions to this literature have focused on increasing returns to scale (Romer, 1986) and spillovers from technological change (Romer, 1990).

was too slow to be consistent with the 1970 version of the Solow model, but was consistent with the augmented version.

Finally, Nasrul Islam (1995) exploited an important feature of the Summers and Heston (1988) data set overlooked in prior empirical studies. That panel-data set contained benchmark comparisons of levels of national product at five-year intervals, beginning in 1960 and ending in 1985. That made it possible for Islam to test an assumption maintained in growth regressions, such as those of Mankiw and associates. Their study, like that of Romer (1987), was based on cross sections of growth rates. Both studies assumed identical technologies for all countries included in the Summers-Heston data sets.

Substantial differences in overall levels of productivity among countries have been documented by Denison (1967), Christensen, Cummings, and Jorgenson (1981), and, more recently, Dougherty and Jorgenson (1996). By introducing econometric methods for panel data, Islam (1995) was able to allow for these differences in technology. He corroborated the finding of Mankiw et al. (1992) that the elasticity of output with respect to capital input coincided with the share of capital in the value of output. That further undermined the empirical support for the existence of the increasing returns and spillovers analyzed in the theoretical models of Romer (1986, 1990).

In addition, Islam (1995) found that the rate of convergence of productivities among countries in the Summers and Heston (1988) data set was precisely that required to substantiate the *unaugmented* version of the Solow model (1970). In short, "crazy explanations" for the productivity slowdown, such as those propounded by Romer (1987, 1994), are not required to explain the complexities of panels of data for advanced and developing countries. Moreover, the model did not require augmentation, as suggested by Mankiw et al. (1992). However, differences in technology among these countries must be taken into account in econometric modeling of differences in growth rates.

The conclusion from Islam's (1995) research is that the Solow model is an appropriate point of departure for modeling the endogenous accumulation of tangible assets. For this purpose it is not essential to endogenize human-capital accumulation as well. The rationale for this key empirical finding is that the transition path to reach balanced growth equilibrium requires decades after a change in policies, such as tax policies, that affect investment in tangible assets. By comparison, the transition after a change in policies affecting investment in human capital requires as much as a century.

Islam's conclusions have been strongly reinforced in two important papers by Charles Jones (1995a,b) testing alternative models of economic growth based on endogenous investment in new technology. Jones (1995a) tested models proposed by Romer (1990), Grossman and Helpman (1991), and Aghion and Howitt (1992). The Jones model is based on an endogenous growth rate, proportional to the level of resources devoted to research and development (R&D). Jones (1995a) demonstrated that this implication of the model was contradicted by evidence from the advanced countries that conduct the great bulk of research and development. Although these countries have steadily increased the resources devoted to R&D, growth rates have been stable or declining.

Jones (1995b) also tested models of endogenous investment in new technology proposed by Romer (1986, 1987), Lucas (1988), and Rebelo (1991), so-called AK models. These models feature a growth rate that is proportional to investment rate, and Jones (1995b) has shown that there are persistent changes in investment rates for advanced countries, but there are not persistent changes in growth rates. Jones concluded that "both AK-style models and the R&D-based models are clearly rejected by this evidence" (p. 519). Jones (1995a) suggested, as an alternative approach, models that make investment in new technology endogenous, but preserve the feature of the Solow model that long-run growth rates are determined by exogenous forces. We shall consider the remaining obstacles to implementation of this approach in Section 6.

In summary, the convergence debate has provided an excellent medium for the revival of interest in growth. The starting point for this debate was the revival of Kuznets's program for research on long-term trends in the growth of industrialized countries by Maddison (1982, 1991, 1995). As the debate unfolded, the arrival of successive versions of the Penn World Table engaged the interest of the new entrants into the field in cross-sectional variations in patterns of growth. However, a totally novel element appeared in the form of relatively sophisticated econometric techniques. In the work of Islam (1995), those techniques were carefully designed to bring out the substantive importance of cross-sectional differences in technology. That proved to be decisive in resolving the debate.

4 Endogenous Growth

Despite substantial progress in endogenizing economic growth over the past two decades, profound differences in policy implications militate against any simple resolution of the debate on the relative importance of investment and productivity. Proponents of income redistribution will not easily abandon the search for a "silver bullet" that could generate economic growth without the necessity of providing incentives for investment in tangible assets and human capital. Advocates of growth strategies based on capital formation will not readily give credence to claims of the importance of external benefits that spill over to beneficiaries that are difficult or impossible to identify.

The proposition that investment is a more important source of economic growth than productivity is just as controversial today as it was in 1973. The distinction between substitution and technical change emphasized by Solow (1957) parallels the distinction between investment and productivity as sources of economic growth. However, Solow's definition of investment, like that of Kuznets (1971), was limited to tangible assets. Both specifically excluded investments in human capital by relying on undifferentiated hours of work as a measure of labor input.

Kuznets (1971) and Solow (1957) identified the contribution of tangible assets with increases in the stock, which does not adequately capture substitution among different types of capital inputs. Constant quality indices of both capital and labor inputs and investment-goods output are essential for successful implementation of the production approach to economic growth. By failing to adopt these measurement conventions, Kuznets and Solow attributed almost all of U.S. economic growth to the Solow residual.[14]

To avoid the semantic confusion that pervades popular discussions of economic growth it is essential to be precise in distinguishing between investment and productivity. Investment is the commitment of current resources in the expectation of future returns, and it can take a multiplicity of forms. This is the definition introduced by Fisher (1906) and discussed by Samuelson (1961). The distinctive feature of investment as a source of economic growth is that the returns can be internalized by the investor. The most straightforward application of this definition is to investments that create property rights, including rights to transfer the resulting assets and benefit from incomes that accrue to the owners.[15]

Investment in tangible assets provides the most transparent illustration of investment as a source of economic growth. This form of investment creates transferable property rights with returns that can be internalized. However, investment in intangible assets through R&D also creates intellectual property rights that can be transferred through outright sale or royalty arrangements and returns that can be internalized. Private returns to this form of investment – returns that have been internalized – have been studied intensively in the literature surveyed by Griliches (1994, 1995) and Bronwyn Hall (1996).

The seminal contributions of Gary Becker (1993), Fritz Machlup (1962), Jacob Mincer (1974), and Theodore Schultz (1961) have given concrete meaning to the concept of "wealth in its more general sense"

---

[14] The measurement conventions of Kuznets and Solow remain in common use. See, for example, the references given in my article "Productivity and Economic Growth" (Jorgenson, 1990), presented at the jubilee of the Conference on Research in Income and Wealth, held in Washington, D.C., in 1988. For recent examples, see Baily and Gordon (1988), Englander and Mittelstadt (1988), Blanchard and Fischer (1989, pp. 2–5), Baily and Schultze (1990), Gordon (1990), Englander and Gurney (1994), and Lau (1996).

[15] Fisher (1906, ch. 2, pp. 18–40) discussed property rights.

employed by Fisher (1906). This notion of wealth includes investments that do not create property rights. For example, a student enrolled in school or a worker participating in a training program can be viewed as an investor. Although these investments do not create assets that can be bought or sold, the returns to higher educational qualifications or better skills in the workplace can be internalized. The contribution of investments in education and training to economic growth can be identified in the same way as for tangible assets.

The mechanism by which tangible investments are translated into economic growth is well understood. For example, an investor in a new industrial facility adds to the supply of assets and generates a stream of rental income. The investment and the income are linked through markets for capital assets and capital services. The income stream can be divided between the increase in capital input and the marginal product of capital or rental price. The increase in capital contributes to output growth in proportion to the marginal product. This is the basis for construction of a constant quality index of capital input.

Griliches (1973, 1979, 1995) has shown how investments in new technology can be translated into economic growth. An investor in a new product design or process of production adds to the supply of intellectual assets and generates a stream of profits or royalties. The increase in intellectual capital contributes to output growth in proportion to its marginal product in the same way as the acquisition of a tangible asset. However, investments in R&D, unlike those in tangible assets, frequently are internal to the firm, so that separation of the private return between the input of intellectual capital and the marginal product or rental price of this capital is highly problematical. The BLS (1994) and Griliches have provided estimates of the contributions of these investments to economic growth.

Finally, an individual who completes a course of education or training adds to the supply of people with higher qualifications or skills. The resulting income stream can be decomposed into a rise in labor input and the marginal product of labor or wage rate. The increase in labor contributes to output growth in proportion to the marginal product. This provides the basis for constructing a constant quality index of labor input. Although there are no asset markets for human capital, investments in human capital and nonhuman capital have the common feature, pointed out by Fisher (1906), that returns are internalized by the investor.

The defining characteristic of productivity as a source of economic growth is that the incomes generated by higher productivity are external to the economic activities that generate growth. These benefits spill over to income recipients not involved in these activities, severing the connection between the creation of growth and the incomes that result. Because the benefits of policies to create externalities cannot be appropriated, these policies typically involve government programs or activities supported through public subsidies. Griliches (1992, 1995) has provided detailed surveys of spillovers from investment in R&D.[16]

Publicly supported R&D programs are leading illustrations of policies to stimulate productivity growth. These programs can be conducted by government laboratories or financed by public subsidies to private laboratories. The justification for public financing is most persuasive for aspects of technology that cannot be fully appropriated, such as basic science and generic technology. The benefits of the resulting innovations are external to the economic units conducting the R&D, and these must be carefully distinguished from the private benefits of R&D that can be internalized through the creation of intellectual property rights.

An important obstacle to resolution of the debate over the relative importance of investment and productivity is that it coincides with ongoing disputes about the appropriate role for the public sector. Productivity can be identified with spillovers of benefits that do not provide incentives for actors within the private sector. Advocates of a larger role for the public sector advance the view that these spillovers can be guided into appropriate channels only by an all-wise and beneficent government sector. By contrast, proponents of a smaller government will search for means to privatize decisions about investments by decentralizing investment decisions among participants in the private sector of the economy.

Kevin Stiroh and I have shown that investments in tangible assets have been the most important sources of postwar U.S. economic growth (Jorgenson and Stiroh, 1995). These investments appear on the balance sheets of firms, industries, and the nation as a whole as buildings, equipment, and inventories. The benefits appear on the income statements of these same economic units as profits, rents, and royalties. The BLS (1983) compiled an official constant quality index of capital input for its initial estimates of total factor productivity, renamed as multifactor productivity.

The BLS retained hours worked as a measure of labor input until July 11, 1994, when it released a new multifactor productivity measure incorporating a constant quality index of labor input as well as the BEA's (1986) constant quality index for investment in computers. The final step in empirically implementing a constant quality index of the services of tangible assets was incorporation of the Hulten and Wykoff (1982) relative efficiencies into the U.S. National Income and Product Accounts by the BEA (1995). Four decades of empirical research, initiated by Goldsmith's (1955–6) monumental treatise *A Study of Saving*, have provided a sound empirical foundation for endogenizing investment in tangible assets.

---

[16] Griliches (1992) also provided a list of survey papers on spillovers. Griliches (1979, 1995) has shown how to incorporate spillovers into a growth accounting.

Stiroh and I have shown that the growth of labor input is second in importance only to capital input as a source of economic growth. Increases in labor incomes have made it possible to measure investments in human capital and to assess their contributions to economic growth (Jorgenson and Stiroh, 1995). Jorgenson and Fraumeni (1989) extended the vintage accounting system developed by Christensen and Jorgenson (1973) to incorporate these investments. Our essential idea was to treat individual members of the U.S. population as human assets, with "asset prices" given by their lifetime labor incomes. Constant quality indices of labor input are an essential first step in incorporating investments in human capital into empirical studies of economic growth. We implemented our vintage accounting system for both human capital and non-human capital for the United States on an annual basis for the period 1948–84.

Asset prices for tangible assets can be observed directly from market transactions in investment goods; intertemporal capital-asset pricing equations are used to derive rental prices for capital services. For human capital, wage rates correspond to rental prices and can be observed directly from transactions in the labor market. Lifetime labor incomes are derived by applying asset pricing equations to these wage rates. These incomes are analogous to the asset prices used in accounting for tangible assets in the system of vintage accounts developed by Christensen and Jorgenson (1973).

Fraumeni and I have developed a measure of the output of the U.S. education sector (Jorgenson and Fraumeni, 1992b). Our point of departure was that whereas education is a service industry, its output is investment in human capital. We estimated investment in education from the impact of increases in educational attainment on the lifetime incomes of all individuals enrolled in school. We found that investment in education, measured in this way, is similar in magnitude to the value of working time for all individuals in the labor force. Furthermore, the growth of investment in education during the postwar period exceeded the growth of market labor activities.

Second, we have measured the inputs of the education sector, beginning with the purchased inputs recorded in the outlays of educational institutions (Jorgenson and Fraumeni, 1992a). A major part of the value of the output of educational institutions accrues to students in the form of increases in their lifetime incomes. Treating these increases as compensation for student time, we evaluated that time as an input into the educational process. Given the outlays of educational institutions and the value of student time, we allocated the growth of the education sector to its sources.

An alternative approach, employed by Schultz (1961), Machlup (1962), Nordhaus and Tobin (1972), and many others, is to apply the Goldsmith (1955–6) perpetual-inventory method to private and public expenditures on educational services. Unfortunately, this approach has foundered on the absence of a satisfactory measure of the output of the educational sector and the lack of an obvious rationale for capital consumption. The approach fails to satisfy the conditions for integration of income and wealth accounts established by Fisher (1906) and Samuelson (1961).[17]

Given vintage accounts for human capital and nonhuman capital, we (Jorgenson and Fraumeni, 1989) have constructed a system of income, product, and wealth accounts, paralleling the system I had developed with Christensen. In these accounts, the value of human wealth was more than 10 times the value of nonhuman wealth, and investment in human capital was 5 times the investment in tangible assets. We defined "full" investment in the U.S. economy as the sum of these two types of investments. Similarly, we added the value of nonmarket labor activities to personal-consumption expenditures to obtain "full" consumption. Our product measure included these new measures of investment and consumption.

Because our complete accounting system included a production account with "full" measures of capital and labor inputs, we were able to generate a new set of accounts for the *sources* of U.S. economic growth. Our system also included an income and expenditure account, with income from labor services in both market and nonmarket activities. We combined this with income from capital services and allocated "full" income between consumption and saving.[18] This provided the basis for a new "measure of economic welfare" and a set of accounts for the *uses* of U.S. economic growth. Our system was completed by a wealth account containing both human wealth and tangible assets.

We aggregated the growth of education and noneducation sectors of the U.S. economy to obtain a new measure of U.S. economic growth. Combining this with measures of input growth, we obtained a new set of accounts for the sources of growth of the U.S. economy. Productivity contributes almost nothing to the growth of the education sector and only a modest proportion to output growth for the economy as a whole. We also obtained a second approximation to the proportion of U.S. economic growth that can be made endogenous. Within a Ramsey model with separate education and noneducation sectors we find that exogenous productivity growth accounts for only 17 percent of growth.

The introduction of endogenous investment in education increases the explanatory power of the Ramsey model of economic growth to 83 percent. However, it is important to emphasize that growth without endogenous investment in education is measured differently. The traditional framework for economic measurement of Kuznets (1971) and

---

[17] For more detailed discussion, see Jorgenson and Fraumeni (1989).
[18] Our terminology follows that of the Becker (1965, 1993) theory of time allocation.

Solow (1970) excludes nonmarket activities, such as those that characterize the major portion of investment in education. The intuition is familiar to any teacher, including teachers of economics: What the students do is far more important than what the teachers do, even if the subject matter is the theory of economic growth.

A third approximation to the proportion of growth that could be attributed to investment within an extended Ramsey model results from incorporation of all forms of investment in human capital. This would include education, child-rearing, and addition of new members to the population. Fertility could be made endogenous by using the approach of Barro and Becker (1989) and Becker and Barro (1988). Child-rearing could be made endogenous by modeling the household as a producing sector along the lines of the model of the educational sector outlined earlier. The results presented by Jorgenson and Fraumeni (1989) show that this would endogenize 86 percent of U.S. economic growth. This is a significant, but not overwhelming, gain in explanatory power for the Ramsey model.

In summary, endogenizing U.S. economic growth at the aggregate level requires a distinction between investment and productivity as sources of growth. There are two important obstacles to empirical implementation of this distinction. First, the distinctive feature of investment as a source of growth is that the returns can be internalized. Decisions can be successfully decentralized to the level of individual investors in human capital and tangible assets. Productivity growth is generated by spillovers that cannot be captured by private investors. Activities generating these spillovers cannot be decentralized and require collective decision making through the public sector. Successive approximations to the Ramsey model of economic growth increase the proportion of growth than can be attributed to investment, rather than productivity.

5 Econometric Modeling

We are prepared, at last, for the most difficult and least glamorous part of the task of endogenizing economic growth – constructing quantitative models for the analysis of economic policies. The Ramsey growth model of Cass (1965) and Koopmans (1965) requires empirical implementation of two highly problematical theoretical constructs, namely, a model of producer behavior based on an aggregate production function and a model of a representative consumer. Each of these abstracts from important aspects of economic reality, but both have important advantages in modeling long-term trends in economic growth.

My 1980 paper "Accounting for Capital" presented a method for aggregating over sectors. The existence of an aggregate production function imposes very stringent conditions on production patterns at the industry level. In addition to value-added functions for each sector, an aggregate production function posits that these functions must be identical. Furthermore, the functions relating sectoral capital and labor inputs to their components must be identical, and each component must receive the same price in all sectors.[19]

Although the assumptions required for the existence of an aggregate production function appear to be highly restrictive, Fraumeni and I estimated that errors of aggregation could account for less than 9 percent of aggregate productivity growth (Fraumeni and Jorgenson, 1980, table 2.38, lines 4 and 11). In 1987 we published updated data on sectoral and aggregate production accounts in our book *Productivity and U.S. Economic Growth* (Jorgenson et al., 1987). We generated the data for sectoral production accounts in a way that avoids the highly restrictive assumptions of the aggregate production function. These data were then compared with those from the aggregate production account to test for the existence of an aggregate production function. We demonstrated that this hypothesis is inconsistent with empirical evidence. However, our revised and updated estimate of errors arising from aggregation over industrial sectors explained less than 3 percent of aggregate productivity growth over the period of our study, 1948–79 (Jorgenson et al., 1987, table 9.5, lines 6 and 11).

Jorgenson et al. (1987) presented statistical tests of the much weaker hypothesis that a value-added function exists for each industrial sector, but that hypothesis was also rejected.[20] The conclusion of our research on production at the sectoral level was that specifications of technology such as the aggregate production function and sectoral valued-added functions result in substantial oversimplifications of the empirical evidence. However, these specifications are useful for particular but limited purposes. For example, sectoral value-added functions are indispensable for aggregating over sectors, and the aggregate production function is a useful simplification for modeling aggregate long-run growth, as originally proposed by Tinbergen (1942).

Sectoral value-added functions were employed by Hall (1988, 1990a) in modeling production at the sectoral level. In measuring capital and labor inputs, he adhered to the traditional framework of Kuznets (1971) and Solow (1970) by identifying labor input with hours worked, and capital input with capital stock. He found large apparent increasing returns to scale in the production of value added.[21] Producer equilibrium

---

[19] A detailed survey of econometric modeling of production is included in my paper "Econometric Modeling of Producer Behavior" (Jorgenson, 1986). This is also the focus of Solow's 1967 survey article "Some Recent Developments in the Theory of Production." The conceptual basis for the existence of an aggregate production function was provided by Robert Hall (1973).

[20] Jorgenson et al. (1987, table 7.2, pp. 239–41). The existence of an aggregate production function requires *identical* value-added functions for all sectors.

[21] Hall (1990a) reported the median degree of returns to scale in value added for two-digit U.S. manufacturing industries of 2.2!

under increasing returns requires imperfect competition. However, Susanto Basu and John Fernald (1997) have pointed out that the value-added data employed by Hall were constructed on the basis of assumptions of constant returns to scale and perfect competition.

Basu and Fernald (1997) employed the strategy for sectoral modeling of production recommended by Jorgenson et al. (1987), treating capital, labor, and intermediate inputs symmetrically. They estimated returns to scale for the sectoral output and input data of Jorgenson (1990) to be constant. Those data included constant quality measures of capital, labor, and intermediate input. Basu and Fernald (1997) also showed that returns to scale in the production of value added are constant, when value added is defined in the same way as by Jorgenson et al. (1987) and constant quality measures of capital and labor inputs are employed.

Data for individual firms provide additional support for value-added production functions with constant or even decreasing returns to scale. Estimates incorporating intellectual capital have been surveyed by Griliches (1994, 1995) and Hall (1996). These estimates are now available for many different time periods and several countries. Almost all existing studies have employed value-added data for individual firms and have provided evidence for constant or decreasing returns to scale. This evidence is further corroborated by an extensive study of plant-level data by Baily, Hulten, and Campbell (1990) providing evidence of constant returns at the level of individual manufacturing plants.

Turning to the task of endogenizing investments in tangible assets and education, we first review the endogenous accumulation of tangible assets. An important objective of the Christensen and Jorgenson (1973) accounting system was to provide the data for econometric modeling of aggregate producer and consumer behavior. In 1973 we introduced an econometric model of producer behavior (Christensen, Jorgenson, and Lau, 1973). We modeled joint production of consumption and investment goods from inputs of capital and labor services, using data on these outputs and inputs from the aggregate production account.

In 1975 we constructed an econometric model of representative consumer behavior (Christensen, Jorgenson, and Lau, 1975). We estimated this model on the basis of data from the aggregate income and expenditure account of the Christensen and Jorgenson (1973) accounting system. We tested and rejected the implications of a model of a representative consumer. Subsequently we constructed a model of consumer behavior based on exact aggregation over individual consumers that specializes to the representative-consumer model for a fixed distribution of total expenditure over the population of consumers[22] (Jorgenson, Lau, and Stoker, 1982).

Yun and I constructed an econometric model for postwar U.S. eco-

---

[22] A survey of empirical approaches to aggregation was given by Stoker (1993).

nomic growth with endogenous accumulation of tangible assets (Jorgenson and Yun, 1986a,b). Our model of consumer behavior involved endogenous labor–leisure choice, following Tinbergen's (1942) neoclassical econometric model of economic growth. Labor–leisure choice is exogenous in Solow's (1956) neoclassical model. In addition, we employed the Ramsey (1928) representation of intertemporal preferences to model saving–consumption behavior, following Cass (1965) and Koopmans (1965). In Solow's model the saving ratio is exogenous.

Econometric application of Ramsey's model of optimal saving was initiated by Robert Hall (1978), removing the final remaining gap between theoretical and empirical perspectives on economic growth.[23] That occurred only eight years after Solow's (1970) classic exposition of the neoclassical theory of growth! The key to Hall's achievement in 1978 was the introduction of an econometrically tractable concept of "rational expectations" that he combined with Ramsey's theoretical model. Building on Hall's framework, Hansen and Singleton (1982, 1983) have tested and rejected the underlying model of a representative consumer.

Yun and I have revised and updated our econometric model of U.S. economic growth and analyzed the consequences of the tax reform act of 1986 for U.S. economic growth (Jorgenson and Yun, 1990). We have also considered alternative proposals for fundamental tax reform, including proposals now under consideration by the U.S. Congress, such as consumption-based and income-based value-added taxes. We found that the 1986 act resulted in a substantial increase in social welfare. However, we also discovered that several of the alternative proposals would have produced substantially higher gains.

Our econometric model of U.S. economic growth (Jorgenson and Yun, 1990, 1991a,b) provided the starting point for our endogenous growth model for the U.S. economy (Jorgenson and Ho, 1995). While my model with Yun endogenized capital input, the endogenous growth model also endogenizes investment in human capital. This model includes all of the elements of our Ramsey model of U.S. economic growth. However, the new model also includes a highly schematic model of production for the U.S. educational system.

Our production model includes a production-possibilities frontier for the noneducation sector that is analogous to the frontier in my papers with Yun (Jorgenson and Yun, 1990, 1991a). The model also includes a production function for the education sector, with investment in education as the output. The inputs include capital and labor services as well

---

[23] Hall's 1978 paper and his subsequent papers on this topic have been reprinted in his book *The Rational Consumer* (1990b). Hall (1990b) and Deaton (1992) have presented surveys of the literature on econometric modeling of consumer behavior within the Ramsey framework.

as purchases of goods and services from the noneducation sector. For both submodels we allow for exogenous growth of productivity; however, we have shown that this is negligible for the education sector (Jorgenson and Fraumeni, 1992a).

Ho and I have evaluated alternative educational policies through the equivalent variation in wealth associated with each policy (Jorgenson and Ho, 1995). As an alternative case we consider an educational policy that would raise the participation rates and policies, keeping taxes and expenditures constant. Presumably, this would result in a lower level of "quality." We also consider an alternative case that would retain the base-case participation rates, but raise "quality" by increasing expenditures on consumption goods and capital and labor services in the education sector and the corresponding taxes. Hanushek (1994) has shown that the second of these alternative policies, substantial improvement in educational quality through increased expenditure, is closely comparable to the actual educational policy pursued during the 1980s.

Jorgenson and Ho (1995) have shown that increasing participation rates without altering expenditure would produce substantial gains in social welfare. In this sense the quality level of the existing educational system is too high to be cost-effective. On the other hand, increasing the quality with no change in participation rates would result in a sizable loss in social welfare. These results are consistent with the literature on educational production functions surveyed by Hanushek (1986, 1989).[24]

With endogenous accumulation of tangible capital, as in the model of Jorgenson and Yun (1986a), almost three-quarters growth is endogenous. By contrast, the model with endogenous investment in education (Jorgenson and Ho, 1995) accounts for 83 percent of growth. By endogenizing fertility behavior and child-rearing it would be possible, at least in principle, to add an incremental three percentage points to the explanatory power of the Ramsey model of economic growth. Modeling population growth endogenously is clearly feasible. However, the construction of an econometric model with this feature would require considerable new data development and is best left as an opportunity for future research.

In summary, our endogenous models of growth (Jorgenson and Yun, 1986a,b; Jorgenson and Ho, 1995) require the econometric implementation of concepts of an aggregate production function and a representative consumer. While each of these concepts has important limitations,

---

[24] Note that the meaning of "production function" in this context is different from the meaning of this term in our model of the education sector. In Hanushek's terminology the output of the education sector is measured in terms of measures of educational performance, such as graduation rates or test scores. Our terminology is closer to the Hanushek (1994) concept of "value added" by the educational system. The output of the education system is the addition to the lifetime incomes of all individuals enrolled in school.

both are useful in modeling long-run economic trends. Furthermore, these concepts lead, naturally, to a substantial increase in the level of sophistication in data generation, integrating investment and capital into a complete system of national accounts.

6 Conclusion

The key innovation in economic measurement required for endogenizing growth is a wealth account that can be integrated with production and income and expenditure accounts. This encompasses the system of vintage accounts for tangible assets implemented by Christensen and Jorgenson (1973), as well as the vintage accounts for human capital developed by Jorgenson and Fraumeni (1989). These incorporate accumulation equations for tangible assets and human capital, together with asset pricing equations. Both are essential in constructing endogenous models of growth to replace the exogenous models that emerged from the professional consensus of the early 1970s.

The framework for economic measurement developed by Christensen and Jorgenson (1973) and Jorgenson and Fraumeni (1989) incorporates the principal features of the United Nations (1993) *System of National Accounts*. This provides a production account for allocating the sources of economic growth between investment and growth in productivity. It also includes an income-and-expenditure account for analyzing the uses of economic growth through consumption and saving. Alternative policies are ranked by means of equivalent variations in wealth for the representative consumer.

In principle, investment in new technology could be made endogenous by extending the accounting framework to incorporate investment in new technology. The BEA (1994) has provided a satellite system of accounts for R&D based on Goldsmith's (1955–6) perpetual-inventory method, applied to private and public expenditures. Unfortunately, this is subject to the same limitations as the approach to human capital of Schultz (1961) and Machlup (1962). The BEA satellite system has foundered on the absence of a satisfactory measure of the output of R&D and the lack of an appropriate rationale for capital consumption.

The standard model for investment in new technology, formulated by Griliches (1973), is based on a production function incorporating inputs of services from intellectual capital accumulated through investment in R&D. Intellectual capital is treated as a factor of production in precisely the same way as tangible assets are treated by Christensen and Jorgenson (1973). Hall (1993) has developed the implications of this model for the pricing of the services of intellectual-capital input and the evaluation of intellectual-capital assets.[25]

---

[25] These implications of the model are also discussed by Jones and Williams (1996).

Griliches (1973) represented the process of R&D by means of a production function that included the services of the previous R&D. That captures the notion of "standing on the shoulders of giants," originated by Jacob Schmookler (1966) and elaborated by Caballero and Jaffe (1993) and Jones and Williams (1996). Under constant returns to scale this representation also captures the "congestion externality" modeled by Jones and Williams (1996) and Stokey (1995). R&D, leading to investment in intellectual capital, is conducted jointly with production of marketable output, and this poses a formidable obstacle to measuring the output of new intellectual capital.

The model of capital as a factor of production that I first proposed in 1963 has been applied to tangible assets and human capital. However, implementation of this model for intellectual capital would require a system of vintage accounts including not only accumulation equations for stocks of accumulated R&D, but also asset pricing equations. These equations are essential for separating the revaluation of intellectual property due to price changes over time from depreciation of this property due to aging. This is required for measuring the quantity of intellectual-capital input and its marginal product.

Pricing of intellectual capital is the key issue remaining before investment in new technology can be endogenized in quantitative models for the analysis of alternative economic policies. Hall (1993) has constructed prices for stocks of accumulated intellectual capital from stock-market valuations of the assets of individual firms. However, she points out that the high degree of persistence in expenditures on R&D at the firm level has made it virtually impossible to separate the effects of the aging of assets from changes in the value of these assets over time. Her evaluation of intellectual capital is conditional upon a pattern of relative efficiencies imposed on past investments in new technology.

Nonetheless, Hall's pioneering research on pricing of intellectual assets has yielded interesting and valuable insights. For example, the gross rate of return in the computer and electronics industry, including depreciation and revaluation of these assets, greatly exceeds that in other industries. This can be rationalized by the fact that revaluation in this industry, as measured by Hall, is large and negative, mirroring the rapid decline in the price of the industry's output. This is evidence for the empirical significance of the process of creative destruction described by Schumpeter (1942) and modeled by Aghion and Howitt (1992), Stokey (1995), and Jones and Williams (1996). Because revaluation enters negatively into the gross rate of return, this rate of return exceeds that for industries with positive revaluations.

Another important result that emerges for Hall's (1996) survey of gross rates of return to R&D is the repeated finding that investment funded by the federal government has zero private return. Even private firms conducting this research under government contract have been unable to internalize the returns. This has the very important policy implication that public investments in new technology can be justified only by comparisons of the costs and benefits to the government. Measurement of these benefits requires careful case studies like those of civilian space technology by Henry Hertzfeld (1985) and commercial aircraft by David Mowery (1985). Grandiose visions of spillovers from public R&D have been exposed as rapidly fleeting mirages.

The final issue that must be resolved in order to complete the endogenization of economic growth is modeling of spillovers. Griliches (1995) has provided a detailed survey of alternative methods and results, based on the model he originated in 1979. The essential idea is to include aggregate input of intellectual capital, together with the inputs of individual producers, as determinants of output. Unfortunately, this requires precisely the same separation of marginal product and capital input for intellectual capital needed for the identification of returns that can be internalized by the individual producer.

Caballero and Lyons (1990, 1992) have attempted to circumvent the problem of measuring intellectual capital by including aggregate output as a determinant of sectoral productivity. However, Basu and Fernald (1995) have shown that the positive results of Caballero and Lyons depend on the same value-added data employed by Hall (1988, 1990a). Treating capital, labor, and intermediate inputs symmetrically, as in their research on economies of scale, Basu and Fernald have shown that the evidence for spillovers evaporates. This leaves open the question of the importance of spillovers from investment in new technology, which must await satisfactory measures of the output of R&D.

An elegant and impressive application of the Griliches (1979) framework for modeling spillovers across international boundaries has been presented by Coe and Helpman (1995). The key idea is to trace the impact of those spillovers through trade in intermediate goods. For each country the stock of accumulated R&D of its trading partners is weighted by bilateral import shares. However, Keller (1996) has shown that the evidence of spillovers is even more impressive if the bilateral trade shares are assigned randomly, rather than matched with the countries conducting the R&D. Another vision of spillovers can be assigned to the lengthening roll of unproven theoretical hypotheses.

In summary, a great deal has been accomplished, but much remains to be done to complete the endogenization of economic growth. An important feature of recent research has been the linking of theoretical and empirical investigations, as in the seminal papers of Romer (1986, 1987, 1990). This integration need no longer be left to the remarkable coincidence of empirical and theoretical perspectives that led Kuznets (1971) and Solow (1970) to the neoclassical framework. In the absence of a clear and compelling link between the theoretical model and the data-generation process, the breakdown of this framework had left economists without a guide to long-run economic policy for two decades.

Fortunately, a new empirical and theoretical consensus on economic growth would require only a relatively modest reinterpretation of the neoclassical framework established by Solow (1956, 1970, 1988), Cass (1965), and Koopmans (1965). However, the traditional framework of economic measurement established by Kuznets (1961, 1971) and embedded in the U.S. National Income and Product Accounts will have to be augmented considerably. The most important change is a reinterpretation of the concepts of investment and capital to encompass Fisher's (1906) notion of "wealth in its more general sense."

In closing I must emphasize that my goal has been to provide a new starting point in the search for a consensus on economic growth, rather than to arrive at final conclusions. The new framework I have outlined is intended to be open-ended, permitting a variety of different approaches to investment – in tangible assets, human capital, and new technology. There is also ample, if carefully delimited, space within this framework for endogenizing spillovers by using the Lindahl-Samuelson theory of public goods. New entrants to the field will continue to find a plethora of opportunities for modeling economic growth.

References

Abramovitz, M. (1956). Resources and output trends in the United States since 1870. *American Economic Review* 46:5–23.
  (1986). Catching up, forging ahead, and falling behind. *Journal of Economic History* 46:385–406.
Aghion, P., and Howitt, P. (1992). A model of growth through creative destruction. *Econometrica* 60:323–51.
Baily, M. N., and Gordon, R. J. (1988). Measurement issues, the productivity slowdown, and the explosion of computer power. *Brookings Papers on Economic Activity* 2:1–45.
Baily, M. N., Hulten, C. R., and Campbell, D. (1990). Productivity dynamics in manufacturing plants. *Brookings Papers on Economic Activity: Microeconomics* 1:187–267.
Baily, M. N., and Schultze, C. L. (1990). The productivity of capital in a period of slower growth. *Brookings Papers on Economic Activity: Microeconomics* 1:369–406.
Barro, R. J., and Backer, G. S. (1989). Fertility choice in a model of economic growth. *Econometrica* 7:481–502.
Barro, R. J., and Sala-i-Martin, X. (1994). *Economic Growth*. New York: McGraw-Hill.
Basu, S., and Fernald, J. G. (1995). Are apparent productive spillovers a figment of specification error? *Journal of Monetary Economics* 36:165–88.
  (1997). Returns to scale in U.S. production: estimates and implications. *Journal of Political Economy* 105:249–83.

Baumol, W. J. (1986). Productivity growth, convergence, and welfare. *American Economic Review* 76:1072–85.

(1994). Multivariate growth patterns: contagion and common forces as possible sources of convergence. In: *Convergence of Productivity*, ed. W. J. Baumol, R. R. Nelson, and E. N. Wolff, pp. 62–85. Oxford University Press.

Becker, G. S. (1965). A theory of the allocation of time. *Economic Journal* 75:493–517.

(1967). Human capital and the personal distribution of income: an analytical approach. Woytinsky lecture no. 1. Institute of Public Administration, University of Michigan.

(1993). *Human Capital*, 3rd ed. University of Chicago Press.

Becker, G. S., and Barro, R. J. (1988). A reformulation of the economic theory of fertility. *Quarterly Journal of Economics* 103:1–25.

Berndt, E. R. (1991). *The Practice of Econometrics: Classic and Contemporary*. Reading, MA: Addison-Wesley.

Blanchard, O. J., and Fischer, S. (1989). *Lectures on Macroeconomics*. Massachusetts Institute of Technology Press.

Bureau of Economic Analysis (1982). Measuring nonmarket economic activity: BEA working paper 2, Washington, DC: Bureau of Economic Analysis, U.S. Department of Commerce.

(1986). Improved deflation of purchases of computers. *Survey of Current Business* 66:7–9.

(1994). A satellite account for research and development. *Survey of Current Business* 74:37–71.

(1995). Preview of the comprehensive revision of the national income and product accounts: recognition of government investment and incorporation of a new methodology for calculating depreciation. *Survey of Current Business* 75:33–41.

Bureau of Labor Statistics (1983). Trends in multifactor productivity. Bulletin 2178. Washington, DC: U.S. Department of Labor.

(1993). Labor composition and U.S. productivity growth, 1948–90. Bulletin 2426. Washington, DC: U.S. Department of Labor.

(1994). Multifactor productivity measures, 1991 and 1992. News release, USDL 94-327, July 11.

Caballero, R. J., and Jaffe, A. B. (1993). How high are the giants' shoulders: an empirical assessment of knowledge spillovers and creative destruction in a model of economic growth. In: *NBER Macroeconomics Annual 1993*, ed. O. J. Blanchard and S. Fischer, pp. 15–74. Washington, DC: National Bureau of Economic Research.

Caballero, R. J., and Lyons, R. K. (1990). Internal and external economies in European industries. *European Economic Review* 34:805–30.

(1992). External effects in U.S. procyclical productivity. *Journal of Monetary Economics* 29:209–26.

Carson, C., and Landefeld, S. (1994). Integrated economic and environmental satellite accounts. *Survey of Current Business* 74:33–49.

Cass, D. (1965). Optimum growth in an aggregative model of capital accumulation. *Review of Economic Studies* 32:233–40.

Christensen, L. R., Cummings, D., and Jorgenson, D. W. (1981). Relative productivity levels, 1947–1973. *European Economic Review* 16:61–94.

Christensen, L. R., and Jorgenson, D. W. (1969). The measurement of U.S. real capital input, 1929–1967. *Review of Income and Wealth* 15:293–320.
  (1970). U.S. real product and real factor input, 1929–1967. *Review of Income and Wealth* 16:19–50.
  (1973). Measuring economic performance in the private sector. In: *The Measurement of Economic and Social Performance*, ed. M. Moss, pp. 233–338. New York: Columbia University Press.
Christensen, L. R., Jorgenson, D. W., and Lau, L. J. (1973). Transcendental logarithmic production frontiers. *Review of Economics and Statistics* 55:28–45.
  (1975). Transcendental logarithmic utility functions. *American Economic Review* 65:367–83.
Coe, D. T., and Helpman, E. (1995). International R&D spillovers. *European Economic Review* 39:859–87.
Cole, R., Chen, Y. C., Barquin-Stolleman, J. A., Dulberger, E., Helvacian, N., and Hodge, J. H. (1986). Quality-adjusted price indexes for computer processors and selected peripheral equipment. *Survey of Current Business* 66:41–50.
Deaton, A. (1992). *Understanding Consumption*, pp. 76–135. Oxford University Press.
Denison, E. F. (1967). *Why Growth Rates Differ*. Washington, DC: Brookings Institution.
  (1974). *Accounting for United States Economic Growth*. Washington, DC: Brookings Institution.
  (1989). *Estimates of Productivity Change by Industry*. Washington, DC: Brookings Institution.
Domar, E. (1946). Capital expansion, rate of growth and employment. *Econometrica* 14:137–47.
Dougherty, C., and Jorgenson, D. W. (1996). International comparisons of the sources of economic growth. *American Economic Review* 86:25–9.
Douglas, P. H. (1948). Are there laws of production? *American Economic Review* 38:1–41.
Dulberger, E. (1989). The application of a hedonic model to a quality-adjusted index for computer processors. In: *Technology and Capital Formation*, ed. D. W. Jorgenson and R. Landau, pp. 37–76. Massachusetts Institute of Technology Press.
Englander, A. S., and Gurney, A. (1994). OECD productivity growth: medium-term trends. *OECD Economic Studies* 22:111–30.
Englander, A. S., and Mittelstadt, A. (1988). Total factor productivity: macroeconomic and structural aspects of the slowdown. *OECD Economic Studies* 10:7–56.
Fisher, I. (1906). *The Nature of Capital and Income*. New York, Macmillan.
Fraumeni, B. M. (1997). The measurement of depreciation in the U.S. national income and wealth accounts. *Survey of Current Business* 78:1–14.
Gilbert, M., Beckerman, W., Edelman, J., Marris, S., Stuvel, G., and Teichert, M. (1958). *Comparative National Products and Price Levels*. Paris: Organisation for European Economic Cooperation.
Gilbert, M., and Kravis, I. B. (1954). *An International Comparison of National Products and the Purchasing Power of Currencies*. Paris: Organisation for European Economic Cooperation.

Goldsmith, R. (1955–6). *A Study of Saving in the United States*, 3 vols. Princeton University Press.
  (1962). *The National Wealth of the United States in the Postwar Period*. Washington, DC: National Bureau of Economic Research.
Gordon, R. J. (1990). *The Measurement of Durable Goods Prices*. University of Chicago Press.
Griliches, Z. (1960). Measuring inputs in agriculture: a critical survey. *Journal of Farm Economics* 40:1398–427.
  (1973). Research expenditures and growth accounting. In: *Science and Technology in Economic Growth*, ed. B. R. Williams, pp. 59–95. New York: Macmillan.
  (1979). Issues in assessing the contribution of research and development to productivity growth. *Bell Journal of Economics* 10:92–116.
  (1992). The search for R&D spillovers. *Scandinavian Journal of Economics* (*Suppl.*) 94:29–47.
  (1994). Productivity, R&D, and the data constraint. *American Economic Review* 84:1–23.
  (1995). R&D and productivity: econometric results and measurement issues. In: *Handbook of the Economics of Innovation and Technological Change*, ed. P. Stoneman, pp. 52–89. Oxford: Blackwell.
Grossman, G. M., and Helpman, E. (1991). *Innovation and Growth*. Massachusetts Institute of Technology Press.
  (1994). Endogenous innovation in the theory of growth. *Journal of Economic Perspectives* 8:23–44.
Hall, B. H. (1993). Industrial research in the 1980s: Did the rate of return fall? *Brookings Papers on Economic Activity: Microeconomics* 2:289–331.
  (1996). The private and social returns to research and development. In: *Technology, R&D, and the Economy*, ed. B. L. R. Smith and C. E. Barfield, pp. 140–62. Washington, DC: Brookings Institution and American Enterprise Institute.
Hall, R. E. (1971). The measurement of quality change from vintage price data. In: *Price Indexes and Quality Change*, ed. Z. Griliches, pp. 240–71. Cambridge, MA: Harvard University Press.
  (1973). The specification of technology with several kinds of output. *Journal of Political Economy* 81:878–92.
  (1978). Stochastic implications of the life-cycle-permanent income hypothesis: theory and evidence. *Journal of Political Economy* 86:971–87.
  (1988). The relation between price and marginal cost in U.S. industry. *Journal of Political Economy* 96:921–47.
  (1990a). Invariance properties of Solow's productivity residual. In: *Growth/Productivity/Employment*, ed. P. Diamond, pp. 71–112. Massachusetts Institute of Technology Press.
  (1990b). *The Rational Consumer*. Massachusetts Institute of Technology Press.
Hall, R. E., and Jorgenson, D. W. (1967). Tax policy and investment behavior. *American Economic Review* 57:391–414.
  (1969). Tax policy and investment behavior: reply and further results. *American Economic Review* 59:388–401.
  (1971). Applications of the theory of optimal capital accumulation. In: *Tax*

Incentives and Capital Spending, ed. G. Fromm, pp. 9–60. Amsterdam: North Holland.
Hansen, L. P., and Singleton, K. J. (1982). Generalized instrumental variables estimation of nonlinear rational expectations models. *Econometrica* 50:1269–86.
  (1983). Stochastic consumption, risk aversion, and the temporal behavior of stock market returns. *Journal of Political Economy* 91:249–65.
Hanushek, E. A. (1986). The economics of schooling. *Journal of Economic Literature* 24:1141–78.
  (1989). The impact of differential expenditures on school performance. *Educational Researcher* 18:45–51.
  (1994). *Making Schools Work*. Washington, DC: Brookings Institution.
Harrod, R. (1939). An essay in dynamic theory. *Economic Journal* 49:14–33.
Hertzfeld, H. R. (1985). Measuring the economic impact of federal research and development activities. Presented at a workshop on the federal role in research and development, National Academies of Science and Engineering.
Hulten, C. R., and Wykoff, F. C. (1982). The measurement of economic depreciation. In: *Depreciation, Inflation and the Taxation of Income from Capital*, ed. C. R. Hulten, pp. 81–125.
Inter-Secretariat Working Group on National Accounts (1993). *System of National Accounts 1993*, pp. 379–406. New York: United Nations.
Islam, N. (1995). Growth empirics. *Quarterly Journal of Economics* 110:1127–70.
Jones, C. I. (1995a). R&D-based models of economic growth. *Journal of Political Economy* 103:759–84.
  (1995b). Time series tests of endogenous growth models. *Quarterly Journal of Economics* 110:495–526.
Jones, C. I., and Williams, J. C. (1996). Too much of a good thing? The economics of investment in R&D. Unpublished manuscript, Department of Economics, Stanford University.
Jorgenson, D. W. (1963). Capital theory and investment behavior. *American Economic Review* 53:247–59.
  (1966). The embodiment hypothesis. *Journal of Political Economy* 74:1–17.
  (1967). The theory of investment behavior. In: *The Determinants of Investment Behavior*, ed. R. Ferber, pp. 129–56. New York: Columbia University Press.
  (1973). The economic theory of replacement and depreciation. In: *Econometrics and Economic Theory*, ed. W. Sellekaerts, pp. 189–221. New York: Macmillan.
  (1980). Accounting for capital. In: *Capital, Efficiency, and Growth*, ed. G. M. von Furstenberg, pp. 251–319. Cambridge, MA: Ballinger.
  (1986). Econometric modeling of producer behavior. In: *Handbook of Econometrics*, vol. 3, ed. Z. Griliches and M. D. Intriligator, pp. 1841–915. Amsterdam, North Holland.
  (1990). Productivity and economic growth. In: *Fifty Years of Economic Measurement*, ed. E. R. Berndt and J. Triplett, pp. 19–118. University of Chicago Press.
  (1996). Empirical studies of depreciation. *Economic Inquiry* 34:24–42.
Jorgenson, D. W., and Fraumeni, B. M. (1989). The accumulation of human and nonhuman capital, 1948–1984. In: *The Measurement of Saving, Investment,*

and Wealth, ed. R. E. Lipsey and H. S. Tice, pp. 227–82. University of Chicago Press.

(1992a). Investment in education and U.S. economic growth. *Scandinavian Journal of Economics (Suppl.)* 94:51–70.

(1992b). The output of the education sector. In: *Output Measurement in the Services Sector*, ed. Z. Griliches, pp. 303–38. University of Chicago Press.

Jorgenson, D. W., Gollop, F. M., and Fraumeni, B. M. (1987). *Productivity and U.S. Economic Growth*. Cambridge, MA: Harvard University Press.

Jorgenson, D. W., and Griliches, Z. (1967). The explanation of productivity change. *Review of Economic Studies* 84:249–80.

Jorgenson, D. W., and Ho, M. S. (1995). Modeling economic growth. Unpublished manuscript, Department of Economics, Harvard University.

Jorgenson, D. W., Ho, M. S., and Fraumeni, B. M. (1994). The quality of the U.S. work force, 1948–90. Unpublished manuscript, Department of Economics, Harvard University.

Jorgenson, D. W., Lau, L. J., and Stoker, T. M. (1982). The transcendental logarithmic model of aggregate consumer behavior. In: *Advances in Econometrics*, vol. 1, ed. R. L. Basmann and G. Rhodes, pp. 97–238. Greenwich, CT: JAI Press.

Jorgenson, D. W., and Stiroh, K. (1995). Computers and growth. *Economics of Innovation and New Technology* 3:295–316.

Jorgenson, D. W., and Yun, K.-Y. (1986a). The efficiency of capital allocation. *Scandinavian Journal of Economics* 88:85–107.

(1986b). Tax policy and capital allocation. *Scandinavian Journal of Economics* 88:355–77.

(1990). Tax reform and U.S. economic growth. *Journal of Political Economy* 98:151–93.

(1991a). The excess burden of U.S. taxation. *Journal of Accounting, Auditing, and Finance* 6:487–509.

(1991b). *Tax Reform and the Cost of Capital*, pp. 1–38. Oxford University Press.

Keller, W. (1996). Are international R&D spillovers trade-related? An analysis using Monte-Carlo techniques. Unpublished manuscript, Department of Economics, University of Wisconsin, Madison.

Koopmans, T. C. (1965). On the concept of optimum growth. In: *The Econometric Approach to Development Planning*, pp. 225–300. Chicago: Rand McNally.

Kravis, I. B., Heston, A., and Summers, R. (1978). *International Comparisons of Real Product and Purchasing Power*. Baltimore: Johns Hopkins University Press.

Kuznets, S. (1961). *Capital in the American Economy*. Princeton University Press.

(1971). *Economic Growth of Nations*. Cambridge, MA: Harvard University Press.

(1992). Modern economic growth: findings and reflections. In: *Nobel Lectures in Economic Sciences, 1969–1980*, ed. A. Lindbeck, pp. 87–102. River Edge, NJ: World Scientific Publishing.

Lau, L. J. (1996). The sources of long-term economic growth: observations from the experience of developed and developing countries. In: *The Mosaic of Economic Growth*, ed. R. Landau, T. Taylor, and G. Wright, pp. 63–91. Stanford University Press.

Levine, R., and Renelt, D. (1992). A sensitivity analysis of cross-country regressions. *American Economic Review* 82:942–63.
Lindbeck, A. (ed.) (1992). *Nobel Lectures in Economic Sciences, 1969–1980*. River Edge, NJ: World Scientific Publishing.
Lucas, R. E. (1988). On the mechanics of economic development. *Journal of Monetary Economics* 22:2–42.
Machlup, F. (1962). *The Production and Distribution of Knowledge in the United States*. Princeton University Press.
Maddison, A. (1982). *Phases of Capitalist Development*. Oxford University Press.
  (1991). *Dynamic Forces in Capitalist Development*. Oxford University Press.
  (1995). *Monitoring the World Economy*. Paris: Organisation for Economic Co-operation and Development.
Maler, K.-G. (ed.) (1992). In: *Nobel Lectures in Economic Sciences, 1981–1990*. River Edge, NJ: World Scientific Publishing.
Mankiw, G., Romer, D., and Weil, D. (1992). A contribution to the empirics of economic growth. *Quarterly Journal of Economics* 407–37.
Mincer, J. (1974). *Schooling, Experience, and Earnings*. New York: Columbia University Press.
Mowery, D. C. (1985). Federal funding of R&D in transportation: the case of aviation. Presented at a workshop on the federal role in research and development, National Academies of Science and Engineering.
Nordhaus, W. D., and Tobin, J. (1972). *Is Growth Obsolete?* New York: National Bureau of Economic Research. Reprinted (1973) In: *The Measurement of Economic and Social Performance*, ed. M. Moss, pp. 509–32. New York: Columbia University Press.
Pieper, P. E. (1989). Construction price statistics revisited. In: *Technology and Capital Formation*, ed. D. W. Jorgenson and R. Landau, pp. 293–330. Massachusetts Institute of Technology Press.
  (1990). The measurement of construction prices: retrospect and prospect. In: *Fifty Years of Economic Measurement*, ed. E. R. Berndt and J. Triplett, pp. 239–68. University of Chicago Press.
Ramsey, F. (1928). A mathematical theory of saving. *Economic Journal* 28:543–59.
Rebello, S. (1991). Long-run policy analysis and long-run growth. *Journal of Political Economy* 99:500–21.
Romer, P. (1986). Increasing returns and long-run growth. *Journal of Political Economy* 94:1002–37.
  (1987). Crazy explanations for the productivity slowdown. In: *NBER Macroeconomics Annual*, ed. S. Fischer, pp. 163–201. Massachusetts Institute of Technology Press.
  (1990). Endogenous technological change. *Journal of Political Economy* 98:S71–102.
  (1994). The origins of endogenous growth. *Journal of Economic Perspectives* 8:3–20.
Samuelson, P. A. (1961). The evaluation of "social income": capital formation and wealth. In: *The Theory of Capital*, ed. F. A. Lutz and D. C. Hague, pp. 32–57. New York: Macmillan.
Schmookler, J. (1966). *Invention and Economic Growth*. Cambridge, MA: Harvard University Press.

Schultz, T. W. (1961). Investment in human capital. *American Economic Review* 51:1–17.
Schumpeter, J. (1942). *Capitalism, Socialism, and Democracy*, New York: Harper.
Solow, R. M. (1956). A contribution to the theory of economic growth. *Quarterly Journal of Economics* 70:65–94.
    (1957). Technical change and the aggregate production function. *Review of Economics and Statistics* 39:312–20.
    (1960). Investment and technical progress. In: *Mathematical Methods in the Social Sciences, 1959*, ed. K. J. Arrow, S. Karlin, and P. Suppes, pp. 89–104. Stanford University Press.
    (1967). Some recent developments in the theory of production. In: *The Theory and Empirical Analysis of Production*, ed. M. Brown, pp. 25–50. New York: Columbia University Press.
    (1970). *Growth Theory: An Exposition*. Oxford University Press.
    (1988). Growth theory and after. *American Economic Review* 78:307–17.
    (1992). *Growth Theory*, 2nd ed. Oxford University Press.
    (1994). Perspectives on growth theory. *Journal of Economic Perspectives* 8:45–54.
Stoker, T. M. (1993). Empirical approaches to the problem of aggregation over individuals. *Journal of Economic Literature* 31:1827–74.
Stokey, N. L. (1995). R&D and economic growth. *Review of Economic Studies* 62:469–90.
Stone, R. (1992). The accounts of society. In: *Nobel Lectures in Economic Sciences, 1981–1990*, ed. K.-G. Maler, pp. 115–39. River Edge, NJ: World Scientific Publishing.
Summers, R., and Heston, A. (1984). Improved international comparisons of real product and its composition: 1950–1980. *Review of Income and Wealth* 30:207–62.
    (1988). A new set of international comparisons of real product and price levels: estimates for 130 countries, 1950–1985. *Review of Income and Wealth* 34:1–25.
    (1991). The Penn World Table (Mark 5): an expanded set of international comparisons, 1950–1988. *Quarterly Journal of Economics* 106:327–68.
Summers, R., Kravis, I. B., and Heston, A. (1980). International comparisons of real product and its composition, 1950–77. *Review of Income and Wealth* 26:19–66.
Tinbergen, J. (1942). Zur Theorie der Langfristigen Wirtschaftsentwicklung. *Weltwirtschaftliches Archiv* 55:511–49.
    (1959). On the theory of trend movements. In: *Selected Papers*, pp. 182–221. Amsterdam: North Holland.
Triplett, J. (1986). The economic interpretation of hedonic methods. *Survey of Current Business* 66:36–40.
    (1989). Price and technological change in a capital good: survey of research on computers. In: *Technology and Capital Formation*, ed. D. W. Jorgenson and R. Landau, pp. 127–213. Massachusetts Institute of Technology Press.
    (1990). Hedonic methods in statistical agency environments: an intellectual biopsy. In: *Fifty Years of Economic Measurement*, ed. E. R. Berndt and J. Triplett, pp. 207–38. University of Chicago Press.

(1996). Measuring the capital stock: a review of concepts and data needs. *Economic Inquiry* 34:93–115.
United Nations (1968). *A System of National Accounts*. New York: United Nations.
(1993). A System of National Accounts. New York: United Nations.
World Bank (1994). *World Development Report 1993*. Washington, DC: World Bank.
Young, A. (1989). BEA's measurement of computer output. *Survey of Current Business* 69:108–15.

PART FOUR

MICROECONOMIC POLICY

CHAPTER 8

Evaluating the Welfare State

James J. Heckman and Jeffrey Smith

Ragnar Frisch was a leading advocate of national economic planning in the service of the welfare state. His Nobel lecture (1970) stressed the value of interactions between economists and politicians in arriving at politically acceptable and economically viable national plans. A major theme of his lecture was that economists should act in the public interest and in so doing should recognize the diversity of policy objectives advocated by different groups in democratic societies. He made the important distinction between maximizing the mythical welfare function assumed in classical welfare economics and in the classic policy analysis of Tinbergen (1956) and reconciling and satisfying the diverse perceptions and values held by citizens of modern states. He stressed the role of economists in informing policy-makers and the general public about the relevant economic trade-offs and the costs of alternative policies.

Frisch's faith in the power of economics to supply the information required to make informed public choices seems wildly optimistic today,

---

Portions of this study were first presented in the Barcelona lecture to the World Econometric Society (Heckman, 1990b), and some of this material draws from Heckman (1992, 1993), Heckman, Smith, and Clements (1997), and Heckman and Smith (1993, 1995). The ideas not presented in those papers were first presented in informal discussions at a CEMFI conference in Madrid, Spain, in September 1993 and at a workshop at the Institute for Research on Poverty at the University of Wisconsin, Madison, in February 1994 and have been shared with colleagues at the University of Chicago. The research in this chapter was supported by grant NSF-SBR-93-21-048, by the Russell Sage Foundation, and by a grant from the American Bar Foundation. We thank the editor of the Econometric Monograph Series, Alberto Holly, and an anonymous referee for helpful comments, as well as Gary Becker, Olav Bjerkholt, Dragan Filipovich, Lars Hansen, Hidehiko Ichimura, Lance Lochner, Tom MaCurdy, Derek Neal, Robert Pollak, Jose Scheinkman, Chris Taber, and Ed Vytlacil. We also thank the seminar participants at the Oslo meeting in March 1995, as well as colleagues at Columbia University, the University of Chicago, University College London, the Canadian Econometric Studies Group in Montreal (September 1995), and Washington University, St. Louis. Ed Vytlacil is singled out for a particularly close reading.

yet his message remains relevant. Economists are still asked to inform the general public and policy-makers about the likely consequences of alternative social programs. Social-welfare functions do not govern decision making in any democratic society, and it is clear that a variety of criteria are relevant for evaluating alternative policies in democratic societies composed of individuals and groups with diverse values and perspectives.

Coercive redistribution and intervention are defining activities of the welfare state. Principled redistribution and intervention are based on interpersonal comparisons made by governments and groups of individuals in society. Different public policies typically have different consequences for different citizens. Enumerating and evaluating these consequences are important parts of social decision making, and different criteria have been suggested.

This essay presents these criteria and considers the data required to operationalize them. Some are very difficult to implement empirically and so cannot serve as practical guides to social decision making. Other criteria can be implemented, especially if economists have access to microeconomic data, but such data must be supplemented by knowledge of – or assumptions about – the choice processes of the agents being studied or the dependence across potential outcomes associated with different policies and by assumptions that relate partial-equilibrium evaluations to general-equilibrium evaluations. We shall examine alternative sets of identifying assumptions that bound, or exactly produce, the alternative criteria used in evaluating the welfare state.

Frisch was well aware that economists often need to supplement the available data with assumptions in order to evaluate policies. His Nobel lecture emphasized the "lure of unsolvable problems," and he advocated evaluation of policies by making bold assumptions if necessary. His famous article on circulation planning emphasized this point (Frisch, 1934). That essay examined how bold the assumptions have to be to answer major economic evaluation questions given the type of data available in many countries.

This essay considers the general policy-evaluation problem, but focuses most of its attention on a specific version of it that is widely studied in econometrics under the rubric of "the analysis of treatment effects" (e.g., Heckman and Robb, 1985). In this version, a policy has a voluntary component, sometimes called a program, and persons choose to participate in it. A job-training program and a tuition subsidy for college attendance are examples. There may be an involuntary component to the policy as well, such as paying the taxes to finance the voluntary component or facing the wages produced by an increase in the supply of trained workers resulting from the program. Having access to data on the outcomes of participants and nonparticipants simplifies some aspects of the policy-evaluation problem, compared with the case where only participants or nonparticipants are observed, but also raises the problem of self-selection bias.

From information on the program participation decisions of eligible persons, it is sometimes possible to infer their preferences for the outcomes produced by the program. This information is of value in its own right. A strictly libertarian evaluation of a program stops with determining individual subjective valuations for the program being evaluated. Evaluation of the welfare state requires more information. "Objective" evaluations of outcomes supplement revealed-preference information to form the basis for policy discussions and interpersonal comparisons. Even if such "objective" information is available about outcomes under each policy, knowledge of individual preferences for specific programs helps in constructing, or bounding, the distribution of outcomes across alternative policy regimes that is required to implement some of the criteria examined in this essay. In addition, if general-equilibrium effects can be safely ignored, knowledge of the outcomes for self-selected nonparticipants sometimes identifies the distribution of outcomes for society at large in the absence of the program produced by a policy.

In the course of examining these issues, we consider which policy questions conventional econometric "treatment-effect" estimators answer by embedding them in a simple general-equilibrium framework. Most of the standard econometric estimators identify parameters of only limited economic interest, but in certain special cases they provide partial answers to economically interesting questions.

We use data from a social experiment designed to evaluate the gross impact of training on the earnings and employment of participants in order to examine the conflict or consistency among the various criteria that have been proposed to evaluate policies. If all the criteria are in agreement, their multiplicity is not a matter of practical importance. We examine participant evaluations as revealed by their attrition from the program instituted by a policy, by their responses to questionnaires, and by econometric analyses of outcome and participation equations under different identifying assumptions. We find that participant self-assessments disagree with revealed preferences as manifested by choices, and with impacts objectively estimated using experimental data. The criteria do not all agree, and there is scope for seriously conflicting assessments of a program. We also present evidence that favorable cost–benefit assessments of government training programs are considerably weakened once the full cost of raising government revenue is taken into account.

This chapter is organized in the following way: Section 1 presents alternative criteria for evaluating the welfare state and the data required to operationalize them. Both the general case and the specific case of evaluating a program into which agents self-select are examined. Section

2 considers how alternative assumptions about decision processes and access to different sources of microeconomic data aid in the construction of the evaluation criteria. Section 3 examines the economic questions addressed by two widely used econometric evaluation estimators and relates them to a portion of what is required in a comprehensive cost–benefit analysis. Evidence is presented on how the inference from the most commonly used econometric evaluation estimator is modified when direct costs of the program are fully assessed, including the welfare costs of taxes raised to support the program. Section 4 presents empirical evidence on the consistency of alternative criteria derived from evaluations based on "objective" outcomes, evaluations inferred from self-selection and attrition decisions, and self-reported evaluations elicited with questionnaires regarding a prototypical job-training program. The chapter concludes with a summary in Section 5.

1 Alternative Criteria for Evaluating the Welfare State

1.1 *The Origin of the Demand for Evaluations*

Coercive redistribution and intervention are essential activities of the welfare state. Adopting any particular policy with a redistributional component involves weighing the subjective assessments made by different groups regarding the outcomes created by the policy using the political process. Coercion arises because the perceived benefit from a policy does not always equal or exceed its cost for all members of a society. If there were no coercion, redistribution and intervention would be voluntary activities, and apart from the free-rider problem there would be no scope for government activity in orchestrating redistribution and conducting interventions. There would be no need to publicly justify voluntary trades among individuals.

If government is producing a service for which there are good market substitutes, there is no need to resort to an elaborate evaluation procedure for the service. Market prices provide the right measure of marginal gain and cost, unless the usual problems of increasing returns, externalities, or public perception that private preferences are defective lead to mistrust of the signals produced from the market mechanism. The argument that justifies the welfare state denies the use of prices and private evaluations as the sole criteria for evaluation of governmental activities, but recognizes that they may be relevant inputs into the general policy-evaluation process.

The demand for publicly documented evaluations arises from a demand for information by rival parties in a democratic state. Even libertarians who do not accept coercion and who oppose government intervention evaluate policies in order to participate in the political dialogue of the welfare state.

Evaluating the Welfare State

The claims that markets fail or that consumer judgments are faulty often are made without a factual basis. If these claims are false, the case for a welfare state is weakened. In this study, we accept the reality of the welfare state, without necessarily endorsing the arguments for it. We do not consider the quality of the evidence supporting the premises of the welfare state. Instead, we consider the evaluation of specific policy proposals within its framework.

1.2 Alternative Criteria for Evaluating Programs

Let the outcome in the presence of policy j for person i be Y_{ji}, and let the personal preferences of person i for outcome Y be denoted $U_i(Y)$. A policy effects a redistribution from taxpayers to beneficiaries, and Y_{ji} represents the flow of resources to i under policy j. Some persons can be both beneficiaries and taxpayers. All policies we consider are assumed to be feasible. In the simplest case, Y_{ji} is net income after tax and transfers, but it can also be a vector of incomes and benefits, including provision of in-kind services. Many criteria have been proposed to evaluate policies. Let "0" denote the no-policy state, and initially abstract from uncertainty. The standard model of welfare economics postulates a social-welfare function W that is defined over the utilities of the N members of society:

$$W(j) = W[U_1(Y_{j1}), \ldots, U_N(Y_{jN})] \tag{1}$$

Policy choice based on a social-welfare function picks that policy j with the highest value for $W(j)$. A leading special case is the Benthamite social-welfare function:

$$B(j) = \sum_{i=1}^{N} U_i(Y_{ji}) \tag{2}$$

Criteria (1) and (2) implicitly assume that social preferences are defined in terms of the private preferences of citizens, as expressed in terms of their own consumption; this principle is called welfarism (Sen, 1979). They could be extended to allow for interdependence across persons so that the utility of person i under policy j would be $U_i(Y_{j1}, \ldots, Y_{jN})$ for all i.

Conventional cost–benefit analysis assumes that Y_{ji} is scalar income and orders policies by their contributions to aggregate income:

$$\text{CB}(j) = \sum_{i=1}^{N} Y_{ji} \tag{3}$$

Analysts who adopt criterion (3) implicitly assume that outputs are costlessly redistributed among persons via a social-welfare function, or else they accept gross national product (GNP) as their measure of value for a policy.

While these criteria are traditional, they are not universally accepted, and they do not answer all of the interesting questions of political economy or "social justice" that arise in the political arena of the welfare state. In a democratic society, politicians and advocacy groups are interested in knowing the proportion of people who will benefit from policy j as compared with policy k:

$$\text{PB}(j|j, k) = \frac{1}{N} \sum_{i=1}^{N} 1[U_i(Y_{ji}) \geq U_i(Y_{ki})] \tag{4}$$

where "1" is the indicator function: $1(A) = 1$ if A is true; $1(A) = 0$ otherwise. In the median-voter model, a necessary condition for j to be preferred to k is that $\text{PB}(j|j, k) \geq \frac{1}{2}$. Many writers on "social justice" are concerned about the plight of the poor, as measured in some base state k. For them, the gain from policy j is measured in terms of the income or utility gains of the poor. In this case, interest centers on the gains to specific types of persons, such as the gains to persons with outcomes in the base state k less than $\underline{y}$: $\Delta_{jki} = Y_{ji} - Y_{ki} | Y_{ki} \leq \underline{y}$, or their distribution

$$F(\Delta_{jk}|Y_k = y_{k_j}, y_k \leq \underline{y}) \tag{5}$$

or the utility equivalents of these variables. Within a targeted subpopulation there is sometimes interest in knowing the proportion of people who gain relative to specified values of the base state k:

$$\Pr(\Delta_{jk} > 0 | Y_k \leq \underline{y}) \tag{6}$$

In addition, measures (2) and (3) are often defined only for a target population, not for the full taxpayer population.

The existence of merit goods like education or health implies that specific components of the vector Y_{ji} are of interest to certain groups. Many policies are paternalistic in nature and implicitly assume that people make the wrong choices. "Social" values are placed on specific outcomes, often stated in terms of thresholds. Thus one group may care about another group in terms of whether or not they satisfy an absolute threshold requirement,

$$Y_{ji} \geq \underline{y} \quad \text{for } i \in S$$

where S is a target set toward which the policy is directed, or in terms of a relative requirement compared with a base state k,

$$Y_{ji} \geq Y_{ki} \quad \text{for } i \in S$$

Uncertainty introduces additional considerations. Participants in society typically do not know the consequences of each policy for each person. A fundamental limitation in applying these criteria is that, ex ante, these consequences are not known and, ex post, one may not observe all potential outcomes for all persons. If some states are not experienced, the best that agents can do is to guess about them. Even if, ex post, agents know their outcome in a benchmark state, they may not know it ex ante, and they may always be uncertain about what they would have experienced in an alternative state.

In the literature on welfare economics and social choice, one form of decision making under uncertainty has been extensively investigated. The "veil of ignorance" of Vickrey (1945) and Harsanyi (1955, 1975) postulates that decision-makers are completely uncertain about their positions in the distribution of outcomes under each policy, or should act as if they are completely uncertain, and they should use expected-utility criteria (Vickrey-Harsanyi) or a maximin strategy (Rawls, 1971) to evaluate their welfare under alternative policies. This form of ignorance is sometimes justified as an "ethically correct" position that captures how an "objectively detached" observer should evaluate alternative policies even if actual participants in the political process use other criteria. An approach based on the veil of ignorance is widely used in practical work in evaluating different income distributions (Sen, 1973) and requires information only about the marginal distributions of outcomes produced under different policies.

A less high-minded, but empirically more accurate, description of social decision making recognizes that persons act in their own self-interest and have some knowledge about how they will fare under different policies, but allows for the possibility that persons can only imperfectly anticipate their outcomes under different policy regimes. The outcomes in different regimes may be dependent, so that persons who benefit under one policy may also benefit under another. However, agents may not possess perfect foresight. Letting I_i denote the information set available to agent i, agent i will evaluate policy j against k using that information. Let $F(y_j, y_k | I_i)$ be the distribution of outcomes (Y_j, Y_k) *as perceived* by agent i. Under an expected-utility criterion, person i prefers policy j over k if

$$E[U_i(Y_j)|I_i] > E[U_i(Y_k)|I_i]$$

Letting θ_i parameterize heterogeneity in preferences, so that $U_i(Y_j) = U(Y_j; \theta_i)$, and using integrals to simplify the expressions, the proportion of people who prefer j is

$$\text{PB}(j|j, k) = \int 1\{E[U(Y_j|\theta)|I] > E[U(Y_k|\theta)|I]\} dF(\theta, I) \qquad (7)$$

where $F(\theta, I)$ is the joint distribution of θ and I in the population whose preferences over outcomes are being studied.[1] In the special case where $I_i = (Y_{ji}, Y_{ki})$, so that there is no uncertainty about Y_j and Y_k,

$$PB(j|j, k) = \int 1[U(y_j; \theta) > U(y_k; \theta)]dF(\theta, y_j, y_k) \qquad (8)$$

Expression (8) is an integral version of (4) when outcomes are perfectly predictable and when preference heterogeneity can be indexed by vector θ.

Adding uncertainty to the analysis makes it informative to distinguish between ex-ante and ex-post evaluations. Ex post, part of the uncertainty about policy outcomes is resolved, although individuals do not, in general, have full information about what their potential outcomes would have been in policy regimes they have not experienced, and they may have only incomplete information about the policy they have experienced (e.g., the policy may have long-run consequences extending past the point of evaluation). It is useful to index the information set I_i by t, I_{it}, to recognize that information about the outcomes of policies may accrue over time. Ex-ante and ex-post assessments of a voluntary program need not agree. Ex-post assessments of a program through surveys administered to persons who have completed it (Katz et al., 1975) may disagree with ex-ante assessments of the program. Both may reflect honest valuations of the program, but they are reported at times when agents have different sets of information about the program. Before participating in a program, persons may be uncertain of the consequences of participation. Persons who have completed program j may know Y_j, but can only guess at the alternative outcome Y_k, which they have not experienced. In this case, ex-post "satisfaction" for agent i is synonymous with the following inequality:

$$U_i(Y_{ji}) > E[U_i(Y_{ki})|I_{it}] \qquad (9)$$

where t is the post-program period in which the evaluation is made. In addition, survey questionnaires about "client" satisfaction with a program may capture subjective elements of program experience not captured by "objective" measures of outcomes, which usually exclude psychic costs and benefits.

In order to operationalize these notions empirically, it is useful to distinguish the effects of a policy as it impacts the tax-collection system from its effects operating through direct program participation. To this end, it is useful to isolate policy outcomes from alternative revenue-

---

[1] We do not claim that persons will necessarily vote "honestly," although in a binary-choice setting they do, and there is no scope for strategic manipulation of votes (Moulin, 1983). "PB" is simply a measure of relative satisfaction and need not describe a voting outcome where other factors come into play.

neutral programs under the same tax structure and consider the consequences of alternative tax structures separately. In most of the empirical work reported here we are able to measure only the impacts of specific programs on direct participants. We abstract from the tax consequences of financing a program, except when we consider the effect of accounting for full social costs in a cost–benefit analysis of a training program. This approach is justified by two distinct arguments: (a) that the tax consequences of the program being evaluated are slight or (b) that the program's "clients" differ from the taxpayers, and we wish to measure only the welfare gains of the "clients."

1.3 The Domain of the Microeconomic Literature on Self-selection and "Treatment Effects"

The classic macroeconomic general-equilibrium policy-evaluation program considered by Knight (1921), Tinbergen (1956), Marschak (1953), and Lucas and Sargent (1981) forecasts and evaluates the impacts of policies that have never been implemented. To do this requires knowledge of policy-invariant structural parameters and a basis for making proposed new policies comparable to old ones.[2]

The common form of the microeconomic evaluation problem is apparently more tractable. It considers evaluation of a program in which participation is voluntary, although it may not have been intended to be so. Persons are offered a service and may select into the program to receive it. Eligibility for the program may be restricted to subsets of persons in the larger society. Many "mandatory" programs have as an option that persons may attrite from them or fail to comply with program requirements. Participation in the program is equated with direct receipt of the service, and payments of taxes and general-equilibrium effects of the program are ignored.[3]

In this formulation of the evaluation problem, the no-treatment outcome distribution for a given program is used to approximate the distribution of outcomes in the no-program state. That is, the outcomes for the untreated within the context of an existing program are used to approximate outcome distributions when there is no program. This approximation rests on two distinct arguments: (a) that general-equilibrium effects inclusive of taxes and spillover effects on factor and

---

[2] A quotation from Knight is apt: "The existence of a problem in knowledge depends on the future being different from the past, while the possibility of a solution of the problem depends on the future being like the past" (Knight, 1921, p. 313).

[3] The contrast between micro and macro analyses is overdrawn. The studies by Baumol and Quandt (1966), Lancaster (1971), and Domencich and McFadden (1975) were micro examples of attempts to solve what we have called a macro problem. Those authors considered the problem of forecasting the demand for a new good that had never previously been purchased.

output markets can be ignored and (b) that the problem of selection bias that arises from using self-selected samples of participants and nonparticipants to estimate population distributions can be ignored or surmounted.

More precisely, let j be the policy regime we seek to evaluate. Eligible person i in regime j has two potential outcomes: (Y_{ji}^0, Y_{ji}^1), where the superscripts denote nondirect participation ("0") and direct participation ("1"). Noneligible persons have only one option: Y_{ji}^0. These outcomes are defined at the equilibrium level of participation under program j. All feedback effects are incorporated in the definitions of the potential outcomes.

Let subscript "0" denote a policy regime without the program. Let $D_{ji} = 1$ if person i participates in program j. A crucial identifying assumption that is implicitly invoked in the microeconomic evaluation literature is that

$$Y_{ji}^0 = Y_{0i} \tag{A-1}$$

and hence that $F(y_j^0 | D_j = 0, X) = F(y_0 | D_j = 0, X)$ for $y_j^0 = y_0$ given conditioning variables X. The outcome for nonparticipants in policy regime j is the same in the no-policy state "0" and in the state in which policy j is operative. This assumption is consistent with a program that has "negligible" general-equilibrium effects and in which the same structure of tax-revenue collection is used in regimes j and "0."

An additional assumption sometimes invoked is that

$$Y_{ji}^1 = Y_{ji} \tag{A-2}$$

where Y_{ji} is the outcome if the program is universally applied. This entails a different kind of general-equilibrium assumption – this time concerning expansion of program j to universal coverage. Making assumptions (A-1) and (A-2) together strains the imagination, for if a program is sufficiently small that (A-1) is plausible, its universal expansion may make it so large that (A-2) will not be plausible. Nonetheless, taken together, these assumptions, strengthened with additional assumptions about agent self-selection rules, enable analysts to generalize from self-selected samples within a given policy regime to choices across policy regimes. Assumption (A-2) is rarely used and plays only a minor role in this study. Assumption (A-1) plays a much more substantial role in this study and in the microeconomic evaluation literature.

From data on individual program participation decisions it is possible to infer the implicit valuations of the program made by persons eligible for it. These evaluations constitute all of the data needed for a libertarian program evaluation, but something more than these will be required to evaluate programs in the interventionist welfare state. For certain decision rules, it is possible to use the data from self-selected samples to bound or estimate the joint distributions required to implement criterion (4) or (7), as we demonstrate later.

The existence of a voluntary-participation component for a program under policy j creates an option value that for eligible person i is

$$\max\{Y_{ji}^0, Y_{ji}^1\} - Y_{ji}^0 \tag{10}$$

By (A-1) this is the same as $\max\{Y_{0i}, Y_{ji}^1\} - Y_{0i}$, which if strengthened by (A-2) is $\max\{Y_{0i}, Y_{ji}\} - Y_{0i}$. The distribution of the value of this option for those who take it is

$$F(y_j^1 - y_j^0 | Y_j^1 > Y_j^0) \tag{11}$$

For persons interested in the equity of program provisions, it is of interest to examine the dependence between the options offered and the non-participation outcomes, which are assumed to approximate the no-policy outcomes.

People who fear "cream skimming" by program administrators whose performance is evaluated on the basis of the outcomes for the participants they select claim that Y_j^1 and Y_j^0 are strongly positively dependent and that the gross value added, $\Delta_j = Y_j^1 - Y_j^0$, is unrelated or negatively related to Y_j^0. To address these concerns, it is necessary to know the joint dependence between Y_j^0 and Y_j^1 and to compute the dependence between Δ_j and Y_j^0.

2 The Data Needed to Evaluate the Welfare State

To implement criteria (1) and (2), it is necessary to know the distribution of outcomes across the entire population and to know the utility functions of individuals. In the case where Y refers to scalar income, criterion (3) requires only GNP (the sum of the program-j outcome distribution). If interest centers solely on the distributions of outcomes for direct program participants, the measures can be defined solely for populations with $D_j = 1$. Criteria (4), (5), (6), and (8) require knowledge of outcomes and preferences across programs. Criterion (7) requires knowledge of the joint distribution of information and preferences across persons. Tables 8.1A and 8.1B summarize the criteria and the data needed to implement them.

This study has little to say about estimating preference functions or preference heterogeneity. We refer readers to Heckman (1974a) and the comprehensive survey by Browning, Hansen, and Heckman (in press), who have documented the empirical importance of preference heterogeneity. Our focus is on estimating the distributions of outcomes across policy states as a first step toward empirically implementing the full criteria. This more modest objective can be fit into the framework of Section 1 by assuming that utilities are linear in their arguments and identical across persons.

Table 8.1A. *Population Data Requirements to Implement Criterion: General Population (Compulsory Programs); Program j Compared with Program k*

	Cost–benefit criterion	Benthamite criterion	General social-welfare function with interdependent preferences	Selfish voting
Criterion	$E(Y_j) - E(Y_k) \geq 0$	$E[U(Y_j, \theta)] - E[U(Y_k, \theta)] \geq 0$ $E[U(Y_\ell, \theta)] = \int U(y_\ell, \theta) dF(y_\ell, \theta);$ $\ell = j, k$	$W(j) > W(k)$ $W(\ell) = W[U_1(Y_{1\ell}, \ldots, Y_{N\ell}), \ldots, U_N(Y_{1\ell}, \ldots, Y_{N\ell})]; \ell = j, k$[a]	$\int 1\,[U(y_j, \theta) \geq U(y_k, \theta)]$ $dF(y_j, y_k, \theta) \geq 0$
Require	Population means $E(Y_j), E(Y_k)$	$U(Y_\ell, \theta)$ and distribution of $(Y_\ell, \theta), F(y_\ell, \theta); \ell = j, k$	Need each $U_i(Y_{1\ell}, \ldots, Y_{N\ell})$ for all i; need outcomes for each person[b]	Need $U(Y, \theta), F(y_j, y_k, \theta)$[c]
Estimable on aggregate time-series data?	Yes, if data exist on aggregate economy in both regimes and can eliminate trend	No, unless θ is the same for everyone (homogeneity); $U(Y_\ell, \theta)$ known and the moment $\int U(y_\ell, \theta) dF(y_\ell, \theta)$ known or estimable; $\ell = j, k$	No, except in the special cases previously considered	No

[a] This includes the special case where individual utility depends only on individual consumption.
[b] In special cases, summary statistics of the distribution of Y may suffice.
[c] For altruistic voting, U depends on outcomes for other persons, $Y_{1j}, Y_{ij}, \ldots, Y_{Nj}$ or various subaggregators.

Table 8.1B. *Population Data Requirements to Implement Criterion (Voluntary Programs, Conditional on $D_j = 1$); Program j Compared with Program k*

	Cost–benefit criterion	Benthamite criterion	General social-welfare function with interdependent preferences[a]	Selfish voting
Criterion	$E(Y_j\|D_j = 1) - E(Y_k\|D_j = 1)$; what j participants gain over state k	$E[U(Y_j, \theta)\|D_j = 1] - E[U(Y_k, \theta)\|D_j = 1]] \geq 0$ where $E[U(Y_\ell, \theta)\|D_j = 1] = \int U(y_\ell, \theta) dF(y_\ell, \theta\|D_j = 1)$; $\ell = j, k$	$W(j) > W(k)$ $W(\ell) = W[U_1(Y_{1\ell}, \ldots, Y_{N\ell}), \ldots, U_N(Y_{1\ell}, \ldots, Y_{N\ell})]; \ell = j, k$	$\int 1[U(y_j, \theta) \geq U(y_k, \theta)]$ $dF(y_j, y_k, \theta \| D_j = 1) \geq 0$
Require	Population conditional means $E(Y_j\|D_j = 1), E(Y_k\|D_j = 1)$	$U(Y_\ell, \theta)$ for $D_j = 1$; $\ell = j, k$	Need each $U_i(Y_{1\ell}, \ldots, Y_{N\ell})$ for all i for whom $D = 1$; need identity of outcomes for each person	Need $U(Y, \theta), F(y_j, y_k, \theta)\|D_j = 1)$
Estimable on aggregate time-series data?	Yes; if aggregate data for participants exist in both regimes, can eliminate trend	No, unless θ is the same for everyone (homogeneity); $U(Y_\ell, \theta)$ known, and the moment $\int U(y_\ell, \theta) dF(y_\ell, \theta \| D_j = 1)$ is known or estimable; $\ell = j, k$	No, except in the special cases previously considered	No

[a] This criterion is not well defined when restricted to subsets of the population. If only the utility of voluntary participants is considered, some position about the utility of nonparticipants must be taken, and the feedback between participants and nonparticipants must be explicitly modeled. When individual utility depends only on individual consumption, the criterion is well defined.

This section considers the problem of constructing the distribution of (Y_j^0, Y_j^1), the distribution of potential outcomes within policy regime j in which direct participation is voluntary. Extension of the estimates of this distribution to other policy regimes follows by invoking the assumptions discussed in Section 1. We discuss how the widely invoked implicit assumption that responses to program treatment are homogeneous across persons greatly simplifies the construction of the joint distribution of potential outcomes and how explicit assumptions about the structure of voluntary program participation rules aid in identifying or reducing the uncertainty about the distributions of outcomes. We consider the information available from cross-section data, from social experiments, from panel data, and from repeated cross-section data.

2.1 The Microeconomic Evaluation Problem

To simplify the notation, we drop the policy-regime subscript j. All of the distributions we consider in this section are measured within that regime. The extrapolation of within-regime measures to across-regime measures is made using assumptions (A-1) and (A-2) discussed in Section 1. In a regime with voluntary participation, we have access to

$$F(y_t^1 | D = 1, X) \quad \text{and} \quad F(y_t^0 | D = 0, X) \tag{12}$$

the distributions of outcomes for participants and nonparticipants at time t, respectively. These embody both the direct and indirect effects of the program.

The fundamental evaluation problem arises from the fact that we do not observe (Y_t^0, Y_t^1) for anyone – just one coordinate or the other of this pair. Given knowledge of individual preferences, and their joint distribution with the outcomes, all of the policy criteria discussed in Section 1 and summarized in Tables 8.1A and 8.1B can be implemented. Here we focus on recovering $F(y_t^0, y_t^1, D | X)$, from which all of the distributions discussed in Section 1 can be recovered. For evaluating the criteria only for program participants, it is enough to know $F(y_t^0, y_t^1 | D = 1, X)$ – the potential outcomes for participants – or various marginal distributions formed from this distribution.

As previously noted, the different evaluation criteria require different data for their empirical implementation. Cost–benefit analysis can, in principle, be performed using a before–after analysis of aggregate time-series data. However, if a program has a small impact on the economy, and other policies are instituted coincident with the program being evaluated, or if the time series is nonstationary, aggregate data do not offer a reliable source of information.

The missing counterfactual for cost–benefit criterion (3) is the mean $E(Y_t^0)$, or $E(Y_t^0 | D = 1, X)$ if the evaluation is conducted solely for participants. $E(Y_t^1|D = 1, X)$ is produced from data on program participants. Benthamite criterion (2) is more demanding and requires $F(y_t^0|X)$, or $F(Y_t^0|D = 1, X)$ if the criterion is defined only for participants. The voting criterion (8) requires $F(y_t^1, Y_t^0|X)$, or $F(y_t^1, Y_t^0|D = 1, X)$ if the criterion is defined only for participants.

In this section we consider how to use cross-section data, data from ideal social experiments, panel data, and repeated cross-section data to construct the different evaluation criteria. Panel data can be used as repeated cross sections, and repeated cross sections can be used as cross sections. Thus it is natural to start with the cross-section case and then determine how access to other sources of data aids in securing identification of the evaluation criteria presented in Section 1.

2.1.1 Cross-Section Data

From cross-section data on $F(y_t^1|D = 1, X)$, $F(y_t^0|D = 0, X)$, and $\Pr(D = 1|X)$ we cannot directly construct the joint distribution $F(y_t^1, y_t^0, D|X)$. Using $F(y_t^0|D = 0, X)$ to proxy $F(y_t^0|D = 1, X)$ runs the risk of selection bias. Various different identifying assumptions have been used to recover the counterfactual distribution $F(y_t^0|D = 1, X)$ or the joint distribution $F(y_t^1, y_t^0, D|X)$. To simplify the notation in this subsection, we drop the t subscript and assume that (Y^0, Y^1) are measured after the program intervention.

Conditional Independence. One assumption that underlies the *method of matching* postulates conditioning variables X such that

$$F(y^0|D = 1, X) = F(y^0|D = 0, X) = F(y^0|X) \qquad \text{(I-1a)}$$

If this assumption is valid, we can safely use nonparticipants to measure what participants would have earned had they not participated, provided we condition on X. Using "$\perp\!\!\!\perp$" to denote independence, this identifying assumption is equivalent to $Y^0 \perp\!\!\!\perp D|X$. To ensure that (I-1a) has an empirical counterpart, we also assume that

$$0 < \Pr(D = 1|X) < 1 \qquad \text{(I-1b)}$$

over the support of X. This condition ensures that both sides of (I-1a) are well defined, (i.e., that for each X, there are both participants and nonparticipants).[4] For computing counterfactual means, a simpler requirement is

$$E(Y^0|D = 1, X) = E(Y^0|D = 0, X) \qquad \text{(I-2)}$$

---

[4] Failure to satisfy this condition is an important source of failure in the use of matching to evaluate job-training programs (Heckman et al., 1996; in press).

This method underlies the intuitive principle of "controlling on observables" to eliminate selection bias (Heckman and Robb, 1985).

The identification assumption (I-1a) implies that $\Pr(D = 1|X, Y^0) = \Pr(D = 1|X)$ (i.e., that Y^0 does not determine participation in the program), although it does not exclude the possibility that participation in the program is based on Y^1. If we strengthen (I-1a) to read

$$(Y^0, Y^1) \perp\!\!\!\perp D|X \tag{I-3}$$

we can recover $F(y^1|X)$ for the support of X satisfying (I-1b). Thus for the entire population or for the sample conditional on $D = 1$, we can construct the cost–benefit criterion and the Benthamite criterion, but not the voting criterion, because there is no information on the joint distribution of (Y^0, Y^1).

To recover the joint distribution, we need some way to associate values of Y^0 with Y^1. The dummy-endogenous-variables model (Heckman, 1978) assumes that

$$Y^1 = \alpha + Y^0 \tag{I-4}$$

where α is a constant or a function of X. Defining α as the treatment effect, this assumption imposes homogeneity of responses to treatment. Everyone with the same X value benefits or loses by the same amount. A generalization of this method developed by Heckman and Smith (1993) and Heckman, Smith, and Clements (1997c) assumes that the quantiles of Y^1 and Y^0 are the same for each person with the same X. Equating quantiles across the two marginal distributions, we form pairs:

$$\left\{ [y^0(q), y^1(q)] \Big| \inf_{y^0} F(y^0|X) > q \text{ and } \inf_{y^1} F(y^1|X) > q, 0 \leq q \leq 1 \right\} \tag{13}$$

Conditional on X, the quantile ranks are preserved, but the effect of treatment is not necessarily the same at all quantiles. More generally, we could assume that the quantiles are mapped in a general way $q_1 = \varphi(q_0)$, where q_1 is a quantile of Y^1 and q_0 is a quantile of Y^0. The gain to moving from "0" to "1" is

$$\Delta(q_0) = Y^1[\varphi(q_0)] - Y^0(q_0) \tag{14}$$

where $Y_1[\varphi(q_0)]$ is the q_1-th quantile of Y_1 expressed as a function of q_0, and $Y_0(q_0)$ is the q_0-th quantile of Y_0.

If φ is a random function, then the mass at q_0 is distributed to different values of q_1, and $\varphi(q_0)$ has an interpretation as a probability density. If φ is a uniform density mapping of q_0 to q_1 over the interval $[0, 100]$ for all q_0, Y^1 and Y^0 are stochastically independent. Provided the mapping

Evaluating the Welfare State

φ is known, the assumption of conditional independence is sufficient to identify the joint distribution $F(y^1, y^0, D|X)$.[5]

An alternative assumption about the dependence across outcomes is that $Y^1 = Y^0 + \Delta$, where Δ is stochastically independent of Y^0 given X. That is,

$$Y^0 \perp\!\!\!\perp \Delta | X \tag{I-5}$$

This assumption states that the gain from participating in the program is independent of the base Y^0. If (I-3) and (I-5) are invoked jointly, we can identify $F(y^0, y^1|X)$ from the cross-section outcome distributions for participants and nonparticipants and estimate the joint distribution by deconvolution methods.[6]

To see how to use this information, note that

$$Y = Y^0 + D\Delta$$

From $F(y|D = 0, X)$, we identify $F(y^0|X)$ as a consequence of (I-3). From $F(y|X, D = 1)$ we identify $F(y^1|X) = F(y^0 + \Delta|X)$. If Y^0 and Y^1 have densities, then, as a consequence of (I-5), the densities satisfy

$$f_1(y^1|X) = f_\Delta(\Delta|X) * f_0(y^0|X)$$

where "$*$" denotes convolution. The characteristic functions of the three random variables satisfy

$$E(e^{i\ell Y^1}|X) = E(e^{i\ell \Delta}|X)E(e^{i\ell Y^0}|X)$$

Because we can identify $F(y^1|X)$, we know its characteristic function. By a similar argument we can recover $E(e^{i\ell Y^0}|X)$. Then

$$E(e^{i\ell \Delta}|X) = \frac{E(e^{i\ell Y^1}|X)}{E(e^{i\ell Y^0}|X)} \tag{15}$$

and by the inversion theorem (e.g., Kendall and Stuart, 1977) we can recover the density $f_\Delta(\Delta|X)$. We know the joint density

$$f(\Delta, y_0|X) = f_\Delta(\Delta|X)f(y^0|X)$$

From the definition of Δ we obtain

$$f(y^1 - y^0|X)f(y^0|X) = f(y^1, y^0|X)$$

Thus we can recover the full joint distribution of outcomes and the distribution of gains.

---

[5] When φ is random, and the random variables are discrete, the matrix mapping probability of Y^0 into Y^1 must be a Markov matrix to preserve probability. For continuous distributions we need a Markov operator.

[6] Barros (1987) used this assumption in the context of an analysis of selection bias.

Under assumption (I-3), assumption (I-5) is testable. The ratio of two characteristic functions in (15) is not necessarily a characteristic function. If it is not, the estimated density f_Δ recovered from the ratio of the characteristic functions need not be positive, and the estimated variance of Δ can be negative.[7]

In a regression setting in which means and variances are assumed to capture all of the relevant information, this approach is equivalent to the traditional normal-random-coefficient model. Letting

$$Y^1 = \mu_1(X) + U_1, \quad E(U_1|X) = 0$$
$$Y^0 = \mu_0(X) + U_0, \quad E(U_0|X) = 0$$

this version of the model can be written as

$$\begin{aligned} Y &= \mu_0(X) + D[\mu_1(X) - \mu_0(X) + U_1 - U_0] + U_0 \\ &= \mu_0(X) + D[\mu_1(X) - \mu_0(X)] + D(U_1 - U_0) + U_0 \\ &= \mu_0(X) + D\bar{a}(X) + D\varepsilon + U_0 \end{aligned} \quad (16)$$

where $\bar{a}(X) = \mu_1(X) - \mu_0(X)$, and $\varepsilon = U_1 - U_0$. By virtue of (I-3), $(U_0, U_1) \perp\!\!\!\perp D|X$.

We can use nonparametric regression methods to recover $\mu_0(X)$ and $\mu_1(X) - \mu_0(X)$, or we can use ordinary parametric regression methods, assuming that $\mu_1(X) = X\beta_1$ and $\mu_0(X) = X\beta_0$. Equation (16) is a components-of-variance model, and a test of (I-5) is that

$$\begin{aligned} \text{var}(Y|D=1, X) &= \text{var}(Y^0 + \Delta|D=1, X) \\ &= \text{var}(Y^0|X) + \text{var}(\Delta|X) \\ &\geq \text{var}(Y|D=0, X) = \text{var}(Y^0|X) \end{aligned}$$

Under standard conditions, each component of variance is identified and is estimable from the residuals obtained from the nonparametric regression of Y on D and X.

An alternative approach relies only on the information contained in the marginal distributions obtained using the conditional independence assumption to bound the joint distribution conditional on D. The Fréchet (1951) bounds inform us that

$$\begin{aligned} \max\{F(y^0|X) + F(y^1|X) - 1, 0\} &\leq F(y^0, y^1|X) \\ &\leq \min\{F(y^0|X), F(y^1|X)\} \end{aligned} \quad (17)$$

These bounds are purely statistical and assume no information about agent behavior. Combining the bounds with (I-1b) and (I-3) allows us to

---

[7] For the ratio of characteristic functions, $r(\ell)$, to be a characteristic function, it must satisfy the requirements that $r(0) = 1$, that $r(\ell)$ is continuous in ℓ, and that $r(\ell)$ is nonnegative definite. This identifying assumption can be tested using the procedures developed by Heckman, Robb, and Walker (1990).

bound the $(D = 1)$ joint distribution $F(y^1, y^0|X)$. Heckman and Smith (1993) and Heckman et al. (1997c) have demonstrated that in most applications these bounds are not very informative.[8]

Information from Revealed Preference. An alternative approach with a long history in economics uses information on agent choices to recover the population distribution of potential outcomes.[9] Unlike the method of matching, the method based on revealed preference capitalizes on a close relationship between (Y^0, Y^1) and program participation. Participation includes voluntary entry into a program or attrition from it.

The prototypical framework is the Roy (1951) model. In that setup,

$$D = 1(Y^1 \geq Y^0) \qquad (18)$$

If we postulate that the outcome equations can be written in a separable form, so that

$$Y^1 = \mu_1(X) + U_1, \qquad E(U_1|X) = 0$$
$$Y^0 = \mu_0(X) + U_0, \qquad E(U_0|X) = 0$$

then $\Pr(D = 1|X) = \Pr(Y^1 - Y^0 \geq 0|X) = \Pr\{U_1 - U_0 \geq -[\mu_1(X) - \mu_0(X)]\}$. Heckman and Honoré (1990) demonstrated that if $X \perp\!\!\!\perp (U_1, U_0)$, $\text{var}(U_1) < \infty$ and $\text{var}(U_0) < \infty$, and (U_1, U_0) are normal, the full model $F(y^0, y^1, D|X)$ is identified even if we observe only Y^0 or Y^1 for any person and there are no regressors and no exclusion restrictions. If instead of assuming normality, we assume that the supports of $\mu_1(X)$ and $\mu_0(X)$ overlap or contain the supports of U_1 and U_0, the full model $[\mu_1(X), \mu_0(X)]$ and the joint distribution of U_1 and U_0 are nonparametrically identified up to location normalizations. Precise conditions are given in Theorem A-1 in Appendix A.

The crucial feature of the Roy model is that the decision to participate in the program is made solely in terms of potential outcomes. No new unobservable variables enter the model that do not appear in the outcome equations.[10] In this case, information about who participates also informs us about the distribution of the values of the program to

---

[8] An exception is that the bounds for low-probability events are informative.

[9] Heckman (1974a,b) has demonstrated how access to censored samples on hours of work, wages for workers, and employment choices identifies the joint distribution of the value of nonmarket time and potential market wages under a normality assumption. Heckman and Honoré (1990) considered nonparametric versions of this model without labor supply.

[10] We could augment decision rule (18) to be $D = 1[Y^1 - Y^0 - k(Z) \geq 0]$. Provided that we measure Z and condition on it, and provided that $(U_1 - U_0) \perp\!\!\!\perp (X, Z)$, the model remains nonparametrically identified. The crucial property of the identification result is that no new unobservable enters the model through the participation equation. However, if we add Z, subjective valuations of gain $[Y^1 - Y^0 - k(Z)]$ no longer equal "objective" measures $(Y^1 - Y^0)$.

Table 8.2. *What Cross-Section Data Nonparametrically Identify from* $F(y^1|D = 1, X)$ *and* $F(y^0|D = 0, X)$, $\Pr(D = 1|X)$ *under Different Assumptions*

Assumption	Recovers	Behavioral assumption	Criteria recovered
(1) $E(Y^1|D = 1, X) = E(Y^0|X) = E(Y^0|D = 0, X)$ (conditional mean independence)	$E(Y^1 - Y^0|D = 1, X)$ $= E(Y^1 - Y^0|X)$	Y^0 does not determine participation conditional on X	Cost-benefit (for $D = 1$ and total population)
(2) $Y^0 \perp\!\!\!\perp D|X$ (conditional independence)	(1) plus $F(Y^0|D = 1, X)$ $= F(y^0|X)$ $= F(y^0|D = 0, X)$	Y^0 does not determine participation conditional on X	Cost-benefit (for $D = 1$ and total population); Benthamite (for $D = 1$)
(3) $(Y^0, Y^1) \perp\!\!\!\perp D|X$ (conditional independence)	(2) plus $F(y^1|D = 1, X)$ $= F(y^1|X)$ $= F(y^1|D = 0, X)$	(Y^0, Y^1) does not determine participation conditional on X	Cost-benefit and Benthamite (for $D = 1$ and total population)
(4) Assumption (3) plus $\Delta \perp\!\!\!\perp Y^0|X$; $\Delta = Y_1 - Y_0$	(3) plus $F(\Delta|X)$	(Y^0, Y^1) does not determine participation conditional on X	All criteria
(5) Assumption (3) plus quantile assignment rule $q_1 = \varphi(q_0)$; φ may be deterministic or random	Same as (4)	(Y^0, Y^1) does not determine participation conditional on X	All criteria
(6) $E(U_0|X, Z) = M(X)$ and existence of an exclusion restriction (Z doesn't appear in outcome equation), and $E(U_1 - U_0|X, Z, D = 1)$ $= E(U_1 - U_0|X, D = 1)^a$	Same as (1)	$\Delta = Y^1 - Y^0$ doesn't enter agents' decision rule and exclusion restriction (Z does not appear in outcome equation)	Same as (1)
(7) $D = 1(Y^1 > Y^0)$; separability of outcome equations and support condition in Theorem A-1	Same as (4)	Participation solely in terms of (Y^0, Y^1, X); model unobservables are U_0, U_1, X	All criteria
(8) D determined by more general decision rule (separability, independence, and support conditions in Theorem A-2)	$F(y^1, D|X) = F(y^0, D|X)$ for $D = 1$ and $D = 0$	Y^0, Y^1, X, and other factors may determine participation	Cost-benefit and Benthamite (for $D = 1$ and total population)

[a] If the IV assumption is interpreted to be $(U_0, U_1) \perp\!\!\!\perp D|X, Z$, or $(Y^0, Y^1) \perp\!\!\!\perp D|X, Z$, IV is just matching conditional on X and Z, and line (3) applies for this conditioning set.

Evaluating the Welfare State

participants $F(y^1 - y^0 | Y^1 > Y^0, X)$. Thus, we acquire the distribution of implicit values of the program for participants, which is all that is required in a libertarian evaluation of the program. However, as we have stressed repeatedly, evaluation of the welfare state requires information about "objective" outcomes and their distributions, which are needed to make the interpersonal comparisons that are essential features of the welfare state. Only in the Roy model do the "objective" and "subjective" outcomes coincide.

If the Roy model is extended to allow for variables other than Y^0 and Y^1 (and the observed conditioning variables) to determine participation, then the decision rule is changed to $D = 1(IN > 0)$, where $IN = \eta(Y^1, Y^0, V, X)$, and it is not possible to identify the joint distribution $F(u_0, u_1)$ even if the unobservables V, U_0, and U_1 are independent of X. Under conditions similar to those presented in Theorem A-1, Heckman (1990a) demonstrated that in this more general case, provided that some structure is placed on η, we can nonparametrically identify $F(y^0, D|X)$ and $F(y^1, D|X)$, but not the full joint distribution $F(y^0, y^1, D|X)$. A generalization of his proof is given in Theorem A-2 in Appendix A. As soon as the tight link in the Roy model between participation and potential outcomes is broken, we confront the standard evaluation problem that failure to observe both coordinates (Y^0, Y^1) precludes identification of their joint distribution. To identify the full joint distribution of potential outcomes, we can assume the same dependence across quantiles as was previously discussed in the case of econometric matching methods, or we can apply the Fréchet inequalities to bound the joint distributions from the nonparametrically determined marginals.

Thus far we have considered the case in which persons know their own (Y^0, Y^1) in advance of participating in a program. If decision rule (18) is operative in the participant population, this implies that

$$\Pr(Y^1 \geq Y^0 | Y^0 = y^0, D = 1, X) = 1$$

This is a strong form of stochastic dominance. All of the mass of the Y^1 distribution conditional on $Y^0 = y^0$ is to the right of y^0 in the participant population.

More generally, persons may not know (Y^0, Y^1), but may base their participation decisions on unbiased guesses (Y^{0*}, Y^{1*}) about them. We can model this in the following way:

$$Y^{0*} = Y^0 + \varepsilon_0 \quad \text{and} \quad Y^{1*} = Y^1 + \varepsilon_1$$

where $E(\varepsilon_0, \varepsilon_1) = (0, 0)$, $(\varepsilon_0, \varepsilon_1) \perp\!\!\!\perp (Y^0, Y^1)$, and $\varepsilon_0 \perp\!\!\!\perp \varepsilon_1$.

In this case, if $D = 1(Y^{1*} \geq Y^{0*})$, conditioning on realized values produces positive regression dependence between Y^1 and Y^0, so that $\Pr(Y^1 \leq y^1 | Y^0 = y^0, D = 1, X)$ is nonincreasing in y^0 for all y^1. This, in turn, implies that Y^1 is right-tail-increasing in Y^0. That is, $\Pr(Y^1 > y^1 | Y^0 > y^0,$

$D = 1, X)$ is nondecreasing in y^0 for all y^1. Intuitively, the higher the value of y^0, the more the mass in the condition Y^1 distribution is shifted to the right, so that "high values of Y^0 go with high values of Y^1." Y^1 being right-tail-increasing, given y^0, implies that Y^1 and Y^0 (given $D = 1$) are positive-quadrant-dependent, so that $\Pr(Y^1 \leq y^1 | Y^0 \leq y^0, D = 1; X) \geq \Pr(Y^1 \leq y^1 | D = 1, X)$ and $\Pr(Y^0 \leq y^0 | Y^1 \leq y^1, D = 1, X) \geq \Pr(Y^0 \leq y^0 | D = 1, X)$.[11] Common measures of dependence like the product-moment correlation, Kendall's τ, and Spearman's ρ are all positive when there is positive-quadrant dependence. Even under imperfect information, rationality in the form considered here can restrict the nature of the dependence between Y^1 and Y^0 given $D = 1$. Evidence against such dependence is evidence against the income-maximizing Roy model. Even if Y^0 and Y^1 are negatively correlated in the population, they are positively correlated given $D = 1$ if agents are income maximizers. This insight motivates our imposition of positive dependence between Y^0 and Y^1 in participant populations ($D = 1$) to recover the joint distribution $F(y^0, y^1 | D = 1, X)$ in the empirical analysis reported in Section 4.

Identification through the Instrumental-Variable Moment Condition and Extensions of the Condition. Taking (16) as a point of departure, it is possible under conditions we now specify to apply the method of instrumental variables to estimate $E(Y^1 - Y^0 | D = 1, X)$ and $E(Y^1 - Y^0 | X) = E(\Delta | X)$. This allows implementation of the cost–benefit criterion provided that instrumental variables Z exist that satisfy the following conditions:

$$E[U_0 + D(U_1 - U_0) | X, Z] = 0 \quad \text{for identifying } E(Y^1 - Y^0 | X) \quad \text{(I-6a)}$$

or

$$\begin{aligned}&E\{U_0 + D[U_1 - U_0 - E(U_1 - U_0 | D = 1, X)] | X, Z\} = 0 \\ &\text{for identifying } E(Y^1 - Y^0 | X, D = 1)\end{aligned} \quad \text{(I-6b)}$$

A second condition is that D depend on Z:

$$\begin{aligned}&\Pr(D = 1 | X, Z = z) \neq \Pr(D = 1 | X, Z = z') \\ &\text{for some } z \neq z' \text{ for all } X\end{aligned} \quad \text{(I-7)}$$

Under condition (I-6a) we can write

$$E(Y | X, Z) = \mu_0(X) + E(\Delta | X) \Pr(D = 1 | X, Z)$$

Or, under condition (I-6b), we obtain

---

[11] These implications are strict except in the case where Y^0 and Y^1 are binary random variables. In that case, Tong (1980) has shown that these notions of dependence are all equivalent.

Evaluating the Welfare State

$$E(Y|X, Z) = \mu_0(X) + E(\Delta|D = 1, X)\Pr(D = 1|X, Z)$$

Thus the population moment equation that identifies $E(\Delta|X)$ under (I-6a) and (I-7) is

$$E(\Delta|X) = \frac{E(Y|X, Z = z) - E(Y|X, Z = z')}{\Pr(D = 1|X, Z = z) - \Pr(D = 1|X, Z = z')} \quad (19)$$

and the population moment equation that identifies $E(\Delta|X, D = 1)$ under (I-6b) and (I-7) is the same:

$$E(\Delta|X, D = 1) = \frac{E(Y|X, Z = z) - E(Y|X, Z = z')}{\Pr(D = 1|X, Z = z) - \Pr(D = 1|X, Z = z')} \quad (20)$$

To satisfy condition (I-6b), it is required that the standard instrumental-variables condition $E(U_0|X, Z) = 0$ be satisfied and, in addition, that

$$E(U_1 - U_0|D = 1, X, Z) = E(U_1 - U_0|D = 1, X)$$

Notice that condition (I-6b) is still satisfied if $U_1 \equiv U_0$, so the response to treatment in (16) is the same for everyone, as assumed by Heckman (1978). This condition is also satisfied if

$$(U_1 - U_0) \perp\!\!\!\perp (X, Z, D) \quad \text{(I-8)}$$

As a consequence of (I-8),

$$\Pr(D = 1|X, Z, Y^1 - Y^0) = \Pr(D = 1|X, Z, U^1 - U^0)$$
$$= \Pr(D = 1|X, Z)$$

The identifying assumption (I-8) will be satisfied if agents know X and Z but cannot predict $(U_1 - U_0)$ at the time they make their decisions to participate in the program. Condition (I-6b) will also be satisfied if (I-8) is weakened to a statement about mean independence:

$$E(U_1 - U_0|D = 1, X, Z) = E(U_1 - U_0) \quad \text{(I-8)}'$$

which will be satisfied if the unobserved components of the gain do not determine program participation.[12] Condition (I-8) does not rule out that Y^0 determines D, but if Y^0 does determine D, it is required that, given X, Z, and Y^0, Δ does not determine D.

Under condition (I-8), $E(Y^1 - Y^0|D = 1, X) = E(Y^1 - Y^0|X)$. The effect of "treatment" on the "treated" is the same as the effect of taking a person from the population at random and assigning that person to treatment. Moreover, (I-8) ensures that (I-6a) is satisfied as well.

---

[12] See Heckman (1997a) for further discussion of these conditions.

Notice that condition (19) is still satisfied if (I-6a) is weakened to

$$E[U^0 + D(U_1 - U_0) | X, Z] = M_1(X) \tag{I-6a}'$$

and condition (20) still holds if (I-6b) is weakened to

$$E\{U_0 + D[U_1 - U_0 - E(U_1 - U_0|D=1, X)]|X, Z\} = M_2(X)$$

The $M_1(X)$ and $M_2(X)$ terms difference out in the instrumental-variables moment conditions (19) and (20), respectively.

Invoking (I-6) and (I-7) under assumptions (A-1) and (A-2), we can answer the cost–benefit questions for the entire population [if we assume (I-6a)] and for populations for which $D = 1$ [if we assume (I-6b)]. These assumptions are not strong enough to identify the Benthamite criterion or the voting criterion. Recovery of the full joint distribution of (U_1, U_0, D) requires strengthening these assumptions. The conditional independence assumption that justifies matching (I-3) will suffice.

Thus, in place of (I-3), which is defined solely in terms of variables X in the outcome equations, we can assume that access to a variable Z produces conditional independence:

$$(U_0, U_1) \perp\!\!\!\perp D|X, Z, \quad \text{but} \quad (U_0, U_1) \not\!\perp\!\!\!\perp D|X \tag{I-9}$$

Equivalently, we can write

$$(Y_0, Y_1) \perp\!\!\!\perp D|X, Z, \quad \text{but} \quad (Y_0, Y_1) \not\!\perp\!\!\!\perp D|X \tag{I-9}'$$

Under these assumptions we can recover the marginal and joint distributions as discussed in the subsection on conditional independence. Interpreted in this way, the instrumental-variables method generalizes the matching method and extends the identification analysis based on conditional independence in terms of variables in the outcome equation to utilize a larger conditioning set beyond those variables.[13]

2.1.2 Social Experiments

We consider randomization administered at two different points: (a) at entry or the stage where persons have applied to and been accepted into a program and (b) at eligibility. As noted by Heckman (1992) and Heckman and Smith (1993, 1995), and Heckman, LaLonde, and Smith (in press-b), social experiments with randomization administered at the stage where persons have applied to and been accepted into a program recover two marginal distributions conditional on $D = 1$:

$$F(y^1|D=1, X) \quad \text{and} \quad F(y^0|D=1, X) \tag{21}$$

---

[13] Heckman, Ichimura, and Todd (1997b, 1998a) and Heckman et al. (1996; in press-a) have extended matching to consider variables in the program participation equation that are not in the outcome equation.

From such an experiment we obtain a truncated sample, and experiments administered at this stage do not identify $\Pr(D = 1|X)$ (Heckman, 1992; Moffitt, 1992). The identifying assumptions that justify this method are

> Randomization does not change the program being studied (no randomization bias), and no close substitutes for the treatment are available to persons randomized out (no substitution bias). (I-10)

Heckman (1992) and Heckman and Smith (1993) have discussed the need for the absence of substitutes for the program being evaluated and the failure of the no-randomization bias assumption. Heckman et al. (1997a) have provided evidence on the importance of substitution bias in an evaluation of a major job-training program. See also the evidence on these questions assembeled in Heckman et al. (in press-b).

From the conditional distributions it is possible to recover the information required to construct the participant versions of the cost–benefit criterion

$$F(Y^1 - Y^0 | D = 1, X)$$

and the Benthamite criterion. Without further assumptions, social experiments do not recover the joint distribution

$$F(y^0, y^1 | D = 1, X) \qquad (22)$$

Any one of several additional assumptions can be used to supplement the information available from social experiments. The joint distribution (22) can be bounded from the experimentally determined marginals using the Fréchet bounds (Heckman and Smith, 1993; Heckman et al., 1997c). Assumptions can be made about the association of quantile ranks (dependence) between outcomes across distributions to recover $F(y^0, y^1 | D = 1, X)$. An alternative assumption is (I-5).

With these assumptions we can construct or bound all of the evaluation criteria presented in Section 1 for the conditional (on $D = 1$) distribution. Under conditional independence assumption (I-3), it is possible to recover the complete marginal distributions $F(y^1 | D = 1, X) = F(y^1 | X)$ and $F(y^0 | D = 1, X) = F(y^0 | X)$ and bound $F(y^0, y^1 | X)$ using the Fréchet bounds, as well as to identify $F(y^0, y^1 | X)$ by (a) making an assumption connecting the quantiles of the two marginal distributions or (b) assuming, as in (I-5), that gains Δ are unrelated to the base state Y^0.

If decision rule (18) is postulated, we can use the Roy model (under the conditions specified in Theorem A-1) to identify $F(y^0, y^1 | X)$ from the conditional distributions $F(y^0 | D = 1, X)$ and $F(y^1 | D = 1, X)$. Under assumptions (A-1) and (A-2) we can answer the evaluation questions comparing policy j with policy "0" that were posed in Section 1 for the entire population and the conditional (for participants) population.

Under more general participation rules we can apply Theorem A-2 to data from a social experiment with randomization administered at the point of entry into the program to identify $F(y^1, D|X)$ and $F(y^0, D|X)$ for both $D = 1$ and $D = 0$. Thus we can construct the cost–benefit and Benthamite criteria for the general population and for the participant populations, but not the general voting criterion or any other criterion requiring the joint distribution of outcomes.

One advantage of social experiments over conventional microeconomic data augmented with the conditional independence condition (I-3) is that experiments expand the range of the support over which the parameters can be identified. Thus, suppose that Support$(X|D = 1) \neq$ Support$(X|D = 0)$. For the domains of X in which there is no common support, Theorems A-1 and A-2 do not apply, and we cannot use conditional independence assumption (I-3). Randomization guarantees that in the population generating the experimental samples, Support$(X|D = 1)$ will be the same for participants and randomized-out persons. Thus, randomization ensures that the support conditions of Theorems A-1 and A-2 are satisfied for the population of participants. However, it may still happen that the support of X for the population for which $D = 1$ is not the same as the support of X for the whole population. Then, even with experimental data, the parameters of interest are identified only over the available support. For both experimental and nonexperimental data it may be necessary to sample more widely on X coordinates to recover parameters defined for the entire population. Experiments have the advantage that they allow identification of impacts even for persons with values of X such that $\Pr(D = 1|X) = 1$, which is not possible using nonexperimental methods because there is no comparison group.

If randomization is performed on eligibility for the program, we recover $F(y^0|X)$, $F(y^1|D = 1, X)$, and $F(y^0|D = 1, X)$ (Heckman, 1992; Heckman and Smith, 1993; Heckman et al., in press-b). In addition, we recover $\Pr(D = 1|X)$, at least for those values of X possessed by eligible persons. Many would regard $F(y^0|X)$ as a better approximation to the no-policy outcome distribution than the approximation embodied in assumption (A-1). Although both approximations ignore general-equilibrium effects, $F(y^0|X)$ avoids self-selection bias. Randomization at eligibility does not recover the full joint distribution of outcomes unless additional assumptions of the type previously discussed are invoked. Table 8.3 summarizes the information obtained from the two types of experiments.

2.1.3 Panel Data

Panel data provide a new source of identifying information. Participation or nonparticipation outcomes in one period can proxy participation or nonparticipation outcomes in another period. Restoring the t sub-

Evaluating the Welfare State

Table 8.3

Assumption	Behavioral assumption	Recovers	Criteria recovered without further assumptions
Randomization at entry			
No randomization or substitution bias	Same as column 1	$F(y^1 \mid D = 1, X)$, $F(y^0 \mid D = 1, X)$	Cost–benefit and Benthamite criteria for participants ($D = 1$)
Randomization at eligibility			
No randomization or substitution bias	Same as column 1	$F(y^0 \mid X), F(y^1 \mid D = 1, X)$, $F(y^0 \mid D = 1, X)$, $\Pr(D = 1 \mid X)$	Cost–benefit and Benthamite criteria for participants ($D = 1$)

script, panel data allow us to make the following approximations for person i:

$$Y^1_{t'i} \doteq Y^1_{ti} \quad (t \neq t') \tag{I-11a}$$

or

$$Y^0_{t'i} \doteq Y^0_{ti} \quad (t \neq t') \tag{I-11b}$$

Provided that the approximations are valid ("$\doteq$" is "$=$"), we can substitute for the missing counterfactual outcome *for each person* and identify the joint distribution of (Y^0_t, Y^1_t) for different conditioning sets. We can answer all of the questions posed in Section 1 for period-t versions of the criteria presented there. It is the ability to directly estimate the dependence across potential outcomes without invoking additional assumptions that is the distinguishing feature of panel data.

When adding a temporal dimension to the analysis, it is useful to distinguish reversible programs from irreversible programs. Human-capital or personal-investment programs have certain irreversibility features, but it is typically assumed that they have no effect on preprogram outcomes.[14] For such programs, we require $t' < t$ in (I-11), where t is the period of participation. Reversible programs switch on and off and have no lasting effects. Examples may include job subsidies or unemployment-insurance benefits. With reversible programs we can go forward or back-

---

[14] If agents anticipate participation in the program, they may take actions in the preprogram period that distinguish them from nonparticipants. The assumed absence of anticipatory behavior is central to received models of program evaluation.

ward in time in the search for a valid counterfactual state, so that we may have $t' < t$ or $t' > t$ in (I-11). We first consider reversible programs.

Reversible Programs. Nonstationarity in the external environment, the effects of aging and life-cycle investment, and idiosyncratic period-specific shocks render assumptions (I-11a) and (I-11b) suspect. To circumvent these problems, the identifying assumptions usually are reformulated at the population level, and conditioning variables X are assumed that "adjust" $Y_{t'}^0$ and Y_t^0 and $Y_{t'}^1$ and Y_t^1 to equality in distribution or conditional mean and allow for idiosyncratic fluctuations. For simplicity, we conduct only a two-period analysis, but estimation of the necessary adjustments may require more data.[15] The modified identification conditions become

$$F(y_{t'}^0, y_t^1|X) = F(y_t^0, y_t^1|X) \quad (y_{t'}^0 = y_t^0) \qquad \text{(I-11a)}'$$

and

$$F(y_t^0, y_{t'}^1|X) = F(y_t^0, y_t^1|X) \quad (y_{t'}^1 = y_t^1) \qquad \text{(I-11b)}'$$

Weaker versions of (I-11a)' and (I-11b)' that are more commonly used are

$$E(Y_{t'}^0|X) = E(Y_t^0|X) \qquad \text{(I-11a)}''$$

and

$$E(Y_{t'}^1|X) = E(Y_t^1|X) \qquad \text{(I-11b)}''$$

The outcome variables may need to be adjusted for deterministic trends. Heckman and Robb (1985) have considered cases in which common deterministic trends affecting mean outcomes in both the participation and nonparticipation states can be eliminated using multiperiod and multicohort data, assuming that they are restricted to be low-order functions of time or age.[16]

The potential cost of using this information on the missing counterfactual outcomes is the possibility of selection bias. Persons who do not participate in t and participate in t' may be atypical of those who participate in t', especially if their nonparticipation in t is linked to the value of the outcome variable in t. Specifically, we can use (I-11a) to construct all of the counterfactuals in period t conditional on $D = 1$ without any further adjustment if it is further assumed in the reversible case that

---

[15] See Heckman and Robb (1985, pp. 210–15), where these adjustments are discussed in detail. See also Heckman et al. (in press-b).

[16] In the method of "difference in differences" it is assumed that a common trend operates on all persons, irrespective of their participation status. The trend is eliminated from the means by comparing participant change to nonparticipant change. More generally, nonparticipants in t and t' can be used to identify the common trend.

$$F(y_{t'}^0, y_t^1 | D_{t'} = 0, D_t = 1, X) = F(y_{t'}^0, y_t^1 | D_t = 1, X) \quad \text{for } y_{t'}^0 = y_t^0 \quad \text{(I-12a)}$$

We can use (I-11b) to construct all of the counterfactuals in period t conditional on $D = 0$ without any further adjustments if it is assumed that

$$F(y_t^0, y_{t'}^1 | D_t = 0, D_{t'} = 1, X) = F(y_t^0, y_{t'}^1 | D_t = 0, X) \quad \text{for } y_{t'}^1 = y_t^1 \quad \text{(I-12b)}$$

Much less often is it also assumed that $F(y_{t'}^0, y_t^0 | D_{t'} = 0, D_t = 0, X) = F(y_t^0 | D_t = 0, X)$ for $y_{t'}^0 = y_t^0$, or $F(y_{t'}^1, y_t^1 | D_{t'} = 1, D_t = 1, X) = F(y_t^1 | D_t = 1, X)$ for $y_{t'}^1 = y_t^1$, although these assumptions seem equally plausible and are testable. They would require that the $Y_{t'}^1$ and Y_t^1 be perfectly dependent, as are outcomes $Y_{t'}^0$ and Y_t^0.

For means, the weaker versions of (I-12a) and (I-12b) are, respectively,

$$E(Y_t^0 | D_{t'} = 0, D_t = 1, X) = E(Y_t^0 | D_t = 1, X) \quad [\text{for } (I-11a)''] \quad \text{(I-12a)}'$$

and

$$E(Y_t^1 | D_t = 0, D_{t'} = 1, X) = E(Y_t^1 | D_t = 0, X) \quad [\text{for } (I-11b)''] \quad \text{(I-12b)}'$$

These are strong implicit behavioral assumptions. Assumptions (I-12a) and (I-12a)' require that persons who participate in t but not in t' have the same no-treatment mean outcome in t' as persons who take treatment in period t would have in t. It rules out that the switch from $D_{t'} = 0$ to $D_t = 1$ is caused by differences in Y^0 between t' and t. More precisely, it excludes $Y_{t'}^0$ as a determinant of $D_{t'}$. Assumptions (I-12b) and (I-12b)' are comparable assumptions about the lack of influence of $Y_{t'}^1$ in determining participation in t'.

One way to justify these identifying assumptions is to postulate a strengthened form of the conditional independence assumption used to justify matching:

$$(Y_{t'}^{D_{t'}}, Y_t^{D_t}) \perp\!\!\!\perp (D_{t'}, D_t) | X, \quad t \neq t' \quad \text{(I-13)}$$

This condition rules out any dependence between D_t and $D_{t'}$ and the components of $(Y_{t'}^{D_{t'}}, Y_t^{D_t})$ that cannot be predicted by X. This assumption rules out selection on any unobserved components of potential outcomes. It is inconsistent with the Roy model. A weaker version of (I-13) is that conditional on D_t and X, $(Y_{t'}^{D_{t'}}, Y_t^{D_t})$ are independent of $D_{t'}$:

$$(Y_{t'}^{D_{t'}}, Y_t^{D_t}) \perp\!\!\!\perp D_{t'} | X, D_t \quad \text{(I-14)}$$

This condition rules out any dependence between the components of $(Y_{t'}^{D_{t'}}, Y_t^{D_t})$ that cannot be predicted by D_t and X and the random variable $D_{t'}$. (I-12a)' and (I-12b)' can be justified by these assumptions.

We could augment (I-13) or (I-14) to include matching variables Z not included in X. Thus it may happen that (I-13) does not hold, but

$$(Y_{t'}^{D_{t'}}, Y_t^{D_t}) \perp\!\!\!\perp (D_t, D_{t'}) | X, Z \qquad \text{(I-13)}'$$

Similarly, (I-14) may be invalid, but it may happen that

$$(Y_{t'}^{D_{t'}}, Y_t^{D_t}) \perp\!\!\!\perp D_{t'} | X, D_t, Z \qquad \text{(I-14)}'$$

is valid. We could also invoke other assumptions patterned after our cross-section analysis to recover the missing counterfactual state. We could model participation in periods t and t' using dynamic selection models. Each cross-section estimator has a panel-data counterpart, which, for the sake of brevity, we do not develop in this study.

If the date of enrollment into the program is endogenous, it is incorrect to simply condition on it, and conditions (I-13) and (I-14) have to be strengthened in order to avoid building an explicit model of the date of enrollment.[17] Let τ be the date of enrollment into the program. Then to use (I-12a) and (I-12b) without modification, we need to augment the conditional independence assumptions to read

$$(Y_{t'}^{D_{t'}}, Y_t^{D_t}) \perp\!\!\!\perp (D_{t'}, D_t, \tau) | X \qquad (t \neq t') \qquad \text{(I-13)}''$$

or, in the weaker form,

$$(Y_{t'}^{D_{t'}}, Y_t^{D_t}) \perp\!\!\!\perp (D_{t'}, \tau) | X, D_t \qquad (t \neq t')^{[18]} \qquad \text{(I-14)}''$$

These conditions rule out dependence between potential outcomes and the set of participation variables conditional on X [(I-13)″], or dependence between potential outcomes and non-t participation variables conditioned on X and D_t [(I-14)″]. Under either set of assumptions we can ignore the date of enrollment as a factor in producing the counterfactual distributions.

Other types of identifying assumptions could be invoked. Cameron and Heckman (1991a,b) developed a multivariate version of the Roy model that explicitly models τ and showed that its parameters can be identified. Those models are closely related to standard panel-data attrition models (e.g., Ridder, 1990).

The Irreversible Case. In the irreversible case, there are no counterparts for (I-11b)′, (I-11b)″, (I-12b), or (I-12b)′ because there are no observations on treated persons in the preprogram period t'. First consider the

---

[17] In a fully dynamic model in which enrollment dates are endogenous, the date of enrollment would be a further source of information about revealed preferences, which we do not pursue in this study. Qualitatively, it conveys information on subjective evaluations in the same way attrition and self-selection decisions convey information about choices.

[18] The required modification for conditional means is obvious and thus is omitted.

case in which program enrollment date τ is fixed and is common for all persons. The probability space is restricted, so $\Pr(D_{t'} = 1|X) = 0$, and no value of $Y_{t'}^1$ is defined. $F(y_{t'}^0, y_t^1|D_t = 1, X)$ can be identified from $F(y_{t'}^0, y_t^1|D_t = 1, X)$ if the preprogram outcomes of participants have the same relationship to program outcomes in t as their nonprogram outcomes in period t. [This is just assumption (I-12a).] We cannot use (I-12b) to construct $F(y_{t'}^0, y_t^1|D_t = 0, X)$ because no value of $Y_{t'}^1$ is defined. In the irreversible case, we have a truncated sample.

If we invoke a conditional independence assumption and assume a counterpart to (I-12) defined for the reversible case,

$$(Y_{t'}^0, Y_t^1) \perp\!\!\!\perp D_t | X \qquad \text{(I-15)}$$

we can identify the full joint distribution.[19] Otherwise we can identify only the evaluation criteria for the population conditional on $D_t = 1$. Because we know $(Y_{t'}^0, Y_t^1)$ conditional on $D_t = 1$ and X, we can use a vector generalization of Theorem A-2, presented in Appendix A as Theorem A-3, to identify $F(y_{t'}^0, y_t^1|X)$ and $F(y_{t'}^0, y_t^1, D_t|X)$. What is required is a set of X values such that $\Pr(D_t = 1|X) = 0$. Under the assumptions made in Theorem A-3, it is possible to recover the full distribution of outcomes even in the reversible case.

If τ is not the same for everyone, and is random, but $t' < \tau < t$, then to use (I-15) we need to assume

$$(Y_{t'}^0, Y_t^1) \perp\!\!\!\perp D_t, \tau | X \qquad \text{(I-16)}$$

or

$$(Y_{t'}^0, Y_t^1) \perp\!\!\!\perp D_t | \tau, X \qquad \text{(I-16)}'$$

These assumptions enable us to ignore the date of enrollment as a determinant of outcomes in constructing the counterfactual distributions.

Heckman and Robb (1985) discussed more general uses of panel data to proxy unobservables to eliminate selection bias. The leading cases are fixed-effects or autoregressive models that transform equations by differencing or generalized differencing to eliminate unobserved components that would produce selection bias. All of the conventional "proxy-variable" econometric methods that eliminate selection bias through some transformation of the original equations can be shown to be equivalent to constructing counterfactual outcomes (i.e., producing predicted values of the outcomes needed to form the missing component of the

---

[19] This assumption could be augmented to allow for Z to be added to the conditioning set so that we would have $(Y_{t'}^0, Y_t^1) \perp\!\!\!\perp D_t | X, Z$, but (I-15) would be invalid.

counterfactual). More generally, if the original equations are subject to transformations, the previously stated identification conditions apply to the transformed equations (Heckman, 1997b).[20] Summaries of the main identification results for joint distributions and means and marginal distributions that exploit panel data are given in Tables 8.4 and 8.5, respectively.

2.1.4 Repeated Cross-Section Data

Heckman and Robb (1985) demonstrated that all panel-data identification assumptions about means, variances, and covariances have counterparts in repeated cross-section data. Conditional-mean versions of all of the identification assumptions presented in Section 2.1.3 have counterparts in repeated cross sections of unrelated persons sampled from the same populations. We first consider the reversible case.

Identification conditions (I-11a)″ and (I-11b)″ can be defined for a common population and do not require that the same persons be followed over time. The same is true for (I-12a)′ and (I-12b)′ and the other identifying assumptions for conditional means. However, it now becomes necessary to classify persons in t' as program participants or nonparticipants it t. This is not so easy to do in the repeated cross-section case, because different persons are sampled in t and t'. What is lost when the analyst is restricted to using repeated cross-section data is the ability to construct joint distributions (Y_t^0, Y_t^1) without invoking the cross sectional assumptions made in Section 2.1.1.

Without invoking additional assumptions about dependence between the two potential outcomes, the identifying assumptions for conditional means enable us to recover only the cost–benefit and Benthamite criteria, not the voting criterion, which is based on the full joint distribution of potential outcomes. An essential benefit of panel data – that they afford nonparametric identification of the joint distribution of potential outcomes under the identifying assumptions made in Section 2.1.3 – is lost when the analyst has access only to repeated cross-section data.[21] A summary of the main cases for panel data and repeated cross sections is presented in Table 8.5.

---

[20] For example, in the method of fixed effects without regressors, $Y_{it}^1 = \alpha_i + \varphi_i + \varepsilon_{it}$, and $Y_{it}^0 = \varphi_i + \varepsilon_{it}$, where $E(\varepsilon_{it}) = 0$ and $\varepsilon_{it} \perp\!\!\!\perp \varphi_i$, $Y_{it}^0 - Y_{it'}^0 = \varepsilon_{it} - \varepsilon_{it'}$ and $Y_{it}^1 - Y_{it'}^0 = \alpha_i + \varepsilon_{it} - \varepsilon_{it'}$. If $\Pr(D_i = 1 | \varepsilon_{it} - \varepsilon_{it'}) = P$, which is not a function of $\varepsilon_{it} - \varepsilon_{it'}$, we can identify $E(\alpha_i | D = 1) = E(Y_{it}^1 - Y_{it'}^0 | D = 1)$. Observe that P can depend on φ_i; see Heckman and Robb (1985). Heckman (1997b) demonstrated that $Y_{it'}^0$ is properly interpreted as a proxy for Y_{it}^0. If there are regressors, we can modify this example to allow for use of X-adjusted $Y_{it}^1 - Y_{it'}^0$, $[(Y_{it}^1 - X_{it}\beta) - (Y_{it'}^0 - X_{it'}\beta)]$, where for convenience we assume a common β.

[21] The modification of the analysis in this subsection to account for irreversibility is straightforward and thus is omitted.

Table 8.4. *Panel Data Main Cases for Distributions*

Assumption	Behavioral assumption	Recovers	Criteria recovered
(1) $F(y_t^0, y_t^1 \mid X) = F(y_{t'}^0, y_{t'}^1 \mid X)$; $y_t^0 = y_{t'}^0$, and $F(y_t^0, y_t^1 \mid X) = F(y_{t'}^0, y_{t'}^1 \mid X)$; $y_t^1 = y_{t'}^1$	Stationarity or sufficient information to adjust to stationarity Stationarity plus reversibility	Nothing by itself (has no empirical counterpart) Nothing by itself (has no empirical counterpart)	None None
(2) Assumption (1) plus $F(y_t^0, y_t^1 \mid D_{t'} = 0, D_t = 1, X) = F(y_{t'}^0, y_{t'}^1 \mid D_t = 1, X); y_t^0 = y_{t'}^0$	Among participants in t, nonparticipants in t' not different from participants in t'; consistent with both irreversibility and reversibility of program	$F(y_t^0, y_t^1 \mid D_t = 1, X)^a$	All criteria conditional on $D_t = 1$
(3) Assumption (2) plus $F(y_t^0, y_t^1 \mid D_{t'} = 1, D_t = 0, X) = F(y_{t'}^0, y_{t'}^1 \mid D_t = 0, X); y_t^1 = y_{t'}^1$	Among nonparticipants in t, participants in t' not different from nonparticipants in t'; consistent with reversibility of program for general t	$F(y_t^0, y_t^1 \mid X)$	All criteria

[a] We can identify the full distribution using Theorem A-3 proved in Appendix A. Thus if there is a limit set, $\Pr(D = 1 \mid X) = 0$ for $X \in S$, where S is a limit set, we can identify $F(y_t^0, y_t^1 \mid X)$ in that limit set. If there are exclusion restrictions, we can identify this distribution everywhere with additional structure given in Theorem A-3.

Table 8.5. *Panel Data and Repeated Cross Sections, Means and Marginal Distributions*

Assumption	Behavioral assumption	Recovers	Criteria recovered
(1a) $E(Y_t^0|X) = E(Y_{t'}^0|X)$	Stationarity in means or sufficient information to adjust to stationarity; holds in irreversible case	Nothing by itself	None
(1b) $E(Y_t^1|X) = E(Y_{t'}^1|X)$	Same, plus holds in reversible case	Nothing by itself	None
(2a) Assumption (1a) plus $E(Y_{t'}^0|D_{t'} = 0, D_t = 1, X) = E(Y_{t'}^0|D_t = 1, X)$	In mean, among participants in t, nonparticipants in t' not different from participants in t'; holds in irreversible case	$E(Y_t^0|D_t = 1, X)$	Cost–benefit for $D_t = 1$
(2b) Assumption (1b) plus $E(Y_{t'}^1|D_{t'} = 1, D_t = 0, X) = E(Y_{t'}^1|D_t = 0, X)$	In mean, among nonparticipants in t, participants in t' not different from nonparticipants in t'; holds in irreversible case	$E(Y_t^1|D_t = 0, X)$	Cost–benefit for $D_t = 0$
(3a) $F(y_t^0|X) = F(y_{t'}^0|X)$	Stationarity in marginal distribution or sufficient information to adjust to stationarity; holds in reversible case	Nothing by itself	None
(3b) $F(y_t^1|X) = F(y_{t'}^1|X)$	Holds in irreversible case	Nothing by itself	None
(4a) Assumption (3a) plus $F(y_{t'}^0|D_{t'} = 0, D_t = 1, X) = F(y_{t'}^0|D_t = 1, X)$	In distribution, among participants in t, nonparticipants in t' not different from participants in t'; holds in irreversible case	$F(y_t^0|D_t = 1, X)$	Cost–benefit plus Benthamite criterion for $D_t = 1$
(4b) Assumption (3b) plus $F(y_{t'}^1|D_{t'} = 1, D_t = 0, X) = F(y_{t'}^1|D_t = 0, X)$	In distribution, among nonparticipants in t, participants in t' not different from nonparticipants in t'; holds in reversible case	$F(y_t^1|D_t = 0, X)$	Cost–benefit plus Benthamite criterion for $D_t = 0$

3 The Relationship between Traditional Cost–Benefit Analysis and the Parameters Widely Used in the Econometric Evaluation Literature

In this section we relate the parameters estimated in the microeconometric evaluation literature to the parameters needed to perform cost–benefit analysis. We present empirical evidence on the importance of accounting for the direct costs of a program and the marginal welfare costs of taxation in assessing the net benefits of a policy. We follow the literature in cost–benefit analysis and assume that the policy being evaluated has a voluntary component and that valid evaluations of a policy can be derived from looking at the impact of the policy on self-selected participants and nonparticipants.

We postulate the following framework: For a given program associated with policy j there are two discrete outcomes corresponding to direct receipt of treatment ($D_j = 1$, for program participation) and no treatment ($D_j = 0$), and there is a set of program-intensity variables φ_j defined under policy j that affect outcomes in the two states and the allocation of persons to treatment or nontreatment. The program-intensity variables φ_j may be discrete or continuous. Policy "0" is a no-intervention benchmark with program intensity φ_0.

Assuming that costless lump-sum transfers are possible, that a single social-welfare function governs the distribution of resources, and that prices reflect true opportunity costs, traditional cost–benefit analysis (e.g., Harberger, 1971; Boadway and Bruce, 1984) seeks to determine the impact of programs on the total output of society. Efficiency becomes the paramount criterion in this framework, with the distributional concerns assumed to be taken care of through lump-sum transfers and taxes. In this framework, impacts on total output, as in the evaluation criterion (3), are the only objects of interest in evaluating policies.

For policy j, let Y_{ji}^1 and Y_{ji}^0 be individual outputs for person i in the direct-participation state ($D_j = 1$) and direct-nonparticipation state ($D_j = 0$), respectively. The vector of program-intensity variables φ_j operates on all persons within the context of program j, although its effects need not be uniform. It determines, in part, participation in the program. We can write $D_j(\varphi_j)$ as the indicator for participating in program j when the program intensity is φ_j. To simplify notation, we keep implicit any conditioning on personal characteristics that may affect both participation and outcomes. We define $c_j(\varphi_j)$ as the social cost of φ_j denominated in units of output. In general, policies could be designed for specific persons, but we do not consider that possibility here. We assume that $c_j(0) = 0$ and that c_j is convex and increasing in φ_j. The value φ_0 defines another benchmark policy, "0", in which there is no program and therefore no participants. This policy has the associated cost function $c_0(\varphi_0)$.

When $\varphi_j = 0$, there might be effects of policy j on output that would distinguish that policy from the no-policy regime "0." A law that is universally assented to and accepted might raise output at no cost (e.g., adopting a convention about driving on the right-hand side of the road). Output could be different in a policy without the law (policy "0"), but the direct costs of enforcement would be the same under both policies.

Letting $N_1(\varphi_j)$ be the number of direct program participants, and $N_0(\varphi_j)$ the rest of the population, the total output of society under policy j at program-intensity level φ_j is

$$N_1(\varphi_j)E[Y_j^1|D(\varphi_j) = 1, \varphi_j] + N_0(\varphi_j)E[Y_j^0|D(\varphi_j) = 0, \varphi_j] - c(\varphi_j)$$

where $N_1(\varphi_j) + N_0(\varphi_j) = \overline{N}$ is the total number of persons in society. Vector φ_j appears twice in the conditioning arguments: as a determinant of D_j and as a determinant of the output levels in the different states. Vector φ_j is general enough to include financial-incentive variables as well as mandates that assign persons to a particular treatment state. Recall that we keep conditioning on personal characteristics implicit.

Assume, for simplicity, differentiability of the treatment choice and mean-outcome functions, and further assume that φ_j is a scalar, a simplifying assumption that is easily relaxed. The change in output in response to a marginal increase in the policy-intensity parameter φ_j from any given position is

$$M(\varphi_j) = \frac{\partial N_1(\varphi_j)}{\partial \varphi_j}\{E[Y_j^1|D_j(\varphi_j) = 1, \varphi_j] - E[Y_j^0|D_j(\varphi_j) = 0, \varphi_j]\}$$
$$+ N_1(\varphi_j)\left\{\frac{\partial E[Y_j^1|D_j(\varphi_j) = 1, \varphi_j]}{\partial \varphi_j}\right\}$$
$$+ N_0(\varphi_j)\left\{\frac{\partial E[Y_j^0|D_j(\varphi_j) = 0, \varphi_j]}{\partial \varphi_j}\right\} - c_j'(\varphi_j)$$

The first term arises from the change in the number of participants induced by the policy change. The second and third terms arise from changes in output among participants and nonparticipants induced by the policy change. The fourth term is the marginal direct-output cost of the change in the intensity of policy φ_j.

In principle, this measure could be estimated from time-series data on the change in aggregate GNP occurring after the policy-intensity parameter is varied. Under the assumption of a well-defined social-welfare function with interior solutions and the additional assumption that prices are constant at initial values, an increase in GNP at base-period prices will raise social welfare.[22]

---

[22] See, e.g., Laffont (1989, p. 155) or the comprehensive discussion by Chipman and Moore (1976).

Evaluating the Welfare State

If marginal program-intensity changes under policy regime j have no effect on intrasector mean output, the bracketed expressions in the second and third terms are zero. In this case, the parameters of interest are as follows:

(i) $\partial N_1(\varphi_j)/\partial \varphi_j$, the number of people induced into program j by the change in φ_j
(ii) $E[Y_j^1|D_j(\varphi_j) = 1, \varphi_j] - E[Y_j^0|D_j(\varphi_j) = 0, \varphi_j]$, the mean output difference between participants and nonparticipants
(iii) $c_j'(\varphi_j)$, the direct social marginal cost of policy j at program-intensity level φ_j

It is revealing that nowhere in this list do we see the parameters that receive the most attention in the econometric policy-evaluation literature (e.g., Heckman and Robb, 1985). These are as follows:

(a) $E[Y_j^1 - Y_j^0|D_j(\varphi_j) = 1, \varphi_j]$, "the effect of treatment on the treated" for persons in regime j at policy intensity φ_j
(b) $E(Y_j^1 - Y_j^0|\varphi_j = \bar{\varphi})$, where $\varphi_j = \bar{\varphi}$ sets $N_1(\bar{\varphi}) = \bar{N}$; this is the effect of universal direct participation in program j compared with universal nonparticipation in j at a level of program intensity $\bar{\varphi}$
(c) $E(Y_j^1 - Y_j^0|\varphi_j)$, the effect of randomly selecting persons for direct treatment and forcing their compliance with this treatment compared with their position in the no-participation state under policy j at program-intensity level φ_j

Parameter (ii) can be obtained from simple mean differences between the treated and the nontreated. No adjustment for selection bias is required. Parameter (i) can be obtained from knowledge of the net movement of persons into or out of direct participation in the program in response to the policy change, something usually not measured in microeconomic policy evaluations; for discussions of this problem, see Moffitt (1992) or Heckman (1992). Parameter (iii) can be obtained from cost data. It should include the full social costs of the program, including the welfare cost of raising public funds, although these are often ignored.

It is informative to place additional structure on this model. This leads to a representation of a criterion that is widely used in the literature on microeconomic program evaluation and also establishes a link with the discrete-choice literature in econometrics. Assume a binary-choice random-utility framework like that used in the Roy model. Suppose that under policy regime j with program-intensity level φ_j agents make choices to directly participate or not based on net utility and that policies affect participant utility through an additively separable term $k(\varphi_j)$ that is assumed scalar and differentiable. Net utility from participating in the program is $U_j = X + k(\varphi_j)$, where k is monotonic in φ_j and where the joint distributions of (Y_j^1, X) and (Y_j^0, X) are $F(y_j^1, X)$ and $F(y_j^0, X)$, respectively.[23] In the special case of the Roy model, $X = Y_j^1 - Y_j^0$, and $k = 0$. In general, $D_j(\varphi_j) = 1(U_j \geq 0) = 1[X \geq -k(\varphi_j)]$, so that

$$N_1(\varphi_j) = \overline{N} \Pr(U_j \geq 0) = \overline{N} \int_{-k(\varphi_j)}^{\infty} f(x) \, dx$$

$$N_0(\varphi_j) = \overline{N} \Pr(U_j < 0) = \overline{N} \int_{-\infty}^{-k(\varphi_j)} f(x) \, dx$$

The total output is

$$\overline{N} \int_{-\infty}^{\infty} y^1 \int_{-k(\varphi_j)}^{\infty} f(y^1, x|\varphi_j) \, dx \, dy^1$$
$$+ \overline{N} \int_{-\infty}^{\infty} y^0 \int_{-\infty}^{-k(\varphi_j)} f(y^0, x|\varphi_j) \, dx \, dy^0 - c_j(\varphi_j)$$

Under standard conditions[24] we can differentiate under the integral sign to obtain the following expression for the marginal change in output with respect to a change in intensity parameter φ_j within policy regime j:

$$M(\varphi_j) = \overline{N} k'(\varphi_j) f_x[-k(\varphi_j)] \{ E[Y_j^1 | D(\varphi_j) = 1, X = -k(\varphi_j), \varphi_j]$$
$$- E[Y_j^0 | D(\varphi_j) = 0, X = -k(\varphi_j), \varphi_j] \}$$
$$+ \overline{N} \left[\int_{-\infty}^{\infty} y^1 \int_{-k(\varphi_j)}^{\infty} \frac{\partial f(y^1, x|\varphi_j)}{\partial \varphi_j} dx \, dy^1 \right.$$
$$\left. + \int_{-\infty}^{\infty} y^0 \int_{-\infty}^{-k(\varphi_j)} \frac{\partial f(y^0, x|\varphi_j)}{\partial \varphi_j} dx \, dy^0 \right] - c'_j(\varphi_j)$$

where f_x, the marginal density of X, is evaluated at $X = -k(\varphi_j)$.

This model has a well-defined marginal-entry condition: $X \geq -k(\varphi_j)$. The first set of terms corresponds to the gain arising from the movement of persons at the margin (the term in curly brackets) weighted by the proportion of the population at the margin, $f_x[-k(\varphi_j)]$, times the number of people in the population. This term is the net gain from switching from nonparticipant to participant status. The expression in curly brackets in the first term is a limit form of the "local average treatment effect" of Imbens and Angrist (1994). The second set of terms is the within-treatment-status change in output resulting from the change in the program-intensity parameter. This term is ignored in many evaluation studies. It describes how people who do not switch their participation status are affected by the policy change. The third term is the direct marginal social cost of the policy change, which is rarely estimated. At a social planner's optimum, $M(\varphi_j) = 0$, provided standard second-order conditions are satisfied. Marginal benefit should equal marginal cost.

---

[23] These are assumed to be absolutely continuous with respect to Lebesgue measure.
[24] See, e.g., Royden (1968) for the required domination conditions.

Either a cost-based measure of marginal benefit or a benefit-based measure of cost can be used to evaluate the marginal gains or costs of the change in policy intensity.

Observe that the local average treatment effect is simply the effect of treatment on the treated for persons at the margin $[X = -k(\varphi_j)]$:

$$E[Y_j^1|D_j(\varphi_j) = 1, X = -k(\varphi_j), \varphi_j]$$
$$- E[Y_j^0|D_j(\varphi_j) = 0, X = -k(\varphi_j), \varphi_j]$$
$$= E[Y_j^1 - Y_j^0|D(\varphi_j) = 1, X = -k(\varphi_j), \varphi_j]$$

The proof of this result is immediate once it is recognized that the set $X = -k(\varphi_j)$ is the indifference set for this problem. Thus the Imbens and Angrist parameter is a marginal version of the conventional evaluation parameter ("treatment effect on the treated") for gross outcomes. This parameter is but one of the three ingredients required to produce an evaluation of social welfare under the cost–benefit criterion.

The conventional evaluation parameter ("treatment effect on the treated")

$$E[Y_j^1 - Y_j^0|D_j(\varphi_j) = 1, X, \varphi_j]$$

does not incorporate costs, does not correspond to a marginal change, and includes the effect of intramarginal changes. This parameter is, in general, inappropriate for evaluating the effect of a policy change on GNP. However, under certain conditions, which we shall now make precise, it is sometimes informative about the gross gain accruing to the economy from the existence of program j at level φ_j compared with the alternative of shutting it down and switching to policy "0." The social cost associated with policy "0" is $c_0(\varphi_0)$, which we assume to be zero: $c_0(\varphi_0) = 0$.

The appropriate criterion for an all-or-nothing evaluation of a policy at level φ_j is

$$A(\varphi_j) = \{N_1(\varphi_j)E[Y_j^1|D_j(\varphi_j) = 1, \varphi_j]$$
$$+ N_0(\varphi_j)E[Y_j^0|D_j(\varphi_j) = 0, \varphi_j] - c_j(\varphi_j)\}$$
$$- \overline{N}E(Y_0|\varphi_0)$$

In the no-policy regime, there is only one output, Y_0, and everyone is in the no-program state. If $A(\varphi_j) > 0$, total output is increased by establishing program j at level φ_j. In the special case in which the outcome in the nonparticipation state under regime j (Y_j^0) is the same as the outcome in the no-program state (Y_0) for both participants and nonparticipants under regime j, we have

$$E[Y_j^0|D_j(\varphi_j) = 0, \varphi_j] = E[Y_0|D_j(\varphi_j) = 0, \varphi_0] \qquad (23a)$$

and

$$E[Y_j^0|D_j(\varphi_j) = 1, \varphi_j] = E[Y_0|D_j(\varphi_j) = 1, \varphi_0] \qquad (23b)$$

The right-hand sides of both expressions describe hypothetical conditional expectations. The right-hand side of (23a) is what the outcome in the no-program state would be for persons who would not directly participate in the program under policy j with parameters φ_j [i.e., those for whom $D_j(\varphi_j) = 0$]. The right-hand side of (23b) is the corresponding expression for persons who would participate in the program under policy j with intensity parameters φ_j [i.e., those for whom $D_j(\varphi_j) = 1$]. These conditioning statements select out, respectively, nonparticipants and participants in policy regime j and compute the expected values of output in the policy-"0" regime.

Assuming that the probability of participation in regime j under program-intensity level φ_j does not depend on the value of φ_0 in the no-program state,

$$\Pr(D_j = 1|\varphi_j, \varphi_0) = \Pr(D_j = 1|\varphi_j) \qquad (A\text{-}3)$$

then under assumption (A-1) we can use the law of iterated expectations to write

$$E(Y^0|\varphi_0) = E[Y_0|D_j(\varphi_j) = 1, \varphi_0]\Pr[D_j(\varphi_j) = 1|\varphi_j]$$
$$+ E[Y_0|D_j(\varphi_j) = 0, \varphi_0]\Pr[D_j(\varphi_j) = 0|\varphi_j]$$

From (23a) and (23b) and (A-3) we obtain

$$E(Y^0|\varphi_0) = E[Y_j^0|D_j(\varphi_j) = 1, \varphi_j]\Pr[D_j(\varphi_j) = 1|\varphi_j]$$
$$+ E[Y_j^0|D_j(\varphi_j) = 0, \varphi_j]\Pr[D_j(\varphi_j) = 0|\varphi_j]$$

Substituting for $E(Y_j^0|\varphi_0)$ in the expression for $A(\varphi_j)$, we obtain

$$A(\varphi_j) = N(\varphi_j)E[Y_j^1 - Y_j^0|D_j(\varphi_j) = 1, \varphi_j] - c_j(\varphi_j) \qquad (24)$$

which vindicates the use of the parameter "treatment effect on the treated" as an evaluation parameter in the case in which there are no general-equilibrium effects in the sense of assumption (A-1). This important case is applicable to small-scale social programs with partial participation. For evaluating the effects of fine-tuning the intensity levels of existing policies, measure $M(\varphi_j)$ is more appropriate.

3.1 Empirical Evidence on the Importance of Adjusting for Direct Costs and the Welfare Costs of Taxation in Cost–Benefit Analysis

This subsection examines the effects of accounting for both the direct costs and the welfare costs of raising government tax revenue in

Table 8.6. *Benefit Minus Cost Estimates for JTPA under Alternative Assumptions Regarding Benefit Persistence, Discounting, and Welfare Costs of Taxation (National JTPA Study, 30-Month Impact Sample)*

Benefit duration	Direct costs included?	6-month interest rate	Welfare cost of taxes	Adult males	Adult females	Male youth	Female youth
30 months	No	0.000	0.00	1,354	1,703	−967	136
30 months	Yes	0.000	0.00	523	532	−2,922	−1,180
30 months	Yes	0.000	0.50	108	−54	−3,900	−1,838
30 months	Yes	0.025	0.00	433	432	−2,859	−1,195
30 months	Yes	0.025	0.50	17	−154	−3,836	−1,853
7 years	No	0.000	0.00	5,206	5,515	−3,843	865
7 years	Yes	0.000	0.00	4,375	4,344	−5,798	−451
7 years	Yes	0.000	0.50	3,960	3,758	−6,775	−1,109
7 years	Yes	0.025	0.00	3,523	3,490	−5,166	−610
7 years	Yes	0.025	0.50	3,108	2,905	−6,143	−1,268

Notes: (1) "Benefit duration" indicates how long the estimated benefits from JTPA are assumed to persist. Actual estimates are used for the first 30 months. For the 7-year-duration case, the average of the benefits in months 18–24 and 25–30 is used for the benefits in each future period.
(2) "Welfare cost of taxes" indicates the additional cost in terms of lost output due to each additional dollar of taxes raised. The value 0.50 lies in the range suggested by Browning (1987).
(3) Estimates are constructed by breaking up the time after random assignment into 6-month periods. All costs are assumed to be paid in the first 6-month period, while benefits are received in each 6-month period and discounted by the amount indicated for each row of the table.

computing benefit–cost estimates for a prototypical government training program. Accounting for direct costs and the welfare costs of government revenue substantially reduces the estimated returns to government training programs over what is conventionally reported. Our estimates of the difference between costs and benefits for the Job Training Partnership Act (JTPA) program appear in Table 8.6. Benefits are measured using the difference in mean earnings between the experimental-treatment and control groups in the JTPA data, which are described more fully in Section 4 and in Appendix B. Direct costs represent the estimated difference in training costs between the treatment and control groups[25] and are assumed to be incurred within the first

---

[25] Both the impact and cost estimates are drawn from the analysis of Orr et al. (1995). The first row of Table 8.6 corresponds to the case they consider. The impact estimates of Orr

6 months after random assignment. The first row for each demographic group presents the experimentally estimated unadjusted benefits of participation over the 30-month post-random-assignment period for which data are available. Each of the remaining rows of Table 8.6 presents estimates that net out the direct costs of training based on the assumptions stated in those rows about the duration of program benefits (30 months or 7 years), the interest rate used to discount the benefits (zero or 0.025 over 6 months), and the welfare cost of taxation (zero or $0.50 per dollar of revenue).

Three main conclusions emerge from this analysis. First, netting out the direct costs of training is empirically important. For job-training programs, costs are often large relative to the estimated benefits, as is clearly the case for female youth where benefits and costs are roughly equal. Second, accounting for the welfare costs of taxation has a substantial effect on the cost–benefit calculation. For adult females with benefits assumed to last 30 months, and assuming no discounting, netting out the welfare costs of taxation, equal to $0.50 per dollar, changes the difference between costs and benefits from $532 to minus $54. The estimates of the welfare cost of public funds presented in the literature vary over the range from zero to $3.00 per dollar of taxes (Browning, 1987). However, the "consensus value" is less than $1.00 and typically is in the range of $0.30–0.50. If the welfare cost of taxation rises as the amount of taxes raised increases, an issue arises as to whether programs should be evaluated as if each were the first program (so that taxes increase from zero to the level needed to finance the program), the marginal program (so that taxes increase from existing levels by the cost of the program), or some intermediate value. Even more problematic is the case in which the tax effects of groups of programs interact and programs are bundled in the legislative process. In this study we use the marginal cost of funds given the current scale of government, which is appropriate because the scale of the JTPA program is relatively small, and we are evaluating it in isolation from other programs.

A third conclusion from Table 8.6 is that the estimated cost–benefit difference is sensitive to the assumed duration of benefits. The best evidence on the longevity of program benefits is that of Couch (1992). He showed that benefits to adult women from the National Supported Work program remained at the same level for at least 7 years beyond random assignment, so that our estimate for this group is conservative. There is also evidence from the U.S. GAO (1996) that JTPA program benefits

et al. (1995) differ somewhat from those presented by Bloom et al. (1993) because of differences in sample compositions and earnings measures. The remainder of our empirical evidence is based on the Bloom et al. (1993) sample and earnings measure, which we prefer because it does not combine earnings information from different data sources. We use the Orr et al. (1995) data in Table 8.6 because cost estimates are not readily available for the Bloom et al. (1993) sample.

extend at least 5 years after random assignment for a subset of the experimental sample.

4 Evidence on Impact Heterogeneity and the Value of Self-assessments and Revealed-Preference Information

This section of the study addresses three questions. Question (1): What is the empirical evidence on heterogeneity in program impacts among persons? The conventional approach implicitly assumes impact homogeneity conditional on observables. This assumption greatly simplifies the task of evaluating the welfare state. Using data from an experimental evaluation of a prototypical job-training program, we use many of the assumptions presented in Section 2 to bound or identify the joint distribution of outcomes conditional on $D = 1$. We find considerable evidence of heterogeneity of program impacts, so that conventional econometric methods do not take us very far in constructing the evaluation criteria discussed in Section 1. Use of experimental data enables us to avoid the self-selection problems that plague ordinary observational data and simplifies our analysis.

Given our evidence on impact heterogeneity, we ask question (2): How sensitive are the estimates of the proportion of people who gain from the program – what we have called the "voting criterion" – to alternative assumptions about the dependence between Y^0 and Y^1? We find that the estimates are very sensitive to alternative assumptions. At the same time, for adult women, the estimate of those who benefit from the program exceeds 50 percent in every case we consider except one, and it is close to 100 percent in some cases.

Some of the estimates used to answer question (2) assume that Y^0 and Y^1 are positively dependent given $D = 1$. We established in Section 2 that under purposive selection based on outcomes in the treated and untreated states, such dependence among participants arises even if Y^1 and Y^0 are independent or are negatively correlated in the population as a whole. An alternative to imposing a particular decision rule is to infer it from self-assessments of the program. These assessments are all that is required for a libertarian evaluation of the welfare state. We examine the implicit value placed on the program by addressing the following: Question (3a): Are persons who applied to the program and were accepted into it, but then randomized out of it, placed in an inferior position relative to those accepted applicants who were not randomized out? We measure ex-ante rational regret using second-order stochastic dominance, which is an appropriate measure under the assumption that individuals are completely uncertain of both Y^1 and Y^0 before going into the program. We also consider ex-post evaluations of participants by asking question (3b): How "satisfied" are participants with their experience in the program? Self-assessments of programs are widely used in evaluation research (e.g., Katz et al., 1975), but the meaning to be placed on them is not clear. Do they reflect an evaluation of the experience of the program (its process) or an evaluation of the benefits of the program? Our evidence suggests that respondents report a net benefit inclusive of their costs of participating in the program. Groups for whom the program has a negative average impact, as estimated by the "objective" experimental data, express as much (or more) enthusiasm for the program as groups with positive average impacts. A third source of revealed-preference evaluations uses the revealed choices of attriters from the program. Econometric models of self-selection, since Heckman (1974a,b), have used revealed-choice behavior to infer the evaluations people place on programs either by selecting into them or dropping out of them. Finally, we come to question (3c): What implicit valuation of the program do attriters place on it?

4.1   Data

Our estimates are based on data from a recent experimental evaluation of the employment and training programs funded under title II-A of the U.S. Job Training Partnership Act (JTPA) (Orr et al., 1995). This program provides classroom training, on-the-job training, and job-search assistance to the economically disadvantaged. We focus primarily, but not exclusively, on adult women (age 22 and older) for many, but not all, of our analyses. We also present selected results for other demographic groups: adult men (age 22 and older) and male and female out-of-school youth (ages 16–21). Our largest samples are for adult women. Given that many of the adult women in the program are welfare recipients, their experiences with training are of special interest, given recent reforms in the U.S. welfare system. Appendix B describes the JTPA data in greater detail.

4.2   Evidence on Impact Heterogeneity

This subsection presents evidence on variability in the response to training. We find strong evidence against homogeneity. However, unless the dependence across outcomes in the treated and untreated states is very high, the estimated variability in program gains is implausibly large.

Suppose that the JTPA experiment satisfies (I-10). Suppose that there are N treated persons and N nontreated persons. Suppose that the outcomes are continuously distributed. Rank the individuals in each treatment category in the order of their outcome values from the highest to the lowest. Define $Y_{(i)}^j$ as the ith highest ranked person in the j distribution. Ignoring ties, we obtain two data distributions:

Evaluating the Welfare State

Treatment outcome: $F(y^1|D = 1)$ Nontreatment outcome: $F(y^0|D = 1)$

$$\underset{\sim}{Y}^1 = \begin{pmatrix} Y^1_{(1)} \\ \vdots \\ Y^1_{(N)} \end{pmatrix} \qquad \underset{\sim}{Y}^0 = \begin{pmatrix} Y^0_{(1)} \\ \vdots \\ Y^0_{(N)} \end{pmatrix}$$

We know the marginal data distributions $F(y^1|D = 1)$ and $F(y^0|D = 1)$, but we do not know where person i in the treatment distribution would appear in the nontreatment distribution. These distributions can also be defined conditional on X. Corresponding to the ranking of the treatment outcome distribution, there are $N!$ possible patterns of outcomes in the associated nontreatment outcome distribution. By considering all possible permutations, we can form a collection of possible impact distributions, that is, alternative distributions of

$$\underset{\sim}{\Delta} = \underset{\sim}{Y}^1 - \Pi_\ell \underset{\sim}{Y}^0 \qquad (\ell = 1, \ldots, N!)$$

where Π_ℓ is a particular $N \times N$ permutation matrix of Y^0 in the set of all $N!$ permutations associating the ranks in the Y^1 distribution with the ranks in the Y^0 distribution, and $\underset{\sim}{\Delta}$, $\underset{\sim}{Y}^1$, and $\underset{\sim}{Y}^0$ are $N \times 1$ vectors of impacts and treated and untreated outcomes. By considering all possible permutations, we obtain all possible sortings of treatment (Y^1) and nontreatment (Y^0) outcomes, using realized values from one distribution as counterfactuals for the other.

The dummy-endogenous-variable model assumes a constant treatment effect for all persons. This model admits only one permutation: $\Pi = I$ for each X. The best in one distribution is the best in the other distribution. In the common-effect case, Y^1 and Y^0 differ by a constant for each person. A generalization of that model preserves perfect dependence in the ranks between the two distributions, but does not require the impact to be the same at all quantiles of the base-state distribution.

In place of ranks, we work with the percentiles of the Y^1 and Y^0 distributions, which have much better statistical properties (Heckman and Smith, 1993; Heckman et al., 1997c). Equating percentiles across the two distributions, we form the pairs given in expression (13) and obtain the deterministic gain function given in (14). For the case of absolutely continuous distributions with positive density at y^0, the gain function (14) can be written as $\Delta(y^0) = F_1^{-1}[F_0(y^0|D = 1)] - y^0$. We can test nonparametrically for the classic common-effect model by determining whether or not percentiles are uniformly shifted at all points of the distribution. We can form other pairings across percentiles by mapping percentiles from the Y^1 distribution into percentiles from the Y^0 distribution using the map $T: q_1 \to q_0$. The data are consistent with all admissible transformations, including $q_0 = 100 - q_1$, where the best in one distribution

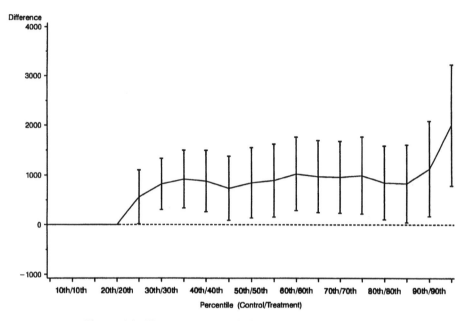

Figure 8.1. Treatment–control differences at percentiles of the 18-month earnings distribution. Perfect-positive-dependence case (adult females): The sample consisted of ABt's experimental 18-month study sample. ABt imputed values were used instead of outlying values. Standard errors for the quantiles were obtained using methods described by Csörgő (1993).

is mapped into the worst in the other. They cannot reject any of these models nor more general models in which Π_ℓ is a Markov transition matrix and we consider all possible Markov matrices.

Figure 8.1 presents empirical evidence on the question of the constancy of the gain effect across quantiles. It shows the estimate of $\Delta(y_0)$ for adult women assuming that the best persons in the "1" distribution are the best in the "0" distribution. More formally, it assumes that the permutation matrix $\Pi = I$. No conditioning is made, so the full sample is utilized. Between the 25th and 85th percentiles the assumption of a constant impact is roughly correct. It is grossly at odds with the data at the highest and lowest percentiles.[26] Heckman et al. (1997c) and Heckman and Smith (1993) have presented a more extensive empirical analysis of this model for different conditioning sets and have reached essentially the same conclusions.

---

[26] Standard errors for the quantiles are obtained using methods described by Csörgő (1993).

4.2.1 Fréchet Bounds

The Fréchet bounds of expression (17) can also be applied to conditional (on $D = 1$) distributions. Both the lower and the upper Fréchet bounds are proper probability distributions. At the upper bound, Y^1 is a nondecreasing function of Y^0. At the lower bound, Y^0 is a nonincreasing function of Y^1. These bounds are not helpful in bounding the distribution of gains $\Delta = Y^1 - Y^0$, although they bound certain features of it. From a theorem of Cambanis, Simons, and Stout (1976), if $k(Y^1, Y^0)$ is superadditive (or subadditive),[27] then extreme values of $E[k(Y^1, Y^0)| D = 1]$ are obtained from the upper and lower bounding distributions obtained from the experimental data.

Because $k(Y^1, Y^0) = Y^1 Y^0$ is superadditive, the maximum attainable product-moment correlation $\rho_{Y^0 Y^1}$ is obtained from the upper-bound distribution, and the minimum attainable product-moment correlation is obtained at the lower-bound distribution. Because var(Δ) is a subadditive function, it is possible to bound the variance of Δ $\{= \text{var}(Y^1) + \text{var}(Y^0) - 2\rho_{Y^0 Y^1}[\text{var}(Y^1)\text{var}(Y^0)]^{\frac{1}{2}}\}$ and thus determine whether or not the data are consistent with the common-effect model in which $Y^1 - Y^0 = \alpha$, a constant, which implies var(Δ) = 0. Kendall's τ and Spearman's ρ also attain their extreme values at the bounding distributions (Tchen, 1980). However, the Fréchet inequalities do not provide bounds on the quantiles of the $\Delta = (Y^1 - Y^0)$ distribution. Only the extreme high and extreme low quantile values are obtained from the Frechet bounds of the joint distribution. Table 8.7 presents the ranges of values of $\rho_{Y^1 Y^0}$, Kendall's τ, Spearman's ρ, and $[\text{var}(\Delta)]^{\frac{1}{2}}$ for the JTPA data for adult women. The ranges are rather wide, but it is interesting to observe that the Fréchet bounds rule out the common-effect model, as var(Δ) is bounded away from zero.[28] They clearly do not rule out the deterministic case of perfect correlation in the ranks across outcome distributions as long as Δ is not a constant.

4.2.2 Sensitivity to Alternative Assumptions about Dependence across the Distributions

Using the sample data, we can pair percentiles of the Y^1 and Y^0 distributions for any choice of rank correlation τ between -1.0 and 1.0.

---

[27] A function $k(x, y)$ is superadditive if $x > x'$, and $y > y'$ implies that $k(x, y) + k(x', y') > k(x', y) + k(x, y')$. Subadditively reverses the inequality. Strict forms of these ideas convert weak inequalities into strong ones.

[28] Heckman et al. (1997c) conducted a Monte Carlo analysis of the standard errors of the standard deviation of Δ. They found that these standard errors did not provide a reliable guide to inferences regarding the null hypothesis that the true impact standard deviation is zero, using inference based on asymptotic normality of the test statistics. However, Monte Carlo estimation of the sampling distribution under the null that var(Δ) = 0 indicates that the null can be rejected in these data at the 0.0001 level.

Table 8.7. *Characteristics of the Distribution of Impacts on Earnings in the 18 Months after Random Assignment at the Fréchet-Hoeffding Bounds (National JTPA Study, 18-Month Impact Sample, Adult Females)*

Statistic	Lower bound	Upper bound
Impact standard deviation	14,968.76 (211.08)	674.50 (137.53)
Outcome correlation	−0.760 (0.013)	(0.998) (0.001)
Spearman's ρ	−0.9776 (0.0016)	0.9867 (0.0013)

Notes: (1) These estimates differ slightly from those reported for $\tau = 1.0$ and $\tau = -1.0$ in Table 8.8 because they were obtained using the empirical CDFs calculated at $100 earnings intervals rather than using the percentiles of the two CDFs. See Heckman, Smith, and Clements (1997) for details.
(2) Bootstrap standard errors in parentheses.

The case of $\tau = 1.0$ corresponds to the case of perfect positive dependence, where $\Pi = I$ and $q_1 = q_0$. The case where $\tau = -1.0$ corresponds to the case of perfect negative dependence, where $q_1 = 100 - q_0$. The first and last rows of Table 8.8 display estimates of quantiles of the impact distribution and other features of the impact distribution for these two cases.

Heckman et al. (1997c) shown how to obtain random samples of permutations conditional on values of τ between 1.0 and −1.0. We display two sets of estimates from their work. The first set assumes positive but not perfect dependence between the percentiles of Y^1 and Y^0, with $\tau = 0.95$. Estimates based on a random sample of 50 percentile permutations with this value of τ appear in the second column of Table 8.8. These results show that even a modest departure from perfect positive dependence substantially widens the distribution of impacts. More striking still are the results in the third column of Table 8.8, which correspond to the case where $\tau = 0.0$. This value of τ is implied by independence between the percentiles of Y^1 and Y^0. Here (as in the case with $\tau = -1.0$) the distribution of estimated impacts is implausibly wide, with large positive values in each distribution often matched with zero or small positive values in the other. However, the conclusion that a majority

Table 8.8. *Estimated Parameters of the Impact Distribution: Perfect Positive Dependence, Positive Dependence with* $\tau = 0.95$, *Independence, and Perfect Negative Dependence Cases (National JTPA Study, 18-Month Impact Sample, Adult Females)*

Statistic	Perfect positive dependence ($\tau = 1.0$)	Positive dependence with $\tau = 0.95$	Independence of Y^1 and Y^0 ($\tau = 0.0$)	Perfect negative dependence ($\tau = -1.0$)
5th percentile	0.00	0.00	−18,098.50	−22,350.00
	(47.50)	(360.18)	(630.73)	(547.17)
25th percentile	572.00	125.50	−6,043.00	−11,755.00
	(232.90)	(124.60)	(300.47)	(411.83)
50th percentile	864.00	616.00	0.00	580.00
	(269.26)	(280.19)	(163.17)	(389.51)
75th percentile	966.00	867.00	7,388.50	12,791.00
	(305.74)	(272.60)	(263.25)	(253.18)
95th percentile	2,003.00	1,415.50	19,413.25	23,351.00
	(543.03)	(391.51)	(423.63)	(341.41)
Percentage positive	100.00	96.00	54.00	52.00
	(1.60)	(3.88)	(1.11)	(0.81)
Impact S.D.	1,857.75	6,005.96	12,879.21	16,432.43
	(480.17)	(776.14)	(259.24)	(265.88)
Outcome correlation	0.9903	0.7885	−0.0147	−0.6592
	(0.0048)	(0.0402)	(0.0106)	(0.0184)

Notes: (1) The values in this table are calculated using percentiles of the two distributions. The perfect-positive-dependence case matches the top percentile in the Y^1 distribution with the top percentile in the Y^0 distribution, the second percentile of the Y^1 distribution with the second of the Y^0 distribution, and so on. The perfect-negative-dependence case matches the percentiles in reverse order, so that the lowest percentile of the Y^0 distribution is matched with the highest percentile of the Y^1 distribution, and so on. The two intermediate cases match the percentiles of the Y^1 distribution with percentiles of a permutation of the Y^0 distribution such that the rank correlation of the matched percentiles has the value indicated.
(2) The perfect-positive- and perfect-negative-dependence cases are based on the single permutation having this characteristic in the sample. The values reported for the intermediate cases represent means of random samples of 50 permutations with the indicated value of τ.
(3) For each case, the difference between each percentile of the Y^1 distribution and the associated percentile of the Y^0 distribution is the impact for that percentile. Taken together, the percentile impacts form the distribution of impacts. It is the percentiles of these impact distributions that are reported in the upper portion of the table. The impact standard deviation, outcome correlation, and percentage positive are calculated using the percentile impacts. The impact standard deviation (S.D.) is the standard deviation of the percentile differences. The outcome correlation is the correlation of the matched percentile from the two distributions. The percentage positive is the percentage of the percentiles impacts greater than or equal to zero.
(4) Bootstrap standard errors in parentheses.

of adult female participants benefit from the program is robust to the choice of τ.[29]

4.2.3 Assuming the Gain Is Independent of the Base

Another source of identifying information for the joint distribution of outcomes and the distribution of impacts postulates that the gain Δ is independent of the base Y^0, so that $Y^0 \perp\!\!\!\perp \Delta | D = 1$. Letting $R = 1$ if a person who applies and is provisionally accepted into the program is randomized into the program, and $R = 0$ if a provisionally accepted applicant is randomized out, $Y = Y^0 + R\Delta$, and $R\Delta \perp\!\!\!\perp Y^0$. Throughout we condition on $D = 1$. This identifying condition will be satisfied if Y^0 is known, but the gain Δ cannot be forecast at the time decisions are made about program participation. This case has been extensively discussed by Heckman and Robb (1985, p. 181), and it produces a model that is intermediate between the common-effect model and the variable-impact model when the impact is anticipated by agents.

Setting $Y^0 = X\beta + U_0$, we obtain a conventional random-coefficient model for a regression: $Y = RY^1 + (1 - R)Y^0 = X\beta + R\Delta + U_0$. Using a components-of-variance model, we can write $E(\Delta) = \bar{\Delta}$ and $\varepsilon = \Delta - \bar{\Delta}$ to obtain

$$Y = X\beta + R\bar{\Delta} + \varepsilon R + U, \qquad E(\varepsilon R + U|X, R) = 0$$

Following the analysis presented in Section 2.1.1, we estimate the variance of ε.

The first row of Table 8.9 presents estimates of the random coefficient based on the identifying assumption $\Delta \perp\!\!\!\perp Y_0 | D = 1$. The evidence supports the hypothesis that $\text{var}(\Delta) > 0$, suggesting that a more elaborate approach to estimating the distribution of Δ based on deconvolution is likely to be fruitful. If we maintain normality of Y^1 and Y^0 (given $D = 1$ and X), the distribution of Δ is normal, with mean $\bar{\Delta}$ and variance $\text{var}(\Delta)$, and deconvolution is easy to perform. Under this assumption we can estimate the voting criterion and determine the estimated proportion of people who benefit from the program.

More generally, it is not necessary to assume that the distribution of Δ is normal. We use the deconvolution procedure discussed by Heckman et al. (1997c) to estimate the distribution of impacts nonparametrically. Table 8.9 presents parameters calculated from this distribution. The evidence suggests that under this assumption, about 43 percent of adult women were harmed by participating in the program. The estimated density is presented in Figure 8.2 and is clearly nonnormal. Nonetheless,

---

[29] Heckman et al. (1997c) presented methods for allowing for mass points of zero earnings in the population, and some evidence derived from such methods. Their qualitative conclusions on variability are similar to ours.

Table 8.9. *Random-Coefficient and Deconvolution Estimates: Impact on Earnings in the 18 Months after Random Assignment (National JTPA Study, 18-Month Impact Sample, Adult Females)*

Analysis	Estimated mean impact	Estimated impact S.D.	Estimated percentage positive
Random-coefficient model	601.74 (201.63)	2,271.00 (1,812.90)	60.45
Deconvolution	614.00	1,675.00	56.35

Notes: (1) Estimated standard errors appear in parentheses, where available.
(2) Random-coefficient model includes race/ethnicity, schooling, and site indicators. Only the treatment coefficient is treated as random.
(3) The estimated impact variance for the random-coefficient model is obtained from a regression of the squared residuals from the corresponding fixed-coefficient model on the treatment indicator.
(4) The estimated percentage positive for the random-coefficient model assumes that Δ is normally distributed.
(5) Mean impact, impact standard deviation, and fraction of positive impacts for the deconvolution case are obtained from the smoothed density. Values for the unsmoothed density differ only slightly from those reported here.

the estimated variance of the nonparametric gain distribution matches the variance for the gain distribution obtained from the random-coefficient model within the range of the sampling error of the two estimates. The estimates of the proportion who benefit are in close agreement across the two models when normality is imposed on the random-coefficient model. The fact that we obtain a positive density indicates that the assumption $Y_0 \perp\!\!\!\perp \Delta | D = 1$ is consistent with the data for women and provides support for the hypothesis that agents do not select into the program based on Δ.

4.3 Evidence from Participant Behavior

4.3.1 Testing for Ex Ante Stochastic Rationality of Participants

If individuals choose whether or not to participate in the program based on the gross gains from the program, if they possess a common, but unknown, concave utility function, and if they know the marginal distributions of outcomes in the participation and nonparticipation states, then second-order stochastic dominance should order the distributions

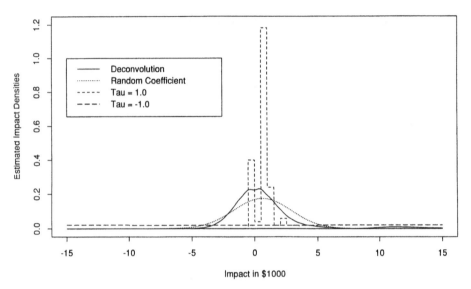

Figure 8.2. Impact densities under alternative identifying assumptions (adult females).

of outcomes for persons who seek to go into the program. For nonnegative y^1 and y^0 this form of rationality implies

$$\int_0^a F_1(y^1|D=1)dy^1 < \int_0^a F_0(y^0|D=1)dy^0 \quad \text{for all } \alpha \in R_+ \quad (25)$$

Draws from the Y^1 distribution produce higher expected utility than draws from the Y^0 distribution among participants. The difference between the two integrals is a measure of regret among persons randomized out from the program and forced into the no-treatment state. This condition may fail for many reasons: Persons may possess more information about their potential outcomes than just the marginal distributions; persons may have different utility functions; and persons may participate in the program on a principle other than expected utility formulated in terms of gross outcomes.

We test condition (25) by comparing the integrals of the empirical CDFs of the control-group and treatment-group earnings distributions for various values of a. Table 8.10 displays the results of tests of the null hypothesis of equality of the integrated distributions in (25) for adult males and females and for male and female youth using self-reported earnings in the 18 months after random assignment. The table shows test results for $\alpha \in \{\$2{,}500, \$5{,}000, \$10{,}000, \$15{,}000, \$20{,}000, \$25{,}000\}$. Standard errors are obtained by bootstrapping. For adult males, the integrated CDF of earnings for the control group exceeds that for the

Table 8.10. *Tests of Second-Order Stochastic Dominance of Experimental-Treatment Group over Experimental Control Group: Earnings in the 18 Months after Random Assignment (National JTPA Study, 18-Month Impact Sample)*

Earnings value (a)	Adult males	Adult females	Male youth	Female youth
2,500	0.8836	1.0296	−0.3357	0.6674
	(0.3162)	(0.2978)	(0.4250)	(0.5094)
	[0.0052]	[0.0005]	[0.4296]	[0.1901]
5,000	1.8067	1.9343	−1.0482	0.7137
	(0.6582)	(0.5955)	(0.9344)	(1.0022)
	[0.0061]	[0.0012]	[0.2620]	[0.4764]
7,500	2.3903	2.7811	−1.8742	0.4428
	(0.9983)	(0.8933)	(1.4610)	(1.4507)
	[0.0166]	[0.0019]	[0.1995]	[0.7602]
10,000	2.9839	3.7315	−2.8489	0.1308
	(1.3334)	(1.1504)	(1.9790)	(1.8486)
	[0.0252]	[0.0012]	[0.1500]	[0.9436]
15,000	4.0191	5.2659	−4.0631	−0.2717
	(1.9826)	(1.5768)	(2.8333)	(2.4032)
	[0.0435]	[0.0008]	[0.1516]	[0.9100]
20,000	4.4428	6.2660	−5.8554	−0.4484
	(2.5434)	(1.8551)	(3.5386)	(2.1750)
	[0.0807]	[0.0007]	[0.0980]	[0.8688]
25,000	4.6171	7.0279	−6.3804	−0.4503
	(2.9192)	(1.9980)	(4.0905)	(2.8641)
	[0.1137]	[0.0004]	[0.1188]	[0.8751]

Notes: (1) The first value in each cell is the difference (control minus treatment) in the integrated CDFs of 18-month earnings. A positive difference indicates that the treatment-group distribution second-order stochastically dominates the control-group distribution. In calculating the integrals, each $100 increment in earnings is normalized to have length one.
(2) Bootstrap standard errors appear in parentheses. Bootstrap standard errors are constructed using 100 samples equal in size to the original sample.
(3) *P* values appear in square brackets.

treatment group at every point, with a *p* value below 0.05 for $a < \$16,500$, and below 0.10 for $a < \$22,500$, which includes most of the supports of the two earnings distributions. The data for adult females provide strong evidence of rational behavior in the sense of (25), passing the test at the 5 percent level or better for every value of a. This evidence suggests that personal objectives and program objectives are aligned for adult women. Results for youth are mixed. For male youth, for whom the mean experimental impact is significantly negative, the difference in integrated CDFs is negative for most values of a, though not statistically significant. For female youth, the difference switches signs at around $a = \$11,000$, but is never close to statistical significance.

4.3.2 Evidence from Self-assessments of Program Participants

Self-assessments of program participants represent an alternative to comparison of observed outcomes as a measure of program impact. Unlike the ex-ante measures based on second-order stochastic dominance, these measures are statements about ex-post expectations. There is no reason that the two measures should agree if people revise their assessments based on what they learn about a program by participating in it. In this section we consider the strengths and limitations of self-reported assessments of satisfaction with the program as evaluation criteria and report on self-evaluations by participants in the JTPA experimental-treatment group. We also consider what can be learned from self-assessment data regarding the heterogeneity of individual treatment effects and the rationality of program participants.

Using participant assessments to evaluate a program has two main advantages relative to the approaches already discussed. First, participants have information not available to external program evaluators. They typically know more about certain components of the cost of program participation than do evaluators. Most evaluations, including the National JTPA Study, do not even attempt to value participant time, transportation, child care, or other costs in evaluating program effectiveness, unless they are paid by the program through subsidies. Participants are likely to include such information in arriving at their self-assessments of the program. Second, participant evaluations provide information about the values placed on outcomes by participants relative to their perceived costs. They have the potential of providing a more inclusive measure of the program's effects than would be obtained from looking only at gross outcomes – one that includes "client satisfaction." To some parties in the welfare state, "customer satisfaction" is an important aspect of a program.

However, participant self-assessments may not be informative on the outcomes of interest to other parties in the welfare state. In evaluations of medical interventions, for example, treatment effects may not be observed by participants or may be difficult for them to assess, compared with what observing scientists might report. Participant assessments of the counterfactual state may be faulty because their judgments are based on inputs or on outcome levels rather than on gains over alternative levels. Persons who choose to go into the program may rationalize their participation in it in responding to questions. In addition, self-assessments, like all utility-based measures, are difficult to compare across individuals.

The top panel of Table 8.11 reports JTPA participant responses to a question about whether or not the program made them better off.[30]

---

[30] The exact wording was "Do you think that the training or other assistance you got from the program helped you get a job or perform better on the job?" The question was asked only of treatment-group members who reported receiving JTPA services.

Table 8.11. *Self-assessments of JTPA Impact: Experimental Treatment Group (National JTPA Study, 18-Month Impact Sample)*

	Adult males	Adult females	Male youth	Female youth
Full-sample percentages				
Percentage who self-report participating	61.63	68.10	62.62	66.29
	(0.81)	(0.68)	(1.29)	(1.09)
Percentage of self-reported participants with a positive self-assessment	62.46	65.21	67.16	71.73
	(1.04)	(0.85)	(1.59)	(1.29)
Overall percentage with positive self-assessments	38.49	44.41	42.06	47.55
	(0.81)	(0.73)	(1.32)	(1.16)
Percentage of self-reported participants with a positive self-assessment by primary treatment received				
None (dropouts)	48.89	51.44	58.90	61.56
	(2.07)	(1.85)	(3.33)	(2.79)
Classroom training in occupational skills	74.10	73.47	72.73	75.28
	(2.15)	(1.36)	(3.60)	(2.30)
On-the-job training at private firm	75.13	78.90	71.00	75.00
	(2.18)	(2.14)	(4.56)	(4.04)
Job-search assistance	59.57	59.80	68.09	68.94
	(2.27)	(2.18)	(3.94)	(4.04)
Basic education	62.96	56.55	70.97	78.44
	(4.67)	(3.84)	(4.09)	(3.19)
Work experience	66.67	68.75	82.76	73.17
	(9.83)	(5.84)	(7.14)	(7.01)
Other	58.47	66.40	62.50	77.98
	(3.65)	(2.98)	(4.77)	(3.99)

Notes: (1) Reported proportions are based on responses to the question "Do you think that the training or other assistance you got from the program helped you get a job or perform better on the job?" This question was asked only of self-reported participants within the treatment group. The overall fraction of positive self-assessments assumes that self-reported nonparticipants would have provided negative self-asssments.
(2) The primary treatment is the one in which the trainee participated for the most hours according to the administrative records of the JTPA sites. Most trainees received only one service; few received more than two. See Smith (in press) for a detailed discussion. Note that for some self-reported participants the JTPA administrative records indicate that no services were received.
(3) Estimated standard errors in parentheses.

Assuming that people answered honestly, and were reporting a gross impact, the self-assessment data clearly contradict the hypothesis of impact homogeneity. For all four demographic groups, 65 to 70 percent of self-reported participants gave positive self-assessments, not the 100 percent or zero percent that would be predicted if impacts were homogeneous. However, if respondents were reporting a perceived net impact, the evidence reported in Table 8.11 does *not* necessarily contradict an assumption of gross impact homogeneity if there was heterogeneity in costs across participants. The entries in the third row of Table 8.11 reveal that the fractions reporting a positive impact were far lower than those obtained from all of the analyses using outcome data. This evidence is consistent with one of two hypotheses: (a) that respondents were reporting net outcomes and that costs borne by participants composed a substantial fraction of gross outcomes or (b) that self-assessments were inaccurate.

The evidence suggests that the self-assessments were at least partly based on inputs received rather than on outputs produced by the program. The lower panel of Table 8.11 shows the fraction of persons receiving each type of training whose self-assessments of the program were positive. The fraction increased with the level of treatment intensity for all four demographic groups. Expensive and more intensive services, such as classroom training in occupational skills (CT-OS) and on-the-job training at a private firm (OJT), elicited a higher proportion of positive self-assessments than did less expensive services, such as job-search assistance (JSA) or basic education. However, the experimental-impact estimates presented by Bloom et al. (1993) revealed that treatment effectiveness and treatment intensity were not positively related. For example, for female youth, classroom training in occupational skills has a more negative mean impact than the less expensive services in the "other-treatment" stream. This evidence suggests that participants may have had difficulty in correctly estimating what would have happened to them in the absence of treatment, and so relied in part on treatment intensity or program inputs as proxies for treatment impact.

Finally, for adult women, we consider how well the self-assessment data match up with the analyses considered in earlier sections. The self-assessment data are not consistent with the assumption of perfect positive dependence in outcomes across the two states. As shown in Figure 8.1, for adult women the JTPA data indicate that perfect positive dependence in outcomes between the treated and untreated states implies a strictly positive impact of the program for about 85 percent of participants – all except those with zero earnings in both states. This value far exceeds the overall self-reported effectiveness rate of 44 percent reported in row 3 of Table 8.11. The 44 percent rate lies below that found even for the case of perfect negative dependence. Overall, the self-reported impact data appear to be too negative when compared with our analyses of the experimental earnings data. This evidence is consistent with participants reporting a net measure, whereas the experimental "treatment effect" measures gross outcomes. The lower positive rating of the program from self-assessment data than from gross outcome data is all the more striking when it is realized that self-assessments were recorded only for people who reported receiving training, whereas the gross outcome data for participants included those who left the program, and the attriters had lower earnings than the nonattriters.

4.3.3 Evidence from Program Dropouts

As a result of the relatively early implementation of random assignment in the JTPA participation process, many treatment-group members never enrolled in the JTPA program and so did not receive JTPA services.[31] In this section we investigate what the information on dropout behavior reveals about treatment heterogeneity and participant rationality. A key limitation in doing this is that the enrollment decision did not depend simply on agent choices, but was a joint decision of the potential participant and of JTPA staff members. The JTPA performance-standards system, which rewards individual training centers based on the labor-market outcomes for their enrollees, provides both a mechanism and incentive for manipulation of the enrollment decision in order to increase center performance.[32] Because we have no data on the preferences of bureaucrats, we ignore this problem and assume that the decisions we observe were solely those of the potential participants.

If anticipated discounted net impacts are the same across all persons, then everyone either participates in the program or drops out of it. The substantial dropout rates reported in the first column of Table 8.12 for all four demographic groups provide evidence that anticipated discounted impacts were heterogeneous.

Next consider the implications of these data for participant rationality. Assume a common discount rate and constant returns per period from the program. Suppose that persons apply and are accepted into the program if $E(\Delta|I) > 0$, where I is the information available at application. Suppose further that Δ is revealed at the time of acceptance into the program, that persons drop out whenever $\Delta \leq 0$, and that $\Delta \perp\!\!\!\perp Y^0$ [this is identifying assumption (I-5)]. If persons entering the program cannot forecast Δ, then, letting $e = 1$ if a person enrolls in the program and $e = 0$ if the person drops out, $E(Y^0|e = 1, D = 1) = E(Y^0|e = 0, D = 1)$, and $E(Y^1|e = 1, D = 1) = E(Y^0|e = 0, D = 1) + E(\Delta|\Delta > 0, D = 1)$.

Table 8.12 presents the mean earnings of JTPA enrollees and dropouts for the 18 months after random assignment for the four demographic groups, along with the experimental impact estimates and the implied differences in Y^0 between the two groups. For adult females and for female youth, the data are consistent with this model, because the dif-

---

[31] Heckman and Smith (1993, 1995) discussed this phenomenon.
[32] This was discussed by Heckman, Smith, and Taber (1998b).

Table 8.12. *Comparisons of Post-Random-Assignment Earnings of Treatment Group Enrollees and Dropouts (National JTPA Study, 18-Month Impact Sample)*

	Percentage dropping out	Mean earnings of enrollees	Mean earnings of dropouts	p value	Mean earnings difference	Experimental impact estimate
Adult males	40.92 (0.72)	13,638 (261)	12,181 (355)	0.0010	1,457 (440)	572 (371)
Adult females	37.39 (0.66)	8,428 (156)	7,947 (244)	0.0975	480 (290)	793 (223)
Male youth	34.83 (1.14)	10,275 (310)	9,442 (441)	0.1231	832 (539)	−801 (475)
Female youth	37.02 (1.04)	6,108 (197)	6,251 (291)	0.6844	−143 (352)	−45 (298)

Notes: (1) The *p* values are from *t* tests of equality of means assuming unequal variances in the two groups.
(2) Mean earnings difference indicates the difference in mean earnings between the enrollees and the dropouts in the experimental treatment group.
(3) Experimental impact estimates differ from those of Bloom et al. (1993) because they are not regression-adjusted and because imputed values for adult female nonrespondents were not used.
(4) Estimated standard errors in parentheses.

ference between the mean earnings of enrollees and dropouts is not statistically distinguishable from the experimental impact estimate. However, the data for adult males and male youth are not consistent with this model.

If, however, we relax the assumption of independence between Δ and Y^0, we can rationalize the male data. Suppose that $\Delta = \Delta(Y^0)$. If $\Delta(Y^0)$ is an increasing function of Y^0, this implies that

$$E(Y^1|e = 1, D = 1) - E(\Delta|\Delta > 0, D = 1)$$
$$= E(Y^0|e = 1, D = 1) > E(Y^0|e = 0, D = 1)$$

which is consistent with the patterns in Table 8.12 for adult males and for male youth.

Another model assumes that the true treatment effect is revealed after random assignment and the net response varies over time. In this case, a person who values only the impacts from the program will remain in it if

$$\sum_{t=1}^{T} \delta^{t-1}\Delta_t > 0$$

Table 8.13. *Six-Month Interest Rates and Discount Factors That Equalize the Discounted Present Value of Mean Earnings of Enrollees and Dropouts in the CT-OS Treatment Stream under Two Assumptions about Benefit Duration (National JTPA Study, 18-Month Impact Sample)*

Parameter	Adult males	Adult females	Male youth	Female youth
Benefits fall to zero after 18 months				
Equalizing r	−0.0627	−0.7720	0.2082	−0.2677
Equalizing δ	1.0669	4.3858	0.8277	1.3656
Benefits continue for 7 years				
Equalizing r	1.1250	0.8720	1.4520	0.9580
Equalizing δ	0.4706	0.5342	0.4078	0.5107

Notes: (1) The CT-OS treatment stream refers to persons recommended for classroom training in occupational skills prior to random assignment in the JTPA experiment. This group comprises roughly one-third of the full experimental sample.
(2) Negative values for the interest rate indicate that positive future preference is required to rationalize choosing the enrollee earnings stream over the dropout earnings stream.
(3) Earnings streams are broken up into 6-month pieces in calculating the discount rates.

where Δ_t is the impact in the tth period after random assignment, and δ is a discount rate. If the inequality is reversed, or becomes an equality, the person drops out.

The implications of this model depend on the temporal pattern of the Δ_t values. For example, in classroom training, where the trainee forgoes earnings initially in order to invest in human capital, we would expect $\Delta_{t'} < 0$ for $t' \le t$, and $\Delta_{t'} > 0$ for $t' > t$, where $t' \le t$ are periods of human-capital accumulation. In the case of a constant Δ, there would be perfect sorting by discount rate into the dropout and enrollee categories. Persons with low δ values would drop out, and those with high δ values would complete the training.

We calculate the interest rate r [where $\delta = 1/(1 + r)$] required to equate the discounted present value of mean earnings in the dropout and enrollment states for persons in the classroom-training treatment stream under two sets of assumptions about the time pattern of impacts more than 18 months after random assignment. The top panel of Table 8.13 shows the interest rate necessary to equalize the present value of dropout and enrollee earnings if the impact falls to zero after 18 months. That these estimated rates are sometimes negative reflects the fact that the returns to training for some groups are insufficient to balance out the earnings lost in the initial period unless there is negative discount rate. The lower panel of Table 8.13 shows the interest rate necessary to equate the present value of dropout and enrollee earnings under the assumption that the impact in the final 6-month period persists through 7 years.

Potential trainees exhibit high rates of time preference. Discount rates of this magnitude have been reported by Thaler (1992). Such high rates are consistent with the view that the poor, who are the primary targets of the JTPA program, are poor because they discount the future heavily.

4.4 Summary of the Evidence on Impact Heterogeneity and Its Consequences

Table 8.14 presents a summary of the main findings of this section: (1) Under a variety of assumptions, we find evidence of heterogeneity in net impacts Δ. (2) The analysis of self-assessments suggests that respondents were reporting impacts different from the "objective" impacts determined from experimental data. This is a further source of heterogeneity and a source of disparity across studies. (3) Departures from high levels of positive dependence between Y^0 and Y^1 produced absurd ranges of impacts on gross outcomes. (The implicit correlations between Y^0 and Y^1 produced under different identifying assumptions are given in the last column of the table.) (4) The ranges of the estimated proportions of people benefiting from the program, in the sense of gross outcomes (the "voting criterion"), varied widely under different assumptions about the dependence in outcomes. The data from the self-report and attrition studies show a lower proportion benefiting – a phenomenon consistent with the hypothesis that net returns (not gross returns) were being reported by participants.

5 Summary

In his Nobel lecture, Ragnar Frisch (1970) recognized the diversity of preferences regarding the outcomes of public policies that characterizes participants in welfare states. This diversity in values gives rise to a multiplicity of criteria for evaluating policies. This study has considered these criteria and presented a formal analysis of the information required to evaluate public policies under different criteria. We have presented the approximations required to go from microeconomic evaluations to conclusions about the general-equilibrium outcomes from alternative policies. We have described conditions under which conventional econometric analyses of "treatment effects" provide part of the information required to conduct general-equilibrium cost–benefit analyses. We note that personal evaluations of policies may not coincide with the evaluations useful in the political arena of the welfare state, and we have presented methods to reveal private or "subjective" evaluations to supplement and complement the "objective" evaluations.

Table 8.14. *Summary of Empirical Evidence on Impact Heterogeneity, the Voting Criterion, and the Dependence between Y^1 and Y^0 (National JTPA Study, 18-Month Experimental-Impact Sample)*

	Description of analysis	Evidence of heterogeneity?	Standard deviation of impacts	Evidence on voting criterion	Dependence between Y^1 and Y^0
Fréchet bounds	Statistical bounds on the joint distribution of outcomes, $F(y^0, y^1 \mid D = 1)$, and on superadditive and subadditive functions of the joint distribution;[a] bounds are like those in (17) but conditional on $D = 1$	Yes; the impact standard deviation is bounded away from zero[b]	Bounded between $675 and $14,969[b]	The bounds do not apply to the indicator function $1(Y^1 \geq Y^0)$, as this function is not superadditive nor subadditive; thus the voting criterion cannot be bounded[b]	Product-moment correlation ρ between Y^1 and Y^0 bounded between −0.760 and 0.998
Perfect positive percentile dependence	Assumes $q_1 = q_0$, where q_1 is a percentile of Y^1 given $D = 1$ and q_0 is a percentile of Y^0 given $D = 1$; conditional on $D = 1$, the counterfactual for each percentile in the Y^1 distribution is the same percentile in the Y^0 distribution	Yes; the impacts vary between zero and $3,250[b]	$1,857[b]	100 percent of participants benefit or are indifferent[b]	Product-moment correlation $\rho = 0.9903$, and Kendall's rank correlation is fixed at 1.00; both are calculated using the percentiles of the two distributions[b]
Perfect negative percentile dependence	Assumes $q_1 = 100 - q_0$, where q_1 is a percentile of Y^1 given $D = 1$ and q_0 is a percentile of Y^0 given $D = 1$; conditional on $D = 1$, the counterfactual for the qth percentile of the Y^1 distribution is the $100-q^{th}$ percentile in the Y^0 distribution	Yes; the impacts vary between −$48,606 and $34,102[b]	$16,432[b]	52 percent positive[b]	Product-moment correlation $\rho = -0.6592$, and Kendall's rank correlation is fixed at −1.00; both are calculated using the percentiles of the two distributions[b]

(*cont.*)

Table 8.14. (cont.)

	Description of analysis	Evidence of heterogeneity?	Standard deviation of impacts	Evidence on voting criterion	Dependence between Y^1 and Y^0
Positive percentile dependence with rank correlation $\tau = 0.95$	Assumes that the percentiles of Y^1 and Y^0 given $D = 1$ have a rank correlation of 0.95; estimates are based on a random sample of 50 such permutations	Yes; the average minimum is $-\$14,504$, and the average maximum is $\$48,544^b$	Average standard deviation of $\$1,857$ (with standard deviation of $\$480)^{b,c}$	Average of 93 percent positive (with standard deviation of $3.88)^{b,c}$	Average product-moment correlation ρ of 0.7885 (with a standard deviation of 0.0402); Kendall's rank correlation τ fixed at 0.95; both are calculated using the percentiles of the two distributions^{b,c}
Independence of percentiles of Y^1 and Y^0, which implies a percentile rank correlation τ of 0.0	Assumes that the percentiles of Y^1 and Y^0 given $D = 1$ have a rank correlation τ of 0.0, which is implied by independence between them; estimates are based on a random sample of 50 such permutations	Yes; the average minimum is $-\$44,175$, and the average maximum is $\$60,599^b$	Average standard deviation of $\$12,879$ (with standard deviation of $\$259)^{b,c}$	Average of 54 percent positive (with standard deviation of $1.11)^{b,c}$	Average product-moment correlation ρ of -0.0147 (with standard deviation of 0.0106); Kendall's rank correlation τ fixed at 0.0; both are calculated using the percentiles of the two distributions^{b,c}
Random-coefficient model	Assumes that $\Delta \perp\!\!\!\perp Y_0 \mid D = 1$	Yes; see Figure 8.2^d	Standard deviation is $\$2,271^d$	If the random coefficient Δ is assumed to be normally distributed, then 60.45 percent have positive impacts^d	The product-moment correlation $\rho = 0.9595^d$

302

	Assumes that $\Delta \perp Y_0 \mid D = 1$		Standard deviation is $1,675[d]	56.35 percent positive[d]	The product-moment correlation $\rho = 0.9774[d]$
Deconvolution		Yes; see Figure 8.2[d]			
Self-assessments	Ex-post self-evaluations by participants based on a survey question regarding whether or not the program provided a benefit	Yes; some participants reported a benefit, and others did not	N.A.[e]	Varies from a low of 39.49 percent positive for adult men to a high of 47.55 percent positive for female youth	N.A.[e]
Dropouts	Attrition decisions after application and acceptance into the program	Yes; there are nonzero attrition rates, and the evidence on the discount rates required to justify a common coefficient model suggests that this model is false	N.A.[e]	Dropping out ranges from a low of 34.83 percent for male youth to a high of 40.92 percent for adult males	N.A.[e]

[a] A function $k(x,y)$ is superadditive if $x > x'$ and $y > y'$ implies that $k(x,y) + k(x',y') > k(x,y') + k(x',y)$. Subadditivity reverses the inequality.
[b] Results are for adult women only. Similar results are obtained for adult men and for male and female youth.
[c] The standard deviation is calculated over the random sample of 50 permutations with the indicated value of τ.
[d] Results are for adult women only. For the remaining demographic groups, $\mathrm{var}(Y^t) < \mathrm{var}(Y^0)$, which indicates that neither the random-coefficient model nor deconvolution is appropriate.
[e] N.A., not applicable.

Implementation of many of the criteria used to evaluate the welfare state requires information on the joint distribution of outcomes across policies. Traditional cost – benefit analysis avoids this problem by assuming that a background social-welfare function automatically solves all of the distributional problems of the welfare state. In this case, which is assumed in much of the microeconometric evaluation literature, simple per-capita measures of economic efficiency based on the change in aggregate output attributable to a policy suffice to evaluate the welfare state. However, even in this case we note that estimators widely used in the econometric evaluation literature do not provide the ingredients required for a comprehensive cost–benefit analysis. In an empirical analysis, we have demonstrated that when conventional estimators are modified to account for direct costs and the welfare costs of taxation, they produce inferences about program impacts very different from those produced using standard econometric methods. We have described conditions under which standard econometric estimators provide reliable answers to well-posed general-equilibrium evaluation questions.

Homogeneity in the response to a policy across persons with the same observed characteristics is the central implicit identifying assumption that underlies most of the widely used econometric policy-evaluation methods. The assumption of response homogeneity greatly simplifies the evaluation problem. Part of the conflict in the estimates produced from different evaluation criteria arises from heterogeneity in the impacts of a given program across persons. We have presented evidence from a major social experiment that heterogeneity in the responses to treatment is an empirically important phenomenon.

An evaluation strategy that properly accounts for individual heterogeneity requires more information than traditional econometric evaluation methods. We have demonstrated how information about participant self-selection choices and program-participation rules aids in identifying the distributions of outcomes across policies and also provides information on personal valuations of program outcomes. We have discussed how social experiments and different types of microeconomic data can be used to identify the criteria considered in this study and how they can be supplemented with additional behavioral and statistical assumptions to construct all of the criteria. Unless special individual decision rules characterize program participation, these sources of data do not resolve the fundamental evaluation problem that persons cannot occupy mutually exclusive outcome states at the same time.

We have applied some of the methods developed in this study to data from a major job-training program. For adult females, we conclude that the program benefited most participants according to the "objective" evaluation criteria based on gross outcomes, but did not benefit a majority of participants according to self-assessments or the revealed-preference behavior of attriters from the program. The disagreement among the alternative criteria highlights the need for providing information about all of them to satisfy the different parties in the welfare state.

Appendix A

Let outcomes Y^1 and Y^0 be written as functions of observed variables X and unobserved variables U_1 and U_0, respectively:

$$Y^1 = g_1(X_1, X_c) + U_1 \tag{A-1a}$$

$$Y^0 = g_0(X_0, X_c) + U_0 \tag{A-1b}$$

where X_1 (a k_1-dimensional vector) and X_0 (a k_0-dimensional vector) are variables unique to g_1 and g_0, respectively, and X_c (a k_c-dimensional vector) includes variables common to the two functions. The variables U_0 and U_1 are unobserved from the point of view of the econometrician. To simplify the analysis, we delete program-specific subscripts.

The decision rule for program participation is given by

$$I = g_I(X_I, X_c) + U_I \quad \text{and} \quad D = 1(I \geq 0) \tag{A-1c}$$

where X_I (a k_I-dimensional vector) consists of measured variables, some of which may appear in X_1 and X_0, and where U_I is unobserved by the econometrician. I is a latent index or net utility of the relevant decision-maker. The joint distribution of (U_0, U_1, U_I) is denoted by $F(u_0, u_1, u_I)$. These variables are statistically independent of (X_0, X_1, X_I, X_c).

The Roy model is a special case of this framework in which selection into the program depends only on the gain from the program. In this case,

$$g_I = g_1(X_1, X_c) - g_0(X_0, X_c) \quad \text{and} \quad U_I = U_1 - U_0$$

For convenience, we write $F(u_0, u_1)$ as the joint distribution of (U_0, U_1).

The following theorem can be proved for the Roy model. It extends and clarifies a theorem presented by Heckman and Honoré (1990).

Theorem A-1. *Let* $Y^1 = g_1(X_1, X_c) + U_1$ *and* $Y^0 = g_0(X_0, X_c) + U_0$. *Assume the following:*

(i) $(U_0, U_1) \perp\!\!\!\perp (X_0, X_1, X_c)$
(ii) $D = 1(Y^1 \geq Y^0)$
(iii) (U_0, U_1) *is absolutely continuous, with* $\text{Support}(U_0, U_1) = R_1 \times R_1$
(iv) *For each fixed* X_c,

$$g_0(X_0, X_c): R_{k_0} \to R_1 \quad \text{for all } X_0$$
$$g_1(X_1, X_c): R_{k_1} \to R_1 \quad \text{for all } X_1$$

and

$$\text{Support}[g_0(X_0, X_c)|X_c, X_1] = R_1 \quad \text{for all } X_c, X_1$$
$$\text{Support}[g_1(X_1, X_c)|X_c, X_0] = R_1 \quad \text{for all } X_c, X_0$$
$$\text{Support}(X_0|X_1, X_c) = \text{Support}(X_0) = R_1 \quad \text{for all } X_1, X_c$$
$$\text{Support}(X_1|X_0, X_c) = \text{Support}(X_1) = R_1 \quad \text{for all } X_0, X_c$$

(v) *The marginal distributions of U_0 and U_1 have zero medians.*

Then g_0, g_1, and $F(u_0, u_1)$ are nonparametrically identified from data on participation choices and outcomes.

Proof. By assumption, we know that for all (X_0, X_1, X_c) in the support of (X_0, X_1, X_c) and for all y,

$$\Pr(Y^1 \leq Y^0 | X_0, X_1, X_c) = \Pr[g_1(X_1, X_c) + U_1 \leq g_0(X_0, X_c) + U_0] \quad \text{(A)}$$

$$\Pr(Y^1 \leq y, Y^1 > Y^0 | X_0, X_1, X_c)$$
$$= \Pr[g_1(X_1, X_c) + U_1 \leq y, g_1(X_1, X_c) + U_1 > g_0(X_0, X_c) + U_0] \quad \text{(B)}$$

$$\Pr(Y^0 \leq y, Y^0 \geq Y^1)$$
$$= \Pr[g_0(X_0, X_c) + U_0 \leq y, g_0(X_0, X_c) + U_0 > g_1(X_1, X_c) + U_1] \quad \text{(C)}$$

Fix X_c. Let $\overline{X}_1$ and $\overline{X}_0$ be in the support of X_1 and X_0, respectively. Using the information in (A), we can define sets of values (X_0, X_1) corresponding to contours of constant probability:

$$S(X_0, X_1 | X_c, \bar{p})$$
$$= \{(X_0, X_1) : \Pr[g_1(X_1, X_c) + U_1 > g_0(X_0, X_c) + U_0]$$
$$= \Pr[g_1(\overline{X}_1, X_c) + U_1 > g_0(\overline{X}_0, X_c) + U_0] = \bar{p}\} \quad \text{(A-2)}$$
$$= \{(X_0, X_1) : g_1(X_1, X_c) + \ell = g_0(X_0, X_c)\}$$

for some unknown constant ℓ.

For any point in S we can use the information in (B) to write

$$\Pr[g_1(X_1, X_c) + U_1 \leq y, U_1 > U_0 + \ell] \quad \text{(A-3)}$$

for all y. Varying X_1 over its full support from assumption (iv), we can find a compensating value X_0 within the set defined by (A-2) so that $\Pr(D = 1|X_1, X_0, X_c) = \bar{p}$ is constant. This keeps fixed the second argument in (A-3). The variation in X_1 produces a set of (y, X_1) values for each value of X_c that identifies the function $g_1(X_1, X_c)$ over the support of X_1, up to an unknown constant. By similar reasoning, we can identify $g_0(X_0, X_c)$ up to an unknown constant using (C) over the support of X_0.

Tracing out (A-3) for all values g_1 and y identifies $F(u_1, u_0 - u_1)$, except for a location parameter. Using (C), we identify $F(u_0, u_1 - u_0)$. The locations of U_0 and U_1 are determined by using the assumption that the medians of U_0 and U_1 are zero, using the marginals obtained by letting $g_0 \to -\infty$ [in (B)] and $g_1 \to -\infty$ [in (C)], respectively. [The information in (B) is actually all we need.] With knowledge of the locations of U_0 and U_1 we can determine the unknown additive constants absorbed in g_1 and g_0. By a standard transformation of variables, we obtain $F(u_0, u_1)$ from either (B) or (C). Since X_c is arbitrary, this completes the proof, because we can recover everything for all X_c. □

The content of this theorem is that if there is sufficient variation in X_1, X_0, and X_c, and if we know that program participation is based solely on outcome maximization, no arbitrary parametric structure on the outcome equations or on the distribution of the unobservables generating outcomes needs to be imposed to recover the full distribution of outcomes using ordinary microeconomic data.

Note that we can obtain $F(y^0|D = 1, X)$ from $F(y^0|D = 0, X)$, where X denotes the full set of conditioning variables. Using the law of iterated expectations,

$$F(y^0|X) = F(y^0|D = 1|X)\Pr(D = 1|X) \\ + F(y^0|D = 0|X)\Pr(D = 0|X)$$

From Theorem A-1 we can recover $F(y^0|X)$. Because we know $\Pr(D = 1|X) = 1 - \Pr(D = 0|X)$, we can recover $F(y^0|D = 1, X)$.

The assumptions made in Theorem A-1 about the supports of X_1, X_0, g_1, g_0, U_1, and U_0 are made for convenience, in an effort to focus on main ideas. Nowhere is it literally required that any function or variable "go to infinity" as some authors have claimed (e.g., Imbens and Angrist, 1994). A version of Theorem A-1 can easily be proved under the following alternative conditions:

$$\text{Support}(U_0) = \text{Support}(U_1) = \text{Support}(g_0) = \text{Support}(g_1)$$

where all of the supports are finite. Under these conditions, and assuming that all of the other conditions hold, it is possible to retrace the argument of Theorem A-1 and produce essentially the same theorem, provided that $\text{Support}(X_0|X_1, X_c) = \text{Support}(X_0)$ and $\text{Support}(X_1|X_0, X_c) = \text{Support}(X_1)$.

In more general cases where the supports of g_0, g_1, U_1, and U_0 do not coincide, or where there are restrictions on the supports of X_1 and X_0, a modified version of the theorem can be proved. It may be possible to construct a set of (X_1, X_0) values that satisfy a condition like (A-2), except now it is no longer necessarily true that we can vary X_1 over its full support within any isoprobability set [the set of values of (X_1, X_0) that set $\Pr(D = 1|X_0, X_1, X_c) = \bar{p}$ for any $\bar{p}$]. That is, for each $\bar{p}$, we are no longer guaranteed to be able to find a compensatory value of X_0 to ensure that for each X_1 we can keep the probability fixed. Suppose $\underline{g}_1 \leq g_1 \leq \bar{g}_1$ and $\underline{g}_0 \leq g_0 \leq \bar{g}_0$. For each X_c and $\bar{p}$, the support of $g_1 - g_0$ is $(\bar{g}_1 - \underline{g}_0, \underline{g}_1 - \bar{g}_0 | X_c, \bar{p})$, provided that Support$(X_0|X_1, X_c)$ = Support(X_0), and Support$(X_1|X_0, X_c)$ = Support(X_1). Only for subsets of the support of X_0 and X_1 can the argument below (A-2) in the proof be invoked. Because $g_0(X_0, X_c)$ and $g_1(X_1, X_c)$ are not necessarily identified over their full support, it follows that we are not necessarily guaranteed to be able to identify $F(u_0, u_1)$ over its full support. Moreover, in general, we shall be able to identify the g_1 and g_0 functions only up to unknown scale parameters. With these qualifications about the support, the conclusions of Theorem A-1, restated to include the restrictions on supports, remain intact.

The Roy model has an unusual structure, because the participation rule and the outcome equations are tightly linked. As a consequence, we can recover the full joint distribution of $F(y^1, y^0|X)$ and the decision rule knowing only conditional distributions (B) and (C) available from cross-section data. For more general decision rules, such as (A-1c), that break the tight link between outcomes and participation decisions, it is not possible to use (B) and (C) to address those questions that can be answered only from the full joint distribution of (Y^1, Y^0). Even access to the data obtained from social experiments – $F(y^0|D = 1, X)$ – does not suffice to solve the fundamental evaluation problem that both Y^0 and Y^1 are never observed for a single person. However, a theorem analogous to Theorem A-1 can be proved that demonstrates that with sufficient variation in the X variables, it is possible to recover $F(y^0|D = 1, X)$ from nonexperimental data. Before presenting a more general version of Theorem A-1, it will be useful to review some recent results on the estimation of nonparametric and semiparametric discrete-choice models that are required in the proof of the theorem.

We consider the nonparametric identification of decision rule (A-1c) under the assumption that

$$(X_I, X_c) \perp\!\!\!\perp U_I \qquad (\text{A-4})$$

The original proof is due to Cosslett (1983), who assumed $g_I = (X_I, X_c)\beta_I$. Matzkin (1990, 1992) considered the more general case that will be used here.[33] In the Roy model, (A-1c) is tightly linked to (A-1a) and (A-1b), and we observe Y^1 and Y^0 in censored samples. In the general case, nonparametric identification of g_I requires a separate argument.

From inspection of

$$\Pr(D = 1|X_I, X_c) = \Pr[g_I(X_I, X_c) + U_I \geq 0] = 1 - F_{U_I}(-g_I)$$

---

[33] Heckman and Taber (1994) surveyed alternative approaches to identifiability in discrete-choice and duration models.

it is clear that without further restrictions on the set of candidate g_I functions, it will be impossible to identify a unique member of the set. For any alternative distribution function F^*, we can define g_I^* so that

$$F_{U_I}(-g_I) = F^*_{U_I}(-g_I^*)$$

with the result that (g_I, F_I) cannot be distinguished from (g_I^*, F_I^*).

Let G be the set of admissible functions. Matzkin (1990) showed that under the independence assumption, if $\bar{g}_I$ is a least-concave representation of $g_I \in G$, then $(\bar{g}_I, \bar{F}_I)$ is identified, where $\bar{F}_I$ is the associated distribution function.[34] Because concavity naturally arises in many economic settings of consumer and producer choice, her assumption is an attractive one. We record Matzkin's basic assumptions, in addition to (A-4):

(M-1) g_I is concave
(M-2)   Support$[g_I(X_0, X_c)] \supset$ Support(U_I)

Theorem M-1 (Matzkin 1). *Under* (M-1) *and* (M-2), $\bar{g}_I$ *and the associated* $\bar{F}_I$ *are identified subject to a scale normalization for* g_I.

Proof. See Matzkin (1990). □

Matzkin (1992) also considered an alternative identifying assumption that can substitute for (M-1) and (M-2).

(M-3)   There exists a subset $\bar{T}$ of the support of $X = (X_I, X_c)$ such that (i) for all $g_{1I}, g_{2I} \in G$, and all $X \in \bar{T}$, $g_{1I}(X) = g_{2I}(X)$, and (ii) for all t in the support of U_I, there exists $X \in \bar{T}$ such that $g_I(X) = t$.

In the estimation of production functions there is a natural set of values $X = 0$ where no input produces no output. Similarly, for cost functions, $c(0) = 0$ is a natural assumption. Matzkin developed a consistent estimator for g_I and F_I under additional assumptions.

Theorem M-2 (Matzkin 2). *Under* (M-2) *and* (M-3), *and with* $X \perp\!\!\!\perp U_I$, (g_I, F_I) *is identified up to a scale normalization for* g_I.

Proof. See Matzkin (1992). □

We use Theorem M-1 or M-2 to claim that we can nonparametrically identify g_I and F_I over the support of the data. Obviously, if

$$0 < \underline{p} \leq \Pr(D = 1 | X_I, X_c) \leq \bar{p} < 1$$

---

[34] A function $\bar{g}_I$ is a least-concave representation of concave function g_I if for any strictly increasing function h such that $h \circ g_I$ is concave, there exists a concave function t such that $h \circ g_I = t \circ \bar{g}_I$. Because g_I is a monotonic transformation of $\bar{g}, g_I$ and $\bar{g}$ must have the same isovalue sets.

and the support of g_I is bounded and strictly contained in the support of U_I, we may be able to identify $F_I(U_I)$ only over a subset of its true support. We are now ready to prove Theorem A-2, which extends and clarifies a result of Heckman (1990a) that generalizes the proof of non-parametric identifiability of the Roy model.

Theorem A-2. *Let (U_0, U_1, U_I) be median-zero, independently and identically distributed random variables with distribution $F(u_0, u_1, u_I)$. Assume structure (A-1a)–(A-1c) and knowledge of $F(y^0|D = 0, X_0, X_I, X_c)$, $F(y^1|D = 1, X_1, X_I, X_c)$, and $\Pr(D = 1|X_I, X_c)$. Assume the following:*

- (a-1) $(U_0, U_I) \perp\!\!\!\perp (X_0, X_I, X_c)$ *or*
- (a-2) $(U_1, U_I) \perp\!\!\!\perp (X_1, X_I, X_c)$;
- (b-1) (M-1) *and* (M-2) *or*
- (b-2) (M-3)
- (c) $\text{Support}(U_I \times U_0) = R_1 \times R_1$
  $\text{Support}(U_I \times U_1) = R_1 \times R_1$; *and*
- (d) $g_I(X_I, X_c) : R_{k_I} \to R_1$ *for all* X_c
  $g_0(X_0, X_c) : R_{k_0} \to R_1$ *for all* X_c
  $g_1(X_1, X_c) : R_{k_1} \to R_1$ *for all* X_c
  $\text{Support}[g_0(X_0, X_c)|X_c] = R_1$ *for all* X_c
  $\text{Support}[g_1(X_1, X_c)|X_c] = R_1$ *for all* X_c
  $\text{Support}(X_0|X_c) = \text{Support}(X_0)$
  $\text{Support}(X_1|X_c) = \text{Support}(X_1)$

Then

- (I) *Under (a-1) or (a-2), (b-1) or (b-2), (c), and (d), F_I and g_I are identified. If (M-1) and (M-2) are used, g_I is understood to be the least-concave version of the original g_I.*
- (II) *Under (a-1), (b-1) or (b-2), (c), and (d), $g_0(X_0, X_c)$ and $F(u_0, u_I)$ are identified over the supports of (X_0, X_c) and (U_0, U_I), respectively.*
- (III) *Under (a-2), (b-1) or (b-2) and (c), $g_1(X_1, X_c)$ and $F(u_1, u_I)$ are identified over the supports of (X_1, X_c) and (U_1, U_I), respectively.*

Proof. Claim (I) is established in the theorems by Matzkin previously summarized.[35] If we establish either the second or third claim, it is clear that the other claim can be proved by a similar argument. We consider only claim (II). Fix X_c. Observe that for X_0, X_I, and X_c in the support of (X_0, X_I, X_c),

$$F(y^0|D = 0, X_0, X_I, X_c) = \frac{\int_{-\infty}^{y_0 - g_0(X_0, X_c)} \int_{-\infty}^{-[g_I(X_I, X_c)]} f(u_0, u_I) \, du_I \, du_0}{\int_{-\infty}^{-[g_I(X_I, X_c)]} f(u_I) \, du_I}$$

---

[35] All that is required to prove claim (I) is $U_I \perp\!\!\!\perp (X_I, X_c)$ and (b-1) or (b-2) from Matzkin.

Evaluating the Welfare State

and further observe that we know the denominator on the right-hand side. Thus we know the left-hand side of

$$F(y^0|D = 0, X_0, X_I, X_c)\Pr(D = 0|X_I, X_c)$$
$$= \int_{-\infty}^{y^0 - g_0(X_0, X_c)} \int_{-\infty}^{-[g_I(X_I, X_c)]} f(u_0, u_I)\, du_I\, du_0$$

Under condition (d), for each X_c, we can vary X_0 freely and trace out $(y_0, g_0 + l_0)$ for each $p = \bar{p} = \Pr(D = 0|X_I, X_c)$. That is, we can vary X_0 as required to fix $F(y^0|D = 0, X_0, X_I, X_c)$ at a given value when y^0 is varied, and in this way we determine g_0 up to scale l_0. Tracing out g_0 for all values of y_0 and X_0 for each value of p identifies $F(u_0|D = 0, X_I, X_c)$ up to scale for u_0. Setting $\bar{p} = 1$ (i.e., letting $g_I \to -\infty$), we obtain $F_0(u_0)$ by virtue of assumption (c). The location of U_0 is obtained from the assumption of a zero median. This pins down the constant l_0 and g_0. With g_0 in hand, we can recover $F(u_0, -g_I(X_I, X_c))$. Varying x_I over its full support, we can identify $F(u_0, u_I)$. As this is true for each value of X_c, we have established (II), and by similar reasoning we can establish (III). Thus we establish the theorem. □

Observe that the theorem can be modified so that the variables in common between g_1 and g_I are different from the variables in common between g_0 and g_I. Furthermore, the supports of U_0, U_1 and the conditional supports of (X_0) and (X_1) do not have to be R_1. It is enough to have Support(U_0) = Support$[g_0(X_0, X_c)|X_c]$ and Support(U_1) = Support$[g_1(X_1, X_c)|X_c]$. Theorem A-2 has a simpler structure than Theorem A-1. A discussion similar to that conducted after Theorem A-1 regarding the support of the X applies.

First, if $0 <$ Support$(p) < 1$, then it is not possible to trace out the full distribution of $F_I(u_I)$, nor is it possible to identify $F_0(u_0)$ using the limit $\bar{p} = 1$. This could happen, for example, if the support of X_I is restricted for all X_c such that

$$\text{Support}[g_I(X_I, X_c)] \subset \text{Support}(-U_I) \quad (A\text{-}5)$$

Under this restriction, it is not possible to trace out the full distribution of U_I. Alternatively, even if the support of X_I is R_{k_I} for all X_c, it is possible that (A-5) is satisfied by virtue of restrictions on the function g_I. Notice also that (A-5) might be satisfied for some values of X_c, but not for others. Similar remarks apply to g_0. Again, restrictions on the range of X_0 may prohibit recovery of $F[u_0|D = 0, g_I(X_I, X_c)]$ even if (A-5) does not hold. Thus it may happen that

$$\text{Support}[g_0(X_0, X_c)] \subset \text{Support}(U_0|g_I + U_I < 0) \quad (A\text{-}6)$$

which might arise because of restrictions on the support of X_0, or because of restrictions on g_0. Even if (A-6) does not hold for some X_c, it may hold for others.

Theorem A-2 is weaker than Theorem A-1. It implies that we can recover $F(u_0|D = 1, X_I, X_c)$ from the available cross-section data, provided that its conditions are satisfied. To see this, recall that we can obtain $F(y^0|X)$ by letting $p \to 1$, which we are free to do because g_I can be varied independently of g_0, and the support of g_I is the whole real line. Because by hypothesis we know $F(y^0|D = 0, X)$, we can apply the identity

$$F(y^0|X) = F(y^0|D = 0, X)\Pr(D = 0|X)$$
$$+ F(y^0|D = 1, X)\Pr(D = 1|X)$$

to solve for $F(y^0|D = 1, X)$ provided that $\Pr(D = 1|X) \neq 0$.

Using nonexperimental data, we are in the same position as we would be in if we ran an experiment that satisfied assumption (I-10) in the text. In particular, we can identify the mean impact of treatment on the treated, $E(Y^1 - Y^0|D = 1, X)$. In the general case covered by Theorem A-2, social experiments do not solve the fundamental evaluation problem that we cannot observe the same person in both states simultaneously, and so cannot observe both components of (Y^0, Y^1).

Collecting all of the subscripted variables into a common vector X, under the conditions of Theorem A-1 it is possible to generalize from the data recovered from a social experiment, $F(y^1|D = 1, X)$, and $F(y^0|D = 1, X)$, combined with data on nonparticipants, $F(y^0|D = 0, X)$, to recover the entire distribution $F(y^0, y^1|X)$ provided that assumption (I-10) is satisfied, and provided that there are no general-equilibrium effects. Thus it is possible to answer all of the questions posed in Section 1 of the text if agents are income maximizers. In the case of the Roy model described by Theorem A-1, social experiments are not required to answer these questions because $F(y^0|D = 1, X)$ is redundant information.

An extension of Theorem A-2 is useful in identifying the full distribution of outcomes conditional on X in the panel-data case when treatments are irreversible.

Theorem A-3. *Let (U_0, U_1, U_I) be median-zero, independently and identically distributed random variables with distribution $F(u_0, u_1, u_I)$. Assume outcome and decision structure (A-1a)–(A-1c) and knowledge of $F(y^0, y^1|D = 1, X_0, X_I, X_c)$ and $\Pr(D = 1|X_I, X_c)$. Assume the following:*

(a) *$(U_0, U_1, U_I) \perp\!\!\!\perp (X_0, X_1, X_I, X_c)$*
(b-1) *(M-1) and (M-2) or*
(b-2) *(M-3)*
(c) *Support$(U_0, U_1, U_I) = R_1 \times R_1 \times R_1$*
(d) *Partition X_I into (X_{II}, X_{I0}, X_{I1}), where X_{II} is a subset of X_I (with k_{II} variables) not in $X_0, X_1,$ or X_c, X_{I0} are variables X_I in common with X_0 (k_{I0} in number), and X_{I1} are variables (k_{I1} in number) in common in X_I and X_1. Partition X_0 into (X_{00}, X_{01}, X_{I0}), where X_{00} is a subset of X_0 (with k_{00} variables) not in X_1 or X_I, and X_{01} is*

Evaluating the Welfare State

the subset of variables (k_{01} in number) in common with X_0 and X_1. Partition X_1 into (X_{11}, X_{01}, X_{I1}), where X_{11} is the subset of k_{11} variables not in common with X_1 and X_I. In this notation, we assume

$g_I(X_{II}, X_{I0}, X_{I1}, X_c) : R_{k_{II}} \to R_1 \quad \text{for all } X_{I0}, X_{I1}, X_c$

$g_0(X_{00}, X_{01}, X_{I0}, X_c) : R_{k_{00}} \to R_1 \quad \text{for all } X_{01}, X_{I0}, X_c$

$g_1(X_{11}, X_{01}, X_{I1}, X_c) : R_{k_{11}} \to R_1 \quad \text{for all } X_{01}, X_{I1}, X_c$

$\text{Support}[g_I(X_{II}, X_{I0}, X_{I1}, X_c) | X_{I0}, X_{I1}, X_c$
$\quad = R_1 \quad \text{for all } X_{I0}, X_{I1}, X_c$

$\text{Support}[g_0(X_{00}, X_{01}, X_{I0}, X_c) | X_{01}, X_{I0}, X_c$
$\quad = R_1 \quad \text{for all } X_{01}, X_{I0}, X_c$

$\text{Support}[g_1(X_{11}, X_{01}, X_{I1}, X_c) | X_{01}, X_{I1}, X_c]$
$\quad = R_1 \quad \text{for all } X_{01}, X_{I1}, X_c$

and

$\text{Support}(X_{II} | X_{I0}, X_{I1}, X_c) = \text{Support}(X_{II})$
$\text{Support}(X_{00} | X_{01}, X_{I0}, X_c) = \text{Support}(X_{00})$
$\text{Support}(X_{11} | X_{01}, X_{I1}, X_c) = \text{Support}(X_{11})$

Then

(I) Under (a) and (b-1) or (b-2), (c), and (d), F_I is identified, and g_I is identified where, if (M-1) and (M-2) are used, g_I is understood to be the least-concave version of the original g_I. (This follows from Theorem M-1.)

(II) Under (a), (b-1) or (b-2), (c), and (d), $g_1(X_1, X_c)$, $g_0(X_0, X_c)$, and $F(u_0, u_1, u_I)$ are identified.

Proof. Claim (I) is established in the same way that claim (II) of Theorem A-2 is established. All that is needed to establish this claim is that $U_I \perp\!\!\!\perp (X_I, X_c)$, (b-1) or (b-2) from Matzkin, and $g_I(X_I, X_c) : R_{k_I} \to R_1$ for all X_c.

Claim (II) is established in essentially the same way that claim (II) of Theorem A-2 is established. From assumption (c),

$$F(y^0, y^1 | D = 1, X_0, X_I, X_c) \Pr(D = 1 | X_I, X_c)$$
$$= \underset{u_0, u_1, u_I}{F} [y^0 - g_0(X_0, X_c), y^1 - g_1(X_1, X_c), -g_I(X_I, X_c)] \quad \text{(A-7)}$$

From condition (d), we can vary the components X_{00}, X_{11}, and X_{II} freely. If we set X_{11} to the value such that $g_1 \to -\infty$, and if we set X_{II} to the value such that $g_I \to -\infty$ [so that $\Pr(D = 1 | X) = 1$], we can trace out $g_0(X_{00}, X_{01}, X_{0I}, X_c)$ given the remaining arguments for each value of the conditioning arguments. [This limit operation "zeros out" the last two arguments of (A-7).] We can repeat this argument for all conditioning subsets and recover $g_0(X_{00}, X_{01}, X_{0I}, X_c)$ up to a constant. Tracing out g_0 for all values of y_0 identifies $F(u_0)$ up to scale. The scale is identified by the median-zero assumption. By a parallel argument, but reversing the roles of X_{11} and X_{00}, and g_1 and g_0, we obtain g_1 and $F(u_1)$. Staying in the set where $\Pr(D = 1|X_I, X_c) = 1$, we can construct $F(u_0, u_1) = F(y_0 - g_0, y_1 - g_1)$ by independently varying g_0 and g_1, which we are free to do as a consequence of assumption (d). More generally, we can repeat this argument for all values of $p = \Pr(U_I > -g_I)$. We can vary x_{II} to offset any changes induced in x_{00} and x_{11}. Thus we can identify

$$F[u_0, u_1, -g_I(X_{II}, X_{I0}, X_{I1}, X_c)] = F(y_0 - g_0, y_1 - g_1 | D = 1, X_I, X_c)$$

and hence we can identify the full joint distribution $F(u_0, u_1, u_I)$ by tracing out X_{00}, X_{11}, and X_{II}. We can do this for all X_{I0}, X_{I1}, X_{01}, and X_c, and hence the theorem is proved. □

Observe that the theorem does not require infinite supports. Thus it is enough to have

$$\text{Support}(U_I) = \text{Support}[g_I(X_{II}, X_{I0}, X_{I1}, X_c | X_{I0}, X_{I1}, X_c)]$$
$$\text{Support}(U_0) = \text{Support}[g_0(X_{00}, X_{01}, X_{I0}, X_c | X_{01}, X_{I0}, X_c)]$$
$$\text{Support}(U_1) = \text{Support}[g_1(X_{11}, X_{01}, X_{I1}, X_c | X_{01}, X_{I1}, X_c)]$$

Appendix B

The data analyzed in this study were gathered as part of an experimental evaluation of the training programs financed under Title II-A of the Job Training Partnership Act (JTPA). The experiment was conducted at a sample of 16 JTPA training centers around the country. Data were gathered on JTPA applicants randomly assigned either to a treatment group allowed access to JTPA training services or to a control group denied access to JTPA services for 18 months. Random assignment covered some or all of the period from November 1987 to September 1989 at each center. In total, 20,601 persons were randomly assigned.

Follow-up interviews were conducted with each person in the experimental sample during the period from 12 to 24 months after random assignment. Those interviews gathered information on employment, earnings, participation in government transfer programs, schooling, and training during the period after random assignment. The response rate for this survey was around 84 percent. The sample used here includes only those adult women who (1) had a follow-up interview scheduled at least 18 months after random assignment, (2) responded to the survey, and (3) had usable earnings information for the 18 months after random assignment.

The sample was chosen to match that used in the 18-month experimental-impact study by Bloom et al. (1993). As in that report, the earnings measure is the sum of self-reported earnings during the 18 months after random assignment. This earnings sum is constructed from survey questions about the length, hours per week, and rate of pay on each job held during this period. Outlying values for the earnings sum are replaced by imputed values as in the impact report. However, imputed earnings values used in the report for adult female nonrespondents are not used.

References

Ashenfelter, O. (1978). Estimating the effect of training programs on earnings. *Review of Economics and Statistics* 60:47–57.
Barros, R. (1987). Two essays on the nonparametric estimation of economic models with selectivity using choice-based samples. Ph.D. dissertation, Department of Economics, University of Chicago.
Baumol, W., and Quandt, R. (1966). The demand for abstract transport modes: theory and measurement. *Journal of Regional Science* 6:13–26.
Bloom, H., Orr, L., Cave, G., Bell, S., and Doolittle, F. (1993). *The National JTPA Study: Title II-A Impacts on Earnings and Employment at 18 Months.* Bethesda, MD: Abt Associates.
Boadway, R., and Bruce, N. (1984). *Welfare Economics.* Oxford, UK: Blackwell.
Browning, E. K. (1987). On the marginal welfare cost of taxation. *American Economic Review* 77:11–23.
Browning, M., Hansen, L., and Heckman, J. (in press). Microdata and general equilibrium models. In: *Handbook of Macroeconomics,* ed. J. Taylor and M. Woodford. Amsterdam: North Holland.
Cambanis, S., Simons, G., and Stout, W. (1976). Inequalities for $E(k(X, Y))$ when the marginals are fixed. *Zeitschrift für Wahrscheinlichskeitstheorie* 36:285–94.
Cameron, S., and Heckman, J. (1991a). A discrete factor structure model for dynamic discrete choice with continuous outcomes. Unpublished manuscript, Department of Economics, University of Chicago.
  (1991b). Dynamic models for panel data. Unpublished manuscript, Department of Economics, University of Chicago.
Chipman, J., and Moore, J. (1976). Why an increase in GNP need not imply an improvement in potential welfare. *Kyklos* 29:391–418.
Cosslett, S. (1983). Distribution-free maximum likelihood estimators of the binary choice model. *Econometrica* 51:765–782.
Couch, K. (1992). New evidence on the long-term effects of employment training programs. *Journal of Labor Economics* 10:380–8.
Csörgö, M. (1993). *Quantile Processes with Statistical Applications.* Philadelphia: Society for Industrial and Applied Mathematics.

Domencich, T., and McFadden, D. (1975). *Urban Travel Demand: A Behavioral Analysis*. Amsterdam: North Holland.

Fréchet, M. (1951). Sur les tableux de corrélation dont les marges sont donnés. *Annales University Lyon* (Sect. A) 14:53–77.

Frisch, R. (1934). Circulation planning: proposal for a national organization of a commodity and service exchange. *Econometrica* 2:274–90.

——— (1970). From utopian theory to practical applications: the case of econometrics. *Les Prix Nobel en 1969*, pp. 213–43. Stockholm: Nobel Foundation.

Harberger, A. (1971). Three basic postulates for applied welfare economics: an interpretive essay. *Journal of Economic Literature* 9:785–97.

Harsanyi, J. (1955). Cardinal welfare, individualistic ethics and interpersonal comparisons of utility. *Journal of Political Economy* 63:309–21.

——— (1975). Can the maximin principle serve as a basis for morality? A critique of John Rawls' theory. *American Political Science Review* 69:594–606.

Heckman, J. (1974a). The effect of child care programs on women's work effort. *Journal of Political Economy* 82:S136–63.

——— (1974b). Shadow prices, market wages and labor supply. *Econometrica* 42:679–94.

——— (1978). Dummy endogenous variables in a simultaneous equation system. *Econometrica* 46:931–59.

——— (1990a). Varieties of selection bias. *American Economic Review* 80:313–18.

——— (1990b). Alternative approaches to the evaluation of social programs: econometric and experimental methods. Barcelona Lecture, World Congress of the Econometric Society.

——— (1992). Randomization and social program evaluation. In: *Evaluating Welfare and Training Programs*, ed. C. Manski and I. Garfinkel, pp. 201–30. Cambridge, MA: Harvard University Press.

——— (1993). The case for simple estimators. Mimeographed manuscript, Department of Economics, University of Chicago.

——— (1996). Randomization as an instrumental variable. *Review of Economics and Statistics* 77:336–41.

——— (1997a). Instrumental variables: a study of implicit behavioral assumptions in one widely-used estimator. *Journal of Human Resources* 32:441–62.

——— (1997b). Constructing econometric counterfactuals under different assumptions. Mimeographed manuscript, Department of Economics, University of Chicago.

Heckman, J., Hohmann, N., Khoo, M., and Smith, J. (1997a). Did we learn the right lesson from the national JTPA study? Substitution bias in social experiments. Mimeographed manuscript, Department of Economics, University of Chicago.

Heckman, J., and Honoré, B. (1990). The empirical content of the Roy model. *Econometrica* 58:1121–49.

Heckman, J., Ichimura, H., Smith, J., and Todd, P. (1996). Sources of selection bias in evaluating programs: an interpretation of conventional measures and evidence on the effectiveness of matching as a program evaluation method. *Proceedigns of The National Academy of Sciences* 93:13416–20.

——— (in press-a) Characterizing selection bias using experimental data. *Econometrica*.

Heckman, J., Ichimura, H., and Todd, P. (1997b). Matching as an econometric evaluation estimator: evidence from evaluating a job training programme. *Review of Economic Studies* 64:605–54.

(1998a). Matching as an econometric evaluation estimator. *Review of Economic Studies* 65:261–94.

Heckman, J., LaLonde, R., and Smith, J. (in press-b). The economics and econometrics of active labor market programs. In: *Handbook of Labor Economics, Vol III*, ed. O. Ashenfelter and D. Card. Amsterdam: North Holland.

Heckman, J., and Robb, R. (1985). Alternative methods for evaluating the impact of interventions. In: *Longitudinal Analysis of Labor Market Data*, ed. J. Heckman and B. Singer, pp. 156–245. Cambridge University Press.

Heckman, J., Robb, R., and Walker, J. (1990). Testing the mixture of exponentials hypothesis and estimating the mixing distribution by the method of moments. *Journal of the American Statistical Association* 85:582–9.

Heckman, J., and Smith, J. (1993). Assessing the case for randomized evaluation of social programs. In: *Measuring Labour Market Measures: Evaluating the Effects of Active Labour Market Policies*, ed. K. Jensen and P. K. Madsen, pp. 35–96. Copenhagen: Danish Ministry of Labor.

(1995). Assessing the case for social experiments. *Journal of Economic Perspectives* 9:85–110.

(1996). Experimental and nonexperimental evaluation. In: *International Handbook of Labour Market Policy and Evaluation*, ed. G. Schmidt, J. O'Reilly, and K. Schömann, pp. 37–88. Cheltenham, UK: Elgar Publishers.

Heckman, J., Smith, J., and Clements, N. (1997c). Making the most out of program evaluations and social experiments: accounting for heterogeneity in program impacts. *Review of Economic Studies* 64:487–535.

Heckman, J., Smith, J., and Taber, C. (1998b). Accounting for dropouts in evaluations of social programs. *Review of Economics and Statistics* 80:1–14.

Heckman, J., and Taber, C. (1994). Econometric mixture models and more general models for unobservables in duration analysis. Mimeographed manuscript, Department of Economics, University of Chicago.

Imbens, G., and Angrist, J. (1994). Identification and estimation of local average treatment effects. *Econometrica* 62:467–71.

Katz, D., Gutek, B., Kahn, R., and Barton, E. (1975). *Bureaucratic Encounters: A Pilot Study in the Evaluation of Government Services*. Ann Arbor, MI: Institute for Social Research.

Kendall, M. G., and Stuart, A. (1977). *The Advanced Theory of Statistics, vol. 1*, 4th ed. London: Griffen.

Knight, F. (1921). *Risk, Uncertainty and Profit*. New York: Houghton Mifflin.

Laffont, J. J. (1989). *Fundamentals of Public Economics*. Cambridge, MA: Massachusetts Institute of Technology Press.

LaLonde, R. (1986). Evaluating the econometric evaluations of training programs with experimental data. *American Economic Review* 76:604–20.

Lancaster, K. (1971). *Consumer Demand: A New Approach*. New York: Columbia University Press.

Lucas, R., and Sargent, T. (1981). Introduction. In: *Essays on Rational Expectations and Econometric Practice*, pp. xi–xl. Minneapolis: University of Minnesota Press.

Mardia, K. V. (1970). *Families of Bivariate Distributions*. London: Griffen.

Marschak, J. (1953). Economic measurements for policy and prediction. In: *Studies in Econometric Method*, ed. W. Hood and T. Koopmans, pp. 1–26. New York: Wiley.

Matzkin, R. (1990). Least concavity and the distribution-free estimation of nonparametric concave functions. Cowles Commission discussion paper.

(1992). Nonparametric and distribution-free estimation of the threshold crossing and binary choice models. *Econometrica* 60:239–70.

Moffitt, R. (1992). Evaluation of program entry effects. In: *Evaluating Welfare and Training Programs*, ed. C. Manski and I. Garfinkel, pp. 231–52. Cambridge, MA: Harvard University Press.

Moulin, H. (1983). *The Strategy of Social Choice*. Amsterdam: North Holland.

Orr, L., Bloom, H., Bell, S., Lin, W., Cave, G., and Doolittle, F. (1995). *The National JTPA Study: Impacts, Benefits and Costs of Title II-A*. Bethesda, MD: Abt Associates.

Quandt, R. (1972). Methods for estimating switching regressions. *Journal of the American Statistical Association* 67:306–10.

(1988). *The Econometrics of Disequilibrium*. Oxford: Blackwell.

Rawls, J. (1971). *A Theory of Justice*. Cambridge, MA: Harvard University Press.

Ridder, G. (1990). Attrition in multiwave panel data. In: *Panel Data and Labor Market Studies*, ed. J. Hartog, G. Ridder, and J. Theeuwes, pp. 45–67. Amsterdam: North Holland.

Roy, A. (1951). Some thoughts on the distribution of earnings. *Oxford Economic Papers* 3:135–46.

Royden, H. L. (1968). *Real Analysis*, 2nd ed. New York: Macmillan.

Sen, A. (1973). *On Economic Inequality*. Oxford: Clarendon Press.

(1979). Strategies and revelation: informational constraints in public decisions. In: *Aggregation and Revelation of Preferences*, ed. J. J. Laffont. Amsterdam: North Holland.

Smith, J. (in press). The JTPA selection process: a descriptive analysis. In: *Performance Standards in a Federal Bureaucracy: Analytical Essays on the JTPA Performance Standards System*, ed. J. Heckman. Kalamazoo, MI: Upjohn Institute.

Tchen, A. (1980). Inequalities for distributions with given marginals. *Annals of Probability* 8:814–27.

Thaler, R. (1992). *The Winner's Curse*. Princeton University Press.

Tinbergen, J. (1956). *Economic Policy: Principles and Design*. Amsterdam: North Holland.

Tong, Y. L. (1980). *Probability Inequalities in Multivariate Distributions*. New York: Academic Press.

U.S. GAO (1996). Job Training Partnership Act: long-term earnings and employment outcomes. GAO/HEHS-96-40. Washington, DC: U.S. General Accounting Office.

Vickrey, W. (1945). Measuring marginal utility by reactions to risk. *Econometrica* 13:319–33.

CHAPTER 9

Frisch, Hotelling, and the Marginal-Cost Pricing Controversy

Jean-Jacques Laffont

> Le meilleur de tous les tarifs serait celui qui ferait payer à ceux qui passent sur une voie de communication un péage proportionnel à l'utilité qu'ils retirent du passage...
>
> Il est évident que l'effet d'un tel tarif serait: d'abord de laisser passer autant de monde que si le passage était gratuit; ainsi point d'utilité perdue pour la société; ensuite de donner une recette toujours suffisante pour qu'un travail utile pût se faire.
>
> Je n'ai pas besoin de dire que je ne crois pas à la possibilité d'application de ce tarif volontaire; il rencontrerait un obstacle insurmontable dans l'improbité universelle des passants, mais c'est là le type dont il faut chercher à s'approcher par un tarif obligatoire.
>
> Jules Dupuit (1849, p. 223)

1 Introduction

In an elegant *Econometrica* paper, Hotelling (1938) provided the appropriate formulas to assess the social costs of marginal departures from marginal-cost pricing when the interrelations between commodities are taken into account. In so doing he generalized the work of Dupuit (1844) and Marshall (1890). But he went further. He advocated marginal-cost pricing for those industries with large fixed costs and more generally increasing returns:

> This proposition has revolutionary implications, for example in electric power and railway economics, in showing that society would do well to cut rates drastically and replace the revenue thus lost by subsidies

---

This essay was written for the Ragnar Frisch Centennial Symposium in Oslo, March 1995. Steinar Strøm's friendly pressure is responsible for its existence. I am grateful to M. Ivaldi for helping me with the simulations and J. Tirole for helpful comments. I thank the participants in the conference for useful discussions, in particular O. Bjerkholt, J. Hausman, J. Heckman, K. Moene, and A. Sandmo. Thanks also to the referee.

> derived largely from income and inheritance taxes and the site value of land. [Hotelling, 1939, p. 151]

In his introduction he suggested that Dupuit had also advocated marginal-cost pricing. A whole generation of economists took that for granted and did not question the historical origin of the policy consisting in pricing commodities at marginal cost and financing the deficit with the general budget.

Ekelund (1968) convincingly demonstrated[1] that Dupuit had never proposed marginal-cost pricing. Actually from the time of Adam Smith (1776) to Edgeworth (1913), most major figures in economics had warned against the dangers of deficits financed by the general budget. Smith (1776) was particularly clear on this point:

> It does not seem necessary that the expence of those public works should be from (that) public revenue.... The greater part of such public works may easily be so managed, as to afford a particular revenue sufficient for defraying their own expence. [p. 682, 1937 edition]

Smith seems to suggest prices proportional to marginal cost, so as to cover costs, what in France we call the Allais rule:

> When the carriages... pay toll in proportion to their weight or their tunnage, they pay... in proportion to the wear and tear. [p. 683]

The reasons given by Smith to motivate his proposal are most interesting. A major argument is an informational one:

> When high roads, bridges, canals... are in this manner made and supported by the commerce which is carried on by means of them, they can be made only where that commerce requires them and consequently where it is proper to make them. [p. 683]

Of course, that is not quite right,[2] but the next argument, a political-economy one, is compelling:

> A magnificent high road cannot be made through a desert country where there is little or no commerce, or merely because it happens to lead to the country villa of the intendant of the province, or that of some great lord to whom the intendant finds it convenient to make his court.

---

[1] According to Ekelund, Dupuit was emphatically opposed to the caprice of political influence in the granting of subsidies. His opposition was based on the belief that the political selection of projects to be subsidized would not be grounded in economic criteria. Dupuit (1844) clearly saw that the usefulness of a road is maximized when its toll is zero: "L'utilité d'une voie de communication est la plus grande possible lorsque le péage est nul" (p. 247). However, he understood the deadweight loss of the financing: "On comprend que pour traiter ainsi la seule question de savoir si on doit ou on ne doit pas établir des péages, il y aurait à examiner par quel impôt ou par quelle aggravation d'impôt ils devraient être remplacés et quels seraient les effets de ces impôts" (p. 247). Dupuit's viewpoint would be formalized by Edgeworth (1913).

[2] It is a sufficient but not necessary test.

> A great bridge cannot be thrown over a river at a place where nobody passes, or merely to embellish the view from the windows of a neighbouring palace. [p. 683]

Smith understood that the decision process for public works must be delegated, and he worried about the incentives created by the delegation of pricing rules to policy-makers.

Note that he did not question the benevolence of the executive power itself, because he relies on it to conduct an appropriate redistribution policy through third-degree price discrimination:

> When the toll upon carriages of luxury, upon coaches, post-chaises, etc. is made somewhat higher in proportion to their weight, than upon carriages of necessary use, such as carts, waggons, etc. the indolence and vanity of the rich is made to contribute in a very easy manner to the relief of the poor. [p. 683]

Walras (1897) essentially followed Smith's point of view ("L'Etat interviendra soit pour exercer lui-même le monopole soit pour l'organiser de façon à ce qu'il soit exercé sans bénéfice ni perte."), without being clear on the allocation of fixed costs in the multiproduct case ("Le monopole des chemins de fer devrait être exercé purement et simplement, soit par l'Etat soit pour son compte, au prix de revient."). However, he mentioned the point of view of Say (1840), who wanted to treat the communication means, roads, canals, and so forth, as public goods, and who therefore proposed marginal-cost pricing (zero price) in a special case.[3]

Walras also considered that communication means could produce some public goods (if only for the armed forces) that would justify subsidies.

Hotelling was aware of a number of criticisms of marginal-cost pricing, but he dismissed them all, on the following grounds: First was the criticism that the financing of deficits induces debatable effects on the distribution of wealth. He argued mainly that the marginal-cost pricing rule would be applied for many different projects, and "a rough randomness in distribution should be ample to ensure such a distribution of benefits that most persons in every part of the country would be better off by reason of the program as a whole" (Hotelling, 1939, p. 259).

Second, in his answer to Frisch (1939), Hotelling (1939) recognized,

---

[3] One motivation for Say was that price equal to average cost may not be sufficient to balance the budget of some projects, despite their social usefulness: "Les frais de confection d'un canal, même les frais indispensables, peuvent être tels que les droits de navigation ne soient pas suffisants pour payer les intérêts de l'avance; quoique les avantages qu'en retirerait la nation fussent très supérieurs au montant de ces intérêts. Il faut bien alors que la nation supporte gratuitement les frais de son établissement, si elle veut jouir du bien qui peut en résulter."

following Lerner (1937), that the income tax he planned to use to finance deficits "is a sort of excise tax on effort and on waiting, ... is to some extent objectionable because it affects the choice between effort and leisure." If that turned out to be a real problem, Hotelling would find an easy escape by appealing to land taxes, externality taxes: "public revenue should be derived primarily from rents of land and other scarce goods, inheritance and windfall taxes, and taxes designed to reduce socially harmful consumption."

Hotelling's argument rested on the assumption that lump-sum taxes somehow exist. In practice, it is recognized that the social cost of public funds is not negligible, ranging from 0.3 in developed countries to more than 1 in developing countries.

A first line of criticism that would eventually be followed, even by great defenders of marginal-cost pricing such as Vickrey, was that even after using land taxes and externalities taxes, the financial needs of the government would be such that distortive taxes would have to be used at the margin. Second-best optimality would then require some form of Ramsey pricing, with the well-known informational difficulties about price elasticities, cream skimming, and bypass.

The third main criticism Hotelling considered concerned the fact that it is necessary to determine whether or not the creation of the project is a wise social policy, and sometimes to select a limited number of proposed investments, corresponding to the available capital, from among a large number of possibilities. He then provided an answer that ignored both incentive and political questions:

> When the question arises of building new railroads, or new major industries of any kind, or of scrapping the old, we shall face, not a historical, but a mathematical and economic problem.... This will call for a study of demand and cost functions by economists, statisticians, and engineers, and perhaps for a certain amount of large scale experimentation for the sake of gaining information about these functions. [1939, p. 269]

The intellectual approach of Hotelling clearly featured the paradigm of the benevolent social maximizer who can become informed by social experimentation. The two main lines of criticism that Hotelling considered and dismissed were related to that point of view. Incomplete information makes lump-sum taxation ineffective and pushes us toward a second-best world, leading to Ramsey pricing. However, the potential lack of benevolence among decision-makers may cause one to question that conclusion.

This introduction leaves us with many questions that we shall consider in turn. First, what is, then, the exact intellectual origin of the policy of pricing at marginal cost, with public funding of deficits? Second, what was the content of the marginal-cost controversy, and what was the role of Frisch in that debate? Third, how can we discuss today the incentives and political-economy issues concerning pricing rules of increasing-returns industries, for simplicity restricting the discussion to natural monopolies?

2   The Marginal-Cost Pricing Rule

Schumpeter attributed to the German economist Launhardt (1885) the paternity of the rule:

> the work of W. Launhardt ... contained the theorem – his argument for government ownership is based upon it – that the social advantage from railroads will be maximized if charges be not higher than – as we should say – marginal cost. It follows from this that the whole overhead would have to be financed from the government's general revenue – the theorem that has been much discussed in our own day after having been independently discovered by Professor Hotelling. [Schumpeter, 1954, p. 948]

The idea also came up in the debates following the discussions of Marshall's idea that decreasing-returns-to-scale industries should be taxed, and increasing-returns-to-scale industries should be subsidized. Pigou (1952) qualified Marshall's suggestion: "provided that the funds for the bounty can be raised by a mere transfer that does not inflict any indirect injury on production" (p. 224). "Those results, ... are results in pure theory" (p. 226). Pigou then raised the question of the practical difficulty of determining the type of returns to scale (the empty-boxes controversy), but hoped that economists would be able to fill those boxes with statistical techniques in the future.

Robinson also clarified some fairly confused discussion:

> The obvious example is a railway system which is working at falling average cost and which is limited to just cover its costs.... The whole problem really boils down to the familiar difficulty that when any concern is running at falling average cost it is impossible to fix a price which both enables it to cover its cost and enables consumers to buy the output whose marginal cost to the firm is equal to the marginal utility to them. The difficulty can be removed by subsidizing the firm.... Whether, on general grounds, such subsidies are desirable, or feasible, is another story. [Robinson, 1934, p. 140]

The idea of pricing at marginal cost and financing the deficit with public money became familiar during the controversy over socialism (Lange and Taylor, 1938; Lerner, 1937). It was even an alleged advantage of public ownership over private ownership, for which subsidies were not even considered.

Finally, we can also note the political-economy defense of marginal-cost pricing by Vickrey:

> Whether the operation is in private or in public hands, if rates are set above marginal cost in an attempt to cover the entire costs of the operation, the solution of the problem of how to fix rates so as to achieve this end with the least possible misallocation of resources calls, at best, for the exercise of very refined judgment, even in a milieu free from contending interests. In practice, moreover, contention by interested parties makes the achievement of a close approach to the best solution even more difficult....
>
> This uncertainty often produces a situation in which it becomes very easy for the decisions to be made primarily on the grounds of political expediency.... Such considerations can be excluded from rate-fixing problems only by setting rates at marginal costs. [Vickrey, 1948, p. 236]

He also voiced a very modern argument from our world of deregulation:

> Subsidized operation at marginal cost will usually eliminate the need that is often felt for surrounding such de facto public monopolies with legal prohibitions against competition. As long as it is necessary to cover costs from revenues, it is often deemed necessary to prohibit private competitors from operating in the same field, in order to prevent "skimming the cream" and impairment of revenues or uneconomical duplication of services....
>
> With rates at marginal cost, however, no such prohibitions would be necessary and, indeed, they would be undesirable.[4] [Vickrey, 1948, p. 237]

3   Frisch's Comment

It is interesting to examine the type of criticism of Hotelling's paper offered by Frisch. It was argued earlier that Hotelling was thinking in terms of an informed benevolent social maximizer. Frisch's comment goes even further, with all the virtue of logic within a well-defined model. Quite rightly within the model he considered, and in the same spirit as Kahn (1935), Frisch (1939, p. 145) pointed out the following:

> The only relevant question is whether the excise taxes are proportional or non proportional to the prices that existed before the imposition of the excise taxes. It is the non proportionality of the excise taxes, and only this, that produces a reduction in satisfaction.

He then claimed that Hotelling had been considering a case of measure zero, that there was a continuum of other systems leading to the same result:

> One consists in telling the individual that under any circumstances his income tax will be so adjusted to the other facts of the situation that his total tax will equal t [i.e., will be constant].

---

[4] Of course, entry is then adequate if entrants have no fixed costs.

And later:

> There exists an infinity of others that are equally good, namely all those whose excise taxes are proportional to the original prices.

Frisch was saying that all decompositions of taxes between excise taxes and income taxes that would keep consumer prices proportional and would raise the same total revenue were equivalent.

Hotelling's answer is also quite interesting. He recognized Frisch's logical point, but criticized the other systems proposed by Frisch on informational grounds that were outside the model: evasion of excise taxes, difficulty in taxing all commodities, nonlinear taxation possibilities with income taxes.

In his 1987 paper in the *New Palgrave*, Vickrey, who wrote 40 papers on marginal-cost pricing, recognized the second-best nature of the problem and the need for taking into account the marginal cost of public funds. Marginal-cost pricing cum funding of the deficit with public funds would have to acknowledge that cost.

The second criticism anticipated by Hotelling was the need for testing the validity of the project. Two questions are raised here: First, assuming costs are imperfectly known, what is the best pricing method? That was the main point raised by Coase (1946). Second, if subsidies are used, one must take into account their rent-seeking implications. Vickrey put it as follows:

> One reason for wanting to avoid such a subsidy is that if an agency is considered eligible for a subsidy much of the pressure on management to operate efficiently will be lost and management effort will be diverted from controlling costs to pleading for an enhancement of the subsidy. [Vickrey, 1987, p. 209]

Hence the tendency to revert to self-financing projects:

> This effect can be minimized by establishing the base for the subsidy in a manner as little susceptible as possible to untoward pressure from management. But it is unlikely that this can be as effective in preserving incentives for cost containment as a requirement that the operation be financially self-sustaining. [Vickrey, 1987, p. 209]

These historical debates show that there are two major arguments against marginal-cost pricing. The first concerns the social cost of public funds, which is not negligible and leads to some form of Ramsey pricing. However, such pricing methods raise informational issues.[5] More importantly Ramsey pricing opens the possibility of political manipulation of price elasticities, as well as the need to control entry (with possibilities of capture) to avoid cream skimming.

---

[5] Laffont and Tirole (1996) have argued that they can be overcome by delegating pricing to the firm through a price cap combined with a profit-sharing scheme.

The second major criticism of marginal-cost pricing is the possibility of political manipulation of fixed costs, which can lead to unwise decisions.

Therefore, it appears that two attitudes are possible. One is to stick to pure theory and conclude that asymmetric information requires Ramsey pricing or some generalized version, such as that developed by Laffont and Tirole (1993). A more policy oriented attitude must take into account political constraints, that is, the fact that the regulatory pricing rules will be mandated by politicians who will have some discretion, because the constitutions, being quite incomplete contracts, cannot control them perfectly.

Such a political economy of pricing is required. Clearly, the various pricing rules are sensitive to different types of political influence, and a complete theory should consider, in each policy case, the most relevant dimensions of discretion. The policy conclusions will certainly be country-specific, industry-specific, because they should, broadly speaking, arbitrate between the inefficiencies of the pricing rules that derive from marginal-cost pricing or Ramsey pricing and the political distortions with which they are associated.

Some might think that it is not politically correct to develop such a theory. Indeed, in his Nobel lecture, Frisch (1970, p. 228) said that "it is not the task for us as econometricians and social engineers to go into a detailed discussion of the political system." Frisch's attitude was based on a quite idealistic view of politicans and of the relationships between economists and politicians. In his Nobel lecture he called for cooperation between them: "This will be of basic importance for clarifying what the political authorities really are aiming at." And later, describing the dialogue between authorities and experts: "the expert will have to end by saying politely: your Excellencies, I am sorry but you cannot have at the same time all these things on which you insist. The excellencies, being intelligent persons, will understand the philosophy of the preference questions." Taking into account interest groups and the private agendas of politicians is necessary to move from the world of pure theory to public policy, as Frisch clearly wished to do.

The next two sections suggest a first step toward such a political economy of pricing rules.[6] They imply a view of the relationships between economists and politicians quite different from Frisch's view.

4 Smith, Edgeworth, Hotelling

Study of the economics of incentives has provided the tools needed for modeling the rents captured by interest groups as functions of the underlying economic parameters. Therefore, this is an essential input into polit-

---

[6] See also Laffont (1996).

The Marginal-Cost Pricing Controversy

ical economy, which is often described as a game of redistribution of rents.[7] We shall now consider some simplified examples of political games in which the "constitutional" choice of the pricing rules for natural monopolies can be discussed.

We have mentioned that Adam Smith proposed to inflate marginal costs proportionally to cover costs. Edgeworth (1913) proposed price discrimination to help cover costs,[8] with less efficiency distortions. Those two approaches have different implications for the efficiency distortions under majority voting, as well as for realization of the project.

We consider a natural monopoly producing q units of a good, with a cost function

$$C = \beta q + k \tag{1}$$

The population of consumers is composed of two types: type 1, in proportion α, with the utility function $S(q)$ for the good produced by the monopoly; type 2, in proportion $1 - \alpha$, with the utility function $\theta S(q)$, with $\theta > 1$, where α takes the value $\alpha^* > \frac{1}{2}$ with probability π, and the value $1 - \alpha^*$ with probability $1 - \pi$.

The policy decisions in this simple model are the production level and the financing of the natural monopoly. There is a party representing the interests of each type of consumer. If $\alpha = \alpha^*$, type 1 is in the majority and makes the policy decisions within the constitutional constraints.

The constitutional constraints are represented by various rules. Consider first the Smith rule: Let q_i be the consumption of type i, $i = 1, 2$. Budget balance is achieved by prices that inflate the marginal cost β by a factor δ such that

$$(\delta - 1)\beta[\alpha q_1 + (1 - \alpha)q_2] = k \tag{2}$$

Consumer optimization leads to

$$S'(q_1) = \delta\beta \tag{3}$$

$$\theta S'(q_2) = \delta\beta \tag{4}$$

The solutions q_1, q_2, and δ are different according to the value of α and therefore according to the type of majority. We index the solutions by superscript i, $i = 1, 2$, depending on the majority. Then the expected welfare[9] is

---

[7] The approach is in the tradition of the VPI school, but we have here a more fundamentalist explanation of rents.

[8] "If a railway cannot be made to pay with rates and fares assigned on the principle of cost of service, it is better that it should practise discrimination than that it should not exist" (p. 223). As we saw earlier, Dupuit was led to a similar idea as an approximation of his ideal pricing.

[9] The welfare criterion is the utilitarian one. Similar reasoning holds for other criteria, such as the Rawls criterion. The index S refers to the Smith rule.

$$W^S = \pi\{\alpha^*[S(q_1^1) - \delta^1 \beta q_1^1] + (1-\alpha^*)[\theta S(q_2^1) - \delta^1 \beta q_1^1]\}$$
$$+ (1-\pi)\{(1-\alpha^*)[S(q_1^2) - \delta^2 \beta q_1^2] + \alpha^*[\theta S(q_2^2) - \delta^2 \beta q_2^2]\} \quad (5)$$

Let $q_1^1(\theta), q_2^1(\theta)$, and $\delta^1(\theta)$ and $q_1^2(\theta), q_2^2(\theta)$, and $\delta^2(\theta)$ be the solutions of (2)–(4) in the cases of majority 1 and 2, respectively. Substituting into W^S, we obtain $W^S(\theta)$. To compare the Smith rule with other rules in the neighborhood of $\theta = 1$, we shall need the derivative of expected social welfare with respect to θ at $\theta = 1$:

$$\frac{dW^S}{d\theta}(\theta) = \pi[-\alpha^* \beta q_1^1 - (1-\alpha^*)\beta q_2^1]\frac{d\delta^1}{d\theta} + \pi(1-\alpha^*)S(q_2^1)$$
$$+ (1-\pi)[-(1-\alpha^*)\beta q_1^2 - \alpha^* \beta q_2^2]\frac{d\delta^2}{d\theta} + (1-\pi)\alpha^* S(q_2^2) \quad (6)$$

For $\theta = 1$, $q_1^1 = q_2^1 = q_1^2 = q_2^2 = \bar{q}$, and

$$\left.\frac{d\delta^1}{d\theta}\right|_{\theta=1} = \frac{(\delta-1)(1-\alpha^*)S'}{(\delta-1)\beta + \bar{q}S''} \quad (7)$$

$$\left.\frac{d\delta^2}{d\theta}\right|_{\theta=1} = \frac{(\delta-1)\alpha^* S'}{(\delta-1)\beta + \bar{q}S''} \quad (8)$$

where S' and S'' (and later S) are evaluated at $\bar{q}$. Hence

$$\left.\frac{dW^S}{d\theta}\right|_{\theta=1} = [\pi(1-\alpha^*) + (1-\pi)\alpha^*]S$$
$$- [\pi(1-\alpha^*) + (1-\pi)\alpha^*]\frac{\beta \bar{q}(\delta-1)S'}{(\delta-1)\beta + \bar{q}S''} \quad (9)$$

Consider now the Edgeworth rule,[10] which we interpret here as second-degree price discrimination: Let (T_1, q_1) and (T_2, q_2) be a non-linear schedule. Incentive compatibility and budget balance[11] require

$$S(q_2) - S(q_1) \leq T_2 - T_1 \leq \theta[S(q_2) - S(q_1)] \quad (10)$$

$$\alpha T_1 + (1-\alpha)T_2 = \beta[\alpha q_1 + (1-\alpha)q_2] + k \quad (11)$$

Under majority 1, the type-2 incentive constraint is binding, and the optimal nonlinear price is the solution of

---

[10] The criticism of the Edgeworth rule that we examine here has been voiced, in particular, by Vickrey (1948).

[11] We assume that we are in a domain of parameter values such that individual rationality constraints are not binding. This will be the case if the valuations of the commodity considered are high enough. See Laffont (1996) for a case where those constraints are taken into account.

The Marginal-Cost Pricing Controversy

$$\max \alpha^*[S(q_1^1) - T_1^1] \tag{12}$$

subject to (10) and (11), yielding

$$S'(q_1^1) = \frac{\alpha^*}{1 - \theta(1 - \alpha^*)} \beta \tag{13}$$

$$\theta S'(q_2^1) = \beta \tag{14}$$

$$T_1^1 = \beta[\alpha^* q_1^1 + (1 - \alpha^*) q_2^1] + k - (1 - \alpha^*) \theta[S(q_2^1) - S(q_1^1)] \tag{15}$$

$$T_2^1 = T_1^1 + \theta[S(q_2^1) - S(q_1^1)] \tag{16}$$

Under majority 2, the type-1 incentive constraint is binding, and the optimal nonlinear price is the solution of

$$\max \alpha^*[\theta S(q_2^2) - T_2^2] \tag{17}$$

subject to (10) and (11), yielding

$$S'(q_1^2) = \beta \tag{18}$$

$$\theta S'(q_2^2) = \frac{\alpha^* \theta}{\theta - (1 - \alpha^*)} \beta \tag{19}$$

$$T_1^2 = \beta[(1 - \alpha^*) q_1^2 + \alpha^* q_2^2] + k - \alpha^*[S(q_2^2) - S(q_1^2)] \tag{20}$$

$$T_2^2 = T_1^2 + S(q_2^2) - S(q_1^2) \tag{21}$$

Then expected welfare is[12]

$$\begin{aligned} W^E = {} & \pi[\alpha^*\{S(q_1^1) + (1 - \alpha^*)\theta[S(q_2^1) - S(q_1^1)] \\ & - \beta[\alpha^* q_1^1 + (1 - \alpha^*) q_2^1] - k\} \\ & + (1 - \alpha^*)\{\theta S(q_2^1) - \alpha^* \theta[S(q_2^1) - S(q_1^1)] \\ & - \beta[\alpha^* q_1^1 + (1 - \alpha^*) q_2^1] - k\}] \\ & + (1 - \pi)[(1 - \alpha^*)\{S(q_1^2) + \alpha^*[S(q_2^2) - S(q_1^2)] \\ & - \beta[(1 - \alpha^*) q_1^2 + \alpha^* q_2^2] - k\} \\ & + \alpha^*\{\theta S(q_2^2) - (1 - \alpha^*)[S(q_2^2) - S(q_1^2)] \\ & - \beta[(1 - \alpha^*) q_1^2 + \alpha q_2^2] - k\}] \end{aligned} \tag{22}$$

and

---

[12] The index E refers to the Edgeworth rule.

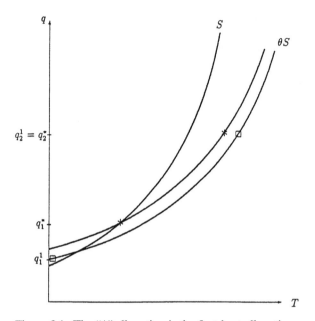

Figure 9.1. The "*" allocation is the first-best allocation most favorable to type 1 given the incentive constraint, that is, $T_2 = T_1 + \theta[S(q_1^*) - S(q_1^*)]$. The "□" allocation that obtains under majority 1 leads to higher welfare for type 1 and lower welfare for type 2 and to more (marginal) price discrimination.

$$\left.\frac{dW^E}{d\theta}\right|_{\theta=1} = [\pi(1-\alpha^*)+(1-\pi)\alpha^*]S \qquad (23)$$

We illustrate in Figures 9.1 and 9.2 the distortions implied by political discrimination. If we continue to assume that when social welfare is maximized, individual rationality constraints are not binding, we obtain the first-best optimal allocation $S'(q_1^*) = \theta S'(q_2^*) = \beta$.

From (13) and (14), $q_1^1 < q_1^*$, $q_2^1 = q_2^*$
From (18) and (19), $q_1^2 = q_1^*$, $q_2^2 > q_2^*$

So political discrimination is excessive in two ways: First, it leads to marginal prices that are different from marginal costs, and it induces larger differences in quantities consumed than at the optimum. Second, it leads to higher differences in utility levels.

Majority 1 tries to use majority 2 to fund the project through the budget-balance equation. The effort to increase this funding, still respecting incentive constraints, leads majority 1 to inflate $\theta[S(q_2) - S(q_1)]$ by decreasing $S(q_1)$ (given that type 2's incentive constraint is binding).

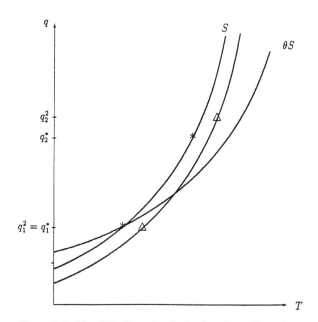

Figure 9.2. The "*" allocation is the first-best allocation most favorable to type 2 given the incentive constraint, that is, $T_2 = T_1 + [S(q_2^*) - S(q_1^*)]$. The "$\Delta$" allocation that obtains under majority 2 leads to lower welfare for type 1 and higher welfare for type 2 and to more (marginal) price discrimination.

Majority 2 must satisfy the type-1 incentive constraint $T_2 - T_1 \geq S(q_2) - S(q_1)$ and therefore chooses, to increase T_1, to increase both T_2 and q_2. Again, this mechanism is less effective when the size of the majority increases and the distortion is decreased.

From the foregoing we can note that the price distortions of the Smith rule concern both types and that they increase with the size of the fixed cost and decrease with the heterogeneity (i.e., θ), because type 2's consume more [see (2)]. The Edgeworth rule introduces a price distortion only for the type who has the majority [see (13) and (19)]. Furthermore, these distortions are higher for both types when heterogeneity is high. They are also higher when the majorities are thin (α^* close to $\frac{1}{2}$).[13]

Intuitively we can expect the Smith rule to be inferior when fixed costs are high, and the Edgeworth rule to be inferior when heteroge-

---

[13] The independence of the Edgeworth rule with respect to the fixed cost is due to the fact that we consider only the case where individual rationality constraints are not binding. This is also the reason that the Edgeworth rule, which finances the project from direct payments from consumers, is first-best optimal if $\theta = 1$.

ity is high and majorities thin. Let us compare those rules more formally.

We denote by η the price elasticity for the Smith rule at $\theta = 1$. From (9) and (23) we immediately obtain the following:

Proposition 1. *For $k > 0$ and $\theta = 1$, the Edgeworth rule is first-best optimal, and the Smith rule is not. For θ close to 1, if*

$$\eta > \frac{\delta}{\delta - 1} \tag{24}$$

the Edgeworth rule's advantage increases with θ. If

$$\eta < \frac{\delta}{\delta - 1} \tag{25}$$

the Edgeworth rule's advantage decreases with θ, suggesting that political second-degree discrimination may become dominated by proportional marginal-cost pricing with budget balance.

When fixed costs decrease, $\delta/(\delta - 1)$ increases, and for a given price elasticity of demand (25) may become satisfied – similarly when the price elasticity decreases.

Therefore, under (25), when heterogeneity increases, the Smith rule gains advantage relative to the Edgeworth rule. Example 1 in Appendix 2 shows that for a high enough heterogeneity, the Smith rule may dominate.

Proposition 2. *For $\theta > 1$ and $k = 0$, the Smith rule is first-best optimal, and the Edgeworth rule is not. Then*

$$\frac{dW^E}{dk} = -1 \tag{26}$$

$$\frac{dW^S}{dk} = -\pi \frac{1}{1 - \dfrac{(\delta - 1)\beta\left[\dfrac{\alpha^*}{-S''(q_1^1)} + \dfrac{1 - \alpha^*}{\theta[-S''(q_2^1)]}\right]}{\alpha^* q_1^1 + (1 - \alpha^*)q_2^1}}$$

$$- (1 - \pi) \frac{1}{1 - \dfrac{(\delta - 1)\beta\left[\dfrac{1 - \alpha^*}{-S''(q_1^2)} + \dfrac{\alpha^*}{\theta[-S''(q_2^2)]}\right]}{\alpha^* q_2^1 + (1 - \alpha^*)q_2^2}} < -1 \tag{27}$$

The Marginal-Cost Pricing Controversy

As k increases, the Edgeworth rule gains advantage relatively to the Smith rule and eventually becomes better. The larger is k, the more useful is price discrimination for covering costs without creating too-large distortions between marginal prices and marginal costs. So despite the fact that second-degree price discrimination opens the possibility of discretionary political discrimination, when fixed costs are large enough, discrimination is better (see Example 2 in Appendix 2).

The distortions due to the discretion embedded in the Edgeworth rule become less damaging than the distortions due to proportional marginal-cost pricing when the fixed cost is large enough. This is simply because they are independent of the fixed cost, as noted earlier.

A way to decrease the discretion embedded in second-degree price discrimination may be to impose a pooling contract (q, T) selected by each majority. To first order around $\theta = 1$, this pooling contract is equivalent to the Edgeworth rule. To second order it is dominated by the Edgeworth rule (see Appendix 1).

A further way to fight discretion is to impose a single quantity transfer and cover costs with a uniform transfer. We refer then to the "egalitarian" rule (using the index Eg). Then $T = \beta q + k$, and expected welfare is

$$W^{Eg} = \{\pi\alpha^* + (1-\pi)(1-\alpha^*) + [\pi(1-\alpha^*)+(1-\pi)\alpha^*]\theta\}S(q) - \beta q - k$$

yielding

$$S'(q) = \frac{\beta}{\pi\alpha^* + (1-\pi)(1-\alpha^*) + \theta[\pi(1-\alpha^*)+(1-\pi)\alpha^*]}$$

and

$$\left.\frac{dW^{Eg}}{d\theta}\right|_{\theta=1} = [\pi(1-\alpha^*)+(1-\pi)\alpha^*]S$$

$$\left.\frac{d^2W^{Eg}}{d\theta^2}\right|_{\theta=1} = [\pi(1-\alpha^*)+(1-\pi)\alpha^*]^2 \frac{S'^2}{(-S'')}$$

For $\theta = 1$, the Edgeworth rule and egalitarian rule coincide, and we immediately obtain the following:

Proposition 3. *In a neighborhood of $\theta = 1$, the egalitarian rule dominates the Edgeworth rule if*

$$[\pi(1-\alpha^*)+(1-\pi)\alpha^*]^2 > \frac{2\alpha^*-1}{\alpha^*}[\pi(1-\alpha^*)+(1-\pi)]$$

This condition holds, in particular, for α^* close enough to $\frac{1}{2}$. If the size of the majority is not large enough, the political distortions of the Edgeworth rule will be greater than the efficiency distortions of the egalitarian rule. Because for θ close to 1 the Smith rule is dominated, the egalitarian rule is then the best rule so far.

Consider now the Hotelling rule (index H) when we take into account the cost of financing the deficit with distortionary taxes. Let $1 + \lambda$ be the cost of public funds. The Hotelling rule is then characterized by

$$S'(q_1) = \beta \tag{28}$$

$$\theta S'(q_2) = \beta \tag{29}$$

plus a cost of public deficit of $(1 + \lambda)k$, and a welfare

$$W^H = E_\alpha\{\alpha[S(q_1) - \beta q_1] + (1-\alpha)[\theta S(q_2) - \beta q_2]\} - (1+\lambda)k \tag{30}$$

$$\frac{dW^H}{dk} = -(1+\lambda) \tag{31}$$

$$\left.\frac{dW^H}{d\theta}\right|_{\theta=1} = [\pi(1-\alpha^*) + (1-\pi)\alpha^*]S \tag{32}$$

Proposition 4. *Suppose that λ is such that the Smith rule and the Hotelling rule coincide for $\theta = 1$. As θ increases, if*

$$\eta > \frac{\delta}{\delta - 1}$$

the Hotelling rule dominates. If

$$\eta < \frac{\delta}{\delta - 1}$$

the Smith rule dominates.

As fixed costs increase, the social costs of the Hotelling rule (due to the distortionary funding) are linear in those costs, whereas those of the Smith rule (due to distortionary pricing) are increasing nonlinearly. For fixed costs low enough, the Smith rule dominates. Also, for θ large enough, the Hotelling rule dominates the Edgeworth rule, which then suffers from high degrees of political discrimination (see Example 1).[14]

---

[14] L. Klein has pointed out to me that the cost of public funds is changing over time, and this might be a problem for the "constitutional" approach. However, it is certainly not changing much, and one could admit, constitutionally, the notion of a λ varying over time with rules contingent on λ. The real difficulty with this would come from the potential discretion embedded in the choice of these values.

5 Project Selection and Pricing Rules

In Section 4 we examined the limits of marginal-cost pricing when public funds are costly. In this case, the cost of funding through indirect taxation must be compared with the distortions due to political discrimination.

Actually, the main criticism voiced against marginal-cost pricing is the political discretion it creates, such that fixed costs can be manipulated to use public funds to finance projects that are not socially valuable.

Suppose, for example, that the fixed cost can take two values, $\underline{k}$ and $\overline{k}$, with probabilities v and $1 - v$, and $\overline{k} > \underline{k}$. Suppose that when $k = \overline{k}$, the project should not be realized with the Hotelling rule, that is,

$$\alpha\{S[q_1(\beta)] - \beta q_1(\beta)\} + (1-\alpha)\{\theta S[q_2(\beta)] - \beta q_2(\beta)\} < (1+\lambda)\overline{k} \quad (33)$$

with

$$q_1(\beta) = \arg\max_q[S(q) - \beta q]$$
$$q_2(\beta) = \arg\max_q[\theta S(q) - \beta q]$$

but that it is realized if funding of the fixed cost is uniform and if type 2 has the majority, because

$$\theta S[q_2(\beta)] - \beta q_2(\beta) - (1+\lambda)\overline{k} > 0 \quad (34)$$

whereas it is not realized if type 1 has the majority:

$$S[q_1(\beta)] - \beta q_1(\beta) - (1+\lambda)\overline{k} < 0 \quad (35)$$

When $k = \underline{k}$ it is realized in both cases. The loss due to political manipulation of the Hotelling rule is then

$$(1-\pi)(1-v)[(1+\lambda)\overline{k} - (1-\alpha^*)\{S[q_1(\beta)] - \beta q_1(\beta)\} \\ - \alpha^*\{\theta S[q_2(\beta)] - \beta q_2(\beta)\}] \quad (36)$$

where $1 - \pi$ is the probability of majority 2.

Under the Smith rule, the project is (here) always realized[15] when it should be:

$$S[q_1(\delta^1\beta)] - \delta\beta q_1(\delta^1\beta) > 0 \quad (<0) \quad (37)$$

if

---

[15] Of course, as already mentioned, this is not always the case. A general theory would take into account the lost opportunities induced by such a rule.

$$(\delta^1 - 1)\beta[\alpha^* q_1(\delta^1 \beta) + (1 - \alpha^*)q_2(\delta^1 \beta)] = \underline{k} \quad (\overline{k}) \tag{38}$$

$$\theta S[q_2(\delta^2 \beta)] - \delta^2 \beta q_2(\delta^2 \beta) > 0 \quad (<0) \tag{39}$$

if

$$(\delta^2 - 1)\beta[(1 - \alpha^*)q_1(\delta^2 \beta) + \alpha^* q_2(\delta^2 \beta)] = \underline{k} \quad (\overline{k}) \tag{40}$$

However, consumption distortions occur, with an expected loss of

$$v\left\{\pi \int_{\beta}^{\delta^1 \beta} [\alpha^* q_1(b) + (1 - \alpha^*) q_2(b)] db \right. \\ \left. + (1 - \pi) \int_{\beta}^{\delta^2 \beta} [(1 - \alpha^*) q_1(b) + \alpha^* q_2(b)] db - \underline{k} \right\} \tag{41}$$

Clearly, depending on the values of π, v, $\underline{k}$, and $\overline{k}$, either of the two regimes can dominate. Suppose we have parameter values such that they are equivalent. Let us see the marginal effect of increases in both fixed costs. For the Hotelling rule,

$$dW^H = (1 - \pi)(1 - v)(1 + \lambda) \tag{42}$$

For the Smith rule,

$$dW^S = -v + v\left\{\pi[\alpha^* q_1(\delta^1 \beta) + (1 - \alpha^*) q_2(\delta^1 \beta)]\beta \frac{d\delta^1}{d\underline{k}} \right. \\ \left. + (1 - \pi)[(1 - \alpha^*) q_1(\delta^2 \beta) + \alpha^* q_2(\delta^2 \beta)]\beta \frac{d\delta^2}{d\underline{k}}\right\} \tag{43}$$

Differentiating (38) and (40) and denoting by η^1 (respectively η^2) the price elasticity of global demand when majority 1 (respectively 2) obtains, we have

$$[\alpha^* q_1(\delta^1 \beta) + (1 - \alpha^*) q_2(\delta^1 \beta)]\beta \frac{d\delta^1}{d\underline{k}} = 1 \bigg/ \left(1 - \frac{\delta^1 - 1}{\delta^1}\eta^1\right)$$
$$[(1 - \alpha^*) q_1(\delta^2 \beta) + \alpha^* q_2(\delta^2 \beta)]\beta \frac{d\delta^2}{d\underline{k}} = 1 \bigg/ \left(1 - \frac{\delta^2 - 1}{\delta^2}\eta^2\right) \tag{44}$$

We obtain, for δ^1 and δ^2 close to 1, the following:

Proposition 5. *The Smith rule dominates the Hotelling rule when fixed costs increase if*

$$(1 - \pi)(1 - v)(1 + \lambda) > \left[\pi \frac{\delta^1 - 1}{\delta^1}\eta^1 + (1 - \pi)\frac{\delta^2 - 1}{\delta^2}\eta^2\right]v \tag{45}$$

In the symmetric case, $\pi = \frac{1}{2}$, and for a constant elasticity, (43) simplifies to

$$(1-v)(1+\lambda) > \eta\left[2 - \frac{1}{\delta^1} - \frac{1}{\delta^2}\right]v \qquad (46)$$

The Hotelling rule is dominated by the Smith rule if the cost of public funds is high, the probability of a bad project is large, and the elasticity of demand is low. Clearly, Smith did not take into account the elasticity of demand (i.e., implicitly assumed a zero elasticity, in which case the superiority of his rule is obvious). Also, we see from (41) that for k small, δ^1 and δ^2 are close to 1, and the efficiency losses of the Smith pricing rule are second-order, whereas the efficiency loss from bad projects being realized remains of the first order.[16]

6 Conclusion

In an indirect way, this essay questions Frisch's view of the relationships between economists and politicians.

In a world of complete information, where transfers between social groups do not carry large deadweight losses, even if the democratic game leads to politicians who favor their electorate, economists should help politicians optimize their objectives. As majorities change, economic agents will see their relative positions change, but the average utility levels will not be too far from optimal.[17]

In a world of asymmetric information and incentive constraints, transfers between social groups may become very costly, leading to poor average performances. The discretion allowed by the constitution enables a majority to capture some rent, but this is very costly for the other group. In this world, two striking results emerge concerning the relationships between economists and politicians.

First, by working for politicians (e.g., by providing information), economists may assist the politicians' agenda of favoring the majority at the expense of other groups, leading to a worse outcome on average.

Second, the economists have an alternative route to enhance public welfare. By suggesting constitutional rules that will decrease the discretion of politicians, even at the cost of some efficiency losses, economists can enhance expected social welfare.[18]

As an example, we have shown that despite inefficiencies in the allo-

---

[16] I thank J. Hausman for this remark.
[17] The argument here requires that the Pareto frontier be fairly flat and that risk aversion be not large.
[18] The budget-balance rule discussed today in the United States is an example of such a rule; see the pioneering work of the VPI school (e.g., Brennan and Buchanan, 1977).

cation of resources it embodies, the constitutional constraint of the Smith rule can improve expected welfare because it dominates alternative rules that would open too-large opportunities for political discrimination. Indeed, it is particularly interesting from a political-economy perspective, because it can prevent both the political manipulations of fixed costs that Smith (1776) was worried about and the cross-subsidies manipulations that Vickrey (1948) emphasized.[19]

Appendix 1

Under the Edgeworth rule, and with majority 1, we have, by differentiating (13) and (14),

$$\left.\frac{dq_1}{d\theta}\right|_{\theta=1} = \frac{1-\alpha^*}{\alpha^*}\frac{S'}{S''}, \quad \left.\frac{dq_2}{d\theta}\right|_{\theta=1} = -\frac{S'}{S''}$$

and the second derivative of welfare with respect to θ at $\theta = 1$, with majority 1, is

$$\frac{(1-\alpha^*)(2\alpha^*-1)}{\alpha^*}\frac{S'^2}{-S''}$$

Similarly, differentiating (18) and (19), we obtain

$$\left.\frac{dq_1}{d\theta}\right|_{\theta=1} = 0, \quad \left.\frac{dq_2}{d\theta}\right|_{\theta=1} = \frac{1}{\alpha^*}\frac{S'}{-S''}$$

as well as a second derivative of welfare

$$\frac{2\alpha^*-1}{\alpha^*}\frac{S'^2}{-S''}$$

and an expected second derivative

$$\left.\frac{d^2W^E}{d\theta^2}\right|_{\theta=1} = \frac{2\alpha^*-1}{\alpha^*}\frac{S'^2}{-S''}[\pi(1-\alpha^*)+(1-\pi)]$$

Under conditions of pooling, majority 1 (i.e., $\alpha > \frac{1}{2}$) solves

$$\max \alpha^*[S(q) - T], \quad T = \beta q + k$$

---

[19] As A. Sandmo pointed out during the conference, the arguments in favor of uniform value-added taxes have the same flavor.

The Marginal-Cost Pricing Controversy

or $S'(q^1) = \beta$ and $T^1 = \beta q^1 + k$. Majority 2 solves

$$\max \alpha^*[\theta S(q) - T], \quad T = \beta q + k$$

or $\theta S'(q^2) = \beta$ and $T^2 = \beta q^2 + k$. Expected welfare is

$$\pi\{\alpha^*[S(q^1) - \beta q^1 - k] + (1 - \alpha^*)[\theta S(q^1) - \beta q^1 - k]\}$$
$$+ (1 - \pi)\{(1 - \alpha^*)[S(q^2) - \beta q^2 - k] + \alpha^*[\theta S(q^2) - \beta q^2 - k]\}$$

$$\left.\frac{dW^P}{d\theta}\right|_{\theta=1} = \{\pi(1 - \alpha^*) + (1 - \pi)\alpha^*\}S$$

From the foregoing,

$$\left.\frac{dq_1}{d\theta}\right|_{\theta=1} = 0, \quad \left.\frac{dq_2}{d\theta}\right|_{\theta=1} = -\frac{S'}{S''}$$

and

$$\left.\frac{d^2W^P}{d\theta^2}\right|_{\theta=1} = (1 - \pi)(2\alpha^* - 1)\frac{S'^2}{-S''}$$

Then

$$\left.\frac{d^2W^E}{d\theta^2}\right|_{\theta=1} - \left.\frac{d^2W^P}{d\theta^2}\right|_{\theta=1} = (2\alpha^* - 1)\left\{\frac{\pi(1 - \alpha^*) + (1 - \pi)}{\alpha^*} - (1 - \pi)\right\}\frac{S'^2}{-S''}$$

$$\geq (2\alpha^* - 1)\pi \frac{1 - \alpha^*}{\alpha^*} \frac{S'^2}{-S''} \geq 0$$

Appendix 2

Example 1

$S'(q) = 10 - q$
$\alpha^* = \frac{3}{4}$
$\beta = 1$
$k = 15$
$\lambda = 0.1$

- For θ large enough, the Smith rule dominates the Edgeworth rule.
- For θ large enough, the Hotelling rule dominates the egalitarian rule and the Edgeworth rule.

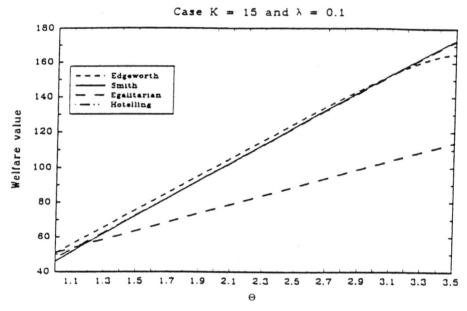

Figure 9.A1. Example 1.

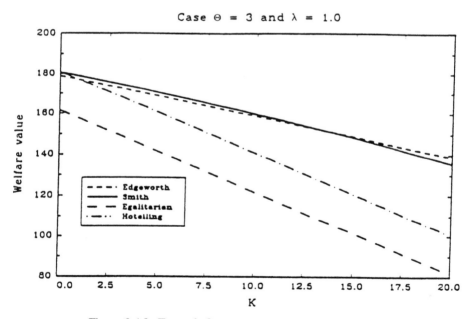

Figure 9.A2. Example 2.

Example 2

$S'(q) = 10 - q$

$\alpha^* = \dfrac{3}{4}$

$\beta = 1$

$\theta = 3$

$\lambda = 1$

- For k large enough, the Edgeworth rule dominates the Hotelling rule, and for k even larger, the Smith rule.

References

Brennan, G., and Buchanan, J. (1977). Towards a tax constitution for Leviathan. *Journal of Public Economics* 8:255–73.

Coase, R. H. (1946). The marginal-cost controversy. *Economica* 13:169.

Dupuit, J. (1844). De la mesure de l'utilité des travaux publics. *Annales des Ponts et Chaussées.*

 (1849). De l'influence des péages sur l'utilité des voies de communication. *Annales des Ponts et Chaussées.*

Edgeworth, F. Y. (1913). Contributions to the theory of railways. *Economic Journal.*

Ekelund, R. B. (1968). Jules Dupuit and the early theory of marginal cost pricing. *Journal of Political Economy* 76:462–71.

Frisch, R. (1939). The Dupuit taxation theorem. *Econometrica* 7:145–50.

 (1970). From Utopian theory to practical applications: the case of econometrics. In: *Les Prix Nobel en 1969*. Stockholm: Nobel Foundation.

Hotelling, M. (1938). The general welfare in relation to problems of taxation and of railway and utility rates. *Econometrica* 6:242–69.

 (1939). The relation of prices to marginal costs in an optimum system. *Econometrica* 7:151–5.

Kahn, R. F. (1935). Some notes on ideal output. *Economic Journal.*

Laffont, J. J. (1996). Industrial policy and politics. *International Journal of Industrial Organization* 14:1–27.

Laffont, J. J., and Tirole, J. (1993). *A Theory of Incentives in Procurement and Regulation.* Cambridge, MA: Massachusetts Institute of Technology Press.

 (1996). Creating competition through interconnection: theory and practice. *Journal of Regulatory Economics* 10:227–56.

Lange, O., and Taylor, F. (1938). *On the Economic Theory of Socialism.* University of Minnesota Press.

Launhardt, W. (1885). *Mathematische Begründung der Volkswirtschaftslehre.* Leipzig: Engelmann.

Lerner, A. (1937). Statics and dynamics in socialist economics. *Economic Journal* 47:253.

McKenzie, L. M. (1951). Ideal output and the interdependence of firms. *Economic Journal* 61:785.

Marshall, A. (1890). *Principles of Economics.* London: Macmillan.
Pigou, A. C. (1952). *The Economics of Welfare*, reprint of the 4th (1932) edition. New York: Macmillan.
Robinson, J. (1934). Mr. Fraser on taxation and returns. *Review of Economic Studies* 1:137–40.
Say, J. B. (1840). *Cours d'Economie Politique*, 7ème partie, ch. 23.
Schumpeter, J. (1954). *History of Economic Analysis.* Oxford University Press.
Smith, A. (1776). *The Wealth of Nations.* Reprinted 1937. New York: Modern Library.
Vickrey, W. (1948). Some objections to marginal-cost princing. *Journal of Political Economy* 56:218–38. Reproduced 1994 in W. Vickrey, *Public Economics*, Cambridge University Press.
  (1955). Revising New York's subway fare structure. *Journal of the Operations Research Society of America* 3:38–69.
  (1987). Marginal- and Average-Cost Pricing. *The New Palgrave*, vol. 3, ed. Eatwell et al., pp. 311–18. New York: Macmillan. Repoduced 1994 in W. Vickrey, *Public Economics*, Cambridge University Press.
Walras, L. (1897). L'Etat et les chemins de fer. *Revue du Droit Public et de la Science Politique*, May-June and July-August. Reprinted 1992 in *August et Leon Walras oeuvres economiques complètes*, vol. 10. Paris: *Economica.*

PART FIVE

ECONOMETRIC METHODS

CHAPTER 10

Scientific Explanation in Econometrics
Bernt P. Stigum

In this essay I shall give a formal account of the meaning of scientific explanations in econometrics. An *explanation* is an answer to a "why" question. It makes clear or intelligible something that is not known or understood by the person asking the question. A *scientific explanation* is an explanation in which the ideas of some scientific theory play an essential role. In econometrics this scientific theory is an economic theory, and the ideas of the theory are used to provide scientific explanations of regularities that econometricians have observed in their data.

There are all sorts of "why" questions, and usually many possible answers to a given question. The questions of interest here concern the occurrence of certain events, such as a sudden sharp drop in prices at the New York Stock Exchange, or the characteristics of observed phenomena (e.g., prolonged periods of severe unemployment in European economies). An answer to the first kind of question might list the causes of the event(s) in question. An answer to the second kind of question might list reasons why the observed phenomena are to be expected.

The form in which the causes of events and the reasons for observed phenomena are listed and used in a scientific explanation will vary among scientists even within a particular discipline. There is, therefore, a need for formal criteria by which we can distinguish between good and bad scientific explanations. These criteria must list the necessary ingredients of a scientific explanation and explicate the ideas of a logically adequate and an empirically adequate scientific explanation.

In this essay I shall give a formal characterization of logically and empirically adequate scientific explanations in econometrics. Both for motivation and for ease of reference, I begin by discussing the useful-

This is an essay that I prepared for the Ragnar Frisch Centennial Symposium in Oslo, March 3–5, 1995. It is based on ideas that I have discussed at length with colleagues in Oslo, Munich, Paris, Oxford, Cambridge, Massachusetts, La Jolla, California, and elsewhere. Special thanks are due to Jon Elster for letting me refer to his unpublished paper "A Plea for Mechanisms." Thanks are also due to two referees and to Alberto Holly and Steinar Strøm for constructive criticisms of an earlier draft of the manuscript.

ness of Carl G. Hempel's deductive-nomological scheme for scientific explanations. Then I present a novel idea concerning the meaning of economic theories, delineate the core structure of theory–data confrontations in economics, and explain what it means to say that a theory is empirically relevant. Finally, I develop my formal account of logically and empirically relevant scientific explanations in econometrics and exemplify it by giving a formal scientific explanation for a phenomenon in financial economics.

1   Formal Characterization of Scientific Explanations

The most influential existing formal characterization of scientific explanations is Carl G. Hempel's *deductive-nomological scheme* (D-N scheme) (Hempel, 1965, pp. 245–51). Hempel insists that a scientific explanation of an event or a phenomenon must have four ingredients: (1) a sentence E that describes the event or the phenomenon in question, (2) a list of sentences $C_1, C_2, \ldots, C_n$ that describe relevant antecedent conditions, (3) a list of general laws $L_1, L_2, \ldots, L_k$, and (4) arguments that demonstrate that E is a logical consequence of the Cs and the Ls. Hempel also insists that such an explanation is *logically adequate* only if at least one L plays an essential part in the demonstration that the *explanandum*, E, is a logical consequence of the *explanans*, the family of Cs and Ls. Moreover, such an explanation is *empirically adequate* only if (i) it is possible, at least in principle, to establish by experiment or observation whether or not the Cs that are used in (4) are satisfied and (ii) the Ls that are used in (4) have been subjected to extensive tests and have passed them all.[1]

Hempel's scheme has attractive features. For example, the Cs and the Ls that explain the occurrence of an event E could have been used to predict the occurrence of E. Also, Hempel and others have used Hempel's scheme to give interesting scientific explanations for events and phenomena in different sciences. Even so, influential philosophers of science have criticized it for many failings and have questioned the possibility of applying it in the social sciences.

One of the failings concerns the logical adequacy of Hempel's scheme. A logically adequate D-N explanation need not explain a thing. For example, a male friend munches pills that women take to avoid having babies. We can use the reputation of the pills to give a logically adequate scientific explanation for why our friend has not had any babies.[2]

Two other failings concern the empirical adequacy of a D-N explanation. First, Hempel's scheme cannot account for the fact that a given

---

[1] Originally, Hempel insisted that the "sentences constituting the explanans must be true" (Hempel, 1965, p. 248).

[2] I have borrowed this example from Bas Van Frassen (1980, p. 106).

"why" question may call for different answers, depending on the context in which it is asked. A valid explanation in one context may be meaningless in another. Just think of pertinent answers to these questions: "Why is Per running?" "Why is the German interest rate rising?" Second, many scientific explanations display vexing asymmetries for which Hempel's scheme cannot account. For example, from the laws of mathematical physics we can deduce that the galaxies are receding from us if and only if the light we receive from them exhibits a shift toward the red end of the spectrum (Van Frassen, 1980, p. 104). Physics and the receding galaxies can explain the red shift. It is difficult to see how physics and the red shift can explain why the galaxies are becoming more distant.

Philosophers question the use of Hempel's scheme in the social sciences because they believe that there are no laws in those sciences. A *law* is a general lawlike statement which insists that individuals or objects of a given kind *must* have certain properties or that individuals or objects of different given kinds *must* be related in a certain way. Also, a general lawlike statement is a law only if it is a logical consequence of an accepted scientific theory and its truth value is independent of place and time. Because there are all sorts of theories in economics, the claim that there are no laws in economics amounts to insisting that there are no theorems in economics whose validity is independent of time and place. That claim cannot be true. To wit: Two of Nassau Senior's fundamental postulates of economics, the first and the last, Gresham's law, and Paul Samuelson's fundamental theorem of consumer choice (cf. B. P. Stigum, 1990, pp. 4, 554, 186) are theorems of economics that many economists believe to be valid irrespective of place and time.

So there are laws in economics, but how prevalent they are is uncertain. Jon Elster believes that economic laws are so rare that economists ought to switch from looking for theorems to looking for what he calls mechanisms. A *mechanism* is a frequently occurring and easily recognizable causal pattern that is triggered under generally unknown conditions. Mechanisms allow us to explain, but not to predict (Elster, 1994, p. 1). Good examples from economics are Kahnemann and Tversky's availability and representativeness heuristics, which people, supposedly, use in uncertain situations to assess likelihoods and make predictions (Kahnemann and Tversky, 1972, pp. 430–54).

E-1.1. We are watching a game of chance in which the probability that a player can win or lose a bet is the same. There are many players, and the game is played many times. We observe that after runs of as much as six wins, about half of the players decrease their bets, and the other half increase their bets. We can use the representativeness heuristics to explain the behavior of the first half, and the availability hypothesis to explain the behavior of the second half. Evidently Kahnemann and Tversky's heuristics cannot be used to predict individual behavior in the given context.[3]

Suppose we were to follow Jon Elster's lead and start looking for mechanisms in economics. Then a question arises: Can we substitute mechanisms for laws in Hempel's scheme and obtain a sound characterization of scientific explanations in economics? The answer depends on our attitude toward the fourth condition of a D-N explanation. If the Cs and the Ls cannot be used to predict the occurrence or being of E, then E cannot be a logical consequence of the same Cs and Ls. Mechanisms cannot be used to predict. Hence we cannot substitute mechanisms for laws in Hempel's scheme unless we change the wording of condition (4) as well.

There are many situations in which the fourth requirement of a D-N explanation seems so strong that rewording is called for. These are, typically, situations in which we are either unable to ascertain the validity of all the Cs or so ignorant about the system under study that we cannot list all the relevant Ls. Good examples from econometrics could include a hypothesis that did not test out and a forecast of economic conditions that failed. For such situations, researchers in artificial intelligence have developed several nonmonotonic logical systems that can be used to justify explanation without prediction. One of these systems is developed in Yoav Shoham's book *Reasoning about Change* (1988). Another system is described in R. Reiter's article "A Logic for Default Reasoning" (1980).

I shall not follow the lead of Reiter and Shoham. Instead, I shall develop my own scheme for scientific explanation. My scheme differs from Hempel's scheme in many ways. My Cs are axioms that delineate properties of a given set of data. Also, my Ls comprise laws and theorems as well as Elster's mechanisms. Finally, my Cs and Ls have many models and allow explanation without prediction. I shall show that my scheme (1) can account for the fact that a given question might call for different answers and (2) can handle some of the vexing asymmetries that have haunted Hempel's scheme.

2   Theory–Data Confrontations in Economics

So much for D-N explanations. In this section I discuss the purport of an economic theory, describe a formal scheme for theory–data confrontations in economics, and explain what it means to say that a theory is relevant in a given empirical context.

---

[3] I have borrowed the idea of the example from Jon Elster, who cited Wagenaar (1988, p. 13) as the original source.

To me, an economic theory is a formal theory concerning some economic situation such as consumer choice of budget or economic growth.

2.1 Formal Theories and Their Models

A *formal theory* is a theory developed by the axiomatic method and consisting of the axioms and all the theorems that can be deduced from them with the help of logical rules of inference. The axioms delineate properties of certain undefined terms that may or may not carry names indicating the interpretations that the originator of the theory intended for them. The theory derived from the axioms is meaningful only if the axioms are consistent in the sense that it is impossible to derive contradictory statements from them. A meaningful theory can be made to talk about many different things simply by giving the undefined terms different interpretations. An interpretation that renders all the axioms true assertions is a *model* of the axioms. The model or, as the case may be, the family of models for which the theory was developed I shall refer to as the *intended interpretation* of the theory.

E-2.1. The following axioms for *choice under uncertainty* concern six *undefined* terms: a universe, an operation, a preference relation, an option, a decision-maker, and a choice function. These terms have the characteristics listed in NM-1–NM-8. In reading the axioms, note that αu is short for $\alpha \cdot u$. Note also that I treat "$\cdot$," "$+$," "$=$," the "$\times$" in $U \times U$, and $[0,1]$ and $(0, 1)$ as *universal* terms. Finally, "$<$" denotes the strict preference relation determined by "$\leqslant$."

NM-1. The *universe* is a system of utilities, U.

NM-2. An *operation* is a function, $f(\cdot)\colon U \times U \mapsto U$, for which there is an $\alpha \in [0, 1]$ such that $f(u, v) = \alpha u + (1 - \alpha)v$ for all $(u, v) \in U \times U$. There is an operation for every $\alpha \in [0, 1]$.

NM-3. A *preference relation* "$\leqslant$" is a complete, reflexive, and transitive ordering of U.

NM-4. If $u, v, w \in U$ and $\alpha \in (0, 1)$, then $u \leqslant v$ if and only if $\alpha u + (1 - \alpha)w \leqslant \alpha v + (1 - \alpha)w$, and $u < v$ implies that $u < \alpha u + (1 - \alpha)v < v$. Also, $u < w < v$ implies that there is an α and a $\beta \in (0, 1)$ such that $\alpha u + (1 - \alpha)v < w$ and $w < \beta u + (1 - \beta)v$.

NM-5. If $u, v \in U$ and $\alpha, \beta \in [0, 1]$, then $\alpha u + (1 - \alpha)v = (1 - \alpha)v + \alpha u$, and $\alpha(\beta u + (1 - \beta)v) + (1 - \alpha)v = \alpha\beta u + (1 - \alpha\beta)v$.

NM-6. An *option* is a member of $\mathcal{P}(U)$, the family of finite subsets of U.

NM-7. A *decision-maker* is a pair $(\leqslant, A)$, where "$\leqslant$" is a preference relation and A is an option.

NM-8. A *choice function* is a function $\mathbb{C}(\cdot)\colon \mathscr{P}(U) \mapsto U$ such that if $A \in \mathscr{P}(U)$ and $v = \mathbb{C}(A)$, $v \geqslant u$ for all $u \in A$.

Axioms NM-1–NM-5 are due to John von Neumann and Oscar Morgenstern. The axioms are called axioms of expected utility, for the reasons listed in Theorem T-1. Von Neumann and Morgenstern gave a proof of T-1 (von Neumann and Morgenstern, 1953, pp. 617–28).

T-1. Suppose that NM-1–NM-5 are valid, and let R denote the set of real numbers. Then there exists a real-valued function $V(\cdot)\colon U \mapsto R$ that satisfies the following conditions: If $u, v \in U$ and $\alpha \in [0, 1]$, $u < v$ if and only if $V(u) < V(v)$, and $V(\alpha u + (1 - \alpha)v) = \alpha V(u) + (1 - \alpha)V(v)$. The function $V(\cdot)$ is uniquely determined up to a positive linear transformation.

I have formulated Axioms NM-1–NM-5 in E-2.1 so that they both accord with the original formulation of these axioms (von Neumann and Morgenstern, 1953, p. 16) and can serve the purposes that I have in mind for them.[4] In current mathematical jargon, Axioms NM-1, NM-2, and NM-5 insist that the universe of utilities with its operations is a mixture space. Also, Axioms NM-3 and NM-4 claim that the universe is endowed with a complete weak-order preference relation that is vNM-independent and Jensen-continuous.

A system of axioms that has a model is consistent. Axioms NM-1–NM-8 have many models. I describe some of them in E-2.2:

E-2.2. We are to describe a family of models of NM-1–NM-8 and begin with the models of NM-1–NM-5: Let $X = \{x_1, \ldots, x_n\}$, and let U denote the set of all probability measures on X. Then $u \in U$ if and only if u is a function, $u(\cdot)\colon X \mapsto [0, 1]$, that satisfies the condition $u(x_1) + \cdots + u(x_n) = 1$. Next, let $R_+ = [0, \infty)$, and let $W(\cdot)\colon X \mapsto R_+$ and $V(\cdot)\colon U \mapsto R_+$ be functions that satisfy this condition: For all $u \in U$, $V(u) = W(x_1)u(x_1) + \cdots + W(x_n)u(x_n)$. Finally, let "$\leqslant$" be a complete, reflexive, and transitive ordering of U that satisfies the following condition: For all $u, v \in U$, $u \leqslant v$ if and only if $V(u) \leq V(v)$. The given U and "$\leqslant$" and the operations on $U \times U$ satisfy NM-1–NM-5. By varying X and $W(\cdot)$, we obtain a family of models of NM-1–NM-5.

We can use the family of models of NM-1–NM-5 to obtain a family of models of NM-1–NM-8 as follows: For each pair $(X, W(\cdot))$ we let a decision-maker be an individual who orders probability distributions on X in accordance with the "$\leqslant$" determined by X and $W(\cdot)$. Also, we insist that this decision-maker, when

---

[4] I have stated the axioms in terms of "$\leqslant$" rather than "$<$." Also, I have added Paul Samuelson's independence condition [$u \leqslant v$ if and only if $\alpha u + (1 - \alpha)w \leqslant \alpha v + (1 - \alpha)w$ for all $\alpha \in (0, 1)$ and $w \in U$] to the original axioms.

faced with an option A, always chooses a probability distribution in A that is maximal in A with respect to "≤." Finally, we let the choice function be a function that records the probability distributions that the individual would choose in the various options in $\mathcal{P}(U)$. By varying X and $W(\cdot)$, we obtain the sought-for family of models of NM-1–NM-8.

I do not know the original intended interpretation of NM-1–NM-8. However, for the purposes of this essay we can think of the family of models delineated in E-2.2 as the intended interpretation of the axioms. In that interpretation the preference order is the preference order of some individual (e.g., a consumer or a bank director). Also, the probability distributions on X are taken to be gambles of various sorts that the same individual might face. Finally, the probabilities of the outcomes of these gambles are the probabilities that the given individual assigns to these outcomes. We presume that if the individual were to choose one gamble from a finite subset of possible gambles, he would always choose a gamble that his preferences ranked the highest.

The universe of an interpretation of a system of axioms is a set of abstract objects. For example, the set of real numbers R is a set of abstract somethings that satisfy a finite set of axioms, such as the eight axioms for the real number system listed by Graves (1956, p. 33). And if the real numbers are abstract objects, then the members of the universes in the models of NM-1–NM-8 (including the consumer and the bank director!) must also be abstract objects. In this essay we shall think of the universe in a model of an axiomatized economic theory as a set of toys in a toy economy. We do not know what these toys look like, but we know that they have the properties that the axioms ascribe to them.

2.2 *The Import of an Economic Theory*

Because the characteristics of toys in a toy economy are rather uninteresting, I must describe, next, what I take to be the import of an economic theory. I begin by saying what I mean by a positive analogy. An *analogy* is a process of reasoning in which objects or events that are similar in one respect are judged to resemble each other in certain other respects as well. A *positive analogy* for a group of individuals $\mathcal{E}$ is a propositional function satisfied by all the individuals in $\mathcal{E}$. A *negative analogy* for $\mathcal{E}$ is a propositional function satisfied by some but not all individuals in $\mathcal{E}$.[5]

My way of looking at an economic theory of some economic situation (e.g., an act or an event or a historical development) is that *the intended interpretation of the theory delineates the positive analogies that the originator of the theory considered sufficient to describe the situation*. Con-

---

[5] I have learned of positive and negative analogies from John M. Keynes (1921, p. 223).

sider, for example, the individual in the intended interpretation of NM-1–NM-8 (i.e., in E-2.2). He orders gambles according to their expected utility. Also, when called upon to choose among gambles in a given option, he always chooses one that has the highest expected utility. To me, that is an *accurate* description of individual behavior in the intended universe of NM-1–NM-8. It provides also a succinct description of a *characteristic feature* of choice under uncertainty in the real world.

My characterization of the meaning of economic theories calls for several remarks. First, the sentences of the intended interpretation of an economic theory are not lawlike statements about matters of fact in the real world. Instead, they are valid assertions concerning matters of fact in a toy economy. Only by confronting the theory with data can we discover where and when the positive analogies that the theory identifies are characteristic features of events and phenomena in the real world.

Second, the characteristic features of a toy economy that an interpreted theory describes are not to be identified with Jon Elster's mechanisms. The characteristic features of events and phenomena in the real world that the originator of a theory has in mind when developing that theory are positive analogies of the events and phenomena in question. In contrast, mechanisms are interesting negative analogies of such events and phenomena. To wit, Elster's own example: "Perhaps for every child who becomes alcoholic in response to an alcoholic environment, another eschews alcohol in response to the same environment" (Vaillant, 1983, p. 65). Here the mechanisms involved are "doing what your parents do and doing the opposite of what they do" (Elster, 1994, p. 1).

Third, my characterization of the import of an economic theory takes exception to two standard conceptions of economic theories. This is exemplified in my view of the intended interpretation of NM-1–NM-8: Expected-utility maximization is a positive analogy of individual behavior under uncertainty. If that is so, it is *wrong* to interpret the theory that we deduce from NM-1–NM-8 as saying that an individual under uncertainty *behaves as if* he were maximizing expected utility. I agree that it is true that an accurate description of the behavior of a given individual would exhibit many negative analogies of individual behavior under uncertainty. Still, I insist that it is *incorrect* to say that the positive analogies that the intended interpretation of NM-1–NM-8 identifies provide an *approximate* description of individual behavior under uncertainty.

2.3   The Core Structure of a Theory–Data Confrontation

The positive analogies of an event or some phenomena that an interpreted economic theory identifies need not have any empirical relevance. To ascertain that the given positive analogies are empirically relevant, we must confront the theory with data. Such theory–data confrontations arise in different contexts and for varied reasons. However, formally speaking, all have the same core structure: two disjoint universes for theory and data, a bridge between the universes, and a sample population.

Let T be an economic theory, and let IT be an interpretation of T. The theory universe for IT is a pair, (Ω_T, Γ_t). Here Ω_T denotes a set of vectors ω_T in a real vector space. The components of ω_T denote so many units of the objects about which IT talks, and Γ_t comprises the family of axioms of IT.

Let T and IT be as before. The data universe for our empirical analysis of IT is a pair, (Ω_P, Γ_p), where Ω_P is a set of vectors ω_P in a real vector space, and Γ_p comprises axioms that delineate the salient characteristics of the components of ω_P. The components of ω_P denote so many units of the individuals that we have observed and the data that we have created with them. Who these individuals are will depend on IT and the original purpose for which they were observed. We use them to create data for the theory–data confrontation. The makeup of the data will depend on IT and the design of our empirical analysis.

Again, let T and IT be as before. The bridge between the theory universe of IT and the corresponding data universe comprises a finite set of assertions. Formally speaking, these bridge principles constitute a family of axioms $\Gamma_{t,p}$ concerning pairs of vectors (ω_T, ω_P) in a subset Ω of $\Omega_T \times \Omega_P$. The members of $\Gamma_{t,p}$ delineate the way in which the components of ω_T are related to the components of ω_P. These relations reflect our own views of the relationships between the variables of IT and our observations. Our views need not be correct. Hence in any empirical analysis of the relevance of IT, the members of $\Gamma_{t,p}$ are as much under scrutiny as are the members of Γ_t and Γ_p.

Finally, the sample population S: In a data confrontation of an economic theory, S is usually a finite set or a denumerably infinite set. Each member of S denotes, say, a firm or a consumer or historical data whose characteristics are of interest. I imagine that we are sampling individuals in S. With each point $s \in S$ we associate a pair of vectors $(\omega_{Ts}, \omega_{Ps}) \in \Omega$. I denote this pair by $\Psi(s)$ and insist that $\Psi(s)$ is the value at s of a function $\Psi(\cdot): S \mapsto \Omega$. I also imagine that there is a probability measure $Q(\cdot)$ on a σ-field of subsets of S, $\mathcal{F}_S$, that determines the probability of our observing an s in the various members of $\mathcal{F}_S$. The properties of $Q(\cdot)$ are determined by $\Psi(\cdot)$ and a probability measure $P(\cdot)$ that assigns probabilities to subsets of Ω. Specifically, there is a σ-field of subsets of Ω, $\mathcal{F}$ and a probability measure, $P(\cdot): \mathcal{F} \mapsto [0, 1]$, such that $\mathcal{F}_S$ is the inverse image of $\mathcal{F}$ under $\Psi(\cdot)$ and such that for all $B \in \mathcal{F}$

$$Q(\Psi^{-1}(B)) = P(B \cap \text{range}(\Psi))/P(\text{range}(\Psi))$$

where $\text{range}(\Psi) = \{\omega = \Omega: \omega \in \Psi(s) \text{ for some } s \in S\}$. Finally, I imagine that we obtain a sample of $\mathbb{N}$ observations from S, $s_1, \ldots, s_N$, in accordance with a sampling scheme $\mathcal{B}$. $P(\cdot)$ and $\mathcal{B}$ determine a probability distribution on subsets of Ω^N. The marginal distribution of the components of ω_P determined by $P(\cdot)$ I shall denote by MPD. The marginal distribution of the sequence of ω_{P_s}s determined by $P(\cdot)$ and $\mathfrak{Z}$ I shall refer to as the data-generating process and denote by DGP.

The sample population does not figure in my following formal account of scientific explanations. However it will play an essential role when we set out to establish the empirical adequacy of a given scientific explanation. I shall have more to say about that in the last part of this chapter.

2.4 The Empirical Relevance of the Intended Interpretation of an Economic Theory

With this formal characterization of the core structure of a theory–data confrontation in hand, I can explicate what it means to say that a theory is "relevant in a given empirical context." I begin with the empirical context. The core structure of a theory–data confrontation is an axiomatic system that has many models. The intended interpretation of (Ω_P, Γ_p) and the sentences that characterize the properties of the MPD delineate the *empirical context* of the system. This empirical context varies with the intended interpretation of the data universe and the MPD.

Next, the relevance of an interpreted theory: Let T, IT, and the core structure of a data confrontation of IT be as described earlier. Also, let IM denote the intended interpretation of the data universe and the MPD. Finally, let $\mathfrak{I}$ denote the family of all sentences about individuals in the data universe and about parameters of the MPD that are logical consequences of Γ_t, Γ_p, $\Gamma_{t,p}$, and the axioms that determine the characteristics of $P(\cdot)$. Then IT is *relevant* in the empirical context that IM delineates if and only if all the members of IM are models of $\mathfrak{I}$.

The relevance criterion on which I insist is strong. So two sober remarks are called for. First, in a given situation we might not be able to check whether or not a member of IM is a model of *all* the sentences in $\mathfrak{I}$. Even when, in principle, we could check them all, we might not have the time and the resources to do it. And if we had the time and the resources, we might find that many of the checks would be inconclusive. They likely would be inconclusive for most "for all" sentences, and chances are that they also would be unconvincing for all sentences concerning parameters of the MPD and the DGP. Certainly an econometrician would be hard put to find an empirical context in which it would be possible to *establish* the relevance of a given IT. In econometrics, the best we can hope for are good statistical grounds for accepting or rejecting the relevance of an interpreted economic theory.

Second, one aspect of my characterization of "relevance in an empirical context" ought not go unnoticed. The family of sentences $\mathfrak{I}$ comprises *all* the sentences on whose validity the relevance of *IT* in the given empirical context depends. Note, therefore, that this family varies with $\Gamma_{t,p}$ and the axioms that determine the properties of $P(\cdot)$. Also, for a given pair $\Gamma_{t,p}$ and $P(\cdot)$, $\Im$ need not contain all the sentences about the data universe and the MPD that are valid in *IM*. This is so because a finite set of axioms, such as Γ_t, $\Gamma_{t,p}$, Γ_p, and the axioms for $P(\cdot)$, might not suffice to give a complete characterization of a given empirical context.

3 Scientific Explanation in Economics and Econometrics

In the case of scientific explanations, the theory–data confrontation consists in finding theoretical explanations for observed characteristics of individuals in a given data universe. This is a complex topic, and so I shall discuss it in stages, beginning with the simplest case.

3.1 *Scientific Explanation: I*

In this section I shall present a formal characterization of scientific explanation in economics for situations in which there is no sample population S, no probability measure $P(\cdot)$ on subsets of Ω, and just one model in the intended interpretation of Γ_p. The situations I have in mind are analogues of the kind of situation for which Hempel developed his D-N scheme (i.e., a situation in which the explanation can be based on physical or economic theories of deterministic character) (Hempel, 1965, p. 351). It is therefore interesting that my characterization of scientific explanations, with the proper translation, can be made to fit Hempel's scheme.

We have observed certain regularities in a set of data, and we search for a scientific explanation for these regularities. Formally, our search can be described as follows:

SE-1.   Let (Ω_P, Γ_p) be some given data universe. Assume that the components of the vectors in Ω_P denote so many units of objects that we have observed and that Γ_p delineates the salient properties of our data. Also, let H be a finite family of assertions concerning Ω_P, and suppose that there is a model of Γ_p, M, in which all the assertions of H are true. We take M to be the intended model of the data universe and assume that H delineates the characteristics of our data that we want to explain. Then to give a scientific explanation of H means to find a theory universe (Ω_T, Γ_t) and a collection of bridge principles $\Gamma_{t,p}$ that link Ω_T with Ω_P such that in the given empirical context H becomes a logical consequence of Γ_t, Γ_p, and $\Gamma_{t,p}$.

Such an explanation is *logically adequate* if H is not a logical consequence of Γ_p alone. It is *empirically adequate* if M is a model of all the logical consequences of Γ_t, $\Gamma_{t,p}$, and Γ_p that concern the components of ω_P.

I have given a detailed example of a scientific explanation in the sense of SE-1 elsewhere (B. P. Stigum, 1995, pp. 595–7). Therefore, to save space, here I shall discuss only how SE-1 relates to Hempel's idea of a scientific explanation. For that purpose I note first that Hempel's Cs, Ls, and E concern individuals in one and the same universe. This universe is in SE-1, my data universe. Next, I note that in SE-1 the members of Γ_p play the roles of Hempel's Cs. Also, when the vectors in Ω_T are translated by $\Gamma_{t,p}$, the members of Γ_t play, in SE-1, the roles of Hempel's Ls. Finally, in SE-1, H has taken the place of Hempel's E. Hence, with the proper translation, SE-1 can be made to fit Hempel's D-N scheme.

My claim that a scientific explanation in the sense of SE-1 can be made to fit Hempel's D-N scheme must not be misunderstood. There is a fundamental difference between SE-1 and Hempel's scheme. To wit: Hempel insists that his Ls be laws (i.e., lawlike assertions that are valid independently of place and time). With such Ls in a scientific explanation he can also insist that the Cs and the Ls give a valid explanation of E only if the occurrence of E could have been predicted from the occurrences of the Cs (Hempel, 1965, pp. 364–76). In contrast, the Ls in SE-1 need not be laws. They can be economic theories. They can also be mechanisms, in the sense given to this term by Elster. This is so because in SE-1 we ask for an explanation of an explanandum, H, in only *one* empirical context. Whether or not the explanans we end up with could have been used to predict the occurrence of H is irrelevant. Also, in *another* empirical context H might not be valid.

The differences in the interpretations of the Ls in Hempel's scheme and the Ls in SE-1 are reflected in my criteria for an explanation to be empirically adequate. Hempel insists that the Ls must have been subjected to extensive tests and have passed them all. I insist only that the *IT* of the theory universe be relevant in the given (!) empirical context in which the explanation is formulated.

My views on the empirical adequacy of a scientific explanation differ from Hempel's ideas. However, they cannot be too different from the views of other leading philosophers of science. The following two observations by Stephen Toulmin and Bas Van Frassen bear witness to that: (i) A law of nature is not an assertion that has a truth value. It is a statement that comes with a list of situations in which it has proved possible to apply it (Toulmin, 1953, pp. 86–7). (ii) We apply theories selectively in scientific explanations. For example, we say that Newton's theory can be used to explain the tides, even though we know that Newton's laws do not satisfy Hempel's criteria for empirical adequacy. Whether or not a theory explains some fact or other is independent of whether or not the real world, as a whole, fits that theory (Van Frassen, 1980, p. 98).

Finally, it is interesting to see how my SE-1 can account for the fact that a given question might call for different answers depending on the circumstances in which it is asked. In SE-1 both the question and the empirical context are given in advance. Without changing H, I can vary the context by varying Γ_p and/or M. Such changes may call for a different scientific explanation of H. Certainly a change in M might require changes in the members of $\Gamma_{t,p}$. There are many other possibilities.

Often vexing asymmetries in scientific explanations can also be eliminated by changing the contexts in which the explanations are given. For example, suppose that the height of a flagpole is recorded by a C, say C_1, in a D-N explanation of the length of the flagpole's shadow. If the length of the shadow has a purpose, we may use the length of the shadow instead of C_1 and insist that the given explanation with the new C provides a D-N explanation of the height of the flagpole.

3.2 Scientific Explanation: II

The situation envisaged in SE-1 is similar to the experimental tests of physical theories that Pierre Duhem described in his book *The Aim and Structure of Physical Theory* (1954, pp. 144–7). It differs, however, from the situations that econometricians usually face when they search for the empirical relevance of economic theories. In SE-1, H is a family of sentences, each one of which has a truth value in every model of (Ω_P, Γ_p), and all of which are true in some model of (Ω_P, Γ_p). In enconometrics, H is often a family of statistical relations. For example, one H might insist that "on the average, families with high incomes save greater proportions of their incomes than families with low incomes." Another H might claim that "the prices of soybean oil and cottonseed oil vary over time as if they were two cointegrated ARIMA processes." When H is a family of statistical relations, a scientific explanation of H must be based on statistical arguments. Such scientific explanations can be characterized as in SE-2:

SE-2. Let (Ω_P, Γ_p) be some given data universe, let $\mathscr{F}_P$ be a σ-field of subsets of Ω_P, let $P_p(\cdot)$: $\mathscr{F}_P \mapsto [0, 1]$ be a probability measure, and let FP denote the joint probability distribution of the components of the vectors in Ω_P that is determined by $P_p(\cdot)$. Also, let H be a finite family of assertions concerning the characteristics of FP. Finally, let $\mathcal{B}$ be a family of models of H, (Ω_P, Γ_p), and the axioms of $P_p(\cdot)$, and suppose that $\mathcal{B}$ is the intended interpretation of H and the data universe. Then, to give a scientific explanation of H means to find a theory universe, (Ω_T, Γ_t), a finite set of bridge principles $\Gamma_{t,p}$, and a probability measure $P(\cdot)$ on subsets of $\Omega_T \times \Omega_P$ such that in the given empirical context H becomes a logical consequence of Γ_t, $\Gamma_{t,p}$, Γ_p, and the axioms of $P(\cdot)$.

Such an explanation is *logically adequate* if H is not a logical consequence of Γ_p and the axioms of $P_p(\cdot)$. The explanation is *empirically adequate* if for all $M \in \mathfrak{B}$, M is a model of all the consequences of Γ_t, $\Gamma_{t,p}$, Γ_p, and the axioms of $P(\cdot)$ that concern properties of FP and the components of the vectors in Ω_P.

It is difficult to give logically and empirically adequate SE-2 explanations of regularities in the kind of data I have in mind for SE-2. So a detailed example is called for. I shall give an SE-2 explanation of regularities in the behavior over time of Treasury-bill yields in the U.S. money market that Hall, Anderson, and Granger (HAG) discovered (Hall, Anderson, and Granger, 1991).

3.3 Treasury Bills and the U.S. Money Market

Roughly speaking, we can think of the relevant part of the U.S. money market as a market in which sellers and buyers meet to determine yields on 21 different securities, 11 pure discount bonds that mature in j months ($j = 1, 2, \ldots, 11$) and 10 one-month pure discount bonds that are to be contracted "now" for purchase $j - 1$ months hence ($j = 2, 3, \ldots, 11$). The market opens every day. Each day the number of participants is large, and no one individual (other than the Treasury) can by his or her own actions influence the level of prices in the market. The market participants manage through bids and offers to determine the day's equilibrium yields on the various securities.

The equilibrium yields on the 21 securities are related. Let $K(j, t)$ be the equilibrium yield at day t of a j-month pure discount bond. Also, let $G(j, t)$ be the equilibrium rate of return from contracting at day t to buy a one-month pure discount bond $j - 1$ months from day t. Then, according to theory, the $K(j, t)$ and the $G(j, t)$ must satisfy equation (1):

$$K(j,t) = (1/j)\sum_{i=1}^{j} G(i,t), \qquad j = 1, 2, \ldots, 11 \tag{1}$$

In studying the behavior over time of the $K(j, t)$, HAG discovered that the yields on Treasury bills moved as if they were realizations of cointegrated $I(1)$ processes. They also observed that the cointegrating vectors for the vector-valued process $K(1, t), \ldots, K(11, t)$ were $(-1, 1, 0, \ldots, 0)$, $\ldots, (-1, 0, \ldots, 1)$. I shall refer to this discovery as the HAG dictum and give a formal scientific explanation of the dictum in Sections 3.4–3.7.

The Treasury-bill market is part of the money market in the United States. The yields in the money market are interrelated. Consequently, when we delineate the relevant positive analogies for the functioning of the Treasury-bill market, we must take into account how the functioning of the remainder of the money market influences the determination of yields in the bill market.

There are many different money-market instruments, even when we

Scientific Explanation in Econometrics 359

distinguish them just by name of issuer and kind of issue (e.g., Treasury versus General Electric, and three-month bills versus six-month bills). There are fabulously many more when we distinguish instruments by maturity as well. For the purposes of this essay it is not necessary to take into account this multiplicity of money-market instruments. So to keep my arguments clear and simple, I shall argue as if there were just two bills and just one other money-market instrument. In due course I shall show that my arguments' gain in clarity will not come at the expense of a reader's loss in insight.

To provide a formal scientific explanation of HAG's dictum, I begin in Section 3.4 by giving an axiomatic characterization of HAG's data universe. In Sections 3.5–3.7 I will describe a pertinent theory universe and formulate bridge principles and probability axioms. At the end I shall assemble all the pieces and build the required explanation.

3.4 HAG's Dictum and the Data Universe

The individuals in HAG's data universe are series of daily bid and asked quotes on 11 Treasury bills: one series for bills with 1 month to maturity, another for bills with 2 months to maturity, and so on to a series with 11 months to maturity. From these series we obtain 11 nominal yield-to-maturity series, $K(j), j = 1, \ldots, 11$, by taking the average bid and asked quotes of the day as the prices of the respective bills and by insisting that the length of a month be 30.4 days.

HAG's sample consisted of 228 observations on each yield series, dating from January 1970 until December 1988. Each observed yield pertained to the last trading day of the month and was taken from the Fama Twelve Month Treasury Bill Term Structure File of the Center for Research in Securities Prices at the University of Chicago.

For the sake of brevity I shall take the yield series, instead of the bid and asked quotes, to be the basic elements of the data universe Ω_P. Also, for the sake of clarity and simplicity, I shall assume that we have observations only on bills of two different maturities (e.g., three- and six-month bills or bills that will mature in one and two months). Since we have monthly observations, I shall take $\hat{K}(1)$ and $\hat{K}(2)$ to denote series of yields of bills that, respectively, mature in one and two months.

With these implicit assumptions in mind, I need only three axioms to characterize the individuals in Ω_P. In the intended interpretation of the axioms the $\hat{y}(j), j = 1, 2$, are auxiliary series that we need to delineate the properties of our data. Also, the numbers in N are taken to denote consecutive "months" beginning at some arbitrary point in time.

D-1. $\omega_P \in \Omega_P$ only if $\omega_p = (\hat{K}(1), \hat{K}(2), \hat{y}(1), \hat{y}(2))$, where $\hat{K}(j) \in (R_+)^N$, $\hat{y}(j) \in (R)^N, j = 1, 2$, and $N = \{0, 1, 2, \ldots\}$.

D-2. For each $\omega_P \in \Omega_P$ and all $t \in N$,

$$\hat{K}(1)_t = \max[\hat{y}(1)_t, 0] \quad \text{and} \quad \hat{K}(2)_t = \max[\hat{y}(2)_t, 0] \qquad (2)$$

where $\hat{K}(1)_t$, $\hat{y}(1)_t$, $\hat{K}(2)_t$, and $\hat{y}(2)_t$ denote the tth components of $\hat{K}(1)$, $\hat{y}(1)$, $\hat{K}(2)$, and $\hat{y}(2)$.

Instead of thinking of ω_P as a quadruple of series, we can think of ω_P in Ω_P as a vector-valued function $(\hat{K}(\cdot, \omega_P), \hat{y}(\cdot, \omega_P)): N \mapsto R_+^2 \times R^2$ defined by equation (3):

$$(\hat{K}(t, \omega_P), \hat{y}(t, \omega_P)) = \omega_{Pt}, \quad t \in N \quad \text{and} \quad \omega_P \in \Omega_P \qquad (3)$$

where ω_{Pt} is the tth component of ω_P. If we think of ω_P in that way, the third axiom concerning the individuals in Ω_P can be stated as follows:

D-3. Let Ω_P be as before, and let the vector-valued function $(\hat{K}, \hat{y})(\cdot)$: $N \times \Omega_P \mapsto R_+^2 \times R^2$ be as described in equation (3). Also, let $\mathscr{F}_P$ be the standard Borel field of subsets of Ω_P. Then there exists a probability measure $P_p(\cdot): \mathscr{F}_P \mapsto [0, 1]$ such that, relative to $P_p(\cdot)$, the probability distributions of the family of random vectors $\{(\hat{K}, \hat{y})(t, \omega_P); t \in N\}$ equal the probability distributions of the random process that generates the individuals in Ω_P.

With Axioms D-1–D-3 in hand, I proceed to formulate the assertion of which I intend to give a scientific explanation.

H. Let $P_p(\cdot): \mathscr{F}_P \mapsto [0, 1]$ be the probability measure on whose existence we insisted in D-3. Also, let the vector-valued function $(\hat{K}, \hat{y})(\cdot): N \times \Omega_P \mapsto R_+^2 \times R^2$ be as described in equation (3). Then, relative to $P_p(\cdot)$, the family of random vectors $\{(\hat{K}, \hat{y})(t, \omega_P); t \in N\}$ satisfies the following conditions:
  (i) For all $t \in N$, $\hat{K}(t, \omega_P) = \max[\hat{y}(t, \omega_P), 0]$, a.e.
  (ii) $\{\hat{y}(t, \omega_P); t \in N\}$ is a vector-valued ARIMA process with one unit root.
  (iii) The components of $\{\hat{y}(t, \omega_P): t \in N\}$ are cointegrated with cointegrating vector $(-1, 1)$; that is, $\{\hat{y}_2(t, \omega_P) - \hat{y}_1(t, \omega_P); t \in N\}$ is a wide-sense stationary process.

The statement H does not sound quite like HAG's dictum. However, if we interpret HAG's assertions with their footnote 5 in mind, we must end up with H as stated. In footnote 5, HAG insist that yields to maturity cannot be integrated processes in the strict sense, because nominal yields are bounded below at zero, whereas integrated processes are unbounded.

3.5 A Theory Universe for the Scientific Explanation of HAG's Dictum

Next I shall describe the theory universe in my scientific explanation of H. For that purpose I need six axioms. In the statement of the axioms, with $j = 1, 2$, the $K(j)$ and $G(j)$ are to be interpreted as the theory universe's series versions of the $K(j, t)$ and $G(j, t)$ that I discussed in my description of the Treasury-bills market. Also, $\eta(j)$ and $u(j)$ are series of error terms, and r is the series of yields to maturity of the one and only non-Treasury-bill security in the money market. Finally, $N = \{0, 1, 2, \ldots\}$ and $\lambda(1), \lambda(2), \Lambda, y(1), y(2),$ and $y(3)$ are series whose meanings are determined by the axioms. The members of N are taken to denote consecutive "months" beginning at some arbitrary point in time.

B-1. $\omega_T \in \Omega_T$ only if $\omega_T \in (R^{15})^N$, and
$$\omega_T = (K(1), K(2), G(1), G(2), r, \lambda(1), \lambda(2), \Lambda, \eta(1), \eta(2), y(1), y(2), y(3), u(1), u(2)).$$

B-2. For each $\omega_T \in \Omega_T$ and $t \in N$,
$$K(1)_t = \max[y(1)_t, 0] \quad \text{and} \quad G(1)_t = K(1)_t \tag{4}$$
$$y(2)_t = \frac{1}{2}[y(1)_t + G(2)_t] \tag{5}$$
$$K(2)_t = \max[y(2)_t, G(2)_t, 0] \tag{6}$$
where $K(j)_t, G(j)_t,$ and $y(j)_t$, respectively, denote the tth components of $K(j), G(j),$ and $y(j), j = 1, 2$.

B-3. For each $\omega_T \in \Omega_T$ and $t \geq 1$,
$$G(2)_0 = \lambda(1)_0, \quad \Lambda_0 = 0, \quad \text{and} \quad G(2)_t = \lambda(1)_t + \Lambda_t \tag{7}$$
where $G(2)_t, \lambda(1)_t,$ and Λ_t, respectively, denote the tth components of $G(2), \lambda(1),$ and Λ.

B-4. For each $\omega_T \in \Omega_T$ and $t \in N$,
$$y(1)_{t+1} = \lambda(1)_t + \eta(1)_{t+1} \tag{8}$$
$$y(3)_{t+1} = \lambda(2)_t + \eta(2)_{t+1} \tag{9}$$
Also, $\eta(1)_0 = 0, \eta(2)_0 = 0$, and there exists a positive pair (y_1, y_3) such that $y(1)_0 = y_1$ and $y(3)_0 = y_3$.

B-5. For each $\omega_T \in \Omega_T$ and all $t \in N$,
$$r_t = \max[y(3)_t, 0] \tag{10}$$

B-6. Let $\lambda = (\lambda(1), \lambda(2))$. There exists a strictly positive 2×2 matrix $\varphi = (\varphi_{ij})$, with largest eigenvalue less than 1, such that for each $\omega_T \in \Omega_T$,
$$\begin{aligned} \lambda'_0 &= \varphi(y(1)_0, y(3)_0)' \\ \lambda'_t - \lambda'_{t-1} &= \varphi((y(1)_t, y(3)_t)' - \lambda'_{t-1}), \quad t \geq 1 \end{aligned} \tag{11}$$

In my scientific explanation of H, the preceding axioms are taken to delineate important positive analogies of the behavior over time of equilibrium yields in the U.S. money market. Some of them (e.g., B-2) describe relationships between different yields that must hold because of the possibilities for arbitrage in the market. Others (e.g., B-4 and B-6) describe essential features of the dynamics of the money market. The following discussion will attest to that.

Axioms B-2–B-6 have logical consequences that are interesting to us. We intend the λ_t of B-6 to represent the theoretical money market's prediction of the most likely value of $(K(1)_{t+1}, r_{t+1})$ conditional upon the observed values of $(K(1)_s, r_s), s = 0, 1, \ldots, t$. That such an interpretation of λ_t is a possibility can be inferred from B-2, B-4, B-5, and Theorem T-1. The latter is a simple logical consequence of B-6.

T-1. Let I be the 2×2 identity matrix. There exists a strictly positive 2×2 matrix $\varphi = (\varphi_{ij})$, with largest eigenvalue less than 1, such that for each $\omega_T \in \Omega_T$ and all $t \in N$,

$$\lambda'_t = \sum_{s=0}^{t} (I - \varphi)^s \varphi(y(1)_{t-s}, y(3)_{t-s})' \qquad (12)$$

HAG claimed that the behavior over time of the yield to maturity on a Treasury bill resembles the behavior of an $I(1)$ process. The possibility of such an interpretation of the pair $(K(1), r)$ and $K(2)$ can be gathered from B-2 and the following three theorems.

T-2. Let φ be the 2×2 matrix of T-1, and let $\eta = (\eta(1), \eta(2))'$. Then, for each $\omega_T \in \Omega_T$,

$$(y(1)_1, y(3)_1)' = \varphi(y(1)_0, y(3)_0)' + \eta_1$$
$$(y(1)_{t+1}, y(3)_{t+1})' = (y(1)_t, y(3)_t)' + \eta_{t+1} - (I - \varphi)\eta_t, \qquad (13)$$
$$t \geq 1$$

T-3. Let φ be the 2×2 matrix of T-1, and let $\xi \in R$ be defined by equations (14):

$$\xi_0 = 0$$
$$\xi_1 = \tfrac{1}{2}[(1 + \varphi_{11})\eta(1)_1 - (1 - \varphi_{11})y(1)_0$$
$$\qquad + \varphi_{12} y(3)_0 + \varphi_{12}\eta(2)_1 + \Lambda_1] \qquad (14)$$
$$\xi_t = \tfrac{1}{2}[(\eta(1)_t - \eta(1)_{t-1}) + \varphi_{11}(\eta(1)_t + \eta(1)_{t-1})$$
$$\qquad + \varphi_{12}(\eta(2)_t + \eta(2)_{t-1}) + \Lambda_t - \Lambda_{t-1}], \qquad y \geq 2$$

Then for each $\omega_T \in \Omega_T$,

$$y(2)_0 = \tfrac{1}{2}[(1 + \varphi_{11})y(1)_0 + \varphi_{12} y(3)_0]$$
$$y(2)_t = y(2)_{t-1} + \xi_t, \qquad t \geq 1 \qquad (15)$$

Scientific Explanation in Econometrics 363

T-4. For each $\omega_T \in \Omega_T$ and all $t \in N$,

$$K(2)_t = \max\{\tfrac{1}{2}[G(1)_t + G(2)_t], 0\} \qquad (16)$$

Finally, HAG insisted that the yields to maturity of Treasury bills are cointegrated and that the spreads between yields of different maturity define the cointegrating vectors. The next theorem establishes the possibility of HAG's dictum being correct in the theory universe. There, yields to maturity on "Treasury bills" might be realizations of cointegrated $I(1)$ processes, and the spread between them might determine their cointegrating relationship.

T-5. Let φ be the 2×2 matrix of T-1. Then for each $\omega_T \in \Omega_T$,

$$y(2)_0 - y(1)_0 = \tfrac{1}{2}[\Lambda_0 + y(1)_1 - y(1)_0 - \eta(1)_1]$$
$$y(2)_t - y(1)_t = \tfrac{1}{2}[\Lambda_t - (1 - \varphi_{11})\eta(1)_t + \varphi_{12}\eta(2)_t], \qquad (17)$$
$$t \geq 1$$

Cointegrated processes have common trends. Looking at the common trend of $y(1)$ and $y(2)$ will provide us with new insight into the dynamics of the theory universe's money market. For that purpose, let

$$CT(R_t) = (\varphi_{11}, \varphi_{12})\left[(y_1, y_3)' + \sum_{s=0}^{t-1} \eta_{t-1-s}\right]$$

Then it follows easily from equations (13), (8), and (7) that

$$y(1)_t = CT(R_t) + \eta(1)_t$$
$$G(2)_t = CT(R_t) + \Lambda_t + (\varphi_{11}, \varphi_{12})\eta_t$$

But if that is so, then the equilibrium condition in equation (5) implies that

$$y(2)_t = CT(R_t) + \tfrac{1}{2}[\Lambda_t + \eta(1)_t + (\varphi_{11}, \varphi_{12})\eta_t]$$

The equations for $y(1)_t$ and $y(2)_t$ justify referring to $CT(R_t)$ as the common trend of these variables. In the complete axiom systems, $CT(R_t)$ behaves as a generalized random walk.

It is interesting to note here that $CT(R_t)$ is a function of $\eta(2)_t$ as well as $\eta(1)_t$. Hence "the other part" of the money market plays an essential part in the construction of the common trend of Treasury-bill yields.

It is also interesting to note that the $y(1)$ and $y(3)$ series need not be cointegrated. In the complete axiom system they will be cointegrated ARIMA processes if and only if there is a pair α_1 and α_2 such that $(\alpha_1, \alpha_2)\varphi = 0$. Then $CT(R_t)$ or some constant multiple of $CT(R_t)$ becomes the common trend of $y(1)$ and $y(3)$.

3.6 Bridge Principles and Treasury-Bill Yields in the Data Universe

So much for Ω_T now. Next I shall write down the bridge principles of my scientific explanation of H and describe several of the properties of Treasury-bill yields in the data universe that we can derive from them and the B axioms. I begin with the bridge principles.

G-1. The sample space Ω is a subset of the cross-product of Ω_T and Ω_P (i.e., $\Omega \subset \Omega_T \times \Omega_P$).

G-2. There exists a 2×2 positive matrix $\Psi = (\Psi_{ij})$, with largest eigenvalue less than 1, such that for each $\omega \in \Omega$,

$$y_0 = \hat{y}_0, \quad u = 0, \quad \text{and} \quad \hat{y}_t - \hat{y}_{t-1} = \Psi(y_t - \hat{y}_{t-1}) + u_t, \quad (18)$$
$$t \geq 1$$

where $\hat{y} = (\hat{y}(1), \hat{y}(2))'$, $y = (y(1), y(2))'$, and $u = (u(1), u(2))'$.

From our characterization of the theoretical universe and from G-1 and G-2 we can derive the following two interesting theorems.

T-6. Let U denote the shift operator, let ξ be as described in equation (14), and let $\varsigma = (\varsigma(1), \varsigma(2)) \in (R^2)^N$ be defined for arbitrary t by equations (19) and (20):

$$\varsigma(1)_t = u(1)_t - u(1)_{t-1} + \Psi_{11}[\eta(1)_t \\ - (1 - \varphi_{11})\eta(1)_{t-1} + \varphi_{12}\eta(2)_{t-1}] + \Psi_{12}\xi_t \quad (19)$$

$$\varsigma(2)_t = u(2)_t - u(2)_{t-1} + \Psi_{21}[\eta(1)_t \\ - (1 - \varphi_{11})\eta(1)_{t-1} + \varphi_{12}\eta(2)_{t-1}] + \Psi_{22}\xi_t \quad (20)$$

Then for each $\omega \in \Omega$

$$\hat{y}_0 = y_0$$

$$[I - (I - \Psi)U^{-1}]\hat{y}_1 = \Psi\begin{pmatrix} \varphi_{11}y(1)_0 + \varphi_{12}y(3)_0 + \eta(1)_1 \\ y(2)_0 + \Lambda_1 \end{pmatrix} + u_1 \quad (21)$$

$$[I - (I - \Psi)U^{-1}](I - IU^{-1})\hat{y}_t = \varsigma_t, \quad t \geq 2$$

T-7. Let ε_t be defined by equation (22) for all $t \in N - \{0, 1\}$:

$$\varepsilon_t = [I - (I - \Psi)U^{-1}]^{-1}\varsigma_t \quad (22)$$

where U is the shift operator and ς is as described in equations (19) and (20). Then for each $\omega \in \omega$ and all $t \in N - \{0, 1\}$,

$$\hat{y}(2)_t - \hat{y}(1)_{t-1} = y(2)_t - y(1)_{t-1} + (-1, 1)\Psi^{-1}(u_t - \varepsilon_t) \quad (23)$$

These two theorems and Theorems T-2, T-3, and T-5 suggest that the y and the $\hat{y}$ series might be realizations of two cointegrated $I(1)$ processes with the same cointegrating vector $(-1, 1)$.

3.7 P Axioms and a Scientific Explanation of HAG's Dictum

To establish that the y and the $\hat{y}$ series in fact are realizations of cointegrated $I(1)$ processes, we must specify the stochastic properties of the components of ω. These properties can be deduced from Axioms P-1 and P-2 and from the conditions we delineated in Axioms B-2–B-6, D-2, G-1, and G-2.

P-1. Let the vector-valued function $(K, G, r, \lambda, \Lambda, \eta, y, u, \hat{K}, \hat{y})(\cdot): N \times \Omega \to R^{19}$ be defined for all $t \in N$ by equation (24):

$$(K, G, r, \lambda, \Lambda, \eta, y, u, \hat{K}, \hat{y})(t, \omega) = \omega_t, \quad t \in N \quad \text{and} \quad \omega \in \Omega \quad (24)$$

Also let $\mathscr{F}$ be a σ-field of subsets of Ω, and suppose that the functions $(K, \ldots, \hat{y})(t, \cdot): \Omega \to R^{19}$, $t \in N$, are measurable with respect to $\mathscr{F}$. There exists a probability measure $P(\cdot): \mathscr{F} \to [0, 1]$ relative to which the family of functions $\{(\hat{K}, \hat{y})(t, \omega); t \in N\}$ has the same probability distributions as the family of functions $\{(\hat{K}, \hat{y})(t, \omega_P); t \in N\}$ in D-3.

P-2. Let $P(\cdot): \mathscr{F} \to [0, 1]$ be as described in P-1. Also let the function $(K, G, r, \lambda, \Lambda, \eta, y, u, \hat{K}, \hat{y})(\cdot): N \times \Omega \to R^{19}$ be as described in equation (24). Then, relative to $P(\cdot)$, the family of functions $\{(\Lambda, \eta, u)(t, \omega); t \geq 1\}$ is a vector-valued wide-sense stationary process the components of which, for each $t \in N - \{0\}$, satisfy the following conditions:

$$E\{\eta(t, \omega) | (y_1, y_3)(0), \ldots, (y_1, y_3)(t-1)\} = 0, \text{a.e.},$$
$$E\{\Lambda(t, \omega) | (y_1, y_3)(0), \ldots, (y_1, y_3)(t)\} = \Lambda(t, \omega), \text{a.e.},$$
$$E\{u(t, \omega) | (y_1, y_3)(0), \ldots, (y_1, y_3)(t)\} = 0, \text{a.e.}$$

With P-1, P-2, and all the other axioms in hand we can give a proof of Theorem T-8. In reading the theorem, note that the random process $\{y(t, \omega); t \in N\}$ is defined on $(\Omega, \mathscr{F})$ and not on $(\Omega_P, \mathscr{F}_p)$. Hence H is not an immediate consequence of T-8 and D-2.

T-8. There exists a probability measure $P(\cdot): \mathscr{F} \to [0, 1]$ that satisfies P-1 and P-2 and is such that the following assertions are true:
  (i) For all $t \geq 1$, with $P(\cdot)$ probability 1,
  $$\lambda(t, \omega) = E\{(y_1, y_3)(t+1) | (y_1, y_3)(0), \ldots, (y_1, y_3)(t)\} \quad (25)$$
  (ii) The family of functions $\{y(t, \omega); t \in N\}$ is a cointegrated $I(1)$ process with cointegrating vector $(-1, 1)$.
  (iii) The family of functions $\{\hat{y}(t, \omega); t \in N\}$ is a cointegrated $I(1)$ process with cointegrating vector $(-1, 1)$.

From T-8 and standard arguments (B. P. Stigum, 1990, pp. 344–7) we can establish the existence of a probability measure $\tilde{P}(\cdot): \mathscr{F}_p \to [0, 1]$ that satisfies the conditions of assertion H. To wit: The family of functions $\{(\hat{K},$

$\hat{y})(t, \omega); t \in N\}$ and $P(\cdot)$ determine the probability distributions of the family of random vectors $\{(\hat{K}, \hat{y}_t); t \in N\}$. These probability distributions, in turn, determine a probability measure $\tilde{P}(\cdot): \mathscr{F}_p \mapsto [0, 1]$ relative to which the family of functions $\{(\hat{K}, \hat{y})(t, \omega_P); t \in N\}$, which we defined in equation (3), satisfies the conditions of H.

The probability measure $\tilde{P}(\cdot)$ need not be the same as the probability measure $P_p(\cdot)$ on whose existence we insisted in D-3. However, according to P-1, the probability distributions of the family $\{(\hat{K}, \hat{y})(t, \omega_P); t \in N\}$ relative to $\tilde{P}(\cdot)$ and $P_p(\cdot)$ are the same. From this and the preceding paragraph, it follows that H is true in all models of D-1–D-3, B-1–B-6, G-1, G-2, P-1, and P-2. Since H is true in some, but not all, models of D-1–D-3, B-1–B-6, G-1, G-2, P-1, and P-2 provide the required scientific explanation of H.

3.8 Concluding Remarks

Before we can use my scientific explanation of H as a scientific explanation of HAG's dictum, several remarks concerning the generality of my explanation and the intended interpretation of $P(\cdot)$ and the components of ω_P are in order.

First, $P(\cdot)$: In the interpretation of the axioms that I intend, the initial conditions on y_1 and y_3; Axioms B-2–B-6, and the properties of $P(\cdot)$ determine the dynamics of equilibrium yields in the money market of my theory universe. The resulting probability distributions of the components of ω_T can be interpreted as conditional distributions determined by sequences of variables that for each and every period specify the supplies of money-market instruments and the characteristics of factors that influence the levels of demand for such securities. They can also be interpreted as marginal distributions in which the previously mentioned conditioning factors have been expected out.

I shall interpret the probability distributions of ω_T as marginal distributions. My reasons for doing that are as follows: It is difficult to think of the supply of Treasury bills in the U.S. money market as being entirely exogenously determined. The term structure of interest rates affects the costs of carrying the public debt. Therefore changes in the term structure will induce the Treasury to make changes in the composition of its outstanding debt and hence in its supply of the various bills. Similarly, it is difficult to see how determinants of demand in the U.S. money market, such as the monetary policy of the Federal Reserve (the Fed), can be characterized as entirely exogenous. In endeavoring to carry out the government's monetary policy, the agents of the Fed interact in interesting ways with the actors in the money market. A fascinating description of this interaction has been provided in Marcia Stigum's extraordinary account of the U.S. money market (M. Stigum, 1990, pp. 390–408). Finally, because HAG did not consider variables other than current and lagged values of the components of K, it is in the spirit of HAG's statistical analysis to interpret the probability distributions of the components of ω_T as marginal distributions in which the actions of the Treasury and the agents of the Fed have been expected out.

Next, the components of ω_P: There is a possibility that my formalization of HAG's dictum is incorrect. For example, it might have been better to insist that $\hat{K}(j)_t = |\hat{y}(j)_t|$, $K(j)_t = |y(j)_t|$, $j = 1, 2$, and $r = |y(3)_t|$. There are many possibilities, and no alternative is obviously better than my choice. So, for now, I shall assume that my H presents the correct formalization of HAG's dictum.

Finally, the generality of my explanation: If my H is a correct rendition of HAG's dictum for two Treasury bills, the generality of my scientific explanation of H must stand or fall on whether or not we lost insight into the workings of the U.S. money market by considering just two bills and one other money-market instrument. Now, it is significant here that Axioms B-2, B-4, and G-2 can easily be generalized to a market with many more securities. From this it follows that our gain in clarity has not been at the expense of a loss in generality.

My scientific explanation of H is logically adequate. Whether or not it is also empirically adequate remains to be seen. To be reasonably certain of the empirical adequacy of B-1–B-6, G-1, G-2, P-1, and P-2 we must get a good idea of $\mathfrak{Z}$, the family of models that constitute the intended interpretation of H and the data universe. The axioms for the data universe, D-1–D-3, describe the relationship between the $\hat{K}$s and the $\hat{y}$s and insist that there is a data-generating process (DGP). H adds to this that the probability distributions of the DGP are such that the components of $\hat{y}$ behave as cointegrated ARIMA processes with one-unit root and cointegrating vector $(-1, 1)$. Finally, as Theorems T-1–T-7 demonstrate, Axioms B-1–B-6, G-1, G-2, P-1, and P-2 impose conditions on the coefficients and the covariance structure of the error terms in the difference equations that determine the behavior of the components of the $\hat{y}$ process. To get a good idea of $\mathfrak{Z}$, we must estimate the values of the components of φ and Ψ and the covariance structure of the ηs, the Λs, and the us. This will require sampling anew in the U.S. money market and carrying out statistical analyses that will involve S, $\mathscr{F}$, and $Q(\cdot)$ in an essential way.

This is not the place to carry out an investigation of the empirical adequacy of my explanation of HAG's dictum. However, it seems relevant to me to indicate how the problems involved in ascertaining the empirical adequacy of an SE-2 explanation can be solved with means that leading time-series analysts have developed during the past 15 years. In the setting of T-8, the probability measure $Q(\cdot)$ on $(S, \mathscr{F})$ and the sampling scheme that was used determine the characteristics of Aris Spanos's Haavelmo distribution (Spanos, 1989, p. 415). That is where the statistical analysis begins. To get a good idea of the family $\mathfrak{B}$ of models that constitute the intended interpretation of H and the data universe, I would begin by imposing conditions on the Haavelmo distribution. Specifically, I would add to P-1 and P-2 conditions on the covariance structure of the family of error terms $\{(\Lambda, \eta, u)(t, \omega); t \geq 1\}$ that would enable me to estimate the parameters in equation (21). The constrained Haavelmo distribution and equation (21) would, in the present setting, constitute David Hendry's GUM (i.e., the most general estimable, statistical model that I believed might contain empirically relevant and interpretable econometric models). From the GUM I would obtain Hendry's congruent model (CM) by statistical reduction (Hendry, 1995, ch. 9). The CM would exhibit the most restrictive assumptions about the probability distributions of the error terms and about the constants in equation (21) that are congruent with the data. In that way the CM would help me delineate the characteristics of $\mathfrak{B}$, which is to be the largest class of models of H and the data universe in which the restrictions that Γ_t, $\Gamma_{t,p}$, Γ_p, and the axioms of $P(\cdot)$ impose on the Haavelmo distribution are valid.

4   Scientific Explanations and Diagnoses

We have established criteria that logically and empirically adequate scientific explanations in econometrics must satisfy. The criteria concern explanations in which the explanandum is a family of assertions about the individuals in a data universe and/or about the parameters of the probability distributions of such individuals. It remains to consider cases where the theory–data confrontation has raised doubts as to the empirical relevance of a given theory and the scientist is asked to explain why.

The third kind of scientific explanation has a characteristic feature. We have found that a logical consequence of many axioms is not valid in a given empirical context. Consequently, at least one of the axioms must lack relevance in this context. We are asked to determine which one (ones) of the many is (are) irrelevant.

It is a difficult task to unmask the irrelevant axioms in a theory–data confrontation. To wit: E-4.1.

E-4.1.   We are attempting to establish the empirical adequacy of my scientific explanation of HAG's dictum. In the process of doing that, we estimate the value of Ψ_{11} in equation (19). The estimate is significantly different from zero and is negative. Because G-2 insists that Ψ be positive, our estimate is inadmissible. Hence, at least one of the 13 axioms of my explanation of HAG's dictum or one of the assumptions concerning the covariance structure of the error terms that we added to P-1 and P-2 must lack relevance in the empirical context of E-4.1. There is no easy way to single out the irrelevant axiom(s) and/or assumption(s).

In cases such as the one envisaged in E-4.1, an appropriate structuring of the statistical analyses might help us single out an appropriate change of axioms and provide us with good probabilistic reasons for carrying out the change. The reader can find an example of such a statistical analysis in chapter 27 of (B. P. Stigum 1990). There I developed a two-stage test of a version of the life-cycle hypothesis in which Milton Friedman's permanent-income hypothesis plays a pivotal role. The lifecycle hypothesis failed the test, and the statistical analysis gave me good probabilistic reasons for blaming the permanent-income hypothesis for the failure.

References

Duhem, P. (1954). *The Aim and Structure of Physical Theory*, trans. Philip P. Wiener. Princeton University Press.
Elster, J. (1994). A plea for mechanisms. Unpublished manuscript, University of Oslo.
Graves, L. M. (1956). *The Theory of Functions of Real Variables*. New York: McGraw-Hill.
Hall, A. D., Anderson, H., and Granger, C. W. J. (1991). A cointegration analysis of treasury bill yields. *Review of Economics and Statistics* 74:116–26.
Hempel, C. G. (1965). *Aspects of Scientific Explanation and Other Essays in the Philosophy of Science*. New York: Free Press.
Hendry, D. (1995). *Dynamic Econometrics*. Oxford University Press.
Janssen, M. C. W., and Tan, Y.-H. (1991). Why Friedman's non-monotonic logic defies Hempel's covering law model. *Synthese* 86:255–84.
Kahnemann, D., and Tversky, A. (1972). Subjective probability: a judgement of representativeness. *Cognitive Psychology* 3:430–54.
Kahnemann, D., and Tversky, A. (1972) Availability: a heuristic for judging frequency and probability. *ORI Research Bulletin*, Vol. 11, no. 6. Oregon Research Institute.
Keynes, J. M. (1921). *A Treatise on Probability*. London: MacMillan.
Nagel, E. (1961). *The Structure of Science*. New York: Harcourt, Brace & World.
Reiter, R. (1980). A logic for default reasoning. *Artificial Intelligence* 13:81–132.
Shoham, Y. (1988). *Reasoning about Change. Time and Causation from the Standpoint of Artificial Intelligence*. Massachusetts Institute of Technology Press.
Spanos, A. (1989). On rereading Haavelmo: a retrospective view of econometric modeling. *Econometric Theory* 5:405–29.
Stigum, B. P. (1990). *Toward a Formal Science of Economics*. Massachusetts Institute of Technology Press.
   (1995). Theory–data confrontations in economics. *Dialogue* 34:581–604.
Stigum, M. (1990). *The Money Market*. Homewood, IL: Dow Jones–Irwin.
Toulmin, S. (1953). *The Philosophy of Science*. New York: Harper & Row.

Vaillant, G. (1983). *The natural History of Alcoholism*. Harvard University Press.
Van Frassen, B. (1980). *The Scientific Image*. Oxford: Clarendon Press.
von Neumann, J., and Morgenstern, O. (1953). *Theory of Games and Economic Behavior*. Princeton University Press.
Wagenaar, W. A. (1988). *Paradoxes of Gambling Behaviour*. Hillsdale, NJ: Lawrence Erlbaum.

CHAPTER 11

An Autoregressive Distributed-Lag Modelling Approach to Cointegration Analysis

M. Hashem Pesaran and Yongcheol Shin

1 Introduction

Econometric analysis of long-run relations has been the focus of much theoretical and empirical research in economics. In cases in which the variables in the long-run relation of interest are trend-stationary, the general practice has been to de-trend the series and to model the de-trended series as stationary autoregressive distributed-lag (ARDL) models. Estimation and inference concerning the long-run properties of the model have then been carried out using standard asymptotic normal theory. For a comprehensive review of this literature, see Hendry, Pagan, and Sargan (1984) and Wickens and Breusch (1988). The analysis becomes more complicated when the variables are difference-stationary, or integrated of order 1 [$I(1)$ for short]. The recent literature on cointegration has been concerned with analysis of the long-run relations between $I(1)$ variables, and its basic premise has been, at least implicitly, that in the presence of $I(1)$ variables the traditional ARDL approach is no longer applicable. Consequently, large numbers of alternative estimation and hypothesis-testing procedures have been specifically developed for the analysis of $I(1)$ variables. See the pioneering work of Engle and Granger (1987), Johansen (1991), Phillips (1991), Phillips and Hansen (1990), and Phillips and Loretan (1991).

In this essay we re-examine the use of the traditional ARDL approach for the analysis of long-run relations when the underlying variables are $I(1)$. We consider the following general ARDL (p, q) model:

This is a revised version of an essay presented at the Ragnar Frisch Centennial Symposium at the Norwegian Academy of Science and Letters, Oslo, March 3–5, 1995. We are grateful to Peter Boswijk, Clive Granger, Alberto Holly, Kyung So Im, Brendan McCabe, Steve Satchell, Richard Smith, Ron Smith, and an anonymous referee for helpful comments. Partial financial support from the Economic and Social Research Council (grant no. R000233608) and the Isaac Newton Trust of Trinity College, Cambridge, is gratefully acknowledged.

$$y_t = a_0 + a_1 t + \sum_{i=1}^{p} \varphi_i y_{t-i} + \boldsymbol{\beta}' \mathbf{x}_t + \sum_{i=0}^{q-1} \boldsymbol{\beta}_i^{*\prime} \Delta \mathbf{x}_{t-i} + u_t \quad (1.1)$$

$$\Delta \mathbf{x}_t = \mathbf{P}_1 \Delta \mathbf{x}_{t-1} + \mathbf{P}_2 \Delta \mathbf{x}_{t-2} + \cdots + \mathbf{P}_s \Delta \mathbf{x}_{t-s} + \boldsymbol{\varepsilon}_t \quad (1.2)$$

where $\mathbf{x}_t$ are the k-dimensional $I(1)$ variables that are not cointegrated among themselves, u_t and $\boldsymbol{\varepsilon}_t$ are serially uncorrelated disturbances with zero means and constant variance-covariances, and $\mathbf{P}_i$ are $k \times k$ coefficient matrices such that the vector autoregressive process in $\Delta \mathbf{x}_t$ is stable. We also assume that the roots of $1 - \Sigma_{i=1}^{p} \varphi_i z^i = 0$ all fall outside the unit circle and that there exists a stable unique long-run relationship between y_t and $\mathbf{x}_t$.

We consider the problem of consistent estimation of the parameters of the ARDL model both when u_t and $\boldsymbol{\varepsilon}_t$ are uncorrelated and when they are correlated. In the former case we shall show that the OLS estimators of the short-run parameters $a_0, a_1, \boldsymbol{\beta}, \boldsymbol{\beta}_1^*, \ldots, \boldsymbol{\beta}_{q-1}^*$, and $\boldsymbol{\varphi} = (\varphi_1, \ldots, \varphi_p)$ are $\sqrt{T}$-consistent, and the covariance matrix of these estimators has a well-defined limit which is asymptotically singular such that the estimators of a_1 and $\boldsymbol{\beta}$ are asymptotically perfectly collinear with the estimator of $\boldsymbol{\varphi}$. These results have the interesting implication that the OLS estimators of the long-run coefficients, defined by the ratios $\delta = a_1/\varphi(1)$ and $\boldsymbol{\theta} = \boldsymbol{\beta}/\varphi(1)$, where $\varphi(1) = 1 - \Sigma_{i=1}^{p} \varphi_i$, converge to their true values faster than the estimators of the short-run parameters a_1 and $\boldsymbol{\beta}$. The ARDL-based estimators of δ and $\boldsymbol{\theta}$ are $T^{3/2}$-consistent and T-consistent, respectively. These results are not surprising and are familiar from the cointegration literature. But more importantly, we shall show that despite the singularity of the covariance structure of the OLS estimators of the short-run parameters, valid inferences on δ and $\boldsymbol{\theta}$, as well as on individual short-run parameters, can be made using standard normal asymptotic theory. Therefore, the traditional ARDL approach justified in the case of trend-stationary regressors is in fact equally valid even if the regressors are first-difference-stationary.

In the case where u_t and $\boldsymbol{\varepsilon}_t$ are correlated, the ARDL specification needs to be augmented with an adequate number of lagged changes in the regressors before estimation and inference are carried out. The degree of augmentation required depends on whether or not $q > s + 1$. Denoting the contemporaneous correlation between u_t and $\boldsymbol{\varepsilon}_t$ by the $k \times 1$ vector $\mathbf{d}$, the augmented version of (1.1) can be written as

$$y_t = a_0 + a_1 t + \sum_{i=1}^{p} \varphi_i y_{t-i} + \boldsymbol{\beta}' \mathbf{x}_t + \sum_{i=0}^{m-1} \boldsymbol{\pi}_i' \Delta \mathbf{x}_{t-i} + \eta_t \quad (1.3)$$

where $m = \max(q, s+1)$, $\boldsymbol{\pi}_i = \boldsymbol{\beta}_i^* - \mathbf{P}_i' \mathbf{d}$, $i = 0, 1, 2, \ldots, m-1$, $\mathbf{P}_0 = \mathbf{I}_k$, where $\mathbf{I}_k$ is a $k \times k$ identity matrix, $\boldsymbol{\beta}_i^* = \mathbf{0}$ for $i \geq q$, and $\mathbf{P}_i = \mathbf{0}$ for $i \geq s$. In this augmented specification, η_t and $\boldsymbol{\varepsilon}_t$ are uncorrelated, and the results stated earlier will be directly applicable to the OLS estimators of the short-run and long-run parameters of (1.3). Once again, traditional methods of estimation and inference, originally developed for trend-stationary variables, are applicable to first-difference-stationary variables. Estimation of the short-run effects still requires an explicit modelling of the contemporaneous dependence between u_t and ε_t. In practice, an appropriate choice for the order of the ARDL model is crucial for valid inference. But once this is done, estimation of the long-run parameters and computation of valid standard errors for the resultant estimators can be carried out either by the OLS method, using the so-called delta method (Δ method) to compute the standard errors, or by the Bewley (1979) regression approach. These two procedures yield identical results, and a choice between them is only a matter of computational convenience.

The use of the ARDL estimation procedure is directly comparable to the semiparametric, fully modified OLS approach of Phillips and Hansen (1990) to estimation of cointegrating relations. In the static formulation of the cointegrating regression,

$$y_t = \mu + \delta t + \boldsymbol{\theta}'\mathbf{x}_t + v_t \tag{1.4}$$

where $\Delta \mathbf{x}_t = \mathbf{e}_t$, and $\boldsymbol{\xi}_t = (v_t, \mathbf{e}'_t)'$ follows a general linear stationary process. In this case the OLS estimators of δ and $\boldsymbol{\theta}$ are $T^{3/2}$- and T-consistent, but in general the asymptotic distribution of the OLS estimator of $\boldsymbol{\theta}$ involves the unit-root distribution as well as the second-order bias in the presence of the contemporaneous correlations that may exist between v_t and $\mathbf{e}_t$. Therefore, the finite-sample performance of the OLS estimator is poor, and in addition, because of the nuisance parameter dependences, inference on $\boldsymbol{\theta}$ using the usual t-tests in the OLS regression of (1.4) is invalid. To overcome these problems, Phillips and Hansen (1990) have suggested the fully modified OLS estimation procedure that asymptotically takes account of these correlations in a semiparametric manner, in the sense that the fully modified estimators have the Gaussian mixture normal distribution asymptotically, and inferences on the long-run parameters using the t-test based on the limiting distribution of the fully modified estimator are valid.

The ARDL-based approach to estimation and inference and the fully modified OLS procedure are both asymptotically valid when the regressors are $I(1)$, and a choice between them has to be made on the basis of their small-sample properties and computational convenience. To examine the small-sample performances of the two estimators we carried out a number of Monte Carlo experiments. Because in practice the "true" orders of the ARDL (p, m) model are rarely known a priori, in the Monte Carlo experiments we also considered a two-step strategy whereby p and m were first selected (estimated) using either the Akaike information criterion (AIC) or the Schwarz Bayesian Criterion (SC), and then the long-run coefficients and their standard errors were estimated using the ARDL model selected in the first step. We refer to these estimators as ARDL-AIC and ARDL-SC. The main findings from these experiments are as follows:

(i) The ARDL-AIC and the ARDL-SC estimators have very similar small-sample performances, with the ARDL-SC performing slightly better in the majority of the experiments. This may reflect the fact that the Schwarz criterion is a consistent model-selection criterion, whereas the Akaike is not.

(ii) The ARDL test statistics that are computed using the Δ method (or equivalently by means of the so-called Bewley regression) generally perform much better in small samples than do the test statistics computed using the asymptotic formula that explicitly takes account of the fact that the regressors are $I(1)$.

(iii) The ARDL-SC procedure, when combined with the Δ method of computing the standard errors of the long-run parameters, generally dominates the Phillips-Hansen estimator in small samples. This is, in particular, true of the size-power performance of the tests on the long-run parameter.

(iv) The Monte Carlo results point strongly in favor of the two-step estimation procedure, and this strategy seems to work even when the model under consideration has endogenous regressors, irrespective of whether the regressors are $I(1)$ or $I(0)$.[1]

The plan of this chapter is as follows: Section 2 examines the asymptotic properties of the OLS estimators in the context of a simple autoregressive model with a linear deterministic trend and the k-dimensional strictly exogenous $I(1)$ regressors. Section 3 considers a more general ARDL model, allowing for residual serial correlations and possible endogeneity of the $I(1)$ regressors, and develops the resultant asymptotic theory. In Section 4 the ARDL-based approach is compared to the cointegration-based approach of Phillips and Hansen (1990). Section 5 reports and discusses the results of Monte Carlo experiments. Some concluding remarks are presented in Section 6. Mathematical proofs are provided in an Appendix.

2 The Lagged-Dependent-Variable Model with Deterministic Trend and Exogenous $I(1)$ Regressors

Initially we consider the simple ARDL $(1, 0)$ model containing $I(1)$ regressors and a linear deterministic trend.

$$\varphi(L)y_t = \alpha_0 + \alpha_1 t + \boldsymbol{\beta}'\mathbf{x}_t + u_t, \qquad t = 1,\ldots,T \qquad (2.1)$$

---

[1] The case where the regressors are $I(1)$ and are cointegrated among themselves presents additional identification problems and is best analyzed in the context of a system of long-run structural equations. On this, see Pesaran and Shin (1997).

where y_t is a scalar, $\varphi(L) = 1 - \varphi L$, with L being the one-period lag operator, $\mathbf{x}_t$ is a $k \times 1$ vector of regressors assumed to be integrated of order 1,[2]

$$\mathbf{x}_t = \mathbf{x}_{t-1} + \mathbf{e}_t \tag{2.2}$$

and $\boldsymbol{\beta}$ is a $k \times 1$ vector of unknown parameters. Suppose that the following assumptions hold:

(A1) The scalar disturbance term u_t in (2.1) is iid $(0, \sigma_u^2)$.
(A2) The k-dimensional vector $\mathbf{e}_t$ in (2.2) has a general linear multivariate stationary process.
(A3) u_t and $\mathbf{e}_t$ are uncorrelated for all leads and lags, such that $\mathbf{x}_t$ is strictly exogenous with respect to u_t.
(A4) The $I(1)$ regressors $\mathbf{x}_t$ are not cointegrated among themselves.
(A5) $|\varphi| < 1$, so that the model is dynamically stable, and a long-run relationship between y_t and $\mathbf{x}_t$ exists.[3]

We shall distinguish between two types of parameters: the parameters capturing the short-run dynamics ($a_0, a_1, \boldsymbol{\beta}$, and φ), and the long-run parameters on the trended regressors, t and $\mathbf{x}_t$, defined by

$$\delta = \frac{a_1}{1 - \varphi}, \quad \boldsymbol{\theta} = \frac{\boldsymbol{\beta}}{1 - \varphi} \tag{2.3}$$

Applying the decomposition $1 - \varphi L = (1 - \varphi) + \varphi(1 - L)$ to (2.1), y_t can be expressed as

$$y_t = \mu + \delta t + \boldsymbol{\theta}' \mathbf{x}_t + v_t \tag{2.4}$$

where

$$\mu = \frac{a_0}{1 - \varphi} - \left(\frac{\varphi}{1 - \varphi}\right)\delta,$$

and

$$v_t = \sum_{i=0}^{\infty} \varphi^i u_{t-i} - \varphi \sum_{i=0}^{\infty} \varphi^i \boldsymbol{\theta}' \mathbf{e}_{t-i}$$

From (2.1) and (2.4) it is clear that y_t and $\mathbf{x}_t$ are individually $I(1)$, but must be cointegrated for (2.1) to be meaningful.[4] Similarly, we obtain

---

[2] Specifications (2.1) and (2.2) can easily be adapted to allow for inclusion of a drift term in the $\mathbf{x}_t$ process. Consider, for example, the process $\Delta \mathbf{x}_t = \boldsymbol{\mu}_x + \mathbf{e}_t$, and note that it can also be written as $\mathbf{x}_t = \boldsymbol{\mu}_x t + \tilde{\mathbf{x}}_t$, where $\Delta \tilde{\mathbf{x}}_t = \mathbf{e}_t$. Therefore, substituting $\mathbf{x}_t$ in (2.1), we have

$$\varphi(L) y_t = a_0 + (a_1 + \boldsymbol{\beta}' \boldsymbol{\mu}_x) t + \boldsymbol{\beta}' \tilde{\mathbf{x}}_t + u_t$$

where $\tilde{\mathbf{x}}_t$ follows an $I(1)$ process without a drift.

[3] Tests of the existence of long-run relationships between y_t and $\mathbf{x}_t$, when it is not known a priori whether $\mathbf{x}_t$ are $I(0)$ or $I(1)$, are discussed by Pesaran, Shin, and Smith (1996).

[4] A relationship between $I(1)$ variables is said to be "stochastically cointegrated" if it is trend-stationary, while "deterministic cointegration" refers to the case where the

$$y_{t-1} = \mu_1 + \delta t + \boldsymbol{\theta}'\mathbf{x}_t + \varkappa_t \tag{2.5}$$

where $\mu_1 = \mu - \delta$, $\varkappa_t = v_{t-1} - \boldsymbol{\theta}'\mathbf{e}_t$, and $\varkappa_t$ is an $I(0)$ process with variance $\sigma_\varkappa^2$.

Our main aim is to derive the asymptotic properties of the OLS estimators of the short-run parameters as well as the long-run parameters in the context of the ARDL $(1, 0)$ model (2.1). For expositional convenience, we transform (2.1) to the partitioned regression model in matrix form as

$$\mathbf{y}_T = \mathbf{Z}_T\mathbf{b} + \mathbf{y}_{T-1}\varphi + \mathbf{u}_T \tag{2.6}$$

where $\mathbf{y}_T = (y_1, \ldots, y_T)'$, $\mathbf{y}_{T-1} = (y_0, \ldots, y_{T-1})'$, $\boldsymbol{\tau}_T = (1, \ldots, 1)'$, $\mathbf{t}_T = (1, \ldots, T)'$, $\mathbf{X}_T = (\mathbf{x}_1, \ldots, \mathbf{x}_T)'$, $\mathbf{Z}_T = (\boldsymbol{\tau}_T, \mathbf{t}_T, \mathbf{X}_T)$, $\mathbf{u}_T = (u_1, \ldots, u_T)'$, and $\mathbf{b} = (\alpha_0, \alpha_1, \boldsymbol{\beta}')'$. Because our main interest is in the long-run coefficients on trended regressors, t and $\mathbf{x}_t$, we also partition

$$\mathbf{Z}_T = (\boldsymbol{\tau}_T, \mathbf{S}_T), \qquad \mathbf{S}_T = (\mathbf{t}_T, \mathbf{X}_T), \qquad \mathbf{b} = \begin{pmatrix} \alpha_0 \\ \mathbf{c} \end{pmatrix}, \qquad \mathbf{c} = \begin{pmatrix} \alpha_1 \\ \boldsymbol{\beta} \end{pmatrix}$$

where the dimensions of $\mathbf{Z}_T$, $\mathbf{S}_T$, $\mathbf{b}$, and $\mathbf{c}$ are $T \times (k+2)$, $T \times (k+1)$, $(k+2) \times 1$, and $(k+1) \times 1$, respectively.

Theorem 2.1. *Under assumptions (A1)–(A5), the OLS estimators of φ and $\mathbf{c} = (\alpha_1, \boldsymbol{\beta}')'$ in (2.6), denoted by $\hat{\varphi}_T$ and $\hat{\mathbf{c}}_T$, respectively, are $\sqrt{T}$-consistent and have the following asymptotic distributions:*

$$\sqrt{T}(\hat{\varphi}_T - \varphi) \overset{a}{\sim} N\left\{0, \frac{\sigma_u^2}{\sigma_\varkappa^2}\right\} \tag{2.7}$$

$$\sqrt{T}(\hat{\mathbf{c}}_T - \mathbf{c}) \overset{a}{\sim} N\left\{0, \frac{\sigma_u^2}{\sigma_\varkappa^2}\boldsymbol{\lambda}\boldsymbol{\lambda}'\right\} \tag{2.8}$$

where $\boldsymbol{\lambda} = (\delta, \boldsymbol{\theta}')'$ is a $(k+1) \times 1$ vector of the long-run parameters on trended regressors, t and $\mathbf{x}_t$, and rank $(\boldsymbol{\lambda}\boldsymbol{\lambda}') = 1$. In addition, the OLS estimator of α_0 in (2.6), denoted by $\hat{\alpha}_{0T}$, is also $\sqrt{T}$-consistent, but has the mixture normal distribution. Defining $\mathbf{h} = (\mathbf{b}', \varphi)'$ and $\mathbf{P}_{\mathbf{Z}_T} = (\mathbf{Z}_T, \mathbf{y}_{T-1})$, and denoting the OLS estimator of $\mathbf{h}$ by $\hat{\mathbf{h}}_T$, the covariance matrix of $\hat{\mathbf{h}}_T$ can be consistently estimated by

$$\hat{V}(\hat{\mathbf{h}}_T) = \hat{\sigma}_{uT}^2 (\mathbf{P}'_{\mathbf{Z}_T}\mathbf{P}_{\mathbf{Z}_T})^{-1}$$

where $\hat{\sigma}_{uT}^2 = T^{-1}(\mathbf{y}_T - \mathbf{P}_{\mathbf{Z}_T}\hat{\mathbf{h}}_T)'(\mathbf{y}_T - \mathbf{P}_{\mathbf{Z}_T}\hat{\mathbf{h}}_T)$, and $\hat{V}(\hat{\mathbf{h}}_T)$ is asymptotically singular with rank equal to 2.

---

cointegrating relation is level-stationary. For a discussion of these two types of cointegrating relations, see Park (1992).

Theorem 2.1 shows that despite the presence of stochastic and deterministic trends in the ARDL model, the OLS estimators of the short-run parameters are $\sqrt{T}$-consistent.[5] The second and more important finding is that the OLS estimators of the coefficients on the trended regressors, α_1 and β, in (2.1) are asymptotically perfectly collinear with the OLS estimator of the coefficient on the lagged dependent variable φ; namely,

$$\sqrt{T}\{(\hat{\mathbf{c}}_T - \mathbf{c}) + \lambda(\hat{\varphi}_T - \varphi)\} = o_p(1) \tag{2.9}$$

One interesting implication of this result is that the t-statistics for testing the significance of individual impact coefficients of the $I(1)$ regressors are asymptotically equivalent, namely, $t_{\hat{\beta}_i} - t_{\hat{\beta}_j} = o_p(1)$ for $i \neq j$, and $t_{\hat{\beta}_i} - t_{\hat{\alpha}_1} = o_p(1)$.[6] Furthermore, $t_{\hat{\beta}_i} - t_{(1-\hat{\varphi})} = o_p(1)$. Relation (2.9), in conjunction with

$$\hat{\lambda}_T - \lambda = \frac{(\hat{\mathbf{c}}_T - \mathbf{c}) + \lambda(\hat{\varphi}_T - \varphi)}{(1 - \hat{\varphi}_T)} \tag{2.10}$$

yields an important result familiar from the cointegration literature, which we set out in the following theorem:

Theorem 2.2. *Under assumptions (A1)–(A5), the ARDL-based estimators of the long-run parameters, given by $\hat{\delta}_T = \hat{a}_{1T}/(1 - \hat{\varphi}_T)$ and $\hat{\theta}_T = \hat{\beta}_T/(1 - \hat{\varphi}_T)$, converge to their true values δ and θ, respectively, at the rates, $T^{3/2}$ and T. Also asymptotically, $T^{3/2}(\hat{\delta}_T - \delta)$ and $T(\hat{\theta}_T - \theta)$ have the (mixture) normal distributions, and therefore*

$$\mathbf{Q}_{\tilde{S}_T}^{1/2}\mathbf{D}_{S_T}^{-1}(\hat{\lambda}_T - \lambda) \overset{a}{\sim} N\left\{\mathbf{0}, \frac{\sigma_u^2}{(1 - \varphi)^2}\mathbf{I}_{k+1}\right\} \tag{2.11}$$

where $\hat{\lambda}_T = (\hat{\delta}_T, \hat{\theta}'_T)'$, $\mathbf{Q}_{\tilde{S}_T} = \mathbf{D}_{S_T}\mathbf{S}'_T\mathbf{H}_T\mathbf{S}_T\mathbf{D}_{S_T}$, $\mathbf{S}_T = (\mathbf{t}_T, \mathbf{X}_T)$, $\mathbf{H}_T = \mathbf{I}_T - \boldsymbol{\tau}_T(\boldsymbol{\tau}'_T\boldsymbol{\tau}_T)^{-1}\boldsymbol{\tau}'_T$, *and* $\mathbf{D}_{S_T} = \text{Diag}(T^{-3/2}, T^{-1}\mathbf{I}_k)$.

The finding that the estimator of θ is T-consistent is known as the "super-consistency" property in the cointegration literature. Because the limiting distributions of $T^{3/2}(\hat{\delta}_T - \delta)$ and $T(\hat{\theta}_T - \theta)$ are (mixture) normal, optimal two-sided inferences concerning δ and θ are possible. Notice also that the covariance matrix of the estimator of λ simply depends on the inverse of the (scaled) demeaned data matrix and the spectral density at zero frequency of $(1 - \varphi L)^{-1}u_t$, namely, $\sigma_u^2/(1 - \varphi)^2$. Once again, this

---

[5] Similar results can be obtained in the case of regressors with higher-order trend terms, such as $t^2, t^3, \ldots$ or $I(2), I(3), \ldots$ variables.

[6] For large enough T we have $t_{\hat{\beta}_i} \approx (1 - \varphi)(\sigma_x/\sigma_u)$. This explains the relatively low t-ratios often obtained for short-run coefficients in ARDL regressions with $I(1)$ variables, especially when φ is close to unity.

finding is in line with the results already familiar from the cointegration literature (see Section 4 for further discussion).

Hypothesis testing on the general linear restrictions involving the (k + 1)-dimensional long-run parameter vector λ can be carried out in the usual manner. Consider the g linear restrictions on λ.

$$\mathbf{R}\lambda = \mathbf{r}$$

where $\mathbf{R}$ is a $g \times (k + 1)$ matrix and $\mathbf{r}$ is a $g \times 1$ vector of known constants. These restrictions can be tested using the Wald statistic,

$$\begin{aligned} W &= (\mathbf{R}\hat{\lambda}_T - \mathbf{r})' \{\mathbf{R}_{\text{Cov}}(\hat{\lambda}_T)\mathbf{R}'\}^{-1} (\mathbf{R}\hat{\lambda}_T - \mathbf{r}) \\ &= (\mathbf{R}\hat{\lambda}_T - \mathbf{r})' \left\{ \frac{(1 - \hat{\varphi}_T)^2}{\hat{\sigma}_{uT}^2} (\mathbf{S}_T' \mathbf{H}_T \mathbf{S}_T) \right\} (\mathbf{R}\hat{\lambda}_T - \mathbf{r}) \end{aligned} \quad (2.12)$$

Of special interest is the t-statistic on the individual coefficients given by

$$t_i = \frac{\hat{\lambda}_{iT} - \lambda_i}{\hat{s}_i}, \quad i = 1, \ldots, k + 1 \quad (2.13)$$

where the standard error of the ith coefficient is consistently estimated by

$$\hat{s}_i = \sqrt{\frac{\hat{\sigma}_{uT}^2}{(1 - \hat{\varphi}_T)^2} (\mathbf{S}_T' \mathbf{H}_T \mathbf{S}_T)_{ii}^{-1}}$$

and $(\mathbf{S}_T' \mathbf{H}_T \mathbf{S}_T)_{ii}^{-1}$ denotes the ith diagonal element of $(\mathbf{S}_T' \mathbf{H}_T \mathbf{S}_T)^{-1}$. By Theorem 2.2, the Wald statistic in (2.12) follows the asymptotic χ^2 distribution with g degrees of freedom, and t_i^2 in (2.13) is distributed asymptotically as a χ^2 variate with one degree of freedom.

It is worth noting that the results in Theorem 2.2 equally apply to the purely autoregressive model with deterministic trend,

$$y_t = \alpha_0 + \alpha_1 t + \varphi y_{t-1} + u_t, \quad t = 1, \ldots, T \quad (2.14)$$

and to the ARDL (1, 0) model without a deterministic trend,

$$y_t = \alpha_0 + \boldsymbol{\beta}' \mathbf{x}_t + \varphi y_{t-1} + u_t, \quad t = 1, \ldots, T \quad (2.15)$$

For completeness, the asymptotic results for these models are summarized in Theorems 2.3 and 2.4.

Theorem 2.3. *Under assumptions* (A1) *and* (A5), *the OLS estimators of* α_0, α_1, *and* φ *in* (2.14), *denoted by* $\hat{\alpha}_{0T}$, $\hat{\alpha}_{1T}$, *and* $\hat{\varphi}_T$, *are all* $\sqrt{T}$-*consistent and asymptotically normally distributed. In addition,* $\sqrt{T} (\hat{\alpha}_{1T} - \alpha_1)$ *and* $\sqrt{T}(\hat{\varphi}_T - \varphi)$ *are perfectly collinear asymptotically, and the covariance matrix of* $(\hat{\alpha}_{0T}, \hat{\alpha}_{1T}, \hat{\varphi}_T)$ *is asymptotically singular with rank equal to* 2. *Furthermore, the estimator of the long-run parameter* δ, *computed by* $\hat{\alpha}_{1T}/(1 - \hat{\varphi}_T)$, *has the following asymptotic distribution:*

$$T^{3/2}(\hat{\delta}_T - \delta) \stackrel{a}{\sim} N\left\{0, \frac{12\sigma_u^2}{(1-\varphi)^2}\right\} \tag{2.16}$$

Theorem 2.4. *Under assumptions* (A1)–(A5), *the OLS estimators of* α_0, β, *and* φ *in* (2.15), *denoted by* $\hat{\alpha}_{0T}$, $\hat{\beta}_T$, *and* $\hat{\varphi}_T$, *are* $\sqrt{T}$-*consistent and have asymptotic (mixture) normal distributions. In addition,* $\sqrt{T}(\hat{\beta}_T - \beta)$ *and* $\sqrt{T}(\hat{\varphi}_T - \varphi)$ *are perfectly collinear asymptotically, and so the covariance matrix of* $(\hat{\alpha}_{0T}, \hat{\beta}_T, \hat{\varphi}_T)$ *is asymptotically singular with rank equal to* 2. *Furthermore, the estimator of the long-run parameter* θ, *given by* $\hat{\theta}_T = \hat{\beta}_T/(1 - \hat{\varphi}_T)$, *has the mixture normal distribution asymptotically, and*

$$Q_{\tilde{X}_T}^{1/2} T(\hat{\theta}_T - \theta) \stackrel{a}{\sim} N\left\{0, \frac{\sigma_u^2}{(1-\varphi)^2} I_k\right\} \tag{2.17}$$

where $Q_{\tilde{X}_T} = T^{-2}\mathbf{X}_T'\mathbf{H}_T\mathbf{X}_T$.

Before considering a more general specification of the ARDL model, we examine the relation between the standard errors of the estimator of the long-run parameter θ obtained from our asymptotic results and the standard errors obtained from the Δ method. For ease of exposition we consider the simple model (2.15) and without loss of generality focus on the case where x_t is a scalar (i.e., $k = 1$). From Theorem 2.4 we have

$$Q_{\tilde{X}_T}^{1/2} T(\hat{\theta}_T - \theta) = \left[\sum_{t=1}^{T}(x_t - \bar{x})^2\right]^{1/2} (\hat{\theta}_T - \theta) \stackrel{a}{\sim} N\left\{0, \frac{\sigma_u^2}{(1-\varphi)^2}\right\} \tag{2.18}$$

where $Q_{\tilde{X}_T} = T^{-2}\sum_{t=1}^{T}(x_t - \bar{x})^2$ and $\bar{x} = T^{-1}\sum_{t=1}^{T}x_t$.[7] Hence a consistent estimator of the variance of $\hat{\theta}_T$ is given by

$$\hat{V}(\hat{\theta}_T) = \frac{\hat{\sigma}_{uT}^2}{(1 - \hat{\varphi}_T)^2} \frac{1}{\sum_{t=1}^{T}(x_t - \bar{x})^2} \tag{2.19}$$

The computation of the variance of $\hat{\theta}_T$ by the Δ method involves approximating

$$\hat{\theta}_T = g(\hat{\mathbf{\Psi}}_T) = \frac{\hat{\beta}_T}{1 - \hat{\varphi}_T}$$

by a linear function of $\hat{\mathbf{\Psi}}_T = (\hat{\beta}_T, \hat{\varphi}_T)'$, and then approximating the variance of $\hat{\theta}_T$ by the variance of the resulting linear function. Denoting the estimator of the variance of $\hat{\theta}_T$ by $\hat{V}_\Delta(\hat{\theta}_T)$, we have

---

[7] In the case where x_t is $I(0)$ we have the same asymptotic result as given by (2.18); that is, since $T^{-1}\mathbf{x}_T'\mathbf{H}_T\mathbf{x}_T = O_p(1)$ and $\sqrt{T}(\hat{\theta}_T - \theta) = O_p(1)$, hence

$$\left(T^{-1}\mathbf{x}_T'\mathbf{H}_T\mathbf{x}_T\right)^{1/2} \sqrt{T}(\hat{\theta}_T - \theta) = \left[\sum_{t=1}^{T}(x_t - \bar{x})^2\right]^{1/2} (\hat{\theta}_T - \theta) \stackrel{a}{\sim} N\left\{0, \frac{\sigma_u^2}{(1-\varphi)^2}\right\}$$

$$\hat{V}_{\Delta}(\hat{\theta}_T) = \left(\frac{\partial g(\hat{\Psi}_T)}{\partial \Psi_T}\right)' \hat{V}(\hat{\Psi}_T) \left(\frac{\partial g(\hat{\Psi}_T)}{\partial \Psi_T}\right)$$

$$= \left[\frac{1}{1-\hat{\varphi}_T}, \frac{\hat{\beta}_T}{(1-\hat{\varphi}_T)^2}\right] \hat{\sigma}_{uT}^2 (\mathbf{R}_T' \mathbf{H}_T \mathbf{R}_T)^{-1} \begin{bmatrix} \dfrac{1}{1-\hat{\varphi}_T} \\ \dfrac{\hat{\beta}_T}{(1-\hat{\varphi}_T)^2} \end{bmatrix}$$

where $\mathbf{R}_T = (\mathbf{x}_T, \mathbf{y}_{T-1})$. After some algebra, $\hat{V}_{\Delta}(\hat{\theta}_T)$ can be expressed as

$$\hat{V}_{\Delta}(\hat{\theta}_T) = \frac{\hat{\sigma}_{uT}^2}{(1-\hat{\varphi}_T)^2}[1, \hat{\theta}_T] \frac{1}{D_T}$$

$$\times \begin{bmatrix} \sum(y_{t-1}-\bar{y})^2 & -\sum(y_{t-1}-\bar{y})(x_t-\bar{x}) \\ -\sum(y_{t-1}-\bar{y})(x_t-\bar{x}) & \sum(x_{t-1}-\bar{x})^2 \end{bmatrix} \begin{bmatrix} 1 \\ \hat{\theta}_T \end{bmatrix} \quad (2.20)$$

where the bar over the variable denotes the sample mean, and

$$D_T = \left[\sum_{t=1}^{T}(x_t-\bar{x})^2\right]\left[\sum_{t=1}^{T}(y_{t-1}-\bar{y})^2\right] - \left[\sum_{t=1}^{T}(y_{t-1}-\bar{y})(x_t-\bar{x})\right]^2$$

Using (2.5), recalling that $\delta = 0$, and defining $\tilde{y}_{t-1} = y_{t-1} - \bar{y}$, $\tilde{x}_t = x_t - \bar{x}$, and $\tilde{\varkappa}_t = \varkappa_t - \bar{\varkappa}$, we also have

$$\tilde{y}_{t-1} = \theta \tilde{x}_t + \tilde{\varkappa}_t \quad (2.21)$$

where $\tilde{\varkappa}_t$ follows a general linear stationary process. Substituting this result in (2.20), we obtain

$$\hat{V}_{\Delta}(\hat{\theta}_T) = \frac{\hat{\sigma}_{uT}^2}{(1-\hat{\varphi}_T)^2}$$

$$\times \frac{\sum_{t=1}^{T}\tilde{\varkappa}_t^2 + (\hat{\theta}_T - \theta)^2 \sum_{t=1}^{T}\tilde{x}_t^2 - 2(\hat{\theta}_T - \theta)\sum_{t=1}^{T}\tilde{x}_t\tilde{\varkappa}_t}{\left(\sum_{t=1}^{T}\tilde{x}_t^2\right)\left(\sum_{t=1}^{T}\tilde{\varkappa}_t^2\right) - \left(\sum_{t=1}^{T}\tilde{x}_t\tilde{\varkappa}_t\right)^2} \quad (2.22)$$

Since $\tilde{\varkappa}_t$ is $I(0)$ and $\tilde{x}_t$ is $I(1)$, using the results familiar in the literature (e.g., Phillips and Durlauf, 1986), we have

$$T^{-1}\sum_{t=1}^{T}\varkappa_t^2 = O_p(1), \quad T^{-2}\sum_{t=1}^{T}\tilde{x}_t^2 = O_p(1), \quad T^{-1}\sum_{t=1}^{T}\tilde{x}_t\tilde{\varkappa}_t = O_p(1)$$

Also, from the result of Theorem 2.4 we know that $T(\hat{\theta}_T - \theta) = o_p(1)$. Hence, taking probability limits of the right-hand side of (2.22) as $T \to \infty$, we have

$$\hat{V}_{\Delta}(\hat{\theta}_T) = \frac{\sigma_u^2}{(1-\varphi)^2} \frac{1}{T^{-2}\sum_{t=1}^{T}(x_t-\bar{x})^2} + o_p(1)$$

Therefore, the standard error for the estimator of the long-run parameter θ, obtained using the Δ method, is asymptotically the same as that given by (2.19), which was derived assuming that x_t is $I(1)$. *One important advantage of the variance estimator obtained by the Δ method over the asymptotic formula (2.19) lies in the fact that it is asymptotically valid irrespective of whether x_t is $I(1)$ or $I(0)$, while the latter estimator is valid only if x_t is $I(1)$.*

The two variance estimators clearly differ in finite samples. Notice that $(\Sigma_{t=1}^{T} \tilde{x}_t \tilde{x}_t)^2$ is asymptotically negligible compared to other terms in (2.22), but it may not be negligible in finite samples, especially when $\tilde{x}_t$ and $\tilde{\tilde{x}}_t$ are correlated. For a comparison of the small-sample properties of the two variance estimators, see the Monte Carlo results reported in Section 5.

3 General Autoregressive Distributed-Lag Models with Deterministic Trend and $I(1)$ Regressors

Thus far we have derived the estimation and asymptotic results for the simple ARDL $(1, 0)$ model under the two strong assumptions (A1) and (A3). These assumptions, however, are too restrictive in the time-series analysis, and so the estimation procedures developed in Section 2 are not expected to be robust to violation of these assumptions, because the limiting distributions of the OLS estimators would then be inconsistent and/or would depend on nuisance parameters.

We first relax assumption (A1) and allow for the possibility of the error process in (2.1) to be serially correlated. To deal with this serial correlation we consider the ARDL (p, q) model[8]

$$\varphi(L)y_t = \alpha_0 + \alpha_1 t + \boldsymbol{\beta}'(L)\mathbf{x}_t + u_t \qquad (3.1)$$

where $\varphi(L) = 1 - \Sigma_{j=1}^{p} \varphi_j L^j$, and $\boldsymbol{\beta}(L) = \Sigma_{j=0}^{q} \boldsymbol{\beta}_j L^j$, and we assume the following:

(A1)′ The scalar disturbance u_t in the ARDL (p, q) model (3.1) is iid $(0, \sigma_u^2)$.

Using the decomposition $\boldsymbol{\beta}(L) = \boldsymbol{\beta}(1) + (1 - L)\boldsymbol{\beta}^*(L)$, where $\boldsymbol{\beta}(1) = \Sigma_{j=0}^{q} \boldsymbol{\beta}_j, \boldsymbol{\beta}^*(L) = \Sigma_{j=0}^{q-1} \boldsymbol{\beta}_j^* L^j$, and $\boldsymbol{\beta}_j^* = -\Sigma_{i=j+1}^{q} \boldsymbol{\beta}_i$, (3.1) can be rewritten as

$$\varphi(L)y_t = \alpha_0 + \alpha_1 t + \boldsymbol{\beta}' \mathbf{x}_t + \sum_{j=0}^{q-1} \boldsymbol{\beta}_j^{*\prime} \Delta \mathbf{x}_{t-j} + u_t \qquad (3.2)$$

---

[8] For convenience we use the same notation u_t for the disturbance terms in (2.1) and (3.1). In practice, the order of the lag polynomials operating on different elements of $\mathbf{x}_t$ could be different. But this does not affect the asymptotic theory presented later.

where we have used $\beta = \beta(1)$. Similarly, applying the decomposition $\varphi(L) = \varphi(1) + (1 - L)\varphi^*(L)$ to (3.2), where $\varphi(1) = 1 - \Sigma_{i=1}^{p}\varphi_i$, $\varphi^*(L) = \Sigma_{j=0}^{p-1}\varphi_j^* L^j$, and $\varphi_j^* = \Sigma_{i=j+1}^{p}\varphi_i$, we have

$$\varphi(1)y_t = \alpha_0 + \alpha_1 t + \boldsymbol{\beta}'\mathbf{x}_t + \sum_{j=0}^{q-1}\boldsymbol{\beta}_j^{*'}\Delta\mathbf{x}_{t-j} - \varphi^*(L)\Delta y_t + u_t \quad (3.3)$$

Also, from (3.1) we obtain

$$\Delta y_t = [\varphi(L)]^{-1}\{\alpha_1 + \boldsymbol{\beta}'(L)\Delta\mathbf{x}_t + \Delta u_t\}$$

Substituting for Δy_t in (3.3), we have

$$y_t = \mu_0 + \delta t + \boldsymbol{\theta}'\mathbf{x}_t + \frac{\left\{\boldsymbol{\beta}^*(L) - \varphi^*(L)[\varphi(L)]^{-1}\boldsymbol{\beta}(L)\right\}'}{\varphi(1)}\Delta\mathbf{x}_t \quad (3.4)$$
$$+ \frac{\left\{1 - (1 - L)\varphi^*(L)[\varphi(L)]^{-1}\right\}}{\varphi(1)}u_t$$

where

$$\mu_0 = \frac{\alpha_0 - \varphi^*(1)\delta}{\varphi(1)}, \quad \delta = \frac{\alpha_1}{\varphi(1)}, \quad \boldsymbol{\theta} = \boldsymbol{\theta}(1) = \frac{\boldsymbol{\beta}}{\varphi(1)}$$

Now it is easily seen that

$$\frac{(1 - L)\boldsymbol{\beta}^*(L) - (1 - L)\varphi^*(L)[\varphi(L)]^{-1}\boldsymbol{\beta}(L)}{\varphi(1)} = \boldsymbol{\theta}(L) - \boldsymbol{\theta}$$

and

$$\frac{1 - (1 - L)\varphi^*(L)[\varphi(L)]^{-1}}{\varphi(1)} = \frac{1 - \{\varphi(L) - \varphi(1)\}[\varphi(L)]^{-1}}{\varphi(1)} = [\varphi(L)]^{-1}$$

where $\boldsymbol{\theta}(L) = \boldsymbol{\beta}(L)/\varphi(L)$. Using these results and the decomposition $\boldsymbol{\theta}(L) = \boldsymbol{\theta}(1) + (1 - L)\boldsymbol{\theta}^*(L)$, where $\boldsymbol{\theta}^*(L) = \Sigma_{j=0}^{\infty}\boldsymbol{\theta}_j^* L^j$ and $\boldsymbol{\theta}_j^* = -\Sigma_{i=j+1}^{\infty}\boldsymbol{\theta}_i$, in (3.4), we obtain

$$y_t = \mu_0 + \delta t + \boldsymbol{\theta}'\mathbf{x}_t + \boldsymbol{\theta}^{*'}(L)\Delta\mathbf{x}_t + [\varphi(L)]^{-1}u_t \quad (3.5)$$

Matching the regressors on the right-hand side of (3.2) with those in (3.5) we finally obtain

$$y_t = \mu_0 + \delta t + \boldsymbol{\theta}'\mathbf{x}_t + \sum_{j=0}^{q-1}\boldsymbol{\theta}_j^{*'}\Delta\mathbf{x}_{t-j} + \varkappa_{0t} \quad (3.6)$$

where $\varkappa_{0t} = \Sigma_{j=q}^{\infty}\boldsymbol{\theta}_j^{*'}\mathbf{e}_{t-j} + [\varphi(L)]^{-1}u_t$. Similarly,

$$y_{t-i} = \mu_i + \delta t + \boldsymbol{\theta}'\mathbf{x}_t + \sum_{j=0}^{q-1}\mathbf{g}_{ij}'\Delta\mathbf{x}_{t-j} + \varkappa_{it}, \quad i = 1, \ldots, p \quad (3.7)$$

where $\mu_i = \mu_0 - i\delta$, $i = 1, \ldots, p$,

$$g_{ij} = \begin{cases} -\theta & \text{if } i > j \\ \theta^*_{j-1} & \text{if } i \leq j \end{cases}, \quad 0 \leq j \leq q-1, \; i = 1, \ldots, p$$

and

$$\varkappa_{it} = \begin{cases} \sum_{j=q-i}^{\infty} \theta^*_j e_{t-i-j} + [\varphi(L)]^{-1} u_{t-i} & \text{for } i \leq q \\ -\theta' \sum_{j=0}^{i-q-1} e_{t-q-j} + \theta^{*\prime}(L) e_{t-i} + [\varphi(L)]^{-1} u_t & \text{for } i > q \end{cases} \quad (3.8)$$

As in the previous section, we rewrite the ARDL (p, q) model (3.2) in matrix notations in the partitioned regression form,

$$\mathbf{y}_T = \mathbf{G}_T \mathbf{f} + \mathbf{Y}_T \boldsymbol{\varphi} + \mathbf{u}_T = \alpha_0 \boldsymbol{\tau}_T + \mathbf{S}_T \mathbf{c} + \mathbf{W}_T \boldsymbol{\beta}^* + \mathbf{Y}_T \boldsymbol{\varphi} + \mathbf{u}_T \quad (3.9)$$

where $\mathbf{y}_T = (y_1, \ldots, y_T)'$, $\mathbf{y}_{T,-i} = (y_{1-i}, \ldots, y_{T-i})'$ for $i = 1, \ldots, p$, $\mathbf{Y}_T = (\mathbf{y}_{T,-1}, \ldots, \mathbf{y}_{T,-p})$, $\Delta\mathbf{X}_{T,-j} = (\Delta\mathbf{x}_{1-j}, \ldots, \Delta\mathbf{x}_{T-j})$ for $j = 0, \ldots, q-1$, $\mathbf{W}_T = (\Delta\mathbf{X}_{T,0}, \Delta\mathbf{X}_{T,-1}, \ldots, \Delta\mathbf{X}_{T,-q+1})$, $\boldsymbol{\tau}_T = (1, \ldots, 1)'$, $\mathbf{t}_T = (1, \ldots, T)'$, $\mathbf{X}_T = (\mathbf{x}_1, \ldots, \mathbf{x}_T)'$, $\mathbf{G}_T = (\boldsymbol{\tau}_T, \mathbf{t}_T, \mathbf{X}_T, \mathbf{W}_T) = (\boldsymbol{\tau}_T, \mathbf{S}_T, \mathbf{W}_T)$, $\mathbf{u}_T = (u_1, \ldots, u_T)'$, $\mathbf{f} = (\alpha_0, \mathbf{c}', \boldsymbol{\beta}^{*\prime})'$, $\mathbf{c} = (\alpha_1, \boldsymbol{\beta}')'$, $\boldsymbol{\beta}^* = (\boldsymbol{\beta}^*_0, \ldots, \boldsymbol{\beta}^*_{q-1})'$, and $\boldsymbol{\varphi} = (\varphi_1, \ldots, \varphi_p)'$. Note that the dimensions of $\mathbf{Y}_T$, $\mathbf{G}_T$, $\boldsymbol{\varphi}$, and $\mathbf{f}$ are $T \times p$, $T \times (k + kq + 2)$, $p \times 1$, and $(k + kq + 2) \times 1$, respectively.

Theorem 3.1. *Under assumptions (A1)' and (A2)–(A5), the OLS estimators of $\boldsymbol{\varphi}$ and $\mathbf{c} = (\alpha_1, \boldsymbol{\beta}')'$ in the ARDL (p, q) model (3.9) are $\sqrt{T}$-consistent and have the following asymptotic distributions:*

$$\sqrt{T}(\hat{\boldsymbol{\varphi}}_T - \boldsymbol{\varphi}) \overset{a}{\sim} N\{\mathbf{0}, \sigma_u^2 \mathbf{Q}_K^{-1}\} \quad (3.10)$$

where $\mathbf{Q}_K$ is the $p \times p$ positive definite covariance matrix of $(\varkappa_{1t}, \varkappa_{2t}, \ldots, \varkappa_{pt})'$ defined by (3.8), and

$$\sqrt{T}(\hat{\mathbf{c}}_T - \mathbf{c}) \overset{a}{\sim} N\{\mathbf{0}, \sigma_u^2 \boldsymbol{\tau}'_p \mathbf{Q}_K^{-1} \boldsymbol{\tau}_p \boldsymbol{\lambda}\boldsymbol{\lambda}'\} \quad (3.11)$$

where $\boldsymbol{\lambda} = (\delta, \boldsymbol{\theta}')'$, $\boldsymbol{\tau}_p$ is the p-dimensional unit vector, and rank $(\boldsymbol{\lambda}\boldsymbol{\lambda}') = 1$. The OLS estimators of α_0 and $\boldsymbol{\beta}^*$, denoted by $\hat{\alpha}_{0T}$ and $\hat{\boldsymbol{\beta}}^*_T$, are also $\sqrt{T}$-consistent and have the mixture normal distributions, asymptotically. The covariance matrix for all the short-run parameters, $\mathbf{h} = (\mathbf{f}', \boldsymbol{\varphi}')'$, is asymptotically singular with rank equal to $kq + 2$ and can be consistently estimated in the usual way by

$$\hat{V}(\hat{\mathbf{h}}_T) = \hat{\sigma}_{uT}^2 (\mathbf{P}'_{G_T} \mathbf{P}_{G_T})^{-1}$$

where $\mathbf{P}_{G_T} = (\mathbf{G}_T, \mathbf{Y}_T)$, and $\hat{\sigma}_{uT}^2 = T^{-1}(\mathbf{y}_T - \mathbf{P}_{G_T}\hat{\mathbf{h}}_T)'(\mathbf{y}_T - \mathbf{P}_{G_T}\hat{\mathbf{h}}_T)$.

From Theorem 3.1 we also find that $\sqrt{T}(\hat{\alpha}_{1T} - \alpha_1)$ and $\sqrt{T}(\hat{\boldsymbol{\beta}}_T - \boldsymbol{\beta})$ are asymptotically perfectly collinear with $\sqrt{T}(\hat{\boldsymbol{\varphi}}_T - \boldsymbol{\varphi})$; that is,

$$\sqrt{T}\{(\hat{\mathbf{c}}_T - \mathbf{c}) + \boldsymbol{\lambda}[\hat{\varphi}_T(1) - \varphi(1)]\} = o_p(1) \quad (3.12)$$

where $\hat{\varphi}_T(1) = 1 - \Sigma_{i=1}^p \hat{\varphi}_{iT}$. It is also straightforward to show that

$$\hat{\lambda}_T - \lambda = \frac{\{(\hat{\mathbf{c}}_T - \mathbf{c}) + \lambda[\hat{\varphi}_T(1) - \varphi(1)]\}}{\hat{\varphi}_T(1)} \tag{3.13}$$

Using Theorem 3.1 and results (3.12) and (3.13), we have the following:

Theorem 3.2. *Under assumptions* (A1)' *and* (A2)–(A5), *the OLS estimators of the long-run parameters*, $\hat{\lambda}_T = (\hat{\delta}_T, \hat{\theta}_T')' = \hat{\mathbf{c}}_T/\hat{\varphi}_T(1)$ *in* (3.9), *converge to their true values at faster rates than the estimators of the associated short-run parameters and follow the mixture normal distribution asymptotically. Therefore,*

$$\mathbf{Q}_{\tilde{S}_T}^{1/2}\mathbf{D}_{S_T}^{-1}(\hat{\lambda}_T - \lambda) \stackrel{a}{\sim} N\left\{\mathbf{0}, \frac{\sigma_u^2}{[\varphi(1)]^2}\mathbf{I}_{k+1}\right\} \tag{3.14}$$

where $\mathbf{Q}_{\tilde{S}_T}$ *and* $\mathbf{D}_{S_T}$ *are as defined in Theorem 2.2.*

Comparing Theorems 2.2 and 3.2, we find that the presence of the $I(0)$ stationary regressors in (3.9) (i.e., additional lagged changes in y_t and the lagged changes in $\mathbf{x}_t$ which are introduced to deal with the residual serial-correlation problem) does not affect the asymptotic properties of the OLS estimator of the long-run coefficients, δ and θ. Therefore, inferences concerning the long-run parameters can be based on the same standard tests as given by (2.12) and (2.13). In this more general case, however, the expression for the asymptotic variance of $\hat{\lambda}_T$ is still given by (2.11), but with $\sigma_u^2/(1 - \varphi)^2$ replaced by the more general expression $\sigma_u^2/[\varphi(1)]^2$.

We now relax assumption (A3) and allow for the possibility of endogenous regressors, but confine our attention to the case where $\Delta \mathbf{x}_t$ can be represented by a finite-order vector AR(s) process,[9]

$$\mathbf{P}(L)\Delta\mathbf{x}_t = \boldsymbol{\varepsilon}_t \tag{3.15}$$

where $\mathbf{P}(L) = \mathbf{I}_k - \sum_{i=1}^s i\,\mathbf{P}_i$, and $\mathbf{P}_i, i = 1, \ldots, s$, are the $k \times k$ coefficient matrices such that the vector autoregressive process in $\Delta\mathbf{x}_t$ is stable. Here $\boldsymbol{\varepsilon}_t$ are assumed to be serially uncorrelated, but possibly contemporaneously correlated with u_t; namely, we assume that $\boldsymbol{\varsigma}_t = (u_t, \boldsymbol{\varepsilon}_t')'$ follows the multivariate iid process, with mean zero and the covariance matrix

$$\Sigma_{\varsigma\varsigma} = \begin{bmatrix} \sigma_u^2 & \Sigma_{u\varepsilon} \\ \Sigma_{\varepsilon u} & \Sigma_{\varepsilon\varepsilon} \end{bmatrix} \tag{3.16}$$

We shall, however, continue to assume that $\text{cov}(u_{t-j}, \varepsilon_{t-i}) = 0$ for $i \neq j$. Notice that despite this assumption the model is still general enough to allow not only for the contemporaneous but also for cross-

---

[9] Our analysis can also allow for the inclusion of lagged Δy_t terms and a drift term in (3.15) without affecting the results presented later. On this, see Boswijk (1995) and Pesaran et al. (1996).

autocorrelations between u_t and $\Delta \mathbf{x}_t$. With assumption (A3) relaxed, the OLS estimators in (3.1) are no longer consistent. To correct for the endogeneity of $\mathbf{x}_t$, we model the contemporaneous correlation between u_t and $\boldsymbol{\varepsilon}_t$ by the linear regression of u_t on $\boldsymbol{\varepsilon}_t$,

$$u_t = \mathbf{d}' \boldsymbol{\varepsilon}_t + \eta_t \tag{3.17}$$

where, using (3.16), we have $\mathbf{d} = \boldsymbol{\Sigma}_{\varepsilon\varepsilon}^{-1} \boldsymbol{\Sigma}_{u\varepsilon}'$, and $\boldsymbol{\varepsilon}_t$ is strictly exogenous with respect to η_t.[10] Substituting (3.15) in (3.17) we obtain

$$u_t = \mathbf{d}' \mathbf{P}(L) \Delta \mathbf{x}_t + \eta_t \tag{3.18}$$

where the $\Delta \mathbf{x}_{t-i}$, $i = 0, \ldots, s$, are also strictly exogenous with respect to η_t. The parametric correction for the endogenous regressors is then equivalent to extending the ARDL (p, q) model (3.2) to the more general ARDL (p, m) specification,

$$\varphi(L) y_t = \alpha_0 + \alpha_1 t + \boldsymbol{\beta}' \mathbf{x}_t + \sum_{j=0}^{m-1} \boldsymbol{\pi}_j' \Delta \mathbf{x}_{t-j} + \eta_t \tag{3.19}$$

where $m = \max(q, s + 1)$, $\boldsymbol{\pi}_i = \boldsymbol{\beta}_i^* - \mathbf{P}_i' \mathbf{d}$, $i = 0, 1, 2, \ldots, m - 1$, $\mathbf{P}_0 = \mathbf{I}_k$, $\boldsymbol{\beta}_i^* = \mathbf{0}$ for $i \geq q$, and $\mathbf{P}_i = \mathbf{0}$ for $i \geq s$.

We now replace assumption (A3) by

(A3)′ The scalar disturbance η_t in (3.19) is iid $(0, \sigma_\eta^2)$, and $\Delta \mathbf{x}_t$ follows the general stationary process given by (3.15). Furthermore, η_t and $\boldsymbol{\varepsilon}_t$ are uncorrelated such that $\mathbf{x}_t$ and the $\Delta \mathbf{x}_{t-j}$, $j = 0, \ldots, m - 1$, are strictly exogenous with respect to η_t in the ARDL (p, m) model (3.19).

There are two main differences between the ARDL models defined by (3.2) and (3.19). Firstly, the order of lagged $\Delta \mathbf{x}_t$ terms in the two models can differ, and secondly, the coefficients on $\Delta \mathbf{x}_t$ terms and their lagged values have different interpretations. Although this alters the dynamic structure of the model, the basic framework for estimating the long-run parameters and carrying out statistical inference on them is the same as before.

Theorem 3.3. *Under assumptions (A3)′, (A4), and (A5), the OLS estimators of the short-run parameters in (3.19), α_0, α_1, $\boldsymbol{\beta}$, $\varphi_1, \ldots, \varphi_p$, $\boldsymbol{\pi}_0, \ldots, \boldsymbol{\pi}_{m-1}$, are $\sqrt{T}$-consistent and asymptotically have the (mixture) normal distributions. Furthermore, $\sqrt{T}(\hat{\mathbf{c}}_T - \mathbf{c})$ is asymptotically perfectly collinear with $\sqrt{T}[\hat{\varphi}_T(1) - \varphi(1)]$, where $\mathbf{c} = (\alpha_1, \boldsymbol{\beta}')'$ and $\varphi(1) = 1 - \Sigma_{i=1}^p \varphi_i$, such that the covariance matrix for the estimators of the short-run parameters is asymptotically singular, with rank equal to $km + 2$. The asymptotic distribution of the OLS estimators of the long-run parameters, $\hat{\boldsymbol{\lambda}}_T = (\hat{\delta}_T, \hat{\boldsymbol{\theta}}_T')'$ $= \hat{\mathbf{c}}_T/\hat{\varphi}_T(1)$ in (3.19), are mixture normal, and therefore,*

---

[10] The relation (3.17) will be exact when the joint distribution of u_t and $\boldsymbol{\varepsilon}_t$ is normal.

$$\mathbf{Q}_{\tilde{S}_T}^{1/2}\mathbf{D}_{S_T}^{-1}(\hat{\lambda}_T - \lambda) \stackrel{a}{\sim} N\left\{0, \frac{\sigma_\eta^2}{[\varphi(1)]^2}\mathbf{I}_{k+1}\right\}$$ (3.20)

where σ_η^2 is the variance of η_t in (3.19), and $\mathbf{Q}_{\tilde{S}_T}$ and $\mathbf{D}_{S_T}$ are as defined in Theorem 2.2.

There are no fundamental differences between the results of Theorems 2.2, 3.2, and 3.3 as far as the estimators of the long-run parameters are concerned. A comparison of (2.11), (3.14), and (3.20) shows that the asymptotic distributions of the estimators of the long-run parameters, $\hat{\lambda}_T$, under various assumptions discussed earlier differ only by a scalar coefficient.

In sum, in the context of the ARDL model, inference on the long-run parameters, δ and θ, is quite simple and requires a priori knowledge or estimation of the orders of the extended ARDL (p, m) model. Appropriate modification of the orders of the ARDL model is sufficient to simultaneously correct for the residual serial correlation and the problem of endogenous regressors. Variances of the OLS estimators of the long-run coefficients can then be consistently estimated either using (3.20) or by means of the Δ method applied directly to the long-run estimators. Alternatively, one could compute the estimates of the long-run coefficients and their associated standard errors using the Bewley (1979) regression procedure. Bewley's method involves rewriting (3.19) as

$$\varphi(L)y_t = \frac{\alpha_0}{\varphi(1)} + \delta t + \theta'\mathbf{x}_t + \frac{1}{\varphi(1)}\sum_{j=0}^{m-1}\pi_j'\Delta\mathbf{x}_{t-j}$$
$$-\frac{1}{\varphi(1)}\sum_{j=0}^{p-1}\varphi_j^*\Delta y_{t-j} + \frac{\eta_t}{\varphi(1)}$$ (3.21)

and then estimating it by the instrumental-variable (IV) method using $(1, t, \mathbf{x}_t, \Delta\mathbf{x}_t, \Delta\mathbf{x}_{t-1}, \ldots, \Delta\mathbf{x}_{t-m+1}, y_{t-1}, y_{t-2}, \ldots, y_{t-p})$ as instruments. It is easy to show that the IV estimators of δ and θ obtained using (3.21) are *numerically* identical with the OLS estimators of δ and θ based on the ARDL model (3.19) and that the standard errors of the IV estimators from Bewley's regression are *numerically* identical to the standard errors of the OLS estimators of δ and θ obtained using the Δ method (e.g., Baardsen, 1989). The main attraction of Bewley's regression procedure lies in its possible computational convenience as compared with the direct OLS estimation of (3.19) and computation of the associated standard errors by the Δ method.[11]

Finally, we note in passing that the results developed in this section also apply to the case where the underlying regressors $\mathbf{x}_t$, given by (3.15),

---

[11] For a computer implementation of the ARDL approach using the Δ method, see Pesaran and Pesaran (1997).

are $I(0)$. (See footnote 7 in Section 2 and the Monte Carlo simulation results in Section 5.)

4 A Comparison of ARDL and Phillips-Hansen Procedures

Here we focus on the case in which there exists a unique cointegrating relation between $I(1)$ variables y_t and $\mathbf{x}_t$, possibly with a deterministic trend. The case in which there are multiple cointegrating relations among $I(1)$ variables presents additional difficulties and will not be discussed here; see Pesaran and Shin (1997) and the references cited therein.

Consider the following cointegrating relation:

$$y_t = \mu + \delta t + \boldsymbol{\theta}'\mathbf{x}_t + v_t \tag{4.1}$$

$$\Delta \mathbf{x}_t = \mathbf{e}_t \tag{4.2}$$

Although the OLS estimator of $\boldsymbol{\theta}$ is shown to be T-consistent (Stock, 1987), it has also been found that the finite-sample behavior of the OLS estimator is generally very poor (e.g., Banerjee et al., 1986). Especially in the presence of non-zero correlation between v_t and $\mathbf{e}_t$, OLS estimators of $\boldsymbol{\theta}$ in (4.1) are often heavily biased in finite samples, and inferences based on them are invalid because of the dependence of the limiting distribution of the OLS estimators on nuisance parameters; for details, see Phillips and Loretan (1991).

Broadly speaking, there are two basic approaches to cointegration analysis: Johansen's (1991) maximum-likelihood approach, and the Phillips-Hansen (PH) fully modified OLS procedure (Phillips and Hansen, 1990).[12] The ARDL approach to cointegration analysis advanced in this chapter is directly comparable to the PH procedure, and we shall therefore concentrate on this method. PH assume that v_t and $\mathbf{e}_t$ in (4.1) and (4.2) follow the general correlated linear-stationary processes[13]

$$v_t = A_1(L)u_t, \qquad \mathbf{e}_t = \mathbf{A}_2(L)\boldsymbol{\varepsilon}_t \tag{4.3}$$

where $\boldsymbol{\varsigma}_t = (u_t, \boldsymbol{\varepsilon}_t')'$ are serially uncorrelated random variables with zero means and a constant variance matrix given by (3.16). Assuming $A_1(L)$ and $\mathbf{A}_2(L)$ are invertible, (4.1) can be approximated as an ARDL specification by truncating the order of the infinite-order lag polynomials $[A_1(L)]^{-1}$ and $[\mathbf{A}_2(L)]^{-1}$ such that $\varphi(L) \approx [A_1(L)]^{-1}$ and $\mathbf{P}(L) \approx [\mathbf{A}_2(L)]^{-1}$, where the orders of the lag polynomials $\varphi(L)$ and $\mathbf{P}(L)$ are denoted by p and s, respectively. Then we obtain the approximate finite-dimensional ARDL (p, m) specification

---

[12] There are also other related procedures, such as the original two-step method of Engle and Granger (1987), the leads and lags estimation procedure suggested by Saikkonnen (1991) and Stock and Watson (1993), and the canonical method by Park (1992).
[13] For more details, see Phillips and Solo (1992).

$$\varphi(L)y_t = \{\varphi(1)\mu + \delta\varphi'(1)\} + \delta\varphi(1)t + \varphi(L)\boldsymbol{\theta}'\mathbf{x}_t \\ + \boldsymbol{\Sigma}_{u\varepsilon}\boldsymbol{\Sigma}_{\varepsilon\varepsilon}^{-1}\mathbf{P}(L)\Delta\mathbf{x}_t + \eta_t \qquad (4.4)$$

where $\varphi'(1) = -\Sigma_{i=1}^{p} i\varphi_i$, $m = \max(p, s+1)$, and, by construction, the $\mathbf{x}_t$ (and the $\Delta\mathbf{x}_t$) are uncorrelated with η_t.[14] Notice that (4.4) is of the same form as (3.19), with the following relations among their parameters: $\alpha_0 = \varphi(1)\mu + \delta\varphi'(1)$, $\alpha_1 = \delta\varphi(1)$, $\boldsymbol{\beta} = \varphi(1)\boldsymbol{\theta}$, $\boldsymbol{\pi}'(L) = \varphi^*(L)\boldsymbol{\theta}' + \boldsymbol{\Sigma}_{u\varepsilon}\boldsymbol{\Sigma}_{\varepsilon\varepsilon}^{-1}\mathbf{P}(L)$, where $\varphi^*(L)$ is defined by $\varphi(L) = \varphi(1) + (1-L)\varphi^*(L)$. Therefore, the ARDL specification (4.4) and the static cointegrating formulation (4.1) and (4.2) represent alternative ways of modelling the serial correlation in the v_t and the endogeneity of $\mathbf{x}_t$.

Here we examine the PH estimation procedure in the context of the ARDL approximation for the y_t process given by (4.4). Assuming that the $\boldsymbol{\xi}_t = (v_t, \mathbf{e}_t')'$ in (4.1) and (4.2) satisfy the multivariate invariance principle, the long-run variance matrix of $\boldsymbol{\xi}_t$ is given by[15]

$$\boldsymbol{\Omega}_{\xi} = \underset{T\to\infty}{\text{Plim}}\left\{T^{-1}\sum_{t=1}^{T}\boldsymbol{\xi}_t\boldsymbol{\xi}_t' + T^{-1}\sum_{j=1}^{\ell}\left[\sum_{t=j+1}^{T}\boldsymbol{\xi}_t\boldsymbol{\xi}_{t-j}' + \sum_{t=j+1}^{T}\boldsymbol{\xi}_{t-j}\boldsymbol{\xi}_t'\right]\right\} \qquad (4.5)$$

where the lag truncation parameter ℓ increases with T such that $\ell/T \to 0$ as $T \to \infty$. We also define

$$\boldsymbol{\Delta}_{\xi} = \underset{T\to\infty}{\text{Plim}} T^{-1}\left\{\sum_{t=1}^{T}\boldsymbol{\xi}_t\boldsymbol{\xi}_t' + \sum_{j=1}^{\ell}\sum_{t=j+1}^{T}\boldsymbol{\xi}_t\boldsymbol{\xi}_{t-j}'\right\} \qquad (4.6)$$

and partition $\boldsymbol{\Omega}_{\xi}$ and $\boldsymbol{\Delta}_{\xi}$ conformably to $\boldsymbol{\xi}_t = (v_t, \mathbf{e}_t')'$,

$$\boldsymbol{\Omega}_{\xi} = \begin{bmatrix} \omega_{vv} & \boldsymbol{\Omega}_{ve} \\ \boldsymbol{\Omega}_{ev} & \boldsymbol{\Omega}_{ee} \end{bmatrix}, \quad \boldsymbol{\Delta}_{\xi} = \begin{bmatrix} \Delta_{vv} & \boldsymbol{\Delta}_{ve} \\ \boldsymbol{\Delta}_{ev} & \boldsymbol{\Delta}_{ee} \end{bmatrix}$$

Although the use of the consistent estimator of the long-run variance matrix may solve the serial-correlation problem of v_t, this does not address the endogeneity problem. To deal with the cross-correlations between v_t and current and lagged values of $\mathbf{e}_t$, PH consider the modified error process, denoted by v_t^+, which is obtained from the regression of v_t on $\mathbf{e}_t$,

$$v_t^+ = v_t - \boldsymbol{\Omega}_{ve}\boldsymbol{\Omega}_{ee}^{-1}\mathbf{e}_t \qquad (4.7)$$

and v_t^+ is not correlated with $\mathbf{e}_t$ by construction. Then the long-run variance matrix of $\boldsymbol{\xi}_t^+ = (v_t^+, \mathbf{e}_t')'$, denoted by $\boldsymbol{\Omega}_{\xi}^+$, is block-diagonal; that is, $\boldsymbol{\Omega}_{\xi}^+ = \text{Diag}(\omega_{v\cdot e}, \boldsymbol{\Omega}_{ee})$, where

$$\omega_{v\cdot e} = \omega_{vv} - \boldsymbol{\Omega}_{ve}\boldsymbol{\Omega}_{ee}^{-1}\boldsymbol{\Omega}_{ev} \qquad (4.8)$$

---

[14] As before, $\eta_t = u_t - \boldsymbol{\Sigma}_{u\varepsilon}\boldsymbol{\Sigma}_{\varepsilon\varepsilon}^{-1}\boldsymbol{\varepsilon}_t$.
[15] The random sequence $\{\boldsymbol{\xi}_t\}$ is said to satisfy the multivariate invariance principle if it is strictly stationary and ergodic, with zero mean, finite variances, and spectral-density matrix $f_{\xi\xi}(\omega) > 0$. See Phillips and Durlauf (1986) for details.

is the conditional long-run variance of v_t given $\mathbf{e}_t$. Combining (4.7) with (4.1) we have the modified "static" cointegrating relation

$$y_t^+ = \mu + \delta t + \boldsymbol{\theta}'\mathbf{x}_t + v_t^+ \tag{4.9}$$

where $y_t^+ = y_t - \Omega_{ve}\Omega_{ee}^{-1}\Delta\mathbf{x}_t$. There is still a bias term remaining in (4.9) because of the correlation between $\mathbf{x}_t$ and current and lagged values of v_t^+, which is given by $\Delta_{ev}^+ = \Delta_{ev} - \Delta_{ee}\Omega_{ee}^{-1}\Omega_{ev}$. Removing this bias leads to the PH fully modified OLS estimators

$$\begin{bmatrix} \hat{\mu}_T^+ \\ \hat{\delta}_T^+ \\ \hat{\boldsymbol{\theta}}_T^+ \end{bmatrix} = (\mathbf{Z}_T'\mathbf{Z}_T)^{-1}\left\{\mathbf{Z}_T'\hat{\mathbf{y}}_T^+ - \begin{bmatrix} 0 \\ 0 \\ \tau_k \end{bmatrix}T\hat{\Delta}_{ev}^+\right\} \tag{4.10}$$

where $\mathbf{Z}_T = (\boldsymbol{\tau}_T, \mathbf{t}_T, \mathbf{X}_T)$, τ_k is the k-dimensional column unit vector, and $\hat{\mathbf{y}}_T^+$ and $\hat{\Delta}_{ev}^+$ are consistent estimators of y_t^+ and Δ_{ev}^+, respectively.

Since the asymptotic distribution of the PH estimators of the coefficients on t and $\mathbf{x}_t$ (standardized by $T^{3/2}$ and T, respectively) is (mixture) normal, we have

$$\mathbf{Q}_{\tilde{S}_T}^{1/2}\mathbf{D}_{S_T}^{-1}(\hat{\boldsymbol{\lambda}}_T^+ - \boldsymbol{\lambda}) \stackrel{a}{\sim} N\{\mathbf{0}, \omega_{v \cdot e}\mathbf{I}_{k+1}\} \tag{4.11}$$

where $\hat{\boldsymbol{\lambda}}_T^+ = (\hat{\delta}_T^+, \hat{\boldsymbol{\theta}}_T^+)'$. This is directly comparable to the asymptotic result in (3.20) obtained using the ARDL estimation procedure. First, we find that the estimators of the long-run parameters obtained using both the ARDL and the PH estimation procedures have the mixture normal distributions asymptotically, and standard inferences on $\boldsymbol{\theta}$ using the Wald test are therefore asymptotically valid. The main difference between the ARDL-based estimators and the fully modified OLS estimators lies in the computation of the long-run variance of the disturbances in the cointegrating regression. In the case of the ARDL estimation procedure the long-run variance is given by $\sigma_\eta^2/[\varphi(1)]^2$, while in the case of the PH estimation procedure the long-run variance is given by $\omega_{v \cdot e}$. But as Theorem 4.1 will show, $\sigma_\eta^2/[\varphi(1)]^2$ and $\omega_{v \cdot e}$ are identical for the ARDL specification (3.19) [or (4.4)].

Theorem 4.1. *In the context of the ARDL specification (3.19) or (4.4), the long-run variance of the Phillips-Hansen modified error process, v_t^+ in (4.9) (denoted by $\omega_{v \cdot e}$), is equal to $\sigma_\eta^2/[\varphi(1)]^2$, which is the spectral density at zero frequency of $[\varphi(L)]^{-1}\eta_t$ in (3.19).*

5   Finite-Sample Simulation Results

In this section, using Monte Carlo techniques, we compare the finite-sample properties of the Phillips-Hansen fully modified estimators of the long-run parameters with the ARDL-based estimators. In the case of the ARDL procedure we consider two different estimators of the variance of the long-run parameter, namely the asymptotic formula (2.19), which is valid only for $I(1)$ regressors, and the Δ-method formula given by (2.20), which is valid more generally, irrespective of whether the regressors are $I(1)$ or $I(0)$. We also include the OLS estimators of the long-run parameters in the static cointegrating relation as a rather crude benchmark of interest.

We consider the following data-generating process (DGP), where the observations on y_t and x_t are generated according to the finite-order ARDL $(1, 0)$ model:

$$y_t = \alpha + \varphi y_{t-1} + \beta x_t + u_t \tag{5.1}$$

$$x_t - \psi x_{t-1} = \rho(x_t - \psi x_{t-1}) + \varepsilon_t \tag{5.2}$$

with $t = 1, \ldots, T$, where (u_t, ε_t) are serially uncorrelated and are generated according to the following bivariate normal distribution:

$$\begin{pmatrix} u_t \\ \varepsilon_t \end{pmatrix} \sim N\left\{0, \Omega = \begin{pmatrix} 1 & \omega_{12} \\ \omega_{12} & 1 \end{pmatrix}\right\} \tag{5.3}$$

We set $\alpha = 0, \beta = 1$, and $\rho = 0.2$ and experiment with the following parameter values: $\varphi = (0.2, 0.8)$, $\omega_{12} = (-0.5, 0.0, 0.5)$, and $T = (50, 100, 250)$.

We carry out two sets of experiments: In the first set (Experiments 1) we fix ψ at 1 and therefore generate x_t as an $I(1)$ process. In the second set (Experiments 2) we set ψ to 0.95 such that x_t is $I(0)$, but with a high degree of persistence. It is worth noting that in general [irrespective of whether x_t is $I(1)$ or $I(0)$], the long-run parameter on x_t in (5.1) is given by

$$\theta = \frac{\beta + (1 - \psi)\omega_{12}}{1 - \varphi}$$

and θ will be invariant to the parameters of the x_t process only if $\omega_{12} = 0$ [i.e., x_t is strictly exogenous in (5.1)] and/or when $\psi = 1$ [i.e., x_t is $I(1)$]. For a more general treatment of this issue, see Pesaran (1997).

Before discussing the simulation results, notice that when $\omega_{12} = 0$ the correct specification is the ARDL $(1, 0)$ model, and when $\omega_{12} \neq 0$ it is the ARDL $(1, 2)$ model (see Section 3). But since, in general, the true order of the ARDL model is not known a priori, we estimated 30 different ARDL models, namely ARDL (p, m), $p = 1, 2, \ldots, 5$, $m = 0, 1, 2, \ldots, 5$, and used the Akaike information criterion (AIC) and the Schwarz criterion (SC) to select the orders of the ARDL model before estimating the long-run coefficients and carrying out inferences. The estimates obtained by these two-step procedures will be referred to as ARDL-AIC and ARDL-SC, respectively.

The simulation results are summarized in Tables 11.1a–f and 11.2a–f for Experiments 1 and 2, respectively. Summary statistics included in these tables are given on page 403.

Table 11.1a. *Small-Sample Performances of Alternative Estimators of the Long-Run Coefficient θ for Experiments 1 ($\psi = 1$, $\varphi = 0.2$, $\theta_0 = 1.25$, $\omega_{12} = 0$)*

	\multicolumn{3}{c}{Estimator}			\multicolumn{3}{c}{t-test}	POWER⁻ 0.95θ₀	POWER⁺ 1.05θ₀
	BIAS	STDEθ	RMSE	MEAN t	STD t	SIZE			
T = 50									
ARDL (1, 0)									
Asymptotic	−0.0024	0.0620	0.0696	−0.0541	1.0829	0.069	0.248	0.260	
Δ method		0.0637		−0.0543	1.0592	0.063	0.235	0.252	
ARDL-AIC									
Asymptotic	−0.0030	0.0583	0.0906	−0.0502	1.3549	0.130	0.304	0.321	
Δ method		0.0647		−0.0497	1.2561	0.108	0.276	0.296	
ARDL-SC									
Asymptotic	−0.0025	0.0608	0.0721	−0.0540	1.1624	0.087	0.261	0.280	
Δ method		0.0628		−0.0546	1.1236	0.077	0.246	0.270	
PH(0)	−0.0081	0.0496	0.0679	−0.1459	1.3011	0.139	0.345	0.388	
PH(5)	−0.0111	0.0510	0.0730	−0.1920	1.4141	0.156	0.337	0.400	
PH(10)	−0.0147	0.0457	0.0738	−0.3036	1.6749	0.213	0.392	0.482	
PH(20)	−0.0187	0.0376	0.0740	−0.4983	2.1263	0.325	0.470	0.598	
PH(40)	−0.0215	0.0286	0.0730	−0.7727	2.8106	0.434	0.572	0.714	
OLS	−0.0241	0.0526	0.0723	−0.4163	1.2328	0.134	0.252	0.432	
T = 100									
ARDL (1, 0)									
Asymptotic	−0.0013	0.0305	0.0337	−0.0460	1.0379	0.062	0.586	0.608	
Δ method		0.0309		−0.0461	1.0254	0.058	0.579	0.602	
ARDL-AIC									
Asymptotic	−0.0013	0.0295	0.0346	−0.0442	1.1205	0.077	0.606	0.624	
Δ method		0.0304		−0.0443	1.0907	0.071	0.588	0.608	
ARDL-SC									
Asymptotic	−0.0014	0.0303	0.0340	−0.0488	1.0534	0.064	0.586	0.611	
Δ method		0.0308		−0.0490	1.0391	0.061	0.578	0.604	
PH(0)	−0.0041	0.0247	0.0336	−0.1486	1.2645	0.125	0.671	0.731	
PH(5)	−0.0044	0.0271	0.0349	−0.1381	1.2052	0.106	0.626	0.689	
PH(10)	−0.0056	0.0259	0.0359	−0.1887	1.3206	0.141	0.642	0.720	
PH(20)	−0.0074	0.0231	0.0368	−0.2943	1.5814	0.204	0.667	0.786	
PH(40)	−0.0095	0.0189	0.0369	−0.4882	2.0106	0.307	0.720	0.853	
OLS	−0.0128	0.0258	0.0364	−0.4428	1.2208	0.133	0.573	0.791	
T = 250									
ARDL (1, 0)									
Asymptotic	−0.0003	0.0123	0.0132	−0.0309	1.0110	0.053	0.978	0.977	
Δ method		0.0124		−0.0308	1.0064	0.052	0.977	0.976	
ARDL-AIC									
Asymptotic	−0.0002	0.0122	0.0134	−0.0280	1.0444	0.062	0.979	0.975	
Δ method		0.0123		−0.0278	1.0344	0.059	0.977	0.974	
ARDL-SC									
Asymptotic	−0.0003	0.0123	0.0132	−0.0307	1.0155	0.053	0.978	0.977	
Δ method		0.0123		−0.0306	1.0105	0.052	0.977	0.976	
PH(0)	−0.0014	0.0100	0.0132	−0.1316	1.2299	0.113	0.983	0.990	
PH(5)	−0.0009	0.0115	0.0134	−0.0766	1.1006	0.076	0.978	0.983	
PH(10)	−0.0011	0.0114	0.0137	−0.0915	1.1429	0.088	0.974	0.984	
PH(20)	−0.0016	0.0109	0.0141	−0.1367	1.2406	0.117	0.970	0.984	
PH(40)	−0.0024	0.0099	0.0144	−0.2320	1.4475	0.170	0.970	0.987	
OLS	−0.0051	0.0104	0.0145	−0.4408	1.2120	0.136	0.967	0.995	

Note: ARDL-AIC and ARDL-SC represent the estimates based on the ARDL model chosen by the Akaike and Schwarz information criteria, respectively, from the set {ARDL (p, m), $p = 1, \ldots, 5, m = 0, \ldots, 5$} specifications. PH($j$) represents the Phillips-Hansen fully modified OLS estimates based on the Bartlett window of size j. See Section 5 text for a more detailed description of the estimators, tests, and summary statistics. The processes generating y and x are given by (5.1) and (5.2). (This Note applies to all the Tables 11.1a–11.2f.)

Table 11.1b. *Small-Sample Performances of Alternative Estimators of the Long-Run Coefficient* θ *for Experiments 1* ($\psi = 1$, $\varphi = 0.2$, $\theta_0 = 1.25$, $\omega_{12} = 0.5$)

	Estimator			t-test				
	BIAS	STDEθ	RMSE	MEAN t	STD t	SIZE	POWER$^-$ 0.95θ_0	POWER$^+$ 1.05θ_0

T = 50
ARDL (1, 2)
| Asymptotic | −0.0002 | 0.0530 | 0.0649 | −0.0078 | 1.1774 | 0.097 | 0.336 | 0.338 |
| Δ method | | 0.0571 | | −0.0069 | 1.1066 | 0.082 | 0.303 | 0.310 |

ARDL-AIC
| Asymptotic | −0.0018 | 0.0496 | 0.0708 | −0.0341 | 1.3943 | 0.150 | 0.383 | 0.396 |
| Δ method | | 0.0542 | | −0.0382 | 1.2871 | 0.121 | 0.356 | 0.362 |

ARDL-SC
| Asymptotic | −0.0023 | 0.0485 | 0.0653 | −0.0410 | 1.3039 | 0.129 | 0.380 | 0.392 |
| Δ method | | 0.0505 | | −0.0408 | 1.2581 | 0.119 | 0.367 | 0.378 |

PH(0)	−0.0042	0.0434	0.0588	−0.0910	1.2967	0.133	0.399	0.434
PH(5)	0.0035	0.0447	0.0619	0.0532	1.3745	0.150	0.435	0.395
PH(10)	0.0066	0.0400	0.0619	0.1367	1.6243	0.205	0.515	0.446
PH(20)	0.0090	0.0327	0.0614	0.2708	2.0904	0.316	0.627	0.529
PH(40)	0.0106	0.0247	0.0604	0.4501	2.7508	0.442	0.724	0.628

| OLS | 0.0120 | 0.0463 | 0.0593 | 0.2287 | 1.2001 | 0.106 | 0.457 | 0.319 |

T = 100
ARDL (1, 2)
| Asymptotic | −0.0011 | 0.0264 | 0.0311 | −0.0315 | 1.0919 | 0.074 | 0.677 | 0.696 |
| Δ method | | 0.0274 | | −0.0304 | 1.0606 | 0.070 | 0.656 | 0.681 |

ARDL-AIC
| Asymptotic | −0.0019 | 0.0257 | 0.0324 | −0.0533 | 1.1657 | 0.091 | 0.683 | 0.715 |
| Δ method | | 0.0266 | | −0.0521 | 1.1288 | 0.083 | 0.667 | 0.699 |

ARDL-SC
| Asymptotic | −0.0033 | 0.0254 | 0.0317 | −0.1033 | 1.1591 | 0.092 | 0.671 | 0.735 |
| Δ method | | 0.0259 | | −0.1013 | 1.1407 | 0.088 | 0.662 | 0.727 |

PH(0)	−0.0034	0.0216	0.0304	−0.1383	1.2796	0.124	0.738	0.806
PH(5)	−0.0005	0.0238	0.0309	−0.0208	1.2166	0.105	0.732	0.740
PH(10)	0.0008	0.0226	0.0313	0.0291	1.3303	0.134	0.756	0.746
PH(20)	0.0023	0.0201	0.0317	0.1150	1.5907	0.197	0.802	0.773
PH(40)	0.0036	0.0162	0.0316	0.2375	2.0547	0.294	0.861	0.823

| OLS | 0.0049 | 0.0228 | 0.0303 | 0.1910 | 1.2145 | 0.108 | 0.799 | 0.713 |

T = 250
ARDL (1, 2)
| Asymptotic | −0.0001 | 0.0106 | 0.0116 | −0.0279 | 1.0200 | 0.056 | 0.988 | 0.986 |
| Δ method | | 0.0108 | | −0.0276 | 1.0091 | 0.054 | 0.988 | 0.984 |

ARDL-AIC
| Asymptotic | −0.0004 | 0.0106 | 0.0118 | −0.0463 | 1.0451 | 0.064 | 0.986 | 0.986 |
| Δ method | | 0.0107 | | −0.0461 | 1.0319 | 0.060 | 0.986 | 0.985 |

ARDL-SC
| Asymptotic | −0.0011 | 0.0105 | 0.0118 | −0.1116 | 1.0405 | 0.062 | 0.987 | 0.989 |
| Δ method | | 0.0106 | | −0.1109 | 1.0333 | 0.060 | 0.986 | 0.988 |

PH(0)	−0.0012	0.0087	0.0116	−0.1368	1.2274	0.111	0.993	0.996
PH(5)	−0.0002	0.0100	0.0117	−0.0354	1.0941	0.077	0.991	0.988
PH(10)	0.0002	0.0099	0.0119	−0.0083	1.1335	0.082	0.990	0.987
PH(20)	0.0006	0.0094	0.0122	0.0258	1.2316	0.109	0.992	0.985
PH(40)	0.0010	0.0085	0.0124	0.0746	1.4446	0.155	0.993	0.986

| OLS | 0.0022 | 0.0091 | 0.0119 | 0.1958 | 1.1825 | 0.107 | 0.995 | 0.986 |

Table 11.1c. *Small-Sample Performances of Alternative Estimators of the Long-Run Coefficient* θ *for Experiments 1* ($\psi = 1$, $\varphi = 0.2$, $\theta_0 = 1.25$, $\omega_{12} = -0.5$)

	Estimator			t-test				
	BIAS	STDEθ	RMSE	MEAN t	STD t	SIZE	POWER⁻ 0.95θ_0	POWER⁺ 1.05θ_0
T = 50								
ARDL (1, 2)								
Asymptotic	−0.0023	0.0524	0.0662	−0.0400	1.2018	0.099	0.347	0.346
Δ method		0.0563		−0.0354	1.1292	0.082	0.317	0.321
ARDL-AIC								
Asymptotic	−0.0014	0.0492	0.0713	−0.0473	1.4301	0.152	0.390	0.401
Δ method		0.0540		−0.0477	1.2905	0.118	0.351	0.367
ARDL-SC								
Asymptotic	−0.0002	0.0515	0.0668	−0.0274	1.2591	0.114	0.360	0.358
Δ method		0.0545		−0.0255	1.1888	0.095	0.336	0.339
PH(0)	−0.0117	0.0441	0.0639	−0.2401	1.3173	0.142	0.380	0.488
PH(5)	−0.0258	0.0486	0.0787	−0.4475	1.4072	0.175	0.325	0.496
PH(10)	−0.0361	0.0456	0.0870	−0.7109	1.6621	0.246	0.355	0.579
PH(20)	−0.0471	0.0394	0.0947	−1.1657	2.1190	0.364	0.406	0.692
PH(40)	−0.0542	0.0311	0.0984	−1.7815	2.7333	0.501	0.491	0.812
OLS	−0.0606	0.0582	0.1009	−0.9327	1.1757	0.192	0.170	0.560
T = 100								
ARDL (1, 2)								
Asymptotic	−0.0007	0.0260	0.0296	−0.0236	1.0836	0.068	0.685	0.696
Δ method		0.0269		−0.0234	1.0515	0.062	0.668	0.680
ARDL-AIC								
Asymptotic	−0.0004	0.0249	0.0307	−0.0239	1.1768	0.097	0.710	0.716
Δ method		0.0259		−0.0240	1.1290	0.086	0.694	0.701
ARDL-SC								
Asymptotic	0.0007	0.0250	0.0299	0.0174	1.1332	0.086	0.724	0.703
Δ method		0.0257		0.0158	1.1056	0.078	0.711	0.690
PH(0)	−0.0044	0.0216	0.0292	−0.1858	1.2470	0.118	0.738	0.808
PH(5)	−0.0077	0.0248	0.0323	−0.2593	1.1730	0.098	0.655	0.781
PH(10)	−0.0115	0.0244	0.0357	−0.3974	1.2758	0.135	0.631	0.811
PH(20)	−0.0168	0.0230	0.0402	−0.6455	1.5064	0.212	0.617	0.858
PH(40)	−0.0224	0.0198	0.0442	−1.0711	1.9059	0.326	0.627	0.912
OLS	−0.0298	0.0286	0.0484	−0.9267	1.1078	0.178	0.393	0.888
T = 250								
ARDL (1, 2)								
Asymptotic	−0.0000	0.0105	0.0115	−0.0050	1.0168	0.056	0.988	0.991
Δ method		0.0106		−0.0049	1.0053	0.053	0.987	0.990
ARDL-AIC								
Asymptotic	0.0002	0.0103	0.0117	0.0087	1.0603	0.061	0.989	0.990
Δ method		0.0105		0.0084	1.0446	0.058	0.988	0.988
ARDL-SC								
Asymptotic	0.0006	0.0101	0.0116	0.0471	1.0637	0.068	0.991	0.990
Δ method		0.0102		0.0466	1.0539	0.065	0.990	0.989
PH(0)	−0.0013	0.0087	0.0115	−0.1378	1.2172	0.113	0.990	0.994
PH(5)	−0.0014	0.0101	0.0118	−0.1122	1.0691	0.068	0.985	0.993
PH(10)	−0.0021	0.0102	0.0124	−0.1671	1.0989	0.078	0.977	0.994
PH(20)	−0.0035	0.0101	0.0136	−0.2857	1.1879	0.108	0.968	0.995
PH(40)	−0.0056	0.0096	0.0154	−0.5046	1.3807	0.170	0.958	0.997
OLS	−0.0119	0.0115	0.0194	−0.9203	1.1137	0.180	0.906	1.000

Table 11.1d. *Small-Sample Performances of Alternative Estimators of the Long-Run Coefficient* θ *for Experiments 1* ($\psi = 1$, $\varphi = 0.8$, $\theta_0 = 5$, $\omega_{12} = 0$)

	Estimator			t-test				
	BIAS	STDEθ	RMSE	MEAN t	STD t	SIZE	POWER$^-$ 0.95θ_0	POWER$^+$ 1.05θ_0
T = 50								
ARDL (1, 0)								
Asymptotic	−0.0244	0.2486	0.3773	−0.1811	1.3950	0.142	0.274	0.332
Δ method		0.3231		−0.1588	1.0951	0.072	0.161	0.245
ARDL-AIC								
Asymptotic	−0.0197	0.2268	0.4161	−0.2150	1.8688	0.224	0.357	0.407
Δ method		0.3103		−0.1924	1.3541	0.128	0.227	0.298
ARDL-SC								
Asymptotic	−0.0235	0.2437	0.3903	−0.1969	1.5126	0.164	0.298	0.350
Δ method		0.3199		−0.1721	1.1649	0.086	0.178	0.263
PH(0)	−1.1527	0.2280	1.3786	−5.2185	3.3720	0.852	0.769	0.910
PH(5)	−0.9850	0.3914	1.2493	−2.6525	2.0803	0.626	0.493	0.752
PH(10)	−0.9915	0.4204	1.2911	−2.5283	2.1741	0.595	0.468	0.711
PH(20)	−1.0968	0.4223	1.4192	−2.9371	2.6879	0.639	0.530	0.728
PH(40)	−1.2228	0.3604	1.5239	−4.1524	3.6499	0.723	0.646	0.791
OLS	−1.3488	0.2873	1.6072	−4.8132	3.0641	0.845	0.767	0.894
T = 100								
ARDL (1, 0)								
Asymptotic	−0.0111	0.1222	0.1524	−0.0995	1.1354	0.088	0.570	0.605
Δ method		0.1406		−0.0910	1.0035	0.055	0.505	0.542
ARDL-AIC								
Asymptotic	−0.0109	0.1173	0.1559	−0.1113	1.2727	0.120	0.594	0.631
Δ method		0.1373		−0.1032	1.0982	0.078	0.519	0.557
ARDL-SC								
Asymptotic	−0.0112	0.1214	0.1548	−0.1061	1.1646	0.094	0.574	0.609
Δ method		0.1399		−0.0969	1.0241	0.060	0.507	0.548
PH(0)	−0.6722	0.1317	0.8221	−4.8927	2.9266	0.862	0.676	0.964
PH(5)	−0.5162	0.2309	0.6673	−2.1405	1.5251	0.527	0.295	0.833
PH(10)	−0.4743	0.2514	0.6448	−1.7892	1.4493	0.426	0.230	0.756
PH(20)	−0.5079	0.2719	0.7115	−1.7609	1.5673	0.414	0.254	0.715
PH(40)	−0.6113	0.2761	0.8307	−2.2095	2.0303	0.522	0.352	0.751
OLS	−0.7984	0.1649	0.9748	−4.6328	2.7775	0.853	0.698	0.947
T = 250								
ARDL (1, 0)								
Asymptotic	−0.0013	0.0493	0.0566	−0.0392	1.0577	0.066	0.970	0.971
Δ method		0.0523		−0.0380	1.0056	0.053	0.962	0.963
ARDL-AIC								
Asymptotic	−0.0012	0.0486	0.0583	−0.0433	1.1060	0.076	0.970	0.968
Δ method		0.0519		−0.0426	1.0420	0.062	0.962	0.959
ARDL-SC								
Asymptotic	−0.0013	0.0492	0.0566	−0.0402	1.0605	0.066	0.970	0.972
Δ method		0.0523		−0.0391	1.0081	0.053	0.962	0.964
PH(0)	−0.3017	0.0593	0.3781	−4.6556	2.7008	0.852	0.611	0.999
PH(5)	−0.2115	0.1030	0.2746	−1.8674	1.2164	0.473	0.314	0.986
PH(10)	−0.1718	0.1085	0.2348	−1.4197	1.0624	0.290	0.332	0.978
PH(20)	−0.1588	0.1142	0.2327	−1.2056	1.0517	0.217	0.366	0.961
PH(40)	−0.1917	0.1265	0.2864	−1.2862	1.1938	0.260	0.349	0.944
OLS	−0.3617	0.0739	0.4534	−4.4773	2.6420	0.844	0.596	0.996

Table 11.1e. *Small-Sample Performances of Alternative Estimators of the Long-Run Coefficient θ for Experiments 1 ($\psi = 1$, $\varphi = 0.8$, $\theta_0 = 5$, $\omega_{12} = 0.5$)*

	Estimator				t-test			POWER⁻ 0.95θ₀	POWER⁺ 1.05θ₀
	BIAS	STDEθ	RMSE	MEAN t	STD t	SIZE			
T = 50									
ARDL (1, 2)									
Asymptotic	−0.0281	0.2138	0.3419	−0.2619	1.5128	0.180		0.329	0.406
Δ method		0.3016		−0.2224	1.1135	0.078		0.186	0.291
ARDL-AIC									
Asymptotic	−0.0081	0.1946	0.3739	−0.1926	1.8997	0.249		0.414	0.445
Δ method		0.2795		−0.1906	1.3497	0.129		0.262	0.342
ARDL-SC									
Asymptotic	−0.0148	0.2058	0.3535	−0.1998	1.6764	0.208		0.377	0.418
Δ method		0.2841		−0.1915	1.2583	0.108		0.232	0.320
PH(0)	−1.0521	0.2057	1.2676	−5.2811	3.4463	0.848		0.763	0.911
PH(5)	−0.8982	0.3524	1.1512	−2.6729	2.1043	0.637		0.492	0.768
PH(10)	−0.9036	0.3773	1.1872	−2.5416	2.1803	0.598		0.466	0.731
PH(20)	−0.9967	0.3769	1.2983	−2.9728	2.7116	0.640		0.530	0.742
PH(40)	−1.1092	0.3206	1.3917	−4.2284	3.6902	0.728		0.641	0.812
OLS	−1.2234	0.2560	1.4665	−4.9168	3.1793	0.836		0.769	0.897
T = 100									
ARDL (1, 2)									
Asymptotic	−0.0141	0.1060	0.1419	−0.1580	1.2264	0.108		0.654	0.704
Δ method		0.1260		−0.1382	1.0487	0.060		0.566	0.629
ARDL-AIC									
Asymptotic	−0.0091	0.1028	0.1477	−0.1223	1.3249	0.134		0.675	0.706
Δ method		0.1225		−0.1117	1.1241	0.081		0.588	0.632
ARDL-SC									
Asymptotic	−0.0040	0.1070	0.1429	−0.0730	1.2447	0.110		0.668	0.677
Δ method		0.1264		−0.0697	1.0721	0.062		0.586	0.606
PH(0)	−0.6110	0.1199	0.7490	−4.8736	2.9267	0.856		0.661	0.970
PH(5)	−0.4687	0.2096	0.6048	−2.1350	1.5118	0.539		0.275	0.854
PH(10)	−0.4302	0.2279	0.5824	−1.7892	1.4352	0.431		0.216	0.780
PH(20)	−0.4613	0.2460	0.6413	−1.7713	1.5587	0.421		0.240	0.746
PH(40)	−0.5561	0.2504	0.7521	−2.2061	1.9845	0.519		0.356	0.767
OLS	−0.7222	0.1484	0.8841	−4.6446	2.8003	0.844		0.685	0.955
T = 250									
ARDL (1, 2)									
Asymptotic	−0.0017	0.0426	0.0500	−0.0639	1.0739	0.070		0.987	0.980
Δ method		0.0459		−0.0611	1.0102	0.055		0.981	0.972
ARDL-AIC									
Asymptotic	−0.0006	0.0423	0.0507	−0.0454	1.1042	0.077		0.987	0.978
Δ method		0.0456		−0.0441	1.0367	0.058		0.982	0.971
ARDL-SC									
Asymptotic	0.0024	0.0436	0.0504	0.0180	1.0585	0.068		0.989	0.975
Δ method		0.0468		0.0144	0.9982	0.052		0.982	0.968
PH(0)	−0.2711	0.0535	0.3438	−4.6110	2.6983	0.848		0.615	0.998
PH(5)	−0.1898	0.0928	0.2491	−1.8488	1.2062	0.467		0.364	0.993
PH(10)	−0.1541	0.0977	0.2132	−1.4035	1.0449	0.281		0.397	0.987
PH(20)	−0.1427	0.1026	0.2126	−1.1924	1.0333	0.210		0.436	0.977
PH(40)	−0.1719	0.1136	0.2610	−1.2689	1.1714	0.251		0.399	0.965
OLS	−0.3234	0.0660	0.4105	−4.4562	2.6611	0.843		0.597	0.996

Table 11.1f. *Small-Sample Performances of Alternative Estimators of the Long-Run Coefficient* θ *for Experiments 1* ($\psi = 1$, $\varphi = 0.8$, $\theta_0 = 5$, $\omega_{12} = -0.5$)

	Estimator			t-test				
	BIAS	STDEθ	RMSE	MEAN t	STD t	SIZE	POWER⁻ 0.95θ_0	POWER⁺ 1.05θ_0
T = 50								
ARDL (1, 2)								
Asymptotic	−0.0351	0.2141	0.3604	−0.2843	1.5817	0.178	0.332	0.420
Δ method		0.3018		−0.2273	1.1431	0.081	0.190	0.286
ARDL-AIC								
Asymptotic	−0.0267	0.1932	0.3823	−0.2711	1.9131	0.255	0.414	0.475
Δ method		0.2766		−0.2284	1.3410	0.131	0.265	0.351
ARDL-SC								
Asymptotic	−0.0421	0.2047	0.3627	−0.3221	1.6632	0.207	0.354	0.452
Δ method		0.2802		−0.2580	1.2294	0.102	0.224	0.338
PH(0)	−1.2738	0.2452	1.5167	−5.3680	3.4405	0.858	0.783	0.912
PH(5)	−1.0925	0.4220	1.3767	−2.7297	2.1095	0.635	0.523	0.754
PH(10)	−1.1009	0.4548	1.4258	−2.5958	2.2140	0.602	0.499	0.707
PH(20)	−1.2209	0.4585	1.5736	−3.0096	2.7512	0.638	0.548	0.726
PH(40)	−1.3569	0.3908	1.6906	−4.2580	3.7440	0.721	0.652	0.790
OLS	−1.4993	0.3142	1.7804	−4.8871	3.0990	0.842	0.778	0.896
T = 100								
ARDL (1, 2)								
Asymptotic	−0.0085	0.1058	0.1410	−0.1100	1.2105	0.099	0.666	0.708
Δ method		0.1265		−0.1004	1.0196	0.056	0.577	0.627
ARDL-AIC								
Asymptotic	−0.0100	0.0998	0.1445	−0.1264	1.3475	0.129	0.695	0.732
Δ method		0.1192		−0.1156	1.1287	0.080	0.605	0.662
ARDL-SC								
Asymptotic	−0.0181	0.1018	0.1424	−0.1962	1.2682	0.117	0.667	0.739
Δ method		0.1196		−0.1736	1.0818	0.073	0.583	0.677
PH(0)	−0.7307	0.1420	0.8912	−4.9305	2.9017	0.864	0.689	0.963
PH(5)	−0.5621	0.2485	0.7219	−2.1668	1.5095	0.541	0.303	0.826
PH(10)	−0.5180	0.2703	0.6995	−1.8204	1.4451	0.436	0.234	0.749
PH(20)	−0.5573	0.2929	0.7748	−1.8001	1.5739	0.421	0.256	0.704
PH(40)	−0.6716	0.2985	0.9076	−2.2454	2.0148	0.523	0.367	0.736
OLS	−0.8716	0.1805	1.0629	−4.6160	2.7321	0.852	0.698	0.948
T = 250								
ARDL (1, 2)								
Asymptotic	−0.0005	0.0425	0.0499	−0.0255	1.0656	0.062	0.986	0.986
Δ method		0.0458		−0.0248	0.9947	0.043	0.979	0.982
ARDL-AIC								
Asymptotic	−0.0013	0.0412	0.0509	−0.0422	1.1162	0.076	0.986	0.986
Δ method		0.0445		−0.0408	1.0395	0.050	0.978	0.980
ARDL-SC								
Asymptotic	−0.0044	0.0413	0.0499	−0.1093	1.0978	0.074	0.984	0.990
Δ method		0.0443		−0.1026	1.0311	0.054	0.978	0.985
PH(0)	−0.3279	0.0638	0.4120	−4.7000	2.7099	0.862	0.595	0.996
PH(5)	−0.2304	0.1105	0.3005	−1.8942	1.2198	0.478	0.285	0.985
PH(10)	−0.1874	0.1161	0.2579	−1.4430	1.0589	0.295	0.287	0.973
PH(20)	−0.1740	0.1220	0.2587	−1.2274	1.0530	0.221	0.324	0.953
PH(40)	−0.2099	0.1359	0.3180	−1.3035	1.2014	0.257	0.304	0.934
OLS	−0.3948	0.0807	0.4964	−4.4736	2.6336	0.853	0.596	0.993

Table 11.2a. *Small-Sample Performances of Alternative Estimators of the Long-Run Coefficient θ for Experiments 2 ($\psi = 0.95$, $\varphi = 0.2$, $\theta_0 = 1.25$, $\omega_{12} = 0$)*

	Estimator			*t*-test				
	BIAS	STDEθ	RMSE	MEAN *t*	STD *t*	SIZE	POWER$^-$ 0.95θ_0	POWER$^+$ 1.05θ_0

T = 50
ARDL (1, 0)
| Asymptotic | −0.0036 | 0.0731 | 0.0793 | −0.0692 | 1.0714 | 0.066 | 0.174 | 0.203 |
| Δ method | | 0.0755 | | −0.0701 | 1.0431 | 0.057 | 0.159 | 0.193 |

ARDL-AIC
| Asymptotic | −0.0036 | 0.0684 | 0.0920 | −0.0679 | 1.3686 | 0.134 | 0.244 | 0.259 |
| Δ method | | 0.0742 | | −0.0689 | 1.2429 | 0.102 | 0.209 | 0.235 |

ARDL-SC
Asymptotic	−0.0040	0.0716	0.0826	−0.0736	1.1721	0.087	0.194	0.222
Δ method		0.0744		−0.0749	1.1178	0.073	0.176	0.211
PH(0)	−0.0113	0.0584	0.0782	−0.1813	1.2873	0.130	0.257	0.320
PH(5)	−0.0171	0.0602	0.0848	−0.2683	1.3992	0.162	0.261	0.347
PH(10)	−0.0229	0.0540	0.0868	−0.4303	1.6533	0.225	0.312	0.435
PH(20)	−0.0288	0.0446	0.0871	−0.6968	2.0671	0.317	0.383	0.561
PH(40)	−0.0319	0.0343	0.0860	−1.0271	2.6683	0.432	0.478	0.671
OLS	−0.0340	0.0620	0.0846	−0.5221	1.1981	0.137	0.166	0.377

T = 100
ARDL (1, 0)
| Asymptotic | −0.0020 | 0.0426 | 0.0462 | −0.0614 | 1.0669 | 0.067 | 0.351 | 0.383 |
| Δ method | | 0.0435 | | −0.0615 | 1.0479 | 0.065 | 0.337 | 0.372 |

ARDL-AIC
| Asymptotic | −0.0020 | 0.0413 | 0.0488 | −0.0601 | 1.1881 | 0.096 | 0.378 | 0.414 |
| Δ method | | 0.0431 | | −0.0591 | 1.1332 | 0.086 | 0.357 | 0.394 |

ARDL-SC
Asymptotic	−0.0023	0.0423	0.0468	−0.0675	1.0893	0.073	0.354	0.393
Δ method		0.0433		−0.0671	1.0664	0.071	0.340	0.383
PH(0)	−0.0072	0.0345	0.0462	−0.2024	1.2900	0.134	0.438	0.551
PH(5)	−0.0092	0.0379	0.0488	−0.2269	1.2595	0.123	0.382	0.505
PH(10)	−0.0125	0.0362	0.0505	−0.3324	1.3766	0.156	0.401	0.562
PH(20)	−0.0165	0.0327	0.0515	−0.5196	1.6101	0.224	0.429	0.640
PH(40)	−0.0202	0.0272	0.0520	−0.8056	2.0194	0.316	0.490	0.748
OLS	−0.0233	0.0361	0.0514	−0.6222	1.2181	0.155	0.305	0.651

T = 250
ARDL (1, 0)
| Asymptotic | −0.0011 | 0.0228 | 0.0237 | −0.0540 | 1.0222 | 0.058 | 0.766 | 0.789 |
| Δ method | | 0.0231 | | −0.0537 | 1.0099 | 0.055 | 0.760 | 0.780 |

ARDL-AIC
| Asymptotic | −0.0009 | 0.0225 | 0.0245 | −0.0485 | 1.0733 | 0.074 | 0.771 | 0.782 |
| Δ method | | 0.0231 | | −0.0472 | 1.0451 | 0.067 | 0.759 | 0.768 |

ARDL-SC
Asymptotic	−0.0011	0.0227	0.0239	−0.0557	1.0324	0.060	0.766	0.786
Δ method		0.0230		−0.0553	1.0193	0.057	0.760	0.778
PH(0)	−0.0047	0.0185	0.0240	−0.2455	1.2413	0.124	0.819	0.909
PH(5)	−0.0044	0.0213	0.0248	−0.1981	1.1302	0.088	0.752	0.847
PH(10)	−0.0060	0.0212	0.0255	−0.2749	1.1668	0.100	0.734	0.859
PH(20)	−0.0087	0.0205	0.0266	−0.4253	1.2492	0.133	0.717	0.890
PH(40)	−0.0119	0.0190	0.0279	−0.6460	1.3971	0.187	0.711	0.920
OLS	−0.0161	0.0192	0.0288	−0.8167	1.1920	0.176	0.666	0.955

Table 11.2b. *Small-Sample Performances of Alternative Estimators of the Long-Run Coefficient θ for Experiments 2 ($\psi = 0.95$, $\varphi = 0.2$, $\theta_0 = 1.275$, $\omega_{12} = 0.5$)*

	\multicolumn{3}{c}{Estimator}			\multicolumn{3}{c}{t-test}	
	BIAS	STDEθ	RMSE	MEAN t	STD t	SIZE	POWER⁻ $0.95\theta_0$	POWER⁺ $1.05\theta_0$
T = 50								
ARDL (1, 2)								
Asymptotic	0.0004	0.0625	0.0742	−0.0157	1.1673	0.092	0.254	0.268
Δ method		0.0681		−0.0154	1.0823	0.071	0.224	0.237
ARDL-AIC								
Asymptotic	−0.0012	0.0581	0.0817	−0.0505	1.4144	0.160	0.323	0.333
Δ method		0.0642		−0.0568	1.2877	0.129	0.283	0.302
ARDL-SC								
Asymptotic	−0.0022	0.0571	0.0736	−0.0600	1.2948	0.126	0.304	0.328
Δ method		0.0597		−0.0594	1.2432	0.115	0.289	0.302
PH(0)	−0.0055	0.0512	0.0677	−0.1250	1.2723	0.122	0.314	0.366
PH(5)	0.0051	0.0526	0.0721	0.0650	1.3665	0.149	0.361	0.336
PH(10)	0.0091	0.0470	0.0720	0.1691	1.6128	0.198	0.448	0.374
PH(20)	0.0123	0.0387	0.0704	0.3148	2.0131	0.303	0.562	0.447
PH(40)	0.0140	0.0296	0.0690	0.4917	2.6267	0.416	0.671	0.554
OLS	0.0149	0.0543	0.0773	0.2431	1.1708	0.100	0.368	0.250
T = 100								
ARDL (1, 2)								
Asymptotic	−0.0008	0.0366	0.0420	−0.0203	1.1131	0.080	0.461	0.469
Δ method		0.0385		−0.0192	1.0631	0.068	0.437	0.443
ARDL-AIC								
Asymptotic	−0.0023	0.0357	0.0442	−0.0595	1.2069	0.106	0.473	0.505
Δ method		0.0376		0.0593	1.1466	0.090	0.446	0.476
ARDL-SC								
Asymptotic	−0.0047	0.0351	0.0424	−0.1170	1.1797	0.100	0.458	0.536
Δ method		0.0361		−0.1141	1.1521	0.094	0.448	0.520
PH(0)	−0.0053	0.0299	0.0403	−0.1705	1.2837	0.130	0.540	0.634
PH(5)	0.0005	0.0330	0.0417	0.0113	1.2449	0.117	0.539	0.528
PH(10)	0.0028	0.0314	0.0422	0.0885	1.3590	0.150	0.580	0.541
PH(20)	0.0053	0.0281	0.0423	0.2002	1.5732	0.197	0.658	0.582
PH(40)	0.0068	0.0233	0.0416	0.3326	1.9610	0.285	0.745	0.648
OLS	0.0085	0.0313	0.0401	0.2608	1.2037	0.112	0.640	0.482
T = 250								
ARDL (1, 2)								
Asymptotic	−0.0005	0.0198	0.0209	−0.0283	1.0388	0.058	0.867	0.876
Δ method		0.0204		−0.0273	1.0087	0.052	0.857	0.862
ARDL-AIC								
Asymptotic	−0.0012	0.0197	0.0126	−0.0634	1.0823	0.067	0.858	0.877
Δ method		0.0204		−0.0629	1.0452	0.058	0.846	0.862
ARDL-SC								
Asymptotic	−0.0037	0.0196	0.0216	−0.1904	1.0619	0.068	0.834	0.908
Δ method		0.0199		−0.1882	1.0427	0.064	0.826	0.902
PH(0)	−0.0038	0.0162	0.0207	−0.2309	1.2317	0.116	0.903	0.952
PH(5)	−0.0001	0.0186	0.0211	−0.0095	1.1180	0.078	0.889	0.890
PH(10)	0.0012	0.0184	0.0215	0.0587	1.1619	0.092	0.900	0.874
PH(20)	0.0027	0.0177	0.0218	0.1445	1.2417	0.109	0.915	0.874
PH(40)	0.0041	0.0164	0.0218	0.2516	1.3865	0.153	0.932	0.877
OLS	0.0059	0.0167	0.0210	0.3436	1.1777	0.108	0.956	0.878

Table 11.2c. *Small-Sample Performances of Alternative Estimators of the Long-Run Coefficient* θ *for Experiments 2 (*ψ *= 0.95,* φ *= 0.2,* θ₀ *= 1.225,* ω₁₂ *= −0.5)*

	Estimator					t-test		
	BIAS	STDEθ	RMSE	MEAN t	STD t	SIZE	POWER⁻ 0.95θ₀	POWER⁺ 1.05θ₀
T = 50								
ARDL (1, 2)								
Asymptotic	−0.0019	0.0618	0.0750	−0.0370	1.2059	0.106	0.261	0.269
Δ method		0.0672		−0.0349	1.1190	0.080	0.231	0.235
ARDL-AIC								
Asymptotic	−0.0012	0.0582	0.0827	−0.0584	1.4449	0.161	0.296	0.319
Δ method		0.0650		−0.0583	1.2759	0.124	0.260	0.279
ARDL-SC								
Asymptotic	−0.0002	0.0610	0.0759	−0.0351	1.2519	0.110	0.270	0.279
Δ method		0.0652		−0.0349	1.1725	0.092	0.247	0.252
PH(0)	−0.0148	0.0518	0.0711	−0.2694	1.2999	0.137	0.272	0.382
PH(5)	0.0364	0.0569	0.0884	−0.5929	1.3653	0.175	0.232	0.435
PH(10)	−0.0516	0.0534	0.0998	−0.9550	1.6038	0.277	0.257	0.545
PH(20)	−0.0666	0.0461	0.1090	−1.5177	1.9610	0.395	0.316	0.693
PH(40)	−0.0752	0.0364	0.1133	−2.2398	2.5062	0.530	0.422	0.810
OLS	−0.0804	0.0678	0.1159	−1.1235	1.0804	0.219	0.099	0.542
T = 100								
ARDL (1, 2)								
Asymptotic	−0.0015	0.0362	0.0414	−0.0395	1.1251	0.083	0.441	0.471
Δ method		0.0380		−0.0372	1.0760	0.077	0.409	0.438
ARDL-AIC								
Asymptotic	−0.0015	0.0346	0.0435	−0.0550	1.2584	0.107	0.477	0.507
Δ method		0.0368		−0.0506	1.2771	0.096	0.437	0.472
ARDL-SC								
Asymptotic	0.0013	0.0349	0.0418	0.0222	1.1740	0.089	0.492	0.476
Δ method		0.0363		0.0201	1.1307	0.081	0.464	0.451
PH(0)	−0.0083	0.0301	0.0408	−0.2577	1.2815	0.133	0.492	0.636
PH(5)	−0.0175	0.0345	0.0476	−0.4592	1.2230	0.132	0.370	0.632
PH(10)	−0.0262	0.0339	0.0541	−0.7225	1.3310	0.189	0.342	0.696
PH(20)	−0.0369	0.0319	0.0617	−1.1483	1.5398	0.291	0.329	0.787
PH(40)	−0.0460	0.0276	0.0675	−1.7668	1.9121	0.437	0.352	0.876
OLS	−0.0539	0.0393	0.0725	−1.3037	1.0515	0.270	0.128	0.836
T = 250								
ARDL (1, 2)								
Asymptotic	−0.0007	0.0195	0.0208	−0.0336	1.0493	0.060	0.849	0.868
Δ method		0.0201		−0.0325	1.0186	0.050	0.837	0.852
ADRL-AIC								
Asymptotic	−0.0001	0.0191	0.0214	−0.0097	1.1059	0.073	0.854	0.864
Δ method		0.0198		−0.0090	1.0653	0.063	0.839	0.847
ARDL-SC								
Asymptotic	0.0013	0.0187	0.0209	0.0635	1.0954	0.073	0.877	0.856
Δ method		0.0191		0.0621	1.0701	0.067	0.868	0.847
PH(0)	−0.0049	0.0161	0.0209	−0.2901	1.2275	0.114	0.869	0.951
PH(5)	−0.0078	0.0190	0.0228	−0.3886	1.0971	0.094	0.768	0.934
PH(10)	−0.0122	0.0193	0.0257	−0.6034	1.1300	0.128	0.712	0.949
PH(20)	−0.0190	0.0193	0.0308	−0.9650	1.2181	0.212	0.622	0.967
PH(40)	−0.0267	0.0186	0.0368	−1.4660	1.3850	0.326	0.540	0.982
OLS	−0.0372	0.0210	0.0444	−1.7193	0.9970	0.394	0.312	0.998

Table 11.2d. *Small-Sample Performances of Alternative Estimators of the Long-Run Coefficient* θ *for Experiments 2* ($\psi = 0.95$, $\varphi = 0.8$, $\theta_0 = 5$, $\omega_{12} = 0$)

	\multicolumn{5}{c}{Estimator}	\multicolumn{4}{c}{t-test}
	BIAS	STDEθ	RMSE	MEAN t	STD t	SIZE	POWER⁻ 0.95θ_0	POWER⁺ 1.05θ_0
T = 50								
ARDL (1, 0)								
Asymptotic	−0.0391	0.2926	0.4506	−0.2390	1.4578	0.170	0.231	0.298
Δ method		0.4045		−0.2060	1.0980	0.079	0.103	0.191
ARDL-AIC								
Asymptotic	−0.0292	0.2660	0.5249	−0.3043	2.0791	0.272	0.330	0.380
Δ method		0.3912		−0.2686	1.4295	0.135	0.166	0.250
ARDL-SC								
Asymptotic	−0.0367	0.2858	0.4674	−0.2555	1.6332	0.192	0.258	0.318
Δ method		0.3983		−0.2213	1.2068	0.092	0.124	0.206
PH(0)	−1.5582	0.2452	1.6902	−6.5953	2.8986	0.964	0.916	0.985
PH(5)	−1.3809	0.4144	1.5486	−3.5302	1.9340	0.800	0.676	0.902
PH(10)	−1.4236	0.4447	1.6114	−3.4380	2.0248	0.772	0.652	0.870
PH(20)	−1.5846	0.4482	1.7724	−3.9655	2.4947	0.814	0.720	0.885
PH(40)	−1.7278	0.3754	1.8918	−5.4744	3.3989	0.884	0.821	0.932
OLS	−1.8212	0.3100	1.9642	−6.0577	2.5381	0.959	0.919	0.982
T = 100								
ARDL (1, 0)								
Asymptotic	−0.0210	0.1702	0.2236	−0.1549	1.2596	0.127	0.360	0.417
Δ method		0.2107		−0.1342	1.0399	0.064	0.236	0.315
ARDL-AIC								
Asymptotic	−0.0212	0.1635	0.2412	−0.1867	1.4637	0.161	0.387	0.447
Δ method		0.2081		−0.1614	1.1624	0.086	0.255	0.339
ARDL-SC								
Asymptotic	−0.0219	0.1690	0.2275	−0.1638	1.2994	0.134	0.365	0.423
Δ method		0.2098		−0.1415	1.0656	0.068	0.238	0.322
PH(0)	−1.1700	0.1639	1.2604	−7.0799	2.4658	0.995	0.934	1.000
PH(5)	−0.9500	0.2858	1.0559	−3.3069	1.4489	0.828	0.578	0.970
PH(10)	−0.9250	0.3141	1.0505	−2.9285	1.4216	0.740	0.483	0.932
PH(20)	−1.0329	0.3460	1.1757	−3.0017	1.5508	0.736	0.508	0.919
PH(40)	−1.2137	0.3481	1.3450	−3.7006	2.0755	0.834	0.647	0.943
OLS	−1.3839	0.2048	1.4847	−6.6914	2.2415	0.995	0.949	1.000
T = 250								
ARDL (1, 0)								
Asymptotic	−0.0064	0.0912	0.1077	−0.0874	1.1433	0.089	0.752	0.766
Δ method		0.1044		−0.0791	1.0031	0.050	0.672	0.700
ARDL-AIC								
Asymptotic	−0.0067	0.0899	0.1115	−0.0979	1.2183	0.105	0.750	0.768
Δ method		0.1044		−0.0884	1.0501	0.057	0.662	0.695
ARDL-SC								
Asymptotic	−0.0068	0.0911	0.1085	−0.0909	1.1532	0.091	0.748	0.768
Δ method		0.1043		−0.0821	1.0104	0.052	0.672	0.700
PH(0)	−0.8446	0.0960	0.8871	−8.6581	2.0763	1.000	0.969	1.000
PH(5)	−0.6267	0.1690	0.6724	−3.6456	1.1470	0.947	0.530	1.000
PH(10)	−0.5634	0.1843	0.6174	−2.9944	1.0978	0.830	0.357	0.998
PH(20)	−0.6039	0.2076	0.6722	−2.8414	1.1335	0.774	0.356	0.994
PH(40)	−0.7512	0.2369	0.8249	−3.1554	1.2912	0.833	0.476	0.995
OLS	−1.0106	0.1190	1.0583	−8.3585	1.8843	1.000	0.987	1.000

Table 11.2e. *Small-Sample Performances of Alternative Estimators of the Long-Run Coefficient* θ *for Experiments 2 (*ψ = 0.95, φ = 0.8, θ₀ = 5.1, ω₁₂ = 0.5*)*

	\multicolumn{3}{c	}{Estimator}	\multicolumn{4}{c	}{*t*-test}	POWER⁻ 0.95θ₀	POWER⁺ 1.05θ₀
	BIAS	STDEθ	RMSE	MEAN *t*	STD *t*	SIZE		
T = 50								
ARDL (1, 2)								
Asymptotic	−0.0347	0.2512	0.4217	−0.3359	1.6517	0.211	0.278	0.384
Δ method		0.3787		−0.2811	1.1552	0.095	0.098	0.238
ARDL-AIC								
Asymptotic	−0.0051	0.2281	0.4675	−0.2470	2.1417	0.288	0.383	0.432
Δ method		0.3493		−0.2415	1.4409	0.147	0.186	0.288
ARDL-SC								
Asymptotic	−0.0106	0.2418	0.4468	−0.2442	1.8404	0.246	0.383	0.432
Δ method		0.3563		−0.2365	1.3067	0.123	0.186	0.288
PH(0)	−1.4516	0.2276	1.5702	−6.6194	2.8536	0.961	0.912	0.984
PH(5)	−1.2795	0.3854	1.4311	−3.5156	1.9012	0.808	0.674	0.903
PH(10)	−1.3147	0.4149	1.4846	−3.3987	1.9703	0.778	0.636	0.879
PH(20)	−1.4631	0.4194	1.6337	−3.8890	2.3792	0.811	0.709	0.887
PH(40)	−1.5993	0.3495	1.7491	−5.4509	3.4065	0.882	0.882	0.932
OLS	−1.6889	0.2839	1.8169	−6.1446	2.5556	0.961	0.918	0.982
T = 100								
ARDL (1, 2)								
Asymptotic	−0.0214	0.1463	0.2065	−0.2057	1.3667	0.150	0.449	0.520
Δ method		0.1895		−0.1757	1.0785	0.073	0.293	0.396
ARDL-AIC								
Asymptotic	−0.0150	0.1415	0.2171	−0.1717	1.5137	0.184	0.489	0.527
Δ method		0.1835		−0.1510	1.1863	0.096	0.338	0.402
ARDL-SC								
Asymptotic	−0.0015	0.1479	0.2091	−0.0749	1.3948	0.153	0.482	0.474
Δ method		0.1897		−0.0761	1.1116	0.076	0.333	0.360
PH(0)	−1.0788	0.1520	1.1596	−7.0322	2.3953	0.992	0.928	1.000
PH(5)	−0.8709	0.2645	0.9634	−3.2714	1.3942	0.840	0.544	0.976
PH(10)	−0.8456	0.2903	0.9552	−2.8961	1.3742	0.742	0.449	0.947
PH(20)	−0.9440	0.3195	1.0700	−2.9732	1.5166	0.736	0.479	0.928
PH(40)	−1.1117	0.3220	1.2283	−3.6630	2.0495	0.839	0.621	0.948
OLS	−1.2707	0.1878	1.3611	−6.6920	2.2028	0.992	0.944	1.000
T = 250								
ARDL (1, 2)								
Asymptotic	−0.0066	0.0791	0.0979	−0.1153	1.1951	0.100	0.848	0.856
Δ method		0.0936		−0.1023	1.0171	0.055	0.768	0.706
ARDL-AIC								
Asymptotic	−0.0027	0.0786	0.0998	−0.0710	1.2348	0.108	0.855	0.846
Δ method		0.0931		−0.0650	1.0473	0.062	0.777	0.782
ARDL-SC								
Asymptotic	0.0062	0.0811	0.0993	0.0393	1.1815	0.092	0.864	0.816
Δ method		0.0954		0.0293	1.0093	0.048	0.791	0.742
PH(0)	−0.7882	0.0888	0.8296	−8.7240	2.1281	1.000	0.958	1.000
PH(5)	−0.5854	0.1559	0.6298	−3.6848	1.1671	0.948	0.490	1.000
PH(10)	−0.5265	0.1698	0.5792	−3.0319	1.1145	0.840	0.320	0.999
PH(20)	−0.5642	0.1909	0.6310	−2.8796	1.1539	0.782	0.321	0.998
PH(40)	−0.7001	0.2178	0.7715	−3.1977	1.3422	0.838	0.456	0.997
OLS	−0.9379	0.1090	0.9843	−8.4561	1.9852	1.000	0.981	1.000

Table 11.2f. *Small-Sample Performances of Alternative Estimators of the Long-Run Coefficient* θ *for Experiments 2* (ψ = 0.95, φ = 0.8, θ₀ = 4.9, ω₁₂ = −0.5)

	Estimator					t-test		
	BIAS	STDEθ	RMSE	MEAN t	STD t	SIZE	POWER⁻ 0.95θ₀	POWER⁺ 1.05θ₀
T = 50								
ARDL (1, 2)								
Asymptotic	−0.0493	0.2500	0.4474	−0.3777	1.7332	0.224	0.286	0.376
Δ method		0.3782		−0.2953	1.1762	0.094	0.116	0.227
ARDL-AIC								
Asymptotic	−0.0350	0.2284	0.4825	−0.3603	2.0905	0.295	0.354	0.441
Δ method		0.3532		−0.2972	1.3778	0.141	0.169	0.287
ARDL-SC								
Asymptotic	−0.0585	0.2404	0.4544	−0.4282	1.8312	0.250	0.296	0.407
Δ method		0.3514		−0.3380	1.2691	0.124	0.141	0.272
PH(0)	−1.6651	0.2566	1.8006	−6.7028	2.8827	0.966	0.921	0.985
PH(5)	−1.4799	0.4340	1.6516	−3.5841	1.8909	0.820	0.704	0.901
PH(10)	−1.5274	0.4672	1.7220	−3.4854	2.0015	0.786	0.674	0.875
PH(20)	−1.7046	0.4729	1.9012	−4.0093	2.4821	0.821	0.734	0.891
PH(40)	−1.8600	0.3960	2.0326	−5.5315	3.4069	0.988	0.831	0.929
OLS	−1.9570	0.3308	2.1081	−6.0698	2.5053	0.962	0.921	0.982
T = 100								
ARDL (1, 2)								
Asymptotic	−0.0219	0.1461	0.2117	−0.2430	1.3749	0.146	0.415	0.512
Δ method		0.1906		−0.1651	1.0636	0.070	0.268	0.371
ARDL-AIC								
Asymptotic	−0.0220	0.1382	0.2304	−0.2201	1.5408	0.182	0.452	0.538
Δ method		0.1805		−0.1874	1.1814	0.102	0.313	0.421
ARDL-SC								
Asymptotic	−0.0384	0.1408	0.2130	−0.3157	1.4223	0.168	0.407	0.558
Δ method		0.1794		−0.2591	1.1240	0.087	0.282	0.435
PH(0)	−1.2356	0.1719	1.3285	−7.1190	2.4378	0.995	0.949	1.000
PH(5)	−1.0023	0.2993	1.1101	−3.3257	1.4319	0.884	0.596	0.971
PH(10)	−0.9764	0.3292	1.1044	−3.9438	1.4008	0.758	0.504	0.939
PH(20)	−1.0922	0.3640	1.2390	−3.0092	1.5276	0.748	0.532	0.926
PH(40)	−1.2862	0.3688	1.4217	−3.6903	2.0508	0.837	0.664	0.946
OLS	−1.4700	0.2186	1.5749	−6.6466	2.1779	0.994	0.960	1.000
T = 250								
ARDL (1, 2)								
Asymptotic	−0.0044	0.0787	0.0960	−0.0793	1.1828	0.099	0.826	0.836
Δ method		0.0931		−0.0716	1.0039	0.052	0.755	0.760
ARDL-AIC								
Asymptotic	−0.0062	0.0762	0.0989	−0.1044	1.2607	0.117	0.826	0.841
Δ method		0.0904		−0.0961	1.0659	0.066	0.755	0.778
ARDL-SC								
Asymptotic	−0.0166	0.0762	0.0975	−0.2383	1.2240	0.114	0.804	0.876
Δ method		0.0890		−0.2096	1.0519	0.068	0.741	0.810
PH(0)	−0.8992	0.1010	0.9423	−8.7563	2.0063	1.000	0.985	1.000
PH(5)	−0.6670	0.1773	0.7131	−3.6962	1.1096	0.962	0.576	1.000
PH(10)	−0.5992	0.1932	0.6540	−3.0365	1.0655	0.856	0.379	0.999
PH(20)	−0.6431	0.2184	0.7136	−2.8767	1.1152	0.797	0.371	0.996
PH(40)	−0.8017	0.2509	0.8782	−3.1827	1.2957	0.846	0.514	0.995
OLS	−1.0815	0.1272	1.1306	−8.3635	1.8121	1.000	0.994	1.000

Autoregressive Distributed-Lag Modelling

BIAS, $\hat{\theta}_R - \theta_0$, where θ_0 is the true value of the long-run coefficient θ, $\hat{\theta}_R$ is the mean of the estimates of θ across replications (i.e., $\hat{\theta}_R = \Sigma_{i=1}^R \hat{\theta}_i/R$), and R is the number of replications

STDE θ, standard error of the estimator $\hat{\theta}_i$ across replications

RMSE, root-mean-square error of $\hat{\theta}_i$, $[R^{-1}\Sigma_{i=1}^R (\hat{\theta}_i - \theta_0)^2]^{1/2}$

MEAN t, average t-statistic for testing $\theta = \theta_0$ against $\theta \neq \theta_0$

STD t, standard deviations of the t-statistic for testing $\theta = \theta_0$ against $\theta \neq \theta_0$

SIZE, empirical size of the t-test of the null hypothesis $\theta = \theta_0$ against $\theta \neq \theta_0$

POWER$^+$, empirical power of the t-test under the alternative $\theta = 1.05\theta_0$

POWER$^-$, empirical power of the t-test under the alternative $\theta = 0.95\theta_0$

The nominal size of the tests is set at 5 percent, and the number of replications at $R = 2,500$.[16]

Tables 11.1a–f summarize the results for the correctly specified ARDL model [namely, the ARDL (1, 0) when $\omega_{12} = 0$, and the ARDL (1, 2) for $\omega_{12} \neq 0$], the estimates based on ARDL-AIC and ARDL-SC procedures, and the Phillips-Hansen fully modified estimators based on the Bartlett window for window sizes 0, 5, 10, 20, and 40, which are reported under PH(0), PH(5), and so forth.

In the case where $\omega_{12} = 0$, the bias of the ARDL estimators is much smaller than that of the PH estimators. The extent of the bias crucially depends on the value of φ, and not surprisingly increases as φ is increased from 0.2 in Table 11.1a to 0.8 in Table 11.1d. Also the RMSE values for the ARDL and PH estimators are very similar when $\varphi = 0.2$, but diverge considerably for $\varphi = 0.8$. As can be seen from Table 11.1d, for $T = 50$ the RMSE of the ARDL estimators is about one-third of the RMSE of the PH estimators. The empirical sizes of the ARDL procedure are much more satisfactory than those obtained using the PH fully modified estimators. When $\omega_{12} = 0$, the sizes of the tests based on the ARDL estimators are generally reasonable and much nearer to their nominal size of 5 percent than are the sizes of tests based on the PH estimators.

The empirical sizes of the tests based on the ARDL estimators computed using the Δ method tend to be much closer to their nominal values than those computed using the asymptotic formula. This is particularly so when T is small. Therefore, in what follows, we shall focus on the ARDL test statistics that are computed using the Δ method.

---

[16] In a very small number of replications, $\varphi(1)$ was estimated to be in excess of 0.99. These cases are not included in the summary results.

Another general feature of the simulation results is the slight superiority of the ARDL-SC method over the ARDL-AIC procedure, which is in accordance with the fact that the SC is a consistent model-selection criterion, while the AIC is not (e.g., Lütkepohl, 1991, ch. 4).

Finally, there is a clear tendency for the tests based on the PH method to over-reject in small samples, and the extent of this over-rejection increases with φ and declines only slowly with sample size T. For example, for $\varphi = 0.8$ and $T = 100$, the empirical sizes of the t-tests based on the PH method exceed 41 percent for all the five window sizes, and even for $T = 250$ do not fall below 20 percent (see the column headed "SIZE" in Table 11.1d). By contrast, the size of the test based on the Δ method in Table 11.1d is reasonable even for $T = 50$. For the correct ARDL $(1, 0)$ specification, the size of the test based on the Δ method is 7.2 percent, and increasing to 12.8 and 8.6 percent for the ARDL-AIC and the ARDL-SC procedures, respectively.

Similar results are obtained in the case where $\omega_{12} = 0.5$, and hence x_t and u_t are contemporaneously correlated. The ARDL estimators are now substantially less biased than the PH estimators (see the column headed "BIAS" in Table 11.1e). Once again the performance of the PH estimators improves with sample size, but very slowly. For $T = 250$ the bias of the PH estimators for the most favorable window size is still around -0.14, but the biases of the ARDL estimators lie between -0.0017 and 0.0024. The size performances of the two test procedures also closely mirror these differences in the degrees of bias of the estimators. The empirical sizes of the tests based on the PH method range between 60 and 85 percent for $T = 50$ and fall to around 21 percent for $T = 250$ and a window size of 20. The size of the tests based on the ARDL procedure, when the Δ method is used to compute the variances, is at most 13 percent for $T = 50$ and lies in the range 5.2 to 7.7 percent when T is increased to 250 (see Table 11.1e).

Because of the large size distortions of the PH procedure, the results presented in Tables 11.1a–f do not allow proper comparisons of the power properties of the two test procedures. But for $T = 250$, where the size distortion of the PH test is not too excessive, the ARDL procedure consistently outperforms the PH method. For example, in the case of $\varphi = 0.8$, $\omega_{12} = 0.5$, $\theta = 5$, and $T = 250$, the power of the ARDL procedure in rejecting the false null hypothesis, $\theta = 0.95\theta_0$, is consistently above 98 percent, while the power of the PH method is at most 62 percent even though its associated size is 85 percent! There seems also to be a tendency for the power function of the ARDL procedure in the case where $\omega_{12} \neq 0$ and T is small to be asymmetric around $\theta = \theta_0$, showing a higher power for the alternatives exceeding θ_0 as compared with the alternatives falling below θ_0.

The results for Experiments 2 with an $I(0)$ regressor are summarized in Tables 11.2a–f. These results are very similar to those obtained for

Experiments 1. The overall performances of the ARDL-based methods with variances estimated using the Δ method are satisfactory for most cases, though slightly worse than those obtained for Experiments 1. (In particular, the biases are slightly larger and the tests are less powerful.) But the performances of the PH estimators are still very poor, especially when T is small.

Overall, the simulation results show that the ARDL-based estimation procedure based on the Δ method developed here can be reliably used in small samples to estimate and test hypotheses on the long-run coefficients in both cases where the underlying regressors are $I(1)$ or $I(0)$. This is an important finding, because the ARDL approach can avoid the pretesting problem implicitly involved in the cointegration analysis of the long-run relationships (Cavanaugh, Elliott, and Stock, 1995; Pesaran, 1997).

Before concluding this section, we note that the comparison of the small-sample performances of the ADRL-based and the PH estimators are not comprehensive in the sense that the DGP we used was biased in favor of the ARDL procedure (Inder, 1993). In this regard, it is more appropriate to consider the relative performances of the ARDL and PH estimators using more general DGPs, such as (4.1) and (4.2), that can allow for moving-average error processes. In the working-paper version of this chapter we also considered Monte Carlo experiments using (4.1) and (4.2) as DGPs. In one set of experiments (called DGP2) we used first-order bivariate vector moving-average processes to generate the errors, v_t and e_t, and in another set of experiments (called DGP3) we generated v_t and e_t according to first-order vector autoregressive processes. Neither of those DGPs allowed transformations of the model so that x_t could become strictly exogenous with respect to the disturbances of the augmented ARDL model. We found that the simulation results based on these DGPs were less clear-cut, but the ARDL-based estimator using the Δ method still outperformed the PH estimator in most experiments, especially for small T. Broadly speaking, the relative small-sample performances of the two estimators seemed to depend on the signal-to-noise ratio, $\text{var}(e_t)/\text{var}(v_t)$, with the ARDL approach dominating the PH method when this ratio was low, and vice versa. This is clearly an area for further research.[17]

6 Concluding Remarks

The theoretical analysis and the Monte Carlo results presented in this chapter provide strong evidence in favor of a rehabilitation of the traditional ARDL approach to time-series econometric modelling. The focus

---

[17] We are grateful to Peter Boswijk and an anonymous referee for drawing our attention to this point.

of this chapter, however, has been exclusively on single-equation estimation techniques, and the important issue of system estimation is not addressed here. Such an analysis inevitably involves the problem of identification of short-run and long-run relations and demands a structural approach to the analysis of econometric models. The problem of long-run structural modelling in the context of an unrestricted var model has been addressed elsewhere (e.g., Johansen, 1991; Phillips, 1991; Pesaran and Shin, 1997). An alternative procedure, which takes us back to the Cowles Commission approach, would be to extend the ARDL methodology advanced in this chapter to systems of equations subject to short-run and/or long-run identifying restrictions (e.g., Boswijk, 1995; Hsiao, 1997). We hope to pursue this line of research in the future to establish a closer link between the recent cointegration analysis and the traditional simultaneous-equations econometric methodology.

Appendix: Mathematical Proofs

For notational convenience we use "$\xrightarrow{p}$," "$\Rightarrow$," and "$\stackrel{a}{\sim}$" to signify the convergence in probability, the weak convergence in probability measure, and the asymptotic equality in distribution. All sums are over $t = 1, 2, \ldots, T$.

In the case where the regressors are stationary, the usual method of deriving the asymptotic distribution of the OLS estimators of the short-run parameters in, for example, (2.1) would be to apply the Slutsky theorem to $(\mathbf{P}'_{Z_T}\mathbf{P}_{Z_T})^{-1}$ and $\mathbf{P}'_{Z_T}\mathbf{u}_T$, separately, where $\mathbf{P}_{Z_T} = (\mathbf{\tau}_T, \mathbf{t}_T, \mathbf{X}_T, \mathbf{y}_{T-1})$, after appropriately scaling it by the sample size. [The appropriate scaling of $\mathbf{P}'_{Z_T}\mathbf{P}_{Z_T}$ in this case is given by $\mathbf{D}_{P_T}\mathbf{P}_{Z_T}\mathbf{P}'_{Z_T}\mathbf{D}_{P_T}$, where $\mathbf{D}_{P_T} = \text{Diag}(T^{-1/2}, T^{-3/2}, T^{-1}\mathbf{I}_k, T^{-1})$.] This procedure cannot, however, be applied to dynamic time-series models with trended regressors (irrespective of whether the trends are stochastic or deterministic), because $\mathbf{P}'_{Z_T}\mathbf{P}_{Z_T}$ does not converge to a nonsingular matrix even if the individual elements of $\mathbf{P}'_{Z_T}\mathbf{P}_{Z_T}$ are appropriately scaled by the sample size.

In what follows, the asymptotic theory will be developed by using the partitioned regression techniques and then writing individual elements of the OLS estimators of the short-run parameters as ratios of random variables, thus avoiding the need to apply the Slutsky theorem to $(\mathbf{P}'_{Z_T}\mathbf{P}_{Z_T})^{-1}$ directly.

Because Theorems 2.1–2.4 are special cases of Theorems 3.1 and 3.2 and can be proved in a similar manner, we omit their proofs to save space.

Proof of Theorem 3.1. Before deriving the asymptotic distributions of the OLS estimators of the short-run parameters in (3.9), we derive some preliminary results. Define

$$\mathbf{q}_{K_T u_T} = T^{-1/2} \mathbf{K}_T' \mathbf{u}_T, \qquad \mathbf{Q}_{K_T} = T^{-1} \mathbf{K}_T' \mathbf{K}_T$$

$$\mathbf{q}_{G_T u_T} = \mathbf{D}_{G_T} \mathbf{G}_T' \mathbf{u}_T = \begin{bmatrix} \mathbf{D}_{Z_T} \mathbf{Z}_T' \mathbf{u}_T \\ T^{-1/2} \mathbf{W}_T' \mathbf{u}_T \end{bmatrix} = \begin{bmatrix} \mathbf{q}_{Z_T u_T} \\ \mathbf{q}_{W_T u_T} \end{bmatrix}$$

$$\mathbf{q}_{G_T K_T} = \mathbf{D}_{G_T} \mathbf{G}_T' \mathbf{K}_T = \begin{bmatrix} \mathbf{D}_{Z_T} \mathbf{Z}_T' \mathbf{K}_T \\ T^{-1/2} \mathbf{W}_T' \mathbf{K}_T \end{bmatrix} = \begin{bmatrix} \mathbf{q}_{Z_T K_T} \\ \mathbf{q}_{W_T K_T} \end{bmatrix}$$

$$\mathbf{Q}_{G_T} = \mathbf{D}_{G_T} \mathbf{G}_T' \mathbf{G}_T \mathbf{D}_{D_T} = \begin{bmatrix} \mathbf{D}_{Z_T} \mathbf{Z}_T' \mathbf{Z}_T \mathbf{D}_{Z_T} & T^{-1/2} \mathbf{D}_{Z_T} \mathbf{Z}_T' \mathbf{W}_T \\ T^{-1/2} \mathbf{W}_T' \mathbf{Z}_T \mathbf{D}_{Z_T} & T^{-1} \mathbf{W}_T' \mathbf{W}_T \end{bmatrix}$$

$$= \begin{bmatrix} \mathbf{Q}_{Z_T} & \mathbf{Q}_{Z_T W_T} \\ \mathbf{Q}_{Z_T W_T}' & \mathbf{Q}_{W_T} \end{bmatrix}$$

where $\mathbf{K}_T = (\varkappa_{1T}, \varkappa_{2T}, \ldots, \varkappa_{pT})$ with $\varkappa_{iT} = (\varkappa_{i1}, \varkappa_{i2}, \ldots, \varkappa_{iT})'$ for $i = 1, \ldots, p$, $\mathbf{D}_{G_T} = \text{Diag}(T^{-1/2}, T^{-3/2}, T^{-1}\mathbf{I}_k, T^{-1/2}\mathbf{I}_{kq})$, and $\mathbf{D}_{Z_T} = \text{Diag}(T^{-1/2}, T^{-3/2}, T^{-1}\mathbf{I}_k)$. Using the results of Phillips and Durlauf (1986), it is easily seen that as $T \to \infty$,

$$\mathbf{q}_{K_T u_T} \xrightarrow{p} \mathbf{q}_{Ku}, \qquad \mathbf{Q}_{K_T} \xrightarrow{p} \mathbf{Q}_K \tag{A.1}$$

$$\mathbf{q}_{G_T u_T} \Rightarrow \mathbf{q}_{Gu} = \begin{bmatrix} \mathbf{q}_{Zu} \\ \mathbf{q}_{Wu} \end{bmatrix}, \qquad \mathbf{q}_{G_T K_T} \Rightarrow \mathbf{q}_{GK} = \begin{bmatrix} \mathbf{q}_{ZK} \\ \mathbf{q}_{WK} \end{bmatrix} \tag{A.2}$$

$$\mathbf{Q}_{G_T} \Rightarrow \mathbf{Q}_G = \begin{bmatrix} \mathbf{Q}_Z & \mathbf{0} \\ \mathbf{0} & \mathbf{Q}_W \end{bmatrix} \tag{A.3}$$

where $\mathbf{q}_{Ku}$, $\mathbf{q}_{Wu}$, $\mathbf{q}_{WK}$, $\mathbf{Q}_K$, and $\mathbf{Q}_W$ are (finite) probability limits of $\mathbf{q}_{K_T u_T}$, $\mathbf{q}_{W_T u_T}$, $\mathbf{q}_{W_T K_T}$, $\mathbf{Q}_{K_T}$, and $\mathbf{Q}_{W_T}$, respectively, and $\mathbf{q}_{Zu}$, $\mathbf{q}_{ZK}$, and $\mathbf{Q}_Z$ are functionals of Brownian motions given by

$$\mathbf{q}_{Zu} = \begin{bmatrix} B_u(1) \\ \int_0^1 r\, dB_u(r) \\ \int_0^1 \mathbf{B}_e'(r)\, dB_u(r) \end{bmatrix}, \qquad \mathbf{q}_{ZK} = \begin{bmatrix} \mathbf{B}_K(1) \\ \int_0^1 r\, d\mathbf{B}_K(r) \\ \int_0^1 \mathbf{B}_e'(r)\, d\mathbf{B}_K(r) \end{bmatrix}$$

$$\mathbf{Q}_Z = \begin{bmatrix} 1 & \frac{1}{2} & \int_1^0 \mathbf{B}_e(r)\, dr \\ \frac{1}{2} & \frac{1}{3} & \int_0^1 r \mathbf{B}_e(r)\, dr \\ \int_0^1 \mathbf{B}_e'(r)\, dr & \int_0^1 r \mathbf{B}_e'(r)\, dr & \int_0^1 \mathbf{B}_e'(r)\mathbf{B}_e(r)\, dr \end{bmatrix}$$

$B_u(r)$ is the scalar Brownian-motion process with variance equal to r times σ_u^2 (since u_t is not serially correlated), $\mathbf{B}_e(r)$ is a k-dimensional Brownian motion on $r \in [0, 1]$ with variance equal to r times the long-run variance of $\mathbf{e}_t$, and $\mathbf{B}_K(r)$ is the p-dimensional Brownian motion on $[0, 1]$ with variance equal to r times the long-run variance of $(\varkappa_{1T}, \varkappa_{2T}, \ldots, \varkappa_{pT})$. The long-run variance of a stochastic process is given by

2π multiplied by the spectral density of the process at zero frequency. Notice that $\mathbf{Q}_Z$ (or $\mathbf{Q}_G$) is of full column rank by assumption (A4), and the elements in $\mathbf{Q}_Z$ involving $\mathbf{B}_e(r)$ are random, even asymptotically.

Because $\varkappa_{1T}, \varkappa_{2T}, \ldots, \varkappa_{pT}$, and $1, t, \mathbf{x}_t, \Delta\mathbf{x}_t, \Delta\mathbf{x}_{t-1}, \ldots, \Delta\mathbf{x}_{t-q+1}$ are all distributed independently of u_t such that $\mathbf{B}_K(r)$ and $\mathbf{B}_e(r)$ are independent of $\mathbf{B}_u(r)$, it follows that

$$\mathbf{q}_{Ku} \stackrel{a}{\sim} N(\mathbf{0}, \sigma_u^2 \mathbf{Q}_\varkappa), \qquad \mathbf{q}_{Gu} \stackrel{a}{\sim} MN(\mathbf{0}, \sigma_u^2 \mathbf{Q}_G) \tag{A.4}$$

where MN denotes the mixture normal distribution. For details concerning the theory of the mixture normal distribution, see, for example, Phillips (1991). However, this (mixture) normality result does not hold in the case of $\mathbf{q}_{GK}$, because $\mathbf{x}_t$ and the $\Delta\mathbf{x}_{t-i}$ ($i = 0, \ldots, q-1$) are correlated with $\varkappa_{it}, i = 1, \ldots, p$.

The OLS estimators of $\mathbf{f}$ and φ in (3.9), denoted by $\hat{\mathbf{f}}_T$ and $\hat{\varphi}_T$, satisfy the relations

$$\hat{\varphi}_T - \varphi = (\mathbf{Y}_T' \mathbf{M}_{G_T} \mathbf{Y}_T)^{-1} (\mathbf{Y}_T' \mathbf{M}_{G_T} \mathbf{u}_T) \tag{A.5}$$

$$\hat{\mathbf{f}}_T - \mathbf{f} = (\mathbf{G}_T' \mathbf{G}_T)^{-1} [\mathbf{G}_T' \mathbf{u}_T - \mathbf{G}_T' \mathbf{Y}_T (\hat{\varphi}_T - \varphi)] \tag{A.6}$$

where $\mathbf{M}_{G_T} = \mathbf{I}_T - \mathbf{G}_T (\mathbf{G}_T' \mathbf{G}_T)^{-1} \mathbf{G}_T'$, with $\mathbf{I}_T$ being the $T \times T$ identity matrix. Using (3.7), $\mathbf{Y}_T$ can be expressed as

$$\mathbf{Y}_T = \mathbf{G}_T \Gamma + \mathbf{K}_T, \tag{A.7}$$

where

$$\Gamma = \begin{bmatrix} \mu_1 & \mu_2 & \cdots & \mu_p \\ \delta & \delta & \cdots & \delta \\ \theta & \theta & \cdots & \theta \\ \mathbf{g}_1 & \mathbf{g}_2 & \cdots & \mathbf{g}_p \end{bmatrix}$$

and $\mathbf{g}_i = (\mathbf{g}_{i0}', \mathbf{g}_{i1}', \ldots, \mathbf{g}_{i,q-1}')'$ is a $kq \times 1$ vector of parameters. Using (A.7) we have

$$\mathbf{Y}_T' \mathbf{M}_{G_T} \mathbf{Y}_T = \mathbf{K}_T' \mathbf{K}_T - \mathbf{K}_T' \mathbf{G}_T (\mathbf{G}_T' \mathbf{G}_T)^{-1} \mathbf{G}_T' \mathbf{K}_T$$

$$\mathbf{Y}_T' \mathbf{M}_{G_T} \mathbf{u}_T = \mathbf{K}_T' \mathbf{u}_T - \mathbf{K}_T' \mathbf{G}_T (\mathbf{G}_T' \mathbf{G}_T)^{-1} \mathbf{G}_T' \mathbf{u}_T$$

where we used $\mathbf{G}_T' \mathbf{M}_{G_T} = \mathbf{0}$. Using (A.1)–(A.3), it can be shown that as $T \to \infty$,

$$T^{-1}(\mathbf{Y}_T' \mathbf{M}_{G_T} \mathbf{Y}_T) = \mathbf{Q}_{K_T} + o_p(1) \xrightarrow{P} \mathbf{Q}_K \tag{A.8}$$

$$T^{-1/2}(\mathbf{Y}_T' \mathbf{M}_{G_T} \mathbf{u}_T) = \mathbf{q}_{K_T u_T} + o_p(1) \xrightarrow{P} \mathbf{q}_{Ku} \tag{A.9}$$

Multiplying (A.5) by $\sqrt{T}$, and using (A.8), (A.9), and (A.4), we obtain (3.10).

Next, substituting $\mathbf{Y}_T$ from (A.7) in (A.6), we obtain

$$\hat{\mathbf{f}}_T - \mathbf{f} = (\mathbf{G}_T'\mathbf{G}_T)^{-1}\mathbf{G}_T'\mathbf{u}_T - \Gamma(\hat{\boldsymbol{\varphi}}_T - \boldsymbol{\varphi})(\mathbf{G}_T'\mathbf{G}_T)^{-1}\mathbf{G}_T'\mathbf{K}_T(\hat{\boldsymbol{\varphi}}_T - \boldsymbol{\varphi}) \quad (A.10)$$

Define

$$\mathbf{d}_T = (\hat{\mathbf{f}}_T - \mathbf{f}) + \Gamma(\hat{\boldsymbol{\varphi}}_T - \boldsymbol{\varphi}) \quad (A.11)$$

Multiplying (A.11) by $\mathbf{D}_{GT}^{-1}$, using (A.1)–(A.3) and (A.10), and applying the continuous-mapping theorem (e.g., Phillips and Durlauf, 1986), it follows that

$$\mathbf{D}_{GT}^{-1}\mathbf{d}_T = \mathbf{Q}_{GT}^{-1}\mathbf{q}_{GT\mathbf{u}T} + o_p(1) \Rightarrow \mathbf{Q}_G^{-1}\mathbf{q}_{Gu} \quad (A.12)$$

Because $\mathbf{q}_{Gu}$ is shown to be mixture normal in (A.4), then

$$\mathbf{Q}_G^{-1}\mathbf{q}_{Gu} \stackrel{a}{\sim} MN(0,\sigma_u^2\mathbf{Q}_G^{-1}), \qquad \mathbf{Q}_{GT}^{1/2}\mathbf{D}_{GT}^{-1}\mathbf{d}_T \stackrel{a}{\sim} N(0,\sigma_u^2\mathbf{I}_{k+kq+2})$$

Next, pre-multiplying (A.12) by the diagonal matrix $\mathrm{Diag}(1, T^{-1}, T^{-1/2}\mathbf{I}_k, \mathbf{I}_{kq})$, we have

$$\sqrt{T}\mathbf{d}_T = \begin{bmatrix} 1 & 0 & 0 & 0 \\ 0 & T^{-1} & 0 & 0 \\ 0 & 0 & T^{-1/2}\mathbf{I}_k & 0 \\ 0 & 0 & 0 & \mathbf{I}_{kq} \end{bmatrix} \mathbf{Q}_{GT}^{-1}\mathbf{q}_{GT\mathbf{u}T} + o_p(1)$$

$$\Rightarrow \begin{bmatrix} 1 & 0 & 0 & 0 \\ 0 & 0 & 0 & 0 \\ 0 & 0 & 0 & 0 \\ 0 & 0 & 0 & \mathbf{I}_{kq} \end{bmatrix} \mathbf{Q}_G^{-1}\mathbf{q}_{Gu} \stackrel{a}{\sim} MN\left\{0, \begin{bmatrix} Q_Z^{11} & 0 & 0 & 0 \\ 0 & 0 & 0 & 0 \\ 0 & 0 & 0 & 0 \\ 0 & 0 & 0 & \mathbf{Q}_W^{-1} \end{bmatrix}\right\} \quad (A.13)$$

where Q_Z^{11} is the (1, 1) element of $\mathbf{Q}_Z^{-1}$. The foregoing result can be rewritten separately for $\hat{\alpha}_{0T}$, $\hat{\mathbf{c}}_T$, and $\hat{\boldsymbol{\beta}}_T^*$ as

$$\sqrt{T}(\hat{\alpha}_{0T} - \alpha_0) + (\mu_1,\mu_2,\ldots,\mu_p)\sqrt{T}(\hat{\boldsymbol{\varphi}}_T - \boldsymbol{\varphi}) = d_{Zu,1} + o_p(1) \quad (A.14)$$

$$\sqrt{T}(\hat{\mathbf{c}}_T - \mathbf{c}) + \lambda\boldsymbol{\tau}_p'\sqrt{T}(\hat{\boldsymbol{\varphi}}_T - \boldsymbol{\varphi}) = o_p(1) \quad (A.15)$$

$$\sqrt{T}(\hat{\boldsymbol{\beta}}_T^* - \boldsymbol{\beta}^*) + (\mathbf{g}_1,\mathbf{g}_2,\ldots,\mathbf{g}_p)\sqrt{T}(\hat{\boldsymbol{\varphi}}_T - \boldsymbol{\varphi}) = \mathbf{Q}_W^{-1}\mathbf{q}_{Wu} + o_p(1) \quad (A.16)$$

where $\boldsymbol{\tau}_p$ is a $p \times 1$ vector of unity and $d_{Zu,1}$ is the first element of $\mathbf{Q}_Z^{-1}\mathbf{q}_{Zu}$. Using (3.10) in (A.15) we obtain (3.11). It is also clear from the foregoing results that the OLS estimators of α_0 and β^* (standardized by $\sqrt{T}$) have (mixture) normal distributions asymptotically.

Finally, using (3.10), (3.11), and (A.13)–(A.16), it is easily seen that a consistent estimator of the variance of $\hat{\mathbf{h}}_T$ is given by $\hat{V}(\hat{\mathbf{h}}_T) = \hat{\sigma}_{uT}^2(\mathbf{P}_{GT}'\mathbf{P}_{GT})^{-1}$, with the rank of $\hat{V}(\hat{\mathbf{h}}_T)$ being equal to $kq + 2$. □

Proof of Theorem 3.2. Partition $\mathbf{d}_T = (a_T, \mathbf{s}_T', \mathbf{w}_T')'$ conformably to $\mathbf{G}_T = (\boldsymbol{\tau}_T, \mathbf{S}_T, \mathbf{W}_T)$; then $\mathbf{s}_T$ is given by

$$\mathbf{s}_T = \sqrt{T}(\hat{\mathbf{c}}_T - \mathbf{c}) + \lambda \boldsymbol{\tau}'_p \sqrt{T}(\hat{\boldsymbol{\varphi}}_T - \boldsymbol{\varphi}) \tag{A.17}$$

Using (A.10) and (A.11), $(\mathbf{s}'_T, \mathbf{w}'_T)'$ can be expressed as

$$\begin{bmatrix} \mathbf{s}_T \\ \mathbf{w}_T \end{bmatrix} = \begin{bmatrix} \mathbf{S}'_T \mathbf{H}_T \mathbf{S}_T & \mathbf{S}'_T \mathbf{H}_T \mathbf{W}_T \\ \mathbf{W}'_T \mathbf{H}_T \mathbf{S}_T & \mathbf{W}'_T \mathbf{H}_T \mathbf{W}_T \end{bmatrix}^{-1} \begin{bmatrix} \mathbf{S}'_T \mathbf{H}_T \mathbf{u}_T \\ \mathbf{W}'_T \mathbf{H}_T \mathbf{u}_T \end{bmatrix}$$
$$- \begin{bmatrix} \mathbf{S}'_T \mathbf{H}_T \mathbf{S}_T & \mathbf{S}'_T \mathbf{H}_T \mathbf{W}_T \\ \mathbf{W}'_T \mathbf{H}_T \mathbf{S}_T & \mathbf{W}'_T \mathbf{H}_T \mathbf{W}_T \end{bmatrix}^{-1} \begin{bmatrix} \mathbf{S}'_T \mathbf{H}_T \mathbf{K}_T \\ \mathbf{W}'_T \mathbf{H}_T \mathbf{K}_T \end{bmatrix} (\hat{\boldsymbol{\varphi}}_T - \boldsymbol{\varphi}) \tag{A.18}$$

Let

$$\mathbf{q}_{\tilde{s}_T \mathbf{u}_T} = \mathbf{D}_{S_T} \mathbf{S}'_T \mathbf{H}_T \mathbf{u}_T, \qquad \mathbf{Q}_{\tilde{s}_T} = \mathbf{D}_{S_T} \mathbf{S}'_T \mathbf{H}_T \mathbf{S}_T \mathbf{D}_{S_T}$$

where $\mathbf{D}_{S_T} = \text{Diag}(T^{-3/2}, T^{-1} \mathbf{I}_k)$. Then it is also easily seen that as $T \to \infty$,

$$\mathbf{q}_{\tilde{s}_T \mathbf{u}_T} \Rightarrow \mathbf{q}_{\tilde{s} u} = \begin{bmatrix} \int_0^1 \left(r - \frac{1}{2} \right) dB_u(r) \\ \int_0^1 \tilde{\mathbf{B}}'_e(r) dB_u(r) \end{bmatrix} \tag{A.19}$$

$$\mathbf{Q}_{\tilde{s}_T} \Rightarrow \mathbf{Q}_{\tilde{s}} = \begin{bmatrix} \frac{1}{12} & \int_0^1 \left(r - \frac{1}{2} \right) \tilde{\mathbf{B}}_e(r) dr \\ \int_0^1 \left(r - \frac{1}{2} \right) \tilde{\mathbf{B}}'_e(r) dr & \int_0^1 \tilde{\mathbf{B}}'_e(r) \tilde{\mathbf{B}}_e(r) dr \end{bmatrix} \tag{A.20}$$

where $\tilde{\mathbf{B}}_e(r) = \mathbf{B}_e(r) - \int_0^1 \mathbf{B}_e(r) dr$ is a k-dimensional demeaned Brownian motion on $[0, 1]$. Since $\tilde{\mathbf{B}}_e(r)$ is also distributed independently of $B_u(r)$, we obtain, as in (A.4),

$$\mathbf{q}_{\tilde{s} u} \stackrel{a}{\sim} MN(0, \sigma_u^2 \mathbf{Q}_{\tilde{s}}) \tag{A.21}$$

Multiplying (A.18) by the diagonal matrix $\text{Diag}(\mathbf{D}_{S_T}^{-1}, T^{1/2})$, using (A.19)–(A.21), and noting that

$$\mathbf{D}_{S_T} \mathbf{S}'_T \mathbf{H}_T \mathbf{W}_T = O_p(1), \qquad T^{-1} \mathbf{W}'_T \mathbf{H}_T \mathbf{W}_T = O_p(1)$$
$$\mathbf{D}_{S_T} \mathbf{S}'_T \mathbf{H}_T \mathbf{K}_T = O_p(1), \qquad T^{-1/2} \mathbf{W}'_T \mathbf{H}_T \mathbf{K}_T = O_p(1)$$

we obtain

$$\mathbf{D}_{\tilde{s}_T}^{-1} \mathbf{s}_T \Rightarrow \mathbf{Q}_{\tilde{s}}^{-1} \mathbf{q}_{\tilde{s} u} \stackrel{a}{\sim} MN(0, \sigma_u^2 \mathbf{Q}_{\tilde{s}}^{-1})$$

and therefore

$$\mathbf{Q}_{\tilde{s}_T}^{1/2} \mathbf{D}_{S_T}^{-1} \mathbf{s}_T \stackrel{a}{\sim} N(0, \sigma_u^2 \mathbf{I}_{k+1}) \tag{A.22}$$

Finally, by (3.13) and (A.15) we have

$$\hat{\lambda}_T - \lambda = \frac{\mathbf{s}_T}{\hat{\varphi}_T(1)} \tag{A.23}$$

Multiplying (A.23) by $Q_{ST}^{1/2} D_{ST}^{-1}$, using (A.22), and noting that $\hat{\varphi}_T(1) \xrightarrow{P} \varphi(1)$, we obtain (3.14). □

Proof of Theorem 3.3 can be established in a similar manner and is omitted to save space.

Proof of Theorem 4.1. Consider the dynamic ARDL (p, m) model (3.19) [or (4.4)] and its static counterpart (4.1). Applying the decomposition $\varphi(L) = \varphi(1) + (1 - L)\varphi^*(L)$ to (3.19) we have

$$y_t = \frac{\alpha_0}{\varphi(1)} + \delta t + \theta' x_t + \frac{\pi'(L)}{\varphi(1)} \Delta x_t + \frac{\eta_t}{\varphi(1)} - \frac{\varphi^*(L)}{\varphi(1)} \Delta y_t \quad \text{(A.24)}$$

Substituting for $\Delta y_t = \delta + \theta' \Delta x_t + \Delta v_t$ from (4.1) in (A.24), we have

$$y_t = \mu + \delta t + \theta' x_t + \frac{\pi'(L)}{\varphi(1)} \Delta x_t + \frac{\eta_t}{\varphi(1)} - \frac{\varphi^*(L)}{\varphi(1)} \quad \text{(A.25)}$$
$$\times (\theta' \Delta x_t + \Delta v_t)$$

Using (A.25), v_t in (4.1) can be expressed as

$$v_t = \frac{\pi'(L) - \varphi^*(L)\theta'}{\varphi(1)} \Delta x_t + \frac{\eta_t}{\varphi(1)} - \frac{\varphi^*(L)}{\varphi(1)} \Delta v_t \quad \text{(A.26)}$$

Defining $\mathbf{k}_t = (\eta_t, v_t, \Delta x_t')' = (\eta_t, v_t, e_t')'$ and

$$\Psi(L) = \left[\frac{1}{\varphi(1)}, \frac{-\varphi^*(L)(1 - L)}{\varphi(1)}, \frac{\pi'(L) - \varphi^*(L)\theta'}{\varphi(1)} \right]$$

then the spectral density of $v_t = \Psi(L)\mathbf{k}_t$ is given by

$$2\pi f_{vv}(\omega) = \Psi(e^{iw}) \text{Var}(\mathbf{k}_t) \Psi'(e^{-iw})$$

where

$$\text{Var}(\mathbf{k}_t) = \begin{bmatrix} \sigma_\eta^2 & \sigma_{\eta v} & \mathbf{0} \\ \sigma_{\eta v}' & \sigma_u^2 & \Sigma_{ve} \\ \mathbf{0} & \Sigma_{ve}' & \Sigma_{ee} \end{bmatrix}$$

Hence the spectral density of v_t at zero frequency is given by

$$2\pi f_{vv}(0) = \frac{\sigma_\eta^2 + [\pi'(1) - \varphi^*(1)\theta']\Sigma_{ee}[\pi(1) - \varphi^*(1)\theta]}{[\varphi(1)]^2} \quad \text{(A.27)}$$

The Phillips-Hansen semiparametric correction is equivalent to removing the second part of (A.27) by subtracting the terms involving Δx_t from v_t. Using (A.26) we have the following expression for the modified disturbance term v_t^+ in the Phillips-Hansen procedure:

$$v_t^+ = v_t - \frac{\pi'(L) - \varphi^*(L)\theta'}{\varphi(1)} \Delta x_t = \frac{\eta_t}{\varphi(1)} - \frac{\varphi^*(L)}{\varphi(1)} \Delta v_t$$
$$= \Psi^+(L)\mathbf{k}_t^+$$

where $\mathbf{k}_t^+ = (\eta_t, v_t)'$ and

$$\boldsymbol{\Psi}^+(L) = \left[\frac{1}{\varphi(1)}, \frac{-\varphi^*(L)(1-L)}{\varphi(1)}\right]$$

Therefore, the spectral density of v_t^+ at zero frequency is given by

$$2\pi f_{v^+v^+}(0) = \boldsymbol{\Psi}^+(0)\mathrm{Var}(\mathbf{k}_t^+)\boldsymbol{\Psi}^{+\prime}(0) = \frac{\sigma_\eta^2}{[\varphi(1)]^2}$$

Using (4.7) we also have

$$f_{v^+v^+}(0) = \mathbf{B} f_{\xi\xi}(0) \mathbf{B}'$$

where $\mathbf{B} = [1, -\boldsymbol{\Omega}_{ve}\boldsymbol{\Omega}_{ee}^{-1}]$. By definition, $\boldsymbol{\Omega}_\xi = 2\pi f_{\xi\xi}(0)$, and

$$2\pi f_{v^+v^+}(0) = \mathbf{B}\boldsymbol{\Omega}_\xi \mathbf{B}' = \omega_{vv} - \boldsymbol{\Omega}_{ve}\boldsymbol{\Omega}_{ee}^{-1}\boldsymbol{\Omega}_{ev} = \frac{\sigma_\eta^2}{[\varphi(1)]^2}$$

Hence, by (4.8), $\omega_{v\cdot e} = \sigma_\eta^2/[\varphi(1)]^2$. $\square$

References

Baardsen, G. (1989). The estimation of long-run coefficients from error correction models. *Oxford Bulletin of Economics and Statistics* 51:345–50.

Banerjee, A., Dolado, J., Hendry, D., and Smith, G. (1986). Exploring equilibrium relationships in economics through statistical models: some Monte Carlo evidence. *Oxford Bulletin of Economics and Statistics* 48:253–77.

Bewley, R. (1979). The direct estimation of the equilibrium response in a linear dynamic model. *Economics Letters* 3:357–61.

Boswijk, H. P. (1995). Efficient inference on cointegration parameters in structural error correction models. *Journal of Econometrics* 69:133–58.

Cavanaugh, C. L., Elliott, G., and Stock, J. H. (1995). Inference in models with nearly integrated regressors. *Econometric Theory* 11:1131–47.

Engle, R. F., and Granger, C. W. J. (1987). Cointegration and error correction representation: estimation and testing. *Econometrica* 55:251–76.

Hendry, D., Pagan, A., and Sargan, J. (1984). Dynamic specifications. In: *Handbook of Econometrics*, vol. 2, ed. Z. Griliches and M. Intriligator, pp. 1023–100. Amsterdam: North Holland.

Hsiao, C. (1997). Cointegration and dynamic simultaneous equations model. *Econometrica*, 65: 647–70.

Inder, B. (1993). Estimating long run relationships in economics. *Journal of Econometrics* 57:53–68.

Johansen, S. (1991). Estimation and hypothesis testing of cointegrating vectors in Gaussian vector autoregressive models. *Econometrica* 59:1551–80.

Lütkepohl, H. (1991). *Introduction to Multiple Time Series Analysis*. Berlin: Springer-Verlag.

Park, J. Y. (1992). Canonical cointegrating regressions. *Econometrica* 60:119–43.

Pesaran, M. H. (1997). The role of economic theory in modelling the long-run. *Economic Journal* 107:178–91.

Pesaran, M. H., and Pesaran, B. (1997). *Microfit 4.0: Interactive Econometric Analysis*. Oxford University Press.

Pesaran, M. H., and Shin, Y. (1997). Long-run structural modelling. Unpublished manuscript, University of Cambridge.

Pesaran, M. H., Shin, Y., and Smith, R. J. (1996). Testing for the existence of a long-run relationship. DAE Working Papers Amalgamated Series, no. 9622, University of Cambridge.

Phillips, P. C. B. (1991). Optimal inference in cointegrated systems. *Econometrica* 59:283–306.

Phillips, P. C. B., and Durlauf, S. N. (1986). Multiple time series regression with integrated processes. *Review of Economic Studies* 53:473–96.

Phillips, P. C. B., and Hansen, B. (1990). Statistical inference in instrumental variables regression with $I(1)$ processes. *Review of Economic Studies* 57:99–125.

Phillips, P. C. B., and Loretan, M. (1991). Estimating long run economic equilibria. *Review of Economic Studies* 58:407–36.

Phillips, P. C. B., and Solo, V. (1992). Asymptotic for linear processes. *Annals of Statistics* 20:971–1001.

Saikkonnen, P. (1991). Asymptotically efficient estimation of cointegration regressions. *Econometric Theory* 7:1–21.

Stock, J. H. (1987). Asymptotic properties of least squares estimates of cointegrating vectors. *Econometrica* 55:1035–56.

Stock. J. H., and Watson, M. W. (1993). A simple estimator of cointegrating vectors in higher order integrated systems. *Econometrica* 61:783–820.

Wickens, M. R., and Breusch, T. S. (1988). Dynamic specification, the long run estimation of the transformed regression models. *Economic Journal* 98:189–205.

CHAPTER 12

Econometric Issues Related to Errors in Variables in Financial Models

G. S. Maddala

1 Introduction

Ragnar Frisch worked with errors-in-variables (EIV) models. Later researchers in econometrics moved the field in the direction of errors in equations. That situation was partially rectified in the early 1970s by the contributions of Goldberger (1972) and Griliches (1974) and later surveys by Griliches (1985) and Chamberlain and Goldberger (1990), but EIV models still occupy a back seat in econometrics. When I was revising my *Introduction to Econometrics* (Maddala, 1992), reviewers unanimously suggested that I drop the chapter on "Errors in Variables" (it is "never used") and add more interesting and useful topics like unit roots and cointegration.

Empirical researchers, however, have to face the problems of errors in variables all the time. This essay discusses that problem in the context of financial models in which proxies are used for unobservables almost all the time. In the following sections we shall discuss this problem with reference to the following topics:

1. tests of the capital-asset pricing model
2. tests of the arbitrage pricing theory, using observed macroeconomic variables as proxies for unobserved factors
3. measuring market responses to corporate pronouncements (dividends, stock splits, etc.), also known as testing signaling models
4. portfolio performance measures

2 Testing the Capital-Asset Pricing Model (CAPM)

This is one area where EIV problems have been extensively discussed in the financial literature. We shall not go into detailed derivations, but shall summarize the main issues. The econometric issues relating to the

---

I would like to thank an anonymous referee and Alberto Holly for helpful comments on an earlier version of this essay.

asset pricing models have been reviewed by Hansen, Heaton, and Luttmer (1995), Ferson and Jagannathan (1996), and Jagannathan and Wang (1996), but not with reference to the EIV problems.

2.1 The Two-Pass Methodology

The CAPM asserts (in its simplest form) that

$$E(R_i) = r + \beta_i[E(R_m) - r]$$

where R_i is the rate of return on security i, R_m is the rate of return on a market portfolio (which is mean-variance-efficient), and r is the riskless rate. The T-bill rate is usually taken as a proxy for r. Tests of the CAPM are usually based on two regressions:

(i) Run a first-pass regression based on time series,

$$R_{it} = \alpha_i + \beta_i R_{mt} + e_{it} \tag{1}$$

to estimate β_i for each security (R_{mt} is usually proxied by the S&P index or a broader index of stocks).

(ii) Using $\hat{\beta}_i$, the estimates of β_i, run a second-pass regression,

$$\bar{R}_i = \gamma_0 + \gamma_1 \hat{\beta}_i + u_i \tag{2}$$

This is the cross-section regression (CSR).

Finally, $\hat{\gamma}_0$ is compared with the risk-free rate r in the period under examination, and $\hat{\gamma}_1$ is compared with $(\bar{R}_m - r)$ for the same period.

Much of the early discussion of the EIV problem was in terms of the CSR equation (2), where $\hat{\beta}_i$, being estimated values of β_i, introduce an EIV problem. Grouping methods have been used for this purpose. We shall discuss those first before moving on to other means for dealing with the EIV problem in estimating equations (2) and (1), in that order.

2.2 Grouping Methods

Grouping methods once were extensively used to deal with the EIV problem in the estimation of equation (2); see, for instance, Black, Jensen, and Scholes (1972), Fama and MacBeth (1973), and, more recently, Fama and French (1992). We shall refer to those papers as BJS, FM, and FF, respectively.

Because grouping methods can be viewed as instrumental-variable (IV) methods, grouping once was expected to solve the EIV problem. There were frequent references to Wald's classic paper in that literature, but the simple grouping method used by Wald was not the one used in those papers. Wald's method consisted of ranking the observations, forming two groups, and then passing a line between the means of the two groups. Wald's procedure amounted to using rank as an instrumental variable, but because rank depends on the measurement error, that could not produce a consistent estimator (a point noted by Wald himself). Pakes (1982) presented more detailed proof to show that the grouping estimator of Wald was not consistent. That problem was pointed out in the finance literature in a more recent paper by Lys and Sabino (1992), although there was no reference in that paper to the work of Pakes (1982).

The method used in FM and FF was not the simple grouping method used by Wald. The procedure was to estimate the betas with, say, monthly observations on the first 5 years and then rank the securities based on those estimated betas to form 20 groups (portfolios). Then the estimation sample (omitting the first 5 years of data) was used to estimate a cross-section regression of asset returns on the betas for the different groups. The statistical properties of this complicated grouping method have not been studied, but it does help to reduce the EIV bias. The argument is as follows:

If $\hat{\beta}_i$ is estimated with an unbiased measurement error v_i then the regression estimate of γ for the model described by equation (2) is given by

$$\text{plim } \hat{\gamma}_1 = \frac{\gamma_1}{1 + [\text{var}(v_i)/\text{var}(\beta_i)]}$$

where $\text{var}(v_i)$ is the variance of the measurement errors, and $\text{var}(\beta_i)$ is the cross-sectional sample variance of the true risk measures β_i. The idea behind the grouping or portfolio technique is to minimize $\text{var}(v_i)$ through the portfolio diversification effect, and at the same time to maximize $\text{var}(\beta_i)$ by forming portfolios by ranking on the β_i measures.

One important point to note in the cross-sectional tests is that grouping to take care of errors in variables is not necessary. The problem here is not the one in the usual EIV models, where the variance of the measurement error is not known. Note that the betas are estimated, but their variance is known. That knowledge was used by Litzenberger and Ramaswamy (1979) (hereafter, L-R) to get bias-corrected estimates. In the statistical literature this method is known as the consistent adjusted least-squares (CALS) method, as discussed by Schneeweiss (1976), Fuller (1980), and Kapteyn and Wansbeek (1984), although the conditions under which the error variances are estimated are different in the statistical literature and the financial literature. The L-R method involves subtracting an appropriate expression from the cross-product matrix of the estimated beta vector to neutralize the impact of the measurement error. The modified estimator is consistent as the number of securities tends to infinity. However, in practice, this adjustment does not always yield a cross-product matrix that is positive definite. In fact, Shanken and Weinstein (1990) observed that in their work and argued that more work is needed on the properties of the L-R method. Banz (1981) also mentioned "serious problems in applying the Litzenberger-Ramaswamy estimator" in his analysis of the effect of firm size.

Besides the L-R method, another promising alternative to the traditional grouping procedure for correcting the EIV bias is the maximum-likelihood (ML) method. Shanken (1992) discussed the relationship between the L-R method and the ML method. In addition to the bias-correction problem there is the problem of correcting the standard errors of the estimated coefficients. Shanken (1992) derived the correction factors for the standard errors in the presence of errors in variables.

2.3 Grouping in the Presence of Multiple Proxies

The foregoing discussion refers to only a simple regression model with one regressor (estimated beta). However, there are models in which several regressors are measured with error. In those cases the number of instrumental variables needed is at least equal to the number of regressors measured with error. An example of multiple proxies was provided by Chen, Roll, and Ross (1986), who used the Fama-MacBeth two-pass procedure. We shall refer to that paper as CRR. They considered five variables describing economic conditions: monthly growth in industrial production, change in expected inflation, unexpected inflation, term structure, and risk premium measured as the difference between the return on low-grade (Baa) bonds and long-term government bonds.

CRR argued (p. 394) that "to control the errors-in-variables problem that arises from the use of beta estimates, and to reduce the noise in individual asset returns, the securities were grouped into portfolios." They used size (total market value at the beginning of each test period) as the variable for grouping. CRR further argued that the economic variables were significant in explaining stock returns, and in addition those variables were "priced" (as revealed by significant coefficients in the second-pass cross-sectional regression). Shanken and Weinstein (1990), however, argued that the CRR results were sensitive to the grouping method used and that the significance of the coefficients in the cross-sectional regression was altered if EIV adjustments were applied to the standard errors.

Shanken and Weinstein (1990) discussed adjusting the standard errors only, but we should be making adjustments for both the coefficient bias and the standard errors. Also, we can use the adjusted least squares, as in the L-R method.

2.4 Maximum-Likelihood (ML) Method

Note that equations (1) and (2) imply the following cross-equation restrictions:

$$a_i = \gamma_0(1 - \beta_i), \quad i = 1, 2, \ldots, N \tag{3}$$

This implies $(N-1)$ restrictions on the parametrics.

Gibbons (1982) suggested that simultaneous estimation of equations (1) and (2) by the ML method, imposing restrictions (3), could avoid the EIV problem in the two-pass estimation method. Shanken (1992) found some support for Gibbons's argument if the maximum-likelihood estimator (MLE) suggested by Gibbons was modified.

In estimating the CAPM model, the EIV problem is created by using the estimated betas in the first stage as explanatory variables in a second-stage cross-section regression. Similar problems arise in the two-pass tests of the arbitrage pricing theory developed by Roll and Ross (1980), Connor and Korajczyk (1988), and Lehmann and Modest (1988), among others.

Although the Gibbons (1982) ML approach avoids the EIV problem introduced by the two-pass method, it does not address the issue of the unobservability of the "true" market portfolio. As pointed out by Roll (1977), the test of the asset-pricing model is essentially a test of whether or not the proxy used for the "market portfolio" is mean-variance-efficient. Gibbons and Ferson (1985) argued that asset-pricing models can be tested without observing the "true" market portfolio if the assumption of a constant risk premium is relaxed. This requires a model for conditional expected returns, which is used to estimate ratios of betas without observing the market portfolio. The problems due to the unobservability of the market portfolio and the EIV problems can be avoided by using one-step methods in which the market portfolio is treated as an unobservable and we have multiple proxies. We discuss models with unobservables in Section 4. The availability of multiple proxies allows us to get around the problem of unobservability of the marked portfolio using the methods described in Section 4.

2.5   The Problem of Mean-Variance Efficiency

As pointed out earlier, Roll (1977) argued that the market portfolio is not observable and also that the test of the CAPM is essentially a test of whether or not the proxy used for the market portfolio is mean-variance-efficient. We have discussed the question of unobservability of the market portfolio and how latent-variable models can be used to address this problem.

As for a test of portfolio efficiency, Shanken (1996) presented a survey of this literature. The test depends on the estimation of the CSR given by (2). Gibbons, Ross, and Shanken (1989), to be referred to as GRS, considered an *excess-return version* of equation (2); that is, R_{it} is the return in excess of the riskless rate, and $E(R_i)$ is the corresponding expected excess return. In this case equation (3) reduces to

$$\alpha_i = 0 \quad \text{for } i = 1, 2, \ldots, N \tag{4}$$

GRS suggested a multivariate test for the joint hypothesis (4). This F-test is also known as the GLS-CSR test (generalized-least-squares cross-section-regression test). This test assumes that the errors in (2) are independent over time and jointly normally distributed. It has been found that the F-test is robust to deviations from normality, but not to conditional heteroskedasticity; see Zhou (1993) and the references there. The problem of serial correlation in errors has not been investigated.

The F-test of GRS failed to reject hypothesis (4) for the portfolios they considered. One problem with the F-test is that the residual covariance matrix of the errors should be invertible. This places restrictions on the number of assets that can be considered, and hence portfolios, rather than individual securities, are used. Issues relating to this problem have been discussed by Shanken (1996, p. 698). Alternative methods that can relax this restriction on the number of assets need to be explored.

Noting that a decade of empirical research, including the exhaustive study by Fama and French (1992), on estimation of the CSR model (2) showed little evidence of a cross-sectional relationship between betas and mean returns, Roll and Ross (1994) argued that the proxies used for the market portfolio were not mean-variance-efficient. They then investigated the question of how far inside the ex-ante efficient frontier the market portfolio can be to get a significant relationship between betas and mean returns.

However, as noted by Roll and Ross (1994, p. 113), the econometric methods used – a pooled time-series cross-section method or GLS method – appear to make a difference in the results (see the GRS results referred to earlier). Shanken (1992) also provided an analysis of the differences in inference provided by the different estimation techniques.

2.6   *Instrumental-Variable (IV) Methods*

IV methods are commonly used to solve the EIV problems. In the case of asset-pricing models, a survey of IV methods has been given by Harvey and Kirby (1996). Some of the recent econometric methods on IV estimation (e.g., Bekker, 1994), however, need to be explored in financial applications. Another problem, noted later in Section 4.3, is that of poor instruments.

2.7   *Bayesian Methods*

Bayesian methods have recently been used in testing asset-pricing models and measuring portfolio efficiency; some examples are the studies by Harvey and Zhou (1990), Kandel, McCulloch, and Stambaugh (1995), and Geweke and Zhou (1995). The econometric issues involved cannot be discussed without going into Bayesian inference in detail, and that will not be attempted here. The use of Bayesian methods in other areas discussed in the following sections still remains unexplored.

3 Factor Analysis with Macroeconomic Variables

In econometric testing of the arbitrage pricing theory (APT), many investigators have suggested that the unobserved factors might be equated with observed macroeconomic variables (e.g., Chen et al., 1986; Chan, Chen, and Hsieh, 1985; Conway and Reinganum, 1988). The papers that have used observed variables to represent the factors have treated those variables as accurate measures of linear transformations of the underlying factors, so that the regression coefficients have been treated as estimates of the factor loadings. However, those observed macroeconomic variables are only proxies for the factors.

Cragg and Donald (1992) developed a framework for testing the APT considering the fact that the factors are measured by the proxies with error. They applied the technique to monthly returns over the period 1971–90 (inclusive) for 60 companies selected at random from the CRSP tape. They considered 18 macroeconomic variables, but found that they represented only four or five factors. The method they used, as outlined by Cragg and Donald (1995), was based on the GLS approach to factor analysis, which is an extension of earlier work by Jöreskog and Goldberger (1975) and Dahm and Fuller (1986). Cragg and Donald argued that there is no way of estimating the underlying factors in an APT model without taking into account that the proxies measure the factors with measurement error. In particular this holds for macroeconomic variables that are possible proxies. However, as argued in previous sections, an alternative method to handle the measurement-error problem is to use the unobserved-components model in which the macroeconomic variables (used as proxies) are treated as indicators of unobserved factors. The LISREL program can be used to estimate this model. The LISREL program handles both the GLS and ML estimation methods. However, the MIMIC models impose more structure than the Cragg-Donald approach. A comparison of the two approaches – the multiple-indicator approach and the approach of factor analysis with proxies for the factors, as followed by Cragg and Donald – is a topic for further research.

4 Response to Corporate Pronouncements: Testing Signaling Models

4.1 *Multiple-Indicator Models*

Several articles in finance have analyzed the responses of the market to unexpected earnings, unexpected dividends, and so on. These variables are unobserved, and it is customary to use some proxies for these variables. Israel, Ofer, and Siegel (1990) discussed several studies that had used change in equity values as a measure of information content of an event (earnings announcement, dividend announcement, etc.) and had used that as an explanatory variable in other equations. All of those studies tested the null hypothesis that there was no information content in the event by testing that the coefficient of the change in equity value was zero. However, those procedures involved an EIV bias. A more reasonable approach is to treat the information content as an unobserved variable and use the MIMIC models. If the unobservable variable occurs in different equations as an explanatory variable (multiple indicators of a latent variable), then one can get (under some identifiability conditions) consistent estimates of the coefficients of the unobserved variable. Such models have been discussed by Zellner (1970), Goldberger (1972), Griliches (1974), and Jöreskog and Goldberger (1975) and have been popularized by the LISREL program of Jöreskog and Sorböm (1989, 1993). These models have also been discussed extensively under various titles: linear structural models with measurement errors, analysis of covariance structures, path analysis, and causal models (Bollen, 1989). Although many problems in finance fall into this category, there have not been many applications of these models in finance. Notable exceptions in corporate finance are the models estimated by Titman and Wessels (1988), Maddala and Nimalendran (1995), and Desai, Nimalendran, and Venkataraman (1996).

Titman and Wessels (TW) investigated the determinants of corporate capital structure in terms of unobserved attributes for which they had indicators or proxies that were measured with error. Maddala and Nimalendran (MN) considered a model to estimate the effects of unexpected earnings on changes in stock prices (P), bid–ask spreads (S), and trading volume (V). Traditionally, unexpected earnings (actual analysts' forecast) ΔE has been employed as a regressor in a regression model to explain the changes in spreads (ΔS) and changes in volume (ΔV) (Skinner, 1991). However, E is an error-ridden proxy for the true (unobserved) expected earning E^*. MN estimated a multiple-indicator model to get around the EIV problem. The specification of their model is

$$|\Delta P| = \alpha_0 + \alpha_1 |\Delta E^*| + \varepsilon_1$$
$$\Delta S = \beta_0 + \beta_1 |\Delta E^*| + \varepsilon_2$$
$$\Delta V = \gamma_0 + \gamma_1 |\Delta E|^* + \varepsilon_3$$
$$|\Delta E| = \delta_0 + \delta_1 |\Delta E|^* + \varepsilon_4$$

where it is assumed that the errors ε_i ($i = 1, 2, 3, 4$) are uncorrelated and are also uncorrelated with $|\Delta E^*|$. There are 10 pieces of information in the variances and covariances of the four observed variables in this model. There are eight regression parameters and four variances. Thus the model is underidentified. But we can set $\delta_0 = 0$ and $\delta_1 = 1$ and get estimates of all the other parameters.

This model gives the effects of earnings surprises on changes in stock prices, bid–ask spreads, and trading volume that are free of the EIV bias present in the other studies. MN found that the EIV biases could be substantial, leading to incorrect inferences. More importantly, MN used the panel structure of their data to obtain within-group and between-group estimates that provided information on the short-term and long-term effects of earnings surprises on the other variables.

4.2 Multiple Signals

The model considered by MN is a model with just one latent variable (or one signal: earnings announcements). Desai, Nimalendran, and Venkataraman (DNV) considered a model with two latent variables – unanticipated dividends and unanticipated stock splits – that were assumed to be uncorrelated. Many papers in finance have suggested that stock splits do not convey more information than dividend announcements. DNV estimated a MIMIC model and observed that even after controlling for the information in dividend announcements, stock splits conveyed significant information to the market.

There are many other areas in finance where the use of MIMIC models can be productive in studying the problem of multiple signals. Some of the recent papers in signaling have argued that management might use a combination of signals to reduce the cost of signaling. In that case the latent variables could be correlated. This problem should be taken into account in the estimation of MIMIC models.

It is also possible that management can signal in a sequential fashion; see John and Mishra (1990) and the references cited there. Many of the signals used by management are dividend changes, stock splits, stock repurchases, restructuring (layoffs, etc.), and insider trading. John and Mishra argued that insider trading is a more direct form of signal. The different signals affect stock prices with different lags. Thus lags should be taken into account in the estimation of signaling models.

4.3 Problem of Poor Proxies and Choice of Proxies

Because the formulation adopted in the MIMIC models amounts to using the proxies as instrumental variables in equations other than the ones in which they occur, the problem of poor proxies is related to the problem of poor instrumental variables, on which there is now considerable literature (e.g., Nelson and Startz, 1990; Maddala and Jeong, 1992; Steiger and Stock, 1997; Dufour, 1994). Therefore the problems associated with the use of poor instruments suggest that caution should be exercised in regard to employing too many indicators. For instance,

Titman and Wessels (1988) used 15 indicators and imposed 105 restrictions on the coefficient matrix. The problems arising from poor instruments are not likely to be revealed when one includes every conceivable indicator variable in the model, as done by Titman and Wessels.

Very often there are several proxy variables available for a single unobserved variable. An example is the work of Datar (1994), who used volume of trading and size (market value) as two proxies for liquidity and argued for the choice of volume as the preferred proxy based on conventional t-tests. The problem of choosing between different proxy variables cannot be dealt with within the framework of conventional analysis. A recent paper by Zabel (1994) analyzed this problem within the framework of likelihood-ratio tests for non-nested hypotheses. However, instead of formulating the problem as a choice between different proxies, it would be advisable to investigate how best to use all the proxies to analyze the effect of, say, "liquidity" on stock returns. This can be accomplished by using the MIMIC model or multiple-indicator-model approach.

Standard asymptotic theory leads us to expect that a weak instrument will result in a large standard error, thus informing us that there is not much information in that variable. However, in small samples a weak instrument can produce a small standard error and a large t-statistic that can be spurious. Dufour (1997) argued that confidence intervals based on asymptotic theory have zero-probability coverage in the weak-instrument case. The question of how to detect weak instruments in the presence of several instruments is an unresolved issue. There have been some studies (e.g., Hall, Rudebusch, and Wilcox, 1994) that have discussed this, but they have relied on an asymptotic test. Jeong (1994) suggested alternative criteria based on an exact distribution. Thus the issue of which indicators to use and which to discard in MIMIC models needs further investigation. It might often be the case that there will be some strong theoretical reasons in favor of some indicators, and these will need to be included (as done in the study by DNV).

4.4 Problem of Nonnormality

The models discussed in previous sections can be estimated by FIML (Aigner and Goldberger, 1977; Aigner et al., 1984; Bollen, 1989). However, if the observed variables have significant excess kurtosis, as is the case with several financial variables, the asymptotic covariance matrix and the χ^2 statistics for model evaluation based on the FIML estimator will be incorrect. These can be obtained by using the asymptotically distribution-free WLS estimation method suggested in Browne (1984). Several statistical packages, including SAS and LISREL, provide FIML estimates and standard errors. LISREL also provides distribution-free WLS estimates and standard errors.

4.5 Nonlinearities and Artificial Neural Networks (ANN)

One other limitation of the models considered in the previous sections is the assumption of linearity in the relationships. The artificial-neural-network (ANN) approach is similar in structure to the MIMIC models (apart from differences in terminology), but allows for unspecified forms of nonlinearity. In the ANN terminology the input layer corresponds to the causes in the MIMIC models, and the middle or hidden layer corresponds to the unobservables. In principle, the model can consist of several hidden or middle layers, but in practice there is only one hidden layer. The ANN models were proposed by cognitive scientists as flexible nonlinear models inspired by certain features of the way the human brain processes information. These models have only recently received attention from statisticians and econometricians. Cheng and Titterington (1994) have provided a statistical perspective, and Kuan and White (1994) have provided an econometrics perspective. An introduction to the computational aspects of these models can be found in the work of Hertz, Krogh, and Palmer (1991).

The ANN is just a kind of black box, with very little said about the nature of the nonlinear relationships. Because of their simplicity and flexibility, and because they have been shown to have some success compared with linear models, ANN models have been used in several financial applications for purposes of forecasting (Trippi and Turban, 1993; Kuan and White, 1994; Hutchinson, Lo, and Poggio, 1994). Apart from the linear–nonlinear difference, one major difference is that the MIMIC models have a structural interpretation, but the ANN models do not. For forecasting purposes, detailed specifications of the structure may not be important. Qi (1996) discussed several financial applications of ANN models (option pricing, bankruptcy prediction, exchange-rate forecasting, and stock-market prediction).

4.6 Signal-Extraction Methods

The signal-extraction problem is that of predicting true values for the error-ridden variables. In the statistical literature this problem has been investigated by Fuller (1990), and in the finance literature it has been discussed by Orazem and Falk (1989), but the setups for those two models were different.

This problem can be analyzed within the context of MIMIC models discussed in previous sections. Consider, or instance, the problem analyzed by Maddala and Nimalendran (1995). Suppose we now have a proxy ΔE for ΔE^* that can be described as

$$\Delta E = \Delta E^* + \varepsilon_4$$

where ΔE is unanticipated earnings. The MIMIC model considered gives us an estimate of $\text{var}(\Delta E^*)$. The signal-extraction approach gives us an estimate of ΔE^* as

$$\Delta \hat{E}^* = \gamma(\Delta E), \quad \text{where } \gamma = \text{var}(\Delta E^*)/\text{var}(\Delta E)$$

Thus, if we have a noisy measure of ΔE^*, then that, in conjunction with the other equations in which ΔE^* occurs as an explanatory variable, enables us to get a predictor for the true ΔE^*. The signal extraction essentially depends on an estimate of γ, and this can be accomplished if we have other variables where ΔE^* occurs as an explanatory variable. Jeong and Maddala (1991) used this procedure in tests of rationality.

4.7 Qualitative and Limited-Dependent-Variable Models

In the signaling models, there are different categories of signals (dividends, stock splits, stock repurchases, etc.). In connection with these models there are the two questions of whether or not to signal and how best to signal. When considering the information content of different announcements (say dividend change or stock split) it is customary to consider only the firms that have sent these signals. But given that signaling is an endogenous event (the firm has decided to signal), there is a selection-bias problem in the computation of abnormal returns computed at the time of the announcement (during the period of the announcement window).

There have been studies (e.g., McNichols and Dravid, 1990) that have considered a matched sample and analyzed the determinants of dividends and stock splits. However, the computation of abnormal returns does not make any allowance for the endogeneity of the signals. In addition, there are some conceptual problems involved with the matched-sample method almost universally used (and universally ignored) in financial research of this kind. The problem here is the following. Suppose we are investigating the determinants of dividends. We have firms that pay dividends, and we get a "matched sample" of firms that do not pay dividends. The match is based on some attributes X that are common to both. Usually the variables X are also used as explanatory variables in a (logit or probit) model to explain the determinants of dividends. Suppose we have a perfect match. Then we have the situation that one firm with the attributes of X has paid dividend, and another with the same attributes of X has not. Obviously, X cannot explain the determinants of dividends. The determinants of dividend payments must be some other variables besides the ones that we use to get matched samples.

The LISREL program can deal with ordinal and censored variables, besides continuous variables. However, combining MIMIC models with selection bias is the more relevant problem in financial applications, as in the example of McNichols and Dravid (1990). This is more complicated if we allow for endogeneity of the signals. It is, however, true that the self-selection model has as its reduced form a censored regression model. Thus the LISREL program can be used to account for selection bias *in its reduced form*. But estimation of MIMIC models with selection bias in the structural form needs further work and is an important problem for future research in signaling models.

5 Bounds Methods and Performance Measurement

Means for obtaining consistent bounds for parameters using direct and reverse regression methods have often been employed to tackle EIV problems (Maddala, 1992, pp. 447–61). These methods have been applied in the financial literature only for problems of performance measurement, but using modifications of the procedures used in the econometric literature. Applications in other areas besides performance measurement have not been investigated yet.

In his 1921 paper in *Metroeconomica*, Gini stated that the slope of the coefficient of the error-ridden variable in a simple regression model lies between the probability limit of the ordinary-least-squares coefficient and the probability limit of the "reverse" regression estimate of the same coefficient. That result, also derived by Frisch (1934), does not carry over to the multiple-regression case in general. The generalization to a multiple-regression case, due to Koopmans (1937), has been discussed, with a new proof, by Bekker, Kapteyn, and Wansbeek (1985). Apart from Koopmans's proof, later proofs have been given by Kalman (1982) and Klepper and Leamer (1984). It has also been extended to equation systems by Leamer (1987).

All these results require that the measurement errors be uncorrelated with the equation errors. Because that assumption is not valid in many applications, there have been many papers that have relaxed that assumption. Erickson (1993) derived the implications of placing upper and lower bounds on this correlation in a multiple-regression model with exactly one mismeasured regressor. Some other extensions of the bounds literature have been given by Krasker and Pratt (1986), who used a prior lower bound on the correlation between the proxy and the true regressor, and Bekker et al. (1985), who used as their prior input an upper bound on the covariance matrix of the errors. Iwata (1992) considered a different problem – the case where instrumental variables are correlated with errors. In that case, the instrumental-variable method does not give consistent estimates, but Iwata showed that tighter bounds can be found if one has prior information restricting the extent of the correlation between the instrumental variables and the regression equation errors.

In the financial literature the effect of correlated errors has been discussed by Booth and Smith (1985). They considered the case of a simple regression where the errors and the systematic parts of both y and x were correlated (all other error correlations were assumed to be zero). They also gave arguments as to why allowing for these correlations is important in financial applications. This analysis has been applied by Rahman, Fabozzi, and Lee (1991) to judge performance measurement of mutual-fund shares, which depends on the intercept term in the CAPM. They derived upper and lower bounds for the constant term using direct and reverse regressions. These results on performance measurement, which are based on the CAPM, thus are subject to criticism of the proxy used for market portfolio. There has also been discussion in the financial literature of performance measurement based on the APT (Connor and Korajczyk, 1986, 1996). In that case, the bounds on performance measurement are difficult to derive. The results of Klepper and Leamer (1984) can be used, but they will be based on the restrictive assumption that the errors and systematic parts are uncorrelated (an assumption relaxed in the paper by Booth and Smith). The relaxation of this assumption is important, as argued in Booth and Smith. Thus, the EIV problems involved with performance measurement remain unsolved.

6 Conclusion

This essay has discussed several econometrics issues related to the EIV problem in financial models. This problem has received a lot of attention in regard to testing of the CAPM, but much of that literature has been based on single-equation methods. That problem has largely been corrected, though some recent papers have used the single-equation method (e.g., Fama and French, 1992). There are still some issues that remain, as noted in several places. Also, apart from the CAPM literature, the EIV problems have been almost completely ignored in other areas of finance.

More attention needs to be devoted to unobservable-variable models and instrumental-variable methods, paying special attention to the problems of choice among multiple proxies and the problem of poor instruments. Also, in the estimation of EIV models, some of the commonly used assumptions about correlations among the errors need to be relaxed, because these are not relevant for financial models.

References

Aigner, D. J., and Goldberger, A. S. (eds.) (1977). *Latent Variables in Socio-Economic Models*. Amsterdam: North Holland.

Aigner, D. J., Hsiao, C., Kapteyn, A., and Wansbeek, T. (1984). Latent variable models in econometrics. In: *Handbook of Econometrics*, vol. 2, ed. Z. Griliches and M. Intriligator, pp. 1321–93. Amsterdam: North Holland.

Banz, R. (1981). The relations between returns and market values of common stocks. *Journal of Financial Economics* 9:3–18.

Bekker, P. A. (1994). Alternative approaches to the distribution of instrumental variable estimator. *Econometrica* 62:657–81.

Bekker, P., Kapteyn, A., and Wansbeek, T. (1985). Errors in variables in econometrics: new developments and recurrent themes. *Statistica Neerlandica* 39:129–41.

Black, F., Jensen, M. C., and Scholes, M. (1972). The capital asset pricing model: some empirical tests. In: *Studies in the Theory of Capital Markets*, ed. M. Jensen, pp. 79–121. New York: Praeger.

Bollen, K. A. (1989). *Structural Equations with Latent Variables*. New York: Wiley.

Booth, J. R., and Smith, R. L. (1985). The application of errors in variables methodology to capital market research. *Journal of Financial Quantitative Analysis* 20:501–15.

Browne, M. W. (1984). Asymptotically distribution-free methods for the analysis of covariance structures. *British Journal of Mathematical and Statistical Psychology* 37:62–83.

Chamberlain, G., and Goldberger, A. S. (1990). Latent variables in econometrics. *Journal of Economic Perspectives* 4:125–52.

Chan, K., Chen, N., and Hsieh, D. (1985). An exploratory investigation of the firm size effect. *Journal of Financial Economics* 14:451–72.

Chen, N. F., Roll, R., and Ross, S. A. (1986). Economic forces and the stock market. *Journal of Business* 59:383–403.

Cheng, B., and Titterington, D. M. (1994). Neutral networks: a review from the statistical perspective (with discussion). *Statistical Science* 9:2–54.

Connor, G., and Korajczyk, R. A. (1986). Performance measurement with the arbitrage pricing theory. *Journal of Financial Economics* 15:373–94.

   (1988). Risk and return in an equilibrium APT: an application of a new methodology. *Journal of Financial Economics* 21:255–89.

   (1996). Arbitrage pricing theory. In: *The Finance Handbook*, ed. R. Jarrow, V. Maksimovic, and W. T. Ziemba. Amsterdam: North Holland.

Conway, D. A., and Reinganum, M. C. (1988). Stable factors in security returns: identification using cross-validation. *Journal of Business and Economic Statistics* 6:1–15.

Cragg, J. G., and Donald, S. G. (1992). Testing and determining arbitrage pricing structure from regressions on macro variables. Discussion paper 14, Department of Economics, University of British Columbia.

   (1995). Factor analysis under more general conditions with reference to heteroskedasticity of unknown form. In: *Advances in Econometrics and Quantitative Economics, Essays in Honor of C. R. Rao*, ed. G. S. Maddala, P. C. B. Phillips, and T. N. Srinivasan. London: Blackwell.

Dahm, P. F., and Fuller, W. A. (1986). Generalized least squares estimation of the functional multivariate linear errors in variables model. *Journal of Multivariate Analysis* 19:132–41.

Datar, V. (1994). Value of liquidity in financial markets. Unpublished Ph.D. dissertation, University of Florida.

Desai, A. S., Nimalendran, M., and Venkataraman, S. (1996). Inferring the information conveyed by multiple signals using latent variables/structural equa-

tion models. Manuscript, Department of Finance, Insurance and Real Estate, University of Florida.
Dufour, J. M. (1997). Some impossibility theorems in econometrics with applications to instrumental variables, dynamic models and cointegration. *Econometrica* 65:1365–87.
Erickson, T. (1993). Restricting regression slopes in the errors-in-variables model by bounding the error correlation. *Econometrica* 61:959–69.
Fama, E. F., and French, K. R. (1992). The cross-section of expected stock returns. *Journal of Finance* 47:427–65.
Fama, E. F., and MacBeth, J. (1973). Risk, return and equilibrium: empirical tests. *Journal of Political Economy* 81:607–36.
Ferson, W. E., and Jagannathan, R. (1996). Econometric evaluation of asset pricing models. In: *Handbook of Statistics. vol. 14: Statistical Methods in Finance*, ed. G. S. Maddala and C. R. Rao, pp. 1–33. Amsterdam: Elsevier.
Frisch, R. (1934). *Statistical Confluence Analysis by Means of Complete Regression Systems*. Oslo: University Institute of Economics.
Fuller, W. A. (1980). Properties of some estimators for the errors-in-variables model. *Annals of Statistics* 8:407–22.
——— (1990). Prediction of true values for the measurement error model. In: *Statistical Analysis of Measurement Error Models and Applications: Contemporary Mathematics*, vol. 112, ed. P. J. Brown and W. A. Fuller, pp. 41–57. Providence, RI: American Mathematical Society.
Geweke, J., and Zhou, G. (1995). Measuring the pricing error of the arbitrage pricing theory. Staff report 789, Research Department, Federal Reserve Bank of Minneapolis.
Gibbons, M. R. (1982). Multivariate tests of financial models, a new approach. *Journal of Financial Economics* 10:3–27.
Gibbons, M. R., and Ferson, W. (1985). Testing asset pricing models with changing expectations and an unobservable market portfolio. *Journal of Financial Economics* 14:217–36.
Gibbons, M., Ross, S., and Shanken, J. (1989). A test of the efficiency of a given portfolio. *Econometrica* 57:1121–52.
Goldberger, A. S. (1972). Structural equation methods in the social sciences. *Econometrica* 40:979–1001.
Griliches, Z. (1974). Errors in variables and other unobservables. *Econometrica* 42:971–98.
——— (1985). Economic data issues. In: *Handbook of Econometrics*, vol. 3, ed. Z. Griliches and M. D. Intriligator, pp. 1465–514. Amsterdam: North Holland.
Hall, A. R., Rudebusch, G. D., and Wilcox, D. W. (1994). *Judging Instrument Relevance in Instrumental Variable Estimation*. Washington, DC: Federal Reserve Board.
Hansen, L. P., Heaton, J., and Luttmer, E. G. J. (1995). Econometric evaluation of asset pricing models. *Review of Financial Studies* 8:237–73.
Harvey, C. R., and Kirby, C. (1996). Instrumental variable estimation of conditional beta pricing models. In: *Handbook of Statistics. vol. 14: Statistical Methods in Finance*, ed. G. S. Maddala and C. R. Rao, pp. 35–60. Amsterdam: Elsevier Science.
Harvey, C. R., and Zhou, G. (1990). Bayesian inference in asset pricing tests. *Journal of Financial Economics* 26:221–54.

Hertz, J., Krogh, A., and Palmer, R. G. (1991). *Introduction to the Theory of Neural Computation*. Reading, MA: Addison-Wesley.

Hutchinson, J. M., Lo, A. M., and Poggio, T. (1994). A non-parametric approach to pricing and hedging securities via neutral networks. *Journal of Finance* 49:851–889.

Israel, R., Ofer, A. R., and Siegel, D. R. (1990). The use of the changes in equity value as a measure of the information content of announcements of changes in financial policy. *Journal of Business and Economic Statistics* 8:209–16.·

Iwata, S. (1992). Instrumental variables estimation in errors-in-variables models when instruments are correlated with errors. *Journal of Econometrics* 53:297–322.

Jagannathan, R., and Wang, Z. (1996). The CaPM is alive and well. *Journal of Finance* 51:3–53.

Jeong, J. (1994). On pretesting instrument relevance in instrumental variable estimation. Unpublished paper, Emory University.

Jeong, J., and Maddala, G. S. (1991). Measurement errors and tests for rationality. *Journal of Business and Economic Statistics* 9:431–9.

John, K., and Mishra, B. (1990). Information content of insider trading around corporate announcements: the case of capital expenditures. *Journal of Finance* 45:835–55.

Jöreskog, K. G., and Goldberger, A. S. (1975). Estimation of a model with multiple indicators and multiple causes of a single latent variable. *Journal of the American Statistical Association* 70:631–9.

Jöreskog, K. G., and Sorböm, D. (1989). *LISREL 7. User's Reference.* Chicago: SSI Inc.

(1993). *LISREL 8. Structural Equation Modeling with the Simplis™ Command Language.* Chicago: SSI Inc.

Kalman, R. E. (1982). System identification from noisy data. In: *Dynamical Systems*, vol. 2, ed. A. Bednarek and L. Cesari. New York: Academic Press.

Kandel, S., McCulloch, R., and Stambaugh, R. F. (1995). Bayesian inference and portfolio efficiency. *Review of Financial Studies* 8:1–53.

Kapteyn, A., and Wansbeek, T. (1984). Errors in variables: consistent adjusted least squares (CALS) estimation. *Communications in Statistics: Theory and Methods* 13:1811–37.

Klepper, S., and Leamer, E. E. (1984). Consistent sets of estimates for regression with errors in all variables. *Econometrica* 55:163–84.

Koopmans, T. C. (1937). *Linear Regression Analysis of Economic Time Series*. Haarlem: Netherlands Economic Institute, DeErven F. Bohn, NV.

Krasker, W. S., and Pratt, J. W. (1986). Bounding the effects of proxy variables on regression coefficients. *Econometrica* 54:641–55.

Kuan, C. M., and White, H. (1994). Artificial neutral networks: an econometric perspective. *Econometric Reviews* 13:1–91.

Leamer, E. (1987). Errors in variables in linear systems. *Econometrica* 55:893–909.

Lehmann, B. N., and Modest, D. M. (1988). The empirical foundations of the arbitrage pricing theory. *Journal of Financial Economics* 21:213–54.

Litzenberger, R. H., and Ramaswamy, K. (1979). The effect of personal taxes and dividends on capital asset prices. *Journal of Financial Economics* 7:163–95.

Lys, T., and Sabino, J. S. (1992). Research design issues in grouping-based tests. *Journal of Financial Economics* 32:355–87.
McNichols, M., and Dravid, A. (1990). Stock dividends, stock splits, and signaling. *Journal of Finance* 45:857–79.
Maddala, G. S. (1992). *Introduction to Econometrics*, 2nd ed. New York: Macmillan.
Maddala, G. S., and Jeong, J. (1992). On the exact small sample distribution of the instrumental variable estimator. *Econometrica* 60:181–3.
Maddala, G. S., and Nimalendran, M. (1995). An unobserved component panel data model to study the effect of earnings surprises on stock prices, volume of trading and bid-ask spreads. *Journal of Econometrics* 68:229–42.
Nelson, C. R., and Startz, R. (1990). Some further results on the exact small sample properties of the instrumental variable estimator. *Econometrica* 58:967–96.
Orazem, P., and Falk, B. (1989). Measuring market responses to error-ridden government announcements. *Quarterly Review of Economics and Business* 29:41–55.
Pakes, A. (1982). On the asymptotic bias of the Wald-type estimators of a straight-line when both variables are subject to error. *International Economic Review* 23:491–7.
Qi, M. (1996). Financial applications of artificial neutral networks. In: *Handbook of Statistics. vol. 14: Statistical Methods in Finance*, ed. G. S. Maddala and C. R. Rao, pp. 529–52. Amsterdam: Elsevier Science.
Rahman, S., Fabozzi, F. J., and Lee, C. F. (1991). Errors-in-variables, functional form, and mutual fund returns. *Quarterly Review of Economics and Business* 31:24–35.
Roll, R. W. (1977). A critique of the asset pricing theory's tests – part 1: On past and potential testability of the theory. *Journal of Financial Economics* 4:129–76.
Roll, R. W., and Ross, S. A. (1980). An empirical investigation of the arbitrage pricing theory. *Journal of Finance* 35:1073–103.
  (1994). On the cross-sectional relation between expected returns and betas. *Journal of Finance* 49:101–22.
Schneeweiss, H. (1976). Consistent estimation of a regression with errors in the variables. *Metrika* 23:101–15.
Shanken, J. (1992). On the estimation of beta-pricing models. *Review of Financial Studies* 5:1–33.
  (1996). Statistical methods in tests of portfolio efficiency: a synthesis. In: *Handbook of Statistics. vol. 14: Statistical Methods in Finance*, ed. G. S. Maddala and C. R. Rao, pp. 693–711. Amsterdam: Elsevier Science.
Shanken, J., and Weinstein, M. I. (1990). Macroeconomic variables and asset pricing: further results. Unpublished manuscript, Department of Economics, University of Southern California.
Skinner, D. J. (1991). Stock returns, trading volume, and bid–ask spreads around earnings announcements; evidence from the NASDAQ national market system. Unpublished manuscript, Department of Economics, University of Michigan.
Steiger, D., and Stock, J. H. (1997). Instrumental variable regression with weak instruments. *Econometrica* 65: 557–86.

Titman, S., and Wessels, R. (1988). The determinants of capital structure choice. *Journal of Finance* 43:1–19.
Trippi, R., and Turban, E. (1993). *Neutral Networks in Finance and Investing.* Chicago: Probus.
Zabel, J. E. (1994). Selection among non-nested sets of regressors: the case of multiple proxy variables. Discussion paper, Tufts University.
Zellner, A. (1970). Estimation of regression relationships containing unobservable independent variables. *International Economic Review* 11:441–54.
Zhou, G. (1993). Asset pricing tests under alternative distributional assumptions. *Journal of Finance* 48:1927–42.
  (1995). Small sample rank tests with applications to asset pricing. *Journal of Empirical Finance* 2:71–94.

CHAPTER 13

Statistical Analysis of Some Nonstationary Time Series

Søren Johansen

1   Introduction

The purpose of this essay is to draw attention to some recent work on the statistical analysis of nonstationary processes that are integrated – in particular, integrated of order 2. A nonstationary process is integrated of order 1 if the differences are stationary, and it is integrated of order 2 if the second differences are stationary. In the analysis of some macroeconomic data, in particular price series, it is found that they are better described as $I(2)$ series than as $I(1)$ series. As an example, take the log of a price index; if the inflation rate is not stationary, it can perhaps be described as $I(1)$, in which case the price series itself will be $I(2)$.

Consider, for illustrative purposes, measurements of the consumer price index in Australia and the United States and the exchange rate and the bond rate from each country. The variables are p_t^{au}, p_t^{us}, exch_t, i_t^{au}, and i_t^{us}, where the first three are in logs. The data are quarterly, 1972:1 to 1991:1, and were kindly provided by Tony Hall. The data were analyzed by Johansen (1996), where indication of $I(2)$ was found.

Figure 13.1 shows the data in levels and differences. Figure 13.2 shows, for U.S. prices, levels, differences, and second differences in the left-hand panel; for comparison, the right-hand panel shows a sequence of independent identically distributed (iid) Gaussian variables and their cumulated sum (which is a random walk) and twice-cumulated sum. The price variable shows a development similar to the twice-cumulated ε over the period, which indicates that the process may be $I(2)$.

The notion of cointegration has become popular since the fundamental work of Granger (1981) and Engle and Granger (1987), and it offers the possibility of describing long-run relations, or long-run equilibria, between nonstationary processes. The notion of $I(2)$ allows us to formulate more complicated long-run relations in the sense that we con-

This essay was presented at the Ragnar Frisch Centennial Symposium in Oslo, March 3–5, 1995.

434 Søren Johansen

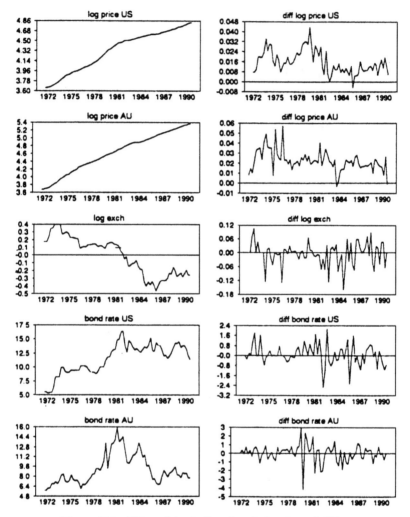

Figure 13.1. U.S. and Australian data in levels and differences.

sider not only linear combinations of levels but also linear combinations of levels and differences. Thus we get the possibility of formulating dynamic long-run equilibria as well as static long-run equilibria (Frisch, 1929).

We can formulate purchasing-power parity as a long-run relation by requiring $p_t^{au} - p_t^{us} - \text{exch}_t$ stationary. In an $I(1)$ model this is formulated as the hypothesis that $(1, -1, -1, 0, 0)$ is a cointegration vector. The hypothesis that the interest-rate differential $i_t^{au} - i_t^{us}$ is stationary is the hypothesis that $(0, 0, 0, 1, -1)$ is a cointegration vector. In the $I(2)$ model such relations need not be stationary, but the linear combinations can

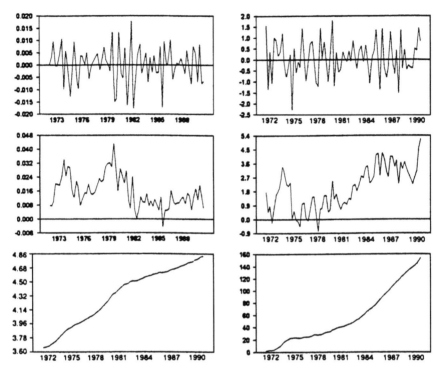

Figure 13.2. The left-hand panel shows U.S. prices in second differences, differences, and levels. The right-hand panel shows a sequence of iid Gaussian variables, their cumulated sum, and twice cumulated sum.

reduce the order of integration from 2 to 1. In that case it is tempting to look for a stationary relation of the form

$$p_t^{au} - p_t^{us} - \text{exch}_t - c\Delta p_t^{us} \tag{1}$$

which involves the levels as well as the differences of the processes.

We give here a brief survey of what has been achieved in the analysis of $I(2)$ processes in a vector autoregressive framework. We start with the basic definitions and give the representations of $I(1)$ and $I(2)$ processes. Then we define the $I(1)$ and $I(2)$ models as submodels of the vector autoregressive model and discuss their estimation by an analysis of the Gaussian likelihood function. Next we treat topics like rank determination and tests of the long-run coefficients and adjustment coefficients and point out the differences and similarities to the $I(1)$ theory.

The theoretical results are from Johansen (1992a, 1995, 1997) and Paruolo (1994, 1996; in press), and the reader is referred to Juselius (1995a,b; in press) for applications and to Johansen (1992b,c) for illustrations.

2 Basic Definitions and Examples

The class of nonstationary processes that we want to model comprises those processes that can be made stationary by differencing. Thus a typical process is a random walk, but any process that can be written as the sum of a random walk and a stationary process should also be included in the definition. This is, of course, a rather simple type of nonstationarity, but we choose it because the processes are well understood and because we already have a statistical theory for their analysis. We begin with two examples.

Example 1. *A moving-average representation:* We consider a four-dimensional process given directly in terms of two random walks $S_{1t} = \Sigma_{i=1}^{t} \varepsilon_{1i}$ and $S_{2t} = \Sigma_{i=1}^{t} \varepsilon_{2i}$ and some iid errors:

$$X_{1t} = S_{1t} + \varepsilon_{3t}$$
$$X_{2t} = S_{2t} + \varepsilon_{4t}$$
$$X_{3t} = S_{1t} - S_{2t} + \varepsilon_{5t}$$
$$X_{4t} = S_{1t} + S_{2t} + \varepsilon_{6t}$$

It is clear that all these processes are nonstationary and that the nonstationarity is caused by the two random walks generated by ε_{1t} and ε_{2t}. Because there are only two such common stochastic trends, we can eliminate these by taking the linear combinations $X_{1t} - X_{2t} - X_{3t}$ and $X_{1t} + X_{2t} - X_{4t}$, which are seen to be stationary. Thus we can transform the processes to stationarity either by taking differences or by taking suitable linear combinations. We say that such processes are integrated of order 1, $I(1)$, and we call the described phenomenon cointegration. Note that once we have found two linear relations that are stationary, then any linear combination of these is stationary as well. Hence the requirement of stationarity of a linear combination is not enough to identify it.

This example is taken from Frisch (1934, p. 80), who used such a set of processes to discuss confluence analysis. He took S_{1t} and S_{2t} to be iid, with a large variance, and he used confluence analysis and bunch maps to find the multicollinear combinations of the variables. The formulation with random walks is another attempt to formulate the concept of a large signal with small noise. Thus, in this sense, cointegration of $I(1)$ variables can be seen as a way of solving the collinearity problem; see Hendry and Morgan (1989) for a recent assessment of confluence analysis.

Example 2. *An autoregressive representation:* We generate the process $X_t = (X_{1t}, X_{2t})'$ by an autoregressive model of order 1. The initial value is X_0, and the equations are

$$\Delta X_{1t} = \alpha_1(X_{1t-1} - X_{2t-1}) + \varepsilon_{1t}$$
$$\Delta X_{2t} = \varepsilon_{2t}$$

If $-1 < 1 + \alpha_1 < 1$, X_t is $I(1)$, and ΔX_t and $X_{1t} - X_{2t}$ are stationary. Thus $I(1)$ variables can be generated by autoregressive processes under suitable conditions on the parameters.

With these two examples as motivation, we now give the basic definitions. The natural definition is that a process is integrated of order 1 if it is nonstationary and the differences are stationary. Such a definition turns out not to be precise enough, and we therefore give a slightly narrower definition. Consider, therefore, a doubly infinite sequence of iid p-dimensional variables ε_t, with mean zero and finite variance. We define a linear stationary process by the expression

$$Y_t = \sum_{i=0}^{\infty} C_i \varepsilon_{t-i}$$

where the coefficient matrices are decreasing exponentially such that the series

$$C(z) = \sum_{i=0}^{\infty} C_i z^i$$

defined for the z complex is convergent for $|z| < 1 + \delta$ for some $\delta > 0$.

Definition 1. *The linear process $Y_t = \sum_{i=0}^{\infty} C_i \varepsilon_{t-i}$ is called $I(0)$ if $C(1) = \sum_{i=0}^{\infty} C_i \neq 0$.*

Definition 2. *The process X_t is called integrated of order 1, $I(1)$, if $\Delta X_t - E(\Delta X_t)$ is $I(0)$.*

In order to explain these definitions, consider the process Y_t, and define $X_t = \sum_{i=1}^{t} Y_i$. By expanding the function $C(z)$ around $z = 1$, we find

$$C(z) = C(1) + (1 - z)C^*(z)$$

for some function $C^*(z)$ given by a power series in a neighborhood of $z = 1$. For the $I(0)$ process $\Delta X_t = Y_t = \sum_{i=0}^{\infty} C_i \varepsilon_{t-i}$ it holds therefore that

$$\Delta X_t = Y_t = C(1)\varepsilon_t + C^*(L)\Delta \varepsilon_t$$

and

$$X_t = \sum_{i=1}^{t} Y_i = C(1) \sum_{i=1}^{t} \varepsilon_i + C^*(L)(\varepsilon_t - \varepsilon_0)$$

Hence the $I(1)$ process X_t contains a random-walk component if $C(1) \neq 0$. It is this type of nonstationarity that we want to call $I(1)$. This explains the condition $C(1) \neq 0$ in the definition of an $I(0)$ process. Thus a linear process with $C(1) = 0$ is not $I(0)$, but of course is still stationary.

We next turn to the definition of cointegration.

Definition 3. *If X_t is $I(1)$ and $\beta' X_t - E(\beta' X_t)$ is stationary, we call X_t cointegrated and β the cointegrating vector. The number of linearly independent cointegrating vectors is the cointegrating rank.*

We shall be particularly concerned with processes that are integrated of order 2, and therefore we give the definition of $I(2)$ processes:

Definition 4. *We call the process X_t integrated of order 2, $I(2)$, if ΔX_t is $I(1)$ or $\Delta^2 X_t - E(\Delta^2 X_t)$ is $I(0)$.*

Thus a log price series p_t is $I(2)$ if the inflation rate Δp_t is $I(1)$. For processes integrated of order 2, the phenomenon of polynomial cointegration can occur; see equation (1).

Example 3. *Define the process X_t by the equations*

$$X_{1t} = \sum_{j=1}^{t} \sum_{i=1}^{j} \varepsilon_{1i} + \sum_{i=1}^{t} \varepsilon_{2i} + \varepsilon_{3t}$$

$$X_{2t} = \sum_{j=1}^{t} \sum_{i=1}^{j} \varepsilon_{1i} - \sum_{i=1}^{t} \varepsilon_{2i} + \varepsilon_{4t}$$

$$X_{3t} = \sum_{j=1}^{t} \sum_{i=1}^{j} \varepsilon_{2i} + \varepsilon_{5t}$$

$$X_{4t} = \sum_{i=1}^{t} \varepsilon_{1i} + \varepsilon_{6t}$$

The process X_t is an $I(2)$ process, even if X_{4t} is only $I(1)$, and $X_{1t} - X_{2t}$ is an $I(1)$ process, so the order is reduced from 2 to 1 by the linear combination $(1, -1, 0, 0)$. In order to obtain stationarity, we consider

$$X_{1t} - X_{2t} - 2\Delta X_{3t}$$

which is seen to be stationary, as are the combinations

$$\Delta X_{1t} - X_{4t} \quad \text{and} \quad \Delta X_{2t} - X_{4t}$$

With this as motivation, we define the notion of polynomial cointegration:

Definition 5. *If X_t is integrated of order 2 and we can find coefficients β_0 and β_1 such that $\beta_1' X_t$ is $I(1)$ and*

$$\beta_1' X_t + \beta_0' \Delta X_t - E(\beta_1' X_t + \beta_0' \Delta X_t)$$

is stationary, we call X_t polynomially cointegrated.

With these definitions in mind, we now want to discuss some statistical models that describe such types of nonstationarity and briefly indicate the statistical analysis and how one makes inferences. Thus we shall discuss the following questions:

1. How can we build statistical models that describe the variations of the data such that the questions of integration and cointegration can be formulated and tested as statistical hypotheses?
2. What are the properties of the processes generated by the statistical models?
3. How can we derive estimators and test statistics from the Gaussian likelihood?
4. How can we make asymptotic inferences under sufficiently weak assumptions on the data-generating mechanism?

These problems have been treated by many authors; see Stock and Watson (1993), Engle and Yoo (1991), Gregoir and Laroque (1993), and Johansen (1994, 1995, 1997). In the following, we focus on the vector autoregressive processes, as these have turned out to be useful in describing the statistical variations of many macroeconomic data series, and because this is the class of models for which we have results based on an analysis of the likelihood function.

3   Representation of Integrated Variables

As the basic model for the stochastic variation of the data, we consider the vector autoregressive equations, and we start by placing conditions on the parameters of the VAR model to ensure that it will generate processes that will be integrated of order i ($i = 0, 1, 2$). We define the autoregressive process with k lags in p dimensions by the equation

$$X_t = \sum_{i=1}^{k} \Pi_i X_{t-i} + \Phi D_t + \varepsilon_t$$

where the errors ε_t are iid, with mean zero and variance Ω, and D_t contains seasonal dummies and a constant term or other deterministic terms that do not grow too fast. It is common practice to reparameterize the model as a reduced-form error-correction model

$$\Delta X_t = \Pi X_{t-1} + \sum_{i=1}^{k-1} \Gamma_i \Delta X_{t-i} + \Phi D_t + \varepsilon_t$$

where $\Pi = -I + \Sigma_{i=1}^{k} \Pi_i$, $\Gamma_i = -\Sigma_{j=i+1}^{k} \Pi_j$, and for later use we let $\Gamma = I - \Sigma_{i=1}^{k-1} \Gamma_i$.

We first discuss under what conditions these equations will generate processes that are $I(0)$, $I(1)$, and $I(2)$, respectively. The conditions involve the characteristic polynomial, where z denotes the complex argument

$$A(z) = (1-z)I - \Pi z - \sum_{i=1}^{k-1}\Gamma_i(1-z)z^i, \quad A(1) = -\Pi$$

so that

$$\frac{dA(z)}{dz} = \dot{A}(z) = -I - \Pi - \sum_{i=1}^{k-1}\Gamma_i[(1-z)iz^{i-1} - z^i], \quad \dot{A}(1) = -\Pi - \Gamma$$

We define $|A(z)| = \det A(z)$.

Theorem 1. *The I(0) theorem: Under the assumption that $|A(z)| = 0$ implies that $|z| > 1$, process $X_t - E(X_t)$ is I(0), and*

$$X_t = A(L)^{-1}(\varepsilon_t + \Phi D_t) = C(L)(\varepsilon_t + \Phi D_t)$$

Here, $C(z) = A^{-1}(z)$ is convergent for $|z| < 1 + \delta$.

The proof of this has been given by Anderson (1971).

Thus we must have roots inside or on the unit circle if nonstationary processes are generated from the autoregressive equations. We are concerned in particular with roots at the point $z = 1$ as a way of generating the type of process that can be made stationary by differencing.

If unit roots ($z = 1$) are allowed, then $\Pi = -A(1)$ is of reduced rank, such that $\Pi = \alpha\beta'$ for α and β of dimension $p \times r$ and rank r, $r < p$. In order to formulate the representation theorem of Granger, we need the concept of the orthogonal complement of a matrix β, and we define $\beta_\perp$ as any $p \times (p-r)$ matrix of full rank such that $\beta'\beta_\perp = 0$.

Theorem 2. *The I(1) theorem: We assume that $|A(z)| = 0$ implies that $z = 1$ or $|z| > 1 + \delta$ and that $\text{rank}(\Pi) = r < p$, such that $\Pi = \alpha\beta'$. A necessary and sufficient condition that X_t is I(1) is that*

$$\text{rank}(\alpha'_\perp \Gamma \beta_\perp) = \text{rank}\left[\alpha'_\perp\left(I - \sum_{i=1}^{k-1}\Gamma_i\right)\beta_\perp\right] = p - r$$

In this case,

$$X_t = C\sum_{i=1}^{t}(\varepsilon_i + \Phi D_i) + C(L)(\varepsilon_t + \Phi D_t) + A$$

where

$$C = \beta_\perp[\alpha'_\perp \Gamma \beta_\perp]^{-1}\alpha'_\perp$$

and where A depends on the initial value X_0. The function $C(z)$ is convergent for $|z| < 1 + \delta$ and satisfies

$$A^{-1}(z) = C\frac{1}{1-z} + C(z), \quad z \neq 1$$

Hence X_t is $I(1)$, and $\Delta X_t - E(\Delta X_t)$ and $\beta' X_t - E(\beta' X_t)$ are $I(0)$. The process is a solution to the reduced-form error-correction model

$$\Delta X_t = \alpha \beta' X_{t-1} + \sum_{i=1}^{k-1} \Gamma_i \Delta X_{t-i} + \Phi D_t + \varepsilon_t \tag{2}$$

The proof has been given by Johansen (1988b, 1991).
The common trends are defined as

$$\alpha'_\perp \sum_{i=1}^{t} \varepsilon_i$$

which are seen to be the random walks that create the nonstationarity in the $I(1)$ process. It is a consequence of the $I(1)$ theorem that the number of unit roots of the characteristic polynomial is $p - r$, that is, equal to the rank deficiency of the Π matrix, and hence is completely described by the value of the characteristic polynomial at the point $z = 1$. This is not so for $I(2)$ processes, where we also need to investigate the derivative of $A(z)$ at $z = 1$.

It follows from Theorem 2 that if we want the equations to generate $I(2)$ processes, we need the matrix $\alpha'_\perp \Gamma \beta_\perp$ to have reduced rank. It turns out that the decompositions of this matrix and the matrix Π give all the linear combinations that are needed to describe the cointegrating and polynomial cointegrating properties of the process. We therefore assume.

$$\Pi = \alpha \beta' \quad \text{for } \alpha \text{ and } \beta \text{ of rank } r < p$$
$$\alpha'_\perp \Gamma \beta_\perp = \xi \eta' \quad \text{for } \xi \text{ and } \eta \text{ of rank } s < p - r$$

We next define, apart from β and α, the new directions

$$\beta^1_\perp = \bar{\beta}_\perp \eta, \quad \alpha^1_\perp = \bar{\alpha}_\perp \xi$$
$$\beta^2_\perp = \beta_\perp \eta_\perp, \quad \alpha^2_\perp = \alpha_\perp \xi_\perp$$

where $\bar{\beta}_\perp = \beta_\perp (\beta'_\perp \beta_\perp)^{-1}$ such that $\beta_\perp^{1'} \beta_\perp^2 = \eta'(\beta'_\perp \beta_\perp)^{-1} \beta'_\perp \beta_\perp \eta_\perp = 0$. The mutually orthogonal directions $(\beta, \beta^1_\perp, \beta^2_\perp)$ define the cointegrating properties of the $I(2)$ process, as we formulate in the next theorem.

Theorem 3. *The $I(2)$ theorem: Assume $|A(z)| = 0$ implies that $|z| > 1 + \delta$ or $z = 1$ and that $\Pi = \alpha \beta'$ is of rank $r < p$. Assume further that $\alpha'_\perp \Gamma \beta_\perp = \xi \eta'$ is of rank $s < p - r$. A necessary and sufficient condition for X_t to be $I(2)$ is that*

$$\text{rank}\left[\alpha_\perp^{2'}\left(\Gamma \bar{\beta} \bar{\alpha}' \Gamma + \sum_{i=1}^{k-1} i \Gamma_i\right) \beta_\perp^2\right] = p - r - s$$

In this case,

$$X_t = C_2 \sum_{i=1}^{t} \sum_{j=1}^{i} \varepsilon_j + C_1 \sum_{i=1}^{t} \varepsilon_i + C(L) \varepsilon_t + A + Bt \tag{3}$$

where A and B depend on initial values X_0 and X_1. The coefficient matrices C_1 and C_2 can be expressed in terms of the parameters of the model. In particular,

$$C_2 = \beta_\perp^2 \left[\alpha_\perp^{2\prime} \left(\Gamma \bar{\beta} \bar{\alpha}' \Gamma + \sum_{i=1}^{k-1} i\Gamma_i \right) \beta_\perp^2 \right]^{-1} \alpha_\perp^{2\prime}$$

The function $C(z)$ is convergent for $|z| < 1 + \delta$ and satisfies

$$A^{-1}(z) = C_2 \frac{1}{(1-z)^2} + C_1 \frac{1}{1-z} + C(z), \quad z \neq 1$$

Hence X_t is $I(2)$, and $(\beta, \beta_\perp^1)'X_t$ is $I(1)$, because $(\beta, \beta_\perp^1)'C_2 = 0$, and finally a calculation shows that $\beta'X_t - \bar{\alpha}'\Gamma\bar{\beta}_\perp^2\beta_\perp^{2\prime}\Delta X_t$ corrected for its mean is $I(0)$. Hence if γ is an $r \times 1$ vector such that $\gamma'\bar{\alpha}'\Gamma\bar{\beta}_\perp^2 = 0$, then $\gamma'\beta'X_t - E(\gamma'\beta'X_t)$ is $I(0)$.

For a proof of this, see Johansen (1992a). In conclusion, we have seen that the vector autoregressive model allows a reduced-rank restriction $\Pi = \alpha\beta'$ such that it describes $I(1)$ processes, and a further reduced-rank restriction $\alpha_\perp' \Gamma \beta_\perp = \varphi\eta'$ such that it generates $I(2)$ processes. We apply these restrictions later to define the $I(1)$ and $I(2)$ models. The $I(2)$ model allows for directions in which the process is $I(2)$, given by $\beta_\perp^2$, other directions in which it is $I(1)$, given by $(\beta, \beta_\perp^1)$, and finally directions β in which the process can be made stationary by taking linear combinations with the differences. The coefficients are functions of the autoregressive parameters.

It is a consequence of this theorem that the unit root of the characteristic polynomial for an $I(2)$ process is $(p - r) + (p - r - s)$. Thus for $I(2)$ processes we cannot check the number of unit roots by inspection of the matrix Π alone. We need to draw into consideration the Γ matrix, that is, not only the value of $A(z)$ but also the derivative of $A(z)$ at $z = 1$, because $A(1) = -\Pi$, and $dA(z)/dz|_{z=1} = -I - \Pi - \sum_{i=1}^{k}\Gamma_i = -\Pi - \Gamma$.

4   Definition of the $I(1)$ and $I(2)$ Models

In this section we define the basic statistical models for describing $I(1)$ and $I(2)$ variables as submodels of the VAR. We consider the equations defining the p-dimensional VAR model in the error-correction form with deterministic term D_t

$$\Delta X_t = \Pi X_{t-1} + \sum_{i=1}^{k-1} \Gamma_i \Delta X_{t-i} + \Phi D_t + \varepsilon_t \tag{4}$$

The ε are independent and have the same Gaussian distribution, with mean zero and variance matrix Ω, and D_t is as before. Moreover, the parameter space is defined by letting

$(\Pi, \Gamma_1, \ldots, \Gamma_{k-1}, \Phi, \Omega)$

vary freely, such that Ω is positive definite and symmetric. Here we specify the Gaussian errors in order to work with the likelihood.

Definition 6. *The I(1) model H_r is defined as a submodel of the VAR by the reduced-rank condition*

$$\Pi = \alpha\beta'$$

where α and β are $p \times r$ ($r \leq p$) matrices and the parameters

$$(\alpha, \beta, \Gamma_1, \ldots, \Gamma_{k-1}, \Phi, \Omega)$$

vary freely.

Note that the models are nested,

$$H_0 \subset \cdots \subset H_r \subset \cdots \subset H_p$$

and that H_0 is the VAR in differences and H_p is the VAR in levels. Section 5 contains a brief discussion of the likelihood analysis leading to reduced-rank regression (Anderson, 1951).

In order to define the I(2) model it is convenient to reparameterize model (4) as follows:

$$\Delta^2 X_t = \Pi X_{t-1} - \Gamma \Delta X_{t-1} + \sum_{i=1}^{k-2} \Psi_i \Delta^2 X_{t-i} + \Phi D_t + \varepsilon_t \qquad (5)$$

where $\Gamma = I - \sum_{i=1}^{k-1}\Gamma_i$, $\Psi_i = -\sum_{j=i+1}^{k-1}\Gamma_j$, $i = 1, \ldots, k-2$.

Definition 7. *The I(2) model $H_{r,s}$ is defined as the submodel of the VAR that we obtain under the reduced-rank conditions*

$$\Pi = \alpha\beta \qquad (6)$$

where α and β are $p \times r$ matrices of full rank, with $r < p$, and

$$\alpha'_\perp \Gamma \beta_\perp = \xi\eta' \qquad (7)$$

where ξ and η are $(p-r) \times s$ matrices, with $s \leq p - r$.

These models are defined by two reduced-rank conditions, but the remaining parameters vary freely; that is, the parameter space is described by the parameters

$$(\alpha, \beta, \Gamma, \Psi_1, \ldots, \Psi_{k-2}, \Phi, \Omega)$$

where the only restriction is (7).

Note that the models are nested as shown in Table 13.1.
Many other models can be defined by specializing the variables D_t. In

Table 13.1. *Relationships between the I(2) models $H_{r,s}$ and the I(1) models H_r for $p = 3$*

r	I(2) models	I(1) models
0	$H_{0,0} \subset H_{0,1} \subset H_{0,2} \subset H_{0,3}$	$\subset H_0$
1	$H_{1,0} \subset H_{1,1} \subset H_{1,2}$	$\subset H_1$
2	$H_{2,0} \subset H_{2,1}$	$\subset H_2$

particular, if $\Phi D_t = \mu$, it is seen from the representation of $I(2)$ processes [see (3)] that

$$X_t = C_2 \sum_{i=1}^{t} \sum_{j=1}^{i} (\varepsilon_j + \mu) + C_1 \sum_{i=1}^{t} (\varepsilon_i + \mu) + C(L)(\varepsilon_t + \mu) + A + Bt$$

Hence μ gives rise to a quadratic trend with a coefficient $\frac{1}{2}C_2\mu$. Thus a submodel of $H_{r,s}$ can be defined by the restriction $\alpha_2'\mu = 0$, which corresponds to assuming that there is no quadratic trend in the process. Similarly, a further submodel is obtained by assuming that $\alpha_1'\mu = 0$.

The likelihood analysis of these models has been given by Johansen (1995, 1997) and Paruolo (1996, in press). The likelihood analysis is not easy, in the sense that there are no simple algorithms for calculation of the maximum-likelihood estimator, and we do not have any information about uniqueness and existence; see, however, Johansen (1997) for an algorithm that seems to work.

The next section contains an analysis of the likelihood function for the $I(1)$ and $I(2)$ models that leads to manageable calculations consisting of repeated applications of reduced-rank regression and that avoids calculation of the second derivative of the likelihood function at each stage.

5 A Statistical Analysis Derived from the Likelihood Function

In the following, we analyze the likelihood function in order to derive estimators. In the $I(1)$ the maximum-likelihood estimator can be calculated by a method called reduced-rank regression, and for the $I(2)$ model it can be shown that an efficient estimator can be based on a two-step reduced-rank regression.

The method of reduced-rank regression is a nonlinear regression [equation (8)] that involves a matrix $\alpha\beta'$ of reduced rank. The method was derived by Anderson (1951) in an investigation of the identification problem for simultaneous equations and later applied in the estimation method LIML. It was applied by Ahn and Reinsel (1988) for stationary processes and by Johansen (1988a) for nonstationary processes as a Gaussian maximum-likelihood estimator.

Because we apply the method repeatedly, we discuss it briefly here. For any three processes U_t, V_t, and W_t, we define

$$S_{uv} = T^{-1}\sum_{i=1}^{T} U_t V_t'$$

$$S_{uv \cdot w} = S_{uv} - S_{uw} S_{ww}^{-1} S_{wv}$$

Let the processes (U_t, V_t, W_t) be related by the equation

$$U_t = \alpha\beta' V_t + \Psi W_t + \varepsilon_t \tag{8}$$

where α and β are $p \times r$ matrices. This is a regression equation, but a nonlinear regression, because the matrix $\alpha\beta'$ has reduced rank and does not vary freely.

Definition 8. *A reduced-rank regression of U_t on V_t corrected for W_t consists of solving the eigenvalue problem*

$$|\hat{\lambda} S_{vv \cdot w} - S_{vu \cdot w} S_{uu \cdot w}^{-1} S_{uv \cdot w}| = 0 \tag{9}$$

for eigenvalues $1 > \hat{\lambda}_1 > \ldots > \hat{\lambda}_p > 0$ and eigenvectors $V = (v_1, \ldots, v_p)$ normalized by $V' S_{vv \cdot w} V = I$. We define the estimators $\hat{\beta} = (v_1, \ldots, v_r)$, $\hat{\alpha} = S_{vu \cdot w} \hat{\beta}$, and $\hat{\Omega} = S_{uu \cdot w} - \hat{\alpha}\hat{\alpha}'$ such that $|\hat{\Omega}| = |S_{uu \cdot w}| \prod_{i=1}^{r} (1 - \hat{\lambda}_i)$.

5.1 The I(1) Analysis

Equation (2) shows that for the I(1) model with Gaussian errors the reduced-rank condition $\Pi = \alpha\beta'$ implies that the maximum-likelihood estimator can be calculated by reduced-rank regression (8) by defining

$$U_t = \Delta X_t, \quad V_t = X_{t-1}, \quad W_t = (\Delta X_{t-1}', \ldots, \Delta X_{t-k+1}', D_t')'$$

The maximized value of the likelihood function can be found to be

$$L_{max}^{-2/T} = (2\pi e)^p |\hat{\Omega}| = (2\pi e)^p |S_{uu \cdot w}| \prod_{i=1}^{r} (1 - \hat{\lambda}_i) \tag{10}$$

This shows that the likelihood-ratio test of H_r in H_p is given by

$$Q_r = -2\log Q(H_r|H_p) = -T \sum_{i=r+1}^{p} \log(1 - \hat{\lambda}_i) \tag{11}$$

The asymptotic distribution of this quantity is a nonstandard distribution that has to be tabulated by simulation. It depends on the number of common trends in the problem and also on the specification of the deterministic terms. The asymptotic distribution of the estimator of β, however, is mixed Gaussian, with the consequence that inference on β can be conducted as if it were asymptotically Gaussian; see section 7.

Thus, once the rank is determined by the preceding test, inference on β can proceed as usual using the asymptotic X^2 distribution, assuming that the correct value of r has been found. A survey of these results is available (Johansen, 1994, 1996), and the details are in the papers by Ahn and Reinsel (1990), Phillips (1991), and Johansen (1991).

5.2 The I(2) Analysis

In (5), only Π and Γ enter the reduced-rank conditions, and the remaining parameters $\Theta = (\Psi_1, \ldots, \Psi_{k-2}, \Phi)$ remain unrestricted. It is therefore convenient to introduce the shorthand notation $Z'_t = (\Delta^2 X'_{t-1}, \ldots, \Delta^2 X'_{t-k+2}, D'_t)$ such that the equations are written as

$$\Delta^2 X_t = \Pi X_{t-1} - \Gamma \Delta X_{t-1} + \Theta Z_t + \varepsilon_t \tag{12}$$

with

$$\Pi = \alpha \beta' \quad \text{and} \quad \alpha'_\perp \Gamma \beta_\perp = \xi \eta'$$

We shall next discuss the two-step procedure, which can be proved to be efficient.

Step 1. We first analyze these equations with reduced-rank regression of $U_t = \Delta^2 X_t$ on $V_t = X_{t-1}$ corrected for $W_t = Z_t$ and ΔX_{t-1}; that is, we disregard the second reduced-rank condition (7). This gives estimates of α and β for each value of r. The remaining part of the analysis assumes that $\alpha, \beta,$ and r are known and that α and β are equal to the estimated values.

Step 2. If (α, β, r) are known, we can reformulate model (12) by multiplying by $(\alpha_\perp, \bar{\alpha})'$, and we find the equations

$$\alpha'_\perp \Delta^2 X_t = -\alpha'_\perp \Gamma \Delta X_{t-1} + \alpha'_\perp \Theta Z_t + \alpha'_\perp \varepsilon_t \tag{13}$$

$$\bar{\alpha}' \Delta^2 X_t = \beta' X_{t-1} - \bar{\alpha}' \Gamma \Delta X_{t-1} + \bar{\alpha}' \Theta Z_t + \bar{\alpha}' \varepsilon_t \tag{14}$$

Here $\bar{\alpha} = \alpha(\alpha'\alpha)^{-1}$, such that $\bar{\alpha}'\alpha = I$ and $\alpha \bar{\alpha}' = \bar{\alpha}\alpha'$ is the projection onto the space spanned by the columns of the matrix α. Next we define $\Omega_{11} = \bar{\alpha}'\Omega\bar{\alpha}$, $\Omega_{12} = \bar{\alpha}'\Omega\alpha_\perp$, $\Omega_{22} = \alpha'_\perp \Omega \alpha_\perp$, $\Omega_{11.2} = \Omega_{11} - \Omega_{12}\Omega_{22}^{-1}\Omega_{21}$, and $\omega = \Omega_{12}\Omega_{22}^{-1}$ and subtract ω times (13) from (14) to obtain the conditional model for $\bar{\alpha}'\Delta^2 X_t$ given $\alpha'_\perp \Delta^2 X_t$ and the past

$$\bar{\alpha}'\Delta^2 X_t = \omega \alpha'_\perp \Delta^2 X_t + \beta' X_{t-1} - (\bar{\alpha}' - \omega \alpha'_\perp)\Gamma \Delta X_{t-1} \\ + (\bar{\alpha}' - \omega \alpha'_\perp)\Theta Z_t + (\bar{\alpha}' - \omega \alpha'_\perp)\varepsilon_t \tag{15}$$

Equations (13) and (15) have independent error terms $\bar{\alpha}'\varepsilon_t$ and $(\bar{\alpha}' - \omega \alpha'_\perp)\varepsilon_t$ by construction. The parameters are

$$(\alpha'_\perp \Gamma, \alpha'_\perp \Theta, \Omega_{22}) \quad \text{and} \quad [\omega, (\bar{\alpha}' - \omega \alpha'_\perp)\Gamma, (\bar{\alpha}' - \omega \alpha'_\perp)\Theta, \Omega_{11.2}]$$

respectively, and it is seen that the two sets of parameters are variation-free, in the sense that for any value of the respective sets of parameters we can still reconstruct the original parameters (Γ, Θ, Ω) for known values of α, β, and r. Thus the equations can be analyzed independently as long as no restrictions are imposed between the sets of parameters. It is furthermore seen that the reduced-rank condition (7) is a restriction of the parameters of (13) because it involves $\alpha'_\perp \Gamma$ only, and the maximum-likelihood estimator of equation (15) is found by a regression of $\bar{\alpha}'\Delta^2 X_t - \beta' X_{t-1}$ on $\alpha'_\perp \Delta^2 X_t, \Delta X_{t-1}$, and Z_t.

In order to analyze (13), we introduce the variables $\beta'\Delta X_{t-1}$ and $\bar{\beta}'_\perp \Delta X_{t-1}$ through the usual trick of writing $I = \bar{\beta}\beta' + \beta_\perp \bar{\beta}'_\perp$, such that

$$\alpha'_\perp \Delta^2 X_t = -\alpha'_\perp \Gamma \bar{\beta}\beta'\Delta X_{t-1} - \alpha'_\perp \Gamma \beta_\perp \bar{\beta}'_\perp \Delta X_{t-1} + \alpha'_\perp \Theta Z_t + \alpha'_\perp \varepsilon_t$$

The reformulation of equation (13) brings into focus the matrix $\alpha'_\perp \Gamma \beta_\perp$, which in the $I(2)$ model is assumed to be of reduced rank. Thus the restriction (7) implies that

$$\alpha'_\perp \Delta^2 X_t = -\alpha'_\perp \Gamma \bar{\beta}(\beta'\Delta X_{t-1}) - \xi\eta'(\bar{\beta}'_\perp \Delta X_{t-1}) + \alpha'_\perp \Theta Z_t + \alpha'_\perp \varepsilon_t \quad (16)$$

Equation (16) is a derived equation for the differences of the process that explicitly contains the parameters ξ and η. This shows that likelihood analysis of (13) or (16) for fixed α, β, and r can be performed by reduced-rank regression of $U_t = \alpha'_\perp \Delta^2 X_t$ on $V_t = \bar{\beta}'_\perp \Delta X_{t-1}$, corrected for W_t, consisting of $\beta'\Delta X_{t-1}$ and lagged second differences and dummies as collected in Z_t. This completes step 2.

What is achieved here by analysis of (13) and (14) is that an equation in differences (16) is derived using the information in the levels matrix $\Pi = \alpha\beta'$. For known values of (α, β, r) this can be analyzed by reduced-rank regression, that is, by an $I(1)$ analysis of a derived model for the differences involving only the errors that enter the common trends (i.e., $\alpha'_\perp \varepsilon_t$).

The likelihood-ratio test $Q_{r,s} = -2\log Q(H_{r,s}|H_r)$ of $H_{r,s}$ in H_r is found by analyzing (16) for $\alpha'_\perp \Gamma \beta_\perp$ of rank $s < p - r$, as well as for $\alpha'_\perp \Gamma \beta_\perp$ unrestricted, that is, $s = p - r$. We then compare the obtained values for the maxima, which have the form (10). Note that the contribution from equation (15) is the same for the analysis of $H_{r,s}$ as for the analysis of $H_{r,p-r}$, because the parameters in the two equations are variation-free. Hence the contribution from (15) to the maximized likelihood function cancels when calculating the likelihood-ratio statistic.

This shows that the likelihood-ratio test has the form

$$Q_{r,s} = -2\log Q(H_{r,s}|H_r) = -T\sum_{i=r+1}^{p}\log(1 - \hat{\lambda}_i)$$

where the $\hat{\lambda}$ terms are calculated from an eigenvalue problem like (9), where $S_{uu \cdot w}$ equals the product moments of $U_t = \alpha'_\perp \Delta^2 X_t$, $S_{vv \cdot w}$ equals the product moments of $V_t = \bar{\beta}'_\perp \Delta X_{t-1}$, and $S_{uv\cdot w}$ equals the mixed moments, all corrected for W_t, consisting of $\beta' \Delta X_{t-1}$ and lagged second differences and dummies; see (16).

Notice that this analysis can easily be modified if we want to restrict the constant term in the analysis of the differences, thereby ruling out the possibility of a quadratic trend. Thus, for instance, if $\Phi D_t = \mu$, the analysis of (16) will involve correcting for the constant term. If we want to restrict this, we assume that $\xi'_\perp a'_\perp \mu = 0$ and perform a reduced-rank regression of $a'_\perp \Delta^2 X_t$ on $(\Delta X'_{t-1} \bar{\beta}_\perp, 1)$ corrected for lagged second differences and $\beta' \Delta X_{t-1}$.

Thus, in summary, we propose to estimate the parameters of the $I(2)$ model $H_{r,s}$ by first estimating model H_r by reduced-rank regression and extracting the estimated values of α and β, as well as the likelihood-ratio statistic for H_r in H_p. Next we derive a model for the differences for each value of r, applying the values found for α and β, and estimate this by reduced-rank regression, which gives the estimates of the remaining parameters and the likelihood-ratio test statistic for $H_{r,s}$ in H_r.

5.3 A Different Parameterization of the $I(2)$ Model

In the investigation of the $I(2)$ model it is natural to find a parameterization that allows the parameters to vary freely, because this makes the analysis of the likelihood function more direct.

Consider a model with two lags and no dummies specified by the equations

$$\Delta^2 X_t = \alpha(\rho' \tau' X_{t-1} + \psi' \Delta X_{t-1}) + \Omega a_\perp (a'_\perp \Omega a_\perp)^{-1} \varkappa' \tau' \Delta X_{t-1} + \varepsilon_t$$

The parameters are

$$(\alpha, \rho, \tau, \varkappa, \psi, \Omega)$$

which vary freely. The coefficient matrix to the levels is $\Pi = \alpha \rho' \tau'$, which is of reduced rank. This shows that the usual parameter β is now written as $\beta = \tau \rho$, and $\beta_\perp$ can be chosen to be $\beta_\perp = (\tau_\perp, \bar{\tau} \rho_\perp)$. In terms of the new matrices, the matrix Γ becomes

$$\Gamma = -\Omega a_\perp (a'_\perp \Omega a_\perp)^{-1} \varkappa' \tau' - \alpha \psi'$$

such that

$$a'_\perp \Gamma \beta_\perp = -\varkappa' \tau' \beta_\perp = -\varkappa'(\bar{\rho}\rho' + \bar{\rho}_\perp \rho'_\perp)\tau' \beta_\perp$$

Because $\beta = \tau \rho$, it follows that $\rho' \tau' \beta_\perp = 0$, such that

$$a'_\perp \Gamma \beta_\perp = -\varkappa' \bar{\rho}_\perp \rho'_\perp \tau' \beta_\perp = \xi \eta'$$

which also has reduced rank, with $\xi = -\varkappa' \bar{\rho}_\perp$ and $\eta = \beta'_\perp \tau \rho_\perp$. Thus we find, after some reductions, that

$$\beta = \tau\rho$$
$$\beta_\perp^1 = \bar\tau\bar\rho_\perp(\bar\rho_\perp\bar\tau'\bar\tau\bar\rho_\perp)^{-1}$$
$$\beta_\perp^2 = \tau_\perp$$

The advantage of this parameterization is that the parameters are freely varying, such that likelihood equations can be analyzed for estimation of the parameters. This way of writing the model is also the starting point for an algorithm for calculating the maximum-likelihood estimator (Johansen, 1997) and is convenient for estimating the parameters under restrictions on the cointegrating relations that reduce the order from 2 to 1, that is, $\tau = (\beta, \beta_\perp^1)$.

6 Determination of the Cointegrating Rank

The limit theory for the test statistics Q_r [see (11)] is well known from the $I(1)$ theory (Ahn and Reinsel, 1990; Phillips, 1991; Johansen, 1988a), provided there are no $I(2)$ components in the system. We can derive the asymptotic distribution of Q_r even if there are $I(2)$ components (Johansen, 1995), and it turns out that the limit distribution depends on the behavior of the deterministic terms. Thus, for instance, there is one limit distribution if $\Phi D_t = 0$, and another if $\Phi D_t = \mu$, and this depends on whether or not the true value of μ gives rise to a trend (Paruolo, 1996).

The limit distribution of $Q_{r,s}$, which is calculated on the basis of a reduced-rank regression of the differences, has the same limit distribution as is known from the $I(1)$ theory, but again the limit distribution depends on how the constant term is specified. Thus there are several possibilities that one should have in mind when testing for cointegrating rank.

In order to formulate a simple result (which is not widely applicable), we assume that $\Phi D_t = 0$.

Theorem 4. *If the rank of α and β is r, and the rank of ξ and η is s, then the test of $H_{r,s}$ in H_p given by $Q_{r,s} + Q_r$ has a limit distribution given by*

$$\mathrm{tr}\left\{\int_0^1(dB_2)B_2'\left[\int_0^1 B_2 B_2' du\right]^{-1}\int_0^1 B_2(dB_2)'\right\}$$
$$+ \mathrm{tr}\left\{\int_0^1(dB)G'\left[\int_0^1 GG' du\right]^{-1}\int_0^1 G(dB)'\right\}$$

where $B = (B_1', B_2')'$, and B_1 and B_2 are independent standard Brownian motions in the s and $p - r - s$ dimensions, respectively. Furthermore $G = (G_1', G_2')'$ is given by

$$G_1(u) = B_1(u) - \left[\int_0^1 B_1 B_2' du\right]\left[\int_0^1 B_2 B_2' du\right]^{-1} B_2(u)$$

$$G_2(u) = \int_0^u B_2(s) ds - \left[\int_0^1 \left(\int_0^s B_2(y) dy\right) B_2(s)' ds\right]\left[\int_0^1 B_2 B_2' du\right]^{-1} B_2(u)$$

This distribution is tabulated by simulation (Johansen, 1995).

This result is not so easy to apply in practice, because the asymptotic distribution of a test statistic depends on the actual rank of the matrices involved, that is, on which of the many submodels holds. We have chosen to formulate the result for the situation where the ranks are the same as the dimensions for $(\alpha, \beta, \xi, \eta)$. If, in fact, any of these ranks is not equal to the dimension, then the distribution is different. Thus even in the limit the test is not similar.

The models $H_{r,s}$ and H_r are formulated as conditions on the dimensions of suitable matrices and hence are nested in the way indicated in Table 13.1. If we ever accept model H_r, we accept that the rank is $\leq r$. Thus, in order to find the rank, we have to reject models $H_s, s < r$.

This gives rise to a procedure whereby we first investigate $H_{0,0}$, then $H_{0,1}$, and so forth, until $H_{0,p-r-1}$. If all these are rejected, we then reject the hypothesis that $r = 0$, and proceed to test $H_{1,0}$ and so forth. The first nonrejected hypothesis determines the values of r and s.

In case the model has a constant or linear drift, a number of different models can be formulated, and the trending behavior has to be determined at the same time as the cointegrating ranks. This has been worked out by Paruolo (1996), and the recent paper by Jørgensen, Kongsted, and Rahbek (1995) contains a formulation that avoids simultaneous determination of the ranks and the order of the trend.

7 Hypothesis Testing on the Cointegrating Parameters

It is easy to formulate the hypotheses known from the $I(1)$ model, such as

$$\beta = H\phi$$

which imposes the same restriction on all cointegration vectors $R'\beta = 0$, where $R = H_\perp$. An example of this hypothesis is given in the illustrative example in Section 1 if we ask whether or not the prices enter only through their differences. In this case we choose $R = (1, 1, 0, 0, 0)'$.

Another hypothesis of interest is

$$\beta = (H_1\phi_1, H_2\phi_2)$$

which allows different restrictions on different cointegrating vectors and hence offers the possibility to test if, say, the PPP relation is stationary or that the interest differential is stationary.

Note that for the $I(2)$ model the other vectors $\beta_\perp^1$ and $\beta_\perp^2$ are defined orthogonal to β, which means that a restriction on β is actually also a restriction on the other vectors. The two-step procedure brings this forward very nicely, because analysis of the last two sets of vectors requires that we have made up our minds about β.

Another natural hypothesis is to investigate whether or not a row in the $\beta_\perp^2$ matrix is zero, which means that the corresponding variable is not $I(2)$ but only $I(1)$. This question is obviously the same as asking if the corresponding unit vector is in the space spanned by the vectors $(\beta, \beta_\perp^1)$. The two-step procedure does not seem to be adequate for estimation under such a constraint.

Finally, it is, of course, of interest to discuss polynomial cointegration more carefully and, for instance, check whether or not the stationary combinations $\beta'X_t - \delta\beta_\perp^{1'}\Delta X_t$ reduce to linear combination of the levels; that is, it is of interest to test the hypothesis that $\varkappa = \bar{\alpha}'T\bar{\beta}_\perp^2 = 0$. Another question that would be nice to answer is how to test identifying restrictions on the combinations $\delta_\perp'\beta'X_t$, which are the combinations that are stationary, without involving differences of the process.

Because the two-step procedure determines β without taking into account the other parameters, it is very easy to derive test statistics for hypotheses on β. It seems not so easy to analyze the likelihood function under restrictions on the other cointegrating vectors, but we can do Wald tests.

It turns out that the asymptotic distribution of $\hat{\beta}$ derived from the $I(1)$ analysis has a mixed Gaussian distribution even if there are $I(2)$ components, and it is in fact efficient; see Johansen (1995, 1997) and Paruolo (in press). This has the implication that likelihood-ratio tests derived for hypotheses on β from the $I(1)$ analysis are still asymptotically χ^2 distributed, even if there are $I(2)$ components in the system. Thus the tests on β are still valid, but of course have a different interpretation, since for $I(2)$ variables $\beta'X_t$ is not in general stationary, only $I(1)$. Thus a test that $i_t^{au} - i_t^{us}$ is stationary in the $I(1)$ model can be formulated as an asymptotic χ^2 test. The test remains valid if in fact there are $I(2)$ variables in the data, but of course the interpretation is different.

A formulation of a result that can be applied both for $I(1)$ variables and for $I(2)$ variables is given below for β normalized by a $p \times r$ matrix c.

Theorem 5. *The asymptotic distribution of $\hat{\beta}_c = \hat{\beta}(c'\hat{\beta})^{-1}$ is mixed Gaussian, with the result that we can treat $\hat{\beta}_c - \beta$ as being asymptotically Gaussian, with a variance matrix estimated by*

$$(I - \hat{\beta}_c c')\hat{\beta}_\perp \left[\hat{\beta}_\perp' \sum_{t=1}^{T} R_t R_t' \hat{\beta}_\perp\right]^{-1} \hat{\beta}_\perp'(I - c\hat{\beta}_c') \otimes (\hat{\alpha}_c'\hat{\Omega}\hat{\alpha}_c)^{-1}$$

where R_t is the residual from a regression of X_{t-1} on the lagged differences and dummies.

As an exemplification of this result, consider the simple case where the model is given by

$$\Delta Y_t = \alpha_1(\beta_1 Y_{t-1} + \beta_2 Z_{t-1}) + \varepsilon_{1t}$$
$$\Delta Z_t = \alpha_2(\beta_1 Y_{t-1} + \beta_2 Z_{t-1}) + \varepsilon_{2t}$$

We normalize β on the vector $c = (1, 0)'$ and write $\beta_c = (1, -\theta)'$, with $\theta = -\beta_2/\beta_1$. Then $Y_t = \theta Z_t + U_t$. The corresponding normalization of α is given by $\alpha_c = (\alpha_1, \alpha_2)\beta_1$. The asymptotic distribution of $\hat{\theta} - \theta$ follows from Theorem 5. We find

$$(I - \beta_c c')\beta_\perp = \begin{pmatrix} 0 & 0 \\ \theta & 1 \end{pmatrix}\begin{pmatrix} \theta \\ 1 \end{pmatrix} = \begin{pmatrix} 0 \\ 1 + \theta^2 \end{pmatrix}$$

and

$$\beta'_\perp R_t = \theta Y_{t-1} + Z_{t-1} = (1 + \theta^2) Z_{t-1} + \theta U_{t-1}$$

Theorem 5 states that the vector

$$\hat{\beta}_c - \beta_c = -\begin{pmatrix} 0 \\ \hat{\theta} - \theta \end{pmatrix}$$

can be treated as asymptotically Gaussian, with variance given by

$$\begin{pmatrix} 0 \\ 1 + \hat{\theta}^2 \end{pmatrix}\left(\sum_{t=1}^{T}(\hat{\theta} Y_{t-1} + Z_{t-1})^2\right)^{-1}\begin{pmatrix} 0 \\ 1 + \hat{\theta}^2 \end{pmatrix}'(\hat{\alpha}'_c \hat{\Omega}^{-1} \hat{\alpha}_c)^{-1} = \begin{pmatrix} 0 & 0 \\ 0 & \hat{\sigma}_\theta^2 \end{pmatrix}$$

where

$$\hat{\sigma}_\theta^2 = (1 + \hat{\theta}^2)^2 \left(\sum_{t=1}^{T}(\hat{\theta} Y_{t-1} + Z_{t-1})^2 \hat{\alpha}'_c \hat{\Omega}^{-1} \hat{\alpha}_c\right)^{-1}$$

$$= \left(\sum_{t=1}^{T}\left(Z_{t-1} + \frac{\hat{\theta}}{1 + \hat{\theta}^2} U_t\right)^2 \hat{\alpha}'_c \hat{\Omega}^{-1} \hat{\alpha}_c\right)^{-1}$$

$$\approx \left(\hat{\alpha}'_c \hat{\Omega}^{-1} \hat{\alpha}_c \sum_{t=1}^{T} Z_{t-1}^2\right)^{-1}$$

Thus the hypothesis that $\beta_1 + \beta_2 = 0$ or, equivalently, that $\theta = 1$ can be tested using the statistic

$$(\hat{\theta} - 1)^2 \sum_{t=1}^{T} Z_{t-1}^2 \hat{\alpha}'_c \hat{\Omega}^{-1} \hat{\alpha}_c$$

which is asymptotically $\chi^2(1)$.

8 Hypothesis Testing on the Adjustment Coefficients

With the two-step procedure it is easy to formulate and test hypotheses on α of the form $\alpha = A\phi$ in the $I(2)$ model, but it is not so easy to interpret what they mean.

In the $I(1)$ model for $X_t = (Y'_t, Z'_t)'$ the test for weak exogeneity of Z_t for β is formulated as a test that $\alpha = (\alpha'_1, 0)'$, and in the $I(2)$ model the corresponding result is that we have weak exogeneity for β if $\alpha = (\alpha'_1, 0)'$ and $\Gamma = (\Gamma'_1, 0)'$ (Paruolo and Rahbek, 1995).

9 Reduction of the $I(2)$ Model to the $I(1)$ Model

It is sometimes possible to reduce the $I(2)$ model to the $I(1)$ model and hence avoid the complicated $I(2)$ analysis. Consider the situation where a price variable seems to cause the other nominal variables to be $I(2)$ in the sense that the real variables are only $I(1)$. It then seems a good idea to transform the system to nominal values, as well as the inflation rate, and continue the analysis with the $I(1)$ analysis. Conditions for this analysis to be efficient can be formulated, and tests are available. In the illustrative example, we could transform the data to the variables $p_t^{au} - p_t^{us}$, Δp_t^{us}, $exch_t$, i_t^{us}, and i_t^{au}. See Juselius (in press) for an analysis of monetary data from this point of view.

10 A Misspecification Test for $I(2)$

After the $I(1)$ analysis is performed, one should plot $\hat{\beta}'X_t$ as a function of time to see that the process appears stationary. Note that this process has not been corrected for deterministic terms, and it is more appropriate to inspect $\hat{\beta}'R_t$, the residuals of $\hat{\beta}'X_{t-1}$ corrected for lagged differences and deterministic terms.

Sometimes $\hat{\beta}'R_t$ appears a lot more like a stationary process than $\hat{\beta}'X_t$. One explanation of this is that there is an $I(2)$ component in the system. If X_t is $I(2)$, then $\beta'X_t$ should not look stationary at all, but because $\beta'X_t$ is polynomially cointegrated with ΔX_t, then $\hat{\beta}'R_t$ is approximately stationary. Thus a striking difference between the graphs of $\hat{\beta}'X_t$ and $\hat{\beta}'R_{1t}$ can indicate $I(2)$-ness.

Before performing the $I(1)$ analysis, we calculated the roots of the characteristic polynomial and noted that some of them were close to $z = 1$. We can also calculate the roots using the coefficients estimated under the $I(1)$ model, that is, after having imposed $p - r$ unit roots. It may turn out that there are still roots close to $z = 1$. This can now have two explanations; the first is that we have not imposed enough unit roots and have determined the rank incorrectly. The rank-determination tests should have taken care of this possibility, although there is a lot of uncertainty in the determination of the rank. The other possibility is that there are $I(2)$ components in the system, because we know that for an $I(1)$ process the number of unit roots plus the cointegrating rank should be the dimension of the process, but for $I(2)$ processes we get more unit roots than are imposed by the Π matrix.

Thus we want to make inference on the roots of the characteristic polynomial. The joint distribution of these is quite complicated, so that Wald tests are, as far as I can see, not feasible. The approach we take is therefore the approach of the likelihood-ratio test, where we formulate hypotheses on the roots.

The misspecification test for the presence of $I(2)$ is based upon the two-step analysis of the $I(2)$ model given earlier, in particular the reduced-rank condition (7).

Theorem 6. *A misspecification test for $I(2)$: Consider model (2), with $\Phi D_t = 0$. Let Q_r denote the likelihood-ratio test of H_r in H_p, and let $c_{p-r}(\delta)$ denote the $1 - \delta$ quantile derived in the $I(1)$ model. Let $Q_{r,s}$ denote the likelihood-ratio test statistic of $H_{r,s}$ in H_r when (α, β, r) are known.*

We choose to accept r cointegrating relations and no $I(2)$ components on the set A_r defined by

$$Q_i \geq c_{p-i}(\delta), \quad i = 0, \ldots, r-1, \ Q_r < c_{p-r}(\delta)$$
$$Q_{r,i} \geq c_{p-r-i}(\delta), \quad i = 0, \ldots, p-r-1$$

This procedure has the properties that

$$\lim_{T \to \infty} P(A_r) = 1 - \delta$$

if H_r holds and there are no $I(2)$ trends. Furthermore,

$$\lim_{T \to \infty} P(A_r) = 0$$

if $H_p \backslash H_r$ holds, and

$$\lim_{T \to \infty} P(A_r) \leq \delta$$

if $H_{r,s}$ holds, $s = 0, \ldots, p - r - 1$.

Thus if the rank of Π is r and there are no $I(2)$ components, the procedure picks out the true value of r with a high probability $(1 - \delta)$. If in fact the cointegrating rank is greater that r, it picks out the value r with limit probability zero. Finally, if there are $I(2)$ components, the procedure will accept no $I(2)$ components with a small probability. The procedure has the advantage that only tables from the $I(1)$ theory are needed in the test.

11 Conclusion

We have given a very brief and concentrated survey of the recent work on $I(2)$ processes for VAR models. Many problems remain unsolved and even unformulated. In my opinion, what remains for the $I(2)$ model to become a useful tool is a flexible algorithm to calculate the maximum-likelihood estimators and hence the test statistics under various restrictions on the many cointegration and adjustment parameters. What is also important is to gain insight into the interpretation of $I(2)$ cointegration, in particular polynomial cointegration. This will come about through application to economic data. An important and difficult problem is to find improved approximations to the small-sample properties of the estimators. This is not only a question of tabulating the limit distribution for smaller values of T but also a problem of the many nuisance parameters that enter the distributions for finite samples. Many of these do not influence the limit distribution, but are important for finite samples. Bartlett correction terms or Edgeworth expansions will be extremely useful for improving our possibilities of making reliable inference for economic data.

References

Ahn, S. K., and Reinsel, C. G. (1988). Nested reduced rank autoregressive models for multiple times series. *Journal of the American Statistical Association* 83:849–56.

(1990). Estimation for partially non-stationary multivariate autoregressive models. *Journal of the American Statistical Association* 85:813–23.

Anderson, T. W. (1951). Estimating linear restrictions on regression coefficients for multivariate normal distributions. *Annals of Mathematical Statistics* 22:327–51.

(1971). *The Statistical Analysis of Time Series*. New York: Wiley.

Engle, R. F., and Granger, C. W. J. (1987). Cointegration and error correction: representation, estimation and testing. *Econometrica* 51:277–304.

Engle, R. F., and Yoo, B. S. (1991). Cointegrated economic time series: a survey with new results. In: *Long-Run Economic Relations. Readings in Cointegration*, ed. C. W. J. Granger and R. F. Engle. Oxford University Press.

Frisch, R. (1929). Statikk og dynamikk i den økonomiske teori. *Nationaløkonomisk Tidsskrift* 67:321–79.

(1934). *Statistical Confluence Analysis by Means of Complete Regression Systems*. Publikasjon nr. 5, Universitets Økonomiske Institut, Oslo.

Granger, C. W. J. (1981). Some properties of times series data and their use in econometric model specification. *Journal of Econometrics* 16:121–30.

Gregoir, S., and Laroque, G. (1993). Multivariate integrated time series: a polynomial error correction representation theorem. *Econometric Theory* 9:329–42.

Hendry, D. F., and Morgan, M. S. (1989). A re-analysis of confluence analysis. *Oxford Economic Papers* 41:35–52.

Johansen, S. (1988a). Statistical analysis of cointegration vectors. *Journal of Economic Dynamics and Control* 12:231–54.

(1988b). The mathematical structure of error correction models. *Contemporary Mathematics* 80:259–386.

(1991). Estimation and hypothesis testing of cointegration vectors in Gaussian vector autoregressive models. *Econometrica* 59:1551–80.

(1992a). A representation of vector autoregressive processes integrated of order 2. *Econometric Theory* 8:188–202.

(1992b). An $I(2)$ cointegration analysis of the purchasing power parity between Australia and USA. In: *Macroeconomic Modelling of the Long Run*, ed. C. Hargreaves, pp. 229–48. London: Edward Elgar.

(1992c). Testing weak exogeneity and the order of cointegration in UK money demand data. *Journal of Policy Modelling* 14:313–35.

(1994). Estimating systems of trending variables. *Econometric Reviews* 13:351–428.

(1995). A statistical analysis of cointegration for $I(2)$ variables. *Econometric Theory* 11:25–59.

(1996). *Likelihood Based Inference in the Cointegrated Vector Autoregressive Model*, 2nd ed. Oxford University Press.

(1997). Likelihood analysis of the $I(2)$ model. *Scandinavian Journal of Statistics* 24:433–42.

Johansen, S., and Juselius, K. (1990). Maximum likelihood estimation and inference on cointegration with applications to the demand for money. *Oxford Bulletin of Economics and Statistics* 52:169–210.

(1992). Structural hypotheses in a multivariate cointegration analysis of the PPP and UIP for UK. *Journal of Econometrics* 53:211–44.

(1944). Identification of the long-run and the short-run structure: an application to the IS-LM model. *Journal of Econometrics* 63:7–36.

Jørgensen, C., Kongsted, H. C., and Rahbek, A. (1995). Trend-stationarity in the $I(2)$ cointegration model. Discussion paper, University of Copenhagen.

Juselius, K. (1995a). On the duality between long-run relations and common trends in the $I(1)$ and $I(2)$ case: an application to aggregate money holdings. *Econometric Reviews* 13:151–78.

(1995b). Do purchasing power parity and uncovered interest rate parity hold in the long run? An example of likelihood inference in a multivariate time series model. *Journal of Econometrics* 69:211–40.

(in press). A structured VAR under changing monetary policies. *Journal of Business and Economic Statistics*.

Pantula, S. G. (1989). Testing for unit roots in time series data. *Econometric Theory* 5:256–71.

Paruolo, P. (1994). The role of the drift in $I(2)$ systems. *Journal of the Italian Statistical Society* 3:65–96.

(1996). On the determination of integration indices in $I(2)$ systems. *Journal of Econometrics* 72:313–56.

(in press). Asymptotic efficiency of the 2 step estimator in $I(2)$ VAR systems. *Econometric Theory*.

Paruolo, P., and Rahbek, A. (1995). Weak exogeneity in $I(2)$ systems. Discussion paper, University of Copenhagen.

Phillips, P. C. B. (1991). Optimal inference in cointegrated systems. *Econometrica* 59:283–306.

Reinsel, G. C., and Ahn, S. K. (1992). Vector autoregressive models with unit roots and reduced rank structure: estimation, likelihood ratio test, and forecasting. *Journal of Time Series Analysis* 13:353–75.

Stock, J. H., and Watson, M. W. (1993). A simple estimator of cointegrating vectors in higher order integrated systems. *Econometrica* 61:783–821.

… PART SIX

MACRODYNAMICS

CHAPTER 14

Frisch's Vision and Explanation of the Trade-Cycle Phenomenon: His Connections with Wicksell, Åkerman, and Schumpeter

Bjørn Thalberg

When Frisch published his famous "propagation and impulse" essay (Frisch, 1933) he had very definite ideas about the descriptive characteristics of the cycle phenomenon, about the method by which the phenomenon ought to be analyzed, and also (albeit not as settled) about the main structure of the economic mechanism that generated the cycles. As to the first point, empirical research in the 1920s by Mitchell, Persons, and others, describing the characteristics of observed time series such as the existence of cycles (or cyclical components) of various lengths (Kitchin, Juglar, Kondratiev) and the structure of leads and lags among central variables over the cycle (the Harvard A, B, and C curves), had left its mark upon the young Frisch. In fact, he had for a brief period (1925–7) taken part in this type of empirical research himself. As described by Andvig (1986), Frisch started his venture into macroeconomics in 1925 by going into advanced time-series analysis, exploring alternative statistical techniques for detecting cyclical components. Over the years Frisch repeatedly expressed (explicitly and implicitly) his steadfast faith in the main results of the Mitchell-Persons kind of empirical research (particularly the existence of cycles of various lengths and the Harvard A, B, and C curves).[1] As to the second point, the question

---

[1] Andvig (1986, p. 77) even indicated that Frisch had, owing to the influence of Mitchell and Persons and his own research on decomposing empirical time series, a "mechanistic" vision of the business cycles.

An example of Frisch's seemingly strong faith in the stylized results of the empirical business-cycle research, including also the existence of the long Kondratiev cycle, is given by Munthe (1994, p. 25). In the summer of 1936, Frisch was asked if the time had come to change from a deficit to a surplus in the budget, as it was observed that the upswing was already on its way. Frisch answered that it was not sufficient to look at the long (8–10 years) cycle, which was then rising; one also had to take account of the much longer (Kondratiev) cycle, which, Frisch claimed, had not then reached its low, and whose turning point might not come before close to the middle of the century.

It may generally be said that Frisch was inclined to believe very strongly in the results of economic theory, and particularly in his own thinking, whether or not supported by econometric studies. This is a trait Frisch shared, I think, with Wicksell and Åker-

of method was early and for many years at the center of Frisch's interests, in regard to both cycle theory and dynamic analysis in general. Andvig (1986, p. 24) described a general program (discovered among Frisch's unpublished papers) that as a young graduate student Frisch had set for himself, namely, to develop, mathematically, methods for static and dynamic analysis, as well as econometrics (continuing the work of Cournot, Jevons, Walras, Pareto, and others). His penetrating works on the concepts of static analysis and dynamic analysis (Frisch, 1929b, pp. 229–72) and of equilibrium and disequilibrium (Frisch, 1936, pp. 100–5) witness his strong interest in basic methodological questions. Moreover, he looked at the problem from an educator's angle. He was deeply concerned about the poor standards in most of the writings in economics at the time, and he crusaded in his writings[2] and in the classroom against loose verbal reasoning and conclusions that could not be verified.

Frisch's university studies in economics of Oslo (1916–19) had, on the whole, not been highly advanced and had not given him much, except (in his own words) that Wicksell was on the reading list. Wicksell's type of analysis by means of well-defined relationships between a few, mostly highly aggregated variables, such as in his "cumulative process" ("the macro theory of the nineteenth century," in the words of Mark Blaug), and Wicksell's methodological approach to cycle theory, as indicated by his rocking-horse analogy, became instrumental in Frisch's development of dynamic theory – a debt he clearly acknowledged.[3] Frisch's vision and explanation of the cycle phenomenon were also influenced by, particularly, Johan Åkerman and Joseph Schumpeter, albeit not as constructively and significantly as in the case of Wicksell. I shall first briefly go into the trade-cycle theory of each of these three economists and seek to assess their influence on Frisch. In the final section I shall comment on Frisch's efforts in his 1933 essay to develop a (first-approximation) trade-cycle model according to his vision.

1 Wicksell's Tentative Trade-Cycle Theory

Wicksell obviously was fascinated by the riddle of the cycle, but his explicit writing on the subject consisted in only one article (of 17 pages):

---

man. Consider the fact that Wicksell explained certain depressions (e.g., the general depression of 1873–97) simply by the failure of banks, or monetary policy, to adjust the bank rate of interest to the decline in the "natural" rate caused by capital accumulation. As to Åkerman, cf. footnote 12.

[2] As, for example, in his very critical and detailed review (Frisch, 1929a) of a textbook by Engländer (1929).

[3] In his essay (Frisch, 1933) he emphasized that he owed the idea of the impulse–propagation dichotomy to Wicksell, and also on various other occasions he expressed his debt to Wicksell: "There is probably no other economist who has had so much influence on my thinking, at least not in monetary theory" (Frisch, 1951, p. 2).

his lecture "Krisernas gåta," given in Oslo 1907 and published in *Statsøkonomisk Tidskrift* the same year, later translated by C. Uhr as "The Enigma of Business Cycles" (Wicksell, 1953, 1965). The article reappeared, under the heading "Note on Trade Cycles and Crises," in a somewhat shortened version in the (posthumous) third (1929) Swedish edition of Wicksell's *Lectures* (English edition: Wicksell, 1935). Wicksell began the note by regretting that he had never found the opportunity to develop further his views on the nature and causes of trade cycles since he had given the lectures in Oslo in 1907. On various other occasions, however, Wicksell made a number of important brief suggestions or polemical remarks on the matter; the most notable example being a footnote in a review article (Wicksell, 1918, p. 71) of K. Petander's thesis "Good and Bad Times" containing Wicksell's profound rocking-horse analogy: "If you hit a rocking-horse with a stick, the movements of the horse will be very different from those of the stick. The hits are cause of the movement, but the system's own equilibrium laws condition the form of the movements." That note was a reflection on the concept of the "cause" of the cycle and also clearly indicated the type of explanation based on the impulse–propagation dichotomy distinguishing between sources of impulses and the propagation mechanisms that carry the effects of the shocks forward in time. The dichotomy was also contained in Wicksell's 1907 lecture, and on several occasions he made use of his physically stable wooden rocking horse. For example, in a seminar on an address by H. Westergaard on economic barometers, Wicksell (1924) sketched his idea about the nature of the impulses: "The difference between (irregular) technical progress and (the more even development of) human wants causes a jerk (impulse) in the organism. This jerk is transformed into a wave that proceeds according to a certain rhythm because of the structure of human society itself." He then continues: "I have many times used the analogy that if one hits a rocking horse with a hammer, the blows may fall quite irregularly and yet the movement of the rocking horse may be more or less regular because of its own form." (See Frisch, 1951, p. 46.)

The rocking-horse analogy contains, in Frisch's words, "the basic principles of the theory of erratic shocks which have come to mean so much in modern economic theory" (Frisch, 1951, p. 46). Wicksell's ideas regarding the nature of the impulses or shocks were, I think, best explained in his 1907 lecture (Wicksell, 1965). He emphasized there that whereas in modern economies aggregate demand grows in a fairly even fashion because of the stable growth of population and real income, technical progress and production are not likely to increase as smoothly. It is, he argued, "in the nature of things that new, great discoveries and inventions must occur sporadically, and that the resulting increase in output cannot take the form of an evenly growing stream like population growth and the increase in consumption demand. As soon as the rate of increase in output begins to lag, a hitch will immediately occur in the growth of the economy. For may part, until I am shown something better, it is in this that I discern the real source of economic fluctuations and crises" (Wicksell, 1965, p. 232). Regarding that sketch of the nature of the irregular impulses and their effects, he commented that "of course this is only the abstract core, the skeleton, of the concrete reality which may assume extremely varied forms in different circumstances." For example, the transition from boom to slump may not have the nature of (deep) crisis, but "a crisis can hardly be avoided if new ventures have been started on a scale that gradually makes the available capital insufficient. And this crisis is reinforced by the psychological factors." Wicksell thus suggested how the amplitude of the fluctuations might depend on specific circumstances. He also suggested how the cyclical fluctuations might be mitigated by banking policy. "In depressed times when they usually suffer from an excess of cash, the banks should reduce their loan rates of interest early and energetically, just as they should raise them early, at the outset of good times, both in order to prevent excessive speculation and unsound ventures and to stimulate saving" (Wicksell, 1965, p. 233).

Whereas Wicksell's concept and explanation of the nature of the impulses that at irregular intervals shock the economy seem clear enough, he did not give an explicit and clear-cut specification of the model of the propagation mechanism. The fact that he used the rocking horse to picture the economy's reaction to impulses implies first that he imagined stability (i.e., that a realistic model of the propagation mechanism should have damped solutions). Moreover, one may add that his vision of the economy reacting cyclically to irregular impulses implicitly implies that the degree of dampening is not extremely strong or extremely weak. (In the first place, the last strike dominates the picture, whereas in the latter case the relative effect of the last strike seems too weak, according to Wicksell's verbal analysis.) Otherwise the field is open to speculation. However, a possibility that presents itself fairly immediately is that his model of the cumulative process may serve as a model of the propagation mechanism. In his study "Wicksell's Business Cycle,"[4] Boianovsky (1993, pp. 53–4) mentions the Swede F. Brock as

---

[4] Incidentally, Boianovsky (1993, p. 23) wrote that Wicksell's trade-cycle theory was not in the spirit of the real-business-cycle theory (RBCT), "apart from the facts that RBCT takes economic growth as its starting point and makes use of the distinction between shocks and propagation mechanisms." It may be of some interest that Wicksell in his 1907 lectures (p. 224) mentioned a possible endogenous source of fluctuations as described by Pareto. "Pareto has in mind an individual who habitually consumes a part of his income and saves the rest. The pleasure of consumption tempts him to increase his consumption, and the feeling of security – tempts him to increase his saving. According to Pareto, these two forces set up a periodically alternating increase and decrease of his consumption and of his saving (or investing) respectively. Now if by chance the behaviour of many individuals is influenced in the same direction, then the consequence would be a wave-like movement in the aggregate." This suggested kind of behavior resembles, to some extent,

"perhaps the first in a long chain of writers to interpret the Wicksellian cumulative process as a business cycle theory." Boianovsky then cited Wicksell's reaction to Brock (Wicksell, 1909, p. 63): In response to Brock, Wicksell pointed out that "I have never tried to explain economic fluctuations, boom and slump, from the much quoted difference between the natural rate of interest and the loan rate, but their real cause lies in the sporadic nature of technical progress itself, supported by certain psychological elements. I well believe that over-speculation and, in connection with it, the sharp breaking between boom and slump, the crisis in the narrow sense, has its roots in the monetary sphere, in a faulty monetary and banking policy." The cause of the cycle was, of course, in Wicksell's view, the impulses rather than the propagation. The quoted passage is not easy to interpret, although it does indicate that it is useful to include the difference between the natural rate and the loan rate of interest in a model of cyclical fluctuations that also aims to explain the severity of downswings. Although many readers may find it difficult to imagine how Wicksell's propagation model should be specified, Frisch certainly looked at the cumulative process (or a natural extension of it) as the basis of Wicksell's vision of the propagation mechanism. In his "cornerstone article" (Frisch, 1951, p. 46) he spoke of the "long chain of Wicksell's thoughts that lead all the way from the ultra-simple abstract assumptions concerning the fundamentals of capital theory, through the somewhat less abstract theory of the cumulative process to a conception of the fully fledged modern society in its progressing and swinging form."

Frisch's account of his interpretation of Wicksell's model of the propagation mechanism was presented in his mimeographed lectures on monetary theory given in Oslo in the autumn of 1935 and later in his "cornerstone article" (Frisch, 1951). The model he attributed to Wicksell was in some respects similar to his own model of the propagation mechanism in his 1933 essay. One may therefore ask if Wicksell's propagation model did, to some extent, serve as a pattern for Frisch's model or if it otherwise influenced Frisch's vision of the cycle mechanism. There may also have been causality in the other direction; that is, Frisch, in his interpretations of Wicksell (1934, and 1951), may have been influenced by his development of his own 1933 model. I shall give a brief exposition of Frisch's account of Wicksell's propagation model, as it appears in the "cornerstone article" (1951), in order to compare it to Frisch's own model later on. (The account Frisch gave in his mimeographed lectures in 1935 was similar to the one given in 1951, but less elaborated.)

The "natural" (or "normal") rate, according to Wicksell, was the "rate of interest at which the demand for loan capital and the supply of savings exactly agree, and which more or less corresponds to the expected yield

the assumption of RBCT that people at times prefer to work long hours and at other times to enjoy more extensively the pleasure of leisure time.

on newly created capital" (Wicksell, 1935, p. 193). In his model of the propagation mechanism, n was assumed to be constant. Frisch began by referring to Wicksell's discussion of the tendency for the marked (bank) rate to gravitate toward the natural (normal) rate, emphasizing that the tendency came about through price movements (Wicksell, 1935, pp. 204–8). Wicksell argued that in a period of expansion, rising prices would increase the need for cash holdings by the public and thereby put a strain on the banks, which would force them to alter their interest rates (p. 206).[5] Denoting the cash holdings of the public by M, and letting d denote the difference between the bank rate r and the natural rate of interest $\bar{n}$ (i.e., $d = r - \bar{n}$), Frisch accordingly assumed that a rise in M would affect d. He made the (strong) assumption that changes in M would affect the acceleration of d [i.e., $\ddot{d} = \theta(\dot{M}/M)$]. He then used the familiar quantity-theory equation $MV = PZ$, where Z denotes output, to derive $\dot{M}/M = \dot{P}/P + \dot{Z}/Z - \dot{V}/V$. Assuming a positive relationship between relative changes in Z and P, he wrote $\dot{Z}/Z = \mu(\dot{P}/P)$. Furthermore, he imagined that velocity V would change with P [i.e., $\dot{V}/V = v(\dot{P}/P)$]. Thus $\dot{M}/M = (1 + \mu - v)\dot{P}/P$. Finally, the relative increase in P would depend negatively on d, that is, the prime relationship of the cumulative process: $\dot{P}/P = -\beta d$. Assuming that β, v, μ, and θ are all constants, we obtain $\ddot{d} = -\beta\theta(1 + \mu - v)d$. The solution of this differential equation in d (as a function of time) is an undamped sinusoidal cycle. Thus, as the natural rate n was constant,[6] and imagining that initially $r < \bar{n}$ (i.e., d is negative), r would increase toward the level of $\bar{n}$ and overshoot, and then move back toward $\bar{n}$ again and overshoot again, and so forth. Frisch was, of course, not wholly satisfied with that solution. That extremely simplified account of cyclical behavior proceeded on the assumption "that there is no friction or similar phenomena which will eventually dampen the oscillations. In reality, such dampening factors are, of course, present" (Frisch, 1951, p. 45). Otherwise he argued that the model, while leaving out many details discussed by Wicksell, brought out "the main structure of the argument."[7] The algebraic solution enabled

---

[5] Cf. Frisch's explanation of his own equation (3).

[6] In this account of Wicksell's propagation mechanism, the natural rate n is assumed to be constant. This is not in conflict with Wicksell's explanation that the cycles are caused by shifts in n (produced by impulses); cf. the impulse–propagation dichotomy. The distinction between impulses and propagation may often help to reconcile seemingly conflicting cycle theories, as Frisch noted (1931a, p. 285).

[7] Wicksell's "equilibrating cumulative process" (i.e., the process that tends to bring about equality between the two rates of interest) was also analyzed by, among others, Patinkin, who concluded that in the case Wicksell assumed, where entrepreneurs anticipate continually rising prices, there may be overshooting; i.e., the return might "be a spiraling one" (Patinkin, 1965, p. 594).

It may also be noted that M. Blaug (1968, p. 633) characterized Frisch's "cornerstone article" (1951) as "very difficult and at times somewhat obscure." He did not explain, but probably he was skeptical of Frisch's bold interpretation of Wicksell's propagation model.

Frisch to conclude that the larger the values of the parameters β, θ, and μ, and the smaller the value of v, the shorter the cycle would be.

2   Åkerman's Thesis "On the Rhythm of Economic Life"

In 1928 Johan Åkerman published his doctoral dissertation, a comprehensive study of the cycle phenomenon.[8] After an examination of earlier theories, he developed his own contribution. His approach was ambitious, as he aimed at a general and simultaneous explanation of the short cycle (three to four years) and the secondary cycle (two to three times longer). Åkerman quoted Wicksell's rocking-horse analogy and restated the impulse–propagation dichotomy, but he wanted to elaborate on the Wicksellian scheme, and he looked for a regular and repetitive factor that could contribute toward an explanation of the regularity and synchronization of the various types of cycles.

Looking at the observed time-series data on pig-iron production, and using Fourier's harmonic analysis, Åkerman argued that upturns and downturns of observed cycles typically start with seasonal fluctuations. The turning of a seasonal curve implies an impulse, triggering through its psychological effects a cyclical upturn or downturn. Thus Åkerman added to the stream of irregular stochastic impulses suggested by Wicksell a very regular kind of impulse that would help explain the shapes and regularities of the cycles. Without such a regular force, he claimed, it would be difficult to explain the observed regularity (Åkerman, 1928, p. 98). A central corollary of his thesis was that there was an exact number of seasonal fluctuations to each primary cycle and an exact number of primary cycles to each secondary one.

Åkerman defended his dissertation in Lund in November 1928, with Ragnar Frisch as the faculty-appointed main examiner. Frisch's evaluation and discussion of the dissertation were published (Frisch, 1931a, pp. 281–300). Frisch criticized Åkerman's descriptions of observed time series for tending to exaggerate the regularity of the cycles and for not, as intended, convincingly establishing a strict synchronization between shorter and longer cycles. However, Frisch's main criticism was strictly theoretical, reflecting also, for the first time, I think, Frisch's own theory of the cycle. His point of departure was the concept of "causation," stressing that Åkerman's thesis failed to provide a basic analysis of that concept. To clarify the concept of causation in cycle theory, it was essential, Frisch maintained, to distinguish between two types of fluctuations:

---

[8] It might be interesting to note that in the 1910s and 1920s, when Wicksell and Åkerman made great efforts to develop cycle theory, their contemporary, Gustav Cassel, in a book published in 1924, as well as in newspapers, claimed that the ordinary cycle phenomenon had ceased to exist in 1914 and had been replaced (up to then) by the phenomena of inflation and deflation (Åkerman, 1928, p. 29).

forced and free oscillations. In the former case, the movements of the variables of the studied system are tied to an outside oscillating force; that is, the periodicity of the system is explained by the exogenous periodicity of this outside force. In a free oscillation, however, the periodicity and some other main properties of the time series in question are explained by the intrinsic structure of the system, a well-known example in physics being the pendulum.[9] In Frisch's view, trade-cycle theory should be about free oscillations. It was only in that case that one could talk about impulses as "causes," and only in that case did the Wicksellian impulse–propagation dichotomy make sense.[10]

Frisch criticized Åkerman for sometimes describing a seasonal fluctuation as a "generating force" or "necessary impulse,"[11] but in other places stressing that seasonal fluctuations do not play the role of a "primary cause," but function more as a sort of metronome, making the swings of the generated fluctuations more distinct (Frisch, 1931a, p. 295).

Frisch did not discuss explicitly what a possible (simplified) formal specification of the model of propagation mechanism implicit in Åkerman's writings would look like – whether it would be linear or nonlinear and whether or not it would display stability. However, it seems that Åkerman, like Frisch, adhered to the axiom of stability, as his discussions were usually in terms of equilibrium and disturbances to and replacements from equilibrium. Åkerman (1934) answered some of the criticism raised by Frisch. He did, on the whole, stick to his main ideas regarding the synchronization between cycles of different lengths and the role of seasonal fluctuations.[12]

---

[9] Incidentally, in the case in which the impact of the impulse is not immediate, but lasts for a significant span of time, Frisch talked about a "half-free swing" (Frisch, 1931b, p. 135).

[10] By adopting this principle, i.e., to consider the cycle as a free swing (under friction), nothing is implied regarding the model of the propagation mechanism, i.e., whether it should be linear or nonlinear, damped or undamped.

[11] In one passage, Åkerman (1928, p. 173) wrote that he sought to modify the Wicksellian trade-cycle theory by replacing the sporadic impulses, i.e., variations in the technological and organizational process, by the regular seasonal fluctuations.

Incidentally, it may be interesting to note a certain difference between Åkerman's and Frisch's general assessments of the works of Wicksell: "I reached the conclusion that whenever a person thinks that he has found an inconsistency or a piece of unclear thinking in Wicksell's work, – the discovery of the fact that Wicksell is, after all, right, will always be a matter of patience and intelligence on the part of the reader" (Frisch, 1952, pp. 654–5). "There has been a tendency to assess post-humous justice to Wicksell, whose work was internationally neglected during his lifetime, by declaring that he was always right – surely an objectionable way of balancing under- and over-appreciation" (Åkerman, 1956, p. 404).

[12] In the 1930s and 1940s Åkerman continued his studies of business cycles and did original work concerning political business cycles. He remained fascinated with the regularities of the cycle phenomenon. For example, using U.S. data for the period 1896–1945 he sketched the following picture: the seasonal variations of one year ("the fundamental

3 Schumpeter's Explanation of the Business Cycle

In developing his cycle theory, Frisch obviously studied Schumpeter's writings on the subject very eagerly and carefully. Significantly, he included in his 1933 essay a section in which he treated Schumpeter's theory of innovations and their role in cyclical movements. Schumpeter summarized, in an article in *Economica* in 1927, his explanation of the business cycle: "arrived at in 1909, first published in 1912 and capable of being compressed into a very few propositions" (Schumpeter, 1927, p. 289). His general approach was clearly stated: "in order to find out whether or not cycles are a phenomenon *sui generis* – arising from within the economic system, we ought, in the first instance, to assume the absence of outside disturbances – non-economic ones, or economic ones which cannot be produced or avoided by economic actions, both of which we are going to call 'casual' – acting on the system" (Schumpeter, 1927, p. 290). Thus Schumpeter, like Wicksell and Frisch, emphasized the impulse–propagation dichotomy and the importance of examining the properties of the propagation mechanism (i.e., of the internal structure of the economy). We should then find, Schumpeter continued, that either the economic system would never evolve that particular kind of inherent fluctuations, in which case outside disturbances would have to be looked upon as responsible, or the economic system would of itself display cyclical fluctuations, in which case we would have to recognize the presence of a problem of a "normal cycle."

Schumpeter then compared his approach to that of Pigou, as stated in *Industrial Fluctuations* (Pigou, 1927). Pigou proceeded, Schumpeter wrote, "to draw a distinction similar to and still fundamentally different from ours. He distinguishes the problem of 'initiating impulses' from what I may term the mechanism of the cycle. His 'initiating impulses' being substantially what I mean by outside disturbances, – and his views seem to us to come close to holding that there are no causes within the system sufficient to produce the cycle and that cycle theory can only consist in describing the mechanism through which initiating impulses act as they arise, some of them sporadically, others periodically." Thus it seems that the ideas of Pigou, Wicksell, and Frisch coincided in that the generating force of the propagation mechanism was not sufficient to produce undamped cycles, although the model of the mechanism could serve to explain the cumulation of the effects of erratic disturbances.

> period of economic activity"); a two-year agricultural cycle; a short industrial cycle of four years, i.e., the political economic cycle (the presidential term); the Juglar cycle, with an average of eight years and the building cycle of 16–18 years. Here the geometrical series stops, Åkerman wrote, even though there may be a secular wave having a length of one generation (Åkerman, 1947, p. 116).

Schumpeter's view was different. Analyzing the way in which booms arose, he wrote that disturbing elements that upset an existing equilibrium may or may not trigger upturns, but if they do, "it is never the mere occurrence of the disturbance which produces them, but a certain attitude of certain people" (Schumpeter, 1927, p. 292). People could react to a disturbance by doing new things or by doing the same things in a new way. And if there were no outside disturbances (i.e., "wars, social unrest, exceptional harvests, and so on"), the "impulse" might be created within the economy. There is always scope for this. Knowledge is always far in advance of actual practice. The fruits of inventions are constantly offering themselves. Hence there are always great prizes to be won by entrepreneurs who have the right attitude and aptitude. Those who have the "willingness and capacity to do new things will always and necessarily find, or be able to create, the opportunity on which to act, being, in fact, itself the one fundamental 'initial impulse'." "In this sense, therefore, I claim 'independence' of the cycle and of those booms and depressions which form the normal cycle, from impulses from without" (Schumpeter, 1927, p. 293). Outside disturbances offered part of the material of which the fabric of every cycle consists, "but which, if absent, would be supplemented by other material always at hand."

"Normal" depressions, Schumpeter continued (1927, p. 294), "are no irregular heap of disturbances, but can be understood as the reaction of business life to the situation created by the boom or more precisely, as the movement of business life towards a new state of equilibrium conforming to the data created by the boom." What happened in a depression would be a consequence of what had happened in the boom (a proposition that most theorists would accept, he claimed). But that did not apply the other way around. One therefore would have explained the cycle when one had explained the boom.

"Normal" booms consisted in carrying out innovations in the industrial and commercial organism. Corroboration was provided, for example, by the fact "of the prominence of the constructional trades, both as to priority in time and as to amplitude of fluctuation, within the events of the cycle." "But innovations would be powerless to produce booms, if they went on continuously in time." One therefore had to ask, "Why is it that industrial and commercial change is not continuously distributed in time, but proceeds by leaps?" The answer was simply that "as soon as any step in a new direction has been successfully made, it at once and thereby becomes easy to follow." Therefore, he continued, "the first success draws other people in its wake and finally crowds of them, which is what the boom consists in" (1927, pp. 296–8).

Turning finally to the influence of banks and "credit-creation," Schumpeter maintained that "booms and consequently depressions are not the work of banks: their 'cause' is a nonmonetary one and entrepreneurs' demand is the initiating cause even of so much of the cycle as can be said to be added by the acts of banks" (1927, p. 306).

In his Section 6, "The innovations as a factor in maintaining oscillations," the last section of his 1933 essay, Frisch briefly considered Schumpeter's explanation of the business cycle. In addition to the source of "energy" that Frisch had analyzed himself (i.e., erratic shocks that serve to keep cyclical fluctuations alive), there was, Frisch wrote, "also present another source of energy operating in a more continuous fashion and being more intimately connected with the permanent evolution in human societies" (Frisch, 1933, p. 203). The nature of that influence could best be analyzed by Schumpeter's theory of innovations and their role in cyclical movements.[13] Schumpeter maintained that new ideas accumulate in a continuous fashion, but are applied on a large scale only during certain phases of the cycle. It is like a force that is released during these phases, and this force is the source of energy that maintains the oscillations. "In mathematical language one could perhaps say that one introduces here the idea of an auto-maintained oscillation" (Frisch, 1933, p. 203).

Frisch then proceeded to explain Schumpeter's idea using a mechanical analogy,[14] (typically) a pendulum. The pendulum was at certain times pushed (Frisch imagined by water streaming from a pipe), so that its movement continued even though friction was present. The water that accumulated in a receptacle above the pendulum represented, Frisch wrote, the Schumpeterian innovations. The water, which at times would descend down the pipe, illustrates that new ideas are utilized in economic life. "This utilization constitutes the new energy which maintains the oscillations."

Frisch's treatment and comments on Schumpeter's cycle theory may seem surprising. Given Frisch's enthusiasm for Wicksell and the rocking-horse analogy, his strong belief in the stability or dampening axiom, and the idea that erratic shocks supply the needed energy to keep cycles alive, one might have expected that Frisch would have gone into some sort of polemics with Schumpeter. After all, Schumpeter's basic theory differed fundamentally from that of Frisch.[15] Schumpter's explanation of the "normal" cycle did not involve disturbances or the stability assump-

---

[13] Note that Schumpeter wrote that "the current periods of prosperity of the cyclical movement are the form progress takes in capitalistic society" (Schumpeter, 1927, p. 295).

[14] Frisch referred to personal correspondence with Schumpeter and claimed that the analogy could be taken as a fair representation (Frisch, 1933, p. 203).

[15] Cf. Schumpeter's claim that Pigou's theory, which basically was in accordance with Frisch's ideas, differed fundamentally from his own. Moreover, Schumpeter emphasized the economic-political advantage of being able to distinguish between a "normal" boom or depression (according to his theory) and "breaks" created by extraordinary disturbances (Schumpeter, 1927, pp. 291, 296).

tion. In the view of Frisch, a model of the propagation mechanism explaining the periodicity of the cycle was missing. In Schumpeter's theory the length of the cycle was stochastically determined. However, Frisch was interested in Schumpeter's ideas on the impulse problem. Frisch's statement that his own theory did not contain the whole explanation, that there was also present another source of energy, may be interpreted to indicate that he felt that Schumpeter's theory could supplement his own theory. Frisch assumed serially uncorrelated shocks, whereas Schumpeter's theory implied some sort of autocorrelated shocks. To use Frisch's mechanical analogy, after a boom it would take some time before a sufficient amount of water would be accumulated in the receptacle to make a new outpouring probable (i.e., the impulses might be autocorrelated to some degree). However, there was no explicit discussion of this matter in Frisch's exposition.

It is interesting to note that Frisch interpreted Schumpeter's theory in light of the central concepts of his own theory (concepts not used by Schumpeter) (i.e., energy, friction, and the freely swinging pendulum). On the whole, the theory advanced by Frisch was (because of its mathematical formalization, its use of central macroeconomic variables, and the introduction of additive stochastic error terms in the structural equations) a more stimulating and fruitful point of departure for subsequent research than was Schumpeter's verbally formulated theory.

4 Frisch's "Propagation and Impulse" Essay

The main purpose of Frisch's 1933 essay was a close mathematical examination of the mechanism by which irregular fluctuations might be transformed into cyclical movements, as suggested by Wicksell's rocking-horse analogy, accompanied by a concrete economic interpretation of that phenomenon (Frisch, 1933, pp. 198–9). The first page summarized Frisch's vision of how the cycle should be explained: External impulses would hit, more or less irregularly, the economic mechanism and initiate swinging movements, which could most plausibly be explained as free oscillations. The periodicity and the dampening tendency of the oscillations would be determined by the intrinsic structure of the economy. Because of frictions, the oscillations generated by the economy's structure would tend to be damped,[16] but the external impulses would provide "energy" to keep the fluctuations alive. That suggested vision was basically the same as was evident from Frisch's article on Åkerman's dissertation (Frisch, 1931a).[17] One may roughly say that Frisch's basic ideas were derived from Wicksell and probably were formed during

---

[16] Or, more specifically, significantly but not extremely damped.
[17] It is also stated (in almost pedantic detail) in Frisch's address to the meeting of Nordic economists in Stockholm (Frisch 1931b).

the time he struggled with Åkerman's attempt to interpret and modify Wicksell.[18]

In his introduction, Frisch also considered some basic methodological principles. He devoted considerable space to explaining that a model of the cycle would have to be determined and that it should be "truly dynamic" ("explaining how a situation grows out of the foregoing").[19] He further stressed that the analysis would have to be of the macrodynamic (as opposed to the microdynamic)[20] type (i.e., intending to give "an account of the fluctuations of the whole economic system taken in its entirety").

As a preliminary step toward developing a model of the propagation mechanism, Frisch then analyzed a simple model of two variables and two equations, containing, inter alia, the acceleration principle. That model led to a first-order differential equation (i.e., it was too simple to generate cyclical fluctuations). Looking to extend the model in order to introduce the possibility of oscillations, Frisch mentioned several alternatives. In the first place, the variables "saving" and "investment" could be included, which was, he wrote, "Keynes's point of view."[21] Moreover, he mentioned, referring to Irving Fisher, the introduction of the existence of "debt" and its influence on the behaviors of consumers and producers; and finally he mentioned the Marxian idea of swings in the distribution of purchasing power between consumers and producers. However, Frisch chose to extend the simple model by introducing Aftalion's distinction between initiating the production of capital goods and the continuing activity needed for completion of those goods. In

---

[18] Frisch mentioned in his 1933 essay the findings from Slutsky's and Yule's experimental studies that some sort of swings will be produced by the accumulation of erratic influences. Obviously, Frisch was very interested in these experiments, but I do not think that they influenced the development of his cycle theory in any significant way. The main ideas were already given in the writings of Wicksell.

Also, I do not think that Frisch's cycle theory was significantly influenced by J. M. Clark, in spite of the Frisch-Clark discussion during the years 1931-2. From that discussion Frisch could have found some good ideas for a better specification of his "consumption equation" (3). But, as described by Andvig (1986, pp. 73-6), Frisch was not as interested in Clark's hypotheses as he was in making his own methodological points.

[19] That was, 60 years ago, an appropriate remark, as witness the many static analyses of business cycles reported by Marschak (1954).

[20] In the 1933 essay Frisch used the term "macro-dynamic," but in his mimeographed lectures from 1934 he used the term "macroeconomic" (Frisch, 1934, p. 8506, the section "Det mikroökonomiske kontra det makroökonomiske synspunkt").

[21] While it was Keynes's point of view, Frisch probably was thinking of the analysis of Wicksell, where saving and investment decisions play a central role. In his article on Wicksell, Frisch (1952, pp. 669-75) argued that to elaborate on Wicksell's ideas, we need a system of concepts where saving can also be different from investment ex post, and that such a system could help to formulate models of macro-dynamics more instructively. However, Frisch never formulated a model of this type.

other words, one should consider the stock of half-finished capital goods in addition to the usual stock of completed capital goods.

5 Frisch's Model of the Propagation Mechanism

Frisch tacitly assumed a closed economy and considered the following three real variables: y, "production starting" of capital goods, producing half-finished capital goods (i.e., flow of capital units entering the production process); z, production of capital goods; x, production of consumption goods. To explain the time paths of those three variables, he operated with the following relationships:

$$y_t = mx_t + \mu \dot{x}_t \tag{1}$$

$$z_t = \int_0^\infty D(\tau) y_{t-\tau} d\tau, \quad \text{where } D(\tau) = 1/\varepsilon \tag{2}$$

that is,

$$\dot{z}_t = (y_t - y_{t-\varepsilon})/\varepsilon \tag{2'}$$

$$\dot{x}_t = c - \lambda(rx_t + sz_t) \tag{3}$$

where the parameters $m, \mu, \varepsilon, c, \lambda, r$, and s are all positive constants. Equation (1) explains the "production starting" of capital goods, with the first term representing replacement investment (in both lines of production), and the second term the acceleration principle, which in this model works solely through variations in consumption. In equation (2) it is assumed that the "advancement function" $D(\tau)$ is constant; that is, each unit of capital is given a constant amount of carry-on activity (and thus value added) over the (constant) production period. Frisch called equation (3) the "consumption equation." It explains, however, the time derivative, not directly the level of production of consumption goods. The idea is that during the upturn, when x and z increase, the need for cash increases, whereas, as a rule, the money supply is not expanded pari passu. This creates a tension that counteracts further expansion. Frisch assumed that consumption would be the first to yield to the cash pressure, so that $\dot{x}$ would decline and perhaps turn negative. Equation (3) was also called "the brake equation."[22]

The model contains some drastic simplifications. For example, each order for capital goods is immediately put into effect, and its completion time is a constant, independent of the phase of the cycle. Moreover, variations in the growth of consumption-goods production are determined

---

[22] "Bremsningsligningen" (Frisch, 1934, p. 8532.3). It is interesting to note that although the model is linear, the construction of equation (3) is such that it introduces virtually a sort of "ceiling" against which an expansion rebounds.

in a conspicuously simple and "mechanical" way. However, Frisch emphasized that the model was of the "first-approximation" type.[23] Considered as such, and remembering that Frisch's main point was methodological, the model may be considered an achievement. Leif Johansen described the model as "much more refined and comprehensive than several later (well-known) dynamic models." However, he thought that the content of equation (3) should be regarded as a supplement to a Keynesian consumption function, rather than as a primary factor in the explanation of consumption (Johansen, 1969, p. 314).

Another kind of critical question, which is raised in the present essay, is whether or not the model was fully in accordance with Frisch's own vision of how the cycle should be explained. I am thinking particularly about the respective roles he envisaged for the propagation mechanism and for the erratic shocks. I shall argue later that such was not the case.

Frisch ascribed the acceleration principle (1) to Clark, his equation (2) to Aftalion, and the idea of the variable *encaisse désirée*, represented here by the expression ($rx + sz$) in equation (3), and the monetary tension during upswings to Walras.[24]

The model seems, intuitively, able to generate cyclical fluctuations. Imagine, for example, that $\dot{x}$ and, according to (1), y increase for some time. Then, given (2), z will also increase after a while. But then ($rx + sz$) will increase, which according to (3) implies that $\dot{x}$ will decline and may easily become negative. Then y, and subsequently z, will also decline, whereby, according to (3), $\dot{x}$ will sooner or later again turn positive.

The model is a mixed system of differential and difference equations and thus is fairly complicated. But Frisch was able to work out the form of the general solution analytically. That is, for the variable time path x,

$$x(t) = x_* + \sum a_k \exp \rho_k t$$

where ρ_k are complex and/or real constants determined by the structural parameters.

In order to study the nature of the solutions, Frisch inserted numerical values for the structural parameters "that may in a rough way express the magnitudes which we would expect to find in actual economic life." His standard numerical example was

---

[23] Frisch's formulations, e.g., about relation (3) (1933, p. 180), "assuming as first approximation the relationship to be linear," might by some readers be interpreted to mean that he was going to relax this simplifying assumption later in the essay. But obviously he was thinking of the concept of a first as distinct from a second- or third-approximation type of model.

[24] He might also have mentioned Wicksell; cf. Frisch's discussion of Wicksell's "equilibrating cumulative process."

$$\varepsilon = 6, \quad m = 0.5, \quad \mu = 10, \quad \lambda = 0.05, \quad r = 2,$$
$$s = 1, \quad c = 0.165$$

Using those numerical values, Frisch found that the solution contained a primary cycle ($k = 1$) with a period of about 8.5 years and secondary and tertiary cycles ($k = 2, 3$) with periods of 3.5 and 2.2 years, respectively. All cycles were heavily damped. Frisch found that result of "considerable interest," as a primary cycle of 8.5 years and a secondary cycle of 3.5 years correspond well to the observed long and short business cycles. Those results were, Frisch thought, "not entirely due to coincidence but have a real significance." The results certainly seem impressive, but also puzzling, in view of the model's drastic simplifications and the fact that the inserted numerical values were very rough guesses. Some of the specified parameter values also seem obscure, particularly the value for ε, which is the period required for completion of capital goods; $\varepsilon = 6$ years seems obviously much too long.[25] Also, the model was primarily intended to demonstrate basic methodological principles, rather than to explain the characteristics of cyclical fluctuations in any detail.[26] But even considered as an experiment of "calibration" (in order to investigate the model's potentiality), the results seem impressive and interesting.[27]

Furthermore, studying and comparing the phases of the generated time paths, Frisch found that the primary, secondary, and tertiary cyclical components all showed distinct patterns of lead–lag relations that accorded well with the Harvard A, B, and C curves. "Production starting" y is the leading variable. When it reaches its peak early in the upturn, $\dot{x}$ is at its maximum, while x is still relatively low. When x reaches its peak, y has fallen off considerably. The carry-on activity z is atypically lagged.

Frisch's numerical illustrations were limited to the specific time paths of the primary, secondary, and tertiary cyclical components. Despite his strong desire, he was unable to work out the total picture (i.e., the sum of all components).

---

[25] As criticized by, inter alia, Tinbergen (1935, pp. 271–2).

[26] The quoted statement, i.e., that result has "real significance," should be seen, I think, as expressing Frisch's excitement with his results, but not really his conviction. Cf., for example, that in his comments to Åkerman, Frisch noted that he did not think the primary cycle and the secondary cycle should be explained in the same way, suggesting that, for example, the length of the primary cycle might be linked to the average lifetime of capital goods, and the length of the secondary cycle to the average construction period (Frisch, 1931a, p. 288).

[27] Andvig suggested that the numerical example might be looked at as a sort of "calibration." "What Frisch seems to have done was just to manipulate the value of the parameters so that the numerical example he studied fitted roughly to his preconceived notion of observed regularities (determined by his statistical decomposing studies, or otherwise)" (Andvig, 1986, p. 102).

6 The Disturbed Case: A "Full" Explanation of the Cycle

Frisch's own example, and many other examples of a similar sort, "show that when an economic system gives rise to oscillations, these will most frequently be damped" (Frisch, 1933, p. 197). It may seem surprising that Frisch so strongly asserted that realistic models produce, as a rule, damped fluctuations. Econometric studies were rare at the time, and he gave no references. One may speculate that his conviction originated from a common and general idea that most economic systems ought to imply stability, because the reality that we observe is, as a rule, stable. It could also be that Frisch envisaged competition from an alternative kind of basic cycle theory not based on the stability axiom and the Wicksell-Frisch approach and that he therefore wanted to stress very strongly the plausibility of his own approach (cf. the earlier quotation where Frisch indicated that Schumpeter introduced the idea of an auto-maintained oscillation).[28]

Thus it seemed natural to Frisch to take up the study of how more or less irregular impulses that "hit" the economic system are transformed into cycles. For technical reasons, in his 1933 essay he was not able to demonstrate this idea by means of his model of the propagation mechanism. He applied instead a model of the freely swinging pendulum that produced a damped sine curve. Imagining that the pendulum was hit by a series of erratic shocks, he computed a curve that displayed persistent and quasi-regular cycles.

Frisch also discussed analytically the nature of the solution for the disturbed case (i.e., how the shocks are formally transformed into cycles). The system of weights in the cumulation of the effects of the disturbances was, he showed, given by the shape of the (undisturbed) solution of the model of the propagation mechanism; Thus the structure of that mechanism should have a significant influence on the final result.

In his lectures in Oslo during the autumn of 1933 and the spring of 1934, Frisch continued his discussion of how undamped cycles could be explained by his theory. He was then able to display the result of an experiment with his own model of the propagation mechanism. He operated with additive erratic terms in equations (1) and (3), remarking that in the first place it seemed reasonable to disregard disturbances in the carry-on activity (Frisch, 1934, p. 8536.2). He also observed that the amplitudes of the generated fluctuations were more affected by the disturbances on the consumption side than by those on the investment side (which was mainly due to the very high value assigned to the

---

[28] An example that Frisch's strong emphasis on dampedness did have an impact on his readers was provided by Samuelson (1974, p. 10). Because of Frisch, Samuelson fell into the dogma "that all economic business cycle models should have damped roots," a dogma that, Samuelson wrote, slowed down his recognition of important nonlinear models.

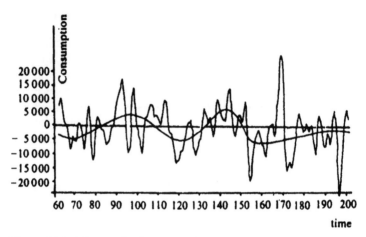

Figure 14.1. Time path of consumption.

parameter μ). He displayed a single computed time path for consumption (as deviations from its equilibrium value), which is reproduced in Figure 14.1. It was possible, Frisch asserted, clearly to distinguish in that time path, which was undamped, the 8.5-year cycle component, as well as, to some extent, the 3.5-year component.[29] He did not, however, seek to substantiate that assertion.[30]

7 Some Concluding Remarks

As explained earlier, Frisch was strongly influenced by Wicksell's writings on the cycle phenomenon, and he may have been influenced by Åkerman's interpretation and elaboration of Wicksell's ideas. Frisch was also very interested in Schumpeter's cycle theory, devoting a section of his essay to it. However, his own theory does not seem to have been influenced by Schumpeter.

Wicksell did not claim to have given a complete explanation of the cycle, but only to have pointed out "a necessary and hitherto often neglected clue to a full explanation" (Wicksell, 1935, p. 209). Wicksell

---

[29] The figure also shows a moving-average curve that has a periodicity of about 50 years.
[30] I have tried to replicate Frisch's computation, using the same values for the parameters. However, in his mimeographed lectures in 1934 he did not give much information about his computation of the path of x (Figure 14.1). There is no information as to the size and duration of the shocks, so I had to guess. My simulated path of consumption x resembled that of Frisch, but the adherent correlogram did not indicate any distinct periodicity. Again, Frisch's claim that the 8.5- and 3.5-year components could be distinguished (in Figure 14.1) might be seen as an expression of his excitement with the result, not to be taken literally (cf. note 26).

seems to have believed that sooner or later there would be a definitive theory of business cycles, as he concluded his review of Petander's book by wondering if Petander's name will be remembered when the definitive theory of crises and business cycles is finally established (Wicksell, 1918, p. 75). Frisch, however, certainly felt that he had in principle solved the problem of how to account for the cyclical fluctuations. The solution should rest upon a "synthesis between the stochastical point of view, and the point of view of rigidly determined dynamic laws" (the deterministic model of the propagation mechanism). He also believed that the periodicity of the cyclical fluctuations should not be linked to any exogenous periodic or quasi-periodic variable, but explained by the model of the propagation mechanism as a "free swing." The structural equations of the economy should explain the average periodicity, the tendency toward dampening (the stability axiom), and several important "stylised facts" of empirical business-cycle study, such as a typical lead–lag structure (the Harvard A, B, and C curves). Exogenous impulses, on the other hand, should explain the maintenance of cyclical fluctuations and, moreover, largely determine their amplitude. They should also account for the irregular and unpredictable character of observed cycles. The assumptions Frisch made in his 1933 essay were derived from that suggested vision.

Velupillai (1992, p. 58) noticed "implicit nonlinearities – especially in terms of the monetary factors – in the most elementary version of the core model" in Frisch's 1933 essay and argued that Frisch, instead of adopting a formula for a freely swinging pendulum (which produces only a damped sine curve), should rather have used a nonlinear version of the formula that had been advocated by Le Corbeiller and Hamburger. However, the pendulum fits the stability axiom (and the rocking-horse picture) perfectly well. Frisch did not say that the model of the propagation mechanism should in principle be linear. But it suited his argument. For one thing, the turning points of the cycle were automatically explained by the model and did not need any particular consideration. Also, if he were to relax his first-approximation assumptions of linearity, he would have to find ways to ensure damping.

Moene and Rødseth mentioned that "Haavelmo criticised the view that a dynamic theory explaining business cycles should have a solution with oscillations. This was (1940) still a common opinion, held even by his teacher Frisch" (Moene and Rødseth, 1991, p. 181). I cannot find any evidence that Frisch thought that the model of the propagation mechanism had to produce oscillations for "technical" reasons (i.e., in order to obtain cycles in the disturbed case). To Frisch that assumption expressed, I think, part of his vision of how the cycle should be explained, that is, endogenously, within a model of the propagation mechanism.

There is also the question of whether or not Frisch's model of the propagation mechanism was adequate in various aspects. Zambelli has conducted a number of computer simulations and found that only in the case of extreme initial conditions does it generate oscillations. The damping is too strong (Zambelli, 1992). With the help of a modern computer I have tried to continue Frisch's numerical experiments where he, for technical reasons, had to stop (Thalberg, 1990). For one thing, I have found that in the disturbed solutions the three variables display, as a rule (and even for small shocks), different and seemingly fairly independent fluctuations. Frisch obviously wanted to see the lead–lag structure, where y leads x, and z is a lagged, as part also of the disturbed solution. Or at least he expected to find some fair degree of synchronization between variations in these three variables. Thus, Frisch would certainly have been dissatisfied with the outcome of the simulations, because they do not quite comply with his preconceived vision, and probably would have looked for amendments. In general, if a model of the propagation mechanism does not knit the variables firmly together, the disturbed solution can easily diverge sharply from the undisturbed one. Confronted with this problem, Frisch probably would have stumbled across the "multiplier." Naturally the link between the investment activity and consumption had to be strengthened. I have shown that this and/or a few other extensions can provide more satisfactory results (Thalberg, 1990).

Rau (1974) discussed the merits of the Frisch approach compared with explanations based on the time paths of exogenous variables. He referred to the experiments reported by Adelman and Adelman (1959), who found that only by incorporating stochastic shocks in the structural equations of the Klein-Goldberger model were they able to explain observed cycles. Rau also recalled results by Zarnowitz "that non-stochastic simulations, given exogenous variables as they actually occurred, underestimated the extent of actual fluctuations." Rau therefore favored the Frisch approach (Rau, 1974, p. 68).

In contrast to Frisch's stability axiom, a model may tend to generate explosive paths of its endogenous variables, while incorporating nonlinear elements that keep its movements within relevant bounds. For a review of the development (in the 1930s and 1940s) of models of this kind, which produce self-generating undamped cycles, and which constitute a serious challenge to the Wicksell-Frisch approach, I refer to Lawrence Klein's Chapter 15 in this volume, particularly Section 3. Whether or not alternative approaches can give more realistic models, with erratic shocks not having to play the role envisaged by Frisch, is not only an empirical issue but also a question of what we demand of our theory. But much modern analysis is conceptually in accordance with Frisch and Wicksell. The discussions often focus upon the nature of the impulses or shocks behind observed macroeconomic variability, which is studied within a framework using an impulse–response type of analysis.

References

Adelman, I. (1960). Business cycles – endogenous or exogenous? *Economic Journal* 70:783–96.
Adelman, I., and Adelman, F. L. (1959). The dynamic properties of the Klein-Goldberger model. *Econometrica* 27:596–625.
Åkerman, J. (1928). *Om det ekonomiska livets rytmik*. Stockholm.
— (1934). *Konjunkturteoretiska problem*. Lund.
— (1947). Political economic cycles. *Kyklos* 1:107–17.
— (1956). The cumulative process. In: *25 Economic Essays in Honour of Erik Lindahl*, pp. 393–412. Stockholm.
Andvig, J. C. (1986). Ragnar Frisch and the Great Depression: a study in the interwar history of macroeconomic theory and policy. Ph.D. thesis, Norwegian Institute of International Affairs, Oslo.
Blaug, M. (1968). *Economic Theory in Retrospect*. London: Heinemann.
Boianovsky, M. (1993). Wicksell's business cycle. Research paper series no. 46, Faculty of Economics and Politics, Cambridge University.
Engländer, O. (1929). *Theorie der Volkswirtschaft. Erster Teil. Preisbildung und Preisaufbau*. Wien: Verlag von Julius Springer.
Evans, M. K. (1969). *Macroeconomic Activity: Theory, Forecasting and Control*. New York: Harper & Row.
Frisch, R. (1929a). Økonomisk teori. *Statsøkonomisk Tidskrift* 43:229–72.
— (1929b). Statistikk og dynamikk i den økonomiske teori. *Nationaløkonomisk Tidskrift* 67:321–79.
— (1931a). Johan Åkerman: Om det ekonomiska livets rytmik. *Statsvetenskaplig Tidskrift* 34:281–300.
— (1931b). Konjunkturbevegelsen som statistisk og som teoretisk problem. In: *Förhandlingar vid Nordiska Nationalekonomiska Mötet i Stockholm, juni 1931*, pp. 127–68, 224–34. Stockholm: Ivar Haeggströms Boktryckeri och Bokförlags A.B.
— (1933). Propagation problems and impulse problems in dynamic economics. In: *Essays in Honour of Gustav Cassel*, pp. 171–205. London: George Allen & Unwin.
— (1934). Forelesninger over makrodynamikk (Lectures on macrodynamics). Mimeographed paper, University of Oslo.
— (1935). Pengeteori. Mimeographed, partly handwritten manuscript, University of Oslo.
— (1936). On the notion of equilibrium and disequilibrium. *Review of Economic Studies* 3:100–5.
— (1951). Knut Wicksell: a cornerstone in modern economic theory. Memorandum from the Institute of Economics, University of Oslo, December 15, 1951. Also published (1952) as Frisch on Wicksell. In: *The Development of Economic Thought*, ed. H. W. Spiegel, pp. 652–99. New York: Wiley.
Haavelmo, T. (1940). The inadequacy of testing dynamic theory by comparing theoretical solutions and observed cycles. *Econometrica* 8:312–21.
Johansen, L. (1969). Ragnar Frisch's contribution to economics. *Swedish Journal of Economics* 71:302–24.
Marschak, J. (1954). A cross section of business cycle discussion. *American Economic Review* 35:268–81.

Moene, K. O., and Rødseth, A. (1991). Nobel Laureate Trygve Haavelmo. *Journal of Economic Perspectives* 5:175–92.
Munthe, P. (1994). Ragnar Frisch, Ole Colbjørnsen og Arbeiderpartiets kriseplaner. Unpublished manuscript, University of Oslo.
Patinkin, D. (1965). *Money, Interest and Prices*. New York: Harper & Row.
Pigou, A. C. (1927). *Industrial Fluctuations*. London: Macmillan.
Rau, N. (1974). *Trade Cycles: Theory and Evidence*. London: Macmillan.
Samuelson, P. A. (1974). Remembrances of Frisch. *European Economic Review* 5:7–23.
Schumpeter, J. A. (1927). The explanation of the business cycles. *Economica*, December, pp. 286–311.
Thalberg, B. (1990). A reconsideration of Frisch's original cycle model. In: *Nonlinear and Multisectoral Macrodynamics. Essays in Honour of Richard Goodwin*, ed. K. Velupillai, pp. 96–117. London: Macmillan.
Tinbergen, J. (1935). Annual survey: suggestions on quantitative business cycle theory. *Econometrica* 3:241–308.
Velupillai, K. (ed.) (1992). *Nonlinearities, Disequilibria and Simulation*. London: Macmillan.
——— (1992). Implicit nonlinearities in the economic dynamics of 'Impulse and propagation'. In: *Nonlinearities, Disequilibria and Simulation*, ed. K. Velupillai, pp. 57–71. London: Macmillan.
Wicksell, K. (1907). Krisernas gåta. *Statsøkonomisk Tidsskrift* 21:255–86.
——— (1909). Penninggränta och varupris. *Ekonomisk Tidskrift* 45:61–6.
——— (1918). Karl Petander: 'Goda och dåliga tider'. *Ekonomisk Tidskrift* 11:66–75.
——— (1924). Comments on H. Westergaard. Om økonomiske barometre. *Nationalekonomiska Föreningens Förhandlingar Ekonomisk Tidskrift* 26:85–96.
——— (1935). *Lectures on Political Economy. Vol. 2: Money*. London: Routledge & Kegan Paul. Translated from Wicksell's *Förelesningar*, 3rd ed., 1929. Lund.
——— (1953). The enigma of business cycles. *International Economic Papers* 3:58–74.
——— (1965). *Interest and Prices*. New York: A. M. Kelley.
Zambelli, S. (1992). The wooden horse that wouldn't rock: reconsidering Frisch. In: *Nonlinearities, Disequilibria and Simulation*, ed. K. Velupillai, pp. 27–54. London: Macmillan.

CHAPTER 15

Ragnar Frisch's Conception of the Business Cycle

Lawrence R. Klein

1 Propagation Problems

There is no doubt in my mind that the most important paper in Ragnar Frisch's impressive bibliography is his paper on "dynamic economics" in the Cassel Festschrift (Frisch, 1933). I cannot imagine a course of lectures in macroeconomics that would omit significant consideration of that paper. For me it is simply a favorite, and for many it is his most celebrated work.

There are problems with that paper, at the levels of *specification* and empirical *measurement*, but the conceptual contribution was overwhelming – to look at the dynamics of the macroeconomy in terms of an internal mechanism related to economic response characteristics and an external mechanism related to random shocks. In later treatments of this subject we have come to rely more heavily on nonrandom exogenous impulses, to a large extent caused by economic policy, but they can easily be incorporated into Frisch's framework.

That paper was based on three equations. In Frisch's numbering system in his Section 4, they were (2), (3.3), and (4):

$$\dot{x} = c - \lambda(rx + sz) \quad \text{(encaisse désirée)} \tag{2}$$

$$y = mx + \mu\dot{x} \quad \text{(production and capital)} \tag{3.3}$$

$$\varepsilon \dot{z}_t = y_t - y_{t-\varepsilon} \quad \text{(capital starting and carry-on activity)} \tag{4}$$

where y is production of capital goods, x is national consumption (also called national income by Frisch), and z is carry-on activity.

The numerical system, with $c = 0$ in (2), is written equivalently as

$$\begin{aligned} y &= 0.5x + 10\dot{x} \\ \dot{x} &= -0.1x - 0.05z \\ -6\dot{z}_t &= y_{t-6} + 0.5(x_t + z_t) \end{aligned} \tag{24}$$

Before we consider the solution of this system, let us consider the economic meaning of its structure.

Frisch called the consumption equation, representing macroeconomic behavior of consumers (households), by a term borrowed from Walras – *encaisse désirée* – to show the need for cash to pay for transactions in consumer goods x and producer goods y. Some aspects of social accounting were treated carefully in Frisch's exposition, but the niceties of nominal and real social accounting were not spelled out. To some extent, real or inflation-adjusted relationships were not sharply distinguished from nominal relationships.

The production relationship was essentially an accelerator equation derived from Wesley Mitchell, J. M. Clark, and, to some extent, A. Aftalion. Fundamentally, equation (3.3) is a production function relating capital to output. In this equation the production of capital goods (a flow) consists of one term that is proportional to output and a term that is proportional to the rate of change of output, $\dot{x}$, to represent the incremental capital goods needed to produce incremental output. It should be noted that Frisch's thinking throughout that paper entailed a 10:1 capital–output ratio (or icorr ratio). I shall return to this empirical point later.

Frisch was mindful of capital consumption in his analysis, and also of the relationship between the capital-goods sector and the consumer-goods sector. Capital is needed in order to produce capital and also to produce consumer goods. Frisch referred to Marx for profit and production incentives, but not for intersectoral schemes of reproduction. At about that time, Griffith Evans, one of the early members and fellows of the Econometric Society, was developing models that explicitly took account of the inputs required for production of capital goods and of the subsequent use of capital to produce consumer goods (Evans, 1934).

The final equation describes the relationship among *capital starting*, the *advancement* function, and *carry-on activity*. Equation (4) relates carry-on activity to the difference in capital-goods outputs at times t and $t - \varepsilon$. The total length of the period from $t - \varepsilon$ to t includes the planning phase for major projects and actual production activity in the capital-goods sector.

Given these three equations, Frisch was ready to make judgmental estimates of important parameter values, but the fact that he searched for a complete-system explanation for business cycles is in itself interesting. In the first place, it indicated an attachment to the Walrasian idea of having as many equations as variables (i.e., in showing *determination* of the values of variables). Frisch found solutions; he did not stop at the point of counting equations and unknown variables. In addition, he laid out the goal of examining the cyclical properties of the variables.

In that respect, his discussion of the analyses of Wesley Mitchell and J. M. Clark is interesting. He obviously drew on the work of those two, but they were not in the emerging mainstream of econometrics; they conducted quantitative analyses, but did not use mathematics in a formal sense. They knew well the time-series, lead–lag properties of consumption and capital production, but Frisch questioned their implied causal interpretation and stated explicitly that equation (3.3) "is only one equation between two variables. Consequently many types of evolutions are possible." It is a pity that so many econometricians of the present generation still try to discern causality by manipulating two time series. In that early paper, Frisch stressed over and over again the need to specify a complete system in order to study the dynamics of the macroeconomy and understand its cyclical mechanism.

Having specified a model and justified it in terms of a-priori economic analysis, he set out to place numerical values on the structural coefficients $\varepsilon, \mu, m, r, s$, and λ in order to see what kind of dynamic path (cycles) could be generated by his three-equation system. He acknowledged the tentative nature of his assumptions:

> At present I am only guessing very roughly at these parameters, but I believe that it will be possible by appropriate statistical methods to obtain more exact information about them. I think, indeed, that the statistical determination of such structural parameters will be one of the main objectives of the economic cycle analysis of the future. [Frisch, 1933, p. 185]

Again, it is a pity that many in the present generation of macroeconomists, like the time-series analysts mentioned earlier, do not stick more closely to Frisch's line of thought, but rather guess at parameter values, instead of using the vast amount of information and facilities that are now available for parameter estimation that could provide the "*real explanation of the movements*" that Frisch was trying to interpret in his pioneering article.

What can be said about Frisch's rough guesses for the parameter values in his system? The average lag between the start of planning for capital-goods production and completion was put at 3 years, because he considered the average to be one-half the maximum lag, which he put at 6 years; therefore $\varepsilon = 6.0$. He assumed $\mu = 10.0$, implying a capital–output ratio that was extremely large. Something closer to 2.0 would seem to have been more plausible. The value placed on m is interpreted as the direct and indirect yearly depreciation on the capital stock. If $\mu = 10$ and $m = 0.5$, I estimate the depreciation coefficient as 0.05 in relation to the capital stock. This *is* a plausible rate, but it comes from the product of a very small output–capital ratio (reciprocal of icorr) and a very large depreciation share in total production ($m = 0.5$). Something closer to 0.1 would be a preferable choice.

Little thought was put into the choice of parameter values for λ (0.05), r (2), and s (1); they represent coefficients of activity variables in relation to the rate of change in consumption. Frisch emphasized their roughness, but regarded them as unimportant in his study of cycles.

The main finding of Frisch's research was that cycles could be generated from this mixed difference-differential-equation model, but that they likely would be highly damped. A second finding was that three cycles were discerned in the solutions, worked out by Harald Holme and C. Thorbjörnsen. One cycle length corresponded to the classic business cycle, just over 8 years in length, and others to the shorter inventory cycles, between 2 and 4 years. By changing some of the guesses about parameter values, he detected only moderate changes in cycle length, but strong changes in the damping measures. Although Frisch was enthusiastic about his main findings, he did foresee the need for further research into a more elaborate model to deal with the savings–investment discrepancy, indebtedness, and the exploitation of monthly data in order to focus better on the short cycles.

Those were all plausible judgments regarding further research, but I believe that his efforts would have been better rewarded if he had looked more closely at certain possible extensions of his model, that is, if he had

1. allowed for exporting and importing (the European economies were very *open*),
2. introduced an explicit financial sector,
3. allowed for capital–labor substitution,
4. allowed for explicit determination of wage rates, interest rates, and price levels, and
5. introduced fiscal-policy variables, with some exogenous variables.

Jan Tinbergen's parallel work at about the same time did find very interesting cyclical results for both The Netherlands and the United States, but he used statistical inference for realistic parameter estimation.

2 Impulse Problems

The equation system (2), (3.3), and (4) or (24) is linear, and the cyclical results studied numerically by Frisch were all damped, implying that the cycles would eventually die out. That was the point at which Frisch's contribution turned out to be even more important than simply showing that it is indeed possible to construct economic models of simultaneous equations that are capable of generating business cycles. He showed how the models could be extended, by making them stochastic instead of deterministic, so that they would be capable of generating *maintained* cycles.

Frisch wrote that "when an economic system gives rise to oscillations, these will most frequently be damped. But in reality the cycles we have occasion to observe are generally not damped." He explained the mechanism for maintenance of the cycle by adding random impulses to his deterministic model. His physical examples are very instructive, especially the rocking horse ("If you hit a wooden rocking horse with a club, the movement of the horse will be very different from that of the club.") and the pendulum, which he conceived to be kept in cyclical motion not only by being hit by a club but also by an automatically functioning mechanical hydraulic device. Those ideas were suggested by Knut Wicksell and Johan Åkerman; Frisch's relationships to them are explained in detail by Bjørn Thalberg in Chapter 14 in this volume. But for the formal mathematics of generating cycles through the summation of random shocks, Frisch was inspired by the work of Eugen Slutsky (1937) and G. U. Yule (1927).

Broadly speaking, Slutsky and Yule independently showed that certain iterated moving averages of random numbers, in a time series, approached a cyclical limit. It was Frisch's inspiration to show how their theorems could be combined with Wicksell's earlier suggestion of propagation and impulse effects and could be put into a mathematical theory of a maintained cycle. In terms of linear difference equations, that could be expressed in the following way.

We define a linear model

$$A(L)y_t + B(L)x_t = e_t$$
$$L^j y_t = y_{t-j}, \quad L^j x_t = x_{t-j}, \quad L^j e_t = e_{t-j}$$

where L is a displacement operator, $A(L)$ is a square-matrix polynomial operating on a vector of dependent variables, $B(L)$ is a rectangular-matrix polynomial operating on a vector of independent variables, and e_t is a vector of random disturbances. The solution to this system can be expressed as

$$y_t = K\lambda^t - [A(L)]^{-1}B(L)x_t + [A(L)]^{-1}e_t$$

where λ is a vector of the (distinct) characteristic roots of the system, and K is a matrix that depends on the initial conditions of the system.

It can be shown that the expression

$$[A(L)]^{-1}e_t$$

is made up of moving totals of random errors e_t. This is a general, linear-economic system representation of the Slutsky-Yule principles. We can, in fact, write the expression as

$$y_{it} = \sum_{s=0}^{\infty} \sum_{j=1}^{np} \frac{\lambda_j^{s+np-1}}{\prod_{j \neq k}(\lambda_j - \lambda_k)} e_{i,t-s}, \quad i = 1, 2, \ldots, n$$

where e_{it} is the ith element of e_t, and y_{it} is the ith element of y_t. If the system is damped, these weighted sums are very much like moving averages, and as Frisch showed in an example, they have a distinctly cyclical time shape.

Frisch was thus able to argue that damped cycles generated by a deterministic linear dynamic model could be kept alive if disturbed by random impulses. In later generations, econometricians equipped with appropriate hardware and software have demonstrated this point over and over again. Indeed, stochastic simulation of dynamic macroeconometric models is an important analytical tool for many purposes, cyclical analysis being just one. Through stochastic simulation we can now construct tolerance intervals for forecasting from highly complicated dynamic models.

In this representation of Frisch's view of economic periodicity, I have added independent (exogenous) variables to the system; they act upon the solution in the same way as random errors. Frisch looked to Schumpeter's theory of innovations as indicative of his impulse effect, but I would not want to treat this purely as a random process. Also, there are public economic policies, not discussed by Frisch in his 1933 paper, but fully appreciated by him, as well as external effects of the world economy if the systems are to be opened to trade and capital flows. The time paths of the independent variables thus make up significant parts of the solution.

3 Some Comparisons with Frisch's Contemporaries

In a formal mathematical sense, Frisch put a great deal of emphasis on the mixed difference-differential property of his dynamic system. This property generalizes and enriches the solution, but is not a central issue of theoretical model properties. The main point of Frisch's system was to have damped cycles that could be kept alive by superimposing additive random impulses. That can be achieved with differential-equation systems, with difference-equation systems, or with mixed systems.

It is interesting that at the Leyden meetings of the Econometric Society in 1933, Michal Kalecki presented a mixed differential-difference-equation system, and Frisch, with Harald Holme, offered a comprehensive analysis of the solution (Frisch and Holme, 1933). Two aspects of Kalecki's model are of interest. One is that the equations of the model, from a substantive point of view, provide, in my opinion, a complete anticipation of the Keynesian system, when the latter is cast in mathematical form as by, say, J. R. Hicks or Oskar Lange. Frisch did not appreciate this aspect of Kalecki's model, as I can assert on the basis of conversations that I had with Frisch in Oslo in 1947.

Apart from the mathematics of the solution, Frisch was mainly interested in the way in which Kalecki obtained a maintained cycle (i.e., by restricting some parameters of his model to take on particular values). This is a "knife-edge" solution and is arbitrary in a model where the parameters are unknown and are estimated with a great deal of uncertainty. Frisch argued that Kalecki should "accept any damping which the empirically determined constants will entail and then explain the maintenance of the swings by erratic shocks." That followed directly from the argument of the paper in the Cassel volume. Frisch was quite right about that, but the relationship of the Kalecki model to the Keynes model raises other issues that are relevant for the use of models to deal with the policy approach suggested by Keynes to alleviate the economic difficulties of the Great Depression in both Europe and North America.

There are at least four other models that have attempted to explain cyclical properties of an economic system that merit comparison with Frisch's attempt. Three of these are based on nonlinearities, and a fourth shows how a linear-accelerator model can be combined with another feature of the Keynesian system to generate cycles.

When Frisch, within the framework of linear systems, considered only the two equations

$$y = mx + \mu\dot{x}$$
$$\dot{x} = c - \lambda(rx + sy)$$

he found only a trend solution for this first-order differential-equation system. He considered three generalizations that might produce oscillations:

1. Keynes's (circa 1933) point of view, distinguishing between savings and investment
2. Irving Fisher's introduction of debt
3. Karl Marx's point of view about increasing income inequality

But instead of following any of those generalizing paths, all of which have some promising ideas, he turned to Aftalion, adopting the distinction between production starting and carrying-to-completion activity in capital-goods supply. That introduced a finite lag and took his analysis to an order higher than first order, an order that could generate cycles.

It can be said that Paul Samuelson took up the Keynesian suggestion, but followed the Keynes of 1935 rather than the Keynes of 1933 or earlier. In the later Keynesian theory there is indeed an important distinction between savings and investment; they represent choices of two different decision-makers in the macroeconomy. Samuelson followed Frisch and his predecessors who developed the accelerator theory of investment, but Samuelson introduced time delays into a consumption function (instead of using a transformation to a savings function) and a rate of change into an investment function of the accelerator type in order to obtain a higher-order system that permitted the existence of conjugate complex roots for a periodic solution (Samuelson, 1939). That early paper by Samuelson was as important and as frequently cited in his career as Frisch's "propagation problems and impulse problems" paper was in his.

Samuelson cited the possibility of real roots (no cycles), divergent complex roots (explosive cycles), convergent complex roots (damped cycles), and unit complex roots (maintained cycles). It was not, however, a theory of maintained cycles, because the complex roots with unit absolute value constituted only a knife-edge solution.

Samuelson, however, pointedly criticized another kind of maintained cycle that did not rest on a knife-edge solution. Francis Dresch (my teacher and a student of G. C. Evans) proposed the following simple theory of price determination in individual markets:

When accumulated inventory stocks [supply in excess of demand, $S(\tau) - D(\tau)$] rise, price falls, and when stocks decline, price rises. This equation can be written as

$$\dot{p} = -\lambda \int_{-\infty}^{t} [S(\tau) - D(\tau)]d\tau$$
$$\ddot{p} = -\lambda[S(t) - D(t)]$$

If $S(t)$ and $D(t)$ are each linear functions of $p(t)$, we get

$$\ddot{p} = \lambda[(d_0 + d_1 p) - (s_0 + s_1 p)]$$
$$= \lambda(d_0 - s_0) + \lambda(d_1 - s_1)p$$

The characteristic equation is

$$p^2 = \lambda(d_1 - s_1)$$

Because $\lambda(d_1 - s_1) < 0$ for conventionally sloped supply and demand functions, the only solution consists of a pair of conjugate complex roots with unit modulus, in other words, a pure cycle. It is not a matter of restricting the values of certain unknown parameters, as in the Frisch–Kalecki dispute. In this case, the cycle is in price, not in macroeconomic activity, but it is an interesting case. It turns out to be the same equation mentioned by Thalberg for cycles in the discrepancy between the bank rate and natural rate of interest.

Samuelson argued that Dresch's solution lacked plausibility because it implied that the variance of price, in a stochastic version of the basic equation, would increase with the passage of time, which was unrealistic (Samuelson, 1947). It is a well-known property of linear dynamic systems, difference or differential, that if characteristic roots lie on the unit circle, the variance of the solution will not remain finite as time increases indefinitely. Dresch's theory needed modification for the linear case in order to introduce damping with a nonsustained cycle (or no cycle at all).

It is of further interest that Kalecki, in developing a dynamic process for generating the lognormal distribution of income, also encountered a case of increasing variance of the distribution of income for exactly the same reasons, although there were no complex roots involved. Kalecki (1945) introduced a modification, as did Samuelson, in order to change the dynamic process by reducing the absolute value of the characteristic root.

This brings me to consideration of another approach to Frisch's problem, which is how to construct a dynamic system with a maintained cycle. An approach that I do not find in Frisch's writings is the consideration of nonlinear dynamics for generating a sustained cycle. But at least three other contemporaries developed some interesting theories by following that line – in contrast with Kalecki's restrictions or Frisch's resort to stochastic impulses.

Nicholas Kaldor's theory of the trade cycle, published at the onset of World War II, is an extremely interesting case (Kaldor, 1940). His model consists of four equations:

$$S_t = f(Y_t) \quad \text{(savings function)}$$
$$I_t = g(Y_t, K_{t-1}) \quad \text{(investment function)}$$
$$\Delta Y_t = \lambda(I_t - S_t) \quad \text{(output-adjustment function)}$$
$$K_t = K_{t-1} + I_t \quad \text{(definition of capital stock, recursive)}$$

The nonlinear (or one linear, one nonlinear) savings and investment functions depend positively on income and, in the case of investment, negatively on capital stock. We could call this an accelerator-multiplier model by noting that the investment function is a version of the *flexible* accelerator, while the savings function is the conventional one used in simple multiplier theory. Except for the lag structure, this part of Kaldor's system is closely related to Samuelson's "interactions" model, cited earlier. The third equation is an output-adjustment equation, which states that output tends to rise if investment exceeds savings, and fall if the reverse is true.

For the model to move in cycles, certain conditions must be met, namely, the nonlinearities must be such that the S_t and I_t functions intersect in three places, with a middle intersection exhibiting

$$\frac{df}{dY} < \frac{\partial g}{\partial Y}$$

while at the outer extremities the intersections must exhibit

$$\frac{df}{dY} > \frac{\partial g}{\partial Y}$$

Further,

$$\frac{\partial g}{\partial K} < 0$$

indicating that capital accumulation depresses investment, and the intersection (or tangency) of the two curves f and g at the left extremity is in the negative half-plane.

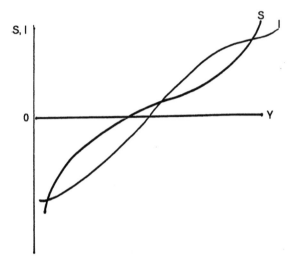

Figure 15.1. Kaldor model.

In words and pictures (Figure 15.1), the model works as follows: If we consider the intersection of the two curves at the middle crossing point, any disturbance will move the system away from the unstable equilibrium. At the upper right intersection, any disturbance moves the system back toward the stable crossing point, but lowers the investment function because capital stock is expanding. The lowering continues until the two curves are tangent, which locates an unstable equilibrium, and the output level falls toward the lower left intersection. Here, investment is negative, and the investment function shifts upward until a new tangency point is found (below the zero line), and the unstable tangency point moves output back toward the upper right intersection point, and so forth. The system has a limit cycle and is not a knife-edge solution.

Are the nonlinear curves plausible and related to a-priori economic analysis? Yes, they can readily be rationalized. When incomes are very low, people tend to dissave and maintain customary life-styles. When incomes are very high, people tend to save the excess and also to maintain conventional life-styles. There is good household-budget information to support this kind of nonlinearity for savings. As for capital formation, there are floors and ceilings. At the bottom, investment cannot be reduced below full depreciation rates, and at the top it is difficult to exceed full capacity utilization.

At a 1955 conference in Paris, in which Ragnar Frisch was also participating, I presented estimates from the Kaldor type of model (Klein

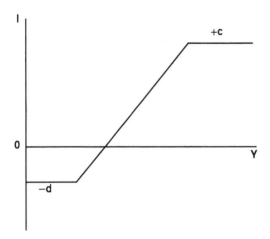

Figure 15.2. Nonlinear investment function ($-d$, maximum-depreciation floor; $+c$, full-capacity ceiling).

et al., 1956)[1] showing that it was possible to fit a model of the Kaldor type to U.S. data. In a later study, we prepared a simulation model of the Kaldor system, fitted to updated U.S. statistics (Klein and Preston, 1969).[2] The computer simulation of that model exhibited a limit cycle, just as the graphic description suggested it should. But there is an interesting additional feature of this system that is of importance for Frisch's view of the business cycle. A maintained cycle generated by a linear model has increasing variance, as Samuelson and others have shown. But stochastic shocks added to a *nonlinear* limit cycle can produce a bounded variance.

Two other nonlinear models that combine investment equations with floors and ceilings also produce limit cycles, and they bear some similarities to the Kaldor model. They both have conventional Keynesian consumption functions, and they both define output as the sum of consumer spending and enterprises' capital formation (investment), but they introduce nonlinearities in the investment function of the accelerator type by imposing abrupt floors and ceilings. They do so not in the smooth continuous transition that is implied by Kaldor's nonlinear investment function but, in effect, in the form shown in Figure 15.2. When capital is

---

[1] Frisch raised some questions about estimation methods, particularly the convergence of the estimation process for autoregressive adjustment of residuals, and the uniqueness of the estimates. He did not question the meaningfulness of the Kaldor model.

[2] See also Kosobud and O'Neill (1972), who presented a general analytical proof of the simulation results.

not being fully depreciated or utilized at full capacity output, it depends linearly on output along the upward-sloping line. This kinked relationship is drawn for a given stock of capital, which is also a variable in the Hicks and Goodwin systems. Along the middle linear segment, investment is undertaken according to the flexible-acceleration hypothesis. In many respects, this kinked relationship can be regarded as a piecewise-linear approximation to Kaldor's investment function. The consumption functions for the models of Hicks and Goodwin are linear. In the Kaldor model, it does not matter, as far as establishing a limit cycle is concerned, whether or not both relationships (savings and investment) are curved, as long as they intersect in three places, with the center intersection being unstable, and the functions shift appropriately as capital stock is built up or drawn down.

These nonlinear models (Kaldor, Hicks, Goodwin) were all discussed in detail at the Paris conference in 1955. It is also of interest to note that Maurice Allais presented his own nonlinear model of the business cycle at that conference; his limit cycle was built around *l'encaisse globale désirée*, a concept that Frisch used in his paper in the Cassel volume.

In the discussion of the Allais paper presented at the conference there was an interchange with Frisch on the effect of random impulses generated by Slutsky's theorem. Allais contended that Slutsky did not provide a model of economic cycles nor advance an explanation of the cycle phenomenon. He regarded his model as the central phenomenon, with the probabilistic process as something added on.

Frisch argued that the solution of a linear dynamic model provided an aggregation that created just the sort of cycle whose existence we were trying to demonstrate. He argued that econometricians should use conventional statistical tests and not rely purely on judgmental parameters or intuition. "It is always the combination of theory and empiricism that assures progress."

In further discussion, when I proposed the ability to predict as the test of theory, Allais objected on the grounds that there are two distinct kinds of models – explanatory models and predictive models. I personally do not believe in that distinction when a predictive model is successfully used over and over again to produce a truly testable distribution of prediction errors. Frisch agreed with my viewpoint concerning prediction, but distinguished two types of prediction: a meteorologist's prediction and a physicist's prediction, where the latter prediction can undergo laboratory testing. He went on to say that the latter sort of prediction is what we should be trying to do in econometrics, because he felt that we were entering more and more into a planned economy. As ever, Frisch was pointing to studies of repercussion and thought that we should be concentrating on research efforts in that direction.

4 Macroeconomic Policy

In addition to his deep interest in the theory of business cycles, Frisch participated in public discussion of economic policy to deal with severe cyclical problems of the day. In 1932 he gave three radio lectures in a university series, later published (1947) as a little book, *Noen Trekk av Konjunkturlaeren*. In the next year he published another little book, *Sparing og Cirkulasjons Regulering*. I had a private discussion with him, one of many during a year's scholarly visit to Oslo, about Keynesian economics and countercyclical stabilization policy. Frisch told me then that he independently had some of the same ideas as Keynes for policies to help to pull an economy out of depression.

From a theoretical point of view, there is no doubt in my mind that he fully appreciated Keynes's theoretical message; this is not to say that he agreed with it, but he fully understood what Keynes was saying, which was not generally the case in the 1930s and 1940s. It comes through clearly in *Noen Trekk av Konjunkturlaeren* and also in the discussions among Nordic economists held near Lillehammer in early 1948.

In thinking about the heated discussion that has recently taken place between Paul Samuelson (1995) and Don Patinkin (1995) on the question of the original innovator of the Keynesian revolution, I thought that it might be interesting to see if Frisch was another contender for the priority of discovery.

It is my opinion that Kalccki fully and independently built a mathematical model that contains all the essentials that are in the mathematical models of Keynes constructed by Lange and Hicks. But Frisch, when studying Kalecki's dynamic models, was interested only in the difference-differential-equation specification and in the knife-edge cyclical solution chosen by Kalecki. He did not go deeply into the economic substance of Kalecki's model and did not pick up the thread in 1948 when I discussed Kalecki's model with him.

In now reading *Sparing og Cirkulasjons Regulering*, however, I find some very interesting passages that indicate to me that Frisch fully understood the paradox of thrift.[3] In the opening chapter of that little tract (37 pages), Frisch posed a question: "What is saving?" He then distinguished between individuals' saving and social (society's) saving. If an individual saves by reducing consumption, he can improve his own balance sheet by placing funds in a financial intermediary (bank), but, Frisch said, "the only way the society as a whole can preserve the fruits of saving, is by investment in real goods." Frisch, of course, realized that investment makes future production possible, and he also allowed for balance-of-payments changes in an open economy.

---

[3] Olav Bjerkholt kindly assisted me in detailed translation of crucial passages from Norwegian into English.

Clearly the Keynesian distinction between the act of saving and the act of investment was fully understood by Frisch, as was the institutional and market mechanism by which savings flow into investment. Keynes felt that the "building of pyramids" could be of help in the process of equating saving and investment and thereby lifting an economy from depression, but Frisch's thinking did not go in that direction. I believe that was so because Frisch was so thoroughly schooled in the supply side as well as the aggregate demand side of the economy. In fact, Frisch dismissed pure inventory buildup as being of "no importance as a means to increase welfare and promote production."

Viewing the world economic situation of 1932–3, Frisch, in *Sparing*, wrote as follows: "Looking objectively at the situation in the world today, it is clearly the latter case of the effect of saving which is now taking place. Consumption has everywhere been drastically reduced, but this 'saving' has in no way resulted in increased production of tools, machinery, or similar goods. On the contrary, production has gone down everywhere. The productive forces have not been channeled in new directions, but have rather been destroyed. The 'saving' has been fictitious, because there have not been investment possibilities in viable enterprises."

I draw the following inferences from these (and other) comments by Frisch in that tract: If individuals try to save more, the whole society may end up by saving less if there is no investment offset to their attempted additional saving. This, indeed, is the paradox of thrift, and I believe that Frisch, as early as 1933, reasoned through this sequence of events just as we do today in teaching macroeconomics, especially the economics of Keynes.

In order to state these general propositions, one must have in mind a simple model that is equivalent to an elementary Keynesian system with a linear savings function whose intercept is lowered, while investment remains unchanged and savings are equated to investment. Frisch did not express these thoughts in mathematical terms, but his literary reasoning followed the same stream of thought.

Frisch told me that he had some of the same policy prescriptions in mind as did Keynes during the Great Depression. In matters of policy, he wrote that one should not blame the citizen who "saves" in order to make ends meet: "The tragedy is in the system." He went on to say that "the reproach should be directed towards those who are ultimately responsible for those parts of the system where the effects of the 'saving' is particularly apparent, namely the monetary system, ... They have done nothing to investigate, without prejudice, whether there are new rational monetary and credit instruments that perhaps could halt the destruction of capital that 'saving' now calls forth." Here he clearly meant saving that is not channeled into investment; that is why he wrote 'saving'.

He cited the fiscal as well as monetary authorities for not acting: "And not even from those who are responsible for fiscal affairs does it seem that we can hope for much assistance. They let the state finances drift in the great overall struggle. The government flounders blindfolded, trying to strengthen the fiscal budget without even stating the problem of the overall budget for the society, i.e. the balance sheet for the economy as a whole."

In the next chapter, he has a section on cooperation between the treasury and monetary authorities. He wants the latter to ease credit conditions and is quite explicit on fiscal policy: "What the state must do in a depression period is to take in less from taxation of people than they pay out in expenditures. . . . First and foremost, in depression times, the state should provide tax relief." Frisch did not formally introduce money demand and supply relationships, but he stated in no uncertain terms that fiscal and monetary authorities should work together in order to put more purchasing power (effective demand) in the hands of people.

When Ragnar Frisch told me privately that he had many of the Keynesian-type ideas at the beginning of the Great Depression, I did not immediately follow up the investigative trail, but I am pleased, on this occasion, to have revisited our conversations and worked through his writings of 1932-3 – to find that he really was thinking along the same lines that we associate with Keynes in order to pull the large industrial countries out of their deep slump.

References

Evans, G. C. (1934). Maximum production studied in a simplified economic system. *Econometrica* 2:37–50.
Frisch, R. (1933). Propagation problems and impulse problems in dynamic economics. In: *Economic Essays in Honour of Gustav Cassel*, pp. 171–205. London: George Allen & Unwin.
Frisch, R., and Holme, H. (1935). The characteristic solutions of a mixed difference and differential equation occurring in economic dynamics. *Econometrica* 3:225–39.
Kaldor, N. (1940). A model of the trade cycle. *Economic Journal* 50:78–92.
Kalecki, M. (1945). On the Gibrat distribution. *Econometrica* 13:161–70.
Klein, L. R., Buckberg, A., Gyorki, L., and Runyon, H. (1956). Quelques aspects empiriques du modèle de cycle économique de Kaldor. In: *Les modèles dynamiques en économétrie*, pp. 127–43. Paris: CNRS.
Klein, L. R., and Preston, R. S. (1969). Stochastic nonlinear models. *Econometrica* 37:95–106.
Kosobud, R., and O'Neill, W. (1972). Stochastic implications of orbital asymptotic stability of a nonlinear trade cycle model. *Econometrica* 40:69–86.
Patinkin, D. (1995). On the chronology of the *General Theory*. In: *Economics, Econometrics and the LINK*, ed. M. Dutta et al., pp. 21–34. Amsterdam: Elsevier.

Samuelson, P. A. (1939). Interactions between the multiplier analysis and the principle of acceleration. *Review of Economic Statistics* 21:73–8.
  (1947). *Foundations of Economic Analysis*. Cambridge, MA: Harvard University Press.
  (1995). Who innovated the Keynesian revolution? In: *Economics, Econometrics and the LINK*, ed. M. Dutta et al., pp. 3–19. Amsterdam: Elsevier.
Slutsky, E. (1937). The summation of random causes as the source of cyclic processes. *Econometrica* 5:105–46. (First published, 1927, by the Conjuncture Institute of Moscow.)
Yule, G. U. (1927). On a method of investigating periodicity in disturbed series. *Transactions of the Royal Society, London* A226:267–98.

CHAPTER 16

Business Cycles: Real Facts or Fallacies?

Gunnar Bårdsen, Paul G. Fisher, and
Ragnar Nymoen

1 Introduction

Conflicting views on the causes and nature of business-cycle fluctuations usually can be attributed to different beliefs about the adjustments of prices and wages. For example, Kydland and Prescott (1990) – KP hereafter – concluded that U.S. prices had been countercyclical since 1954 and interpreted that as evidence against demand-driven models of the cycle. Those findings were based on the innovative "stylized-facts" method of KP, as further developed (Kydland and Prescott, 1991) and contrasted with the econometric "system-of-equations" approach of Koopmans (1947, 1949).

The main reason for KP's dismissal of econometric models seems to have been that results derived from system-of-equations models were model-dependent and represented biased evidence on the nature of business-cycle fluctuations (e.g., the "myth" that prices behave procyclically). As an alternative, KP offered their own stylized-facts method, which involved only a minimum of assumptions, thus allowing the data to speak directly, instead of through the veil of an econometric model. KP applied a filtering technique known in the economics literature as the Hodrick-Prescott (HP) filter to the raw data in order to identify and remove the trend in the individual series. The filtered or "cyclical" series were then used to analyze business-cycle fluctuations by calculation of bivariate correlations between, say, de-trended prices and GDP at

---

We would like to thank Sigbjørn A. Berg, Clive W. J. Granger, Kåre Johansen, Tor J. Klette, Bjørn Naug, Torsten Persson, and Paul Søderlind for helpful comments, as well as participants at seminars given at the University of Stockholm, the University of Trondheim, the Norwegian School of Economics and Business Administration, the Bank of England, the Central Bank of Norway, the Norwegian School of Management, and the 8th Nordic Symposium on Multivariate Cointegration Analysis. We would also like to thank an anonymous referee for detailed and helpful comments. The views expressed are those of the authors and should not be interpreted as reflecting those of the Bank of England or the Central Bank of Norway. The research was partly financed by SNF project 2550.

different leads and lags. The full set of bivariate correlations constituted the stylized facts.

Stylized-facts methods have been successful in attracting the interest of business-cycle analysts. Blackburn and Ravn (1992) found results for the United Kingdom that were consistent with the KP results: that prices are countercyclical, and that the real wage is procyclical. Other studies using the stylized-facts approach conveyed a more mixed picture; see Brandner and Neusser (1992), Danthine and Girardin (1989), Correia, Neves, and Rebelo (1992), Englund, Persson, and Svensson (1992), and Schlitzer (1993). Although some of those studies found countercyclical prices, an even more conspicuous finding was that correlations changed over sample periods and across countries. Thus Englund et al. (1992), using Swedish data for 128 years, found unstable correlations between wages and GDP output. For a much shorter sample period, and using quarterly data, Blackburn and Ravn (1992) found large fluctuations in the correlation between prices and output.[1] Building on a multicountry study, Andersen (1994, pp. 18–19) reported instabilities both across time and between countries. Instabilities of that kind obviously represent a problem for business-cycle analysis, because to constitute stylized facts, the "statistical properties of cyclical fluctuations must remain broadly invariant to the passage of time" (Blackburn and Ravn, 1992, p. 393).

KP made no distinction between the system-of-equations approach advocated by Koopmans and modern econometric models and methods. In this essay we reconsider the econometric approach of explaining business-cycle correlations, taking account of the past 10–15 years of methodological debate and subsequent developments; see Granger (1990) and Banerjee et al. (1993, ch. 9) for discussion and overview. One product of this debate has been renewed interest in several of the concepts and problems that figured markedly during the formative years of econometrics (Morgan, 1990, pp. 262–3). They include dynamic systems, which were essential to Tinbergen's models in the 1930s but died away under the weight of static Keynesian systems, and the concept of autonomy of relationships, which was introduced by Ragnar Frisch (1938, 1948) and further discussed and refined by Trygve Haavelmo (1944).[2]

Broadly speaking, a relationship is more autonomous the wider the range of circumstances under which the relationship is valid. Several aspects of the concept of autonomy have reappeared in discussions of "exogeneity," "fragility," and "structure" (e.g., Engle, Hendry, and Richard, 1983; Pagan, 1987; Hendry, 1993). Relationships with low degrees of autonomy Frisch and Haavelmo called confluent relation-

---

[1] Between −0.8 and 0; see Blackburn and Ravn (1992, fig. 5).
[2] See Morgan (1990, ch. 4.4) on Frisch's views of Tinbergen's (first) League of Nations report, and see Aldrich (1989) for a history of the concept of autonomy. An excellent discussion of autonomy is available in Johansen, 1977, ch. 4.4.

ships. Today the distinction between autonomous and confluent relationships is drawn in several contexts, such as between identified cointegration relationships and spurious regressions (Hendry and Morgan, 1989; Hendry, 1993).

In this essay we demonstrate that system-of-equations models have much to offer in explaining business cycles generally and specifically in resolving the puzzles that have arisen from applications of stylized-facts methods. A main theme in our account is that whereas regime shifts and structural breaks will necessarily induce changes and fluctuations in bivariate correlations, that is not necessarily true for econometric relationships. Thus, invoking Frisch's terminology, the KP bivariate correlations constitute relationships that are confluent *relative* to econometric relationships – they are less autonomous. Conversely, changing correlations constitute information that is vital for the discovery of structure in the form of stable and invariant econometric relationships (i.e., relationships with a certain degree of autonomy).

Central to our approach is the notion of *structure* as the set of invariant features of the economic mechanism (Hendry, 1993; Morgan and Hendry, 1995). Invariance under extensions of the information set (time, regime, sources of information) is a key property of structure. Conversely, discovering structure implies a certain degree of autonomy. Necessary attributes of structure are testable (e.g., stability), even if sufficient ones are not. Hence claims of structural interpretation of *models* can be tested; Ericsson and Irons (1994) have collected several practical examples. However, models are simple constructs relative to the complex real systems they mimic, so we can determine only partial structure, and invariance properties are always relative.

The rest of this chapter is organized as follows. Section 2 briefly reviews the use of the HP filter in extracting trends. The use of simple bivariate cross-correlations of de-trended data to analyze business cycles has been shown to yield results that are nonrobust and may actually hide existing structure. We end Section 2 with a brief account of our method. Section 3 describes a theoretical wage–price model that we find to have the potential to encompass both the empirical results of KP and the earlier results they rejected.

In Section 4, the model derived in Section 3 is estimated using both Norwegian and United Kingdom data. The empirical models are stable and convey partial structure in the form of identified cointegrated relations. The marginal analysis of these econometric models reported in Section 5 shows that the observed cross-correlations of macroeconomic variables depend entirely on the original source of the cyclical fluctuation. We argue that because observed business cycles during the past 50 years have arisen from many different sources, it is not surprising that it is possible to obtain apparently contradictory bivariate correlations. Furthermore, we are able to account for unstable correlations by means of stable econometric models. Section 6 offers a brief summary and conclusions.

2 Business-Cycle Analysis

We start by giving a critical account of the stylized-facts method and then sketch the ingredients in an alternative econometric approach to business-cycle analysis.

2.1 The KP Approach

The studies cited earlier generated cross-correlations from de-trended data using the HP filter, which identifies a time-varying trend based on the following minimization:

$$\min_{\tau_i} \sum_{t=1}^{T} (y_t - \tau_t)^2 + \lambda \sum_{t=2}^{T-1} [(\tau_{t+1} - \tau_t) - (\tau_t - \tau_{t-1})]^2 \qquad (1)$$

for $i = 1, \ldots, T$, where y_t is the series of interest, τ_t is the trend, and λ is a positive parameter to be determined.[3] The first part of equation (1) encourages the trend to follow the actual series, and the second part is minimized if the trend behaves smoothly. Several potential problems with the statistical properties of the filter have been discussed by King and Rebelo (1993), Harvey and Jaeger (1993), and Cogley and Nason (1995). For example, Cogley and Nason (1995) have shown that when applied to persistent data series, the HP filter can generate spurious cycles. This is worrisome, because experience shows that many macroeconomic series appear to be well approximated by stochastic trends. Despite these reservations, the filter can be useful in analyzing business cycles (see Section 4). Our point here is simply that its limitations need to be recognized, and interpretations adjusted accordingly.

Computing cross-correlations, at different leads and lags, is the second step in the stylized-facts method and is our main concern here. There is always a limit to the usefulness of bivariate correlation techniques, especially when dealing with two variables that are both endogenous to the macroeconomy. It is by no means obvious that real GDP should have a stable correlation coefficient with any of the variables examined by KP (production inputs, output and income components, monetary aggregates, the price level, real wages).

In the following, we concentrate on the cyclical properties of nominal wages and prices and of real wages. Our own computations of the GDP–inflation correlations show the expected instability and thus corroborate the findings of others (e.g., Andersen, 1994, fig. 2.2). The same

---

[3] Kydland and Prescott (1990, p. 8) concluded that $\lambda = 1600$ is a "reasonable" value for U.S. log GNP.

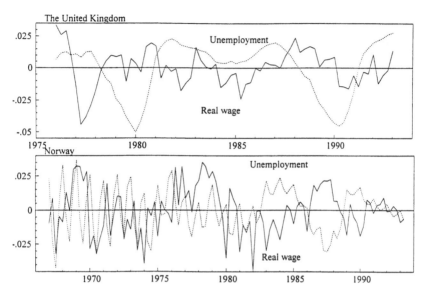

Figure 16.1. Deviations from HP trends for unemployment and real wage (scales adjusted).

is true for real wages and unemployment, which is more relevant in light of the model of price–wage adjustment discussed later. Figure 16.1 shows that HP cycles for consumer real wages and unemployment, using quarterly data for Norway and the United Kingdom.[4] We then consider the correlation between de-trended unemployment and real wages at time t and at four-period leads and lags of real wages. We compute *rolling* correlation coefficients, using a fixed window width of 32 quarters. The results of these exercises are reported in Figure 16.2. The correlation coefficients are numerically unstable, and they even change sign over the sample periods.

One might suspect that perhaps the window width of eight years is too small to obtain robust information. However, very little improvement in the results is obtained when the correlations are computed *recursively*, as Figure 16.3 demonstrates. One possible interpretation of graphs like Figures 16.2 and 16.3 is that there is little structure to discover; the cyclical properties of real wages evidently are very transient, and little can be learned, at least with linear models. However, that is too pessimistic, because bivariate correlations may actually hide structure. To see this, note that the correlation r_{yx}^2 can be written as

$$r_{yx}^2 = \hat{\beta}\hat{b} \qquad (2)$$

---

[4] In estimating the trends, we use $\lambda = 1600$.

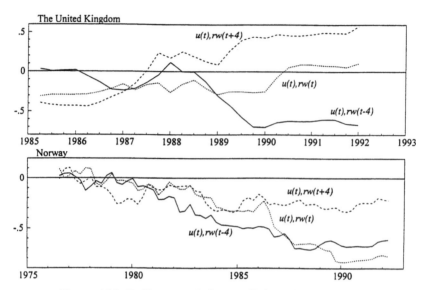

Figure 16.2. Rolling correlation coefficients between unemployment and real wage, using a window width of 32 quarters.

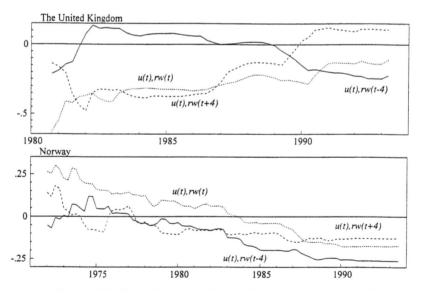

Figure 16.3. Recursive correlation coefficients between unemployment and real wage, using a starting period of 12 quarters.

where $\hat{\beta}$ is the OLS estimate from the regression model

$$y_t = \alpha + \beta x_t + \varepsilon_{w,t} \tag{3}$$

and $\hat{b}$ is the estimate from the inverse regression

$$x_t = a + by_t + \varepsilon_{y,t} \tag{4}$$

Instability in r_{yx}^2 does not in itself imply that $\hat{\beta}$ is recursively unstable – it is possible that all instability in the correlation coefficient is matched by the inverse regression estimate $\hat{b}$. In this (possibly rare) case, equation (3) is invariant to the regime shift made manifest by the instability in the correlation coefficient, and hence it can be claimed that equation (3) has a structural interpretation. Note that it is the occurrence of regime shifts that makes it possible to discover the structural nature of (3); hence they represent useful information, not a nuisance. Conversely, the correlation coefficient is nonstructural by definition and therefore is unlikely to be stable even when the underlying behavior is invariant.

In practice we shall not often expect to discover structure from simple bivariate regressions like equation (3). But the same logic holds for multivariate models, with r_{yx} interpreted as a partial correlation coefficient. Thus, changes in correlations are what make it possible to refute the idea that an estimated relationship represents structure (i.e., the relationship breaks down). Nonrejection of invariance over the sample strengthens the claim of a structural interpretation, although any invariance property of econometric models is always relative to a set of interventions; thus autonomy and structure are relative concepts (Haavelmo, 1944; Hendry, 1993).

2.2 A Macroeconometric Approach

In the rest of this chapter we set out to investigate whether or not econometrics can help resolve the puzzles that have arisen from modern business-cycle analysis and elucidate the cyclical properties of aggregate wages and prices. Before we set out, it may be helpful to summarize our approach under the following three headlines.

2.2.1 Multivariate Framework

We use a multivariate framework, as opposed to the KP bivariate framework. The outlines of the models that we estimate follow from a simple theoretical model discussed in Section 3. In economics we cannot carry out true laboratory experiments to isolate cause and effect. In interpreting the data, we need to allow for all possible influences – hence the prevalence of multivariate equation systems. As we shall see in Section 3, the observed correlations can depend entirely on the source of stochastic variation. In particular, the trend estimation using the HP filter smooths over different cycles, and the estimated correlation coefficients represent average relationships. Hence a demand-driven contraction is treated identically as a supply-driven contraction, even though the signs of bivariate correlations may be reversed.

2.2.2 Cointegration Analysis

Experience shows that actual data for wages and prices contain stochastic trends, in such a way that, for example, wages w_t are integrated of order 1, which we write as $w_t \sim I(1)$. Postulated relationships between $I(1)$ variables may prove to be spurious, but this possibility can be tested by using cointegration analysis (Engle and Granger, 1987; Johansen, 1988). In a multivariate setup there may be more than one relationship holding between the $I(1)$ variables; hence there is a problem of identifying the structural cointegration vectors, a problem that is related to Frisch's confluence analysis (Hendry and Morgan, 1989). Identification of cointegration vectors draws on the subject matter of economic theory and thorough testing of the relevant restrictions on the cointegration space (Johansen and Juselius, 1992). Inclusion of empirically valid long-run cointegration relationships in the model of cyclical price behavior is important for theory consistency, and it identifies a separate propagation mechanism: equilibrium correction with respect to underlying equilibrium relationships. Finally, inclusion of identified cointegrating relationships enhances structure, in that they remain invariant to expansions of the information set (e.g., Hendry, 1993; Banerjee et al. 1993, ch. 9.2).

2.2.3 Simultaneous-Equations Model

Embedding identified cointegration vectors in dynamic adjustment equations brings the analysis into $I(0)$ space and ensures economic interpretability and econometric stability of the steady state of the system. The importance of this stage thus lies in the possibility that the simultaneous-equations model can parsimoniously encompass the unrestricted reduced form (Hendry and Mizon, 1993; Bårdsen and Fisher, 1995).

3 A Theoretical Model of Wage–Price Adjustment

In this section we set out a simple model of wage and price interactions that might account for the correlation results reported by KP. We use a wage–price system for an open economy, based on theories of imperfect competition in goods and labor markets. The model is adapted from Kolsrud and Nymoen (in press), who discussed its dynamic properties in more detail. The variables used are nominal wages W, retail prices P, productivity *PR*, the import-price deflator *PI*, the unemployment rate *U*, the employers' tax rate *T*1, the income-tax rate *T*2, the tax rate on the retail price basket *T*3, and the deviation *gap* of output from the trend. Lowercase letters denote logs, except that (for convenience) $ti = \ln(1 + Ti)$, $i = 1, 3$, and $t2 = \ln(1 - T2)$.

Theories of wage formation (e.g., Carlin and Soskice, 1990; Lindbeck, 1993) state that the bargained nominal wage level depends on

- firm-side variables (e.g., productivity, producer prices, and the payroll-tax rate)
- factors affecting workers' take-home pay (e.g., consumer prices and the income-tax rate)
- labor-market pressure
- institutional features (e.g., the existence of centralized wage-bargaining institutions and the degree of mismatch)

These items are represented by the following textbook wage equation:

$$w_t^* = \alpha_1 pp_t + (1 - \alpha_1)p_t + \theta_1 pr_t - \beta_1 t1_t - \varkappa_1 t2_t - \zeta_1 u_t, \\ 0 \leq \alpha_1 \leq 1, \; \beta_1, \theta_1, \varkappa_1, \zeta_1 \geq 0 \tag{5}$$

We have in mind a loglinear relationship; hence w_t^* denotes the logarithm of the predicted wage level. The variables pp_t, pr_t, and $t1_t$ represent the firm-side variables. Institutional and structural features are reflected in the coefficients of (5). Changes in the impact of institutions on wage setting can therefore be tested by looking at the empirical stability of (5) over the sample period. To simplify the exposition, we shall, in the following, set $\theta_1 = 1$ and $\varkappa_1 = 0$. Both restrictions are tested and accepted for the empirical models in Section 4.

In an economy with imperfect competition, firms set their equilibrium prices to reflect a constant markup m_2 over normal unit-labor costs:

$$pp_t^* = m_2 + w_t - pr_t + t1_t \tag{6}$$

Equation (6) is kept deliberately simple. For example, the pricing-to-market hypothesis suggests that producer prices depend on competing prices in addition to unit labor costs (cf. Naug and Nymoen, 1996). However, in the following sections we focus on the modeling of consumer-price behavior, and in that equation a separate pricing-to-market coefficient would not be identifiable.

Wage growth is a function of expected-price growth, Δp_{t+1}^e and Δpp_{t+1}^e, and last period's deviation from the desired wage level [i.e., equation (5)]:

$$\Delta w_t = c_1 + \gamma_{1,1}\Delta p_{t+1}^e + \gamma_{1,2}\Delta pp_{t+1}^e - \delta_1(w - w^*)_{t-1} + \varepsilon_{1t}, \\ 0 \leq \gamma_{1,1} + \gamma_{1,2} \leq 1, \; \delta_1 \geq 0 \tag{7}$$

Superscript e denotes "expectation," and ε_{1t} is an error term. As already noted, integratedness of the price and wage series is an important assumption underlying our work. Consequently, Δw_t, Δp_{t+1}^e, and Δpp_{t+1}^e are all assumed to be stationary $I(0)$, and furthermore (7) can become a balanced equation only if $(w - w^*)_{t-1} \sim I(0)$; that is, the wage level predicted by theory is *cointegrated* with the actual wage level; see Banerjee et al. (1993) for an exposition. Conversely, the equilibrium-correction term $\delta_1 (w - w^*)_{t-1}$, with $\delta_1 > 0$, is implied by cointegration. Hence, in the empirical sections we first test that (5) is indeed a valid cointegrating equation before we proceed to the dynamic equation (7).

In the short run (i.e., the capital stock is fixed) the marginal-cost curve is upward-sloping, and hence an increase in output exerts a positive pressure on prices. The variable gap_t represents the deviation of log output from trend. In addition, product price inflation is governed by expected-wage growth in excess of productivity growth $\Delta (w - pr)_{t+1}^e$, as well as by corrections from last period's deviation from the equilibrium price:

$$\Delta pp_t = c_2 + \gamma_2 \Delta(w - pr)_{t+1}^e - \delta_2 (pp - pp^*)_{t-1} + \zeta_2 gap_{t-1} + \varepsilon_{2t}, \quad (8)$$
$$0 \leq \gamma_2 \leq 1, \delta_2, \zeta_2 \geq 0$$

Theoretical models of price adjustment under imperfect information lead to expressions similar to (8). For example, if the information setup is such that agents get to know the optimal full-information price only with a lag, then it is rational to adjust current prices with respect to the difference between the optimal and actual prices in period $t - 1$ (Andersen, 1994, ch. 6.3).

The model is closed in two steps. First, the import price in domestic currency pi_t is treated as exogenous in the consumer-price-index equation, together with the indirect-tax rate $t3_t$:

$$p_t = \eta pp_t + (1 - \eta) pi_t + t3_t, \quad 0 < \eta < 1 \quad (9)$$

Second, expectations develop according to

$$\Delta pp_{t+1}^e = \Delta pp_t$$
$$\Delta p_{t+1}^e = \Delta p_t \quad (10)$$
$$\Delta(w - pr)_{t+1}^e = \Delta(w - pr)_t$$

One interpretation of (10) is that forward-looking aspects of price and wage adjustments arise from data-based predictors rather than model-based (e.g., rational) predictors (Campos and Ericsson, 1988). For an integrated process x_t that is $I(d)$, a simple forecast is obtained from $\Delta^{d+1} x_{t+1} \approx 0$. For $d = 1$, that implies $\Delta x_{t+1}^e = \Delta x_t$ or that $x_{t+1}^e = x_t + \Delta x_t$. The term x_{t+1}^e is unbiased if Δx_t is $AR(q)$ with symmetrical error process, and can be "rational" if information is costly; see Hendry and Ericsson (1991) for a discussion. However, if agents do act on model-based expectations, (10) is obviously wrong, and the Lucas critique applies. Ultimately, it is an empirical question whether or not structural models must build on the theory of dynamic optimizing behavior and model-consistent rational expectations.

The theoretical model (5)–(10) is easily condensed to a simultaneous-equations model for wages and consumer prices:

$$\Delta w_t = -\delta_1[(w - p - pr) + (a_1 - \alpha_1)(pi - p) + \zeta_1 u \\ + \beta_1 t1 + a_1 t3]_{t-1} + c_1 + (\gamma_{1,1} + g_{1,2})\Delta p_t \\ - (g_{1,2} - \gamma_{1,2})\Delta pi_t - g_{1,2}\Delta t3_t + v_{wt} \quad (11)$$

$$\Delta p_t = -\delta_2[(1 - \eta)(p - pi) - \eta(w - p - pr + t1) - t3]_{t-1} \\ + \eta\zeta_2 gap_{t-1} + \eta(c_2 + \delta_2 m_2) + g_2\Delta(w - pr)_t \\ + (1 - \eta)\Delta pi_t + \Delta t3_t + v_{pt} \quad (12)$$

where $a_1 = \alpha_1/\eta$, $g_{1,2} = \gamma_{1,2}/\eta$, $g_2 = \gamma_2\eta$, $v_{wt} = \varepsilon_{1t}$, and $v_{pt} = \eta\varepsilon_{2t}$.

Equation (11) is a wage equation in the equilibrium-correction form introduced by Sargan (1964). We have derived it with reference to theories of wage bargaining. The equation also embodies earlier "conflict" theories of inflation (Nymoen, 1990, ch. 1). Equation (11) represents a generalization of conventional Phillips curves, entailing that the only wage-equilibrating mechanism is the rate of unemployment, where there is a unique natural rate of unemployment that depends only on the parameters of the wage and price equations. Equation (12) is a cost-markup price equation, where the markup is a positive function of output fluctuations.

The main relevance of the model (11) and (12) is that it implies that correlations between output and inflation, and between wages and unemployment, are *nonstructural* and will depend on where shocks arise and on the propagation mechanisms embodied in the model dynamics (Frisch, 1933).

As a reminder of the importance of the origin of shocks consider first the situation where markets are imperfectly competitive and prices exceed marginal costs, so that a positive *demand shock* might be expected to induce increased supply even at the initial price level. Hence, productivity will pick up, and this may induce an initial tendency for prices to be countercyclical. However, if the change in output then induces an increase in employment, unemployment will start to fall, wages will pick up, and eventually prices will also rise and inflation will become procyclical. Hence, in this scenario, both nominal and real wages are procyclical, but out of phase. However, these responses can be reversed if there is a strong effect of excess demand in price formation (e.g., if the demand shock occurs in a "heated" situation where marginal costs are rising very sharply). Excess demand will push up prices and wages, and we shall observe a *positive*, procyclical, correlation between inflation and output. Depending on the wage pressure stemming from reduced unemployment, real wages can go either way.

Suppose now that we see a *supply-side shock* that increases wage costs: c_1 goes up. Real wages rise, so employment and output fall. Prices will then catch up to restore profit margins, and eventually the system will revert either to the starting point or to a new natural rate, depending on the permanence of the shock – assuming a noninflationary policy response. We shall then have observed a *negative*, countercyclical, correlation between inflation and output.

A first point to make about propagation mechanisms is that an inherent property of dynamic systems is that the short-run response of an endogenous variable to a shock is different from the long-run response, determined by the steady-state solution of the system. To find the steady state in our case, we follow Kolsrud and Nymoen (in press) and solve for the *producer* real wage $w_{p,t} = w_t - pp_t - pr_t$ and the real exchange rate $pi_{p,t} = pi_t - pp_t$. Kolsrud and Nymoen (in press) showed that the producer real wage $w_{p,t}$ is negatively related to unemployment in the medium run. However, if $0 \leq \alpha_1 < 1$, the steady-state producer real wage is shown to be independent of the level of unemployment. In other words, the predicted short-run responsiveness of producer real wages is larger than long-run responsiveness. The same is true for inflation: A negative short-run effect from a rise in unemployment follows directly from markup pricing. However, in a steady state we have, by definition, $\Delta pi_p = \Delta pi - \Delta pp = 0$, and thus $\Delta p = \Delta pi$, saying that inflation is unresponsive to unemployment and the output gap in the long run, despite being positively related to domestic-demand pressure in the short and medium terms. As a final example, anticipating the analysis of the empirical models later, consider the steady-state solution for *consumer* real wages[5]

$$(w - p - pr) = \frac{c_1/\delta_1 + \alpha_1(c_2/\delta_2 + m_2)}{1 - \alpha_1} - \frac{1}{(1 - \alpha_1)\delta_1}\Delta pr$$

$$- \frac{(1 - \gamma_{1,1} - \gamma_{1,2})/\delta_1 + [(1 - \gamma_2)\alpha_1]/\delta_2}{1 - \alpha_1}\Delta pi \qquad (13)$$

$$- \frac{\zeta_1}{1 - \alpha_1}u + \frac{\alpha_1 - \beta_1}{1 - \alpha_1}t1$$

The degree of long-run real-wage responsiveness to unemployment is

$$\zeta_1/(1 - \alpha_1)$$

Depending on the structural parameters, this magnitude can be larger or smaller than the degree of short-run responsiveness $\delta_1\zeta_1$. The latter case

---

[5] That is, for fixed growth rates of productivity (Δpr) and import prices (Δpi), fixed tax rates t_1 and t_3, constant rate of unemployment, and *gap* = 0.

is referred to as "wage hysteresis," following Nickell (1987), and is seen to be encompassed by our model of wage–price dynamics.

Within this framework we can conclude that there is no unique correlation between output fluctuations and price inflation or between unemployment and real wages. Both the source of shocks and the persistence of the shocks matter. This result is hardly new (e.g., Andrews et al., 1985) and could be stated for any (pairwise) correlation between price and quantity.

In the following we investigate the idea that simple and aggregate systems of equations can encompass any "fact" based on filtering and cross-correlations. In order to demonstrate this in practice, the two next sections present estimation and simulation results based on Norwegian and United Kingdom data.

4 Econometric Wage and Price Models for the United Kingdom and Norway

In this section we summarize the results from applying the macroeconometric approach set out in Section 2.2 to the modeling of open-economy wages and prices. Elsewhere (Bårdsen, Fisher, and Nymoen, 1998) we have analyzed the wage–price process in Norway and the United Kingdom. We rely heavily upon the econometric results from that paper to illustrate our points.

4.1 The United Kingdom

In the data set for the United Kingdom, the wage variable, w, is average actual earnings. The price variable, p, is the retail-price index, excluding mortgage interest payments and the "community charge." The nonmodeled variables consist of employers' taxes $t1$, indirect taxes $t3$, mainland productivity pr, import prices pi, the unemployment rate u, and a measure of the output gap (gap) approximated by mainland GDP cycles estimated by the HP filter. Finally, two dummies are included to take account of income policy events – see the Appendix for precise details.

The estimated equilibrium of the model, by means of the Johansen procedure, is given as

$$w = p + pr - t1 - 0.065u + \text{constant} \tag{14a}$$

$$p = 0.89(w + t1 - pr) + 0.11pi + 0.6t3 + \text{constant} \tag{14b}$$

Wages are homogeneous in consumer prices. The elasticity of productivity is also unity. According to (14), all changes in employers' taxes ($t1$) are reflected in wages in the long run. The estimated wage-moderating effect of unemployment seems reasonable, compared to what others have found for U.K. manufacturing data. For example, Rowlatt [1987, eq.

Table 16.1. *The Model for the United Kingdom*

The wage equation

$$\widehat{\Delta w_t} = \underset{(0.075)}{0.187}\Delta w_{t-1} + \underset{(0.039)}{0.332}(\Delta_2 p_t + \Delta pr_t) - \underset{(0.100)}{0.341}\Delta^2 t1_t$$
$$- \underset{(0.064)}{0.162}\Delta_2 t3_t - \underset{(0.023)}{0.156}(w_{t-2} - p_{t-2} - pr_{t-1} + t1_{t-2} + 0.065 u_{t-1})$$
$$+ \underset{(0.071)}{0.494} + \underset{(0.003)}{0.013}BONUS_t + \underset{(0.001)}{0.003}IP4_t$$

$\hat{\sigma} = 0.45\%$

The price equation

$$\widehat{\Delta p_t} = \underset{(0.149)}{0.963}\Delta w_t - \underset{(0.118)}{0.395}\Delta pr_t + \underset{(0.059)}{0.153}\Delta(p + pr)_{t-1} - \underset{(0.019)}{0.044}\Delta u_{t-1} + \underset{(0.092)}{0.536}\Delta t3_t$$
$$- \underset{(0.047)}{0.480}\left[p_{t-1} - 0.89(w + t1 - pr)_{t-2} - 0.11 pi_{t-2} - 0.6 t3_{t-1}\right]$$
$$+ \underset{(0.099)}{0.238}gap_{t-1} - \underset{(0.131)}{1.330} - \underset{(0.005)}{0.019}BONUS_t - \underset{(0.001)}{0.005}IP4_t$$

$\hat{\sigma} = 0.71\%$

Diagnostic tests
Overidentification $\chi^2(16) = 24.38\ [0.08]$
AR1–5 $F(20, 94) = 0.97\ [0.50]$
Normality $\chi^2(4) = 3.50\ [0.48]$
Heteroskedasticity $F(84, 81) = 0.63\ [0.98]$

Notes: The sample is 1976(3) to 1993(1), 67 observations. Estimation is by FIML. Standard errors are in parentheses below the estimates. The symbol $\hat{\sigma}$ denotes the estimated percentage residual standard error. The *p* values for diagnostic tests are in brackets.

(20)] implied a long-run elasticity of −0.08, whereas for Nickell [1987, eq. (22)] the estimate is −0.104 (i.e., for a fixed long-term unemployment proportion). The appearance of the rate of unemployment u_t in (14a) is consistent with $u_t \sim I(1)$ and cointegrating with wages, prices, and productivity. On the other hand, if w_t, p_t, and pr_t cointegrate, u_t can nevertheless be in the levels part of the wage model, as a separate $I(0)$ variable, which is also consistent with (14a).

According to equation (14b), prices are partly adjusted for changes in the indirect-tax rate. Furthermore, prices are set as a weighted average of markup over labor costs and import prices. Compared with the corresponding Norwegian estimates presented later in equation (15), it is interesting to note how the size and therefore the openness of the economy are reflected in this weighted average.

The estimated dynamic model for the United Kingdom is given in Table 16.1, and Figure 16.4 shows one-step residuals and residual standard errors – $\{y_t - \hat{\beta}_t x_t\}$ and $\{\pm 2\hat{\sigma}_t\}$ in standard notation – for each equation. The third panel records Sargan's (1964) test of overidentifying restrictions against its 5 percent critical value for every sample size [1976(3)–1984(3), 1976(3)–1984(4), . . . , 1976(3)–1993(1)]. Following

Business Cycles: Facts or Fallacies? 513

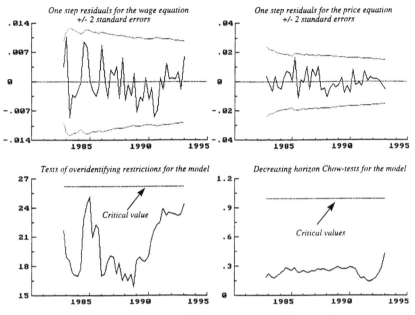

Figure 16.4. Recursive stability tests for the U.K. model.

Hendry and Mizon (1993), the interpretation of an insignificant Sargan statistic is that the model in Table 16.1 encompasses the underlying VAR system. Finally, the fourth panel shows the "breakpoint" Chow statistic for the sequence [1984(3)–1993(1), 1984(4)–1993(1), ..., 1992(4)–1993(1), 1993(1)] for the model in Table 16.1.

The model in Table 16.1 is estimated by FIML. The model equilibrium is incorporated into the dynamic model as equilibrium-correction terms to represent the adjustment to disequilibria, and their importance is clearly shown. In addition to the equilibrium-correction term, wages are driven by growth in consumer prices over the last two periods and by productivity gains. With an elasticity estimate of 0.66 and a standard error of 0.039, short-run homogeneity is clearly rejected. The negatively estimated coefficient for the change in the indirect-tax rate ($\Delta t3_t$) is surprising at first sight, but inspection of (11) shows that the result is in accordance with theory: Consumer prices respond when the tax rate is increased [cf. the price equation (12)], which in turn is passed on to wages. Hence, the net effect of a discretionary change in the indirect-tax rate on wages is estimated to be effectively zero in the short run and positive in the intermediate and long terms. The effect of an increase in the payroll-tax rate is to reduce earnings, both in the short and long terms.

According to the second equation in Table 16.1, prices respond sharply (by 0.96 percent) to a 1 percent change in wage costs. Hence short-run homogeneity is likely to hold for prices. In addition to wage increases and equilibrium-correction behavior, price inflation is seen to depend on the output gap, as captured by the variable *gap*.

Finally, note that the two income policy dummies, *BONUS* and *IP4*, are significant in both equations, albeit with different signs. Their impact in the first equation is evidence of wage-raising income policies, and their reversed signs in the price equation indicate that these effects were not completely anticipated by price-setters.

The diagnostics reported at the bottom of Table 16.1 give evidence of a well-determined model. In fact, Figure 16.4 shows that the model encompasses the underlying system for almost every sample size. Hence the model constitutes a valid parsimonious model of the underlying reduced-form system. The diagnostics are vector tests and hence multivariate tests on the residuals of the model; see Doornik and Hendry (1994) for details.

4.2   Norway

In the Norwegian data set, the wage variable w is average hourly wages in the mainland economy (i.e., excluding the North Sea oil-producing sector and international shipping). The productivity variable pr is defined accordingly. The price index p is measured by the official consumer-price index, and pi again denotes import prices. The unemployment variable u is defined as a "total" unemployment rate (i.e., including labor-market programs).

The other nonmodeled variables are normal working time h_t and the indirect-tax rate $t3$. The change in the length of the working day Δh_t captures wage compensation for reductions in the length of the working day (Nymoen, 1989b). Income policies and direct price controls have been in operation on several occasions during the sample period. Two intervention variables, *WD* and *PW*, and one impulse dummy, $d80q2$, are used to capture the impact of these policies. Finally, $d70q1$ is a VAT dummy. We use seasonally unadjusted quarterly data, so the estimated model includes three seasonal dummies ($S_i, i = 1, 2, 3$).

Cointegration analysis yields the following estimated long-run relationships:

$$w = p + pr - 0.08u + \text{constant}$$

$$p = t3 + 0.65(w + t1 - pr) + 0.35pi + \text{constant}$$

which are remarkably close to the corresponding results for the United Kingdom. The import-price index is attributed a larger weight in the Norwegian price equation, which is reasonable. It is interesting that the estimated unemployment elasticity is only marginally larger (in absolute value) than in the United Kingdom model. This finding contradicts the widely held view that Nordic wages are extremely responsive to changes in unemployment; see the elasticities reported by Layard, Nickell, and

Table 16.2. *The Estimated Model for Norway*

The wage equation

$$\widehat{\Delta w_t} = \Delta p_t - \underset{(0.027)}{0.104}\Delta_2(w - p - pt)_{t-1} - \underset{(0.035)}{0.104}\Delta pi_t - \underset{(0.190)}{0.728}\Delta(t1_t + t1_{t-2})$$
$$- \underset{(0.085)}{0.496}\Delta t3_{t-2} - \underset{(0.102)}{0.294}\Delta h_t - \underset{(0.0193)}{0.131}[(w - p - pr)_{t-2} + 0.08 u_{t-1}]$$
$$- \underset{(0.016)}{0.106} + \underset{(0.009)}{0.027} D80q2_t - \underset{(0.004)}{0.021} WD_t - \underset{(0.010)}{0.046} D70q1_t + \underset{(0.003)}{0.021} PD_{1t}$$
$$- \underset{(0.005)}{0.022} S_{1t} + \underset{(0.008)}{0.041} S_{2t} + \underset{(0.005)}{0.009} S_{3t}$$

$\hat{\sigma} = 0.92\%$

The price equation

$$\widehat{\Delta p_t} = \underset{(0.015)}{0.115}\Delta[w_t + (w - 0.5pr)_{t-1}]$$
$$- \underset{(0.008)}{0.090}[p_{t-3} - 0.65(w_{t-3} + t1_{t-3} - pr_{t-2}) - 0.35 pi_{t-1} - t3_{t-2}]$$
$$+ \underset{(0.016)}{0.066} gap_{t-1} + \underset{(0.001)}{0.013} + \underset{(0.004)}{0.050} D70q1_t - \underset{(0.002)}{0.013} PD_{1t}$$
$$- \underset{(0.002)}{0.001} S_{1t} - \underset{(0.002)}{0.004} S_{2t} - \underset{(0.002)}{0.005} S_{3t}$$

$\hat{\sigma} = 0.39\%$

Diagnostic tests
Overidentification $\chi^2(41) = 36.31$ [0.68]
$AR1-5\ F\ (20, 162) = 0.97$ [0.51]
Normality $\chi^2(4) = 3.78$ [0.44]
Heteroskedasticity $F\ (168, 99) = 0.84$ [0.85]

Notes: The sample is 1967(4) to 1993(2), 103 observations. Estimation is by FIML. Standard errors are in parentheses below the estimates. The symbol $\hat{\sigma}$ denotes the estimated percentage residual standard error. The p values for diagnostic tests are in brackets.

Jackman (1991, ch. 9, table 2). Our estimates correspond much better with those of Nymoen (1990, table 4.1), who estimated a long-run elasticity of -0.13 on a similar aggregate data set. Johansen (1995) found the same long-run wage responsiveness to unemployment as we do, albeit for annual observations of manufacturing wages. Earlier models of manufacturing wages had obtained somewhat stronger wage responsiveness; Nymoen [1989a, eq. (16)] reported the estimated elasticity as -0.21, and Calmfors and Nymoen (1990, table 7) found -0.17 on annual data.

The estimated dynamic model is shown in Table 16.2. There is considerable within-sample constancy, as Figure 16.5 shows. This suggests invariance to such "shocks" as the credit-market liberalization that occurred in the early 1980s, the 50 percent reduction in oil prices in 1986, and the changes in exchange-rate regime in the late 1980s.

The *wage equation* in Table 16.2 imposes short-run homogeneity with respect to consumer prices. At first glance this suggests real-wage rigidity. However, closer inspection of the equation shows that this is not the case in general: The wage equation includes an indirect-tax rate with a

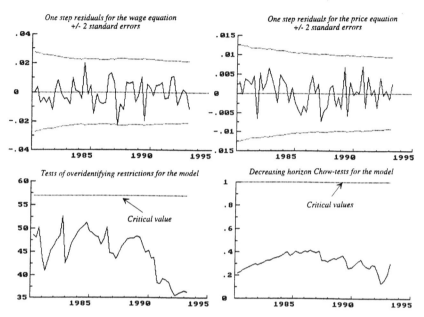

Figure 16.5. Recursive stability tests for the Norwegian model.

negative sign, a negative coefficient of the VAT dummy ($D70q1_t$) and (ceteris paribus) positive effects of price controls (PD_t). Hence discretionary policies have clearly succeeded in affecting consumer real-wage growth over the sample period. However, without such policies, Norwegian aggregate wages *do* seem to react very quickly to "normal" or expected consumer-price increases. Import-price growth is likely to be the most important "unexpected" part of price inflation, so given the unit coefficient on Δp_t, it is not surprising that Δpi_t is attributed a negative estimated coefficient. The equilibrium-correction term is highly significant, with a t value of -6.8. Finally, the change in normal working time Δh_t enters as expected in the wage equation (i.e., with a negative coefficient).

From the second part of Table 16.2 we find that, in addition to equilibrium correction and the dummies representing income policy, price inflation is significantly influenced by wage growth and excess demand. The overall speed of adjustment seems to be slower for Norwegian consumer prices than for U.K. retail prices.

5   Simulating the "Stylized Facts"

The estimated wage–price models described in the preceding section are stable, data-coherent models estimated by FIML. The models can be thought of as the structural forms of restricted open VAR systems. The

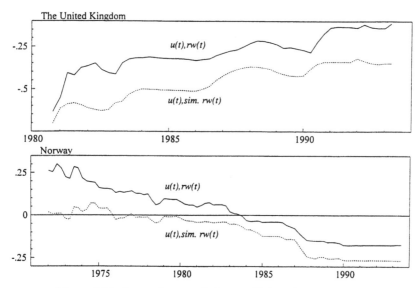

Figure 16.6. Recursive correlation coefficients between unemployment and real wage, and between unemployment and simulated real wage, using a starting period of 12 quarters.

nonmodeled variables are unemployment, productivity, import prices, and tax rates on employment and consumer prices. In this section the relevance of the estimated structure (propagation) and the importance of the nonmodeled variables (impulses) are illustrated with the aid of simulation exercises. First, Section 5.1 demonstrates the models' ability to match both sample paths and moments. Against that background, Section 5.2 shows how different paths of the nonmodeled variables can generate different correlations in the data.

5.1 Matching Trends and Moments

An econometric model of $I(1)$ variables that is data-coherent must reproduce the trends in the modeled variables: nominal prices and wages. Given the homogeneity restrictions, the models must also track the trend in the implied real wage $w_t - p_t$. Hence, dynamic simulation of the two models produces a "good fit" for the real wage in the two countries, reflecting the numerical as well as statistical significance of the nonmodeled variables in Tables 16.1 and 16.2.

It is less obvious that econometric models will necessarily reproduce those features of the data that were not taken into account during the modeling process. Hence we attempt to reproduce the nonconstancy of the bivariate correlations using the dynamic-simulation results for real wages. This is demonstrated in Figure 16.6, which shows how the models reproduce the recursive correlation coefficients. The instability of the bivariate correlations is just as evident with the simulated data from the two constant-parameter models, thus illustrating the nonstructural nature of "stylized facts."

5.2 Matching Correlations with the Cycle

The high contributions from the nonmodeled variables to the close match between the predicted and observed correlations make it interesting to examine the partial dynamic responses of earnings, prices, and real wages to shocks in these "exogenous" variables. The nonmodeled variables are by no means independent of each other, and this makes the partial responses something of a thought experiment rather than a realistic counterfactual simulation. Nevertheless, the results prove to be a useful diagnostic in understanding why certain cross-correlations are observed.

We have undertaken a variety of simulations and report just two. Both can be thought of as resulting from a cycle in output taking the form of a sine wave with a 1 percent amplitude, with the period of the cycle (frequency) to be varied:

1. a cosine wave in the log of the unemployment rate, with amplitude of 10 percent – hence a 1 percent amplitude in the level of the rate around a base value of 10 percent unemployment – for the United Kingdom, and with an amplitude of 5 percent for Norway. This implicitly assumes that the output cycle is totally reflected in employment, with no change in recorded productivity.
2. a sine wave in recorded productivity, with an amplitude of 1 percent. This implicitly assumes that employment and hence unemployment remain constant.

Ideally we would use a closed macroeconomic model to isolate the independent sources of economic fluctuations (changes in policy variables, external events, demographic and technology trends, etc.). However, that would serve to cloud the issue, and we concentrate on the transmission of real shocks to prices, which covers some of the major debating points when examining business-cycle correlations. To complete this assumption and to preserve homogeneity in nominal variables, we assume that import prices remain fixed to their foreign-currency values (p^f) and that the exchange rate (ex) adjusts instantaneously to changes in domestic prices. This allows us to substitute out the import price for domestic prices plus a real-exchange-rate term (rex). Effectively, we are introducing a third equation ($pi_t = p_t^f - ex_t \equiv p_t + rex_t$).

The wavelength of the shock is variable. The current cycle in most western countries will have a period not far short of 10 years, and so this

Business Cycles: Facts or Fallacies? 519

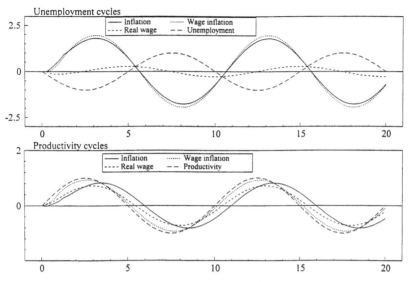

Figure 16.7. Unemployment and productivity 10-year cycles in the U.K. model.

is our base case. But some cycles are shorter, and so we have experimented with the case of four cycles in 10 years as well.

5.2.1 The United Kingdom

Taking the United Kingdom 10-year cycle in unemployment first, unemployment is negatively correlated with price and wage inflation. The real wage is relatively constant and is out of phase (Figure 16.7). When the input cycle is productivity, then both wage and price inflations are procyclical but weaker, and the real-wage response is procyclical and significantly larger. Hence the correlation of cycles in activity with cycles in the real wage depends entirely on whether or not fluctuations in output lead to fluctuations in employment or measured productivity.

The results of a shorter input cycle are depicted in Figure 16.8. Taking the unemployment cycle first: Price and wage inflations are now so much out of phase that they appear to lead unemployment. Real wages are still countercyclical, but out of phase compared with the pattern for the long input cycle in Figure 16.7. As regards the productivity cycle, the real-wage response is now practically zero.

These results are sufficient to demonstrate that the correlations of endogenous variables are sensitive to the nature of the shock, including the periodicity. Further experiments with other shocks, such as the real exchange rate or an autonomous shock to wages, demonstrate that a wider range of correlations is possible. We also note in passing that the

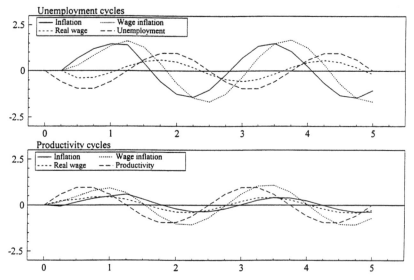

Figure 16.8. Unemployment and productivity 2.5-year cycles in the U.K. model.

results depend slightly on whether the input cycle is started up from cold or is the continuation of an existing cycle.

5.2.2 *Norway*

Having demonstrated the sensitivity of partial correlations within one country, the main interest in examining a second country is the fact that we have similar structures yielding different results. The inflation responses in Norway are smaller, despite very similar long-run elasticities (by constraining the real exchange rate to be constant)[6] and a large *real-wage* response. The dynamics of the response are also much more lagged.

Comparing Figures 16.7 and 16.9 we find that the inflation response is more vigorous for the United Kingdom, and the real-wage response is stronger and procyclical in Norway. Note that this emerges despite the fact that the long-run wage responses are estimated to be quite similar in both systems. This highlights the importance of considering both wage and price formations when predicting real-wage behavior over the cycle. The more muted responsiveness in U.K. real wages is explained by our estimation results. In terms of the structural parameters in equations (11)

---

[6] The smaller shock compensates for the nonlinearity in the association of output with the unemployment rate. But this does not explain the totality of the smaller inflation response.

Business Cycles: Facts or Fallacies? 521

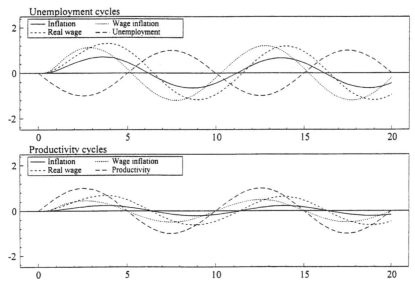

Figure 16.9. Unemployment and productivity 10-year cycles in the Norwegian model.

and (12), the estimation results tell us that the price equilibrium correction δ_2 and the simultaneous pass-through of wages on prices g_2 are much higher in the United Kingdom than in Norway. Conversely, expected inflation has a greater impact ($\gamma_{1,1} + g_{1,2}$) on Norwegian wages than on U.K. wages. As a result, U.K. nominal wage claims are almost instantaneously canceled by price adjustment. Against the background of a more open economy and the institutional setup in Norway (e.g., more centralization and coordination), this explanation has some credibility.

In summary, these diagnostic simulations confirm that even when underlying behavior is invariant, we can expect to observe quite different correlations of macroeconomic variables over the business cycle, depending on the nature and source of the shocks that disturb the system.

6   Discussion and Summary

A set of "stylized facts" in the form of univariate and bivariate moments summarizes salient properties of marginal and bivariate distributions that are of interest to business-cycle analysis. A primary use of the correlations is the calibration of real-business-cycle (RBC) models. They represent key "facts" that the theoretical model of interest should be able to account for.

Calibration gives rise to a range of methodological and technical issues (e.g., the absence of measures of sampling uncertainty and of statistical-evaluation criteria), and on several fronts progress appears to have been made; see Canoe, Finn, and Pagan (1994), Eichenbaum (1995), and Wickens (1995) for discussion. So far, less attention has been paid to the validity of the assumption that the correlations are stable over time. Therefore, a new kind of problem is posed by the empirical instability of the correlations, which has now been demonstrated for several of the correlations used for the evaluation of RBC models; see the results for price/wage output correlations by Blackburn and Ravn (1992), Englund et al. (1992), and Andersen (1994, pp. 18–19), as well as our own results for Norway and the United Kingdom in Section 2. An immediate concern is that reliance on the correlations per se in RBC analysis is apt to generate fragile results. Indeed, as pointed out by Hendry (1995), the current practice of matching subsets of moments that are inherently nonconstant induces a sample-dependence problem for the very models that originated from a desire to avoid exactly this difficulty.

We have concentrated on the correlations (r_{yx}) between real wages and the unemployment cycle and have demonstrated that econometric modeling can determine (partial) structure and resolve the puzzle of unstable r_{yx} values. A simple theory model of wages and prices that allows imperfect competition elucidates why there is no reason to expect a consistent pattern of bivariate correlations. Each cycle is likely to reflect different shocks to the economic system – both the signs and magnitudes of the correlations will depend on the implicit shocks. The textbook suggestions of procyclical price variations originate from analysis of demand-led business cycles. Some of the recent cycles in many countries appear to have had major contributions from external or supply-side shocks. It is therefore hardly surprising that observations from different samples yield different bivariate correlations.

The real issue of interest is to identify which shocks cause which correlations and how these combine to explain the historical record. There is more than one possible approach to resolve this question. We have chosen the route of specifying and estimating structural econometric models, based on the encompassing of VAR systems. We have focused on the responses of nominal variables to real shocks; hence we have constructed partial wage and price systems for the United Kingdom and Norway.

Our econometric estimates yield stable, data-coherent models that, as we show, are able to explain the unstable observed correlations in the data sample. For several of the key parameters, the estimates for the United Kingdom and Norway are surprisingly similar in appearance. Simulation results from the estimated models reveal that the observed correlations between the cycle, inflation and real wages will depend entirely on the nature of the real shock – we concentrate on whether the output shock affects productivity or unemployment. The correlation also depends on the frequency of the shock and varies across countries because of the different dynamic adjustment processes.

These results demonstrate that even when the underlying behavior is invariant, we cannot expect to observe consistent pairwise correlations either in macroeconomic time series or in cross-country comparisons. It is nevertheless possible to capture such complicated movements in the data by the use of systems-of-equations models, ideally in a closed model of the macroeconomic system.

Appendix: Data Definitions

Small letters denote the natural logarithms of the variables.

A.1   United Kingdom

All variables are seasonally adjusted except for the retail-price index. ONS is the Office for National Statistics (formerly the CSO).

W	wages: index of actual quarterly average earnings. ONS identifier DNAB.
P	Retail-Price Index. ONS identifier CHAW.
PR	non–North Sea productivity. ONS identifiers CKJL/DYDC.
PI	price deflator for expenditure on imported goods and services. ONS identifiers DJBC/DJDJ.
U	unemployment rate: registered number of unemployed. ONS identifier BCJE.
gap	output gap defined as log of non–North Sea GDP (NNO) deviations from trend, where the trend is estimated by the HP filter using $\lambda = 1600$. ONS identifier for NNO: CKJL.
T1	employers' tax rate: $(GTAY + AIIR + TSET)/[34.203 * DNAB * (BCAD + BCAH)/1000]$, which are ONS identifiers apart from *TSET*, which is receipts of selective employment tax. *GTAY* and *AIIR* give employers' National Insurance and other contributions, and the last term gives the aggregate employed salary bill.
T3	tax rate on the Retail-Price-Index basket, excluding mortgage interest payments. This tax rate is derived from the Bank of England's spreadsheet for construction of RPIY (Beaton and Fisher, 1995).
BONUS	impulse dummy for retimed bonus payments brought forward one month before a general election; takes the value 1 in 1992(1) and −1 in 1992(2).

*IP*4   income policy dummy; zero after 1979(2). Source: Whitley (1986).

A.2   Norway

W   nominal mainland hourly wages. Source: Quarterly National Accounts (QNA).

P   Consumer-Price Index; 1991 = 1. Source: Norges Bank's database of economic time series.

PR   mainland-economy value added per man-hour at factor costs; million 1991 Norway krone (NOK). Source: QNA.

PI   deflator of total imports; 1991 = 1. Source: QNA.

gap   output gap defined as mainland GDP deviations from trend, where the trend is estimated by the HP filter using $\lambda = 1600$; million 1991 NOK. Source: QNA.

*T*1   employers' tax rate. Source: RIMINI database. RIMINI is the Central Bank of Norway's quarterly econometric model.

U   rate of unemployment: registered unemployed plus persons on labor-market programs as a percentage of the "labor force." The labor force is calculated as employed wage earners plus unemployment. Source: QNA and RIMINI database.

*T*3   indirect-tax rate. Source: RIMINI database.

H   normal working hours per week.

*D*80*q*2   dummy for lifting of wage freeze; 1 in 1980(2), zero otherwise.

WD   composite dummy for wage freeze; 1 in 1979(1), 1979(2), 1988(2), and 1988(3).

*D*70*q*1   VAT dummy; 1 in 1970(1), zero otherwise.

PD   composite dummy for introduction and lifting of direct price regulations; 1 in 1971(1), 1971(2), 1976(4), 1979(1); −1 in 1975(1), 1980(1), 1981(1), 1982(1); zero otherwise.

References

Aldrich, J. (1989). Autonomy. *Oxford Economic Papers* 41:15–34.

Andersen, T. M. (1994). *Price Rigidity. Causes and Macroeconomic Implications*. Oxford: Claredon Press.

Andrews, M. J., Bell, D. N. F., Fisher, P. G., Wallis, K. F., and Whitley, J. D. (1985). Models of the UK economy and the real wage employment debate. *National Institute Economic Review* 112:41–52.

Banerjee, A., Dolado, J. J., Galbraith, J. W., and Hendry, D. F. (1993). *Cointegration, Error Correction and the Econometric Analysis of Non-stationary Data.* Oxford University Press.

Bårdsen, G., and Fisher, P. G. (1995). The importance of being structured. Arbeidsnotat 1995/2, Research Department, Central Bank of Norway.

Bårdsen, G., Fisher, P. G., and Nymoen, R. (1998). Modelling wages and prices in the United Kingdom and Norway. Unpublished manuscript.

Beaton, R., and Fisher, P. G. (1995). The construction of RPIY. Working paper series 28, Bank of England.

Blackburn, K., and Ravn, M. O. (1992). Business cycles in the United Kingdom. *Economica* 59:383–401.

Brandner, P., and Neusser, K. (1992). Business cycles in open economies: stylized facts for Austria and Germany. *Weltwirtschaftliches Archiv* 128:67–87.

Calmfors, L., and Nymoen, R. (1990). Nordic employment. *Economic Policy* 5:397–448.

Campos, J., and Ericsson, N. R. (1988). Econometric modeling of consumers' expenditure in Venezuela. International finance discussion paper 325, Board of Governors of the Federal Reserve System.

Canoe, F., Finn, M., and Pagan, A. R. (1994). Evaluating a real business cycle model. In: *Nonstationary Time Series Analysis and Cointegration*, ed. C. P. Hargreaves, ch. 8. Oxford University Press.

Carlin, W., and Soskice, D. (1990). *Macroeconomics and the Wage Bargain.* Oxford University Press.

Cogley, T., and Nason, J. M. (1995). Effects of the Hodrick-Prescott filter on trend and difference stationary time series: implications for business cycle research. *Journal of Economic Dynamics and Control* 19:253–78.

Correia, I. H., Neves, J. L., and Rebelo, S. (1992). Business cycles from 1850 to 1950: new facts about old data. *European Economic Review* 36:459–67.

Danthine, J. P., and Girardin, M. (1989). Business cycles in Switzerland: a comparative study. *European Economic Review* 33:31–50.

Doornik, J. A., and Hendry, D. F. (1994). *PcFiml 8.0: Interactive Econometric Modelling of Dynamic Systems.* London: International Thomson Publishing.

Eichenbaum, M. (1995). Some comments on the role of econometrics in economic theory. *Economic Journal* 105:1609–21.

Engle, R. F., and Granger, C. W. J. (1987). Co-integration and error correction: representation, estimation and testing. *Econometrica* 55:251–76.

Engle, R. F., Hendry, D. F., and Richard, J.-F. (1983). Exogeneity. *Econometrica* 51:277–304.

Englund, P., Persson, T., and Svensson, L. E. O. (1992). Swedish business cycles: 1861–1988. *Journal of Monetary Economics* 30:343–71.

Ericsson, N. R., and Irons, J. S. (1994). *Testing Exogeneity.* Oxford University Press.

Frisch, R. (1933). Propagation problems and impulse problems in dynamic economics. In: *Economic Essays in Honour of Gustav Cassel*, pp. 171–205. London: George Allen and Unwin.

  (1938). Statistical versus theoretical relationships in economic macrodynamics. Memorandum, *League of Nations.* Reprinted in *Autonomy of economic relationships*, memorandum 6. November 1948. Oslo: Universitetets Socialøkonomiske Institutt.

(1948). Repercussion studies at Oslo. *American Economic Review* 38:367–72.

Granger, C. W. J. (1990). General introduction: Where are the controversies in econometric methodology? In: *Modelling Economic Series. Readings in Econometric Methodology*, ed. C. W. J. Granger, pp. 1–23. Oxford University Press.

Haavelmo, T. (1944). The probability approach in econometrics. *Econometrica (Suppl.)* 12:1–118.

Harvey, A. C., and Jaeger, A. (1993). Detrending, stylized facts and the business cycle. *Journal of Applied Econometrics* 8:231–47.

Hendry, D. F. (1993). The roles of economic theory and econometrics in time series econometrics. Paper presented at the European meeting of the Econometric Society, 1993.

(1995). Econometrics and business cycle empirics. *Economic Journal* 105:1622–36.

Hendry, D. F., and Ericsson, N. R. (1991). Modelling the demand for narrow money in the United Kingdom and the United States. *European Economic Review* 35:833–81.

Hendry, D. F., and Morgan, M. (1989). A re-analysis of confluence analysis. *Oxford Economic Papers* 41:35–52.

Hendry, D. F., and Mizon, G. E. (1993). Evaluating dynamic econometric models by encompassing the VAR. In: *Models, Methods and Applications of Econometrics*, ed. P. C. B. Phillips, pp. 272–300. Oxford: Basil Blackwell.

Johansen, K. (1995). Norwegian wage curves. *Oxford Bulletin of Economics and Statistics* 57:229–47.

Johansen, L. (1977). *Lectures on Macroeconomic Planning. 1. General Aspects.* Amsterdam: North Holland.

Johansen, S. (1988). Statistical analysis of cointegration vectors. *Journal of Economic Dynamics and Control* 12:231–54.

Johansen, S., and Juselius, K. (1992). Testing structural hypotheses in a multivariate cointegration analysis of the PPP and the UIP for UK. *Journal of Econometrics* 53:211–44.

King, R. G., and Rebelo, S. T. (1993). Low frequency filtering and real business cycles. *Journal of Dynamics and Control* 17:207–31.

Kolsrud, D., and Nymoen, R. (in press). Unemployment and the open economy wage–price spiral. *Journal of Economic Studies*.

Koopmans, T. C. (1947). Measurement without theory. *Review of Economic Statistics* 29:161–72.

(1949). The econometric approach to business cycle fluctuations. *American Economic Review* 39:64–72.

Kydland, F. E., and Prescott, E. C. (1990). Business cycles: real facts and a monetary myth. *Federal Reserve Bank of Minneapolis*.

(1991). The econometrics of the general equilibrium approach to business cycles. *Scandinavian Journal of Economics* 93:161–78.

Layard, R., Nickell, S., and Jackman, R. (1991). *Unemployment*. Oxford University Press.

Lindbeck, A. (1993). *Unemployment and Macroeconomics*. Massachusetts Institute of Technology Press.

Morgan, M. S. (1990). *The History of Econometric Ideas*. Cambridge University Press.

Morgan, M. S., and Hendry, D. F. (1995). *The Foundations of Econometric Analysis*. Cambridge University Press.
Naug, B., and Nymoen, R. (1996). Pricing to market in a small open economy. *Scandinavian Journal of Economics* 98:329–50.
Nickell, S. (1987). Why is wage inflation in Britain so high? *Oxford Bulletin of Economics and Statistics* 49:103–28.
Nymoen, R. (1989a). Modelling wages in the small open economy: an error-correction model of Norwegian manufacturing wages. *Oxford Bulletin of Economics and Statistics* 51:239–58.
   (1989b). Wages and the length of the working day: an empirical test based on Norwegian quarterly manufacturing data. *Scandinavian Journal of Economics* 91:599–612.
   (1990). *Empirical modelling of wage-price inflation and employment using Norwegian quarterly data*. Ph.D. thesis, University of Oslo.
Pagan, A. (1987). Three econometric methodologies: a critical appraisal. *Journal of Economic Surveys* 1:3–24.
Rowlatt, P. A. (1987). A model of wage bargaining. *Oxford Bulletin of Economics and Statistics* 49:347–72.
Sargan, J. D. (1964). Wages and prices in the United Kingdom: A study of econometric methodology. In: *Econometric Analysis for National Economic Planning*, ed. P. E. Hart, G. Mills, and J. K. Whitaker, pp. 25–63. London: Butlerworth.
Schlitzer, G. (1993). Business cycles in Italy: a retrospective investigation. Temi di discussione 211, Banca d'Italia.
Whitley, J. D. (1986). A model of incomes policy in the UK 1963–79. *Manchester School* 44:31–64.
Wickens, M. (1995). Real business cycle analysis: a needed revolution in macroeconomics. *Economic Journal* 105:1637–48.

PART SEVEN

MACROECONOMIC PLANNING

CHAPTER 17

The Influence of Ragnar Frisch on Macroeconomic Planning and Policy in Norway

Petter Jakob Bjerve

1   Introduction

To understand why and how Ragnar Frisch influenced macroeconomic planning and policy, his basic political and professional views must be kept in mind. He was very critical toward the free market system, about which he expressed moral indignation. Thus in 1932 he observed that "it is an unworthy situation that people amidst a world of real abundance shall live in an economic system that with regular intervals creates suffering and anxiety for almost all groups of the population" (Frisch, 1932a, p. 139). In 1949 he made the observation that "the mass unemployment prevailing in most countries during the 1930s, led to a monstrous situation. Standards of living declined in the midst of plenty. Food and other consumption goods were deliberately destroyed while people hoped and prayed that something would turn up that would finally allow them to use their own labour for the satisfaction of their own wants" (Frisch, 1949b, p. 4). Such situations had to be prevented by "some sort of overall national planning," without which a "simultaneous realization of social justice and a high rate of economic growth is impossible" (Frisch, 1963a, p. 21).

Frisch was convinced that to make such a combination possible, economists could play a major role. Their role should be to clarify the state of the economy and to explore the means required to achieve goals determined by policy-makers. Economists should not impose their own preferences upon the politicians. He emphasized the moral importance of this distinction in many contexts. Already in one of his early courses at the University in Oslo, Frisch urged the students to distinguish sharply between scientific statements and value judgments. His presentation of

---

My sincere thanks to the many Norwegian economists who commented on drafts of this essay. I benefited from their experience in planning and policy, in particular, when reformulating the section on macroeconomic planning models. They also suggested a number of improved formulations. In this respect I am greatly indebted to Olav Bjerkholt for his help.

this issue, influenced by Max Weber, made a strong impression on many of his students and was later incorporated in his textbook on production theory (Frisch, 1946a, pp. 7–10; 1965a, pp. 5–8). It had an important impact as a moral guide for their advice on government policy.

The main professional interest of Frisch was economic theory, and he preferred to spend his time on theoretical work. He used to illustrate his policy function in military terms: He should himself represent the "heavy artillery," and his pupils were the "infantry" or "foot soldiers." His influence on policy should be exerted through his pupils. They should be armed with the best possible tools for design of policy. After the Second World War the theory of macroeconomic policy decisions became his major interest.

The influence of Frisch on macroeconomic planning and policy in Norway was manifest in several ways. One was the development of conceptual systems (Section 2). Results from that activity were instrumental in preparing numerical national accounts and corresponding projections designated "national budget" (Section 3). Frisch followed up his conceptual work by constructing macroeconomic models that can be regarded as precursors of the system of models applied by the Norwegian government today (Section 4). In addition, he exerted important personal policy influence through his students by teaching and organization of research and through politicians by disseminating economic information and by advisory activities (Section 5). Ragnar Frisch had extraordinary vision and ambition, as revealed by confrontations with reality (Section 6). The economic effects of the influence of Frisch are not discussed.

2 Conceptual Systems

In 1932, Ragnar Frisch, in his inaugural lecture as a professor at the University of Oslo, predicted that "we shall obtain a theory which is sufficiently complicated to be able to serve as a recipient for the concrete observation material and at the same time we shall obtain observations which are explicitly planned and carried out with the object of fitting them into the theoretical structures" (Frisch, 1932b, p. 100). In accordance with that vision he worked to develop three different systems of macroeconomic concepts.

The first system was presented in 1939 at a meeting of Nordic statisticians. The purpose of the system was to facilitate a numerical description of the economic structure of Norway. Three years later he published another system whose original purpose was to provide definitions of relationships in macroeconomic theory. That was designated the economic-circulation system (Ecocirc system). A third system, published in 1952, was intended to provide definitional relationships for analyses of monetary liquidity and was presented as an accounting system for the financial transactions between different sectors of the Norwegian economy. At that time he had worked on macroeconomic concepts and their relationships since the late 1920s.

2.1 *Structural National Accounts*

In 1936 Frisch published, together with two colleagues, a plan for a structural survey of the Norwegian economy. In a section of that plan, obviously written by Frisch, the purpose of national accounting was defined as "coordinating the most important data to be collected for the structural survey in such a manner that they appear as parts of a whole. The national accounts shall provide the same kind of survey for the entire country as that which the balance account and the profit and loss account of the ordinary bookkeeping provides for the individual establishment. Thus, it is the economic viewpoint of the establishment that appears in the forefront" (Frisch, Keilhau, and Wedervang, 1936, p. 29). This implied that the economic structure was to be described in great detail. Funds were granted, and in 1937 work on structural national accounts began at the Institute of Economics, University of Oslo, under the supervision of Frisch. He had two to four assistants at his disposal, mainly for data work.

According to the report on the Nordic meeting, Frisch stated that in 1939 the conceptual work was far advanced, whereas empirical work had been limited mainly to an exploration of the data sources available (Frisch, 1940).[1] The conceptual system arrived at was very ambitious. Three examples may illustrate this:

1. Regarding valuation of the entries to be included in the national accounts, Frisch mentioned three principles that were of particular interest (viz., actual costs, market prices, and discounted value of prospective results). Basically the accounting would be made at actual costs, but a system of supplementary accounts would indicate income and wealth according to the two other principles of valuation.
2. Each establishment would be cross-classified by industry and the form of its organization. For industry classification, a standard developed by the League of Nations would be applied. The classification by organizational form was developed by the Insti-

---

[1] At that meeting, Frisch presented quite an advanced definition of national accounting: "By national accounts we mean not only a survey of national income in a certain year and the national wealth at a given point of time, but a fairly complete survey of the entire economic activity in a year, presented in such a manner that the relationships in which we are particularly interested, show up by the necessity of bookkeeping. For instance, the change of wealth shall by bookkeeping necessity conform with the data on income, consumption and saving" (Frisch, 1940, pp. 141–2).

tute of Economics. Each cell of the cross-classification was designated a structural sector, which again might be divided into so-called individual sectors. (For some sectors, even a classification of establishments by size might be attempted.)
3. For each sector, large or small, data would be organized by a standard system of "business accounts." Two main characteristics of this system are mentioned in the report, namely, that it had separate accounts for real and for financial stocks and flows, and that production accounts would show value added as a balancing item. In total the system consisted of 127 accounts summarized into 14 main accounts. Data for the country as a whole would be obtained by adding up pyramidically the accounts for all structural sectors. These data would, inter alia, provide information for each of a large number of sectors on the national product broken down by consumption, internal net investment, and net investment abroad. In addition, opening and closing balances would show data on both real and financial capital broken down by kind.[2]

The system was never published in all its detail, but typewritten presentations are available at the Institute of Economics. These presentations show that Frisch was ahead of his time in several respects, inter alia, by making the distinction between institutional (organizational) and functional (industrial) sectors, by distinguishing sharply between real and financial stocks and flows, and by introducing the concept of human capital (Bjerve, 1940, p. 84).

2.2 The Ecocirc System

In 1933 Ragnar Frisch recommended the establishment of national accounts "to get a basis for evaluating the real economic weight of the arguments that are being made in the economic debate" (Frisch, 1933b, p. 36). Thus the purpose of the accounts envisioned at that time was macroeconomic analysis. He dealt with this in several series of lectures (during 1928–29, 1933–34, 1935, and 1940), in the introduction to his famous Cassel article (Frisch, 1933a), in a seminar during the spring of 1942 with several university teachers participating, and afterward in a number of meetings with some of them. Finally, in the fall of 1942 major

---

[2] At the time when numerical national accounting was initiated in accordance with the system described, Frisch had developed a simpler conceptual system that was presented in mimeographed form: Et generelt monetært begrep- og symbolsystem (A general monetary system of concepts and symbols). This system would have been suitable as a framework for calculating data for the purpose of macroeconomic analysis, but for the structural survey a much more detailed system was chosen.

Table 17.1. *A Simplified Version of the Ecocirc System for the Real Economy*

Entries	Production Debit	Production Credit	Utilization of resources Debit	Utilization of resources Credit	Application of income Debit	Application of income Credit	Increase in capital Debit	Increase in capital Credit
Gross product		A	A					
Input of commodities	H			H				
Value added	E					E		
Depreciation					D			D
Gross investment			J				J	
Consumption			C		C			
Real tax			T		T			
Net export surplus			A^{ex}				A^{ex}	
Saving					S			S
Sum	$H + E = A$		$A = H + J + C$ $+ T + A^{ex}$		$D + C + T + S$ $= E$		$J + A^{ex} = D$ $+ S$	

Note: In this table, $E - D$ = net product R; $J - D$ = net investment; A^{ex} = exports A^{ex+} − imports A^{ex-}.

conclusions were summarized in a mimeographed presentation (Frisch, 1942). The conceptual system arrived at was the Ecocirc system. A detailed description of the development of this system has been presented (Bjerve, 1986, 1996).

A simplified version of the Ecocirc system is exhibited in Table 17.1, which shows a set of accounts, the column sums of which indicate major definitional relationships.[3] All entries in these accounts represent flows of real objects (i.e., objects that would exist even in an economy without ownership). The stock of such objects is designated real capital K. The Ecocirc system also includes concepts and definitional relationships for stocks and flows of financial objects (i.e., objects that would not exist in an economy without ownership). This system is designed analogously with the system of real concepts. The financial flows are symbolized by boldface letters (e.g., **R** for net financial income). The stock of financial objects is designated financial capital **K**. The most interesting definitional relationships, including both real and financial concepts, are the following:

Real capital K + Financial capital **K** = Total capital
Net real product R + Net financial income **R** = Total income
Net real investment I + Net financial investment **I** = Total investment
Net real saving S + Net financial saving **S** = Total saving

[3] Frisch also exhibited these relationships by means of a graph (the Ecocirc graph).

Total investment + Total capital gains + Total revaluation of capital = Increase in total capital

In developing the Ecocirc system, Frisch emphasized the need for standardization "aiming at several things: the logical content of the concepts, the terminology, the mathematical presentation by means of letters and formulas, the presentation by an Ecocirc-Graph, and finally the bookkeeping by means of a system of accounts" (Frisch, 1942). Such a standardization might facilitate comparison of the conceptual systems of different authors. Perhaps Frisch even hoped that his standardized concepts would be adopted by other theorists. Some comparisons were actually made (Bjerve, 1944a,b).

The Ecocirc system presented in 1942 was designed so as to be applicable for any economic sector. It did not show intersectoral (from whom to whom) flows, for instance, flows between government and other sectors. This weakness was partly remedied in 1948 by a new version of the Ecocirc system that had separate accounts for the private sector and government sector (Aukrust, Bjerve, and Frisch, 1948a). Consequently, that version also included transfer of income between the two sectors and the concept of disposable income. That change had already been made in 1946 by the Ministry of Finance (Finans- og tolldepartementet, 1946, p. 11).

The Ecocirc system may be regarded as an aggregate form of the structural accounts described earlier, implying far lower data requirements for calculation of numerical national accounts. But Frisch probably felt that a conceptual system of this kind, which he had developed quite far already in 1935, would not be suitable for structural analysis.

2.3   *Intersectoral Financial Accounts*

Frisch dealt with conceptual systems for the accounting of financial stocks and flows, both during the 1930s and after the war. Most of that work, in contrast to the two other systems, was aimed at showing the flows between major sectors of the economy, calculated as net changes in the financial stocks. At the end of 1932 he prepared a memorandum in which he, inter alia, by means of two alternative tables, demonstrated how the increase in deposits and the increase in loans for the banking system as a whole were related to each other and were dependent upon the change in cash holdings by the public (Frisch, 1951a, pp. 3, 11–19). One of his conclusions was that if the cash holdings were constant, an increase in loans would create an equally large increase in deposits. If the increased lending resulted in greater productive activity, the cash holdings were likely to be augmented, and consequently the deposits would increase correspondingly less than the loans. In lectures later in the 1930s Frisch dealt with such relationships by applying a simple system for financial accounting, with separate accounts for government,

Bank of Norway, other banks, and a residual sector. The financial flows included, inter alia, the increases in loans, deposits, and cash holdings. By means of that system, he demonstrated, inter alia, that increased lending might create increased deposits and that a government deficit-financed by internal loans would not increase the net debt for the country as a whole.

After the war, systems of financial accounts were developed further. In the spring of 1946 Frisch was approached by the Ministry of Finance for advice on the development of financial accounts. The outcome was a dummy table in which changes in financial assets and liabilities were cross-classified by type and major sectors of the economy. Calculation of these changes was also attempted, but without success. For such a purpose, concepts and classifications of the credit-market statistics at that time differed too much for different groups of credit institutions, and even for some institutions within the same group.

In the early 1950s, Frisch, in cooperation with Arne Amundsen, prepared a more advanced system of intersectoral financial accounts (Frisch, 1952b). A simplified version is presented in Table 17.2, where claims of each sector are indicated in the columns, and debts are indicated in the rows. The upper part of the table shows domestic, and the lower part foreign, claims and debts and cash. In addition, he presented an identical cross-classification for the *grants* of credit, so that for each sector the sum of all kinds of grants could be added to the total net claims and cash. Subclassifications for the government sector, the banks, and other sectors were also presented. Data for 1948 were roughly calculated by Arne Amundsen, but he concluded that sufficiently reliable data could not be obtained until a coordination of the statistics on claims and debts had been carried out.

2.4 *Evaluation*

It may seem surprising that Frisch spent as much energy as he did over a long period of time developing conceptual systems that today may appear trivial. However, in the 1930s such systems were being discussed at length by other macroeconomic theorists. In particular, the relationship between investment and saving was often confused.

The conceptual contribution of Frisch to national accounting was parallel to similar efforts by outstanding economists in other countries, for instance, M. Copeland, S. Kuznets, and W. Leontief in United States, C. Föhl and E. Schneider in Germany, J. M. Keynes in the United Kingdom, and E. Lindahl in Sweden. But Frisch, already in his 1928–29 lectures, had succeeded in defining a system of macroeconomic concepts that in essence anticipated modern national accounts (Bjerve, 1996, p. 4). In the 1930s he developed that system further, inter alia, by making the distinction between real and financial stocks and flows and between institutional and functional sectors. After the war the major ideas of his

538   **Petter Jakob Bjerve**

Table 17.2. *Changes in Claims and Debts by Kind and by Sector*

Financial objects	Sectors				
	Government	Bank of Norway	Other banks	Other sectors[a]	All sectors

Internal claims
  Government
  Bank of Norway
  Other banks
  Other sectors[a]					

Total internal claims					

Net internal claims
  (sum of columns
  minus sum of rows)
Norwegian claims on
  foreign countries
–Foreign claims on Norway
Notes (including gold
  and coins)					

Total net claims and cash					

[a] Including government enterprises.

Ecocirc system reached economists beyond Norway and indirectly led to a revision of the United Nations standard national accounts in 1968 (Aukrust, 1994, pp. 52–3).

In Norway, the conceptual systems of Frisch provided definitions and definitional relationships required for building the macroeconomic models to be discussed later. Moreover, they improved macroeconomic thinking, not only of economists but also among policy-makers and others. In those ways the systems had an important impact on Norwegian planning and policy.

3   Utilization of the Systems of Concepts

3.1   *Numerical National Accounts*

The numerical work on structural national accounts was discontinued when the university was closed by the German occupation authorities in the fall of 1943 and was not resumed after the liberation of Norway. When evaluating the results of that work, Frisch concluded that "it was never completed in the sense that it covered the entire economy, but for some sectors numerical accounts were prepared, and for the sector 'official and semi-official banks' the results were particularly satisfactory" (Frisch, 1948a, p. 2). In fact, only a very small part of the economy was covered by data, mostly for one year, and a printed publication was issued only for shipping (Rossen, 1942).

For a strange reason, calculations based on the Ecocirc system could, in the fall of 1943, be initiated by the Central Bureau of Statistics (recently renamed Statistics Norway). At that time the occupation authorities had requested the bureau to provide data that after a German victory could justify claims against the Allies for war damage in Norway. Thereby the director of the bureau, Gunnar Jahn (who was a top member of the secret resistance movement) felt authorized to initiate calculations of the annual national product by industry for 1935 and subsequent years and calculation of the reduction in real capital from 1939 on caused by war damage and significant German appropriation of Norwegian resources.

For that work, a group of recently graduated economists was recruited. All of them had thorough knowledge of the Ecocirc system, and two had even worked for Frisch both on structural accounting and on the Ecocirc system. This explains why, in addition to the national product and the reduction in real capital, calculations were made for exports and imports, the German use of goods and services, and the residual consumption (public and private) for the years 1940–43. Thus, more comprehensive data than originally envisaged were calculated for both supply and demand of resources in that period (Statistisk Sentralbyrå, 1946). Those data enabled the Ministry of Finance, after the war, to calculate ever more detailed numerical national accounts as a basis for its national budgeting, to be described later.

Parallel with those calculations, the Central Bureau of Statistics was developing new and much more detailed numerical national accounts. Data from those accounts were published in 1952, replacing the calculations of the ministry. The new accounts were also designed in conformity with the Ecocirc system, but in addition the input–output work of Wassily Leontief and the national accounts designed by Richard Stone were used. For prospective planning it was particularly important that they included annual interindustry tables prepared as an integral part of the national accounts (Bjerkholt, 1995). Those tables, and a much more detailed table later prepared for 1954, were utilized for work on planning models, both by Frisch and by the research department of the bureau. (The national accounts were extended from covering 34 production sectors for 1948 to 123 sectors for 1954.) The new accounts did not include data on intersectoral financial flows.

3.2   *The National Budget*

In February 1946 the Ministry of Finance presented to the Storting (parliament) a white paper on the national budget (i.e., a budget for the country as a whole, projecting major magnitudes of the national accounts) (Finans- og tolldepartementet, 1946). The budget was based on national-accounts data for 1944, calculated in cooperation with the Central Bureau of Statistics, and included alternative projections of the national product and its major components for 1946 and for the period 1946–50. Its purpose was to provide a basis for the design of macroeconomic policy during the years of reconstruction.

Additional national budgets for 1947 and subsequent years were prepared in much greater detail and applied both for design of policy and for coordination of the many policy instruments that were used in the postwar economy, and they were presented to the Storting as annual programs for macroeconomic policy. The preparation of these budgets was to a large degree delegated to the ministries in charge of macroeconomic policy instruments. They elaborated so-called sub-budgets in conformity with the Ecocirc system, and these were submitted as policy proposals to the Ministry of Finance, which in turn adjusted them so as to fit into the national budget as a whole. The final decisions on these adjustments were made by the cabinet in cooperation with the ministries concerned, after deliberations in a cabinet committee. This method of successive approximations toward the final national budget by means of decentralized administrative adjustments was applied in the elaboration of 14 annual national budgets and three so-called long-term programs (which in fact represented national budgets for periods of four years).

After that decentralization of national budgeting, the Ecocirc system became an important means of making the various sub-budgets consistent. In each ministry taking part in the budgeting process, economists with thorough knowledge of the system either carried out the budgeting themselves or were given sufficient logical control of this work. The concepts and definitions of the Ecocirc system were in a sense a common language understood by all civil servants involved.

3.3   *The Credit Sub-budget*

Because of the lack of coordinated credit-market statistics, many years passed before financial sub-budgets could be included in the national budget. Such coordination was initiated by the Central Bureau of Statistics in 1952. Standards were prepared for the definition and classification of claims and debts by type, and of debtor and creditor sectors by kind of economic activity. Those standards were made obligatory for all institutions that supplied data for credit-market statistics. Thereby the different types of such statistics could be combined and coordinated within a comprehensive system of financial accounts, and quite reliable data could be obtained. Among the information provided were data on the change in total loans issued by all credit institutions, broken down by groups of such institutions and by debtor sectors.

In a preface to the publication in which standardized credit-market statistics were first published, the bureau acknowledged that "the accounting framework is greatly influenced by the theoretical work of Professor Ragnar Frisch on the financial circulation analysis" (Statistisk Sentralbyrå, 1957, p. 6). In fact, the main difference compared with the accounting system presented in Table 17.2 was a more detailed classification of sectors and of claims and debts.

The standardized credit-market statistics enabled the Ministry of Finance to present, from the end of 1955, annual credit sub-budgets of the national budget. Those budgets indicated the maximum increase in loans that the major groups of credit institutions were allowed to issue and were used as a basis for direct control of credit, as long as such control was maintained.

3.4 Evaluation

Even though Frisch was not successful in his attempts at establishing numerical national accounts, his conceptual systems, in particular the Ecocirc system, promoted the work on numerical national accounts in the Central Bureau of Statistics and on the national budget in the Ministry of Finance. Without the Ecocirc system, the national budget could not have been initiated as early as it was, and consequently the coordination of macroeconomic policy instruments could not have become as effective as it actually turned out during the first postwar years.

Evaluating this influence of Frisch, one must be aware that Norwegian economists during the war did not receive information on the development of national accounts in Anglo-American countries. Without the work of Frisch, they would, at the end of the war, have been several years behind in applying such accounts as a basis for planning and policy.

Frisch neither established the organization of national budgeting nor developed the method of successive administrative approximations for such budgeting. Work on the national budget was initiated by Erik Brofoss, the minister of finance of the first Labour government after the war. He was a pupil of Frisch and learned about the Ecocirc system and the existing national-accounts calculations after his return in 1945 from London, where he was a department chief in the Norwegian government administration in exile, and where he most likely got information on macroeconomic projections made by the British government (Bjerve, 1991). However, the designation "national budget" for such projections was coined by Frisch and suggested to Brofoss either directly or indirectly.[4]

---

[4] Frisch coined the terms "national accounts" and "national budget" in respectively 1933 and 1940, as the first in Norway, if not in the world. He used the designation "national accounts" in Frisch (1993b, p. 36) and "national budget" at a staff meeting on January 29, 1940, from which a record exists.

4   Macroeconomic Models

Planning in the form of national budgets was for many years carried out entirely by means of the administrative method. During the 1950s, interindustry tables of national accounts were utilized to improve some of the administrative calculations, though not to replace them. Replacement began in 1960 by means of model computations. From then on, a gradual transition took place by using numerical models in the national budgeting instead of the administrative method, although not entirely. That development was, during the first couple of postwar decades, indirectly influenced by Frisch, partly by way of his models and partly by his training of and cooperation with model builders in the Central Bureau of Statistics and the Ministry of Finance.

4.1   *The Frisch Models*

Frisch was clearly pleased with the national budgeting. In an address at the beginning of 1947, he said that "at present the national budget plays a very large role in the whole financial policy of our country." As a result of national accounting work, "the foundation was laid and trained personnel available" at the time when the national budgeting "was launched on a large scale by our Ministry of Finance in 1945" (Frisch, 1947, p. 1). In addition, he mentioned that the Institute of Economics had begun work on a project to "find out what will happen when certain measures, such as fiscal measures or definite wage policies or the like, are applied to the economic system." He further observed that the studies were "modelled over the burning economic problems of our Norwegian community today" and that "most important, is the analysis of the *structural relations* that connect these various variables in the national budgeting system."

Important progress on that project was made during 1947 and 1948. At that time Frisch was a member of the United Nations Subcommission on Employment and Economic Stability.[5] At a meeting of that group in the fall of 1947 he became dissatisfied with the discussion, which, in his opinion, focused too much on "the evils of inflation." He felt that to improve the debate a macroeconomic model ought to be presented to the subcommission (Bjerve, 1989, p. 198). At the next meeting, in the spring of 1948, Frisch presented a note, "A System of Concepts describing the Economic Circulation and Production Process" (Aukrust et al.,

---

[5] At the end of 1946, the government appointed Frisch as the Norwegian member of the UN Commission for Economy and Employment, of which he was elected chairman. That commission, at a meeting in the middle of 1947, established two subcommissions, one on employment and economic stability. Frisch became a member of that subcommission, but was not elected its chairman.

1948a). Probably as a justification for that note he later explained that the work at the Institute of Economics on conceptual systems "had all the time been inspired by the idea that this was only a stepping stone to a study of the *structural* relations (production relations, consumption relations etc.) of the economy" (Frisch, 1948a, p. 3).

At the end of 1948, Frisch published a first model, the main purpose of which was analysis of the effects of changed price subsidies, clarifying the "*numerical relationships* existing between price level, subsidies, income distribution etc." (Frisch, 1948b, p. 1). That model consisted of 20 variables between 13 independent definitional relations (i.e., the model had 7 degrees of freedom).[6] A few months later Frisch completed a considerably extended model including both definitional and structural relationships, later designated "the Submodel" (Frisch, 1949a). A paper describing that model was presented to a meeting of the subcommission in the spring of 1949, but the participants showed no enthusiasm for it.

Frisch did not attend subsequent UN meetings, but concentrated on model work. In the fall of 1949 he gave a brief progress report admitting that the model system developed thus far was simple and that the data used were in part only rough estimates, "yet the system does give valuable information of a kind hitherto not available,... extensive tables have been computed which indicate what effects are to be expected on various aspects of the Norwegian economy if a given system of price-wage-tax-subsidy measures is applied" (Frisch, 1949b).

In February 1950 he presented a plan for future model work, organized by projects such as indicated in Table 17.3, informing that the Central Bureau of Statistics would cover projects 2B and 3, in cooperation with the Institute of Economics[7] (Frisch, 1950a, p. 3). That had already been discussed with the director of the bureau, who was interested in such an arrangement. Frisch would himself be in charge of the theory of models, and the institute would be responsible for projects 1A, 1B, and 2A.

The model aimed at was then designated the "decision model," which he later defined as "a theoretical model supported by empirical evidence and constructed with the specific object in mind of discussing the probable consequences of alternative courses of action" (Frisch, 1955, p. 4), and still later as "an analytical framework to achieve *coordination* and *system* in the many-sided discussions on basic goals of economic policy

---

[6] At that time a change in the existing price subsidies in Norway was a major policy issue, and a committee had been appointed to clarify the problems implied by that policy (Aukrust, Haavelmo, and Hiorth 1948b).

[7] Frisch strongly supported the establishment of a research department in the bureau in 1950. Building numerical planning models was from the beginning a major objective of that department, and development of statistics required for such modeling became an important objective for the other departments.

Table 17.3. *Projects for Work on Decision Models*

Theory of the decision model	1. The consumption economy	1A. Mathematical-statistical computations on consumption and labor input
		1B. Investigations by surveys on consumption and labor input
	2. The production economy	2A. Investigations on the production elasticities in individual industries
		2B. Interindustry analysis
	3. The monetary economy	3. Circulation of financial objects

and the means (instruments) that can be used for realizing these goals" (Frisch, 1958, p. 277).

Cooperation between the Institute of Economics and the Central Bureau of Statistics became quite close from the early 1950s onward. Soon it was extended to the Ministry of Finance, whose main role was to clarify how the models should be constructed in order to improve national budgeting. Frisch was instrumental in organizing this tripartite cooperation. He initiated the establishment of several committees for this purpose, and a large number of meetings were held. Quite often Frisch himself took an active part in them. Thereby he received factual information from the two other parties, and they in return were informed about the work going on at the institute and were stimulated by contact with Frisch (Bjerkholt and Longva, 1980, pp. 12–14).

Frisch had a relatively large staff assisting him in model building during the 1950s and early 1960s. Most assistants were doing numerical work (including collection of data) and elaborating classifications, but some were also doing more advanced analysis.[8] Three major numerical models were constructed, subsequent to the Submodel:

1. the Median model (Frisch, 1956)
2. the Refi model (Frisch, 1959a)
3. the Channel model (Frisch, 1960)

Those models had definitional relationships corresponding to those of the new national accounts and structural relationships for production that were estimated on the basis of the input–output data for these

---

[8] In the middle of 1952 as many as six research associates were engaged in such work. In addition, a clerical staff carried out extensive computations for the purpose of model building.

accounts. The Median model, in addition, had structural relationships for the consumption by different groups of households. The Refi model was extended to include financial definitional relationships of the kind that Frisch had published in 1952 and structural relationships that enabled analyses of the financing of real investments, which had to be exogenously determined. The Channel model also had investment relationships required to determine real investments endogenously (Edvardsen, 1970; Frisch, 1959a, 1960). Those models were considerably more detailed and required more data than the numerical models presented by other economists at that time, such as those by J. Tinbergen and H. Theil.

From the mid-1950s onward Frisch became more and more interested in supplementing his models with macroeconomic preference functions to avoid reliance on target-setting, which he felt was a primitive way of planning.[9] As a consequence, he engaged himself heavily in programming techniques for solving the equation systems of such models, not only the linear programming developed by Dantzig and others but also more complex methods.

None of the macroeconomic models constructed by Frisch was directly used in designing policy. For such a purpose their structural relationships were too roughly calibrated. To a large extent the parameters required were guessed. Frisch used to consult economists both at the institute and in the government on such parameters, often about their probable upper and lower limits. Then he used the numbers that he found most reasonable. Frequently he used alternative sets of numbers in order to determine which of them would generate the most realistic results. Frisch was not interested in accuracy, but first and foremost in obtaining the parameters desired.

He also made attempts at statistical data collection. Thus the institute conducted a household survey by means of interviewers, but returns were obtained from far fewer respondents than anticipated. Technical data collected from establishments and technicians were used for estimating production functions, and an investigation of private investment in real capital was made on the basis of the official manufacturing statistics (Sevaldson, 1953). When interindustry data became available, Frisch made extensive use of them, but most of the other data that he applied for estimation of structural relationships were rather unreliable.

4.2   *Separate Production and Consumption Models*

In the early 1950s the Central Bureau of Statistics invited Frisch to a meeting to discuss the model building at its research department. He was

---

[9] According to Johansen (1973), one reason for that change in interest was that Frisch "considered the problem of avoiding depressions as solved and raised the ambitions to a higher level."

informed that the department planned to develop, first, a production model based on interindustry tables and, later, hopefully, engage in the building of additional partial models. Frisch objected to such a step-by-step strategy. He was in favor of a more general approach, developing a comprehensive model system and estimating all its structural relations.[10] Nevertheless, Frisch, to a considerable extent, assisted the bureau in its model work.

In 1951, experimental-model computations were carried out using an interindustry table for 1938 (Aukrust and Frisch, 1951). As soon as such a table for 1948 was completed and arranged in nearly triangular form by the Central Bureau of Statistics, an inversion of it was carried out. Later, Frisch showed how the inverted matrix could be used in analysis and planning by calculating the effects on production and imports of given alternative changes in consumption, investment, and exports (Frisch, 1952c).[11] Similarly, the price consequences of alternative changes in cost components were computed. The results of those computations were presented in the form of tables that Per Sevaldson later designated "tables of effects." Such tables were frequently used by the Ministry of Finance to improve the reliability of national budget calculations. Toward the end of the 1950s, input–output computations were made to check the consistency of such calculations.

During most of the 1950s the Central Bureau of Statistics focused its model building on use of the interindustry tables (Bjerve, 1954). Comprehensive analyses were made in order to clarify the theoretical and empirical validity of the assumptions on which the interindustry analysis was based (Sevaldson, 1960). The leader of that project, Per Sevaldson, had worked for Frisch as a student. After years of preparation he developed a comprehensive production model based on an interindustry table for 1954. In 1954 the bureau recruited Arne Amundsen, who for five years had worked under Frisch. He developed a model of private consumption based partly on household surveys carried out by the bureau and partly on national-accounts data, utilizing a method developed by Frisch (Amundsen, 1957). Both of those models were, to some degree, used for national budgeting in the late 1950s in order to improve

---

[10] This attitude was similar to that characterizing his prewar attempt at preparing numerical national accounts. In both cases he was overambitious. It reflected a difference of attitude between Frisch and the bureau toward reliability of the data to be used. Whereas Frisch, as just mentioned, did not care much about reliability, the bureau naturally wanted to base its models on statistics of relatively high reliability.

[11] The inversion of the 34-sector interindustry table for 1948 was carried out by the Institute of Economics and the Central Bureau of Statistics in cooperation, each institution being responsible for about half of the computations. Two operators in each institution completed the operation in two weeks, using electric desk calculators (already at that time Frisch expressed great interest in the new electronic computers available in the United States).

the estimates of some national budget entries, without changing the administrative method substantially.

It may also be of interest to mention that Atle Elsås of the Ministry of Finance, clearly inspired by Frisch, constructed a model that could be used to calculate the combined effects of tax policy and monetary policy on private consumption, private real investment, and imports. Its definitional relations were largely copied from the financial accounts designed by Frisch. That model was to some extent used in the national budgeting for 1959. Frisch himself presented the model in a separate memorandum (Frisch, 1959b).

4.3 The MODIS Models

A breakthrough for the use of numerical models in macroeconomic planning and policy occurred in 1960 when Sevaldson and Amundsen combined the production and consumption models into one, adding a few institutional relationships (Sevaldson, 1962). The variables and the definitional relationships were the same as those of the national accounts. The model, designated MODIS (MOdel of DISaggregated type), could be used for computing most of the gross national product, total imports, and most of private consumption at given magnitudes of other demand components and the industrial output that is determined by capacity limits. Those computations were made by means of the first-generation Deuce computer (English Electric), which the Central Bureau of Statistics had acquired in 1958. MODIS was completed early enough to be used for preparing the national budget for 1961.[12] A prerequisite for that breakthrough was the pioneering model work of Frisch, aiming at a combination of corresponding models. He had explained that "it is of the greatest importance as soon as possible to integrate the demand side and the production side into a more comprehensive model" (Frisch, 1953, p. 16).

After 1960, extended versions of MODIS were successively developed. In addition, a number of special-purpose models were constructed by the Central Bureau of Statistics (Bjerve, 1976). Some of them were integrated with the existing MODIS version.[13] The MODIS models

---

[12] Administrative estimates were nevertheless made for checking purpose, and they corresponded well with the model estimates. For subsequent years the Ministry of Finance collected calculations of exogenous variables made by other ministries, and when the model computations had been made, the ministries concerned were asked to verify that the results appeared reasonable.

[13] The last version of MODIS, first used in 1974, contained flows of about 200 kinds of commodities in 150 industries. As many as about 2,000 variables were considered exogenous, including those determined by the government. In 1988 that version was replaced by a more aggregated model, but even that was large compared with models used in other countries at that time.

were more and more extensively used in macroeconomic planning, instead of the administrative method for computing national budget magnitudes. From 1968 onward, long-term projections were made for production, employment, and investment in different industries by means of a general-equilibrium model originally developed by Leif Johansen (1960).

4.4 Evaluation

The application of numerical models for planning and policy began at a relatively early date in Norway. That was, to a high degree, due to the influence of Ragnar Frisch. He convinced economists taking part in the national budgeting that the administrative method applied should be supplemented and to some extent substituted by model computations.

The model building at the Central Bureau of Statistics was inspired by the early model work of Frisch. Furthermore, it was facilitated by the training that the model builders gained at the Institute of Economics and by the assistance they got from Frisch, inter alia, on matrix inversions. In addition, the tripartite cooperation organized by him influenced the model development and thereby contributed to an improvement of macroeconomic analysis and planning.

Although the major numerical models constructed by Frisch were not directly applied for planning and policy purposes, to some degree they provided guidance for building the models actually used. Thus the combining of separate production and consumption models into the first MODIS model was clearly guided by the Median model. The possible guidance of the other Frisch models is less clear, but they may have indicated what kind of variables and structural relationships should be included in successive MODIS models. In these ways, the Frisch models may be considered as prerequisites for the numerical models actually applied. However, the extensive work of Frisch on programming and interviewing techniques remained academic and hardly influenced Norwegian planning and policy, except that it clarified the concepts of "goals" and "targets."

The model work of the Central Bureau of Statistics during the 1950s and early 1960s was also facilitated by model developments in other countries, particularly by the interindustry models constructed by Wassily Leontief (Bjerkholt, 1992). However, the system of numerical models applied in Norway today could hardly have been developed as early as it was without the model work of Frisch. Thereby he exerted significant influence on Norwegian planning and policy.

5 Personal Policy Influence[14]

5.1 *Teaching and Research*

The influence on planning and policy that Ragnar Frisch exerted through his students was, of course, first and foremost by teaching at the University of Oslo, where he was the dominating force. He also played a major role in reforming the study of economics and in establishing the Institute of Economics at the university, which were important prerequisites for his achievements in organization of economic research.[15]

Frisch was not always well prepared for his lectures. At times the students were more like observers in his study than listeners to a formal lecture. But in return they experienced the fascination and, not least, the inspiration of watching the genius at work. The students who saw his face shining when he found fine formulations would never forget it. His professional enthusiasm was pervasive.

Before World War II and until the university was closed by the occupation authorities, the competence of his students on macroeconomic policy was developed primarily by study of Keynes's general theory and of publications by Danish and Swedish economists, such as Kjeld Philip and Gunnar Myrdal. However, the conceptual frameworks presented to them by Frisch promoted their understanding of those publications.

The teaching of Frisch during the postwar years was to a high degree focused on macroeconomic planning and policy. His lectures were often recorded by one of his students and, after being corrected by himself, published as memoranda from the Institute of Economics, in mimeographed form.[16] Those were made available at low cost to the students and contributed a great deal to their education.

A reformed study program in economics was adopted by the Storting in 1935. It required five years of study and qualified one for a master's degree (cand. oecon.). That implied access to the civil service on equal

---

[14] A more detailed presentation of this influence has been published (Bjerve, 1995).
[15] These activities were inspired by his belief that economists in the future would be "an important factor in eliminating maladjustments between fundamental economic factors and assure a smooth and progressive utilization of resources" (Frisch, 1946b, p. 1) and that they could and should play a decisive role in achieving those goals and in preventing the "monstrous situation" of the 1930s from being repeated. Many of the economists studying in the 1930s were motivated by a concern for the high level of unemployment, by a desire to get a better knowledge of its causes, and perhaps even by a hope of becoming able to contribute to its prevention. Similarly, during the 1940s the serious postwar economic problems caused by the German occupation, and later the need for reconstruction, motivated the study of economics. Thus, during those periods the students were particularly receptive to the teaching and training of Frisch.
[16] From May 1947 to November 1964 no less than 240 memoranda were issued, varying in size from 2 to 250 pages. Most of them were written by Frisch, and some by him in cooperation with one of his associates.

terms with the study of law and attracted a greater and perhaps more interested group of students at a time of increasing concern for economic and social problems.

At the same time, the curriculum was extended and modernized, with particular emphasis on economic and statistical theory. By several series of lectures, Frisch gradually improved the curriculum substantially. By partly applying mathematics, he also made the presentation substantially more precise than that of ordinary textbooks at the time (Frisch, 1946c).

Shortly after the war, Frisch presented a plan for economic research and teaching in Norway (Frisch, 1945, p. 2), pointing out that both the government and the private sector now wanted to "use economists to a much larger extent than before. There is a need for people with a broad theoretical knowledge on a modern basis and with acquaintance of the characteristics of Norwegian economy and social structure." That view was followed up in 1953 when a revision of the curriculum was made that allowed the students to choose between different subjects, while a large basic group of subjects remained as a common requirement.[17]

The Institute of Economics was established January 1, 1932, with Ragnar Frisch and one of his colleagues, Ingvar Wedervang, as leaders. In a report on achievements of the institute presented at the end of 1941, Frisch pointed out that it had made possible "a scientific recruitment and the creation of a scientific milieu in the field of economics which would have been inconceivable without this activity" (Frisch, 1941, p. 7). Among the 22 economists working at the institute during the period 1947–48 through 1952–53, as many as 8 became professors, and 2 assistant professors.

A large percentage of the economists graduating after the middle of the 1930s went into the civil service. Gradually they achieved such competence that quite a few were appointed to high or the highest positions, to a large extent replacing retiring lawyers who previously had had a virtual monopoly on such positions.[18] Some of them also were appointed to political positions, mostly for short periods. As many as 13 became members of the cabinet; 1 even became prime minister, and 7 were

---

[17] The idea behind that change was, according to Frisch, that economics had become such a wide field of subjects that "no single person can command it. A cooperation is needed between persons who, each of them commanding their specialities, at the same time have so much common ground that they can understand each others language" (Frisch, 1958). However, the revision was also a result of pressure from the students, who wanted a choice of subjects.

[18] In particular, this occurred in the Ministry of Finance, where a number of economists were appointed for national budgeting during the first postwar decade, and later also for fiscal budgeting and other work. At the end of 1962 as many as four of seven top positions in this ministry were occupied by economists (Lie, 1995, p. 350).

ministers of finance. Thus, many of the students of Frisch became members of his "infantry."

5.2   Information and Advice

The policy influence of Frisch through politicians began in the early 1930s. His first contact with the mass media probably occurred in October 1931, when he gave a newspaper interview on the occasion of Norway leaving the gold standard. Shortly afterward he published an article in the same newspaper advocating an expansionary policy to fight the Depression. From then on, Frisch presented a large number of interventions in the public debate on macroeconomic issues (newspaper articles, expository articles in weekly and monthly periodicals, and public lectures on the radio as well as to audiences at various places around the country).

A series of newspaper articles published by Frisch in 1933 triggered an invitation from the Labour Party to participate in the preparation of a proposal for financing an expansionary Crisis Program.[19] First he attended a party conference on that issue, and later Frisch, together with some of the leading party members, held further meetings that resulted in the final bank-and-finance chapter of the Crisis Program. That chapter has been characterized as "indisputably Frisch's" (Andvig, 1986, pp. 366, 378–80). At the request of the party leader Johan Nygaardsvold, Frisch even authored a Labour Party statement to the parliamentary Committee of Finance on May 5, 1934.

In March 1935 the Labour Party came into power, and the next month Frisch was appointed a member of the Monetary Committee,[20] replacing one of the members who had become minister of finance. In an annex to a report by that committee, Frisch published, in November 1935, a presentation on open-market operations (Frisch, 1935) that clearly explained the effects of such operations. The government later changed the law on the Bank of Norway so as to allow open-market operations.

---

[19] Those articles were based on a confidential memorandum distributed to distinguished politicians and bankers, describing "the injury and suffering" caused by the economic situation, sketching its causes and making proposals for action (Frisch, 1951a, pp. 3, 11–19). He even invited some of them to private meetings on the memorandum. Those meetings were not successful. Frisch characterized them as "running the head against the wall." In the memorandum, Frisch recommended the creation of new purchasing power: "The logical rational solution is that the central government acts to create this new purchasing power and makes use of it on the strategically decisive point: in the consumption." He also made several policy proposals, inter alia, on the use of treasury bills to finance budget deficits and the establishment of a directorate with the power to counteract business cycles independently of the government authorities.

[20] Established by the Ministry of Finance April 6, 1932 "for reporting on matters concerning economic and monetary policy." Referred to as the Monetary Committee.

Shortly after the war the Labour Party won a majority in the parliament and adopted a macroeconomic policy that Frisch fully supported and partly influenced. In February 1946 he took part in drafting the first budget speech of Erik Brofoss, and later he was very active as a member of the Monetary and Financial Council (successor to the prewar Monetary Committee).[21]

A part of the budget speech outlined a monetary and financial policy that to a high degree was pursued during the first postwar decade and that, inter alia, required maintenance of the direct price and quantity regulations introduced during the war. Frisch was a member of a group drafting that part, and a number of formulations obviously were his.[22]

The Monetary and Financial Council during 1946 discussed credit policy at several meetings chaired by the minister of finance himself. Frisch supported the low-interest policy already adopted and agreed with the majority of the council that it required a direct restriction of lending.

During the period 1950–52 the council prepared three reports. In the first, Frisch made some observations of his own on introduction of an income tax based on consumption units and on potential income rather than actual income, as well as on wage compensation (Frisch, 1950b). In the second, he, together with three other members, advised against applying special benefits as a part of a wage agreement (Frisch, 1951b). In the third report, the majority of the council, to which Frisch belonged, recommended that credit rationing be introduced, that lending of the state banks be financed by loans from the central government, and that the commercial and savings banks be obliged to buy quotas of government bonds at a low rate of interest (Penge- og Finansrådet, 1952).[23] Those recommendations were later implemented.

From 1952 onward the Monetary and Financial Council held no meet-

---

[21] Frisch was also a member of the Foreign Exchange Committee, established in August 1945, which unanimously proposed a 20 percent increase in the exchange rate toward the pound sterling (Valutakomiteen av august 1945). He was very active in the deliberations of that committee and wrote a substantial part of the premises for the proposal. However, the cabinet decided to maintain the existing exchange rate.

[22] Examples of such formulations "to the extent that a budget deficit of the central government is financed by internal loans, they have no direct consequence for the real national wealth. Whether such a deficit indirectly will result in an increase or decrease of this wealth, depends on how the government uses the borrowed money." "Therefore it is a misunderstanding when it sometimes is said that the raising of an internal government loan means imposing burdens on future generations." "However, the government debts have importance for the distribution of the real wealth and the real income in society" (Brofoss, 1946).

[23] As a basis for this report the Central Bureau of Statistics, in cooperation with Frisch and Leif Johansen, made forecasts of bank liquidity by means of a model with definitional relationships of the financial accounts and with some roughly calibrated structural relationships (Bjerve, 1956).

ings, being dissolved in 1955. Afterward, Frisch was not a member of any government committee. His advisory role had terminated.

Later in the 1950s Frisch experienced growing discontent with Norwegian planning and policy and in the early 1960s disassociated himself from the Labour Party.[24] Even though the government accepted important recommendations of the Monetary and Financial Council that Frisch supported, other aspects of the macroeconomic policy disappointed him, for instance, that the interest level was allowed to increase and that the quantitative restrictions on foreign trade and real investment were gradually abolished. The fact that the Labour government and the economists in charge of planning did not apply his models may also partly explain his discontent.[25]

5.3   *Evaluation*

By his teaching and research Ragnar Frisch influenced the thinking of an entire generation of Norwegian economists. Many of them became "foot soldiers" in his fight for improved macroeconomic planning and policy, and Frisch, to some degree, even ensured that they were placed in strategic positions.[26] Thereby, through his pupils, he exerted an important indirect influence on planning and policy in the postwar years (Bjerve, 1989).

The informative activities of Frisch undoubtedly contributed to better understanding of the functioning of the economy and of current economic problems, but some proposals for new schemes and institutions were too complex and too impractical to be accepted.[27] The expansionary macroeconomic policy that Frisch, in the early 1930s, advised the Labour Party to carry out was only to a slight degree adopted by the

---

[24] Thus, in 1965 he published 12 articles in the Socialistic Left Party's newspaper, where he criticized heavily, even furiously, a number of aspects of recent Labour Party policy (Frisch, 1965b, pp. 2, 22). Even more polemical was his fight during the 1960s and early 1970s against Norwegian membership in the European Economic Community. In that debate he did not always distinguish sufficiently between scientific statements and value judgments (Frisch, 1963b).

[25] One indication of this is the fact that when a coalition cabinet of parties to the right of the Labour Party came into power during a short period in 1963, Frisch, two days before its term of office began, offered to become its advisor on macroeconomic policy. He expressly mentioned economic programming as one kind of possible advice (Lyng, 1973, pp. 197–8).

[26] In a letter to Erik Brofoss dated March 13, 1950, Frisch expressed the view that the research department to be established in the Central Bureau of Statistics "must be a scientific centre" and then added that "you will certainly not take me amiss that I currently keep an eye on the young economists who constitute the entire scientific milieu, and that I at any time try to explore the possibilities that are available to promote the scientific development for each of them, considering his special abilities and interests."

[27] In the early 1930s he even recommended replacement of the free market by a moneyless barter system (Munthe, 1992, pp. 99–134).

Labour government that gained power in 1935. However, the majority government formed by the Labour Party in 1945 carried out such a policy with the support of Frisch, inter alia, in the Monetary and Financial Council (Det norske Arbeiderparti, 1945). After 1952 his advice had hardly any influence on macroeconomic policy. Thus his influence through politicians terminated at a relatively early time.

6   Visions and Ambitions versus Reality

Ragnar Frisch was an economist with grand visions and extraordinary ambitions, as evidenced in the preceding sections. In conclusion, it may be of interest to confront some of his visions and ambitions with the reality. His vision of being himself the "heavy artillery," and his pupils "the infantry," agreed well with reality. The vision of complementary development of theory and of the data observed was also quite in harmony with the actual development, at any rate in macroeconomics. The contributions of economics and economists to humanity have not become as great as Frisch envisioned; at any rate, his vision of politicians and experts sitting together in a conference, computing an optimal policy by means of models, continues to be a dream (Frisch, 1952a, p. 20). Obviously, his conception of party policy was too simple. This is not the least reflected in Frisch (1970).

The political ambitions of Frisch increased over time, from keeping secret his contacts with the Labour Party in the early 1930s to offering advice even to a government to the right of that party in 1963. Frisch was very satisfied with the macroeconomic policy views of the Labour Party during the first half of the 1930s, and he praised the reforms implemented during the second half, when the party was in power. In particular, he lauded Prime Minister Johan Nygaardsvold "by whose side" he had fought (Frisch, 1965b). The most important reason for his growing discontent from the early 1950s on seems to have been economic liberalization. Frisch was convinced that to achieve a combination of social justice and a high rate of economic growth, many instruments of economic policy were required. That belief was based on "the general mathematical principle" that "if a function is maximized under certain restrictions (in this case that some instruments are not permitted) one will *never* be able to achieve a higher maximum than if these restrictions *are removed*" (Frisch, 1962, pp. 1, 3).

Frisch was an outstanding thinker and a vast source of inspiration. He had an abundance of ideas, remarkable ability to generalize, extraordinary capacity for work, and almost inexhaustible energy. But perhaps because of that greatness, his professional ambitions tended to exceed the possibilities. For instance, his macroeconomic concepts, terminology, and symbols were not adopted as international standards, such as he perhaps hoped. The accounting system developed for the purpose of structural analysis was too comprehensive and detailed to be numerically applied. Also, in the building of macroeconomic models his ambitions carried him away from achieving practical results, particularly in constructing numerical welfare functions.[28] Nevertheless, many of his ambitions also turned out to conform well with reality.

References

Amundsen, A. (1957). Vekst og sammenhenger i den noske økonomi 1920–1955 (Growth and interdependence in the Norwegian economy). *Statsøkonomisk Tidsskrift* 71:121–58.

Andvig, J. C. (1986). *Ragnar Frisch and the Great Depression*. Oslo: Norwegian Institute of International Affairs.

Aukrust, O. (1994). The Scandinavian contribution to national accounting. In: *The Accounts of Nations*, ed. Z. Kennesey, pp. 16–65. Amsterdam: IOS Press.

Aukrust, O., Bjerve, P. J., and Frisch, R. (1948a). A system of concepts describing the economic circulation and production process. Memorandum, March 8, 1948, Institute of Economics, Oslo.

Aukrust, O., and Frisch, R. (1951). Prøverekning på numerisk løsning av kryssløpslikningene (Experimental computations on a numerical solution of the inter-industry equations). Memorandum, February 18, 1951, Institute of Economics, Oslo.

Aukrust, O., Haavelmo, T., and Hiorth, O. (1948b). PM om stabiliseringspolitikken (P.M. on the stabilization policy), November 8, 1948. Mimeographed manuscript. Oslo.

Bjerkholt, O. (1992). Hvordan kryssløpsanalysen kom til Norge (How the inter-industry analysis came to Norway). In: *Mennesker og modeller. Livsløp og Kryssløp*, pp. 43–63. Samfunnsøkonomiske studier 78. Oslo: Statistisk Sentralbyrå.

(1995). When input–output analysis came to Norway. *Structural Change and Economic Dynamics* 6:319–30.

Bjerkholt, O., and Longva, S. (1980). MODIS IV. A model for economic analysis and national planning. Samfunnsøkonomiske studier 43. Oslo: Statistisk Sentralbyrå.

Bjerve, P. J. (1940). Utredning om regnskapet for struktursektoren Bankvirksomhet – Stat (Explanation of the accounts for the structural sector banking activity – government). Unpublished manuscript, Oslo.

(1944a). Grafisk framstilling av sirkulasjonssystemet til Föhl (Graphical presentation of Föhl's circulation system). *Nordisk Tidsskrift for Teknisk Økonomi* 1941:101–3.

(1944b). Økosirksystemet og realsirkulasjonen i "The General Theory of Employment, Interest and Money" (The Ecocirc system and the real circu-

---

[28] Nevertheless, even at the end of his career Frisch maintained that without models with welfare functions, "there are so many things we shall be cut off from doing in advanced planning analyses, that we must engage on this task the sooner the better" (Bjerve and Frisch, 1971).

lation in "The General Theory of Employment, Interest and Money"). *Statsøkonomisk Tidsskrift* 58:1–25.

(1954). Kryssløpsforsking i Statistisk Sentralbyrå (Inter-industry research in the Central Bureau of Statistics). *Statistisk Tidskrift* 3:3–15.

(1957). Forecasting bank liquidity. *Income and Wealth*, ser. 6, ed. M. Gilbert and R. Stone, pp. 52–77. London: Bowes & Bowes.

(1976). *Trends in Norwegian Planning 1945–1975*. Oslo: Statistisk Sentralbyrå.

(1986). Ragnar Frisch og Økosirksystemet (Ragnar Frisch and the Ecocirc system). *Sosialøkonomen* 40:17–23, 26–30.

(1989). *Økonomisk planlegging og politikk. (Economic Planning and Policy).* Oslo: Det Norske Samlaget.

(1991). Korfor fekk vi nasjonalbudsjettet? (Why did we get the national budget?). *Norsk Økonomisk Tidsskrift* 105:77–96.

(1995). *The Influence of Ragnar Frisch on Macroeconomic Planning and Policy in Norway*. Oslo: Statistics Norway.

(1996). *Contributions of Ragnar Frisch to National Accounting*. Oslo: Statistics Norway.

Bjerve, P. J., and Frisch, R. (1971). Økonomisk teori og økonomisk politikk (Economic theory and economic policy). Radio conversation, Oslo: H. Aschenhoug & Co. July 5, 1970. Published in *Økonomi og politikk. 15 artikler*, pp. 5–13.

Brofoss, E. (1946). *Norges økonomiske og finansielle stilling (The Economic and Financial Position of Norway)*. Oslo.

Edvardsen, K. (1970). A survey of Ragnar Frisch's contribution to the science of economics. *De Economist*, 118:175–208.

Det norske Arbeiderparti (1945). *Arbeidsprogram (Work Program)*. Oslo: DNA.

Finans- og tolldepartementet (1946). *Nasjonalregnskapet og nasjonalbudsjettet. Særskilt vedlegg nr. 11 til statsbudsjettet (Ministry of Finance: The National Accounts and the National Budget. Separate Enclosure no. 11 to the Central Government's Budget)*. Oslo.

Frisch, R. (1932a). Verdensøkonomien i efterkrigstiden. Konjunkturene (The world economy in the post war years. The business cycles). Universitetets radioforedrag, pp. 79–139. Oslo.

(1932b). New orientation of economic theory. Economics as an experimental science. *Nordic Statistical Journal* 4:97–111.

(1933a). Propagation problems and impulse problems in dynamic economics. In: *Economic Essays in Honour of Gustav Cassel*, pp. 171–205. London: George Allen & Unwin.

(1933b). *Sparing og cirkulasjonsregulering (Saving and Circulation Planning)*. Oslo: Fabritius og Sønners Forlag.

(1935). Open market operations og deres virkninger på banksystemet. Bilag 4 til Innstilling om Markedsoperasjoner avgitt av Komiteen til utredning av økonomiske og pengepolitiske spørsmål (Open market operations and their influence on the banking system. Annex 4 to Report on Market operations submitted by The Monetary Committee), pp. 43–60. Oslo.

(1940). Nasjonalregnskapet (National accounts). Beretning om Det 3. nordiske statistikermøte i Oslo. (Report from the 3rd Nordic meeting of statisticians in Oslo). June 28–9, 1939. Oslo.

(1941). P.M. om arbeidet ved Universitetets Økonomiske Institutt og ved Koordineringsavdelingen av den Økonomiske Strukturoversikt for Norge (P.M. on the work at the Institute of Economics, University of Oslo, and at the Coordination Section of the Structural Economic Survey of Norway). Oslo.

(1942). Noen innføringsmerknader om Økosirk-Systemet (Det økonomiske sirkulasjonssystem) [Some introductory remarks on the Ecocirc system (The economic circulation system)]. Oslo. A shorter version was published in *Ekonomisk Tidskrift* 45:106–21.

(1945). Økonomisk forskning og undervisning i Norge (Economic research and teaching in Norway). *Statsøkonomisk Tidsskrift* 59:101–12.

(1946a). *Innledning til produksjonsteorien*. (*Introduction to the Theory of Production*), 7th ed. Oslo: SSSS-trykk.

(1946b). The responsibility of the econometrician. *Econometrica* 14:1–4.

(1946c). *Notater til økonomisk teori* (*Notes on Economic Theory*). 3rd ed. Oslo: SSSS-trykk.

(1947). The economist and the world problems of the day. Address to the International Economic Club, Lake Success, February 3, 1947. Also in *American Economic Review* 48:367–72.

(1948a). Work on national accounting done at the University Institute of Economics, Stencil-memo, December 22, 1948, University Institute of Economics. Oslo.

(1948b). Subsidielikningssystemet (The system of subsidy equations). Memorandum, December 9, 1948, Institute of Economics, Oslo.

(1949a). Price-wage-tax policies as instruments in maintaining optimal employment. Memorandum of March 28, 1949. Oslo. Also published as a United Nations document (E/CN1/Sub 2/13 1949) 18 April 1949. Later published in *Metroeconomica* 7:111–36.

(1949b). Work done and work planned at the University Institute of Economics, Oslo. *Stimulator* 3:4–10.

(1950a). Hovedsynspunkter for arbeidet med den økonomiske samgripingsanalyse (Decisjonsmodellen) [Main views of the work on the economic analysis of interrelationships (Decision Model)]. Memorandum, February 3, 1950, Institute of Economics, Oslo.

(1950b). Sœruttalelser i Penge- og Finansrådets innstilling 30. august (Special comments in the report of the Monetary and Financial Council). St. prop. nr. 129 (1950), Annex 10-11. Special comments together with Gunnar Bøe Annex 27-32. Oslo.

(1951a). Statens plikt til cirkulasjonsregulering (Nedtegnet i hast 10.-12. desember 1932) [The government's duty to circulation planning (written in a hurry December 10–12, 1932)]. Memorandum, Institute of Economics, January 11, 1951. Oslo.

(1951b). Sœruttalelse i Penge- og Finansrådets innstilling, 15. oktober 1951 (Special comments in the report of the Monetary and Financial Council), pp. 40–1. Oslo.

(1952a). Økonomisk demokrati (Economic democracy). Memorandum, October 16, 1952, Institute of Economics, Oslo.

(1952b). Betalingsmiddelforskyvninger mellom sektorer i et lands næringsliv (Shifting of payments between sectors in the industry life of a country), pp. 68–82. Oslo. Report, January 13, 1952, Monetary and Financial Council, Oslo.

(1952c). Reperkusjonsanalytiske problemer som kan studeres på grunnlag av vare- og tjenestetilgangen oppdelt etter tiltrekningsandeler, hovedkategorier av goder og næringssektorer (Problems of repercussion analysis that can be studied on the basis of the supply of goods and services divided by estimation shares, major categories of goods and industrial sectors). Memorandum, November 6, 1952, Institute of Economics, Oslo.

(1953). Samfunnsmodell anvendt i en analyse av hvordan de økonomiske faktorer griper inn i hverandre. (Model of the society applied in an analysis of how the economic factors are interrelated). *Stimulator* 6:5–19.

(1955). From national accounts to macro-economic decision models. In: *Income and Wealth*, ser. 4, ed. M. Gilbert and R. Stone, pp. 1–26. London: Bowes & Bowes.

(1956). Submodell, Medianmodell og Refi-modell. (Submodel, median model and REFI model). Memorandum, January 2, 1956, Institute of Economics, Oslo. See also memoranda of October 21, 1956, February 5, 1957, June 4, 1957.

(1957). Oslo decision models. Memorandum, June 4, 1957, Institute of Economics, Oslo.

(1958). Økonomikkens landevinninger i nyere tid (Recent progress in economics). *Statsøkonomisk Tidsskrift* 72:263–86.

(1959a). Aggregat-Refi-Modeller (Aggregate REFI models). Memorandum, April 20, 1959, Institute of Economics, Oslo. See also memoranda of June 29, 1959, November 17, 1959, February 19, 1960, June 27, 1960. Printed (1961) in *Bulletin de L'institut International de Statistique*, 33 session, Paris, pp. 1–11, and (1966) in *Problems of Economic Dynamics and Planning, Essays in Honour of Michal Kalecki*, ed. T. Kowalik, pp. 133–56. Elmsford, NY: Pergamon.

(1959b). Elsås-modellen og dens utbygging for programmeringsformål (The Elsås model and its extension for programming purpose). Memorandum, March 15, 1959, Institute of Economics, Oslo.

(1960). Synopsis of a channel model for macroeconomic programming. Memorandum, August 23, 1960, Institute of Economics, Oslo. See also memoranda of May 13, 1961, October 20, 1961, October 3, 1963. Printed (1962) in *Europe's Future in Figures*, ed. R. C. Geary, pp. 248–87. Amsterdam: North Holland.

(1962). Prinsipiell diskusjon om makroøkonomiske virkemidler (A discussion on principles as regards macroeconomic instruments). Memorandum, December 7, 1962, Institute of Economics, Oslo.

(1963a). An implementation system for optimal national economic planning without detailed quantity fixation from a central authority. In: *Abstracts of the 3rd International Conference on Operational Research, Oslo*, pp. 20–59. London: Dunod.

(1963b). Hva saken gjelder (What the case concerns). Oslo: A. S. All-trykk.

(1965a). *Theory of Production*. Dordrecht: Reidel.

(1965b). Politikk i pakt med framtiden (Policy in keeping with the future). Oslo: Orientering.

(1970). *Co-operation between Politicians and Econometricians on the Formalization of Political Preferences.* Stockholm: Federation of Swedish Industries.

Frisch, R., Keilhau, W., and Wedervang, I. (1936). *Plan til en økonomisk struktu-*

rundersøkelse for Norge (*Plan for a Structural Survey of Norway*). Oslo: Fabritius & Sønners boktrykkeri.
Johansen, L. (1960). *A Multi-Sectoral Study of Economic Growth*. Amsterdam: North Holland.
— (1973). Ragnar Frisch (1895–1973). *Economics of Planning* 11:1–3.
Lie, E. (1995). *Ambisjon og tradisjon. Finansdepartementet 1945–1965* (*Ambition and Tradition. The Ministry of Finance 1945–1965*). Oslo.
Lyng, J. (1973). *Vaktskifte. Erindringer, 1953–1965.* (*Changing of the Guard. Memories*). Oslo: Cappelen.
Munthe, P. (1992). *Norske økonomer* (*Norwegian Economists*). Oslo: Universitetsforlaget.
Penge- og Finansrådet (1952). Innstilling 13. januar (Report of the Monetary and Financial Council, 13 January). Oslo.
Rossen, S. (1942). Koordinerte regnskaper for skipsaksjeselskap (Coordinated accounts for shipping). In: *Statistisk månedsskrift*, pp. 23–147. Oslo kommunale statistiske kontor.
Sevaldson, P. (1953). Notat om Forskningsplanmøte på Sosialøkonomisk Institutt (Note about a meeting on research planning at the Institute of Economics, 26 June). Unpublished manuscript.
— (1960). Kryssløpsanalyse av produksjon og innsats i norske nœringer 1954 (Input–output analysis of Norwegian industries, 1954). Samfunnsøkonomiske studier 9. Oslo: Statistisk Sentralbyrå.
— (1962). En produksjons-konsum-kryssløpsmodell for økonomisk planlegging (A production consumption input–output model for economic planning). *Statsøkonomisk Tidsskrift* 76:69–98.
Statistisk Sentralbyrå (1946). *Nasjonalinntekten i Norge 1935–1943* (*National Income in Norway*). Oslo.
— (1957). Kredittmarkedsstatistikk (Credit market statistics). NOS XI 281. Oslo.
Valutakomiteen av august 1945 (1945). Innstilling (Report from the Foreign Exchange Committee of August 1945). Oslo.

CHAPTER 18

How Frisch Saw in the 1960s the Contribution of Economists to Development Planning

E. Malinvaud

1   Motivations and Limitations

Two considerations motivate this essay: First, the author may have testimony to give about Ragnar Frisch. Second, the history of economic ideas should analyze those views about planning that were influential during the third quarter of this century, particularly in Western Europe. During the 1950s and early 1960s, European economists involved in setting up national accounts and macroeconomic programming often met for a week or so, in conditions very different from those prevailing in the large, short gatherings now common for international scientific interchange. A group of some 30 participants would discuss at length issues raised by their work. The younger ones would receive advice from a few dominant personalities, who would also at times embark on lengthy debates with each other. The atmosphere was friendly and open.

Ragnar Frisch was almost always present at the many such meetings I went to during that period; he, of course, marked them by his interventions. After a while I thought I could fairly well predict some of his comments, even some with which I disagreed. But other comments were truly unpredictable and surprising. The differences in approach and temper between Frisch and such people as Richard Stone, Jan Tinbergen, or Herman World were also worth noting. Because I am one of the few living non-Norwegian economists who had such an acquaintance with Frisch, I feel a duty to provide whatever information I can regarding that extraordinary man.[1]

This essay was a contribution to the Ragnar Frisch Centennial Symposium in Oslo, March 3–5, 1995. This revised version has benefited from discussion at the symposium, from documentation provided by Olav Bjerkholt, and from suggestions by Peter Hammond.

[1] I do not think, on the other hand, that I have any direct testimony to give about the role of Frisch in the Econometric Society, which I joined 20 years after its foundation, nor in the editorship of *Econometrica*. Perhaps I should just mention that he never interfered, so far as I remember, with my work as European co-editor of the journal from 1954 to 1964, even though my appointment had been part of the package for solving the tension

Frisch on Economists and Development Planning

The present and future generations of economists ought to find it instructive to reflect on the "planning movement," which was supported with enthusiasm by part of the European economic profession in the first two or three decades after the Second World War. I see it as an important and relevant subject for the history of economics. What was really thought and achieved by proponents of the movement? What remains valid? How can one explain the errors made at the time?

Ragnar Frisch clearly shared in that enthusiasm. Beginning in the late 1940s he turned almost all his research toward the issues raised by the operation of economic planning. Historians of the movement ought to pay a good deal of attention to him. Working in France, being involved in planning, being sympathetic to most of the ideas prevailing in my country about it, and meeting Frisch on problems related to this work, I should again be an interesting non-Norwegian witness to the matter.

Among others, a particularly significant opportunity to understand Frisch's views was offered to me by a study week on "the econometric approach to development planning" held at the Pontifical Academy of Sciences in October 1963. The meeting was attended by 18 rather well known economists, including some much involved in planning methods, such as W. Leontief, P. C. Mahalanobis, R. Stone, and H. Theil, as well as Frisch and myself. The agenda fitted so well with Frisch's ideas that it could have been drafted by him (probably the organizer, the statistician and pontifical academician Boldrini, had taken advice from Frisch). The agenda started with the following three paragraphs:

> Modern economies are extremely complex and both theory and practice show that the free play of individual choice does not guarantee, as used to be thought, favourable results for the community.
>
> Once this is admitted it is obviously necessary to provide suitable informative and control instruments and fix the targets which the economy is aiming at.
>
> From these requirements was born econometrics, which uses the statistical and mathematical methods both in the theoretical study of economic phenomena and in the formulation of directives for economic policy and development planning.

The proceedings of the meeting were published in two volumes, with an extensive report of the discussions. I have looked carefully at them in order to refresh my memory about the event, which I consider important for my subject. But this essay cannot aim at providing a faithful historical account of the points it discusses. In particular, I was not in a position to survey the available literature, even the part written in the

---

between the Chicago office on one side and Frisch and some other European members of the society on the other.

English language.[2] Here I shall make reference to what I was able to read. But my recollection of what I perceived to be Ragnar Frisch's attitudes ought to be confirmed by others before it can be accepted. This text is no more than the testimony of an individual witness.

2   The Intellectual Climate

The preceding quotation from the introduction to the Vatican study week may look queer when read today. The positive tone means that its author considered the statements as indisputable. Indeed, it would no longer be possible to so write now; but it was possible in the early 1960s, particularly in Western Europe. Any history of the planning movement must take the change in intellectual climate into account, because the climate of the time had implications, and the change requires explanation.

Here I should like first to show briefly how the prevailing ideas gave a broad justification to the kind of research Frisch did after the war. But I should also like to raise two questions: Why is it that Frisch apparently showed so little motivation for writing on issues that were then the objects of attention among other economists also concerned in planning? What explanation can one give for the errors in judgment that were part of the postwar European intellectual climate and that many, including Frisch, found so painful to recognize?

Members of the planning movement shared an awareness of market failures, and they had confidence in planning as a tool for managing the economy in rich countries and promoting development in poor ones. Socialist and Christian thinkers saw failures in an inequitable distribution of welfare, in an inefficient allocation that neglected collective infrastructures and services, and finally in a lack of spontaneous stabilization, which the Great Depression had vividly illustrated. Dissatisfaction would have been vain if possibilities for improvement had not been seen. But Keynes had provided a rationale for macroeconomic policies; Beveridge had drawn ambitious projects for the "welfare state" that were widely imitated; the war economy had proved that large productive sectors could be planned; the Swedish socialist model was functioning; the USSR seemed to be performing well, both in launching *Sputnik* and producing sophisticated arms and in apparently quickly raising the standard of

---

[2] As is well described by Bjerkholt (1995), Frisch left unpublished, or even incomplete, many of his writings. The proceedings of the Vatican study week give an amusing proof of that. Clearly space was not a problem, since M. Allais's article covers 282 pages. The article by Frisch is only 8 pages long. But it ends with the following note showing the distress of the editor: "The verbatim record of the technical parts of Professor Frisch's presentation is not given here. Nor are the several mimeographed documents distributed by Professor Frisch reproduced. This material will subsequently be coordinated by Professor Frisch and published by him separately."

living of its populations; and so on. In Western Europe, planners often had the experience of working in the public sector and were aware of "government failures," but enlightened planning was perceived as the way to remedy those failures. For most European economists the question was not whether or not planning was good, but rather which form of planning was best: authoritative or indicative? On quantities or through prices? For the whole economy or only "the public sector"? And so on.

There was considerable agreement on the notion that a central role in the planning work was to be played by macroeconomic projections, which would provide the reference for whatever policy studies or detailed planning could be entertained and worked out. But the level of detail of such projections and the type of modeling that would underlie them were important subjects to be discussed. To those subjects Frisch was devoting his research.

If the then-prevailing ideology can be so described when seen from a distance, it would be wrong to speak of unanimity among economists. On the contrary, a minority containing some prominent figures was arguing against planning. Among supporters, more or less fundamental divergences in approach also existed. It is surprising that Ragnar Frisch, who had large intellectual concerns and was at times outspoken, should have taken so little part in some of the disputes.

The most debated issues had somewhat shifted. They no longer bore so much on the feasibility of rational resource allocation under socialism; there was a literature on this subject from von Mises (1981) to Lange (1936–37) and Lerner (1944); it was not fully conclusive but had shown that the subject was not simple. For most economists the main question was rather whether or not socialist planning was compatible with democracy. In a widely read pamphlet, Hayek (1944) had argued for a negative answer. But particularly at the time of the first postwar Labour government in the United Kingdom, a number of English writings had appeared, presenting conditions under which reliance could be placed on "planism by inducement," to be preferred to "planism by direction" (Meade, 1948; Lewis, 1948), to quote just two well-known economists. Although on a more technical tone criticisms were also raised later by Russian economists concerning the deficiencies of planning in the USSR (e.g., Kantorovitch, 1965).

Ragnar Frisch could not ignore those various writings, which had to do with the application of the methods on which he was working. Why is it that he so seldom discussed them or referred to them? We can think of possible specific explanations: He did not like the Walrasian general-equilibrium approach that was used in the debate about the feasibility of socialist planning. (But why so?) He had much less confidence than other economists in prices as instruments for the implementation of plans (a subject to which we shall return). Do the proceedings of the Vatican study week give a sign in favor of the last hypothesis?[3]

The Vatican discussion of Frisch's contribution was opened by Maurice Allais, who disputed the idea that planning could do any good. His conclusion stated: "For me, Frisch's paper appears as a long and convincing demonstration of the practical impossibility of planning in Frisch's sense." Although Frisch answered some points concerning the preference function (to which we shall return), he neglected those about feasibility. Because Allais had earlier criticized some factual statements as being just Frisch's opinion, Frisch did not want to enter into an argument; his answer was short: "My paper presents what I personally think is the most appropriate procedure for constructing a national economic decision model. It represents my personal creed at this stage." Very often in international meetings, Frisch appeared to me careful to avoid anything that could have fueled a political discussion.

A surprising clue to explain why Frisch did not examine at length the feasibility of economic planning was given, in a somewhat different context, by Leif Johansen (1974), who wrote: "Ragnar Frisch was of course aware of these difficulties, but he did not yield to them. One of his favorite maxims was that the difference between a manageable and an impossible problem is merely that it takes a little longer time to solve the latter." Could even a clever man get away in conscience with such a gross conjuring trick?[4]

The favor with which economic planning was viewed in many circles during the 1950s and 1960s had to do with the interpretation of the then-available factual information. As I suggested earlier, that information was often received as showing that planning did perform well. Frisch certainly had no doubt about that, and he wrote that "it suffices [for the Soviets] to let the West continue in its stubborn planlessness. It will then rapidly be lagging behind economically and will in due time fall from the tree like an overripe pear" (Frisch, 1962, p. 257). He was also quoted by Allais as having said in the Vatican study week that "the centralized

---

[3] Perhaps the hypothesis also has a part to play in the fact that Frisch apparently ignored, in his writings, Oscar Lange, who had written about market socialism, had been associated with the Cowles Commission and hence with the Econometric Society from 1939 to 1945, had been Frisch's substitute as acting editor of *Econometrica* from 1942 to 1946, was later promoting econometrics and quantitative economic programming, served (like Frisch) as a planning adviser in India, and finally was involved in Warsaw in actual economic planning. Lange had always had strong political motivations, probably was much less of a democrat than Frisch, and at times could not speak out freely in postwar Poland. It is also true, however, that Lange was less interested than Frisch in mathematical programming techniques and more interested in the theoretical study of economic systems, of socialist systems in particular.

[4] About the awareness of difficulties, I can quote here Frisch (1962) writing on "the main types of problems we encounter when we face the tremendous task of optimal economic programming in all its complexity" (p. 262).

economies had grown faster than the market economies." But such statements were not particular to him – far from it.

When we reflect today on what now appears to have been a major factual error, we have to recognize that the performance of the formerly centrally planned economies was much poorer during the last three decades than before. We also have to recognize the difficulty of objective international comparisons, even within the family of Western developed market economies; a significant part remains subjective in the more difficult cases; present assessments may be biased in the reverse direction because of the swing of the pendulum of public opinion. However, it is fair to say that many Western intellectuals were fooled by deliberate misinformation. That was partly their fault: They were careless in accepting official data coming from totalitarian regimes; they did not want to closely study the rare dissenting evidence, which would have weakened their own views.

3 Search for a Better Economic System

Let us now consider in broad terms the views of Ragnar Frisch about the desirable transformation of Western economies. My query may be somewhat unfair, because an independent professor is not required to have clear views on everything. On the other hand, some of his statements against the existing state of affairs were so strong that they called for explanations on how to improve on it.

Before anything else we must remember that Frisch was a true and unfailing democrat. This emerges from his writings in many brief hints with unambiguous connotations. It is also testified by his students. For instance, writing about his teaching and his general philosophy, Bjerkholt and Longva (1980) have the following sentence, which makes the point and actually goes beyond: "He had a never faltering and strong belief in the possibilities for improving the material conditions of mankind as well as promoting a true democracy by appropriate use of scientific economic programming at the national and international level" (p. 14). That position inspired his attachment to the neutrality of economists and to the role of politicians as responsible for the choice of priorities.

Frisch insisted on the point whenever he discussed the preference function. For instance: "We as scientific analysts are perfectly neutral ... regarding what the preference function ought to be. This is a matter to be decided by the politician" (PAS, 1965, p. 107). But he also wanted to strongly rebut the statements made by Allais, in his comments to both Stone's and Frisch's papers, according to which the author of a decision model, as opposed to the author of a forecasting model, cannot be neutral. At a point he went beyond purely logical argument and said: "For centuries there has been a tendency to define neutrality in economics by saying that any analysis which takes the free market system as an axiom is "neutral", but any analysis that has the audacity of questioning the free market system is not "neutral", but "political" and should therefore not be allowed to enter into the ivory tower of the scientist.... Today we have to recognise the fact that there are *other economic systems* that are "in the air" and must be discussed by us as social engineers" (PAS, 1965, p. 1220).

Ragnar Frisch clearly was not satisfied with the actual form taken by "the free market economy," a historical form that he used to call "unenlightened financialism," suggesting in a single phrase that the move from "enlightened despotism" had been politically good but economically damaging. His criticism concerned the efficiency and equity of the system rather than, as we might be inclined to think today, its stability. According to Leif Johansen (1973), Frisch reoriented his modeling work after the 1940s in part because "he considered the problem of avoiding depressions as solved." The following quotation well reveals his state of mind in 1960: "If it is at all possible to save the Western democracies, we must find a way to safeguard the freedom and ethical and moral dignity of the individual in the true spirit of the age of enlightenment and at the same time achieve full and effective use of all resources, natural as well as human know-how. This goal can never be reached through unenlightened financialism, but it has become technically possible since the advent of the electronic computer and the econometric methods" (Frisch, 1962, p. 258). Also interesting is the following: "I will state a personal belief that 100 years from now our grand-children will devote practically all their efforts to the study of those models that deviate from the free market system. They will use only an infinitesimal amount of their energy discussing such things as, say, the stability of the equilibrium in a free market system" (PAS, 1965, p. 1221).

Again, the views and projects of Frisch did not look extravagant at the time. For instance, Richard Stone wrote: "The imperfections of *laissez faire* as a mode of economic organisation are so glaring that it has been either thrown out altogether, as in socialist countries, or modified out of all recognition by state intervention even in countries devoted to the principle of free enterprise. So angry have men been of the abuses, injustices and waste of resources... that they have shown very little appreciation of the good points of the system they were destroying.... The purpose of this paper is to discuss how economic models might help us to reconcile the advantages of central planning with those of individual initiative" (PAS, 1965, p. 4). Also, in a different context: "The purpose of the model is to explore the problems of economic growth in Britain with the object of finding means to make the rate of growth higher than it has been in the past.... Since we are contemplating the possibility of a rate of economic growth as much as two to three times as high as the present one..." (Stone and Brown, 1962, p. 288).

Unfortunately, Ragnar Frisch did not go very far into defining the alternative economic system that would have had his preference. He gave only a few hints in this respect. Firstly, considering what others said or wrote at the time, it is remarkable to note that Frisch did not see the problem of developing countries as having been essentially different from that of Western democracies. On the contrary, the "Oslo channel model," presented as suited for the latter, had grown out of the consulting work done in Egypt on the evaluation of development projects. Frisch's message, both in India and Egypt, was something like the following: "your country has good prospects provided your economy is planned in a wise way, i.e. with a global plan based on optimality computations."[5]

Secondly, Frisch had serious reservations about the widely held idea of relying on "decentralization through prices." The following quotation is perfectly clear in this respect: "The endless discussions amongst Soviet economists on how the prices ought to be fixed indicate the complexity of this matter. From my long-time study I have reached three rather definite conclusions. First, in any economy where one formulates preferences about the goals to be attained... it is *impossible* to leave the prices alone. They have to be tampered with. Second, even the strictest direct control over prices in all parts of the economy is *not sufficient*.... Third, actual prices... can only be fixed after a system of shadow prices has been found through the optimum solution of a... model which is formulated in *technical units only*" (Frisch, 1962, p. 268).

The last condition refers to Frisch's conception of there being two stages in planning: first, selection of the optimum solution; second, its implementation. We shall return to this conception, which he stated many times. For the time being, we must note that the idea of economists working out the quantitative objectives to be achieved by an optimal plan carries with it the notion of a rather technocratic economic system, even if one says that economists act as neutral experts, given the preferences of political authorities. How such a system could be accepted as a permanent component of a democracy was never explained by Frisch, so far as I know.

Ragnar Frisch lived long enough to realize that the economic systems of Western democracies were not evolving in the direction he was favoring, but rather were reverting to "unenlightened financialism." The ideological evolution within his profession was also moving away from his

---

[5] See Frisch (1960, 1965). The first reference is a selection of memoranda written by Frisch during his stay in India from the end of 1954 to the spring of 1955. It turns out to be a study on how linear programming can be used for national economic planning. Technical problems are discussed at length. The somewhat more general first essay, on "Planning in underdeveloped economy," is only 12 pages long.

views. To a large extent, that must explain why he grew increasingly critical in scientific meetings, and no doubt elsewhere.

4   Econometrics and the Need for Planning

The quotation at the end of the first section of this essay presents econometrics as *the* instrument for the formulation of development plans. Such an association between econometrics and planning was often made by Frisch in the last decades of his life, but he had a rather personal selection of those parts of econometrics that were really useful for planning. It is part of the subject of this essay to note which parts he was *not* interested in, whereas many of his colleagues working on planning felt differently. The two most significant ones concern macroeconometric models, of the type particularly promoted by Jan Tinbergen and Lawrence Klein, and decision rules under uncertainty. On the other hand, we must carefully look here at Frisch's conception of the proper decision models for planning.

At the Vatican study week Franklin Fisher gave a paper on "dynamic structure and estimation in economy-wide econometric models." In the discussion, the longest intervention was made by Frisch. Surprisingly, his main point was to dispute the relevance of looking for unbiased estimators and to insist on the importance of the purpose for which the estimate was going to be used. Clearly, he was not much interested in the models being studied, a kind that he often called "growth models." That lack of interest must be related to three aspects of Frisch's ideas.

In the first place, according to him, development planning required decision models, which he sharply opposed to the most commonly used econometric models mainly intended to make projections. "In most countries, the shift [toward a decision] viewpoint is based on a sort of half-logic which I have never been able to understand and which, I think, will never be able to yield fundamental solutions. On the one hand one . . . tries to make projections. . . . On the other hand one will *afterwards* try to use such projections as a basis for decisions" (Frisch, 1962, pp. 252–3). He later granted in the same text that a decision model could be obtained if "the possible decisions were built in *explicitly* as essential variables." Undoubtedly that rule was applied in the models that he discussed in the 1940s with his students, probably not so different from Tinbergen's "growth models," although they early turned toward the analysis of more structural problems, such as the effects of price controls and tax policy or monetary policy on investment, consumption, imports, and employment.[6] Thus the logic of mathematical programming was

---

[6] The work done by Frisch on economic policy immediately after World War II and later is reported in Johansen (1969, pp. 309–13). That article gives some indication of the models Frisch was considering during successive periods. In the first half of the 1950s

introduced in his work and progressively became dominant. In the 1960s his preferred decision models were of a quite different type, which we shall examine in a moment.

In the second place, he did not believe macroeconomic time series could provide the information needed for the models he was considering: "Such series are irrelevant for a great number of the estimates of the equations that enter into the equational system we have to use in development planning" (PAS, 1965, pp. 457–8). The main source of information contemplated by him was engineering data, which he viewed as having a fair degree of accuracy (as pointed out by Bjerve, Chapter 17, this volume, Frisch was not very demanding in terms of accuracy). Interview data would also play a part in the determination of the preference function to be maximized.

In the third place, Frisch seemed to me to be sharing an attitude that I often met at that time among people working for planning or economic policy analysis, namely, a tendency to underestimate the need for in-depth studies of economic behavior. Because in any case an important private sector would remain, reactions of the private economy had to be taken into account; but existing knowledge about them was weak and deserved extensive research. Macroeconometric models certainly were not providing the only tool to be used in that research, but they did contribute to it. If I am right, Frisch paid little attention in the 1960s to that need for a better econometric knowledge of economic behavior. For someone who when young had been writing on the estimation of demand and supply laws, this looked to me like a surprising attitude. Probably he thought that sufficient knowledge existed concerning the main economic behaviors for calibration of whatever was needed in his models. Alternatively, he may have left to others the pursuit of a line of research he was no longer working on.

The discussion by Frisch of another paper given at the Vatican study week was revealing of another surprising lack of interest. Henri Theil spoke of "decision rules and simulation techniques in development programming" and explained how the certainty equivalence property could be used in order to cope with the fact that decisions have to be made under conditions of uncertainty; he also explained that because the proper model was dynamic, one had to determine not only the first-period decision but also the decision rule for subsequent periods, or equivalently the maximizing strategy, of which the first-period decision was a part. Frisch apparently did not understand the point, or at least did

---

they were extended input–output models, which inspired those, called MODIS, built and used in the Norwegian administration. In the latter part of the 1950s they had turned into comprehensive programming models. Interest in developing economies then led to adapting the models toward the task of evaluating investment projects, as we shall see. Additional information can be found in Chapters 1 and 17, this volume.

not accept the proposed dynamic programming solution, for he said: "Regarding the very principles of using rules of strategy, I really doubt whether that is a practical proposition in actual economic planning. To me it would seem much more efficient, much more practical, to use what I call... the principle of moving planning" (PAS, 1965, p. 496).[7] My comment about this point may have to do with the fact that the strategic aspect of planning under uncertainty became an important part of accepted wisdom in France under the leadership of P. Massé (1965).

The first objective of the models on which Frisch was working during the 1960s was simultaneous evaluations of many investment projects, among which one had to choose those to be carried out. Such was the main planning problem of Egypt as he had perceived it in Cairo, where indeed, among other projects, construction of the High Dam on the Nile was contemplated. After Dorfman's paper dealing with public-investment projects at the Vatican study week, Frisch said that "there are certain things that can... be included in a project description, and which can be specified without relating this project to other projects.... But there are other effects... which can only be described by considering this project as part of the whole economy. Here is where the economists come into the picture. Some of these effects... are very difficult to trace. This is just the *raison d'être* of the complete decision model" (PAS, 1965, p. 221).

Also in a different context, distinguishing his decision models from the more common and "passive" growth models, he wrote that "we have to consider a *great number* of... decisional parameters, for instance those characterizing many different types of investment and their relations to the current account activity of many different domestic sectors.

---

[7] A background for clarifying Frisch's position is supplied by his long article listed here as Frisch (1963), an article to which Johansen (1969) drew attention precisely because it deals with "strategies" for controlling a dynamic economy. Frisch there discussed a linear model inspired by the familiar multiplier-accelerator theory, with the addition of "autonomous investment" H_t and of a "government strategy with respect to current account expenditure," actually a rule giving government consumption G_t as a linear function of output Y_{t-1} and Y_{t-2}. The bulk of the article deals with the mathematical solution of the dynamic model, for the case of a rule with fixed coefficients. In the last part on "the programming approach" Frisch shows a definite preference for the situation in which the government would control the series of autonomous investment, either fully or through "its simultaneous probability distribution." In the absence of such a real control, he proposes a "moving optimization," in fact an expenditure rule giving the coefficients to apply in the computation of G_t; these coefficients would then depend on the last actually realized output growth rate. His heuristic argument looks to me as being motivated by a concern for sustainability, as well as for growth. He ends up with: "The above expenditure rule is as good a rule as can reasonably be deviced. But the rule only leads to protection against decline, not to real progress.... If the model should have been able to display a driving force for progress, it would have been necessary to add a relation that indicates an effect of government current expenditure on autonomous investment."

These remarks will apply in all countries, less developed and more developed" (Frisch, 1962, pp. 262–3).

So, large programming models were being contemplated, all the more so as Frisch did not want to neglect the regional dimension. But models cannot be large enough to cover everything. The aggregation problem had to be faced. Frisch touched on it many times. He had some ideas on how to cope with it; for instance, "it is wanted to consider not only a detailed list of specific projects but also groups of projects, i.e. aggregation of projects into *channels*, each channel being defined by certain average project characteristics" (Frisch, 1962, p. 272). In broader terms, his attitude was marked by two beliefs: (1) Aggregation always means a loss of accuracy, so that as long as it remains manageable, thanks to modern computing equipment and expertise, a wisely chosen, more detailed model is always an improvement. (2) There are no general rules on how best to avoid aggregation errors, so that the econometrician has to be pragmatic. I am not able to say more here, but I suspect the research memoranda available in Oslo contain a number of developments of the approaches explored by Frisch in order to tackle the aggregation problem.

5 Optimization

"To develop a technique of discussing feasible policy alternatives ... is one of the most burning needs in economic policy making. ... When the effort to map out a spectrum of feasible alternatives has gone on for a while, the conclusion will inevitably force itself ... that the number of alternatives is so great that it is impossible to keep track of them simply by listing them and looking at them. It will be understood that one needs an analytical technique for picking that one – or those – alternatives that are in some sense of the word the optimum ones. This leads directly to ... mathematical programming" (Frisch, 1962, pp. 253–4). This quotation conveys two ideas that are not equivalent: (1) There are too many feasible alternatives. (2) One needs to find the optimum one. In the 1960s, mathematical programming was seen at times as implied by the second idea, but at times also as a way of coping with the difficulty stressed by the first idea. Frisch had no opposition to the latter notion, but he was more interested in the direct determination of the optimum.

The objective function that the program had to maximize was most often presented as being "the preference function" of the political authority. The economists were serving as neutral experts and had to adopt whatever preferences the authority might have; they were then in a position to directly determine the preferred policy alternative from all the feasible ones. Starting from these principles, Frisch spent much of his time working on two technical problems: how to elicit the preference function, and how to compute the optimum of the program. The second problem falls completely outside the scope of this essay. But the approach recommended for solution of the first problem has to be briefly considered, in particular but not only because it was one of the research fields in which Frisch worked over and over again during the last two decades of his life.

He held the view that a program of well-planned interviews with politically responsible persons was the best approach in order to select the preference function for use in planning models. Johansen (1974) gave two examples in which Frisch actually used the approach. In 1948 or so, he interviewed, probably several times,[8] the minister of finance, with a number of questions related to the allocation of national product (14 variables were involved). In a paper read in Sweden in 1971 he reported the results of interviews with a high-ranking civil servant in the Norwegian Ministry of Finance; five variables were used, representing unemployment, the growth rate of national product, a measure of inequality in the distribution of income, the rate of inflation, and the trade balance. Of course, Frisch did not expect the authorities to express their preferences in the form of the objective function required for mathematical programming. He developed methods for, on the one hand, selecting questions that would make sense, be easily understood by the interviewed person, and reveal his preferences, while on the other hand constructing a preference function consistent with the answers. These methods were discussed in Johansen's article.

Certainly Frisch knew that his work could be considered only as exploratory. The preference function exhibited in his examples involved definitely fewer variables than would have been necessary for a real application of his programming models for the selection of development projects. He could not ignore, either, the rather special position of a respected professor interviewing people who, although endowed with high responsibilities, were disposed to give some of their time, so expressing their gratitude as well as their preferences. A large acceptance and diffusion of his general views about economic planning had to occur before one could seriously entertain the practical application of his methods.

Among those working on economic planning in the 1960s the consensus enlightened view was somewhat different. According to it, econ-

---

[8] Ragnar Frisch insisted on the idea of an iterative process in discussion with the policymaker. For instance, at the Vatican study week, Koopmans said that "when a policy maker is asked for his preferences, [he should] be given a chance to see the implications of confronting those preferences with the econometrician's model of the structure, so that he knows what is implied in the first indication of his preferences." Frisch entirely agreed and added: "But it is essential that the process be iterative in terms of *complete* optimal solutions and if you are going to have any complete solution, you must start by a preference function, trying to lead the politician's mind completely away from his preconceived ideas of the structure" (PAS, 1965, p. 1224).

omists, acting as neutral experts, would be able to specify a number of preference functions whose set would correctly span the family of those that political authorities could have. That specification would mainly come from the economists' knowledge of what was taken to be important in their country, as revealed by oral or written declarations as well as by earlier policy choices. Each one of the preference functions in the set would be used in turn as the objective function of the program, so selecting the corresponding "optimum," which should rather be called the congruent privileged alternative. The political authorities would then be presented the full set of privileged alternatives and would choose one of them. In other words, the set of preferences functions would lead to a good representation of the set of relevant efficient solutions.

Frisch was not opposed to that consensus view. Considering how economic policy ought to be discussed in a democracy, he wrote, and underlined, "It is alternative optimal solutions and not alternative specific measures that should form the object of public debate" (Frisch, 1962, p. 256).

6   Implementation

Ragnar Frisch used to distinguish two problems in economic planning: selection and implementation. Selection was the determination of the optimum, which is what has been considered so far here and about which most of Frisch's writings on planning were concerned.

The separation between the two problems was justified as convenient in practice, because in that way "the biggest advantages of a precise quantitative analysis [of selection] can be gained" and "the selection problem can be studied without stating a priori the kind of economic institutions (competitive markets or central controls etc.) one is prepared to accept." Frisch recognized that the separation had a cost, but he sometimes drew surprising conclusions from the remark. The following quotation (Frisch, 1962, p. 267) is worth noting: "After the selection problem has been solved, one will take up the implementation problem. If on scrutiny one should find that practical difficulties of implementation under an existing institutional, administrative and financial set-up make it impossible to reach the high goals... which have emerged as feasible from the selection viewpoint, two ways are open: either to try to change the... structure so as to make the high goals attainable, or to... acquiesce to lower goals. In the latter case the computation of the difference between the two results will furnish a sound piece of information."

Frisch did not explain how to determine the solution that would be implementable with actual institutions, though reaching only "lower goals." We should say today that he did not work out the second-best solution. [Johansen (1974) remarked that Frisch hardly wrote on implementation; he pointed out that even when Frisch had chosen to deal with "an implementation system for optimal national economic planning" at the third international conference on operations research, held in Oslo in 1963, the proceedings published only "Part I – Prolegomena: Selection".] He was, however, very modern in spirit when stressing that the difficulties in implementation arose mainly from incentive incompatibility.[9] That was the message of the published part of his paper at the Vatican study week. In order to survey that (short) part, I shall let Frisch speak as he did in 1963. Here are a few extracts from his text, in the order in which they appear (PAS, 1965, pp. 1197–204):

> What I am going to present to you today is in all humility a frontal attack on a ghost. . . . I think it is fair to say that the free market system has two advantages: (1) its simplicity and (2) its effort-releasing effect. But it has one fundamental shortcoming: it does not assure the realization of *specific* preferences. . . . The purpose of wise planning is to realize many special goals, while retaining as many as possible of the advantages of the competitive system. We wish to search for some better economic system. . . . But in that search, we encounter a ghost that has been haunting all of us for the last generations. . . .
>
> This ghost is human nature itself. Many people . . . can be induced to make a personal effort only if thereby they can obtain some tangible advantage. . . . The historical challenge, facing us as economists and social engineers, is to help the politicians work out an economic system built upon a set of incentives, under the impact of which the economic activity will be satisfactory. . . . We must find a means of circumventing the human obstacle to human progress. . . .
>
> The more spectacular deviation from the traditional market economy is found in the centrally steered economies of the East. . . . But the same ghost has acted in his typical manner also. . . .
>
> The suggestion I have to make regarding ways and means of finally killing the ghost . . . is a suggestion as to *a way of thinking* which I believe is a *conditio since qua non* for real progress. . . . We must begin by making a clear-cut and precise distinction between two phases of the steering work: the selection and the implementation. . . . The implementation analysis is a study of the kinds of national or international institutions most helpful in bringing about *that particular constellation* of the national or world economy which has emerged as the optimal one in the selection analysis, or at least to bring about a close approximation to that constellation.

After that statement, the last page of the text deals with selection analysis.

Confidence was once again expressed in the ability of economists and

---

[9] In his writings from the same period, references to incentive effects were not narrowly limited to planning. One could survey these writings in order to spot where he had the insight into the later view of incentive compatibility as a major part of economic research. Once more in his life he exhibited a shrewd heuristic understanding that some questions were important for economic theory.

econometricians to serve as "social engineers." But no method was given for implementation analysis. Undoubtedly, Ragnar Frisch in his seventies felt that his agenda was unfinished, particularly in this respect.

When listening to Frisch 30–40 years ago, I often found his introductions more interesting than what followed. Like his Norwegian students, I was fascinated by many of his ideas about our discipline, its relevance and its scientific methodology; but I could also be worried about what I perceived to be a lack of realism; in particular, I could be irritated when he began to discuss the technical details of mathematical programming, on which he spent so much of his time and effort.[10] Great men may have their weaknesses.

References

Bjerkholt, O. (1995). Ragnar Frisch: the originator of econometrics. In: *Foundations of Modern Econometrics: The Selected Essays of Ragnar Frisch*, ed. O. Bjerkholt, pp. xiii–lii. Aldershot: Edward Elgar.

Bjerkholt, O., and Longva, S. (1980). *MODIS IV – A Model for Economic Analysis and National Planning*. Oslo: Central Bureau of Statistics.

Frisch, R. (1960). *Planning for India – Selected Explorations in Methodology*. Calcutta: Indian Statistical Institute.

(1962). Preface to the Oslo channel model: a survey of types of economic forecasting and programming. In: *Europe's Future in Figures*, ed. R. C. Geary, pp. 248–86. Amsterdam: North Holland.

(1963). Parametric solution and programming of the Hicksian model. In: *Essays on Econometrics and Planning*, pp. 45–82. Calcutta: Eka Press.

(1965). Planning for the United Arab Republic. *Economics of Planning* 5:29–42.

Hayek, F. (1944). *The Road to Serfdom*. London: Routledge & Kegan Paul.

Johansen, L. (1969). Ragnar Frisch's contribution to economics. *Swedish Journal of Economics* 71:302–24.

(1973). Ragnar Frisch (1895–1973). *Economics of Planning* 2:1–2.

(1974). Establishing preference functions for macroeconomic decision models. Some observations on Ragnar Frisch's contributions. *European Economic Review* 5:41–66.

Kantorovitch, L. (1965). *The Best Uses of Economic Resources*. Oxford: Pergamon.

Lange, O. (1936–37). On the economic theory of socialism. *Review of Economic Studies* 3(1):53–71 and 4(2):123–42.

Lerner, A. (1944). *The Economics of Control: Principles of Welfare Economics*. New York: Macmillan.

Lewis, W. A. (1948). *The Principles of Economic Planning*. London: Allen & Unwin.

---

[10] The following statement of Johansen (1974) vividly echoes that irritation: "The main ideas in his works ... often do no stand out clearly because he treated technical and practical details at such great length" (p. 542).

Massé, P. (1965). *Le plan ou l'anti-hasard*. Paris: Gallimard.
Meade, J. (1948). *Planning and the Price Mechanism*. London: Allen & Unwin.
PAS (1965). *The Econometric Approach to Development Planning*. Citta del Vaticano: Pontificia Academia Scientiarum.
Stone, R., and Brown, J. (1962). A long-term growth model for the British economy. In: *Europe's Future in Figures*, ed. R. C. Geary. Amsterdam: North Holland.
von Mises, L. (1981). *Socialism: An Economic and Sociological Analysis*, 3rd English edition. Indianapolis: Liberty Classics.

CHAPTER 19

On the Need for Macroeconomic Planning in Market Economies: Three Examples from the European Monetary Union Project

A. J. Hughes Hallett

1   Introduction

However deep the economic recession may have been in the 1930s, those were extraordinarily productive years for economists. In 1933 Frisch founded the Econometric Society and, along with it, many of the formal methods we now use to analyse the working of our economies and the impact of economic policies. Then in 1936 Keynes published his general theory, and Tinbergen published the world's first econometric model. Both events were ultimately dedicated to providing the theoretical justification (in the first case) and the practical means (in the second) for adopting and evaluating active interventionist policies for achieving society's economic targets.

Since then, neoclassical economics, particularly that with a "freshwater" American flavour, has mounted a major counterchallenge in favour of noninterventionism, arguing that if markets work efficiently then they will adjust automatically. Therefore, if policy is needed, it is for reasons of redistribution; or because markets fail; or because there are specific restrictions or externalities in people's behaviour that prevent prices adjusting by enough; or because there are inherent lags in information collection and decision making. In such cases there will be a case for policy, but only for purposes of increasing supply-side responsiveness, of correcting market failures, of increasing market efficiency in terms of speeding up responses and improving price signals, or of removing externalities and noncooperative inefficiencies in national policy-making. Hence, even under this paradigm there is considerable need for, and scope for, policy interventions in a fully functioning market economy. My purpose in this essay is to show that the need for policy has not been overtaken or rendered irrelevant by the neoclassical paradigm.

I am grateful to an anonymous referee and to Roger Sandilands, John Ireland, and especially Maria Demertzis for their comments and suggestions. But the usual disclaimer applies with added force, because they may not always have agreed with the interpretations offered here.

This holds true for the monetary union proposed for Europe in particular, despite the many neoclassical features assumed by that regime. Indeed, left to itself, a monetary union will actually have the effect of exaggerating the restrictions, externalities, and market inefficiencies in the national economies because the process of market integration will spread the effects of market failures all around the system, and because it may well slow down the adjustment responses at the same time.

A discussion of economic planning in a market-economy context is of particular interest because Frisch himself had such a strong interest in economic policy and was a stern critic of the embryonic "European union" of his day. What would his policy analysis have made of the monetary-union proposal? Would it appear beneficial? If not, what policies would be needed to make it work successfully?

In fact, Frisch opposed the European Economic Community (EEC) as it then was, claiming in his pamphleteering work that it represented nothing more than "conservatism, capitalism and catholicism." By that, I think he meant the following:

1. *Conservatism*: an obsession with inflation aversion at the cost of output and employment. In modern language, an overriding concern with credibility and the financial markets, with too little attention to performance on the real side and fiscal sustainability. This amounts to a type of policy failure, and we shall illustrate it with examples of the fiscal difficulties which a monetary union would introduce.
2. *Capitalism*: an assumption of perfectly clearing markets, ignoring the inherent constraints on market behaviour and the need for some social objectives. We shall illustrate this with examples from labour-market aggregation with immobility and the tendency for factor price equalization to worsen inflation. Market failures therefore.
3. *Catholicism* (in the sense of "universality," without religious connotations): an overemphasis on centralized, rule-based decision making, without much care for redistribution and incentive compatibility. This can be illustrated using the differential impacts of an exchange-rate regime dedicated to Europe-wide targets, on the different participant countries.

These labels are of course just metaphors; they are not intended to represent precise philosophical or religious concepts.

2   Frisch's Theory of Economic Policy: Then and Now

Frisch's concept of economic policy and planning was based on his classification of variables into targets and instruments. The target variables would be assigned ideal values that the planner would like to reach. But it might not be technically feasible to reach all those target values in every period. In that case the target variables would need to be embedded within a preference function that would describe how the failure to reach one target value should be traded off, at the margin, against the failure to reach another target value. That would allow policy-makers to create a welfare-optimizing package of policies (Frisch, 1969). That, of course, comes close to the traditional Tinbergen-Theil "flexible-target" concept of economic planning: First you decide where you would like to go, then you pick a sequence of policy values that, when constrained by a model of feasible economic performance, can be expected to steer the economy as closely as possible to that path. It is important to say that although that approach was developed in the literature by Tinbergen (1952) and Theil (1964), it was first proposed and then used by Frisch in his work for the United Nations (Frisch, 1949).

How well has Frisch's target-instrument approach to economic design survived? The recent literature would give the impression that it has been overtaken and replaced by the more formal techniques of control engineering and optimal-control theory (e.g., Pindyck, 1973; Aoki, 1976; Chow, 1976). But the simplicity of the Frisch approach and the ease with which it can be extended to deal with problems of risk sensitivity, multiple policy-makers, and forward-looking and nonlinear behaviour have ensured that it is still widely used in practice – both in economic problems and outside (Hughes Hallett, 1989). This section illustrates some of those features, so that we will be in a position to use Frisch's approach to analyse his other great policy concern: economic integration in Europe.

Fixed Targets. The simplest version of Frisch's approach starts with a conventional econometric model:

$$Y_t = \sum_{j=1}^{\ell} \pi_{1j} Y_{t-j} + \sum_{j=0}^{k} \pi_{2j} X_{t-j} + e_t \qquad (1)$$

where Y_t are g endogenous variables, x_t are n policy instruments, and e_t are noncontrollable random variables. Y_t itself will contain a subset of m policy targets y_t; the remaining elements of Y_t will be nontargets; and e_t will be composed of variables exogenous to both the policy-makers and the model (including the model's disturbance terms).

Given (1), a naive policy choice would be to pick x_t so as to reach the desired target values y_t^d in each period $t = 1, \ldots, T$, each time taking all lagged values as fixed and setting the e_t variables at their expected values. Deleting the nontarget equations from (1), the required interventions are

$$X_t^* = \tilde{\pi}_{20}^{-1}(y_t^d - a_t) \qquad (2)$$

where

$$a_t = \sum_{j=1}^{k} \pi_{1j} Y_{t-j} + \sum_{j=0}^{k} \pi_{2j} X_{t-j} + E_t(e_t)$$

is a known vector at the start of period t, and $\tilde{\pi}_{20}$ contains just m rows from π_{20} in (1). Of course, (2) exists only if $m = n$ and $\tilde{\pi}_{20}$ is nonsingular. Under these conditions, y_t^d will be achieved exactly (in expectation) period by period. In time this became known as Tinbergen's theory of economic policy.

Policy Effectiveness. A second and more important point is that by concentrating on the conditions for $\tilde{\pi}_{20}$ to have an inverse, we force policy-makers to distinguish clearly between targets and instruments and prevent them from trying to "decouple" their policies by assigning instruments to targets on a 1-to-1 basis. This is a matter of policy effectiveness. By focusing on the condition that $\tilde{\pi}_{20}$ should possess an inverse, rather than replacing $\tilde{\pi}_{20}$ by a diagonal assignment matrix, each policy instrument will be given its own level of specification while correctly allowing for its interactions with the other instruments. The instruments will then be coordinated correctly. Otherwise we would deny ourselves Pareto efficiency by failing to coordinate our domestic-policy instruments properly. And that would simply result in a decline in the effectiveness of our policy instruments (Cooper, 1969).

Flexible Targets. The fixed-target approach can be criticized because there is nothing to restrain the cost of intervening nor to ensure that the interventions will be politically and administratively feasible. Similarly there is no mechanism to take account of the predictable dynamic effects after each intervention, nor is there any mechanism for dealing with uncertainty or multiple policy-makers in any systematic way. Fortunately all these features can be incorporated by introducing explicit preference functions, as Frisch had suggested. The details were worked out by Theil (1964).

Let the planning priorities be represented by a normalized quadratic function of the deviations of the target and instrument variables from their ideal values, y_t^d and x_t^d, respectively, up to an arbitrary planning horizon $t = 1, \ldots, T$. Define $\tilde{y}_t = y_t - y_t^d$ and $\tilde{x}_t = x_t - x_t^d$ to be those policy "failures" or deviations. The objective is then to minimize

$$w = \frac{1}{2}(\tilde{y}'B\tilde{y} + \tilde{x}'A\tilde{x}) \tag{3}$$

where $\tilde{y}' = (\tilde{y}_1', \ldots, \tilde{y}_T')$ and $\tilde{x}' = (\tilde{x}_2', \ldots, \tilde{x}_T')$. Theil specified A and B to be positive semidefinite and symmetric matrices, because society's true collective preferences cannot be known a priori and can at best be specified as an implicit performance index $w = w(\tilde{y}, \tilde{x})$ that is convex, that is twice differentiable, and that satisfies the usual axioms. Hence (3) is a second-order approximation to $w(\tilde{y}, \tilde{x})$, where[1]

$$Q = \frac{\partial^2 w}{\partial z \partial z'}, \quad Q = \begin{bmatrix} B & 0 \\ 0 & A \end{bmatrix}, \quad z = \begin{bmatrix} y \\ x \end{bmatrix} \quad (4)$$

which allows the numerical values of the relative priorities to vary with activity levels (Hughes Hallett, 1979). This is an important point, because Frisch argued that policy-makers would not know how to specify their priorities exactly ab initio, but would have to discover them on the basis of trial and error, or introspection (Frisch, 1957). He also argued that an appropriate social-welfare objective would be an aggregate of the preferences of the different decision-making groups in society, not just of the politicians in power at some given moment. An aggregate of these different preferences cannot be specified a priori, but must be built up from the participants' underlying preferences (Hughes Hallett, 1991).

The targets themselves are governed by a dynamic model such as

$$y_t = f(y_t, y_{t-1}, x_t, e_t) \quad (5)$$

where e_t are exogenous (random) variables. Under suitable nonsingularity conditions, the first-order approximation

$$y = Rx + s \quad (6)$$

where

$$R = \begin{bmatrix} R_{11} & & & 0 \\ \cdot & \cdot & & \\ \cdot & & \cdot & \\ \cdot & & & \\ R_{T1} & \cdot & \cdot & \cdot & R_{TT} \end{bmatrix}$$

contains the dynamic policy multipliers $R_{tj} = \partial y_t/\partial x_j$ for $t \geq j$, and zeros elsewhere. The noncontrollable elements are represented by $s' = (s'_1, \ldots, s'_T)$, where

$$S_t = \sum_{j=1}^{t} (\partial y_t/\partial e_j)e_j + (\partial y_t/\partial y_0)y_0$$

Deleting the nontarget rows from (6) will produce a small set of constraints from even the largest models.

Now, substituting $\tilde{y} = R\tilde{x} + c$ into (3), where $c = s - y^d$, yields the constrained objective function

---

[1] The zero restrictions in Q are for notational convenience only and assume additive separability between targets and instruments. This is a plausible assumption, but it is not a necessary one. The more general specification is dealt with by Theil (1964).

$$w = \frac{1}{2}\tilde{x}'K\tilde{x} + k'\tilde{x} + \left[b'c + \frac{1}{2}c'Bc\right] \qquad (7)$$

where $K = R'BR + A$ and $k = R'Bc$. The optimal decisions are therefore

$$x^* = x^d - K^{-1}k \qquad (8)$$

In order to deal with uncertainty, the policy-maker is assumed to replace the objective function by its expected value $E_t(w) = E(w|\Omega_t)$ and optimize that conditional on the currently available information Ω_t. But at $t = 1$,

$$E_1[w(u, x)] - w[E_1(y), x] = \frac{1}{2}\left\{E_1(s'Bs) - E_1(s)'BE_1(s)\right\} \qquad (9)$$

Hence (9) is invariant to the choice of x so long as the variance-covariance matrix of s is independent of x. Hence the optimal certainty-equivalent decisions are given by (8), with $E_1(s)$ replacing s within c and k. Consequently the initial calculations [i.e., (8), with $E_1(s)$] give first-period certainty-equivalent decisions, but the list of *implemented* decisions x_t^*, taken from each of the subsequent revisions with respect to Ω_t, $t = 2, \ldots, T$, in turn, is multiperiod certainty-equivalent. In modern terms, first-period certainty equivalence means optimal open-loop decisions, whereas multiperiod certainty equivalence implies closed-loop control, because the revisions take place as often as the data availability and the decision machinery permit.

Risk Sensitivity. Extensions to remove the risk neutrality implied by (9) have been discussed by Hughes Hallett (1984). A more general formulation would represent the expected value of some utility function $u(w)$ by a combination of all the moments of w, $E_t + \Sigma a_j \mu_j$, where $\mu_j = E_t[w - E_t(W)]^j$ for $a_j \geq 0$ and $j \geq 2$. As an approximation, we might consider

$$\min_x \left\{\alpha E_t(w) + \frac{1}{2}(1 - \alpha)V_t(w)\right\}, \qquad 0 \leq \alpha \leq 1$$

where α is a risk-aversion parameter. The solution can be written as Theil's decision rule (8), but with transformed preference parameters for A and B (Hughes Hallett, 1984). This reparameterization has the effect of penalizing the high-risk targets more heavily and the instruments less heavily and of introducing asymmetric penalties to compensate for asymmetrically distributed shocks.

Forward-looking Expectations. Forward-looking expectations can also be handled in this framework simply by solving the model numerically to obtain a matrix of dynamic multipliers for (6), which is not block-lower-triangular. Inserting (6) and (3) in the usual way yields (11) as the optimal decision rule, with a modified, nontriangular R matrix (Ghosh, Gilbert, and Hughes Hallett, 1987).

Decentralized Decision Making. The remaining sources, of uncertainty in (8) are policy variables in the hands of other national decision-makers. Suppose there are two decision-makers, with their own (private) objective functions

$$w^{(i)} = \frac{1}{2}\left(\tilde{y}^{(i)'} B^{(i)} \tilde{y}^{(i)} + \tilde{x}^{(i)'} A^{(i)} \tilde{x}^{(i)}\right), \quad i = 1, 2 \tag{10}$$

where $A^{(i)}$ and $B^{(i)}$ are positive definite and symmetric. The constraint set (6) must be partitioned between the targets of the two players:

$$\tilde{y}^{(i)} = R^{(i,1)} \tilde{x}^{(1)} + R^{(i,2)} \tilde{x}^{(2)} + c^{(i)}, \quad i = 1, 2 \tag{11}$$

Here $R^{(i,i)}$ describes domestic-policy responses, and $R^{(i,j)}$ spillovers from "abroad." Player i would substitute (11) into (10) to obtain his optimal reaction function:

$$\tilde{x}^{(i)*} = -\left[R^{(i,i)'} B^{(i)} R^{(i,i)} + A^{(i)}\right]^{-1} R^{(i,i)'} B^{(i)} \left(c^{(i)} + R^{(i,j)} \tilde{x}^{(j)}\right) \tag{12}$$

If player j does the same, then the solution of a two-player game (the Nash equilibrium), using (12) and its counterpart for $\tilde{x}^{(j)}$, is

$$\begin{bmatrix} I & -D^{(1)} \\ -D^{(2)} & I \end{bmatrix} \begin{bmatrix} \tilde{x}^{(1)} \\ \tilde{x}^{(2)} \end{bmatrix} = \begin{bmatrix} F^{(1)} & c^{(1)} \\ F^{(2)} & c^{(2)} \end{bmatrix} \tag{13}$$

where $F^{(i)} = -(R^{(i,i)'} B^{(i)} R^{(i,i)} + A^{(i)})^{-1} R^{(i,i)'} B^{(i)}$ and $D^{(i)} = F^{(i)} R^{(i,j)}$, for $i, j = 1$ and 2.

Cooperation. Frisch (1934) stressed the importance of coordination between policy-makers and actors who have different goals or priorities in the economy. This can be accommodated by solving

$$\min_{x^{(1)}, x^{(2)}} \left\{ w = \alpha w^{(1)} + (1 - \alpha) w^{(2)} \right\} \tag{14}$$

subject to (11). Pareto-optimal solutions will be obtained for each value of $0 < \alpha < 1$. But *incentive-compatible* solutions are only those that belong to the core subset, or strictly dominant subset, of that Pareto-optimal set – marked as *CD* on the "contract curve" in Figure 19.1, where *N* marks the outcomes of the noncooperative decisions obtained from (13).

More generally, incentive compatibility is used to secure gains for both players individually (not just on average) over the best that could be obtained by noncooperative decision making, that is, points in the whole area *NCD*, although preferably on the frontier *CD*. Outside that domi-

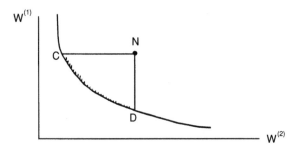

Figure 19.1. Contract curve.

nant set, one player will lose out and will revert to noncooperative policies. The cooperative regime then becomes unsustainable.

Nonlinear Behaviour. What happens if the targets respond to the policy instruments in a nonlinear way: $y = f(x, e)$? The constrained objective function (3) becomes

$$w = \frac{1}{2}\{[f(x,e) - y^d]'B[f(x,e) - y^d] + \tilde{x}'A\tilde{x}\} \quad (15)$$

The Newton-Raphson optimization procedure, with α_k chosen to ensure that $w(x_{k+1}) \leq w(x_k)$, at each step is

$$x_{k+1} = x_k - \alpha_k G_k^{-1} g_k \quad (16)$$

where $G_k = R'_k BR_k + A$ and $R_k = [\partial f/\partial x]_{x_k}$, and the gradient vector is

$$g_k = R'_k B[f(x_k, e) - y^d] + A\tilde{x}_k \quad (17)$$

But at the minimum of (15), $g_k = 0$. That implies

$$x_{k+1} = x^d - (R'_k BR_k + A)^{-1} R'_k Bc_k \quad (18)$$

because $f(x_k, e) = R_k x_k + s_k$, where $s_k = [\partial f/\partial e]_{x_k}$ and $c_k = s_k - y^d + R_k x^d$. That, of course, is just Theil's solution applied to a linearization of the model about x_k and e. The new policy x_{k+1} then implies a new linearization, and so on iteratively until convergence in R_k. If convergence difficulties arise, (18) may be accelerated as

$$\tilde{x}_{k+1} = -\alpha_k (R'_k BR_k + A)^{-1} R'_k Bc_k + (1 - \alpha_k)\tilde{x}_k \quad (19)$$

But that, in turn, is just the Newton algorithm again, because $s_k = y_k - R_k x_k$.

Thus the Frisch approach is actually the same Newton algorithm recommended in the recent literature for the control of nonlinear models. It involves a two-part iteration: a "prediction" phase to get $R_k = \partial y/\partial x_k$, alternating with a "control" phase to get x_{k+1} given R_k and s_k. Convergence depends on evaluating the roots of $[\partial R_k/\partial x] \cdot [\partial x_k/\partial R]$ along the iteration path (Brandsma, Hughes Hallett, and Windt, 1984). The first component depends only on the model, but the second depends on the priorities in (3). That brings out the interaction between economic feasibility and political preferences quite clearly.

3 When Is Monetary Union Desirable? Political versus Economic Benefits

What would Frisch's concept of policy analysis say about monetary union? Almost any analysis would contrast the microeconomic (market-efficiency) gains with the macroeconomic adjustment costs.[2] But in a single-market economy with free access and perfect competition, market efficiency will already be at a peak. So we need only to compare macroeconomic performance in and out of the union, given a fully competitive market economy.

Following Alesina and Grilli (1992, 1993) we write each country's welfare (loss) function according to the Barro-Gordon model:

$$w^i = \frac{1}{2}\left[p_i^2 + \beta_i(y_i - \bar{y}_i)^2\right] \tag{20}$$

where p_i is inflation, y_i is output, $\bar{y}_i$ is the desired level of output in country i, and β_i is the *relative* priority that country i attaches to stabilizing output. Output itself will then be determined by an expectations-augmented Phillips curve:[3]

$$y_i = (p_i - q_i) + v_i \tag{21}$$

where $q_i = E(p_i)$ is the anticipated inflation in country i, and v_i is a country-specific shock with mean zero and variance σ_i^2. This Phillips curve is expressed in deviations about the long-run, full-capacity, or "natural" level of output.

Minimizing (20) subject to (21) is the appropriate approach, because the monetary-union debate has largely been concerned with the trade-off between inflation and losses in output – the official aim being to secure price stability in the first place, together with a reasonable rate of growth if that can also be achieved (Giavazzi and Pagano, 1988; EEC, 1990). The standard (time-consistent) solution to this problem is given by

---

[2] There are also some macroeconomic gains from, e.g., exchange-rate stability. But as these affect market efficiency, they are counted as part of the microeconomic benefits here. In practice, market efficiency may not be as high as assumed in this idealized picture of the single market, but it is clearly the intention that it should be.

[3] Barro and Gordon (1983). The fact that y_i is defined as a deviation from its natural rate here is consistent with (20), because if y_i is such a deviation, then so is $\bar{y}_i$. But if y_i is in natural units in (20), then so is $\bar{y}_i$.

$$p_i = \beta_i \bar{y}_i - \frac{b_i}{1 + \beta_i} v_i \qquad (22)$$

The corresponding output level is

$$y_i = \frac{v_i}{1 + \beta_i} \qquad (23)$$

with variance $\sigma_{y_i} = \sigma_i^2/(1 + \beta_i)^2$. But if a monetary union is formed, the European authorities will have to pick a common inflation-monetary policy to minimize the Europe-wide loss function

$$w_E = \frac{1}{2}\left[p_E^2 + b(y_E - \bar{y}_E)^2\right] \qquad (24)$$

on behalf of each country involved. European output will then follow the European Phillips curve driven by the common inflation rate

$$y_E = p_E - q_E + u \qquad (25)$$

Minimizing (24) subject to (25) yields the union-wide outcomes

$$p_E = b\bar{y}_E - \frac{b}{1 + b} u \quad \text{and} \quad y_E = \frac{u}{1 + b} \qquad (26)$$

with output variance $\sigma_y^2 = \sigma_u^2/(1 + b)^2$. In this setup, b is the relative priority the European authorities place on output stability versus inflation, and u is the common (union-wide) shock.

The advantage (or otherwise) in joining the monetary union is now shown by comparing country i's expected welfare losses in and out of the union. Substituting (22) and (23) into the national loss function (20), and then (26) into (20), yields

$$E(w^i) = \frac{1}{2} E\left\{\left(B_i \bar{y}_i - \frac{\beta_i}{1 + \beta_i} v_i\right)^2 + \beta_i\left(\frac{1}{1 + \beta_i} v_i - \bar{y}_i\right)^2\right\} \qquad (27)$$

$$E(w_E^i) = \frac{1}{2} E\left\{\left(b\bar{y}_E - \frac{b}{1 + b} u\right)^2 + \beta_i\left(v_i - \frac{b}{1 + b} u - \bar{y}_i\right)^2\right\} \qquad (28)$$

respectively. After some manipulation, we have

$$E(w_E^i - w^i) = \frac{1}{2}\left\{\bar{y}^2(b^2 - \beta_i^2)\right.$$

$$+ (1 + \beta_i)\left[\left(\frac{b}{1 + b}\right)^2 \sigma_u^2 - \left(\frac{\beta_i}{1 + \beta_i}\right)^2 \sigma_i^2\right]$$

$$\left. - 2\beta_i\left[\left(\frac{b}{1 + b}\right)\text{cov}(u, v_i) - \left(\frac{\beta_i}{1 + \beta_i}\right)\sigma_i^2\right]\right\} \qquad (29)$$

where $\text{cov}(u, v_i) = \rho_i \sigma_u \sigma_i$, and ρ_i is the correlation coefficient between u and v_i.

This expression represents the net gain from joining the union. If it is negative, country i's losses will be lower (and its welfare higher) if it joins the union; but if it is positive, country i will be better off out of the union. These net benefits, however, can be decomposed into two elements; the political (based on the different relative preferences, b and β_i) and the economic (based on the differences between the average and country-specific output shocks, u and v_i). Obviously any decision to join the union will depend on both elements, but to see their effects we must separate them.

To get at the political element, we eliminate the economic differences by supposing $u = v_i$ [i.e., $\sigma_i^2 = \sigma_u^2 = \text{cov}(u, v_i)$]. Then (29) becomes

$$\begin{aligned} E(w_E^i - w^i) &= \frac{1}{2}\left[\bar{y}^2(b^2 - \beta_i^2) + \sigma^2\left(\frac{b}{1+b} - \frac{\beta_i}{1+\beta_i}\right)\right. \\ &\quad \left. \times \left(\frac{1+\beta_i}{1+b}b - \beta_i\right)\right] \\ &= \frac{1}{2}\left[\bar{y}^2(b^2 - \beta_i^2) + \frac{\sigma^2(b - \beta_i)^2}{(1+b)^2(1+\beta_i)}\right] \end{aligned} \qquad (30)$$

Thus, on purely political grounds, it will be beneficial to join a monetary union only if its policy-makers are *more* conservative (inflation-averse) than you; $b < \beta_i$. On this particular point, therefore, Frisch might appear to have been wrong. He was right to say that any monetary union worth joining would be very conservative. But far from being a reason not to join, this extra conservatism is necessary so that an improvement in inflation performance might outweigh any deterioration in output stability. On the other hand, this point can be sustained only in a world of identical shocks, responses, and structures. In practice that will not be the case.[4] So whether or not conservatism still will lead to welfare improvements when there are asymmetries between economies will depend on whether the political elements are reinforced or offset by the economic elements in (29), that is, on the political-economic interactions emphasized in Section 2.

To get at the economic components of (29), on the other hand, we must eliminate the political elements. Setting $b = \beta_i$ yields

$$\begin{aligned} E(w_E^i - w^i) &= \frac{1}{2}\left[\left(\frac{b^2}{1+b}\right)(\sigma_u^2 + \sigma_i^2 - 2\rho_i\sigma_u\sigma_i)\right] \\ &= \frac{1}{2}\left[\left(\frac{b^2}{1+b}\right)\text{var}(u - v_i)\right] \geq 0 \end{aligned} \qquad (31)$$

---

[4] See, for example, the empirical evidence of Bayoumi and Eichengreen (1994) and Demertzis, Hughes Hallett, and Rummel (1996).

Hence on macroeconomic-stabilization grounds, joining a monetary union is *always* disadvantageous irrespective of the relative size and variability of the shocks in the domestic economy compared with those elsewhere in the union. So it does not matter if union shocks are "smoother" or smaller; it is simply that they will become more difficult to absorb (Hughes Hallett and Vines, 1993).

In fact, the only asymmetry that matters is the degree of *correlation* between the domestic shocks and those in the rest of the union. If the shocks are perfectly correlated ($\rho_i = 1$), then monetary union is at its most attractive, and domestic policy-makers should be indifferent (on economic grounds) between joining and not joining. But if they are uncorrelated, or strongly negatively correlated (implying strong asymmetries), then monetary union is at its most unattractive, and policy-makers would regard it as being harmful *unless* the degree of extra conservatism were very strong or the impact of the economic asymmetries were pretty weak. So Frisch may have been right after all; it all depends on whether or not the conservative political advantages outweigh the economic disadvantages.

4 The Need for Policy in Market Economies

Example 1: *Conservatism Implies the Need for a Planned Fiscal Policy in a Monetary Union*[5]

The Maastricht treaty states that no country shall be allowed to run a fiscal deficit larger than 3 percent of its GNP, nor a debt above 60 percent of GNP. That implies a significant restriction on the ability to use fiscal policy, because all the European Union (EU) economies (Luxembourg excepted) have already found it necessary to exceed the deficit limit in recent years; and all but three have exceeded the debt limit as well. Indeed Belgium, Italy, and Greece have debt ratios of 120 percent or more.[6]

There are many reasons why a monetary union might impose limits on fiscal policy:

1. The first is the conservatism inherent in the incentives to form a union. We have just seen that countries will wish to form a

---

[5] Adapted from Hughes Hallett and Ma (1997).

[6] Ironically, given Frisch's views, Norway's economic performance in late 1996 was by far the best in Europe and significantly better than the specified convergence criteria for monetary union. Its debt is negative (−1.7 percent of GNP), its budget is actually in surplus at 4 percent of GDP, price inflation is lower than anywhere in the EU (1.2 percent), and interest rates are only fractionally above German rates. The irony here is that if Norway had joined the union in 1996, then by lowering the average of the three best inflation rates it would actually have caused many of the "core" countries to fail the convergence criteria and possibly leave the union.

union only if it adopts stronger anti-inflationary policies than they would have adopted themselves. The result will be lower inflation, but some short-term output losses. That change in mix might well tempt countries to use their fiscal policies more vigorously to minimize those losses. At the same time, having a single currency will remove the opportunity for adjustments in *relative* monetary policies in countries that have different structures and response rates, or that are subject to different shocks. That will also make countries likely to use fiscal policies to compensate, that is, to create some regional stabilization power (there being no fiscal-federalism in the treaty). Thus there is a risk that countries will be tempted into *unsustainable* fiscal positions because they will find that they have to use fiscal policies "excessively," either in aggregate or relative to the average, in order to compensate for the inherent conservatism of the single monetary policy (Hughes Hallett and Vines, 1993). Presumably the "two-speed" proposal, and now the Stability Pact, were designed to rule out such excessive fiscal policies, albeit at some cost to output, employment, or output capacity (Hughes Hallett and McAdam 1998; in press).
2. The tendency to more active, but decentralized, fiscal policies in a single European capital market carries with it the incentive for uncoordinated expansions. In fact, there is an overexpansion bias, leading to crowding out and higher interest rates even for the more disciplined. In a single capital market, those who expand fiscally will not bear the full cost of their own deficit financing, because the interest-rate rises will be moderated by being shared by others. Hence, in a noncooperative world, each will overexpand, causing unnecessary crowding out that will damage the union as a whole and generate spillovers that will threaten the policies of countries with questionable fiscal sustainability. This is a market failure that could be overcome by explicit coordination.
3. Even if policy-makers do not impose fiscal limits directly, the financial markets may try to produce the same effect by imposing default-risk premia on excessive borrowers. And because of the risk of pressure on other countries to mount a bailout, or because the possibility of a large default might "persuade" the authorities to monetize the debt or inflate it away rather than face a liquidity crisis across the European capital markets, these risk premia are likely to prove contagious for other countries. The markets would fear, in particular, that the reduced external discipline on individual members of the union, coupled with tighter monetary controls from the centre, would again trigger an overexpansion bias that would not be properly priced into

the union's overall fiscal stance. That signals market responses to a market failure, and fiscal policies must be designed to meet it.
4. The burden of these remarks is that excess debts, rather than a potentially transient deficit, is the real indicator of fiscal difficulties. In that case we need to examine fiscal planning for controlling debt levels. In practice, of course, policy-makers have almost always concentrated on controlling deficits instead, and an analysis of that case can be found elsewhere (Hughes Hallett and McAdam, 1998), emphasizing a different theme, namely, the importance of maintaining coordination between fiscal policies.

To illustrate the importance of these points, we examine the trade-off between fiscal discipline and the other targets of the proposed monetary union. This we do with a game-theoretic version of Frisch's policy analysis applied to a monetary union of two countries. The details, and the economic model, are specified in Appendix 1. The main points are that one of the two countries has an excessive debt ratio, and one does not. Both have the ordinary targets specified in the treaty (price stability and output growth). There is a single currency and one monetary policy, and there are decentralized but cooperatively chosen fiscal policies. The high-debt country is given a certain period of time to work off its excessive debt. That is because the treaty recognizes that the immediate imposition of those limits in each and every period would be unrealistic. Instead, small excesses may be allowed, provided that they are "demonstrably temporary and subject to substantial and continuous decline, so as to approach the specified limits at a satisfactory pace," although "temporary," "substantial," and "a satisfactory pace" remain open to interpretation. That suggests that "soft" rather than "hard" fiscal limits would be applied in practice.

We examine the case in which one country (Germany) has a debt ratio of 40 percent, and the other (Italy) a ratio of 100 percent. Italy is given 5 years for its ratio to reach 60 percent, where the ideal adjustment path is to pro-rate that ratio down in equal steps. There are no other shocks. The results are set out in Table 19.1. They show that it is very difficult to reduce the debt ratio without building up problems elsewhere. Whereas fiscal cuts will produce budgetary surpluses that will reduce the debt level, they will also produce output losses that will reduce the GNP level at the same time. If the ratio's denominator is pushed down faster than its numerator, the ratio will actually rise instead of fall. That would make it impossible to meet the required debt limit, and any subsequent attempt to do so would produce further rises in the debt ratio, a downward spiral in output, and eventual collapse. This will always be the case if the model has *short-run* fiscal-to-output multipliers greater than unity, as it does

Table 19.1. *Full EMU: 5-Year Debt Reduction*

		1	2	3	4	5
German economy						
Output	%	6.33	1.41	0.89	2.28	5.36
CPI inflation	D	0.95	4.70	3.46	3.50	4.75
Real money supply	D	4.13	0.55	0.73	2.34	5.24
Real exchange rate	%	13.51	11.87	9.61	6.13	0.86
Wealth	%	1.45	1.78	2.01	2.60	4.00
Nominal exchange rate	%	13.51	17.87	19.55	19.82	19.60
Real interest rate	D	−1.62	−2.21	−3.42	−5.18	−8.11
g	%	0.14	0.08	0.06	0.05	0.05
Current account	%	0.43	−1.11	−1.97	−2.72	−3.77
Investment	%	1.01	1.38	2.14	3.24	5.07
Italian economy						
Output	%	−1.93	0.80	1.88	3.14	5.76
CPI inflation	D	0.95	0.94	2.45	3.47	4.96
Real money supply	D	−4.13	−0.06	1.72	3.20	5.64
Real exchange rate	%	13.51	18.47	18.00	14.55	8.91
Wealth	%	0.87	7.43	16.45	26.54	37.54
Nominal exchange rate	%	13.51	17.87	19.55	19.82	19.60
Real interest rate	D	4.99	−0.43	−3.38	−5.55	−8.38
g	%	−1.35	−6.33	−8.25	−8.64	−8.50
Current account	%	3.99	6.26	6.61	5.96	4.70
Investment	%	−3.12	0.27	2.11	3.47	5.24

Note: Welfare-function values for first 5 years: Germany 74.87, Italy 298.23, Europe 395.91. D, absolute deviation from equilibrium path; %, proportional deviation from equilibrium path.

here. Hence, even if the fiscal multipliers go to zero, any attempt to clear the debt burden by fiscal consolidation is bound to produce this apparently perverse result and hence instability. This observation leaves open three options:

1. If the long-run multipliers are small, then creating a fiscal surplus and sitting it out would eventually lead to a lower debt level, with a roughly unchanged level of output. But that leaves output losses along the way.
2. It would be more effective to run a fiscal deficit instead, because although that would add to the debt, it would expand output by even more. Hence the debt ratio would fall. But that implies extra inflation along the way.
3. The third and most effective strategy is to combine monetary expansion with a fiscal surplus. If the monetary expansion is suit-

ably strong, that will allow then output to expand while also cutting into the level of debt. That is the fastest way to bring the debt ratio down. However, the fiscal-contraction–monetary-expansion combination will induce a depreciation in the external, European Currency Unit (ECU) exchange rate, implying extra inflationary pressure. The key is therefore to get the *balance* between fiscal and monetary policies right.

These adjustment strategies highlight an important trade-off: Faster corrections of the debt ratio come at the cost of higher inflation and larger currency depreciations. This need not interfere with the central bank's day-to-day management of the ECU exchange rate. But it does mean that the fiscal authorities could always bail out their indebted national governments and remove the risk of default by manipulating the ECU's intended parity value. Over the long term that would undermine the central bank's inflation policy, which in turn would introduce an inflation-risk premium in interest rates in place of any default-risk premium. These two risk premia are opposing indicators of credibility – that in monetary policy and financial variables versus that on the real and fiscal-policy side. Thus conservatism has its price too.

Table 19.1 demonstrates this speed-of-reduction–adjustment-costs trade-off very clearly. Italian policy operates on both the top and the bottom of its debt ratio. The economy runs a fiscal surplus, starting at 1.5 percent of GNP and building up to 8.5 percent by year 5. That implies a sharp contraction. But it is more than offset by monetary expansion in both real and nominal terms. As a result there is some inflation, so that real interest rates fall further below their equilibrium starting values than do nominal interest rates. This fiscal-contraction–money-expansion mix also causes the external exchange rate to depreciate in years 1 and 2. Consequently there is appreciable inflation, which is still increasing in year 5.

Now we come to the monetary-union part of the story. The overexpansion in this scenario is not solely the result of Italian policy; part of it is a result of spillovers from Germany. There are no fiscal contractions there. But the existence of a single monetary policy ensures that Germany is obliged to share in a monetary relaxation that Italy has to have in order to prevent an uncontrolled deflation spiral. As a result, output also expands in Germany, and that combined with the joint monetary expansion ensures that inflation persists too. Output expansion and the shared inflation then spill back to Italy. Monetary union therefore worsens the trade-off because Germany has to accept an inappropriate monetary policy, which in turn dilutes the conservatism that was the advantage of the union in the first place. This explains why Germany has favoured a "two-speed" regime.

Example 2: *Capitalism Implies the Need for Policies to Create Greater Flexibility in the Labour Markets*[7]

The single European market introduces a difficult problem in the European labour markets. There will be full and flexible movement in the goods and capital markets, and hence rapid market clearing on a partial-equilibrium basis. But labour markets will remain segmented and subject to persistent disequilibria. Legislating to remove barriers does not ensure mobility; that is a necessary but not sufficient condition for equilibrium. Similarly, rigidities derived from labour-market regulation, plus political pressure for factor-price equalization, will interfere with wage flexibility. Consequently it is possible that the single market programme will actually have the effect of *worsening* economic performance as the single market in goods and capital exaggerates the rigidities in the labour markets and spreads their consequences all around the system, especially if one of the consequences of economic union is Europe-wide wage settlements in different industries so that all workers in a given industry receive broadly similar wages regardless of productivity differences. That would create new market failures and extend old ones. As a result it would be preferable to intervene to redress the disequilibria through extra wage–price flexibility or by rebalancing the expenditure patterns. This example demonstrates the need for such interventions.

Suppose two countries, A and B, decide to form an economic union, in which the labour force is divided equally between two labour markets. The average rates of unemployment and wage inflation are given by

$$U = \frac{1}{2}(u_A + u_B), \quad \dot{W} = \frac{1}{2}(\dot{w}_A + \dot{w}_B) \tag{32}$$

For the moment we shall assume that identical Phillips-curve relationships hold between $\dot{w}_A$ and u_A, and between $\dot{w}_B$ and u_B. If unemployment is the same in both markets, then $\dot{w}_A = \dot{w}_B$. The relation between the union-wide aggregates $\dot{W}$ and U will then be identical with that between their regional counterparts, $\dot{w}_i$ and u_i.

But if unemployment in the two regions is different (e.g., $u_A < u_B$ in Figure 19.2), and corresponds only *on average* to a natural rate of $U = a$ and constant wage inflation W_c, then the outcome will be different. The

---

[7] Adapted from Demertzis and Hughes Hallett (1995b). None of these examples is watertight in the sense of exclusively representing one of the metaphors without elements from the others. This one, in particular, shows free-market aggregation as a centralizing tendency without attention to the distributional consequences. So it is a bit "catholic" too. But this is an endogenous response – catholicism by default. That contrasts with the next example, which deals with a policy response, i.e., catholicism by design, which supplies the missing element of authoritarianism.

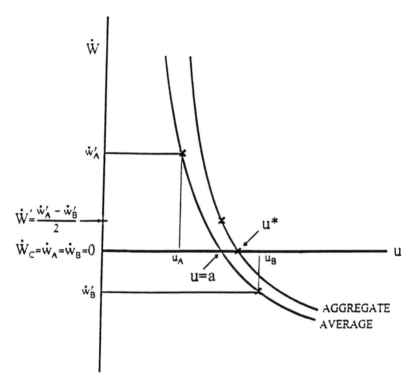

Figure 19.2. Aggregation of nonlinear Phillips curves.

average unemployment rate $(u_A + u_B)/2$ will generate $\dot{w}_A = 0$ in A and $\dot{w}_B = 0$ in B. But that's as if the unemployment were fully redistributed between A and B (i.e., as if wage bargaining took place in a single market with *perfect* mobility). If the markets are segmented by a lack of labour mobility, then u_A will generate $\dot{w}'_A$, and u_B will generate $\dot{w}'_B$. For the union as a whole, the outcome will therefore be positive wage inflation at the average natural rate $U = a$, because $\dot{W}' = (\dot{w}'_A + \dot{w}'_B)/2 > 0$. Similarly, the natural rate of unemployment will rise from $U = a$ to $U = U^*$. These movements give the *aggregate curve* in Figure 19.2, when u_A and u_B are varied with a fixed disparity between them. The aggregate inflation–unemployment outcomes are Pareto-inferior and lie along a curve to the northeast of the average of the national outcomes. In addition, the greater the disparity in the underlying unemployment rates, the greater the northeasterly displacement. That is because wages increase faster in the market with excess demand (where $u < a$) than they fall in the market with excess supply (where $u > a$). Hence across the union as a whole, wage inflation will be higher at any average level of unemployment, and for a constant rate of inflation the natural rate of unemployment will have to rise from $U = a$ to $U = U^*$.

Theory. We can now calculate how market aggregation can affect both the sacrifice ratio and the position of the inflation–unemployment trade-off. Consider an economic union containing n distinct labour markets, with rates of unemployment and wage changes u_i and $\dot{w}_i$ for $i = 1, \ldots, n$. Let a_i be the weight of the ith economy, defined as total employment in region i as a proportion of total employment in the union as a whole. Thus $\Sigma a_i = 1$, and $\Sigma a_i u_i = U$ is the union employment rate. Suppose that wage adjustments in each labour market follow a standard inflation-compensated Phillips curve:

$$\dot{w}_i = a + k\dot{P} + \beta f(u_i) \tag{33}$$

where $\dot{P}$ is the anticipated rate of change in the union price index. That is the fundamental relationship described by Alogoskoufis and Smith (1991), but as yet without dynamics, because the expectations terms still have to be defined. It can be derived either from Phillips's own work or from Alogoskoufis and Smith's two-country model with rational expectations of future prices (Alogoskoufis and Smith, 1991, pp. 1257, 1264). We further assume that unemployment exerts negative and convex pressure on wage formation: $f'(u_i) < 0$ and $f''(u_i) \geq 0$. The aggregate wage change over all regions is now

$$\dot{W} = \sum_{i=1}^{n} a_i \dot{w}_i = a + k\dot{P} + \beta \sum_{i=1}^{n} a_i f(u_i) \tag{34}$$

Expanding $f(u_i)$ around the aggregate unemployment rate U and summing over regions,

$$\sum a_i f(u_i) = f(U) + \sum_{j=2}^{\infty} \sum_{i=1}^{n} \frac{a_i (u_i - U)^j}{j!} \frac{d^j f(U)}{dU^j}$$

$$= f(U) + \frac{1}{2} s^2 \frac{d^2 f(U)}{dU^2} + \frac{1}{6} \mu_3 \frac{d^3 f(U)}{dU^3} \tag{35}$$

$$+ \frac{1}{24} \mu_4 \frac{d^4 f(U)}{dU^4} + \ldots$$

where $s^2 = \mu_2$, and where $\mu_j = \Sigma a(u_i - U)^j$ for $j \geq 1$ define the (weighted) sample moments from the regional distribution of unemployment rates. Hence, substituting (35) in (34),

$$\dot{W} \simeq a + k\dot{P} + \beta f(U) + \beta \left[\frac{1}{2} s^2 \frac{d^2 f(U)}{dU^2} \right.$$

$$\left. + \frac{1}{6} \mu_3 \frac{d^3 f(U)}{dU^3} + \frac{1}{24} \mu_4 \frac{d^4 f(U)}{dU^4} + \ldots \right] \tag{36}$$

Thus any disparity among unemployment rates (i.e., $s^2 \neq 0$) will put upward pressure on inflation. Similarly, the tendency of unemployment rates to become bunched together in some places, and spread out in others, will increase that pressure if the asymmetries in the unemployment distribution and the responsiveness of wages to increasing levels of excess demand are negative and decreasing, or (less probably) positive and increasing (i.e., when μ_3 and $\partial^3 f/dU^3$ reinforce one another). Finally, any tendency for unemployment rates to spread evenly over a wide range or to bunch together into two or more distinct groups (μ_4 large) will also increase the upward pressure on wages.

To complete this model we must specify $f(U)$ explicitly. For maximum flexibility, we adopt a Box-Cox transformation and allow the data to pick the best-fitting specification:

$$f(U) = a + \beta \log U, \quad \text{with } \beta < 0, \text{ if } \lambda = 0 \tag{37}$$

or

$$f(U) = a + \beta U^{-\lambda}, \quad \text{with } \beta > 0, \text{ if } \lambda > 0 \\ \text{and } \beta < 0, \text{ if } \lambda < 0 \tag{38}$$

Our estimation for the pre-1993 European Union countries accepted $\lambda = 1$. In that case, (36) implies

$$\dot{W} = a + k\dot{P} + \frac{\beta}{U} + \beta \frac{s^2}{U^3} - \beta \frac{\mu_3}{U^4} + \beta \frac{\mu_4}{U^5} + \ldots, \quad \beta > 0 \tag{39}$$

Hence the impact of the moments diminishes as their degree of order increases, but whether or not it will do so rapidly will depend on both the size of those moments and the level of unemployment.

Taken together, the moments of the unemployment dispersion effects imply a shift in the Phillips-curve trade-off and a change in its slope.

Change in Slope. From (39), ignoring μ_3 and higher moments for the moment,

$$\dot{W} = a + k\dot{P} + \frac{\beta}{U} + \beta \frac{s^2}{U^3}, \quad \beta > 0 \tag{40}$$

The slope of the original curve (i.e., ignoring the distribution of unemployment) is

$$\frac{d\dot{W}}{dU} = -\frac{\beta}{U^2} \tag{41}$$

But after economic integration the new slope will be

$$\frac{d\dot{W}}{dU} = -\frac{\beta}{U^2}\left(1 + \frac{3s^2}{U^2}\right) \tag{42}$$

Hence the new slope is therefore unambiguously steeper than the old one.

Shift Effect. The vertical shift, as a result of having accounted for the structural differences in unemployment, is $\beta s^2/U^3$ at each level of unemployment. Although this shift reduces asymptotically as U increases, it is always positive and implies an unambiguous deterioration in the position of the trade-off between $\dot{W}$ and U. A constant level of inflation will therefore be associated with a high level of unemployment. In short, the sacrifice ratio has become worse both in the sense that it now needs a greater increase in the rate of inflation to secure a unit reduction in the rate of unemployment, and because this less favourable trade-off now happens at a higher level of unemployment for every given rate of inflation.

The lesson here is that policy is needed even in a free-market context – one cannot simply rely on market forces to produce good inflation and employment outcomes. In Frisch's terms, we need an extra instrument to control the distribution of unemployment. More important, perhaps, this example also shows that policy evaluations must be able to accommodate changes in market behaviour (in this case, a change in slope as well as location). On the other hand, those changes have proved entirely systematic and predictable, so that, unlike in Lucas's critique, one can base corrective policies on them. Thus Frisch's concern with shifting behavioural relationships when policy regimes change (Andvig, 1988) is an important but essentially resolvable aspect of the problem.

Estimation. A standard short-run specification of the Friedman-Phelps type would be

$$\dot{W}_t = \beta_0 + \beta_1 \sum \alpha_i f(u_{it}) + \beta_3 \dot{P}_t + \beta_4 (\dot{W}_t^e - k_0 \dot{P}_t^e) + e_t \quad (43)$$

where actual and expected wage changes are now measured as deviations from actual and expected price changes (Brechling, 1974). Internal consistency requires $k_0 = \beta_3$, because otherwise the aggregate Phillips curve could never tend to any steady state. Moreover, $\beta_4 = 1$ would make this trade-off vertical.

Next we impose rational expectations on all the expected values that go into the wage-formation process. For quarterly data, that implies[8]

$$\left. \begin{array}{l} \dot{W}_t^e = \dot{W}_{t+4} - \xi_{t+4} \\ \dot{P}_t^e = \dot{P}_{t+4} - \xi_{t+4} \end{array} \right\} \text{ where } \xi_t \text{ and } \zeta_t \text{ are white noise}$$

A series of non-nested tests established that the best functional form was given by[9] $\lambda = 1$, and therefore $f(u_{it}) = 1/u_{it}$. Hence

---

[8] Expectations are derived today about tomorrow's variables, but expressed on an annual basis. *Annual* wage-bargaining rounds therefore lie behind this specification.
[9] For details of these tests and other estimation details, see Demertzis and Hughes Hallett (1995a).

$$\dot{W}_t = \beta_0 + \beta_1 \sum \alpha_i/u_{it} + \beta_3 \dot{P}_t + \beta_4(\dot{W}_{t+4} - \beta_3 \dot{P}_{t+4}) + v_t \quad (44)$$

where $v_t = e_t - \beta_4 \xi_{t+4} + \beta_4 \beta_3 \zeta_{t+4}$. Equation (44) was estimated by the general-method-of-moments (GMM) technique to account for both the implicit simultaneity between $\dot{P}_t$ and $\dot{W}_t$ and a moving-average error term, using a sample of quarterly data for the EU economies over the period 1975–92. This produced the following results (t ratios in parentheses):[10]

$$\beta_0 = 1.471 \ (4.34) \qquad \beta_3 = 0.945 \ (16.24)$$
$$\beta_1 = 12.642 \ (1.65) \qquad \beta_4 = -0.28 \ (-1.03)$$

The estimates produced are heteroskedasticity- and MA(4)-consistent. The test of overidentifying restrictions confirmed the validity of the instruments and the model specification, with a value of $\chi^2_{(5)} = 4.02$, which is highly insignificant at both the 1 percent and 5 percent levels.

Results. All the parameter estimates have the expected signs and significance.[11] Now, inserting figures for the moments of the unemployment distribution into (39), term by term, starting with the second moment and setting $\beta = 12.642$, gives us the *increase* in wage inflation arising from a poor (and deteriorating) distribution of unemployment rates, all other factors remaining constant. The total increases and their composition by factor are given for the first quarter of each year in Table 19.2a. We take such increases to be a measure of the inefficiencies caused by labour immobility, because in a single market for goods and capital they show how much lower wage inflation would have been had labour been perfectly mobile at the levels of aggregate demand and unemployment that ruled at the time.

Wage-Inflation Effects

Table 19.2a shows, first of all, that the skew and spread factors contribute less than half as much as the variance components and that they offset one another. Hence the variance is what matters. The second point is that the extra upward pressure on wages has increased over the period

---

[10] IMF, Datastream data are used for all 1994 EU member countries, excluding Portugal and Luxembourg. Despite the later entry of Greece and Spain into the community, their data are considered since 1975 on the basis that, in the process of preparing their economies for entry, they would take into consideration European policies and therefore be affected by them. All the estimates reported here are in natural units; $\dot{W} = 1$ implies a 1 percent increase in wages per quarter.

[11] See Demertzis and Hughes Hallett (1995a) for a more detailed report on the econometric specification and comparisons with the other possible specifications. But for our purposes, it is sufficient to note that this specification was preferred in terms of significance, diagnostic checks, and the plausibility of the parameter estimates.

Table 19.2a. *Impact of the Distribution of Unemployment Rates on Inflation and the Natural Rate of Unemployment in the EU, 1983–92*

	\multicolumn{3}{c}{Contribution of}			Extra
	s^2	μ_3	μ_4	Combined	inflation (% p.a.)
83Q1	0.078	−0.030	0.023	0.071	0.28%
84Q1	0.090	−0.044	0.035	0.081	0.32%
85Q1	0.100	−0.058	0.053	0.095	0.38%
86Q1	0.097	−0.055	0.052	0.094	0.38%
87Q1	0.087	−0.038	0.036	0.085	0.34%
88Q1	0.083	−0.036	0.031	0.078	0.31%
89Q1	0.099	−0.036	0.032	0.095	0.38%
90Q1	0.126	−0.041	0.039	0.124	0.50%
91Q1	0.139	−0.054	0.052	0.137	0.55%
92Q1	0.134	−0.051	0.060	0.143	0.57%

1988–92, starting with an additional 0.3 percent on the *annual* wage-inflation rate in 1988, but accelerating to add an extra 0.6 percent by the start of 1992.[12] That indicates significant market inefficiencies (failures), because that was a period of *increasing* market integration. The third point is that the pressure for higher wage rises is evidently unstable. That instability reflects the changing impact of the underlying demand pressures: wage pressures rising as unemployment gets more unequal in boom periods, but falling as the average level of unemployment rises in recession.

Impact on the Natural Rate of Unemployment

By contrast, Table 19.2b shows the additions to the natural rate of unemployment to be fairly stable. These figures have been obtained by solving our preferred model for the rate of unemployment consistent with an unchanged rate of wage inflation, and then computing the increase in that unemployment rate as a result of introducing the second, third, and fourth moments of the unemployment distribution in (39). The aggregate unemployment rate will in fact lie 0.7–0.8 percentage points higher than otherwise. That represents roughly 1.7 million extra unemployed across the EU by 1992. The costs of labour immobility in Europe (increasing inefficiencies as markets integrate) are therefore one possible explanation of the persistence of European unemployment over the

---

[12] In timing, this might be associated with German unification; but from its size it has clearly affected all of Europe, not just East Germany.

Table 19.2b. *Impact of the Distribution of Unemployment Rates on Inflation and the Natural Rate of Unemployment in the EU, 1983–92*

	U^3/B	ds^2	$-d\mu_3/U$	$d\mu_4/U^2$	Extra unemployment (% pts)
83Q1	0.07687	7.95	−3.11	2.34	0.55
84Q1	0.06937	11.05	−5.36	4.25	0.69
85Q1	0.06379	13.42	−7.89	7.18	0.81
86Q1	0.06329	13.36	−7.64	7.17	0.82
87Q1	0.06417	12.34	−5.41	5.12	0.78
88Q1	0.06872	10.56	−4.56	3.95	0.68
89Q1	0.07302	9.86	−3.58	3.17	0.69
90Q1	0.07751	9.35	−3.04	2.93	0.72
91Q1	0.08103	8.65	−3.34	3.23	0.69
92Q1	0.07234	10.36	−3.95	4.68	0.80

Note: By equation (39), $dU^* = U^3[ds^2 - d\mu_3/U + \partial\mu_4/U^2]/\beta$ gives $\dot{w} = 0$, where $B = U^4 + 3U^2s^2 - 4U\mu_3 + 5\mu_4$ for an average unemployment rate U.

past decade. Given tight inflation control, those costs will obviously appear in the form of higher unemployment. Hence capitalism, in a regime of incomplete or incompletely free markets, has its price too.

Example 3: *Catholicism Implies the Need for Policies that Will Ensure Incentive-Compatible Outcomes for All Participants*[13]

The centrepiece of monetary union in Europe will be the single currency and a single monetary policy. The major gain is expected to derive from the closer coordination that this will induce in the economic performance of the participants. But in practice, in a world of economies with different structures and preferences and subject to different shocks, this coordination may come at a considerable cost – as we saw prior to the collapse of the European Monetary System (EMS) in 1992/3. Such a regime may be designed to create better outcomes for the union on average because it centralizes policy-making on one policy instrument. But a single instrument can successfully serve only one target at a time – in this case a union-level target rather than the national targets that make up the union target. That is a restriction on the policy mechanism that is bound to be "authoritarian" in that it necessarily imposes greater externalities on the participants than they would have chosen individually or collectively – externalities that are not properly internalized in

---

[13] Based on Hughes Hallett and Ma (1996).

the policy-selection process. The point, therefore, is to show that adopting a centralizing regime, such as the EMS or EMU, actually implies market restrictions that, even if they help society as a whole (as a catholic administration would argue), will have distributional consequences that need to be corrected for the benefit of those damaged by the additional unpriced externalities. Thus, we must have incentive compatibility if coordination is to work – an idea implicit in Frisch's "circulation planning" (Frisch, 1934).

To demonstrate this point, we compare fully cooperative policies designed to be incentive-compatible and noncooperative policies, with a number of alternative regimes for the four main European countries in the early 1990s. Those alternative regimes are as follows:

A Hard-Target-Zone Regime. The leading central bank exploits its reputation for credible monetary policies. The remaining countries act as followers, with reaction functions determined by their commitment to stay within set exchange-rate bands without realignment. Countries are forced to tie their hands to German monetary policy. Arguably this was the position in Europe until the suspension of the EMS regime in 1993, when German policy became too tight to be sustained in a Europe undergoing recession.

The Domain Solution. If the goal is to improve European economic performance, then it would be better to have the Germans target *average* European variables directly and have the other countries target deviations from the average using the instruments remaining at their disposal, all of this happening under an agreed set of preferences. Those preferences might be the original German preferences or non-German preferences or some compromise between the two. In this scenario the Germans extend the domain of their policies to all of Europe, instead of simply following their own national goals and forcing the other countries to follow suit. That allows policy-makers to account for differences in structure and shocks, while retaining the effectiveness of German policy design in their own economies.

Variants of the Domain Solution. We consider three variants. In the first variant, each country makes its decisions, subject to the constraints of the domain solution, but according to its own national preferences, while the lead country (Germany) has to design policy for the system's averages at the system's average preferences. The results are then evaluated using national preferences to show the incentives for individual countries to follow this decision strategy. The second variant is to evaluate those same results at the average of the national preferences to show the incentives for adopting this strategy when policy-makers wish to improve the social welfare of the system as a whole. The third variant is then the one foreseen in the Maastricht treaty. Here a domain solution is created by using the lead country's preferences (in this case Germany's preferences) for policy selection, but national preferences to evaluate each country's projected outcomes.

The impact of these different regimes is calculated using an empirical multicountry model, the IMF's MULTIMOD, over a 6-year period, 1990–96, which includes German unification and a significant recession. Each of the G7 countries has a specific set of targets, priorities, and information and wishes to minimize the impact of those events on its target variables. The details of the general problem specification are given in Appendix 2. The European countries, however, are required to stay within the 2.5 percent bands of the EMS in all cases; the only thing that distinguishes one regime from another is the definition of the objectives or their relative priorities, or the parities within EMS bands. And unless otherwise stated, the United Kingdom and Italy realign their official parities down in 1992, as happened, but then stay in the ERM. Finally, all the simulations are "open-loop" in that they use the initial information set and that the policy projections are not revised again. Policy revisions are not relevant here, because we wish to compare decision strategies ex ante, as they would have appeared when policy-makers had to make a choice between them.

Tables 19.3 and 19.4 report the results. The regimes covered are (1) *our reference solution*, optimal noncooperative (Nash-equilibrium) policies under national preferences and ideal values, (2) the *domain solution*, as described earlier, but with respect to the price targets only, and (3) *explicit cooperation* among G7 countries, using a weighted average of the objective functions, with weights chosen to ensure incentive compatibility for each participant.

Noncooperative Policies. The reference solution shows that optimization, even on a noncooperative basis, would produce significant improvements over the historically chosen policies. In the non-European economies, these improvements come largely from reducing the volatility of the target variables and stabilizing monetary policy. That implies a more active use of fiscal policy in order to absorb external shocks.

In Europe, Germany (like the United States and Japan) does not change its policies much in the reference solution. There is some tightening of German fiscal policy (a less ambitious reunification programme), which allows a small relaxation in monetary policy. The results are decreases in growth and in inflation. France benefits from this easier German policy, being able to reduce interest rates a little and expand fiscally to produce slightly higher growth for no extra inflation. The United Kingdom and Italy, meanwhile, enjoy significant gains in stability on the real side, at the cost of much greater volatility in monetary policy. However, some small relaxation of monetary policy, for the same

Table 19.3. *Expected Objective-Function Values ("The Costs to Go") under Four Basic Decision Schemes (1990–96)*

	Baseline values	Reference solution (simulation A)	Domain solution (simulation B) Standard case National preferences	% improve	"The Social Welfare of Europe" case European preferences	% improve	Domain solution under German preferences (simulation C) National preferences	% improve	G7 cooperation (simulation E) National preferences	% improve
USA	22.09	11.07	10.91	+1.4	10.91	+1.4	10.96	+0.1	10.55	+4.7
Japan	23.02	10.12	10.28	−1.6	10.28	−1.6	10.21	+0.1	8.52	+15.8
Canada	60.55	28.92	28.48	+1.5	28.48	+1.5	28.54	+1.5	22.79	+21.2
Germany	63.06	57.23	87.92	−53.4	45.22	+21.0	70.16	−22.6	43.55	+23.9
UK	232.06	160.08	124.34	+22.3	134.70	+15.8	133.15	+16.8	152.24	+4.9
France	66.83	48.09	18.28	+62.0	17.72	+63.1	26.96	+43.9	36.50	+24.1
Italy	135.39	104.53	72.11	+31.0	81.69	+21.9	81.65	+21.9	95.23	+8.9

Notes:
1. The German objective-function value for the domain solution using *average* European preferences or the average of the non-German preferences was 31.89 (compare column 4) or 18.86 (compare column 1), respectively.
2. "European preferences" means each European economy uses the European average of the preference weights in its objective function to evaluate the domain solution.
3. Improvements are relative to the reference (noncooperative) solution.
4. Bargaining weights for simulation E were U.S. = 0.59, Japan = 0.09, Canada = 0.02, Germany = 0.09, UK = 0.08, France = 0.07, and Italy = 0.06.

Table 19.4. *Mean and Variance Outcomes of the Optimized Policies: Basic Decision Procedures, 1990–96*

	Reference solution (simulation A)		Domain solution (simulation B)		Domain solution (simulation C)		G7 (simulation E) cooperation	
	Mean	Variance	Mean	Variance	Mean	Variance	Mean	Variance
USA								
GṄP	2.28	0.85	2.28	0.82	2.28	0.83	2.21	1.01
Ṗ	3.42	1.19	3.39	1.21	3.38	1.22	3.21	1.07
G/Y	18.90	1.39	18.91	1.39	18.92	1.40	18.8	1.24
RS	4.45	0.00	4.45	0.00	4.44	0.00	4.25	0.00
Japan								
GṄP	2.49	0.90	2.50	0.92	250	0.91	2.48	0.85
Ṗ	1.89	0.43	1.89	0.44	1.88	0.44	1.79	0.40
G/Y	15.33	2.27	15.32	2.31	15.32	2.29	15.38	2.29
RS	3.89	0.05	3.89	0.05	3.89	0.04	4.00	0.00
Canada								
GṄP	2.26	1.77	2.28	1.66	2.28	1.70	2.61	1.74
Ṗ	3.41	4.68	3.41	4.69	3.40	4.70	3.51	4.04
G/Y	22.68	0.87	22.67	0.85	22.67	0.86	23.37	3.37
RS	5.24	0.08	5.24	0.08	5.24	0.08	5.01	0.23
Germany								
GṄP	1.47	1.34	2.17	1.05	1.86	0.94	1.76	0.94
Ṗ	3.05	0.58	3.79	1.53	3.53	1.27	3.29	1.44
G/Y	21.14	1.88	21.54	1.44	21.11	1.90	20.48	4.16
RS	7.48	1.22	6.08	0.18	6.41	0.32	5.70	3.22
UK								
GṄP	1.53	1.24	1.82	0.77	1.77	0.87	1.72	1.40
Ṗ	4.92	6.08	5.21	6.19	5.13	6.10	4.93	6.66
G/Y	24.81	1.49	24.94	1.10	24.96	1.12	24.33	0.93
RS	7.72	16.74	7.08	13.16	7.21	13.95	6.17	4.66
France								
GṄP	2.00	0.67	2.37	0.50	2.31	0.50	2.10	0.38
Ṗ	2.86	0.23	3.20	0.28	3.14	0.26	2.79	0.17
G/Y	21.65	0.52	21.79	0.38	21.81	0.39	21.01	0.61
RS	6.95	6.56	6.02	2.47	6.16	2.88	5.28	0.21
Italy								
GṄP	2.21	0.66	2.63	0.44	2.57	0.46	2.48	0.60
Ṗ	5.34	1.10	5.71	1.23	5.65	1.18	5.28	0.77
G/Y	19.82	0.45	20.07	0.33	20.09	0.34	19.16	0.47
RS	8.01	13.94	7.40	10.00	7.52	10.42	6.64	3.23
Europe Average								
Ṗ	3.91	0.60	4.37	0.68	4.24	0.60		

or slightly expanded fiscal policy, is possible. That yields gains in growth, and only minor increases in inflation.

The Domain Solution. Evaluating the domain solution at the original national preferences (columns 2 and 3 of Table 19.3) shows that the three follower economies (France, Italy, and the United Kingdom) gain substantially over our noncooperative reference solution. France gains disproportionately, with a 62 percent improvement; Italy is next best, with a 31 percent gain, and the United Kingdom gains by 22 percent. Thus France gains by two or three times as much as the other two. That is to be expected, because France was highly deflationary in the noncooperative case, being the only one of the three not allowed an exchange-rate realignment in 1992/3. As a result, relaxed controls on individual price levels mean that larger rises in Germany (or Italy and the United Kingdom) can be balanced against small falls in France to get stable prices *on average*. This relaxation is bound to produce the biggest benefits to the otherwise highly deflationary France. By contrast, Italy and the United Kingdom realigned their currencies down in 1992, and that has its own inflationary consequences. That implies less opportunity for balancing price rises against price falls.

By contrast, for Germany it matters where the improvements in France, Italy, and the United Kingdom appear. If, as here, they are in higher growth at the cost of somewhat higher inflation, then Germany will also enjoy faster growth at higher prices, both from spillovers through the usual trade and monetary linkages and through the monetary-policy relaxation that is the consequence of targeting average rather than purely German price stability. So Germany gets gains in one target (growth), but losses in the other (inflation); and if the penalties on the latter are large enough, then German preferences will register an overall loss. And that is the case here. Inflation, per percentage point, is penalized at five times the rate for failing to achieve adequate rates of growth. The result is to cause a 53 percent deterioration in German objectives. That gives an idea of the magnitude of the *disincentive* that the Germans would have to face if they were to give up their national objectives for the sake of helping the rest of Europe.

The Domain Solution and Incentive Incompatibility. These gains have been generated by a domain solution applied to inflation targets only. One might think that extending the domain mechanism to the remaining targets would produce better outcomes for growth as well as inflation. But in view of Frisch's analysis, it would necessarily make Germany worse off in terms of its own preferences, unless the spillovers from better performances elsewhere in Europe were very substantial, because we would in effect be adding extra targets to Germany's optimization problem without supplying extra instruments. In other words, unless the spillover benefits to Germany are large relative to these sacrifice losses in its own targets, the problem with the domain solution will always be a conflict between gains on average versus incentive incompatibility for the policy leader. That would reinforce German fears that concessions to Europe would simply damage German domestic targets.

Germany Helps Optimize a Social-Welfare Function for Europe. If, less plausibly, improvements in the European aggregates are taken to be the real aim of the member countries, then the incentive-incompatibility difficulty disappears. Evaluating our "inflation-only" domain solution at the European average of the national preference weights, to imply some commitment to a better performance across Europe as a whole,[14] gives the outcomes in column 5 of Table 19.3. Those outcomes show a Pareto improvement, that is, gains for each participant over raw noncooperation, as well as gains in terms of European aggregates. Catholicism, apparently, works only if you believe in it totally.

But it is important to notice that this solution actually requires a shift in the German *relative* priorities, not just the addition of extra target variables in the form of European averages. In other words, the Germans will have to regard a better European performance as a target in its own right, not just as an intermediate target that is useful because it makes it easier to achieve their own national targets. That is because, to get a shift in the relative priorities, German policy-makers have to show some concern for other goals, as yet unspecified, so that when the new goals are included among the German objectives, changes will appear in the relative priorities assigned to the existing goals. Simply redefining the target variables in order to introduce some new intermediate targets within the existing priority scheme won't do it. On the other hand, the Germans are perfectly entitled to ask their partners for a matching shift in preferences in return. Transferred conservatism is also necessary therefore.

An EMU (or Maastricht-consistent) Domain Solution. If the previous solutions have been politically infeasible, at least in terms of Germany's losses, then the obvious remedy is a domain solution with German preferences. That would minimize the incentive-incompatibility problem, as well as represent a neat political bargain: The Germans would be allowed to retain their strong anti-inflation preferences so long as they took other (European) inflation rates into consideration. More important, this would be the main precondition for EMU, as foreseen in the Maastricht

---

[14] This is an example of why Frisch argued that implicit preferences should be used for macroeconomic planning, the problem here being one of determining the appropriate aggregation.

treaty, which specifies that German policy preferences and design should be applied to the targets of the union as a whole.

Table 19.3, however, shows that even this solution is not incentive-compatible. Germany still loses by 22 percent compared with the reference (noncooperative) policies. The other European countries continue to make nice gains, albeit smaller than in the other solution. But the important point is that the Bundesbank's fears of extending their domain of policy are realized: Germany itself will be made worse off. Put another way, in order to make EMU incentive-compatible it is actually necessary to make the European central bank *more* conservative than, not just as tough as, the Bundesbank in its anti-inflation preferences/credentials. But the consequences of that latter point are clear to see in Table 19.4. Everybody gets significantly slower growth – particularly Germany – for only small reductions in the inflation rate. In other words, policy-makers will have to do something more than just integrate their policy-making and economies if they are to generate improvements for all participants.

A Hard-Exchange-Rate Regime. At the time of the 1992 currency crises, many argued that currency realignments would be counterproductive and should be avoided. The loss of policy credibility, the rise of inflationary expectations, and the inflation of domestic-currency import prices would, it was argued, combine to increase actual inflation in the devaluing countries – and hence lead to even higher interest rates or inflation and a second devaluation. Others went further, arguing that the best response was to "harden" the parities and narrow the exchange-rate bands in order to secure the benefits of monetary credibility (e.g., Thygesen, 1993).

We have examined these claims by rerunning the reference solution in which the United Kingdom and Italy are forbidden to realign their currencies in 1992. They are obliged to hold to bands of deutsche marks (DM) 2.95 ± 2.5 percent for the pound and DM 1.33 ± 2.5 percent per 1,000 lire, instead of 2.43 ± 2.5 percent and 0.993 ± 2.5 percent, respectively. The result is disastrous for all four European economies, not just for the two denied realignment. Compared with the realignment case, Germany is 120 percent worse off, France 25 percent, the United Kingdom 500 percent, and Italy 1,000 percent worse off. These are very substantial losses, equivalent to output losses of 4.4 percent each year in Germany, 1.8 percent in France, and 13.5 percent and 16.4 percent in the United Kingdom and Italy, if every other variable remains at its reference-solution level. The sizes of the U.K. and Italian losses give an idea of the damage that those economies were suffering through misaligned real exchange rates. No country can withstand losses on that scale. Similarly, the size of the German losses explains why the German government was happy to recommend realignment; the cost of providing noninflationary credibility with locomotive power for the rest of Europe was simply too expensive domestically. Finally, the relatively small losses in France confirm why French policy-makers thought they could get away with not realigning. The costs to France (although non-negligible) would not be huge if no one else realigned; but relative to this case, significant gains would appear if others did realign and France did not have to. They therefore attempted to free-ride, believing they would gain from the (monetary) credibility of their existing policies, not realizing that that would leave them all the more exposed in terms of lost real credibility when everyone else had realigned but they had not – since the deflationary pressures would then become concentrated entirely within France. The final crisis of 1993 was therefore no surprise.

In this counterfactual, the most dramatic changes occur in the United Kingdom and Italy. There are massive increases in instability as recession, an overvalued exchange rate, and high interest rates, and hence losses in real credibility, drive things downward (Table 19.4). There are no inflationary problems (prices fall by 2–3 percent each year), but interest rates have to rise to levels not seen since the late 1970s. Real interest rates are therefore very high. That generates a persistent recession (output falls 0.5–1 percent each year, down 2–3 percent on the realignment case). Fiscal policy expands sharply to offset that, but to no avail. Germany meanwhile is left to counter the effects of that expansion on its own, so interest rates rise still further. The net effect is some countervailing growth in Europe, but also some local inflation. The increases in target failures (but decreases for the instruments) show the Germans beginning to lose control of the situation. France meanwhile sits by, suffering only minor adjustments to its growth and inflation targets. Clearly there is no incentive for this regime.

5   Conclusion: A Tale of Two Marxes

The lesson from this review of Frisch's approach to economic planning is that it remains in robust health. Its application to the European monetary-union project has shown that

1. too much conservatism, with its anti-inflation bias, raises output losses and increases fiscal uncertainty
2. too much capitalism, with its belief in perfectly competitive markets, overlooks the costs and inefficiencies of imperfect market interactions
3. too much catholicism, in the sense of centralization, may make for more effective policies in aggregate. It also gives a false sense of infallibility, and those who do not benefit directly may wish to leave

These examples have also shown the importance of Frisch's distinction between "selection" and "implementation"; that is, between the way policies are chosen and the regimes in which they are designed to operate. Frisch thought it was a matter of first choosing policies and then engineering institutional or operational changes to get better results (Andvig, 1988). However, it seems that Frisch got the sequencing wrong. Because the choice of regime has, if anything, a larger impact on the policies chosen than vice versa, it would be important to choose both policies and regime jointly.

Finally, and more controversially, monetary union suffers from two internal contradictions. Article 103(1) of the Treaty on European Union demands the adoption of "an economic policy" for all states based on "the definition of common objectives." The Frisch analysis of economic policy shows that this can happen only if everyone adopts the same preferences and is treated the same even if they have different structures. A monetary union will also tend to promote factor-price equalization. Hence the first contradiction: It is almost as if the interstate relationships have to be run on Marxist lines, whereas the intermarket and intramarket relations are designed to be run on capitalist (i.e., free-market) lines. These two elements will have difficulty in coexisting, and if policies are set centrally, then it is the free-market benefits that will suffer.

But there is another contradiction that is more important. What the conservatism example shows is that the system itself is going to stand or fall on another famous "Marxist" principle, the one popularized by the actor Groucho Marx.[15] It states that you will want to join a union only if that union is more conservative than yourself. But by the same token, the existing members will not accept you into the club because that would dilute its conservatism and thereby remove the incentive for them to remain as members. One by one they would want to leave. So you might want to join a union that was more conservative, but you would be acceptable only in one that was less conservative. In other words, Frisch's view that conservatism lies at the heart of European union was correct, for without it there would be no union, but with it the process of accepting members reduces the incentive for others to join or remain. A union constructed on this basis surely contains the seeds of its own dissolution.

Appendix 1

The model is in levels, and all variables are expressed in deviations from their long-run (equilibrium) growth paths. All U.S. variables are exogenous and are therefore suppressed. The mark and lira exchange rates are each expressed in terms of the dollar, rather than bilaterally. Parameters have been chosen so as to correspond in a stylized fashion with reality:

---

[15] Groucho's aphorism was "I don't care to join a club that is prepared to have me as a member."

1. The Keynesian multiplier has a value of 2.0.
2. The marginal propensity to import is 0.25 in both countries.
3. At the margin (that is, in variations around the equilibrium growth paths), 72 percent of Italian and German trade is trade between themselves. This means that the *marginal* propensity of each to import from the other is 18 percent, and 7 percent from elsewhere.
4. Trade elasticities are of a standard size: The sum of the price elasticities of demand for exports and imports is 2.5. This means that a 1 percent depreciation of the mark, not matched by a change in the lira, would, ceteris paribus, improve the German current-account balance by 2.5 percent of the initial level of exports (or 0.625 percent of GDP).

Equations (1) and (1*) show the determination of aggregate demands. The real-exchange-rate terms show the effects on the home-country trade balance of home-country and foreign-country exchange rates. The y^* term shows Italian demand for German exports, and vice versa in equation (1*). Equations (2) and (2*) are the Phillips curves, which contain effects in both the level of and change in output. Equations (3) and (3*) relate consumer prices to output and import prices (which are influenced by both exchange rates). Equations (4) and (4*) show current-account evolution, and equations (5) and (5*) show investment. Together they show national wealth inclusive of interest payments, (6) and (6*). Equations (7) and (7*) show exchange-rate determination under perfect capital mobility under model-consistent expectations. Equation (8) and (8*) are public-sector debt identities.

The Model

In these equations, a "+1" subscript denotes a forward-looking variable.

$$
\begin{aligned}
&(1)\ y = 1.25a - 0.90a^* + 0.36y^* + 2.0\text{inv} + 2.0g \\
&(1^*)\ y^* = 1.25a^* - 0.90a + 0.36y + 2.0\text{inv}^* + 2.0g^* \\
&(2)\ p_{+1} = p + pc - pc_{-1} + 0.5y + 0.3(y - y_{-1}) \\
&(2^*)\ p^*_{+1} = p^* + pc^* - pc^*_{-1} + 0.5y^* + 0.3(y^* - y^*_{-1}) \\
&(3)\ pc = p + 0.25a - 0.18a^* \\
&(3^*)\ pc^* = p^* + 0.25a^* - 0.18a \\
&(4)\ ca = 0.625a - 0.45a^* - 0.25y + 0.18y^* \\
&(4^*)\ ca^* = 0.625a^* - 0.45a - 0.25y^* + 0.18y \\
&(5)\ \text{inv} = -0.625(r - p_{+1} + p) \\
&(5^*)\ \text{inv}^* = -0.625(r^* - p^*_{+1} + p^*) \\
&(6)\ w = (1 + r)/(p/p_{-1})w_{-1} + ca + \text{inv}, \quad w_0 = 0 \\
&(6^*)\ w^* = (1 + r^*)/(p^*/p^*_{-1})w^*_{-1} + ca^* + \text{inv}^*, \quad w^*_0 = 0 \\
&(7)\ a_{+1} = a + (r - p_{+1} + p) \\
&(7^*)\ a^*_{+1} = a^* + (r^* - p^*_{+1} + p^*)
\end{aligned}
$$

(8) $b = (1 + r)b_{-1} + pd$
(8*) $b^* = (1 + r^*)b^*_{-1} + pd^*$

An asterisk denotes an Italian variable; variables without asterisks are German variables.

Endogenous variables

y	output
p	output prices
pc	consumer prices
ca	current balance
inv	investment
w	wealth
a	real exchange rate in $ terms
b	public-sector debt

Policy instruments

g	net fiscal expenditures
r	nominal interest rate
pd	primary deficit

Policy Multipliers under EMU

	1	2	3	4	5	6
Fiscal stance						
incremental	1.63	−0.58	−0.23	−0.03	−0.02	−0.01
cumulative	1.63	1.05	0.82	0.79	0.78	0.77
Interest rates						
incremental	0.52	0.04	0.04	0.02	0.02	0.01
cumulative	0.52	0.56	0.60	0.62	0.64	0.65

The Objectives

$U = \Sigma'[\Delta pc^2 + \alpha y^2 + \beta w^2 + \gamma r^2 + \delta g^2]$ for Germany, where $\alpha = \delta = 1, \beta = 0.1, \gamma = 0$. All variables are deviations from their equilibrium growth paths.

$U^* = \Sigma[\Delta pc^{*2} + \alpha y^{*2} + \beta w^{*2} + \gamma r^{*2} + \delta g^{*2}]$ for Italy.

Monetary Union

Optimize an equally weighted combination of U and U^* (to create *cooperatively* chosen fiscal policies), subject to a single monetary policy. The instruments are thus $r = r^*, g$, and g^*. Identical dollar exchange rates for the lira and mark, to create a single currency (ECU) that can float against the dollar. The lira and mark exchange rate is never altered. Because the optimization algorithm is restricted to be *time-consistent*, this constitutes a single currency. Policies are optimized over 60 periods (the long run), but results are quoted only for the first 5 periods.

Appendix 2

The Model

To explore the interdependence and interactions between the European economies, we have used one of the better-known empirical multicountry models: the IMF's MULTIMOD, which contains linked models for each of the G7 countries (the United States, Japan, Canada, Germany, France, Italy, and the United Kingdom). It also contains fully specified models for the smaller EU economies as a bloc (the "rest of the EMS") and for the rest of the OECD. There are also models for OPEC and for Africa, Asia, and Latin America. Each of these national or regional models is linked to the others through bilateral trade flows, capital movements, and exchange rates that in turn influence domestic financial markets.

The models' specifications explain the main expenditure categories and production flows in each country, from which employment, investment, prices, interest rates, and exchange rates are determined. Financial markets, trade flows, and capital movements (including loans and interest payments) are included. Trade is divided into three markets: oil, primary commodities, and manufactured goods. The oil market contains an exogenous real price, demand driven by activity levels in each country, and supplies that clear the market. Perfectly flexible prices clear the commodity markets, where demands are driven by activity levels and supplies by prices and a predetermined capacity. Manufactured goods are produced and traded everywhere. Aggregate demand is then built up from consumption (based on current and expected future earnings, asset values), investment (based on market evaluations of firms' current and expected future earnings), trade, and the net fiscal position. This determines output in the short run. Long-run or potential output is determined by a production function, so capacity utilization (the ratio of actual to potential output) can vary. Domestic-output prices are subject to a Phillips curve and the state of the labour markets, such that the higher the capacity utilization, the greater the inflation pressure.

In the government sector, non-ERM exchange rates are determined by open interest parities and the *expected* depreciations consistent with a complete model solution. The non-German ERM rates, however, are obliged to stay within a 2.5 percent band around preassigned parity values. Monetary policy, for ERM members, therefore consists of forcing interest rates to follow a reaction function that targets the given DM parity and maintains the currency within its band. For other countries, and for Germany, a preassigned monetary growth rate is targeted, with interest rates set to gradually reduce the gap between actual and targeted money growth. Likewise tax rates adjust to eliminate the gap between actual and targeted debt levels, subject to an intertemporal budget constraint. Fiscal expenditures are therefore also partly exogenous and partly endogenized. A full description of MULTIMOD's properties and simulation characteristics has been given by Masson, Symanski, and Meredith (1990).

The Policy Preferences

Tables 19.A1–19.A4 summarise the reference-solution preferences over the declared targets and instruments of policy: output growth (GDP), inflation ($\dot{P}$), aggregate fiscal expenditures as a proportion of GNP (G/Y), and short-term interest rates (RS). The ideal values are set at levels rather better than recent experience. Because they are infeasible, but represent the sort of value that the policy-makers themselves say they wish to aim for, they should not prove very controversial. Our *relative* priorities are set so that each percentage-point failure (in each variable in each period) is penalized equally, except for German inflation, which is penalized at five times that rate. That is a plausible starting point, given that all policy variables are measured in equivalent units.

The Baseline and Information Set

All the simulations that follow work from a baseline composed of the historical values of the model's variables plus projections forward to some terminal point (in this case 40 years from our start date of 1990). The model is solved sufficiently far ahead so as to remove any influence of the terminal conditions. We report results for the period 1990–96 inclusive. The baseline itself is identical with that used by the IMF in its own work; the endogenous and exogenous variables are made to follow the 1993 projections in the IMF's *World Economic Outlook*. Forward-looking expectations are then solved to be equal to the outcome projected for the relevant future period.

The Exchange-Rate Regime

With the exception of Germany, which floats the deutsche mark against outsiders, each ERM country is obliged to accept its official 1990 parity against the deutsche mark and to maintain its 2.5 percent band around that for the duration of the simulation (1990–96). However, Italy and the United Kingdom are allowed to realign their currencies down during 1992, from DM 1.33 ± $2\frac{1}{2}$ percent to 0.993 ± $2\frac{1}{2}$ percent per 1,000 lire, and from DM 2.95 ± $2\frac{1}{2}$ percent to 2.43 ± $2\frac{1}{2}$ percent per pound, roughly as happened. But for the purposes of this essay, both currencies are required to stay within the ERM system after 1992. France, of course, is allowed no realignments; we retain 3.35 ± 2.5 percent francs per deutsche mark throughout and do not attempt to include the 1993

Table 19.A1. *Reference Simulation A (G7 Nash Solution for Open-Loop Policies)*

	1990	1991	1992	1993	1994	1995	1996
Predicted targets							
United States							
GDP	1.225	0.746	2.403	2.644	3.107	2.848	2.969
P	5.469	4.280	3.252	3.029	2.714	2.307	2.896
$/ECU	1.282	1.211	1.292	1.163	1.129	1.095	1.075
Japan							
GDP	3.770	3.756	2.214	1.613	1.487	1.946	2.675
P	2.556	2.619	1.342	1.508	1.281	1.332	2.565
Canada							
GDP	0.577	0.515	1.641	2.973	3.107	3.432	3.597
P	5.764	7.022	3.222	2.759	1.307	1.662	2.162
Germany							
GDP	2.278	1.363	1.584	−0.822	1.062	2.025	2.788
P	2.554	3.403	4.290	3.688	2.771	2.318	2.307
M	12.516	7.112	15.010	5.665	4.960	5.276	5.418
United Kingdom							
GDP	0.735	−0.017	0.666	1.491	2.263	2.594	2.944
P	9.488	6.719	2.560	2.654	3.718	4.783	4.484
DM/£	2.894	2.872	2.663	2.423	2.457	2.447	2.451
France							
GDP	2.499	1.978	1.824	0.473	1.600	2.819	2.777
P	3.544	3.421	2.963	2.714	2.315	2.338	2.707
DM/FFr	0.294	0.291	0.296	0.293	0.292	0.295	0.295
Italy							
GDP	2.019	2.284	1.426	0.954	2.352	3.207	2.997
P	6.330	6.985	5.222	5.363	4.882	3.805	4.774
DM/lira	1.323	1.309	1.226	0.969	0.993	1.010	1.013
Optimized instruments							
United States							
G/GDP	19.324	21.008	19.553	18.829	18.019	17.977	17.614
RS	4.489	4.358	4.439	4.476	4.458	4.425	4.524
Japan							
G/GdP	13.232	13.333	15.881	16.887	16.751	16.017	15.179
RS	4.222	4.057	3.732	3.661	3.698	3.838	4.012
Canada							
G/GDP	22.656	23.849	23.816	22.860	22.397	21.771	21.396
RS	5.568	5.678	5.066	5.160	4.924	5.097	5.159
Germany							
G/GDP	18.650	20.630	20.641	22.914	22.201	21.705	21.228
RS	7.178	8.535	9.224	7.851	6.817	6.321	6.413
UK							
G/GDP	22.911	25.611	26.467	25.755	24.678	24.248	23.976
RS	11.775	7.704	14.930	4.411	4.877	5.212	5.133
France							
G/GDP	20.776	21.812	22.114	22.791	21.959	21.116	21.009
RS	6.806	7.797	12.219	6.632	4.992	5.064	5.115

Table 19.A1. *Continued*

	1990	1991	1992	1993	1994	1995	1996
Italy							
G/GDP	19.025	19.460	20.535	20.874	19.994	19.387	19.468
RS	7.732	9.035	15.975	5.957	6.141	5.625	5.635

Notes: GDP, growth rate; P, inflation rate; G/GDP, government current expenditure/GDP ratio; RS, nominal short-term interest rate; M, nominal money growth rate. Objective-function values: US, 11.07; Japan, 10.12; Canada, 28.92; Germany, 57; UK, 160.08; France, 48.09; Italy, 104.53.

Table 19.A2. *Policy Preferences, 1990–96: Ideal Values*

	$\dot{G}DP$ (%)	$\dot{P}$(%)	G/Y (%)	RS (%)
United States	3.0	2.7	19.0 → 17.6	4.5
Japan	3.0	1.5	14.8 → 15.1	4.0
Canada	3.0	2.0	22.6 → 2.17	5.0
Germany	3.0	2.0	20.6 → 21.2[a]	6.0
UK	3.0	4.0	22.8 → 24.0	5.0
France	3.0	2.0	21.3 → 21.0	5.0
Italy	3.0	4.0	20.1 → 19.6	6.0

Note: $\dot{G}DP$ and $\dot{P}$ in percentage growth per annum; G/Y, government expenditures as percentage of national income; RS in percentage points.
[a] Via 22.6 in 1991/2; the actual and baseline figures are rather higher.

Table 19.A3. *Policy Preferences, 1990–96: Relative Priorities*

	$\dot{G}DP$	$\dot{P}$	G/Y	RS
US	1	1	1	1
Japan	1	1	1	1
Canada	1	1	1	1
Germany	1	5	1	1
UK	1	1	1	1
France	1	1	1	1
Italy	1	1	1	1

Table 19.A4. *Policy Preferences, 1990–96: ERM Parities/Weights*

	1990	1991	1992	1993	1994	1995	1996
DM/£	2.95	2.95	2.95	2.43	2.43	2.43	2.43
(weight)	(1,500)	(1,000)	(1,000)	(1)	(1)	(1)	(1)
Fr/DM	3.35	3.35	3.35	3.35	3.35	3.35	3.35
(weight)	(100,000)	(100,000)	(200,000)	(100,000)	(1)	(1)	(1)
Lira/DM	0.748	0.748	0.748	1.007	1.007	1.007	1.007
(weight)	(5,000)	(5,000)	(5,000)	(1)	(1)	(2,000)	(2,000)

Note: The bands of ±2.5 percent are maintained throughout.

widening of the bands to 15 percent. The figures are summarized in Table 19.A4 together with the penalty-function weights that are necessary to keep the currencies within their 2.5 percent bands. Notice, in that table, the extreme pressure on the French franc in 1990–93, as reflected in the huge penalties necessary to maintain the franc's bands (20 to 200 times greater than those necessary to hold the pound and lira in place). Moreover, the pressure on the realigned pound and lira evidently vanishes in 1992, although the lira weakens again from 1995.

This completes the baseline and reference-solution ERM specification; the remaining currencies are free to float.

References

Alesina, A., and Grilli, V. (1992). The European Central Bank: reshaping monetary politics in Europe. In: *Establishing a Central Bank: Issues in Europe and Lessons from the U.S.*, ed. M. Canzoneri, V. Grilli, and P. Masson, pp. 49–77. Cambridge University Press.

  (1993). On the feasibility of a one speed or multispeed monetary union. *Economics and Politics* 5:145–65.

Alogoskoufis, G., and Smith, R. (1991). The Phillips curve, the persistence of inflation and the Lucas critique: evidence from exchange rate regimes. *American Economic Review* 81:1254–75.

Andvig, J. C. (1988). From macrodynamics to macroeconomic planning. *European Economic Review* 32:495–502.

Aoki, M. (1976). *Optimal Control and Systems Theory in Dynamic Economic Analysis*. Amsterdam: North Holland.

Barro, R., and Gordon, D. (1983). Rules, discretion and reputation in a model of monetary policy. *Journal of Monetary Policy* 12:101–21.

Bayoumi, T., and Eichengreen, B. (1994). Shocking aspects of European Monetary Unification. In: *Adjustment and Growth in the European Monetary Union*, ed. F. Giavazzi and F. Torres, pp. 193–240. Cambridge University Press.

Brandsma, A. S., Hughes Hallett, A. J., and v. d. Windt, N. (1984). Optimal economic policies and uncertainty: the case against policy selection by nonlinear programming. *Computers and Operational Research* 11:179–97.

Brechling, F. (1974). Wage inflation and the structure of regional unemployment. In: *Inflation and Labour Markets*, ed. D. Laidler and D. Purdy, pp. 197–226. Manchester University Press.

Chow, G. C. (1976). The control of nonlinear econometric systems with unknown parameters. *Econometrica* 44:685–95.

Cooper, R. N. (1969). Macroeconomic policy adjustment in interdependent economies. *Quarterly Journal of Economics* 83:1–24.

Demertzis, M., and Hughes Hallett, A. J. (1995a). Is the natural rate of unemployment a useful concept for Europe? In: *The Natural Rate Hypothesis after Twenty-five Years*, ed. R. Cross, pp. 315–45. Cambridge University Press.

(1995b). On measuring the costs of labour immobility and market heterogeneity in Europe. Discussion paper 1189, Centre for Economic Policy Research, London.

Demertzis, M., Hughes Hallett, A., and Rummel, O. (1996). Is a 2-speed system the answer to the conflict between the German and the Anglo-Saxon models of monetary control? In: *Competition and Convergence in Financial Markets: The German and Anglo-American Models*, ed. S. Black and M. Moersch, pp. 247–94. Amsterdam and New York: North Holland.

EEC (1990). One market, one money. European economy no. 44, EC Official Publications, Luxembourg.

Frisch, R. (1934). Circulation planning. *Econometrica* 2:259–337.

(1949). A memorandum on price-wage-tax subsidy policies as instruments in maintaining optimal employment. UN document E(CNI/Sub2/13, April), United Nations, New York.

(1957). The multiplex method for linear and quadratic programming. Socio-Economic Institute, University of Oslo (21 January 1957); reported in C. van Eijk and J. Sandee (1959) Quantitative determination of an optimum economic policy. *Econometrica* 27:1–13.

(1969). From utopian theory to practical applications: the case of econometrics. In: *Nobel Lectures in Economic Science, 1969–1980*, ed. A. Lindbeck. London: World Scientific Publishers.

Ghosh, S., Gilbert, C. L., and Hughes Hallett, A. J. (1987). *Stabilising Speculative Commodity Markets*. Oxford University Press.

Giavazzi, F., and Pagano, M. (1988). The advantage of tying one's hands: EMS discipline and central bank credibility. *European Economic Review* 32:1055–82.

Hughes Hallett, A. J. (1979). Computing revealed preferences and the limits to the validity of quadratic objective functions for policy optimisation. *Economics Letters* 2:27–32.

(1984). Optimal stockpiling in a high risk commodity market: the case of copper. *Journal of Economic Dynamics and Control* 8:211–38.

(1986). International policy design and the sustainability of policy bargains. *Journal of Economic Dynamics and Control* 10:467–94.

(1989). Econometrics and the theory of economic policy: the Tinbergen-Theil contributions 40 years on. *Oxford Economic Papers* 41:189–214.

(1991). On decision making by committee. *Economics of Planning* 24:107–20.
Hughes Hallett, A., and McAdam, P. (1998). Fiscal deficit reductions in line with the Maastricht criteria for monetary union: an empirical analysis. In: *The New Political Economy of EMU*, ed. J. Frieden, D. Gros, and E. Jones. Denver, CO: Rowman and Littlefield.
  (in press). Implications of the growth and stability pact: Why the growth element is important. In: *Fiscal Aspects of European Monetary Integration*, ed. A. Hughes Hallett, M. Hutchison, and S. E. H. Jensen. Cambridge University Press.
Hughes Hallett, A. J., and Ma, Y. (1996). Transatlantic policy coordination with sticky labour markets: the reality of the real side. In: *The New Transatlantic Economy*, ed. M. Canzoneri, W. Ethier, and V. Grilli. Cambridge University Press.
  (1997). The dynamics of debt deflation in a monetary union. *Journal of International and Comparative Economics* 5:1–29.
Hughes Hallett, A. J., and Vines, D. (1993). On the possible costs of European monetary union. *The Manchester School* 61:35–64.
Masson, P., Symanski, S., and Meredith, G. (1990). MULTIMOD Mark II: a revised and extended model. Occasional paper 70. Washington, DC: IMF.
Pindyck, R. S. (1973). Optimal policies for economic stabilisation. *Econometrica* 41:529–59.
Theil, H. (1964). *Optimal Decision Rules for Government and Industry*. Amsterdam: North Holland.
Thygesen, N. (1993). Towards monetary union in Europe – reform of the EMS in the perspective of monetary union. *Journal of Common Market Studies* 31:447–72.
Tinbergen, J. (1952). *On the Theory of Economic Policy*. Amsterdam: North Holland.

Author Index

Aarum, T., 5
Abramovitz, M., 207, 212–13
Adelman, F. L., 480
Adelman, I., 480
Afriat, S. N., 69, 70, 114
Aftalion, A., 88n17, 92n20, 473, 484
Aghion, P., 214, 227
Ahn, S. K., 444, 446, 449
Aigner, D. J., 423
Åkerman, J., 45, 48, 51, 462, 467–8, 472, 478
Alesina, A., 585
Allen, R. G. D., 54, 61–2, 69, 73
Alogoskoufis, G., 595
Alt, F., 60
Altonji, J. G., 158
Amoroso, L., 27, 37, 48
Amundsen, A., 546
Andersen, T. M., 500, 502, 508, 522
Anderson, H., 358
Anderson, T. W., 444, 440, 443
Andrews, M. J., 511
Andrews, W. H., Jr., 87, 171–3
Andvig, J. C., 12, 461–2, 551, 597, 609
Angrist, J., 278–9
Antonelli, G. B., 61
Aoki, M., 579
Arellano, M., 179, 180
Arrow, K. J., 66, 67
Atkinson, A. B., 150
Attanasio, O. P., 161
Aukrust, O., 536, 537, 542, 546

Baardsen, G., 386
Baily, M. N., 223
Balk, B. M., 72
Banerjee, A., 387, 500, 506
Banks, J., 151, 152, 154–6, 159, 163
Banz, R., 416–17
Bårdsen, G., 506, 511
Barro, R. J., 221
Bartels, R., 84
Basu, S., 223, 228

Baumol, W. J., 212–13
Beaton, R., 523
Becker, G. S., 216, 221
Bekker, P., 426
Bergson, A., 62, 65, 70
Bewley, R., 373
Bierens, H. J., 151
Birck, L. V., 61
Bjerkholt, O., 539, 544, 548, 565
Bjerve, P. J., 16, 535, 536, 537, 541, 542, 547, 553
Black, F., 415
Blackburn, K., 500, 522
Blundell, R. W., 149, 151, 155–6, 159, 161, 180, 186
Boadway, R., 275
Boianovsky, M., 464–5
Bollen, K. A., 421, 423
Bond, S., 179, 180, 186
Booth, J. R., 427
Bortkiewicz, L. von, 27, 32, 36–7, 42, 53, 67–70
Boswijk, H. P., 406
Bover, O., 180
Bowley, A. L., 27, 32–3, 37, 38, 40, 63, 71–2
Brandner, P., 500
Brandsma, A. S., 585
Brechling, F., 597
Bresciani-Turroni, C., 54
Breusch, T. S., 371
Brown, B. W., 120
Brown, J., 566
Browne, M. W., 423
Browning, M. J., 149, 156, 251
Bruce, N., 275
Brynjolfsson, E., 171
Burns, A., 35
Buscheguennce, S. S., 69

Caballero, R. J., 227–8
Calmfors, L., 515
Cambanis, S., 287

Author Index

Cameron, S., 270
Campbell, D., 223
Campos, J., 508
Cannan, E., 40
Canoe, F., 522
Carlin, W., 507
Carver, T. N., 37, 40–1
Cass, D., 208, 210, 221, 224, 229
Cassel, G., ix, 37
Cavanaugh, C. L., 405
Chamberlain, G., 178–9, 414
Chamberlin, E. H., 33n13
Chan, K., 420
Chen, N. F., 417, 420
Cheng, B., 424
Chipman, J. S., 93n23
Chow, G. C., 579
Christensen, L. R., 150, 208–9, 214, 219, 223, 226
Chuprov, A., 32
Clark, J. B., 37
Clark, J. M., 37, 40, 88–90, 484
Cobb, C. W., 169
Coe, D. T., 228
Cogley, T., 502
Colson, C., 36
Connor, G., 418, 427
Conway, D. A., 420
Cooper, R. N., 580
Copeland, M., 537
Correia, I. H., 500
Cosslett, S., 308
Couch, K., 282
Cournot, A., 30
Cowles, A., 42–3, 46–7, 55
Cragg, J. G., 420
Crepon, B., 179
Csörgő, M., 286n26
Cummings, D., 214

Dahl, C., 128
Dahm, P. F., 420
Danthine, J. P., 500
Darmois, G., 45
Datar, V., 423
David, H. T., 46
Davidson, R., 84
Deaton, A., 112, 150, 154–5, 160
Debreu, G., 77
del Vecchio, G., 37, 45
Denison, E., 212–14
de Pietri-Tonelli, A., 37
Desai, A. S., 421
Diamond, P., 112
Diewert, W. E., 69–70
Dillon, J. L., 169
Divisia, F., 27, 31–2, 36, 38, 43–5
Domar, E., 204
Donald, S. G., 420
Dougherty, C., 214

Douglas, P. H., 169, 171–2, 209
Dravid, A., 425–6
Dresch, F., 490
Dreze, J., 173
Dufour, J. M., 422, 423
Duhem, P., 357
Dupuit, J., 319
Durlauf, S. N., 380, 409

Edgeworth, F. Y., 59, 320, 327
Eichenbaum, M., 522
Eichhorn, W., 72
Ekelund, R. B., 320
Elliott, G., 405
Elster, J., 347, 352
Engle, R. F., 371, 433, 439, 500, 506
Englund, P., 500, 522
Erickson, T., 426
Ericsson, N. R., 501, 508
Evans, G. C., 37, 484
Ezekiel, M., 33n13, 37, 54

Fabozzi, F. J., 427
Falk, B., 424
Fama, E. F., 415, 419, 427
Fanno, M., 45, 54
Feller, W., 93n23
Fernald, J., 223, 228
Ferson, W. E., 415, 418
Fiebig, D. G., 84
Finn, M., 522
Finney, F. L., 140
Fisher, I., 27, 30–3, 36–7, 38, 42–3, 50, 59, 67, 72–3, 216–17, 220, 473
Fisher, P. G., 506, 511, 523
Föhl, C., 537
Fraumeni, B. M., 219–22, 225–6
Fréchet, M., 258
French, K. R., 415, 419, 427
Fry, V., 149
Fuller, W. A., 416, 420, 424
Fuss, M., 174

Gately, D., 128
Geweke, J., 419
Ghosh, S., 583
Giavazzi, F., 585
Gibbons, M. R., 418
Gilbert, C. L., 583
Gini, C., 37, 50, 87
Girardin, M., 500
Goldberger, A. S., 414, 420, 421, 423
Goldsmith, R., 208, 218, 219, 226
Gomulka, J., 150
Goodwin, R. M., 94, 494
Gorman, W. M., 148, 154
Granger, C. W. J., 358, 371, 433, 500, 506
Graves, L. M., 351
Greenan, N., 171
Gregoir, S., 439

Author Index

Griliches, Z., 170, 171, 178, 179, 187, 188, 189, 190, 195–7, 207–10, 216–18, 223, 226–7, 228, 414, 421
Grilli, V., 585
Grossman, G. M., 214
Guldberg, A., 5

Haavelmo, T., 11, 18, 21, 46, 87, 94, 500, 505
Haberler, G., 68–70
Hall, A. D., 358
Hall, A. R., 423
Hall, B. H., 171, 179, 186, 189, 216, 223, 226–7
Hall, R. E., 148, 156, 188, 208, 210, 222, 224, 228
Hansen, A. H., 31n8, 46–8, 54, 88
Hansen, B., 371, 373–4, 387
Hansen, L. P., 224, 415
Hanushek, E., 225
Harberger, A. C., 275
Hardle, W., 117, 151, 153
Harrod, R., 46, 204
Harsanyi, J., 247
Harvey, A. C., 502
Harvey, C. R., 419, 502
Hausman, J., 112–14, 120, 151, 179
Hawtrey, R., 40
Hayek, F. A., 563
Hayes, K., 113
Heady, E. O., 169
Heaton, J., 415
Heckman, J. J., 148, 156, 242, 251, 259, 263–6, 268, 270–2, 277, 285–6, 288, 290, 310
Hellerstein, J. K., 171
Helpman, E., 214, 228
Hempel, C. G., 346–7, 355–6
Hendry, D., 368, 371, 436, 500, 501, 505, 508, 513
Hertz, J., 424
Hertzfeld, H., 228
Heston, A., 206, 212, 214
Hicks, J., 45, 46, 48, 55, 62n5, 94, 494–5
Hinshaw, R., 99
Hitt, L., 171
Ho, M. S., 207, 224–5
Hoch, I., 173, 178
Holme, H., 94, 488
Honoré, B., 259
Hotelling, H., 26, 38, 74–6, 94, 319–22, 325
Houthakker, H., 62n5
Howitt, P., 214, 227
Hsiao, C., 406
Hsieh, D., 420
Hughes Hallett, A. J., 581, 582, 583, 585, 588, 589, 590
Hulten, C., 210, 218, 223
Hutchinson, J. M., 424

Imbens, G., 278–9
Inder, B., 405
Irons, J. S., 501
Islam, N., 206, 214–15
Israel, R., 421
Iwata, S., 426

Jaeger, A., 502
Jaeger, O., 5, 8, 9
Jaffe, A. B., 227
Jagannathan, R., 415
Jensen, M. C., 415
Jeong, J., 422, 423, 425
Jerison, M., 151
Jevons, W. S., 30–1, 59
Johansen, K., 515
Johansen, L., 548, 564, 566, 572, 573
Johansen, S., 371, 406, 433, 435, 439, 442, 444–6, 449, 451, 475, 506
John, K., 422
Johnsen, S., 16
Jones, C. I., 214–15, 227
Jordan, C., 32–3, 74
Jöreskog, K. G., 420, 421
Jørgensen, C., 450
Jorgenson, D. W., 150, 169, 206–10, 214, 218–26
Juselius, K., 435, 453, 506

Kahn, R. F., 324
Kahnemann, D., 347
Kaldor, N., 491–4
Kalecki, M., 45, 488–91, 495
Kalman, R. E., 426
Kandel, S., 419
Kantorovich, L., 563
Kapteyn, A., 416, 426
Katz, D., 248, 284
Keane, M. D., 179
Keilhau, W., 10
Kemmerer, E. W., 40
Kendall, M. G., 257
Keynes, J. M., 37, 55, 69, 473, 489, 495–7, 537, 549, 562, 577
King, R. G., 502
Kirby, C., 419
Klein, L. R., 22, 174, 188, 492–3
Klepper, S., 426, 427
Klette, T. J., 188, 195–7
Kmenta, J., 173
Knight, F. H., 33n13, 249
Kolsrud, D., 506, 510
Kondratieff, N. D., 52–3
Kongsted, H. C., 450
Konüs, A. A., 67–70
Koopmans, T. C., 10, 82, 87, 208, 210, 221, 224, 229, 426, 499
Korajczyk, R. A., 418, 427
Krämer, W., 84
Krasker, W. S., 426

Kravis, I., 206, 212
Krishna, K. L., 178
Krogh, A., 424
Kuan, C. M., 424
Kuznets, S., 204–7, 210, 212–13, 216, 220, 222, 228–9, 537
Kydland, F. E., 499

Laffont, J.-J., 326
LaLonde, R., 264
Lange, O., 21, 55, 323, 495, 563
Laroque, G., 439
Lau, L. J., 150, 223
Launhardt, W., 323
Leamer, E. E., 83–4, 426, 427
Leavens, D. H., 47
Le Corbeiller, P., 45
Lee, C. F., 427
Lehmann, B. N., 418
Leontief, W., 55, 80–1, 537, 539, 548, 561
Lerner, A. P., 46, 322, 563
Leser, C., 150
Lewbel, A., 151, 156
Lewis, A., 563
Li, K. C., 119
Lichtenberg, F. R., 171
Lindahl, E., 12, 537
Lindbeck, A., 204, 507
Linton, O., 117
Litzenberger, R. H., 416
Lo, A. M., 424
Longva, S., 544, 565
Loretan, M., 371, 387
Lotka, A., 93n23
Lowell, M. C., 84
Lucas, R. E., Jr., 215, 249
Lütkepohl, H., 404
Luttmer, E. G. J., 415
Lyons, R. K., 228
Lys, T., 416

McAdam, P., 590
MacBeth, J., 415
McCulloch, R., 419
McFadden, D., 66, 112, 174
Machlup, F., 216, 219, 226
MacKinnon, J. G., 84
McNichols, M., 425–6
MaCurdy, T. E., 156
Maddala, G. S., 414, 421, 422, 424–6
Maddison, A., 206, 212, 215
Mahalanobis, P. C., 561
Mairesse, J., 170, 171, 178, 179, 186, 187, 189, 197
Maler, K.-G., 204
Malinvaud, E., 561
Malmquist, S., 70
Mankiew, N. G., 213–14
Marschak, J., 31n8, 44, 45, 48, 54, 56, 82, 87, 171–3, 249

Marshall, A., 5, 12, 30, 83, 319
Massé, P., 570
Matzkin, R., 308–9
Mayer, H., 36
Meade, J., 46, 563
Meghir, C., 149, 156, 159
Meier, G. M., 98
Menderhausen, H., 72, 171
Menger, Karl, 26–7
Mill, J. S., 99
Mills, F. C., 26, 33n13, 35n15, 46, 54, 56
Mincer, J., 216
Mishra, B., 422
Mitchell, W. C., 33, 36, 484
Mizon, G. E., 506, 513
Modest, D. M., 418
Moene, K. O., 479
Moffitt, R., 265, 277
Moore, H. L., 33n13, 37
Moret, J., 36
Morgan, M. S., 436, 500, 501, 506
Morgenstern, O., 350
Mortara, G., 55
Mowery, D., 228
Mudgett, B. D., 87
Muellbauer, J., 150, 154–5
Mundlak, Y., 169, 173, 178, 189
Myrdal, G., 12

Nason, J. M., 502
Naug, B., 507
Nelson, C. R., 422
Nelson, W. F. C., 47
Nerlove, M., 188
Neumark, D., 171
Neusser, K., 500
Neves, J. L., 500
Newey, W. K., 123, 142, 144–5, 151
Neyman, J., 46
Nickell, S. J., 149, 158, 511, 512
Nimalendran, M., 421, 424
Nordhaus, W., 207, 210, 219
Nymoen, R., 506, 507, 509, 510, 511, 514, 515

Ofer, A. R., 421
Ogburn, W. F., 26, 40
Ohlin, B., 37
Olley, S., 190–4
Orazem, P., 424
Ore, O., 26, 46–7
Ostberg, D. R., 140

Pagan, A., 371, 500, 522
Pagano, M., 585
Pakes, A., 190–4, 416
Palmer, R. G., 424
Pareto, V., 30, 59–60
Paruolo, P., 435, 444, 449, 450, 451, 453

Author Index

Pashardes, P., 151
Patinkin, D., 495
Persons, W. M., 33n13, 37
Persson, T., 500
Pesaran, M., 387, 390, 405, 406
Phillips, P. C. B., 371, 373–4, 380, 387, 406, 408–9, 446, 449
Pigou, A. C., 37, 69, 323, 469
Pindyck, R. S., 579
Pischke, J.-S., 162
Poggio, T., 424
Polak, R. A., 70
Pollak, J. J., 98
Porter-Hudak, S., 113
Pott-Buter, H. A., 151
Powell, J. L., 151
Pratt, J. W., 426
Prescott, E. C., 499
Preston, I., 159
Preston, R. S., 493

Qi, M., 424

Rahbek, A., 450, 453
Rahman, S., 427
Ramaswamy, K., 416
Ramsey, F., 210, 224
Rau, N., 480
Ravn, M. O., 500, 522
Rawls, J., 247
Rebelo, S., 215, 500, 502
Regev, H., 190
Reiersol, Olav, 16, 82, 84, 87
Reinganum, M. C., 420
Reinsel, C. G., 444, 446, 449
Reiter, R., 348
Ricci, U., 36
Richard, J.-F., 500
Ridder, G., 270
Rietz, H. L., 36
Ringstad, V., 170, 178, 188
Robb, R., 242, 268, 271, 290
Robertson, D. H., 12
Robin, J.-M., 155
Robinson, J., 323
Robinson, P., 116, 135
Rodseth, A., 479
Rogers, J. H., 26
Roll, R., 417–20
Romer, D., 213
Romer, P., 213–15, 228
Roos, C. F., 26–7, 31n7, 36, 37–40
Rorty, M. C., 26
Rosen, H., 113
Rosenstein-Rodan, P. N., 45
Ross, S. A., 417–20
Rossen, S., 539
Rowlatt, P. A., 511
Roy, A., 259
Roy, R., 45, 55

Rudebusch, G. D., 423
Rueff, J., 36
Runkle, D. E., 179

Sabino, J. S., 416
Samuelson, P. A., 49, 62n5, 67, 70, 72–3, 93n23, 94, 114, 209–10, 216, 220, 489–90, 495
Sargan, J., 371, 509
Sargent, T., 249
Say, J. B., 321
Schlitzer, G., 500
Schmookler, J., 227
Schneeweis, H., 416
Schneider, E., 537
Scholes, M., 415
Schonheyder, K., 8
Schultz, H., 26, 35, 36, 37, 45, 69
Schultz, T. W., 216, 219, 226
Schumpeter, J. A., 12, 26–7, 34, 37, 38–40, 45, 56, 227, 469–72
Sevaldson, P., 546, 547
Shanken, J., 416–19
Shephard, R. W., 70
Shewhart, W. A., 26, 48
Shin, Y., 387, 406
Shoham, Y., 348
Siegel, D. R., 421
Simons, G., 287
Singleton, K. J., 224
Skinner, D. J., 421
Slutsky, E., 32–3, 37, 42, 49, 94, 487
Small, K., 113
Smith, A., 320–1, 338
Smith, J., 259, 264–6, 285–6
Smith, R., 497, 595
Snyder, C., 26, 54
Solow, R. M., 174, 188, 204–7, 209–10, 214, 216, 221–2, 224, 228–9
Sorböm, D., 421
Soskice, D., 507
Spanos, A., 367
Sraffa, P., 45, 55
Staehle, H., 45, 55, 69, 87
Stambaugh, R. F., 419
Stamp, J. C., 55
Startz, R., 422
Steiger, D., 422
Stern, N. H., 150
Stigum, B. P., 347, 356, 365, 369
Stigum, M., 366
Stiroh, K., 218–19
Stock, J. H., 387, 405, 422, 439
Stoker, T. M., 223
Stokey, N. L., 227
Stone, R., 83, 208, 539, 561, 566
Stout, W., 287
Strotz, R. H., 148
Stuart, A., 257
Subramanian, S., 72

Author Index

Summers, R., 206, 212, 214
Svensson, L. E. O., 500
Swamy, S., 70, 72

Taussig, F. W., 40–1
Taylor, F., 323
Tchen, A., 287
Thalberg, B., 95, 480
Theil, H., 561, 569, 579, 580
Throne Holst, J., 10–11
Thygesen, N., 607
Tinbergen, J., 39, 45, 48, 209, 222, 224, 241, 249, 577, 579, 580
Tintner, G., 94–5, 169
Tirole, J., 326
Titman, S., 421, 423
Titterington, D. M., 424
Tobin, J., 207, 210, 219
Toulmin, S., 356
Tout, H., 48
Trippi, R., 424
Turban, E., 424
Tversky, A., 347

Uzawa, H., 66

Vaillant, G., 352
Van Frassen, B., 347, 356
Varian, H., 114
Vartia, Y., 113
Velupillai, K., 479
Venkataraman, S., 421
Vickrey, W., 247, 323–5, 338
Vines, D., 588, 589
Voeller, J., 72
von Mises, L., 563
von Neumann, J., 350

Wald, A., 72, 87
Walker, M. B., 120

Walras, L., 30, 44, 321
Wang, Z., 415
Wansbeek, T., 416, 426
Watson, M. W., 439
Waugh, F. V., 84–5, 84–6
Weber, B., 151, 161
Wedervang, I., 9, 10–11, 23, 26–7
Weil, D., 213
Weinberger, O., 45
Weinstein, M., 416–17
Wessels, R., 421, 423
Westergaard, H., 36
White, H., 424
Whitley, J. D., 524
Wickens, M. R., 371, 522
Wicksell, K., 12, 30, 95, 462–7, 472–3, 478–9
Wiener, N., 26
Wilcox, D. W., 423
Willassen, Y., 87
Williams, J. C., 227
Willig, R., 112
Wilson, E. B., 26–7, 35–6, 41
Windt, N. v. d., 585
Wold, H., 83
Wold, K. G., 16
Working, H., 33n13, 79–80, 150
Wykoff, F. C., 210, 218

Yntema, T. O., 55
Yoo, B. S., 439
Young, A., 33
Yule, G. U., 94, 487
Yun, Kun-Young, 206, 223–5

Zabel, J. E., 423
Zambelli, S., 480
Zawadzki, Wl., 27, 37
Zellner, A., 173, 177, 421
Zhou, G., 419

Subject Index

acceleration principle (J. M. Clark), 88–90
accounts, Norway's national: Frisch's Ecocirc system, 534–6, 538–41; Frisch's intersectoral flows concept, 536–7; Frisch's plan to describe structure of Norway's economy, 533–41; numerical, 538–41; work on structural, 533–4
aggregation: of production function, 221–2; over sectors, 221
allocation, intertemporal: based on Euler equation, 156–63; of Frisch, 148–9
arbitrage pricing theory, 420
artificial-neural-network (ANN), 424
asset pricing models, using Bayesian methods for, 419–20
autonomy of relationships, concept of Frisch and Haavelmo, 500–1
autoregressive distributed-lag (ARDL) models: AIC Monte Carlo experiments, 373–4; compared with Phillips-Hansen procedures, 387–405; with deterministic trend and $I(1)$ regressors, 381–7; finite-sample simulation results, 389–405; general, 371–3, 381–2; lagged-dependent-variable model, 374–81; SC Monte Carlo experiments, 373–4
autoregressive representation of nonstationary process, 436–7

bunch analysis (Frisch), 87
business-cycle analysis: autonomous and confluent relationships concepts, 500–1; cointegration analysis, 506; Frisch's model with shocks, ix, 90–5; KP stylized-fact method (Kydland-Prescott), 502–5; macroeconomic approach to, 505–6; multivariate framework, 505–6; of Pigou, 469; simultaneous-equations model, 506; stylized-facts method, 499–500, 502–5, 516–23; system-of-equations approach, 499–501; use of HP filter in, 502; wage–price adjustment model, 506–16
business cycles: Frisch's models to generate, 486–7; summation of random shocks to generate, 487–8
business-cycle theory (*see also* shocks, or impulses): of Åkerman, 467–8, 472; Allais's nonlinear model, 494; Frisch's contribution to, 88–95; Frisch's criticism of Åkerman's, 467–8; Frisch's idea of internal and external mechanisms, 483–6; Frisch's interpretation of Schumpeter's, 471–2; Frisch's model, ix, 90–5; Frisch's model of propagation mechanism, 473–6; of Kaldor, 94, 491–4; Kalecki's system, 488–91, 494–5; of Mitchell and J. M. Clark, 484–5; real-business-cycle theory, 464n4; and of Samuelson, 489–90; Schumpeter's explanation of, 94, 469–72; of Tinbergen, 486; of Wicksell, 462–7, 478–9

capital-asset pricing model (CAPM): correcting for EIV using maximum likelihood, 417–18; testing, 414–15
capital theory (Frisch), 88–95
circulation planning (Frisch), 95–9, 242, 601
coercion in welfare state intervention and redistribution, 244
cointegration: in business-cycle analysis, 506; cointegrating rank, 449–50; defined, 438; definition in nonstationary processes, 438–9; hypothesis testing on parameters of, 450–2; in nonstationary processes, 433–4; polynomial, 438; of variables, 436; vectors, 434, 450–2
confluence analysis (Frisch), ix, 78–84, 86–8, 506; use of nonstationary processes in, 436

626 Subject Index

constant elasticity of substitution (CES) (Arrow-Solow), 66
consumer demand: Frisch's sequential approach to analysis of, 147–9; gasoline demand application, 126–33; testing conditions of, 124–6
consumer surplus: in estimating demand function for gasoline, 132; estimation of, 112, 115–21; kernel and series estimators, 133–45
cost–benefit analysis: adjusting for direct and welfare costs of taxation, 280–3; data required for, 254–64; parameters needed to perform, 275–80; traditional, 275
cumulative process (Wicksell's model), 464–5

data (*see also* time series): to evaluate public policy, 242–3; to evaluate welfare state, 251–74; Frisch's choices for analysis, 569; implementation of Frisch's ideas for collection of, 545; microeconomic panel data in production function analysis, 174–99; need for better and more, 198–9; panel data to evaluate welfare state policy, 266–74; repeated cross-section data, 272, 274; in theory–data confrontations, 352–4; using cross-section data, 255–64; using panel data, 266–74
data sources: for analysis of Engel curve, 151, 155; for estimating demand functions for gasoline, 126; for evidence of heterogeneity of JTPA program impact, 284, 314–15; Penn World Table, 213, 215
deadweight loss (DWL): in estimating demand function for gasoline, 133–4; measure of, 112–13
decision making: Frisch's postwar work on models for, 17–20; under uncertainty, 247–9
deductive-nomological (D–N) scheme, 346–7, 355–6
demand (*see also* elasticities of demand; supply): Frisch's contribution to functions of, 78–84; price elasticities (Frisch), 148–50; want-independent (Frisch), 147
demand curves: Leontief's solution, 79–83; nonparametric regression models to estimate, 111–15; parametric form, 114; Schultz's contribution, 79
demand functions: complete scheme of computing (Frisch), 76–8; in estimating consumer surplus, 115–21; estimating welfare measures from estimates of, 113; parametric and nonparametric, 114–15, 126–33

dependence, 287–90
distribution theory, asymptotic, 133–45
dynamic analysis (Frisch), 462

Ecocirc system, Norway, 534–6, 538–41
econometrics: Frisch's definition, vii, 28–9; scientific explanation in, 355–68
Econometric Society: early years, 38; editorial policy for *Econometrica*, 46–52; election of Fellows, 52–5; founding (1930), 26–8, 37–8
Economic and Monetary Union (EMU), limits on fiscal policy under, 588–93
economic growth: constant quality indices to measure, 209–10, 217–19; endogenization of, 207–8, 211–15, 221–9; investment and productivity as sources of, 215–21; Kuznets's theory of, 205–6, 212; modeling spillovers to endogenize, 228–9; Ramsey model of optimal growth, 208, 210, 220–1; Solow residual, 216; Solow's model of, 205–7, 210–11, 213–14; system of accounts to measure, 208–9, 219–20, 226
economic planning (*see also* circulation planning (Frisch); fiscal policy; macroeconomic planning): European postwar, 562–5; Frisch as advocate of national, 241; Frisch's target-instrument approach to, 578–85; in market-economy context, 578; Tinbergen-Theil flexible-target concept, 579
economics: Frisch's contribution to welfare, 73–6; neoclassical, 577–8; scientific explanation in, 355–68; static and dynamic laws of (Frisch), ix, 88–95, 462; theory–data confrontations in, 348–55
elasticities of demand: complete scheme to compute own- and cross- (Frisch), 76–8; of Frisch, 148–9; Frisch intertemporal allocation approach, 148–50; Slutsky substitution elasticities, 154–6; using nonparametric Engel curve analysis, 149–54
elasticities (Slutsky), 149–50, 154–6
encaisse désirée (Frisch's consumption equation), 483–4
Engel curve: in applied microeconomic research, 150–1; nonparametric, 150–3
equilibria, long-run dynamic and static (Frisch), 434, 462
errors-in-variables (EIV): in capital-asset pricing model (CAPM), 414–15; Frisch's work with, 414; grouping methods with simple regression model, 415–17; grouping with measurement of several regressors, 417; instrumental-variable methods to solve problems of, 419; interpreting results of panel data

Subject Index

with, 182–7; later work with, 414; methods to obtain parameter bounds, 426–7; performance measurement models, 426–7; signaling models, 420–6
expenditure function (Frisch), 63

factor analysis, 420
fiscal policy: for Economic and Monetary Union, 588–93; potential for limits imposed by monetary union, 588–92
Fréchet bounds, 258–9, 265, 287–8, 301
Frisch, Ragnar: academic positions and teaching at University of Oslo, 7–9, 11–14, 16–17, 20–3; advanced studies of, 6–7, 462; as advocate of national economic planning, 241; Åkerman's influence on, 462, 478; contributions to utility theory, index numbers, and welfare economics, 59–78; criticism of free market system, 531, 566, 574; criticism of Hotelling's marginal-cost theory, 324–5; experiences during World War II, 14–16; game-theoretic version of policy analysis applied to monetary union, 590–2, 609–11; influence on policy in Norway, 549, 551–3; lectures in economics, 11–14; Norwegian economists' influence on, 553; opposition to EEC, 578; policy analysis applied to monetary union, 585–8; political ambitions, 554–5; postwar plan for economic research and teaching, 550; role in Econometric Society, 26–9; Schumpeter's influence on, 462; Slutsky's influence on, 487; student years, 4–6; target-instrument approach to economic planning, 578–85; use of mathematical programming, 19–20, 571–2, 575; view of economic behavior analysis, 569; view of preference function, 565, 571–2; Wicksell's influence on, 95, 462, 472–3, 478; work for United Nations, 542–3, 579
Frisch-Waugh theorem, 84–6

heterogeneity: evidence of variability in response to job training, 283–305; impact of programs on people, 283–4
Hodrick-Prescott (HP) filter: in analysis of business cycles, 502–3; as detrending technique, 499
Houthakker-Hicks-Samuelson theorem, 62n5
human capital investment, 216–17, 219–21, 227

impulses, *see* shocks, or impulses
independence: assumptions in analysis of variability of response to job training, 290–1; conditional, 255–9, 269–70; Frisch's concept of want-independence, 76–8
index number theory, Frisch's contribution to, 62–73
innovations (Schumpeter's theory), 488
input–output models (Frisch); median model, 17; Oslo channel model, 18; refi model, 18
Institute of Economics, University of Oslo: achievements of, 550; cooperation with Central Bureau of Statistics, 544; establishment of and Frisch's role at, 9–11, 19; influence of, 548–9; work on conceptual systems, 543; work on structural national accounts, 533–4, 542
instrumental-variable (IV) methods, 419
investment: accelerator theory of, 489; defined, 216; as source of economic growth, 215–21, 226

job training: evidence on variability of response to, 283–305; self-assessment of participants, 294–7

kernel estimator: of consumer surplus at particular income and covariate values, 133–45; in estimating demand functions for gasoline, 127, 129–30, 132; in estimation of asymptotic variance, 121–4; estimation of consumer surplus, 116–18
Keynesian theory: distinction between savings and investment, 489; evidence of Frisch's understanding of, 495–6; Frisch's teaching of, 549; Keynesian multiplier, 95
knots: defined, 118; in estimating demand function of gasoline, 127–9, 131

likelihood function, 444–9
Lindahl-Samuelson theory of public goods, 229

Maastricht treaty, 588
macroeconomic models: of Frisch, 542–5; numerical models of Frisch, 17–19, 544–8
macroeconomic planning: European postwar, 562–5; Frisch's work in and influence on, ix–x, 532, 549
macroeconomic theory: Frisch's conceptual systems in, 532–3; Frisch's interest in and teaching of, 12, 532; of Keynes, 95–6, 562, 577
marginal-cost pricing: arguments against, 325–6; Edgeworth's rule, 328–34, 338–41; egalitarian rule, 333–4, 339–40; Hotelling's criticism of, 319–22; Hotelling's rule, 334–7, 339–41;

Subject Index

Launhardt's rule, 323; Smith's rule, 320–1, 327–8, 331–7, 339–40; Vickrey's argument for, 323–5
matching and conditional independence assumption, 255–9, 269–70
mathematical programming, 19–20, 571–2, 575
maximum-likelihood method to correct for EIV in CAPM, 417–18
mechanisms (*see also* propagation mechanism): in economics, 347–8; Frisch's idea of internal and external business cycles, 483; structure of economic, 501
median model, 17, 544
MODIS models, 547–8
monetary union (*see also* Economic and Monetary Union [EMU]): Frisch's concept of policy analysis applied to, 585–8; Frisch's opposition to European, x, 578–9; labor markets under, 593–4; limits on fiscal policy under, 588–93; need for policy in market-oriented, 577–8; potential limits on fiscal policy under, 588–92
moving-average representation (nonstationary processes), 436
multicollinearity: defined, 86; Frisch's study of, 78–9; indication of, 87

National Income and Product Accounts, United States, 208, 210–11
nonstationary process: integrated of order (1) and order (2), 433, 437–8; made stationary by differencing, 436–9

Oslo channel model, 18–19

path independence: of consumer surplus from price path, 124–5; of demand function, 113; testing of, 124
Phillips-Hansen procedures, 387–405
portfolio efficiency: test for, 418–19; using Bayesian methods, 419–20
power series: as approximating function, 118; in estimating demand functions for gasoline, 127, 132
preference function: Frisch's approach to selection of, 572–3; Frisch's view of, 565, 571
preferences: diversity related to public policy outcomes (Frisch), 300; nonparametric analysis of consumer, 148–54; revealed preferences, 283–300
price series, integrated, 433–5
pricing, *see* marginal-cost pricing
production function: aggregate, 221–2; approaches and problems in identification of, 187–97; Cobb-Douglas, 169, 172, 213; components of error in, 175–7; criticism of Douglas's work, 171–5; estimates using different data cuts, 180–7; as framework for analysis, 170–1, 199; of Frisch's business-cycle theory, viii, 483–4; marginal-productivity theory, 174; panel data to estimate, 174–87; problems in estimating, 194–9; simultaneous-equations method, 171–3; u as errors in, 172–3, 175
propagation mechanism: conceptions of Pigou, Wicksell, and Frisch, 469; Frisch's interpretation of Wicksell's, 465–7; Frisch's model of, ix, 93–5, 473–8, 480, 509; in wage–price adjustment model, 509–10; Wicksell's idea of, 464–5
public policy: criteria for evaluation of welfare state, 244–51; enumerating and evaluating consequences of, 242; Frisch's concept of economic, 578–9; Frisch's influence on, 549, 551–4

Ramsey model of optimal growth, 208, 210, 220–1, 224
random walk of nonstationary processes, 436, 441
real-business-cycle model (RBC): calibration of, 521–2; link of business-cycle model to, ix, 90–5
refi model, 18, 544
relationships: autonomous, 500–1; confluent, 501
research, economic: Frisch's business-cycle model, 90–5; Frisch's method and direction for empirical, 30–1; Frisch's postwar plan for, 550
Rockefeller Foundation, 9–11, 19
Roy model, for cross-section data, 259, 261–2, 265

scientific explanation: defined, 345; in economics and econometrics, 355–68; Hempel's deductive-nomological scheme, 346–8, 356
selection bias: using cross-section data, 255–9; using panel data, 268
self-interest, 247–9
self-selection, 249–51
separability: additive and homothetic, 148; Frisch's application of, 148; prices under (Gorman), 148
series estimators: of consumer surplus at particular income and covariate values, 133–45; consumer surplus estimation, 118–19; in estimating demand functions for gasoline, 127; for estimation of asymptotic variance, 121–4
shocks, or impulses: Åkerman's conception of, 467; Frisch's definition, 94; Frisch's

Subject Index 629

illustration of effect of random, 94–5; Schumpeter's idea of responses to, 470; transformed into cycles (Frisch), 477; in wage–price adjustment model, 509–11; Wicksell's ideas related to, 463–5
signaling models, 420–6
simultaneous-equation method and other solutions to estimate production function, 171–94
skewness concept, 97
Solow residual, 216
spillovers, 228–9
splines: in estimating demand function for gasoline, 127, 129, 131–2; regression splines as approximating functions, 118
static analysis (Frisch), 462
stochastic simulation, 488
supply, Frisch's contribution to function of, 78–84
supply curves: Leontief's solution, 79–83; Schultz's contribution, 79
System of National Accounts, United Nations, 208, 226

taxation, direct and welfare costs, 280–3
time series (*see also* cointegration; variables): Frisch's analyses of, viii–ix, 12, 33–4, 90, 461; Frisch's view of macroeconomic, 569; iterated moving averages of random numbers (Slutsky and Yule), 487; price series as $I(1)$ and $I(2)$, 433
trade-cycle theory, *see* business-cycle theory

uncertainty, 247–9
utility, Frisch's consumer demands related to marginal, 147–8
utility function, equilibrium or indirect (Allen), 61–2

utility theory: complete scheme (Frisch), 76–8; Frisch's work on, 59–67

value-added functions, sectoral, 221–3
variables (*see also* errors-in-variables (EIV); instrumental-variable (IV) methods): factor analysis with macroeconomic, 420; Frisch's examination of cyclical properties of, 484–5; Frisch's use of cointegration of, 436; instrumental, 262–4; in market-signaling models, 420–6; as targets and instruments (Frisch), 578
variables, integrated: analysis of $I(1)$ and $I(2)$ in likelihood function, 444–8; $I(1)$ and $I(2)$ as submodels of the VAR, 442–4; representation of, 439–42
variance, asymptotic, 121–4
vector autoregression (VAR) model: conditions on parameters of, 439–42; $I(1)$ and $I(2)$ variables as submodels of, 442–4

wage–price model of adjustment, 506–11; analysis of Norway data, 514–16; analysis of United Kingdom data, 511–14
Walras's law, 96
welfare state: coercive redistribution and intervention as activities of, 242, 244; cost–benefit analysis of programs, 275–83, 304; criteria for evaluating public policy in, 244–51; data required to evaluate, 251–74; econometric analysis of programs, 275–83, 304; Frisch's advocacy of economic planning in, 241; intervention as activity of, 244; redistribution activity of, 244
welfarism principle, 245

For EU product safety concerns, contact us at Calle de José Abascal, 56–1°,
28003 Madrid, Spain or eugpsr@cambridge.org.

www.ingramcontent.com/pod-product-compliance
Ingram Content Group UK Ltd.
Pitfield, Milton Keynes, MK11 3LW, UK
UKHW040413060825
461487UK00006B/487